DESIRE and DENIAL

DESIRE and DENIAL

Celibacy and the Church

by Gordon Thomas

LITTLE, BROWN AND COMPANY
BOSTON   TORONTO

FIRST EDITION

Library of Congress Cataloging-in-Publication Data

Thomas, Gordon.
  Desire and denial.

  Bibliography: p. 525
    1. Celibacy—Catholic Church—Case studies.
  2. Catholic Church—Clergy—Sexual behavior—Case
  studies.   3. Nuns—Sexual behavior—Case studies.
  I. Title.
  BV4390.T52   1986   262′.14   86-151
  ISBN 0-316-84097-1

MV

Designed by Jeanne F. Abboud

PRINTED IN THE UNITED STATES OF AMERICA

For
EDITH

*and her determination that
no one would take unfair
advantage or distort reality
for any reason.*

Research Coordinator:
Augustina Bunn

Researchers:

Paula Anderson	(*United States*)
Andrew Budd	(*United States*)
Patricia Crichton	(*Spain*)
Christine Gurmann	(*Austria*)
Patrick Jenkinson	(*Ireland*)
Harald Kraner	(*West Germany*)
Maria Kraner	(*France*)
Cheryl Lawrence	(*Belgium/Netherlands*)
Gabrielle Redden	(*Italy*)
Sabine Schmidt	(*United Kingdom*)
Jane Watson	(*Philippines*)
John Williams	(*Central/South America*)

Research by
CLARISSA McNAIR

Special thanks to

HIS EMINENCE, CARDINAL FRANZ KÖNIG, ARCHBISHOP OF
VIENNA
HIS GRACE, ARCHBISHOP GAETANO ALIBRANDI, APOSTOLIC
NUNCIO TO IRELAND
MONSIGNOR EMERY KABONGO, PERSONAL PRIVATE SECRETARY
TO HIS HOLINESS, POPE JOHN PAUL II
MONSIGNOR JOHN MAGEE, PONTIFICAL MASTER OF
CEREMONIES
FATHER SEAN MACCARTHY, VATICAN RADIO
FATHER LAMBERT GREENAN, EDITOR, ENGLISH-LANGUAGE
EDITION, *L'OSSERVATORE ROMANO*
FATHER GEORGE TAYLOR, PARISH PRIEST

and

THE ONE HUNDRED AND SEVENTY-FIVE PRIESTS AND NUNS IN
BELGIUM, GERMANY, GREAT BRITAIN, FRANCE, HOLLAND,
IRELAND, ITALY, AND THE UNITED STATES WHO
CONTRIBUTED THEIR THOUGHTS.

above all to

FATHER SEAMUS BRESLIN
VICTORIA, SISTER SARAH JOHN
FATHER PHILIPPE
CLARE, SISTER MARY LUKE
ANDREW
AND THEIR LOVED ONES

All gave of their lives and time unsparingly.

NOTE TO THE READER:

All the people in this book are real. Nevertheless, I felt duty bound to protect some of their secrets; where appropriate, their recognizable identities are among them. In providing this necessary shelter I do not believe I violate a duty to the truth or compromise any of the admirable rules for writing authentic nonfiction as stated by Macaulay: "A perfect historian must possess an imagination sufficiently powerful to make his narrative affective and picturesque. Yet he must control it so absolutely as to content himself with the materials which he finds and to refrain from supplying deficiencies by additions of his own."

Those whose experiences are related here will become known to you in exactly the same way as they see and recognize themselves. They, of course, created or were caught up in the situations which finally allowed light to emerge from the darkness that has surrounded their chosen way of life for centuries. They are part of the mystery, if that is the word, of how priests and nuns of the most powerful religion in the world — the Holy Roman Catholic and Apostolic Church — cope with their sexual needs, having taken sacred vows of celibacy and chastity.

The solutions, perhaps not surprisingly, will confirm suspicions, create dismay, and even arouse shock or anger; the more so because the men and women in these pages reveal such intimate truths about themselves and their brothers and sisters in Christ. But behind their more obvious motives for breaking silence is also something else. It is the realization that religion must exact its penalty and claim its victims. In that sense their story is that of all of us.

All biblical quotations are from either the Douay Bible or the Jerusalem Bible.

†

Contents

CONTENTS

†

THE POPE'S CELIBATES

Vows can't change nature.

— ROBERT BROWNING

CHAPTER 1

†

The Lessons for Today

About remaining celibate, I have no directions from the Lord but give my own opinion.

When the Apostle Paul announced that to the Christians in the promiscuous city of Corinth, he unwittingly sowed the seed for an unprecedented crisis that today permeates the Roman Catholic Church. Beneath the panoply of the papacy, behind the wealth, power, and influence of the Holy See, is a profound struggle, one that is of crucial concern to its million and a half priests and nuns, its 810 million members, and to many beyond its fold. At stake is the future direction of a still powerful, dynamic, yet deeply perturbed and confused institution. The unexpected source of the attack has heightened the dismay and disruption throughout the universal Church.

For centuries successive pontiffs have applied a substantial portion of their energies to confronting their external enemies of atheism, secularism, and nihilism. These traditional bogeymen of Rome remain a threat, surfacing in a number of guises: opposition to the Church's rigid position on abortion and birth control; Third World demands to adapt the Church's rituals and procedures to local rites; a wide range of questions affecting family life and morality. Among them are divorce, remarriage, and the religious education of children in a neopagan world, so that they will never forget that being a good Catholic means accepting the dogma that the Church is the moral conscience of society. These remain substantial, perplexing, and explosive matters.

To them has been added a new, growing, and increasingly powerful challenge from within the Church, one that comes from its priests and nuns. Their confrontation stems from a tumultuous upheaval that began during the Second Vatican Council (1962–1965). The changes wrought by that policy-setting gathering of bishops were the most radical in the history of the Church. Centuries of tradition were reinterpreted. Clergy and sisters who once had obediently submitted their minds and wills to Church-defined faith and morals now rebelled. They demanded to be freed from one of the most profound constraints ever set by Rome. They wanted to be allowed to live full and open sexual lives. Refused, some resigned from religious life; more now continue to do so.

For a Church that has survived persecution, wars, and schism, the challenge was, and remains, stunning in its implications: as Catholicism approaches its third millennium it could find itself so seriously depleted within its ranks that it will no longer be able to function effectively. The worldwide number of candidates for the priesthood in 1985 was 71,000 — a decline of 40 percent from what it had been annually in the pre–Vatican Two era. Undoubtedly more dismaying for Rome is that for every young man who wishes to enter Holy Orders another has applied to leave. All the available evidence points to an ever-widening gulf between a predominantly patriarchal pontificate and its clergy and sisters: many find that while they can continue to live up to their pledge of poverty, they can no longer, in all conscience, promise obedience to vows of celibacy for priests and chastity for nuns. They point out that a celibate is someone who has simply decided not to marry; on the other hand religious chastity, far from being a Catholic innovation, is based upon the Mosaic commandment that forbade adultery and sexual licentiousness. Those nuns and priests insist that this commandment does not exclude them from satisfying their sexual needs; that only the Church, for its own ends, has misinterpreted the original meaning of the Law of Moses.

Many of Pope John Paul II's concerns and actions since coming to office in 1978 have been part of a grand strategy to highlight the distinctions between the clergy and the laity. Fired by his own unquestionably determined belief in the tradition of religious life, he has set out to tighten his authority over his flock and to apply punitive sanctions to those who will not bend to his demand that for them sexual abstinence is a lifelong commitment. The pontiff insists that for a priest celibacy is what distinguishes him from all other men. Sisters, once they have taken their solemn vows, are equally embraced by Catholicism's distinctive nonsexual system. The Pope has repeatedly stressed there can be no argument about a decision originally made at a time when the Catholic Church was a totally dominant institution and had no difficulty in enforcing its holy writ. He insists that celibacy remains nonnegotiable. For nine centuries the Church has maintained its hold over both clergy and sisterhood by commanding that "service in moral leadership" depends on the total sacrifice of all sexual desires.

But modern biblical scholarship and, in the wake of the Second Vatican Council, a growing informed critical attitude among young priests and nuns have meant that the word of Rome, and particularly the view of Pope John Paul, are not accepted with the blind obedience of old.

Twenty years after Vatican Two there has been a significant change in the educational levels among rank-and-file priests and nuns. Surveys in the United States and Europe show that clergymen and sisters are now generally more highly educated than their bishops. One poll of American nuns revealed that 65 percent held master's degrees and 25 percent possessed doctorates. In contrast only 24 percent of U.S. bishops have master's and 10 percent have doctorates. Better equipped to think, young priests and nuns continue to challenge with a skill that leaves their superiors baffled and bewildered — and often forced to fall back on the all-too-true argument that confrontation within the Church is driving the laity away in unprecedented numbers. Gallup polls in 1985 showed that only half of the 70 million Catholics in the United States attended Mass in a typical week, a decline of 74 percent over thirty years. In West Germany the attendance figures have declined by 70 percent over twenty years. In France only two Catholics in every ten regularly attend Mass. The overriding reason given for not attending church is a general dissatisfaction with the way priests conduct themselves; that, in seeking for sexual emancipation, to be no longer denied the freedom to express natural desires, to be released from social constraints, many priests in the eyes of their congregations have lost those unique values and norms that set them apart and have demeaned the office of the priesthood. At the same time these priests have raised doubts about many of the other great ideologies upon which Rome has ruled. The clergy's repeated response is that they have lost patience with the way their personal lives are mismanaged by Rome. Priests often reinforce this claim with the argument that Jesus had no sympathy for the views of the religious aristocracy of His day. For them the Vatican is no different from the Sadducees whom Christ challenged. The priests believe they would have His support in challenging, by word and deed, the existing Roman ecclesiastical establishment's right to deny them sexual freedom.

A growing number find themselves in the unenviable position of being virtually forced to remain in a job that demands control over their sexuality. While nuns who find this intolerable can generally be dispensed from their vows without trouble, priests, on the direct order of the Pope, can be released from their sacred promises only after they have personally petitioned Rome.

In practice the number of priestly dispensations worldwide has dropped from a peak of 15,000 in 1975 to under 500 annually a decade later. Yet the extent of the problem can be partly gauged from the fact that the two Vatican Sacred Congregations responsible for processing petitions admitted in 1986 they had received almost 250,000 submissions since 1980 from nuns and priests. Nine out of ten applicants gave as their reason for wanting to be dispensed an inability to cope with the Church's treatment of their sexuality. A growing number, without waiting to be formally refused, have left Holy Orders, returning themselves to the world without any help from the Church on resettlement, and many have found themselves living off welfare payments. In the United States there are an estimated 5,000 priests in this position — men who have walked out, since Vatican Two, to marry or live openly as homosexuals. There are just as many who have opted out in Europe.

Those who wish to leave the priesthood, yet who remain in the Church, do so for many reasons. Anxiety is one. A survey of Mississippi priests showed that an overwhelming percentage of those asking to be dispensed said they would leave only with Rome's approval; many claimed that a priest who walks out on his vocation in the South is looked upon with the same suspicion as an ex-convict. A desire to remain under the religious umbrella of the Church is another powerful reason to wait for Rome's nod. Surveys in the United States, Spain, France, Holland, and West Germany identify this as a common response. Priests who want to resign hesitate to do so without Vatican approval because they would otherwise be denied the right to marry within the Church or receive Communion. For committed Catholics these are powerful reasons to soldier on, however unhappily. Others admit that having applied for laicization, they have hesitated because the priesthood does offer job security for life, a higher standard of living than most comparable workers enjoy, and fringe benefits that can include vacations, extensive wardrobes, membership in a whole range of clubs, a car, and bank loan facilities — all provided by grateful parishioners.

Priests who have abandoned their vocations without Vatican approval are understandably envious of Catholic clergy in the Philippines. There, a recent study reveals that half the priests have "a lasting relationship with a woman and the communities they serve accept this fact without difficulty." Their cardinal, Archbishop Jaime Sin, has given no indication he would be able, or wish, to change this situation. His office has indicated that while His Eminence does not personally approve, these liaisons have a long tradition and form part of the local culture. The happy position of their Filipino colleagues can only increase the tendency of those who have petitioned Rome to see themselves as victims of a religious demand that is not only capricious and seemingly selective, but outmoded in an age when restraint over sexual activity has been redefined and relaxed in the secular world.

The lobbyists against celibacy claim that the Church has failed to understand why religious men and women have come to see they must interpret their own lives through the experiences of Jesus Christ; they say there must be more attention given to social psychology, not only to philosophy and theology; there must be a greater understanding of the priest and nun in his or her biological and psychological dimensions. The Church, the traditional champion of human rights, must stop suppressing that most basic of all freedoms — the sexual drive. Jesus, they add, would have been appalled over the way they are treated. He had never intended them to be denied the right to love fully. They see it as a Roman decision, maintained as part of the Church's coercive and repressive power.

In the face of such attacks, the order from the Vatican is to close ranks, to fall in behind the Pope's stark reminder that the priesthood is forever. Jesus, the Pope insists, would have expected nothing less.

While the Gospels reveal Jesus as a compassionate, caring, loving, affectionate, demonstrative, exciting, captivating, and warm person — all qualities that make His sexuality human in the best sense of the word — and describe how He repeatedly touched people, either physically, psychologically, or spiritually, none of the Apostles makes any specific reference to the sort of sexual life Jesus expects from those who answer the call to follow Him. While notably Matthew and Luke point to the fact that Jesus was a sexual being — implicit in their recounting of His humanity — it has been left to Paul to set down his own views on celibacy in those words in the Letter to the Corinthians.

Paul points out twice more to the Corinthian Christians that he is merely expressing his personal ideas, and they should not think they are being handed on from Jesus. This careful caveat, one of the few disclaimers the Bible contains, seems unlikely material to have created a contemporary crisis both within and without the celibate community. Yet his handful of words has, close to two thousand years later, unleashed a sexual revolution within the Church, one that not only continues to have a direct effect on the lives of every priest and nun and the laity for whom they are spiritually responsible, but also has reached beyond to become an examination of religion itself in present-day culture.

Just as marriage is challenged — having become more of a social rather than a sacramental institution, a convenience to be disposed of when it has served its purpose — so mandatory celibacy is rejected. Its opponents argue it is rooted in an elitist group of sexually maladjusted men and women who are forcing others to achieve sexual fulfillment by stealth and who live in an unhealthy fantasy world of sublimation created by suppression in the name of sacrifice. The supporters of celibacy reiterate that it is the highest form of Christian perfection; that abstinence is the noblest form of love; that it is the ultimate way to express a life in Christ.

Both sides draw comfort from the words of Paul, claiming in common that while indeed the Apostle insists his views are his own, he was undoubtedly reflecting the thoughts of Christ. While it is a matter for fierce but moot debate on how much Paul might have been influenced by Jesus on this issue, the whole question of celibacy has become a complex interchange between modern culture and medieval religious values developed from mankind's more ancient religions: Hinduism, Buddhism, and Judaism.

Five thousand years before Paul addressed the Corinthian Christians there were celibates in India. Judaic belief is partly focused on the premise of the "impurity" of women: at one time only men who eschewed sex were believed to be exalted enough to serve as rabbis. Like much else that it has absorbed and adapted from other religions, the Roman Catholic Church has embraced and developed the concept of celibacy for its priests and nuns. In the first three hundred years of its existence, the Church placed few restrictions upon its clergy in regard to marriage. Celibacy was, as Paul indicated, a matter of choice. Then, in the year 305, the Council of Elvira in Spain held a lengthy discourse on the theme that continence is a more holy state than marriage, citing in support the words of Jesus as recorded by Matthew: *"There are eunuchs who have made themselves that way for the sake of the kingdom of heaven. Let anyone receive it who can."*

The Elvira Council, while not forbidding marriage, passed the first decree on celibacy. It required "bishops, priests, and all who serve the altar to live, even if already married, in continence." Twenty years later, at the Council of Nicaea summoned by the Emperor Constantine, the Pope and his bishops considered banning priests from marrying but decided not to do so. It was not until the decretal of Pope Siricius in 385 that the Church first commanded celibacy for bishops, priests, and deacons, and even the separation of those already married. A priest has "always to offer sacrifice for the people, must always pray, and therefore always abstain from marriage." This prohibition coincided with the spread of monasticism, replacing martyrdom as the ultimate witness to Christ. During the fourth and fifth centuries Mary's popular appeal greatly increased, and her virginity became widely accepted, providing a still more secure basis, in the teaching of the Church, for its priests and later its nuns to accept compulsory celibacy. But there still were married clergy, who in theory remained continent. Then the First Lateran Council in 1123 absolutely forbade clergy to marry and again decreed that those who had must dissolve their unions. From then on celibacy has been extolled by Rome as even more perfect than marriage: those who embrace it are exalted as consecrated men and women, living sacrifices, the embodiment of everything that is sacred in His name. It is, nevertheless, a matter of clerical rather than divine law, and as a result to question celibacy has often been seen as a challenge to the Church's authority.

Yet men and women who promise to give up sexual involvement too often find they have not lost the urge for it. Sublimating normal desires has led to intriguing revelations. Solid psychological evidence now supports an old suspicion: boys and young men with a feminine perception of themselves tend to be attracted to a vocation, and the long years of religious formation often reinforce this pattern. One survey of priests in 1984 revealed that only two out of every ten priests actually saw themselves as masculine, while four out of ten admitted to a strong feminine identification. Father Jaime Filella, a Jesuit professor of psychology, concluded from his own findings in the matter that, on a global scale, only approximately half as many priests see themselves as masculine compared with those who view themselves as feminine. That could mean that close to a quarter of a million Catholic clergy have clinically defined feminine-type personalities. Another Catholic psychologist, Father Donald Goergen, who has done impressive pioneer work in the field, has suggested that many of the problems of priestly celibates stem from their psychologically feminine-oriented ministry together with an inability to integrate the simultaneous needs of being spiritual and fully sexual.

Psychological screening of seminarians is still relatively recent. Even those drawn to the priesthood who are psychologically no different from other boys of the same age find that, because of the lengthy period of formation (seven years), the atmosphere of suppressed sexuality in the normal seminary, and the isolation from female company, they are gradually fashioned in a feminine pattern. Forty seminarians surveyed in Rome in 1984 admitted that after two or more years of living in formation houses they felt less masculine and more feminine. There is no reason to believe this to be an isolated example. Further, clinical research suggests the hypothesis that after ordination priests develop feminine traits because the expectations their parishioners have of them are very clear-cut: to love others, to understand them, to be gentle, meek, and kind. These qualities fit the classic social stereotype of femininity. While they are worthwhile attributes for any cleric, some psychologists argue that in the case of Catholic priests these virtues can lead to a psychological imbalance caused by one significant factor. Unlike the clergy of other Christian denominations who are allowed, and generally encouraged, to marry, the Roman priest is denied the emotionally balancing effect of a wife and children. The result, too often, is that the value of being the proverbial gentle, meek, and mild person can become warped, allowing positive qualities to assume a negative light.

Psychiatrists, along with the more liberal of the Church's theologians and, of course, nuns, believe this tendency could explain why some priests, after a period of celibacy, compensate with an excessive exercise of power. The sisters, in particular, claim that much priestly authority is designed to suppress the position of women in the Church. They say that this, in part, explains why the number of women leaving religious life is statistically far greater than men. A common refrain among nuns is that priestly domination of an organization known as "Mother Church" indicates a well-entrenched fear of women that the Pope, for all his veneration of the Virgin, is encouraging. They insist that his pontificate has deliberately developed a religious organization that is more male-oriented now than in living memory.

While the overall criticism of the present papacy is more widespread than that directed against previous ones in this century — wherever John Paul goes he is increasingly challenged on such issues as the ordination of women, divorce, and contraception — the issue within the clergy and sisterhood of whether celibacy should once more be optional overrides all others. So far the Pope has steadfastly refused to be moved on the subject. All the signs are that he will remain resolute.

To strengthen his hold on this, the most sensitive of all the areas in which he is challenged, the pontiff has created a core of like-minded tough disciplinarians in the Curia, the Church's bureaucracy. Further afield, he has changed the makeup of hierarchies, especially in the United States and the great center of European dissension, Holland. The Pope's intention has been to end what he sees as a test of wills over sexuality in the celibate life.

In Britain the normally indulgent hierarchy has been nudged by the Vatican into taking a firmer line with its more radical clergy and sisterhood. Ireland's 26,000 priests and nuns found themselves in 1986 with a hierarchy determined to show them that there would be no more talk of Irish women being ordained; they would steer clear of political office; religious orders would regain lost discipline. Yet the Irish Church, one of the most conservative in the Catholic fief, continues to face a falling away. Matters were not helped by the Pope's appointment in 1985 of a tough traditionalist to the country's most powerful diocese, Dublin. From the outset the Archbishop made it clear that he had scant sympathy for any priest who wanted to renounce his calling on grounds of being unable to cope with celibacy. Soon there was a growing number of diocesan priests agonizing about leaving — men also fearful of the Archbishop's power to affect their survival in secular life. In a nation where the Church still wields real influence, this is an important consideration. These unhappy priests take no comfort in knowing that in Italy and France the decline is even greater. There priests regularly walk off the job.

In 1966 the resignation rate of priests in the United States was minuscule — one half of one percent. A decade later the figures had increased by eleven times, with twice as many priests in religious orders leaving than diocesan clergy. Order men — the priests, monks, and brothers living in communities — have, like the sisters in their convents, historically been more conscious of their sacred vows. In one U.S. poll taken in 1983, 94 percent of the priests and nuns surveyed said an inability to live within the vows of celibacy or chastity was their reason for leaving.

The American seminary statistics are now a cause of abiding concern for Rome. From a high of almost 49,000 seminarians in 1965, the number dropped, twenty years later, to under 12,000 — a decline of 75 percent. In 1966 there were 183 high school seminaries in the United States; in 1986 there were barely thirty.

If present trends continue, according to a study by Professors Richard A. Schoenherr and Annemette Sorensen of the University of Wisconsin, there will be only 21,000 diocesan priests and 13,000 Order priests remaining in the United States by the year 2000 — a decline of over 40 percent from the 1985 figures.

Nor have the convents escaped. Europe and North America are filled with Mother Houses that were built to hold hundreds, but that now count themselves fortunate to have a mere handful of sisters. More than 60,000 nuns have left their orders in America since 1966. The worldwide figure is above 300,000. Since Vatican Two one in every five nuns has given up. Again, the most significant reason has been an unwillingness or inability to cope with the vow of chastity. Again, the most frequently stated reason that women do not enter religious life is that the Church has no understanding of their sexual needs, let alone of how difficult it often is for them to deny those desires.

Not surprisingly, those who argue the case for celibacy — including the Pope, his cardinals and bishops, and a significant percentage of priests and nuns — are over the age of fifty, a time when the prospect of a first marriage statistically falls away dramatically. Equally, priests and sisters under the age of forty — still a child-bearing time for women — interpret the Apostle Paul's words to support their argument that compulsory celibacy is no longer to be desired or admired. These religious men and women — particularly in the United States, Holland, and West Germany, once bastions of traditional Catholic thinking but now at the forefront of reform — argue that celibacy is not only a barrier to normal pleasure, satisfaction, and happiness, but can lead to serious, sometimes permanent, psychological damage.

They point to the increasing number of priests and nuns receiving psychiatric treatment to help cope with the effects of celibacy. No reliable figures are publicly available for the numbers in therapy, but there is a widespread belief among the clergy and sisterhood that these statistics are stored on the state-of-the-art computers in the Vatican's Statistics Office, and are so embarrassingly large that a policy decision has been made to suppress them. It is nevertheless reasonable to assume that each of Rome's close to three thousand dioceses has its quota of priests and nuns hospitalized on any given day with some aspect of what might be termed "the celibate syndrome."

Biofeedback research into a person's ability to exercise voluntary control over many physiological functions that until recently were considered almost totally beyond control has shown that priests and nuns often have a highly developed ability to fantasize sexually for lengthy periods in what is known as the "twilight" state of drowsy pre-sleep; in this condition the necessary volition that makes for a Church-defined "sin" is absent. Nevertheless, psychiatrists as far apart as Dublin, New Orleans, Boston, and Munich have reported that since the short but revolutionary pontificate of Pope John XXIII (1958–1965) a growing number of priests and nuns have been receiving treatment for sexual problems, and that this has increased dramatically since Pope John Paul II assumed office.

Patients have understandably wondered why the Church, so compassionate in other ways, does not accept that denial has left them emotionally impaired. They find it unrealistic and painful to accept that surrendering their right to sexual fulfillment is a matter of grave consequence, but a necessary sacrifice in the service of God. They can no longer be comforted, for instance, by the claim of Saint John Chrysostom that the "root and flower of virginity is a crucified life," or, almost a millennium later, by Pope Paul VI's insistence, in 1975, that the celibacy and chastity of Catholic priests and nuns are "happy and easy sacrifices."

For them the words of the Apostle Paul are more soothing and offer more hope:

It is a good thing for a man not to touch a woman; but since sex is always a danger, let each man have his own wife and each woman her own husband. The husband must give his wife what she has the right to expect, and so too the wife to her husband. The wife has no rights over her own body; it is the husband who has them. In the same way the husband has no rights over his body; the wife has them. Do not refuse each other except by mutual consent, and then only for an agreed time, to leave yourselves free for prayer; then come together again in case Satan should take advantage of your weakness to tempt you.

While Catholic feminists, who include an ever-increasing number of nuns, object to Paul's claim that a woman has no bodily rights, the great majority of those opposed to compulsory celibacy interpret his words as meaning that the only way to handle the "danger" of sex is to be able to enter into a monogamous relationship; to turn back the clock eight hundred years before the Lateran Council forbade priests to marry. Persuasive though the argument is, it has been applied only to the clergy. No one, not

13

even the most outspoken of the sisterhood, is seriously suggesting there could be married nuns.

More important, Paul is clearly saying throughout his advice to the Corinthians, as well as in his other writings, that the manner in which a person handles his or her body — and he makes no distinction between those in religious life and the laity — is an analogy for Christ's love for the Church. Throughout the Pauline epistles runs a continuous refrain: a full understanding of sexuality is possible only when it is equated with the relationship Christ has with the Church, and the act of human lovemaking is the closest and most fitting description of that divine bond.

The claim advanced by those priests favoring the abolition of compulsory celibacy is that they, as the representatives on earth of the Vicar of Christ, should be allowed freely to express their sexuality in His name. They argue that celibacy should not be seen merely as a "Catholic Question" but placed in a wider arena, where religion, culture, and humanity interact. Some further point out that in the Eastern Orthodox Church, separated from the Church of Rome by the schism of 1054, the priests and deacons are usually married men, although they may not marry *after* ordination.

The challenge to the present pontificate — with its widespread and still undeniably effective apparatus of religious control — is therefore all the more dramatic. Encouraged by such boldly dissident theologians as Hans Küng and Edward Schillebeeckx, committed men and women increasingly defy the Church's position. It is a revolution that goes to the core of the concept of Catholicism as a divine autocracy. There is no doubt that the Pope sees the drive for optional celibacy and a general loosening of the sexual reins within the Church as part of a wider campaign to introduce secularization into the Church and to imperil the very certitudes on which Rome stands or falls.

There are others who argue that the Church must urgently reexamine its position on all sexual matters if it is to avoid a schism that could leave it more depleted and locked into its own fortress mentality than at any time since Jesus said to Simon, "You are Peter, and on this rock I will build my Church."

Sex, the great leveler, is attacking that rock.

Church doctrine, like statistics, tells only part of the story. Behind it are the flesh and blood, and often the pain and bewilderment, of men and women trying to keep their vows to live chaste lives. Even the most committed find it is a daily struggle, one that continues to haunt them as long as their bodies continue to respond to sexual stimuli. The Church freely acknowledges it was never meant to be easy.

This is the story — the first of its kind — of how supremely hard it is for any priest and nun to live by a man-made rule the sort of life that challenges the law of nature. The biographies of five people make up the story. Each person is chosen because he or she is representative of the complex and often disturbing issues raised by the demands of sexuality in celibacy.

In the 1940s, when Father Seamus Breslin's vocation began — and with it our story — there were no detectable signs that the Church's autocratic attitude toward the sexuality of its membership was about to be challenged. Seamus Breslin found himself embraced, and was happy to be so, by a religious system that used time-tested formulas of social control. Celibacy was compulsory. There was no more to be said. As a seminarian, he received one of the finest educations of the day, but no formal instruction on how to cope with his private passions. He had to make his own rules. Hundreds of thousands of young men found themselves facing the sort of dilemmas he faced. Not all coped as he did; many became marked for life because of their guilt about their sexuality.

Father Breslin had established his personal guidelines by the time the first strong conflicts over sexual attitudes within the Church began to surface in the late 1950s. While he remains convinced those guidelines on what was a "sin" saved his vocation, allowing him to remain a priest while coping with the demands made on him as a man, countless thousands of his fellow priests and nuns had known no other recourse than to suppress their sexuality. They found themselves in a state of personal crisis, as the sexual revolution within the Church changed their perception of what might be permissible.

Victoria — Sister Sarah John — entered religious life at a time when the demands for change had become vociferous at various levels of the Church's organizational structure. These would affect forever her attitudes and behavior, making her part of the pressure for reform of celibacy. Remarkable though her story is, it is not unique. She represents a turning point in the moral attitudes of so many nuns and priests of the generation who followed Father Breslin into the religious life.

The challenge and demand posed by the likes of Victoria meant that successive pontiffs found themselves engulfed by a crisis that would not respond to traditional methods of control. By the 1960s, when Father Philippe — the third of our principal characters, and in every sense a remarkable priest — entered Holy Orders, the protest movement within its fold was part of a general anti-authority challenge that was worldwide.

Father Breslin's guidelines for coping with his sexuality, which had seemed daring and innovative only a few years before, appeared mild and ineffectual compared with the behavior of a generation of seminarians and postulant nuns who increasingly felt that the Church must no longer be allowed to set its face against their right to express freely their sexuality.

Long before he was ordained, Father Philippe had come to the conclusion, shared by many of his peers, that the Church still clung to the dogma of the early fathers; that for a priest or a nun the body is nothing more than a casing for the soul. He began to see, through his own experiences, that his bodily demands were of great importance, and that he could not function properly as a priest without taking them into account. Like Victoria, Father Philippe found himself in direct conflict with the kind of traditional Roman Catholic mentality Father Breslin possesses. The disparity between their views is an image of the conflict between all those nuns and priests who demand ever more sexual freedom and those who believe that the limit has been reached.

Clare — Sister Mary Luke — whose life in religion forms a fourth segment of our story — embarked upon her commitment at a time in the 1970s when the sheer speed of change had engendered deepening and demoralizing horror in her superiors. In the short period between Father Breslin's settling into his ministry and Clare's taking her vow of celibacy, little more than twenty years, the sexual revolution within the Mother of all Churches was given full vent in the wake of Vatican Two. Father Breslin, by then middle-aged and burdened by accumulated experience and pain in coping with his sexuality, found the freedoms expressed in the Council decrees left him disappointed, surprised, and angry. Like many others, he wondered if all his years of struggling to remain true to his vow of celibacy had any real purpose.

Committed young nuns like Clare found they suddenly had difficulty in understanding their sexual role. Close in age to Father Philippe and Victoria, Clare nevertheless found herself in many ways in sympathy with priests like Father Breslin. Like him, she felt their world was no longer secure.

Nor did Clare, and a great many like her, feel they were encouraged to redress the balance by Rome's reinforcement of discipline: its reminder that the priesthood is forever; that it is not for women; that celibacy and chastity are a "sign of the freedom that exists for the sake of service."

Those words of Pope John Paul have not halted the debate, reduced the physical tensions, or stemmed the attempts by a militant clergy and sisterhood to complete the dismantling of Roman authority over them in sexual matters.

When Andrew — the last of our case studies — entered religious life, doing so more than forty years after Father Breslin had entered his seminary, he found himself, in the 1980s, in a Church of depopulated seminaries and convents, political bishops, nuns like Victoria, who openly enjoy sexual activities, and priests like Father Philippe, who slept with parishioners. While Father Breslin doggedly clung to his way of life, Clare increasingly began to lose faith in an organization that she felt gave little evidence of being the Church of Jesus.

To these conflicting and typical attitudes, Andrew brings his own viewpoint, one also not uncommon. He does not wish to see the Church return to the sexual feudalism that had dominated the formation of the religious men and women of Father Breslin's generation. Equally, he remains uncertain whether full sexual freedom — of the kind advocated and practiced by Father Philippe and Victoria — is what the Church must espouse. All Andrew knows is that for him, and those whom he represents — well educated before entering seminary life, sexually experienced, worldly — the need for change is not a matter of debate. The question is, what form should change take?

Heading for ordination, Andrew remains uncertain about the sorts of freedom he would like to see, apart from optional celibacy for the priesthood. A growing number of seminarians share his view. It is one that, nearly forty years on into his ministry, arouses Father Breslin's sympathy, though like a great many of his age, he feels he has lived a life of celibacy too long to want to change.

Separated not only by age and a training that, in Andrew's case, is far more sophisticated than the one Father Breslin received, all these men and women are nevertheless closely linked by a fierce determination: to do all they can personally to ensure that their Church, and religion itself, are not irrevocably harmed by the events of the past forty years — the seminal period of a unique sexual revolution. Clare shares that view; and, in spite of their own actions, so do Father Philippe and Victoria. What makes their testimony so remarkable is that it reflects the attitude of all those religious men and women trying to live with their desires and denials.

Essentially the people in these pages are intensely private persons. They would never have agreed to open their lives to public scrutiny if they were not convinced that their experiences, individual as they are, could benefit others. All have worked hard to reproduce the three-dimensional feel of what they underwent, to make their stories quintessential and, though very different in detail, to provide a view of that quasi-mystical state called religious celibacy. A story of intense personal experience, this is also one about growth and profound change brought about by the mystery of spiritually dying and then coming alive again.

†

IMAGES
YESTERDAY

In a higher world it is otherwise;
but here below to live is to change,
and to be perfect is to have changed often.

— JOHN HENRY NEWMAN

CHAPTER 2

†

A Way of Life

H e continues to watch.
A younger priest, less experienced, might have come forward at once, overanxious to be involved, perhaps even eager to be done and on his way. Father Seamus Breslin knows that some priests, like some doctors, are reluctant to stay long near the dying because they like to talk to people in terms of cure. But he has lost count of the number of persons he has helped to die in peace by this, the thirty-ninth year of his ministry. Yet even now as he stands here, he wonders how much longer it will be possible for him, for any priest, to retain the final custody over the dying. The sisterhood's campaign to admit women into the ranks of the Catholic clergy is mounting. For Father Breslin a nun nowadays often denotes a revolutionary in a habit trying to edge that much closer to taking over the functions of a priest — hoping, among other things, to administer the last rites he is about to give.

The very idea of a woman's holding such power and authority makes Father Breslin tremble. He clasps his hands tightly together to control the shaking, his mind fighting off old and familiar anxieties. Father Breslin is sixty-three years old. Apart from some distant cousins, he has no living relatives to share his sorrow over the changes predicted: Church-recognized divorce, contraception, ordained women priests, optional celibacy.

The physicians he has seen over the years have warned him such thoughts can bring on another bout of depression. The last psychiatrist explained that depression is a chemical happening in his brain, as mysterious as transubstantiation. Father Breslin had disliked the analogy. Transubstantiation is something wonderful and pure, that sacred moment when the Eucharistic bread and wine change in essence, though not in appearance, into Christ's Body and Blood. What happens in his brain is something else: an invisible evil substance is released, powerful enough to all but extinguish his life force; a poison that feeds on memory and experience, gnaws away at his spirit, and bows it down through despair. The psychiatrist prescribed a drug, explaining it should help restore the electrolytic balance in his brain.

He had taken a tablet only a few hours ago and he suspects he sounded doped when he answered the call from the hospital. The news that Eileen's time has finally come rapidly cleared his mind and brought into focus the promise he had made to her. *You will die in peace because I will be there to see you do.* Dealing with death is something no seminary taught. The closest Father Breslin ever came as a student to realizing what is involved was an oblique reference from a tutor that neither the sun nor death can be looked at with a steady eye. It took him years to synthesize death and an awareness of death, to recognize that the customs and rituals surrounding the act of dying serve two purposes: to try to reduce its frightening aspects by placing it in a recognizable system of values, and to support those who are about to be bereaved. Both ideals are linked by the concept of a life after death. It is one of his many skills that he has always managed to make the words associated with dying sound as if he had never used them before. He recognizes this is another way to ward off the spiritual numbness and intellectual immobility that plague so many priests who cannot fully accept that the reasons for entering the priesthood are often not the ones for staying.

Standing in the doorway, he is a short, slight figure, with a face dominated by sharply intelligent eyes. They are gauging the correct moment for him to intervene. Eileen's heartbeats continue moving across the monitor positioned near the bed; blips pulsing on the screen, reducing her grasp on life to an endless trace. She has cancer and an acute heart condition. It has been a long and painful illness, but now it is ending. Eileen is forty-six years old, a wife for twenty-five of them, the mother of four grown children. Her husband and three sons are grouped around the bed. Her daughter, working abroad, has been summoned. Father Breslin is certain she will arrive too late. The emotions aroused by approaching death are already settling over this hospital room. He can detect the fear, sorrow, despair, and helplessness of the family and the resignation of the doctor and nurse. While he well understands their responses, they do not for a moment unduly concern him. It is Eileen who matters now.

Father Breslin has visited her regularly during her months in the hospital, reminding Eileen that her faith asserts she will not wholly die; that when the time comes God will receive her. He has restated his belief that dying interrupts life, that it should be seen as a return to a wanted and familiar world. He has told Eileen, in a dozen ways, that her own strong religious conviction is the best preparation for the life hereafter and that it will actually protect her from any fear of death. She must look upon her dying as not the end but the beginning of a fuller life. It has, nevertheless, taken him several talks to foster the idea that she must accept, in the final stages of her illness, the possibility of a growing and inevitable sense of separation from her family, doctors, and nurses. He has explained it might be the only way they could tolerate what is happening to her. Their distancing could show itself in private whispering, hollow cheerfulness, halting conversations, and perhaps even downright avoidance. Hard though it would be to bear, he has urged her not to look upon their disengagement as heartless or cruel, but to see it as another part of the inevitable process of dying — to be accepted in the comforting context that temporal life on earth is only an aspect of total human existence.

Driving to the hospital, he remembered how Eileen once said she was glad to be a Catholic because it gave her a priest with no emotive ties other than to his ministry. She had surprised him. Until then he never thought of Eileen as having even a rudimentary interest in his vocation. But she spoke feelingly and knowledgeably about the holiest and greatest of celibates — saints such as Francis; that their apostolic deeds and writings were influenced by their complete consecration to God. Because it is what he suspected Eileen wished, Father Breslin had picked up on her words, espousing the attraction of the celibate life; how it binds a person to God, Christ, Church, and ministry in a distinctive way. She had listened to him carefully, her eyes solemn. Afterward, she had smiled, satisfied. And, smiling too, he had thought: *How could I have even had the notion of telling her otherwise? Of explaining that celibacy is a continuing education in human frailty?* That would have given her too great a glimpse into his mind.

Father Breslin knows she senses his presence now. Her eyes, pupils dilated with pain-killing drugs, drift from the monitor toward where he stands in his surplice and stole. The family gathered around the bed are caught in some deep, primitive, and instinctive ritual. Her husband holds Eileen's hands, his fingers barely brushing her skin, as if he is afraid even such contact might cause her pain. The eldest son is at the foot of the bed, head bowed, a hand resting on the bedding, close to his mother's feet. This contact, too, is light yet deeply poignant. The other two sons stare silently at their mother, almost as if no words can communicate their true feelings, as if this most simple and powerful kind of human contact needs none.

Eileen's eyes turn back to the monitor. Father Breslin suspects that the medical equipment surrounding the bed, machines that click and ping, provide desperate confirmation for the family that all is not yet lost; that active measures are still being taken to keep Eileen's death at bay. He steps toward the bed. He walks slowly, careful to avoid the cables on the floor. He skirts a red-painted surgical cart. This is the "crash cart," the ultimate emergency aid in this aseptic world. The top shelf is clear, a work space for the variety of materials on the two lower shelves. Here are drugs to help stimulate cardiac output. Here are sponges, tourniquets, solutions, syringes, needles, probes, suction catheters, airways, an aspirator, and a defibrillator — a boxlike instrument capable of giving a powerful electric shock to start a stopped heart beating again. He reaches the bed.

All those around instinctively draw back. As they edge past him, none of them speaks. The doctor, nurse, and family retreat to the corridor, taking with them the air of barely suppressed frustration which Father Breslin long ago recognized is associated with the reluctance of the dying to succumb. Eileen, like so many others, in spite of all his preparation, is unwilling to surrender to her inevitable fate; she is simply fearful of being torn from life. Her distress is all the more harrowing for its silence and has affected both the doctor and nurse; he has taken refuge in too professional a calm; she is close to tears. In turn their discomfort has entangled itself in the grief of the family. Father Breslin suspects that deep down, they all know they have been looking at their own ultimate fate. But this stark, sterile, and brightly lit room is not the place for such thoughts.

The life-support equipment has leads that run to sensors attached to Eileen's chest and tubes connected to needles in each arm.

Father Breslin bends over Eileen and says in a soft and clear voice that he will give her the Viaticum, Holy Communion for those close to death. She will also receive the final anointing. He takes a wafer from its case and makes the sign of the cross before Eileen's face, aware of how little time he has. After murmuring a prayer, he bends closer to listen. From Eileen's lips comes a weak "Amen." He places the wafer upon her waiting tongue and gently closes her lips over the Host. She stares at him, too weak to swallow. He gently lifts her chin, allowing the wafer to slide down her throat. He takes from a pocket a tiny silver vial containing holy oil, unscrews the tip, and presses a thumb against the opening, moistening the skin. He places his thumb on her forehead and the palms of her hands, murmuring further prayers as he does so. After the rites are over, Father Breslin places her rosary in her hand. He glances at the monitor. The blips seem slower and weaker. He hurries to the door.

The family, followed by the doctor and nurse, return to the bedside. Eileen's husband resumes holding her hand, fingering the rosary beads and praying softly. His sons stand at his shoulder. Father Breslin is beside them. Across the bed the doctor and nurse stare intently at the screen. Suddenly, strange-looking, irregular beats appear. A red light flashes on the machine. The doctor checks Eileen's pulse. A straight, unbroken line has replaced the blips. The light no longer flashes. The nurse looks at Eileen's husband.

"She's gone."

The family turn and stare at Father Breslin, who offers his first words of reassurance.

"She has found God's peace."

He nods to the doctor and nurse to leave. They take the crash cart with them.

The silence in the room is broken when Eileen's husband says, without a trace of bitterness or self-pity, that Father Breslin should be glad he will never feel the pain of losing a loved wife.

Father Breslin remains silent. How can he explain to anybody at the best of times, let alone at this moment, that for him the past is a potent aphrodisiac; that somewhere in his subconscious those halcyon summers of long ago still live on; that while outwardly he appears barely to tip the scales at his emotional weight, inwardly he still carries those secret memories.

He begins to comfort Eileen's family. Just as he has helped her to die, so he has prepared, in these past months, her loved ones to face the painful and difficult adjustment her death will bring. He has urged them to recognize, and resist, an impulse to isolate themselves. In their close-knit community it would be especially sad if they turned away the helpful intentions of their relatives and friends. And if some do not rally around, it will be because they will not know what to do or say.

Father Breslin continues now in the same positive vein. His voice is calm and certain, devoid of any pity, but filled with a deep sense of sympathy. He urges them to see that Eileen's death must not be felt solely as a terrible blow. Nor must they blame themselves or those who have cared for her, the doctors and nurses. No one could have done more. There must be no displaced anger. Above all, there must be no temptation to turn away from God. He does not ask them, he says, to understand death but only to accept it.

Father Breslin pauses, waiting for his words to register. He is a fine judge of how long to remain silent and when to offer another constructive thought. The one he selects is something he had discussed with Eileen, shortly after the doctors told her, in their oblique way, there was no hope.

Looking down at her still face, he recalls the words she had quoted back at them. They were the ones used by the condemned Socrates before going to his death. In a voice exactly pitched to reach only the silent group beside the bed, Father Breslin recites: *"Now is the time that we were going, I to die and you to live. But which of us has the happiest prospect is unknown to anyone but God."*

Then quietly, without fuss, he detaches himself from the bedside tableau, leaving the others grouped stiffly silent. He knows that for the moment there is no more he can do. Out in the corridor he is an isolated figure in black. Doctors and nurses nod to him as they pass. They instinctively know the reason for his presence. He is part of the sudden sound of grief coming from the room he has left.

Other priests Father Breslin knows would have returned to offer further condolence. He walks on, out of the hospital. The family, he is certain, will draw sympathy and strength from one another. This is not the time for outsiders to be part of the shedding of tears. Besides, crying at this stage is more than part of the social catharsis of mourning; it demonstrates an acceptance of Eileen's death. It is a healthy sign.

Driving back to the parochial house, he ponders that flat and unequivocal statement of Eileen's husband about loving and losing a woman. How could any one of his parishioners even begin to suspect that, emotionally exhausting though it is, his committed involvement with them is also a safety valve for his own daily struggle to accept that the total celibacy the Church demands from him is neither based upon antisexual asceticism nor totally repressive, but rather is a condition that has allowed him an opportunity to achieve a higher state of Christian perfection?

He has never told anybody about his doubts that he has squandered that chance; that he once carried forward this failure year after year like a bad debt which will never be honored. How could he begin to tell anyone that for so long he had dangled on the rope of conscience? That he has thought he would never be able to exorcise that ghost with the capacity to recall his past desires and denials?

He has often wondered where she is and who she is with. Whether, if he had behaved differently, he would not now be returning to a loneliness which, in spite of all his efforts, he cannot totally pray away. Whenever he thinks about her, he always comes back to Kierkegaard's dictum: *To cheat oneself out of love is the most terrible deception: it is an eternal loss for which there is no reparation, either in time or in eternity.*

He wonders, again, where she is.

† † †

Victoria is late: not that she minds. She has been making well-managed entrances all her life. She assumes her lateness will give Paul, her host, more time to explain to his other guests about her. He is protective in that way, and she is glad of his sensitivity.

In the cab ride across the city, she has mused again on how prurient some people are when they learn her profession. If she were a psychiatrist — work for which she has certain basic educational qualifications — or a model — she has the figure and walk — Victoria knows people would not ask her to explain how she differentiates between sexual love and genital sex or where she stands on mortification of the flesh and the Pope's latest reminder that masturbation is still a mortal sin. And, of course, nobody would ask her about chastity; but because of who she is, they do.

Once, such questions made her feel uncomfortable; she believed they were put by people merely trying to shock her. But Victoria has, from the outset, answered them truthfully; trying not to sound too detached, defensive, or, above all, pious. Removing misunderstandings, she believes, is one of her talents.

Another is her clothes sense. Tonight, Victoria wears a Dior scarf around her neck, a Thai silk blouse, and a fashionable three-quarter-length skirt with matching blue shoes. She is tall and lightly tanned. She wears no makeup, jewelry, or flowers in her hair; nothing to detract from her natural good looks. Though graying, she looks younger than her forty-five years.

Paul is waiting for her at the door to the apartment he has scalloped out and remodeled from a slum attic. Following him around and being introduced to his guests, she is impressed with how well he now handles his homosexuality. Victoria believes a deeper understanding of her own sexual needs enabled her to help him overcome a broken marriage and a number of gay encounters before he settled into a relationship with his live-in lover, Mario.

Paul introduces her to a dress designer who makes a modest living copying Paris originals. He admires her blouse. Paul ushers her to a group listening to an actor describe why he has refused yet another offer from Hollywood. Victoria knows the man's only source of income is dubbing English-language films into Italian.

Finally, she reaches Jim, standing by a window, holding a glass of white wine for her. He is strongly built with a clean complexion and a face whose handsomeness owes more to his honestly happy smile than to its angular features. Jim combs his hair the way he has since he was a college freshman, parted on the left, with a cowlick that continues to defy a comb. He wears loafers, a sports shirt, and white linen pants. He does not look his age — close to fifty.

Victoria positions herself almost protectively, her back to the room, screening Jim from any guest who might wish to intrude. Accepting her wine, she kisses him on the mouth.

After a few moments of exchanged pleasantries, their conversation turns to an article just published in one of the specialist journals they both read. It confirms their own observations: a high percentage of those in religious life have no clear idea of how to handle their emotional and physical demands; a common problem among these celibates is their inability to integrate the simultaneous demands of being totally committed spiritual people and fully sexual persons.

Jim is almost enraged by John Paul II, the Polish-born Pope who, by a stroke of his pen, soon after being elected in October 1978, ended official dispensation from the priesthood. For months Jim has been trying to get authoritative figures from the Vatican on the numbers who, without bothering with ecclesiastical formality, have abandoned their vocation. But the Curia remains silent on the matter.

In the immediate wake of the Second Vatican Council, he reminds Victoria, "Christ's anointed on earth had jumped into the secular lifeboats in droves." Twenty years later, now he adds, "The official Church line is that husbands may desert wives and doctors may give up medicine but priests will not be dispensed."

Victoria murmurs: *"Tu es sacerdos in aeternum."*

The words are from the ceremony of ordination and used by a bishop when he places his hands on a man's head, symbolizing he will be a priest forever.

Yet, continues Jim, the desertions go on. Corpus, a Chicago-based organization formed to help those priests who have deserted because they have found the demands of celibacy impossible to follow, estimates there are in the United States alone over five thousand men living in a religious no-man's-land. They have had their priestly facilities withdrawn: no longer can they celebrate Mass, preach publicly, baptize, hear confession, or anoint the dying except in the most extreme circumstances when a priest in good standing is not available. Yet these men, in the eyes of the Church, are still priests; trapped and tethered to a religious system they reject but that will never release them.

"Tu es sacerdos in aeternum." There is a hint of anger and disillusionment in Jim's voice.

Victoria squeezes his arm. She, better than anyone in this room, knows his deep sense of frustration over the situation. She turns the conversation to the growing influence of Dignity, an association of Catholic homosexuals who wish to worship as "dignified gays." She mentions the names of several American bishops who discreetly support the organization. But in Europe, the more conservative hierarchies — among them those of Spain, France, and Ireland — tenaciously cling to the official Catholic teaching, defined in 1975 by the Sacred Congregation for the Doctrine of the Faith, that while homosexual orientation is morally neutral, the genital expression of it in any form is sinful.

She sips her wine and adds her own judgment. "Catch–Twenty-two."

Jim's eyes rest on Paul and Mario. How would they feel, he asks, if they knew that up until a hundred and fifty years ago it was still common practice for the Catholic Church in Europe to approve that homosexuals should be castrated, burned alive, judicially drowned, beheaded, or hanged?

They are still discussing the matter when Paul calls them to dinner. He is a fine cook; the meal is an epicurean delight. Jim and Victoria are at opposite ends of the table. They exchange glances constantly. The conversation, as she expected, has a distinctive undertone. The actor relates that when he was with a touring company he regularly visited gay public baths, because they were always the cleanest.

"Nice soft lighting and music. If somebody gave you the fish-eye you just said, 'I'm resting.' It was an accepted code. Nobody bothered you. Now I guess it's different."

Another guest boasts of his latest acquisition. He had persuaded a sculptor friend to create in solid silver a representation of two young men making love.

"I tell my straight friends it's a surrealist impression of the Alaska pipeline."

Mario, who has recently returned from New York, describes an establishment that must be the ultimate fantasy experience.

"The setup is designed so that you keep on descending to different levels. The more you spend, the further down you go. On one level there's bondage. On another, boys in wet leather. Stage by stage, it gets more exciting . . ."

Paul interrupts to say gay hedonism bores him. Mario looks hurt.

Another guest inquires of Jim if he has read *The Church and the Homosexual*. Jim has. Its author is a respected Jesuit. The essence of his argument is that a man knows he is a true homosexual only when he falls in love with another man; even if he is a priest, the experience should not affect his calling.

Victoria senses the focus of interest switching and narrowing. She is prepared and quotes from Willa Cather's novel *Death Comes for the Archbishop*, citing the words of one of the book's central characters, Father Martinez, who has an illegitimate son.

" 'Celibate priests lose their perceptions. No priest can experience repentance and forgiveness of sin unless he falls into sin.' " Pausing, she looks at Jim.

He completes Martinez's speech. " 'Since concupiscence is the most common form of temptation, it is better to know something about it.' "

The questions come.

Paul keeps a watchful eye, ready to intercede and deflect any inquiry he judges to be too pointedly personal. However, they are all the same, searching enough.

Afterward, on the way back to her apartment, Jim and Victoria agree it has not been hard to convince the other guests that while they frequently share the same bed and kiss or caress, they do not actually make love because she is a professed nun and he is a full-fledged priest.

Jim, however, will not sleep over on this night because in the morning he must celebrate early Mass.

† † †

Some things, he reminds himself, never change. They still call him Father Philippe.

He concentrates on the activities around the altar, conscious of Cap beside him. The boy is five years old, tall for his age, with his mother's fair hair. He is too young to understand the whispering directed at them.

Father Philippe has hardened himself against the tongue-waggers. But it maddens him that they talk about Margot behind his broad back, pointing out that he is not as carefully groomed as before; that his clothes are off the rack instead of custom-made; his after-shave is not the expensive cologne he once imported from Paris. Yet he knows there is still a sense of style about him most of the diocesan priests do not have. He suspects what really offends his detractors is that he has refused to crumble before their hostility by moving out of the parish to escape their gossip. Instead, supported by Margot and her family, Father Philippe has stood his ground; not defiant but determined. Part of his resolve is that he will appear at Mass when they least expect him. The scandalized stares have followed him all the way from the vestibule and past the confession boxes, as he leads Cap, arm protectively around the boy's shoulder, to their seats. Father Philippe senses what they are saying: that he is putting on weight and that his face, which has always been soft and boyish, has suddenly caught up with his forty-five years. That's what happens, he imagines them murmuring to each other, whan a priest does what he has done.

Father Philippe clasps his hands tightly. He is careful that no one, least of all Cap, can see his right thumbnail scraping the skin of his left hand; it's a nervous habit going back to his days as an altar boy. Being a priest had then been Father Philippe's only ambition.

Now, a survey shows that 94 percent of American Catholic boys between fourteen and eighteen have never considered the priesthood. All across the country seminaries stand derelict; not even determined Irish-American mothers or the handsome Roman-collared recruiters can fill them. The great days of the sixties are over; then magnetic cassocked figures rode from school to school delivering their vocational pitch: he who dares to be holy, dares to be different. They made it sound like joining the Green Berets, the favorite service branch of America's first Catholic President.

Father Philippe gazes at the sanctuary windows, sparkling in the diffused morning sun. The light gives the Christ on the stained glass the appearance of being crucified against a purple sky tinged with red, darker than blood. The body is luminous, hanging limply from hands nailed through the palms, the knees bent and weakened, the hair dark and wet from pain. Christ's wounds glow.

In one of his last conversations with the diocesan chancellor he had commended the authenticity of the engraving. The monsignor, of Irish descent, listened with a splintering stare as Father Philippe reminded him that it was generally accepted Christ was nailed through the wrists because His weight would have pulled the nails through His hands. He then explained he was one of those who now believed that Jesus was pinioned through the palms; that His feet were nailed so that they sloped downward. This would force Him to stretch upward, racking the limbs. Father Philippe said this was the unique torture of the Cross. The strain on Christ's outstretched arms would inhibit His lungs, making it impossible for Him to breathe unless He tried to take the strain of hanging on the frame through His knees. But in doing so the pressure of the nails in His feet would become unendurable. The torment of having constantly to rise and fall would have ended only with asphyxiation and death. The chancellor had coldly replied that he should have taken up medicine instead of the priesthood. It was the one time he came close to hating his superior.

Watching him concelebrate Mass with the Bishop, Father Philippe wonders whether the chancellor can ever understand the decision he has made and why the Church has given him no choice. Once more he gazes at the stained glass and its bearded man, almost naked, looking older than his reported thirty-three years. Has the chancellor any idea of what it is like now realistically to follow Christ? Did he not see that celibacy is a lost dream? Was he even remotely aware that there probably isn't a young priest in the whole Catholic world who cannot rationalize a nocturnal emission?

Would the monsignor ever begin to understand the argument that if a priest has never had a relationship with a woman, then he cannot know what he is giving up? Could the chancellor begin to grasp that he comes to Mass to remind him and all those like him, right along the spiritual ladder to Pope John Paul in Rome, that if a bush fire is beaten out in one corner it will often start in another?

The Bishop has recognized a shift is under way, even if it is one he cannot always understand, let alone control. He once said to Father Philippe, when they touched on the subject, that the monolithic and seemingly unmovable edifice of the Church had slipped, almost too swiftly for the eye to see, and it was now trying to extract itself from the trap of history. This, Father Philippe suspects, is why the Bishop has shown him compassion. This morning, as always, he is careful. If he has seen Father Philippe, he offers no recognition. This is part of their unspoken pact.

The preparations at the altar are complete. The Sacred Host has been removed from the tabernacle, itself guarded by a veil before the door, and the sanctuary lamp has its red, perpetual light burning steadily. In orderly file, pew by pew, people approach the altar rail, which separates the sanctuary from the rest of the church.

Father Philippe scoops Cap in his arms and, eyes fixed on the Bishop and chancellor, who are moving back and forth behind the rail dispensing Holy Communion, he joins the lengthening procession. He knows people are genuinely stunned to see him in the line. He ignores them. Instead, Father Philippe reminds himself that Jesus had said at the Last Supper that nothing is impossible to Him or those who follow His teaching. Father Philippe wants to partake in the extraordinary miracle by which He gives His Body and Blood for spiritual nourishment. These and other profound truths manifest themselves through the Holy Eucharist and are at the center of Catholic faith.

Father Philippe is close to the rail. He lowers Cap to the floor and grasps his hand, smiling reassurance. For the moment, every space at the rail is occupied with kneeling supplicants, waiting for either the Bishop or chancellor to pause before them. As they receive the wafer, they rise and leave, their places taken by others. Father Philippe reaches the head of the line.

A space becomes vacant at the chancellor's side of the rail. Father Philippe motions a woman behind him to take it. She steps forward, ignoring him and the child. A communicant rises from before the Bishop. Father Philippe moves swiftly forward, tugging Cap with him, and kneels in the vacant place. The boys stands at his back.

The two priests, working inward from opposite ends of the rail, meet in the middle and then retrace their steps. Shafts of sunlight flood the sanctuary. Through them, high above him, Father Philippe can see the crucified Christ. The effect is dizzying. He quickly lowers his eyes.

The Bishop and chancellor converge. Father Philippe looks up. There is a burning look in the monsignor's eyes. There, too, is that faint and familiar odor from his cassock; the unmistakable mixture of incense, sweat, hospital antiseptic, and the aroma of funeral parlors. Father Philippe remembers the monsignor has had four wake rosaries in the past week.

He can hear the voices softly intoning the hallowed *the Body of Our Lord Jesus Christ* as each wafer is taken from the paten. Father Philippe continues to stare ahead, willing himself that having come this far, he must remain kneeling. The chancellor is three places away. He can sense the man's puffy, red-rimmed eyes on him, not believing Father Philippe is, after all, actually kneeling at the rail. The Bishop reaches him. Impassively, he places a wafer on Father Philippe's tongue and murmurs the incantation. He moves on.

Father Philippe closes his eyes to squeeze back the tears. He experiences no triumph, far from it; only a feeling that, after all, God loves him. For a moment longer he kneels in prayer. He rises to his feet and, holding Cap's hand, walks to their pew.

Father Philippe is an ordained priest, but he knows he will never again say Mass and certainly not in this, his old church. Nor will he publicly recite the Psalms, sit in the priest's box of the confessional, receive new holy oils, or bury the dead. Yet in the eyes of the Church, Father Philippe will remain a priest until he dies or the pontiff in Rome and his advisers change their minds about granting him dispensation.

He suspects not even Margot always understands his feelings. Though he would never hurt her by saying so, he thinks even his wife cannot fully grasp what it feels like for him to be denied a vocation because he has chosen to love her.

Father Philippe has been married twice. With the covert help of the Church, his first union had been dissolved, so that he could return to his ministry. While still a priest in the eyes of the Church, he has wed Margot and fathered two children, Cap and little Daniel.

✝ ✝ ✝

Clare prepares the table with a minimum of fuss, not because she will again eat by herself, or because this is Friday evening, the start of the forty-eight-hour period in her week when she will not be answerable to the clock, school bells, and the repetitive questions of children. She makes the preparation from force of habit; an automatic gathering-up of the past into the present.

The Mistress of Postulants and Novices instilled in her the principle that no matter what the task, it should be carried out with the least commotion. Clare does not need to look at the whitened groove on her left-hand finger to recall the days when it had been covered by the silver wedding band personally blessed by the Bishop. Those were the days she devoutly believed her work was enough to fill her life, and when she was prepared to accept that the all-seeing Mistress had total control, down to the smallest detail; deciding, among other things, when Clare could receive a new pair of shoes, take a bath, or obtain a new toothbrush.

Sometimes she is ashamed of the anger that surfaces in her when she recalls those times. She wonders if it derives from a sense of failure in going back on what originally was meant to be a lifelong commitment. If she had failed, she tells herself, she could not help it. God only knew how hard she had tried. Besides, how could the Mistress have ever understood that Clare wanted to feel entirely responsible for what remained of her life; that she wanted to live with her body and not feel alienated from it.

Clare finishes setting the table. Cup, saucer, and plate are in symmetrical order with the cutlery. This meticulous alignment had once formed part of what the Order's Rule called Preparation. She can never forget the words the Mistress used to expand its meaning:

You must symbolically put your flesh to death, so that your love becomes absolutely focused on God's will.

Love is the word Clare most readily associates with her cloistered life and now resents. From the outset, it was drummed into her, the Mistress emphasizing her points with sharp taps of a ruler on her desk, that all Clare's ideas on love must change. What mattered was being able to love selflessly; being loved in return by any other person was beside the point, indeed was actively discouraged. She must accept the constant presence of only three persons in her life, God, Christ, and the Blessed Virgin Mary; they were the axes of the great Church she had been selected to serve. If ever she felt the onset of loneliness or despair, it could only be because Clare was no longer expressing love the way she should.

Then the Mistress had smiled and delivered words that Clare can, almost fifteen years later, instantly recall, in spite of all that has happened:

You are never alone. God is there. Look at Him and His love as if it were a mirror. When you love God you become His mirror and He becomes yours. To live in God's love is your greatest challenge.

To signify her commitment, Clare accepted that her hair must be covered with tight bands of linen and her body must be enveloped in shapeless cloth. The garments were intended to help her eliminate sensual feelings. On her head, she also wore a veil to proclaim she was consecrated to Christ. She was given a second name, biblical and familiar, and also a number. She was listed in the Order's Name Book as Sister Mary Luke — 136. She was told she must not see this as depersonalizing. She accepted it all as part of relinquishing the past.

Clare voluntarily had agreed to forgo numerous other rights: the freedom to travel at will, to visit or entertain friends as she wished, to go home when she felt like it, to have her family visit her without having to seek special permission. She could not wear, beneath her heavy serge, one single item that could be construed as feminine or frivolous. These restrictions, she was told, were necessary to help her become spiritually formed.

When Clare felt no longer able to meet such requirements, she took with

35

her into the outside world a solid, tangible memory. It was a piece of cardboard upon which she had neatly copied, during Recreation, an extract from Corinthians. For a long time, the card had lain in the back of a drawer, deliberately placed there in an effort to try to forget. One day, responding to another of the impulses the Mistress used to say would be her downfall, she decided to frame the text. Afterward, she had moved the card from room to room; from her bedside table to the kitchen work-top, giving it a few days in each place, before finally placing it on top of the television set. In its present position she can watch the screen while she eats alone from the table she has so carefully set. She knows the words by heart; they form her leitmotiv.

Love is always patient and kind; it is never jealous; love is never boastful or conceited; it is never rude or selfish; it does not take offense, and is not resentful. Love takes no pleasure in other people's sins but delights in the truth; it is always ready to excuse, to trust, to hope, and to endure whatever comes. . . . In short, there are three things that last: faith, hope, and love; and the greatest of these is love.

She has another link with her past in that she is still a virgin. There had been nothing unusual about virginity when she joined the Order at eighteen. Now, it is different; girls frequently have full sexual experience before going into religious life. But at the age of thirty-four she recognizes the reality that she might live the remainder of her life without physically knowing a man. Still, strong within her, more than any other, is the idea the Mistress had promoted:

Sexuality is the enemy of chastity. The demands of the body can be overcome.

Clare was, she now sees, far too young when she committed herself to the concept that chastity can become easier through prayer; that bodily urges can wither and die by the recitation of the rosary.

Because of Tom she now knows differently.

She keeps his photograph out of sight, thumbtacked to the inside of the door of her wardrobe. It depicts a tall, smiling man, not unhandsome, in his early forties.

Clare took the picture some months after leaving the convent. She had saved from her salary as a teacher to buy the camera. She remembers in detail when she snapped him. It was a Saturday morning, outside the city's main art museum. That was also the day she first raised the subject of their relationship and then only to say that she did not want him to think she would ever ask for it to go beyond what he wanted. It really was no different now, she added quickly, than in those days when they first met and she was a nun. Clare wanted him to know that she realized it had to be a relationship without promises, having no real future. She knew she was deceiving herself. It didn't matter.

So it began. They would speak on the phone each Friday evening when she was back from school, agreeing to meet the following day at some place of mutual interest. It could be an art exhibition, a concert hall, a theater. Afterward, they might end up in a pub for a drink and sometimes go on to a restaurant for supper. Because she earned far more than he did, she would insist on paying her way. After some protest he accepted. She would meet Tom each Saturday as if he was enough of a reward for a week of hard work. The traveling and the demands of the classroom left her very tired and emotionally drained. Tom was a reviver. He was understanding and also a good listener.

Gradually she came to realize she wanted more. She wanted to take his arm as they stood waiting to cross a street; to surprise him as they sat in a darkened auditorium, watching a play or listening to a concert, by placing her hand on his knee. Once over dinner she had almost reached across the table and impulsively kissed him. They were in a bistro in an unfamiliar part of the city and had been talking about their childhood — they had had remarkably similar upbringings with loving but firm parents who had steeped them in the fullest meaning of faith. She had known then that she loved him and wanted to tell him and hear his response, to complete the circle. But Clare did none of these things because of who he was.

She began to notice little traits in him. He was at pains never to commit himself fully, always holding back something of himself; yet at the same time he showed he could be vulnerable and needed reassurance. He had a natural radar to detect any threat to his position. All this had only increased her desire for him. At times she felt the tension to be both exquisite and unbearable, and he too must have realized that the space between them was charged with sexuality.

The photograph shows none of this. Nor does it reveal, by as much as a glimpse, anything of the bouts of stress that suddenly began to plague Tom, giving him crippling pains in the back accompanied by blinding headaches. He would then telephone her on a Friday evening and beg off meeting her next day. She would invariably use a consoling voice but all the while she suffered a concealed anguish and that particular disappointment that accompanies unfulfilled love.

It was after the third Friday in a row when he offered a particularly bad headache as an excuse for not meeting that the blow fell. She had been especially solicitous although careful not to go too far. There was certain territory she knew she must never stray into. One forbidden area was to visit him. But next day she had impulsively telephoned him and had been told he had gone away for the weekend. The woman sounded cold and suspicious. Clare risked one more question, asking if Tom had recovered from his sickness. The woman said she must have the wrong number — there was no one sick at this house — and hung up without saying another word. That night Clare dreamed Tom phoned her and explained everything.

It was two weeks later when he did ring. That Friday he said he would pick her up next day and they would drive into the hills. When he collected her in his unwashed car, he wore jeans and a short-sleeved shirt. She had never seen him look more casual or relaxed. She noticed the muscles in his arms and the dark hair covering them. She thought that intellectually he might deny his sexuality but his body confirmed it.

She had known something was seriously wrong when they had driven in silence. Normally he would have found a dozen things to talk about. Abruptly, he had parked on the edge of the road. She thought he had stopped to admire the view of a waterfall cascading in the distance. Instead, he had told her he could no longer meet her. She had asked, in a small voice, why. Tom had restarted the car and driven a full mile before answering. He merely said she should not make it harder than it was.

She had wanted to question him, as though by pushing the knife even deeper into herself she could perform an operation that would cure her forever of love. She wanted to ask him about the weekend when he had lied to her, to confront him with evidence, convicting him in her eyes forever — anything that would force her to recognize the extent of her illusions. Clare had said nothing.

When Tom dropped her off, he said very quietly how she had always known there was a part of his life she could never share and he was grateful that she understood. Then he drove away.

In all the months that followed she has never for a moment considered that she should stop loving him. She has tried to tell herself that she only wishes he would accept her love as a gift. A part of her mind says she has hoped that Tom, of all men, could have done that. Then another part reminds her there must always be pain in loving someone who is already as committed as Tom.

He is a priest.

✝   ✝   ✝

Late though the hour is, past midnight, Andrew continues to write at the desk in his bedroom. From somewhere beyond the massive walls of the seminary, voices on a radio argue. Suddenly they are gone, as an unseen hand switches to a music station. Formulating his thoughts about love into words, Andrew has decided, is even more of a commitment than the sexual act itself. Words transform his physical memories into a permanent record, forcing him to give substance to moments plucked from the recesses of his mind. There are times when he feels he is writing about somebody else. It is one way to dim the pain he experiences when he tries to find new ways of expressing himself about Jane.

He pauses over a sentence. He has been keeping the diary since his first day in the seminary. On its flyleaf he has blocked out the word PRIVATE. The diary is his way of reminding himself that in the rigidly structured routine of the seminary he has managed to "keep a little piece of myself which only the Almighty knows about." The music is lost in a sudden breeze. This is the thunderstorm season; the air is warm and humid.

A Polaroid snapshot of Jane is Scotch-taped to a board festooned with notes from his tutors and his spiritual director. In the photograph she has a halo of blonde hair, generous mouth, slightly crooked because she is smiling. The print is more than three years old. But his images of her remain vivid. This is why he is having to pause constantly and remind himself of his promise of faith.

Below in the street there are voices, hollow and lonely, like fading footsteps in an empty room. Andrew likes the analogy; he writes it down. He can sense the storm brewing. It spurs him on. He wants to be finished before the clouds burst.

He has sometimes wondered what God might think of some of the diary entries. About his admission to a powerful ambition to rise high in the Church, "perhaps even become Pope." Of his confession that he finds some of the other seminarians social bores and a few of the tutors riddled with pointless dogma. He has also confided his own shortcomings: his impatience, his lack of humility and generosity. He has written: "I must give, give, give and keep on giving because that is what the Lord wants of me."

But what, he has also wondered, would God say about his feelings for Jane? She dominates the diary. Her presence is there on page after page: words and descriptions that cause Andrew the kind of emotional pain he has never thought possible. That is why he hesitates over how much he can put on paper. It hurts too much. It also flies in the face of everything he is trying to achieve. He knows that the deeply felt emotions for Jane constantly rise to threaten his progress toward a promising clerical career.

Lightning opens the sky. The thunder rolls in like bombs. Andrew puts down his pen. Storms produce a secret fear in him because of their hidden energy: they make him feel insignificant. The dread is not unlike the feeling he had experienced at the outset of his love affair with Jane. Another fork of lightning and then the rain rushes across the city in great waves before the storm passes quickly.

Then, once more, the physical memory of Jane — the musk of her body, the sheen of her hair, and the smooth hardness of her nipples under his touch — permeates the monastic room. The familiar excitement courses through him. He is a teenager again, no longer a man close to thirty, in his third year of training for the priesthood. He is aware of what is happening. He is also determined this time to stop nature from collecting her dues for being abused and ignored by him. He will not pay the price for his self-imposed chastity and be punished for his celibacy. Andrew remembers what the spiritual director had said:

Temptation is always there. But remember, if you yield, you are breaking a solemn promise to be faithful to God and the Church. Don't see your vocation as the waste of a man. Be realistic. Recognize the challenge. Face the Devil in you, in me, in all of us who have been called.

Andrew goes to the small but select collection of books on the shelves along one wall. They are old friends, the pages well thumbed, some passages underscored. He begins to read a comforting interpretation of Genesis, the very first account of the Creation, the one that says God was clearly concerned about man and aware of his struggles with loneliness. He turns to the New Testament. On a slip of paper between the pages of the Gospel of Matthew he has inserted his own interpretation of the Apostle's views on marriage. "It is not possible for everyone because of its special demands. But neither is celibacy. And Matthew seems to be saying that either is acceptable as long as a person chooses to follow Jesus. But there seems to be a choice. Marriage or celibacy."

He skims one book after another, seeking the confirmation and reassurance he knows they contain. Andrew returns to his desk, pondering, mentally framing a thought, conscious again of Jane. Once more he begins to write, quickly, the way he does when taking notes during lessons on moral theology. "No one can say that sexual abstinence is better than sexual intercourse. Nor is it less perfect. Both intercourse and abstinence are New Testament values. They cannot be presented as the supreme Christian value. That value is giving one's life to Christ. Doing that means the highest form of lasting love is possible. One nothing can shake."

Andrew reads back what he has written. He picks up his pen and adds a sentence. "My love for Jane is lasting."

Andrew stops writing. Tears begin to blot the page. He pushes the diary aside.

A scene from a novel comes into his mind — Huxley's *Point Counter Point*. He recalls it from his university days. A couple had shared a bath and the author said, "Of such is the Kingdom of Heaven." He knows why that image remains vivid when a thousand others have been obliterated under the demands of the seminary. He regularly had shared a bath with Jane. The memory is still fresh in his mind, part of the swirl of images she can still arouse in him. The spiritual director has advised him how to cope:

At these moments ask God to help you. Beg Jesus to intervene. Don't give in. Confront your feelings. Reduce them to the essentials. Down to the choice you have made.

Andrew begins to scribble on a piece of paper, alternatively, *Celibacy. Jane.* Each time he completes either word, he adds a question mark. Then he draws a line through the word and writes the next one. In this way he fills the sheet.

The images grow stronger, detail after detail retained in all its crystal and destroying clarity. He can recall the bedroom they shared, the way she had positioned each item of furniture. Some of it had been there when they rented the apartment: the double bed with a missing leg, propped up with a stack of old textbooks; the faded yellow cotton curtains; the Victorian painting of the Firth of Forth Bridge in the dark wooden frame he thought ghastly but she loved. They had bought a number of items at local sales, bidding against other students from the university, afterward carrying home their purchases in triumph. There was a mahogany cabinet with an inlaid black marble top that she had placed on her side of the bed. In it she stored her curlers, setting lotion, diaphragm, and gel. He would squat naked on the bed and watch her, totally nude, cream and insert the cap. Then he would reach for her.

They had bought a table for his side of the bed, using money from both their grants. On it he had kept the radio that, apart from Jane's photo, is the only visible link with the past. The radio is on his desk, close to the diary in which he has confided so many unsettling remembrances.

There was the hard-back Edwardian dining-table chair they had argued over; he thought the price inflated, she had not. She had placed the chair beneath the bedroom window. They used it as a clotheshorse, dumping their Levi's, T-shirts, and underwear on it when the urge to make love became intense. He had read somewhere that sexual responses are more individual than fingerprints; if this is so, then he is certain they had perfectly matching prints. Their lovemaking was always a secret triumph between them, a communion of bodies and minds, producing a shared sense of wonder and jubilation. In the long deep bath that was big enough for them both, they would soak, bodies pressed together, and they would make love, joined like sea urchins, her eyes closed as though she were alone at the end of some journey. The last time they had bathed together she had begged him not to rush, to see how long he could remain inside her. To encourage him she had whispered those three words that still held him captive. "I love you."

Andrew opens his eyes, brushing away tears with the back of his hand, and rises to his feet. From a jacket he fishes out a handful of coins. He looks at his watch. It is almost one o'clock in the morning. It will be close to midnight where she is.

He begins to pace the room. It is a small, cluttered place, no more than twelve paces by eight. His belongings are scattered everywhere: shoes, shirts, shorts, exercise books, old newspapers, letters. Jane had often complained how untidy he was and he tried to make light of it by saying that being in love makes everyone careless of everything. She had looked at him carefully before turning away. Was that the start, he often wonders, the beginning of the end? He doesn't know. It is one of the many uncertain details about their relationship that even now still haunts him.

He can, he knows, go to the seminary's chapel and pray her away, or at least try to. It is open all night for just such purposes. He knows that several seminarians regularly use it as a refuge from their sexuality. Barefooted, he pads from his cell-like room, hurries down the corridor, past all the other identical rooms. Dark though it is, he knows his way: he has made this journey many times at this hour. He is excited now as he reaches the top of the staircase of this building, which for almost four centuries has housed young men being trained for the priesthood.

He edges down the stairs along which saints and popes have trod, on past the Corridor of the Cardinals. Though it is too dark to see them, he knows the portraits of their Eminences are there on the walls. Finally, he reaches the ground floor. The seminary's public telephone is beside the massive sixteenth-century front door, thick enough to withstand a battering ram. Nothing disturbs the silence. He pauses, breathing slowly, getting his emotions under control. He looks at the coins in his hand. One by one he inserts them into the telephone box. Careful though he is, the noise as each one drops through the slot is loud. But having come this far, nothing will make him stop. He knows he is surrendering all reason, but he is hopelessly consumed. The last coin drops into the box. Andrew begins to dial, slowly, careful not to make a mistake and have to repeat the long sequence of numbers. He knows he should feel guilt, but love, as he once told Jane, can turn him into a monster. He presses the receiver to his ear. He hears a series of clicks. Then silence. He groans aloud; he must have misdialed. He is about to start again when the ringing tone sounds. A sleepy woman's voice answers. With infinite gentleness Andrew kisses the receiver and replaces it, breaking the connection with Jane.

Slowly he retraces his steps, head bowed, dejected. He is shocked and disgusted at his adolescent longing and lust for Jane, more so because she is now another man's wife. Equally, he knows there are inner forces convincing him that a nocturnal telephone call across Europe to hear for a few brief seconds the voice of the girl he rejected to become a priest is one way for him to cope with a life of celibacy.

Safely back in his room, Andrew sits at his desk and records what he has done and how he feels about it. Gradually, self-forgiveness emerges through his words. He has not been himself and God will understand his weakness. This is why Christ died on the Cross, to help sinners like him.

His diary is already filled with questions. He adds more.

"In the end is it like this for every priest and nun? Are the demands on their sexuality not only sacred but cruel? Is it possible to live in the midst of the world without enjoying its pleasures?"

Andrew, as yet, has no satisfactory answers. He wonders if there are any.

†

COMMITMENTS

Marriage has many pains,
but celibacy has no pleasures.
— SAMUEL JOHNSON, *Rasselas*

CHAPTER 3

†

Once a Priest

Seamus Breslin finds pleasure in the most ordinary of things. Among them is awakening promptly and, in the few moments of lying quietly under the bedding, having time to think: trying, as the Dean of Studies repeatedly urges, to see himself as a sentient cog in the vast, intricate machine of life. Rhetoric is one of the Dean's indulgences. The only other one, as far as he knows, is scalding-hot tea, which the man drinks with relish, punctuating his gulping with loud sighs. The sounds of a solitary mind, Seamus has termed it, pleased at his growing ability to judge a personality through careful study.

Observation, he is certain, helps make a good priest, just as much as mastering Latin, Gregorian chant, and the mystery of prayer. While they are important, especially Latin, the language of the Church, they are only a part. So are lilies on the altar at Easter; burning incense; the taste of wine from the chalice; the sadness of so much organ music; the daub of grit on the forehead for Ash Wednesday, a reminder of the mortality of man — that he comes from and will return to dust.

It is what all this combines to create that matters to Seamus: the immensely comforting faith of Catholicism. For as long as he can remember, he has always been stirred by the unchallengeable belief of his faith, with its own language and ritual that distinguish it from all other religions. There is fish on Friday and the sign of the cross to be made when passing a funeral or graveyard: confession and penance; plenary indulgences and papal encyclicals; and over it all, the Holy Father in Rome, a figure almost as mystical as God. It all fuses, he knows, to make Catholicism different. This is why he wants to be a priest. It is no ordinary job.

Seamus firmly believes that the priesthood is all about preparing others here on earth for the life everlasting. He has been told so, in one way or another, on every one of his days in the seminary. Acceptance has made it that much easier to live in this place of rigid moral laws and careful controls.

On the first day the Dean told the newcomers he assumed they fully accepted that sexual abstinence is absolutely necessary. Seamus's spiritual director tried to be more expansive, saying celibacy was ultimately a personal mystery, not to be explained by argument. He added that the only real way to overcome a threat to chastity is through prayer.

This was after Seamus reported an experience that filled him with remorse and the fear he had committed mortal sin. The director questioned him carefully about how deeply asleep he had been before he awoke to find his pajamas sticky with seminal fluid. Satisfied, he told Seamus he had not committed a sin, but experienced a "spontaneous emission." There had been no volition.

Seamus is twenty-one years old on this summer morning and a virgin; he has never taken out a girl or kissed any women except his mother and sisters on their cheeks. Almost all of his heroes and heroines have "Saint" before their names. He still cannot imagine who he'd been dreaming about on that night. This morning he still found a place in his first prayers of the day to express his thanks for another undisturbed sleep.

Afterward he begins to pack carefully his suitcase made of pressed cardboard, because his mother has a passion for neatness. Tidiness is as much a part of Anne Breslin as her bluntness, which is based on her dislike of pretense; as her tenderness, which never verges on the sentimental; as her total belief in the invincibility of the Roman Catholic Church over all other faiths. From her he has acquired a mind marked by civility, mild skepticism, and detachment, joined to an iron will.

He continues to fold and pack underwear, socks, spare white shirts, a black sweater for the cool evenings. On top he places his Bible.

This is his forty-sixth month of training, of commitment to an ideal which he still can only best describe as "a call from God." It singled him out from other young men beyond the walls of the seminary of Clonliffe on the outskirts of Dublin.

In spite of all the long hours he devotes to various sports, he is puny: short and wiry, slope-shouldered and bespectacled. But there is about him an alertness beyond his years. In his time at Clonliffe he has shown that he is nobody's fool and that he suffers fools badly. This sometimes worries him. Those who are forming his religious outlook — the Dean, and his spiritual director, his tutors in theology and liturgy — stress that humility and compassion are among the essentials of a good priest. Yet, try as he may, Seamus will not tolerate stupidity. In this respect he is very much like his father. The thought does not please him.

Nor does he relish the prospect of once again having to deal with his father's merciless questions. On his last visit home his father wanted to know if Seamus didn't at least feel a twinge of longing at the news that one old classmate was getting married and another had fathered a child. Didn't that stir something in him? Fighting down the temptation to tell his father to stop goading, Seamus calmly quoted the words Matthew ascribes to Jesus: *"For there are eunuchs, who were born so from their mother's womb; and there are eunuchs, who were made so by men; and there are eunuchs who have made themselves eunuchs for the kingdom of heaven. He that can take, let him take it."*

It was a mistake. His father hooked his thumbs into his braces and said there was nothing in the Gospels to show that Christ recommended celibacy. In vain, Seamus tried to argue, but his father cut him off, growling about fancy words never winning the day, and went off to the pub. His mother sat in her chair, silent, too proud to show her hurt.

Seamus tucks a pair of shoes into the suitcase; they need mending. But it will be a while longer before he will take them to the cobbler. The family budget is already fully stretched to keep him in Clonliffe.

Battered though it is, the suitcase is unusual in that it has sturdy tin locks, a rarity nowadays. This is the fifth year of World War Two, and metal of any sort from neutral Ireland is being sent to England to help build planes and make bomb casings.

Seamus had been ambivalent about the outcome of the struggle between Hitler's Germany and Churchillian Britain until that day bombs fell on Dublin not far from the seminary. The dust from the debris barely settled before the rumors swirled through the cold and forbidding corridors of Clonliffe. Winston Churchill had personally authorized the air raid as a warning of what would follow unless Ireland openly committed itself to the Allies. Hitler was behind the attack, launching it as a brutal reminder that nowhere in Europe was beyond his reach. There were almost as many rumors as seminarians.

Born and raised in a staunch Republican family; his mind filled with tales of the atrocities committed by Englishmen on Irish soil; aware that his father had supported Franco and Fascism in the Spanish Civil War; convinced that Britain's new partner in the war against Nazism, Russia, is the greatest threat to Catholicism — despite all this, Seamus has surprised himself by having no doubts who dropped the clutch of bombs on Dublin. They were uncaring Nazi pilots, the same sort of fliers he has seen in the movie newsreels attacking Warsaw and Rotterdam. From then on he has been committed to an Allied victory. The strength of his feelings continues to astonish him. He wonders if they are appropriate for a priestly life.

Seamus knows that other, very different, deeply buried emotions also trouble him. One episode disturbed him so much that at the time he felt unable to go to his regular confessor at Clonliffe. Instead, in the semidarkness and total privacy of a confession box in a church he had never before, or since, entered, he accused himself, as rite demands, of mortal sin. After reciting the first part of the Confiteor, the prayer used in the Sacrament of Penance, Seamus confessed how Brigid was the first woman to bring him face to face with sexual temptation.

†

The Mass of Exposition of the Blessed Sacrament, one of the great celebrations in the Catholic calendar, was reaching its climax in the parish church of a County Carlow village. It was the closing ceremony of the *Quarant' Ore*, the Forty-Hour Vigil, throughout which the parishioners took turns continuously praying and singing hymns. Their faith was visible on their faces as they stood packed tight in their pews: row after row of men in blue serge suits, women in print dresses, boys and girls in the garments they wore for First Communion.

To be among them was to remind himself of his roots. Though his parents moved to Dublin when he was a baby, the tug of the land was still in him; he liked nothing better than to feel bog moss under his feet or to smell pungent burning peat. Every year since entering Clonliffe he had come here for the summer, staying on an uncle's farm, training the parish choir for the *Quarant' Ore*, initiating them in the intricacies of Gregorian chanting. He had worked them hard and had been thrilled at how well the villagers had responded: broad country accents had under his tutelage become unified and mellifluous in the responses, introits, and antiphons that had soared to the rafters of this starkly simple place of worship.

Now, as they led the packed congregation in a final hymn, Seamus, watchful as always, ears attuned for a false note, felt intensely proud of what he had achieved with his choir. He had indeed handled them well.

He only wished he could say the same about Brigid. She was, in the front row of the choir, singing in perfect harmony. Her eyes were fixed intently on him. She was petite, the way girls from Carlow often were: jet-black hair, bobbed in the front and falling to her shoulders; velvety black eyes set in an oval face; her skin free of makeup and tanned, for this was August and it had been an exceptionally hot summer for Ireland.

They had known each other for less than a month; twenty-three days, to be exact. But he could remember every one of them, every hour he had spent with this nineteen-year-old who worked in the village store, whose father was dead and mother in domestic service with one of the landed gentry families whose mansions dotted this pleasant countryside.

After the nightly choir practices, he had escorted Brigid home, sweltering in his black clerical suit, cycling through the country lanes that led to her mother's cottage. One night she had told Seamus of her dream of moving to Dublin. To Brigid it was as remote and exciting as the New York, Paris, or London she saw in the weekly film screenings in the church hall. Perhaps, she added, if she came to Dublin, there might be an opportunity for them to meet. She had dropped her gaze to give his discomfort privacy. He remained staring blankly ahead, knowing Brigid could become an occasion of sin. He should tell her, plainly, why they could not meet again.

Next night he took her home once more, pedaling slowly and saying little. Approaching the cottage, she dismounted and he followed, being careful to keep their bicycles between them. She looked at him quizzically and had quietly asked what was the problem. He said there was none, and had laughed, trying to leap over his embarrassment and hating himself even more for not being able to explain. Brigid had looked at him steadily. He had waited for her to say something. Instead, she mounted her bicycle and pedaled away. During the next few days he felt increasingly unsettled. He realized Brigid was endangering the sexual purity the laws of the Church demanded of him. He sensed the threat in her eyes. The knowledge terrified him. His lectures had not prepared him for this. There had been oblique, guarded cautions about temptresses and wanton women sent by the Devil to seduce priests from their celibate calling. He knew she was none of these. Brigid's commitment to her faith was as deep as his own. He could also say, in all truth, that they had not even touched, let alone embraced or kissed.

Yet he also knew that he wanted to hold her in his arms and kiss her with a passion he never realized he possessed. His desire had left him in a state of acute anxiety, mingled with guilt, a sense of failure, a feeling of shame and unworthiness. In a desperate effort to find a solution, he had tried to intellectualize his emotions, applying the same techniques he used successfully in Clonliffe to analyze a scriptural passage. But academic rationalization and being in love, he had discovered, have nothing in common.

Watching Brigid, her eyes intent on him as the hymn reached its final verse, Seamus realized that throughout the entire service his own eyes had never left hers when closed in prayer. Later, outside her cottage, he put down his bicycle. Then, without a smile, with no word, but with great seriousness, he took her hands and gently tried to remove them from her bicycle handlebars. She resisted, gripping the bars tightly, a mildly surprised expression in her eyes. He had fought his shyness, looking hard and steadily at her, feeling as if he was leaping from a precipice, hoping she would catch him, but not knowing if she would.

"Why?" she had asked, holding his gaze.

He could not understand the question, or the sudden tears in his eyes. Why was sadness mingling with his passion?

"Do you really want to?" she asked.

"Of course." He had paused, frightened by his own boldness. "Do you?"

She had not answered, but stood there, stiffly silent, his hands gripping hers. Finally, when she spoke it was softly, like the trembling in her fingers. "Do you want to kiss me?"

Her words shocked him.

She had spoken quickly, sensing her mistake. "Would you like some tea? It'll be okay to come in."

She had turned and he was about to follow when, out of the darkness, a new voice came.

"You'll not be bringing him in! Get to bed, girl."

Seamus had jumped on his bicycle and pedaled away furiously. Long after he was out of earshot, he could still remember the angry voice of Brigid's mother.

Next day he returned to Dublin.

✝

Having unfolded his story to the confessor in that unfamiliar church, Seamus had been reassured by the priest that he had not put his vocation in jeopardy — but that he should look upon the incident as a warning. He was determined that when he returned to his uncle's farm he would avoid not only Brigid but any woman who showed the slightest interest in him.

Now, before taking the slow train to Carlow, he must go home. His mother will be eagerly waiting to hear how the semester had gone. He is less certain about his father's mood. He had lost count of the times he had sat in his seminary room and prayed for God to give his father the strength to stop drinking. His sottishness was casting not only an ever-lengthening shadow over his own life and testing as never before his wife's love, but also filling Seamus with emotions he knew had no place in the heart of any would-be priest. He feels anger, resentment, shame, and guilt over his father. He blames himself for not being more resolute. He should have reasoned with his father, laid out the indisputable evidence, perhaps even begged, done *anything* to make him see reality.

Instead, Seamus had remained silent. In recognizing this, self-recrimination had given way, as it always did, to the bitter knowledge that he was probably the last person in the family able to influence his father. Seamus knew that, apart from the war, there was still no way he could safely discuss any subject with his father without running the risk of provoking one of those sudden, volcanic outbursts. As long as he could remember, these explosions had been the dominant feature of their relationship. They reached far back into his childhood.

Barely eight years old, Seamus had dismantled his father's pocket watch, long defunct anyway, and having replaced the useless workings, was unable to close the case. In his anxiety to do so he clenched it between his jaws, leaving his teeth marks on the casing. That night his father found the watch. He held it up, demanding to know who had dared touch it, let alone bite the case. Seamus, close to terror, blamed one of his sisters. Her teeth did not fit the grooves. He told Seamus to try. His teeth matched the indentations. His father had beaten him mercilessly. Just as he had lost count of the number of times he had prayed for his father, Seamus could not begin to estimate the number of thrashings that had punctuated his upbringing. In his father's eyes his son had, in a sense, been cast as his intimate foe; it was almost as if Kevin Breslin resented the fact that Seamus resembled him only physically.

His dominant characteristics came from his mother. They shared the same determination to see a thing through; they had the same thirst for knowledge. There were other strong ties: God, and a rooted belief that the family was a storehouse of secrets and it was a vital function of each of its members to keep them intact. There could be no greater crime in Anne

Breslin's eyes than to display in public so much as a bone of any family skeleton. Her son had the same passionate conviction.

As usual, Seamus is ready well before the taxi will pick him up. It was not that he is eager to leave Clonliffe for the summer break: far from it. He enjoys seminary life to the full. But he has always had this habit of being prepared well in advance. In a way it has helped him to be a model student from the outset.

†

Geographically, Seamus's journey to Clonliffe has been short — a few miles from the family home in the suburbs of Dublin. Spiritually, his experiences in the seminary have placed an irreversible distance between himself and his past.

The recollections are still clear: playing cricket; in one memorable year coming out tops in mathematics for the entire country's school system; discovering, for the first time, that Lent really meant giving up something precious; learning from an older boy that it was a mortal sin to enter a Protestant church; discovering how to hang his weight between his elbows and knees when he knelt on bare boards during devotions; being instructed by a priest on how to become a dependable altar server; being told by a nun who is a relative that it would be a fine thing to get married one day but even more of a triumph if he became a priest. It was the first time he had heard of religious vocation being placed above wedlock. It was an energizing thought. He began to think seriously about the priesthood, and ponder if God was indeed calling him. It seemed the most natural of things to give what talent he had back to God in the form of religious life. These memories are still in his mind, the charter steps to his final decision. But he sees them now with the detachment that is part of his training.

He has been taught at Clonliffe that while human relationships matter, and are important for both mental and physical reasons, they are ultimately for others. His tutors constantly have reminded him that he is a student on what amounts to sufferance; that the demands for a place in one of Ireland's most distinguished seminaries far exceed availability; that his call from God is no guarantee he has the staying power to survive both the spiritual and physical rigors of seminary life.

The concept of formal training for the priesthood spread after the Council of Trent approved it in the sixteenth century, decreeing that an apprentice to Holy Orders must be at least twelve years old and not a bastard in the literal sense. The same principles were applied at Clonliffe.

Those selected for vocational training were young and hopefully chosen to meet the original requirements of Trent — that a candidate is selected "before the habits of vice take possession of the whole man." Behind this stricture was a logic that had survived four hundred years: that, just as metal tarnishes unless polished, so a boy would be at risk unless kept in a hermetic atmosphere like that of Clonliffe.

The threat of dismissal was constant, ready to be invoked for a long list of infractions: missing chapel; talking during the periods of silence; not knowing the name and history of the saint of the day; failing to make use of every minute of study time; being seen in the company of any woman except a nun or a student's own relative; entering another seminarian's room. In Clonliffe the staff paid particular attention to monitoring all friendships. But no one mentioned a fear of homosexuality. It belonged to the wider taboo on all official discussion on sex. Clonliffe was an authentic asexual haven, a sanctified terrarium where all energies were directed to a common cause — creating worthy successors to the original fisher of men.

Nevertheless, Seamus had managed to establish one friendship; within the bounds of the rules, the relationship was relaxed. In part, Seamus realized, it was because he was so dissimilar to Patrick Gallagher. There was an air of worldliness about Patrick which was not there in the other seminarians. He knew as much about jazz as he did about chant. He had traveled in Europe; he spoke French and Spanish as fluently as he did Gaelic. He made everything he did seem easy, engagingly deprecating his efforts by saying he was making up for misspent years at school. His real gift for Seamus was that he could find out things. Nobody could skim a row of books in the Clonliffe library for facts more quickly than Patrick could.

This, in the end, was how Seamus came to learn a little more about celibacy. Directed by Patrick's unfailing sense of where information was buried in leather-bound tomes that had often lain undisturbed for years, he read about the *brahmacharya* of Hinduism, with its emphasis on total discipline and education; how poverty and celibacy are at the center of Buddhism. He had discovered that during the first three centuries of the Catholic Church, there were almost no barriers placed upon any cleric wishing to marry. He had traced back the earliest legislation to the fourth century, when the Spanish Council of Elvira ordered all clergy to "abstain from their wives." The decree did not actually forbid marriage but merely demanded abstinence. Total celibacy grew only with the rise of monasticism, and the Madonna became the new ideal as Christianity spread throughout the Roman Empire. Her virginity became universally accepted as a Catholic tenet, forming a cornerstone for celibacy.

In the library Patrick had unearthed a dissertation by a former president of Clonliffe, arguing that as well as any form of forbidden physical sex for a priest, there was the equal danger from psychological sex, the emotional attraction of persons for each other; that sensuality engaging the mind was as difficult to handle as were physical urges.

It was Patrick who risked asking about celibacy in the Dean's ordination class. The Dean stared at him in stony disbelief, pinching his nose with his thumb and finger. Finally, answering the question, he said celibacy is a gift. No one refused a gift, especially when it comes from God. They should pray every day to keep it intact.

After the experience with Brigid, Seamus was more determined than ever not to do anything that would put his vocation at risk. Every one of his prayers contained an entreaty to protect him from all mortal sins.

Seamus's formative years passed in an atmosphere where prayer was seen as some mysterious factor working in an unfathomable and unilateral manner, divorced from all other mortal thoughts. It required human coop-eration, but the way it produced results was incomprehensible, much as if the heavens suddenly parted and through the gap God picked up all the messages from earth. These earlier simplistic beliefs sowed in him the seed that all prayer springs from love. At Clonliffe, he had come to realize its wider meaning. In one of his first essays in the seminary he had described prayer:

"Utter and self-giving, with nothing held back. It is the kind of love which always demands giving of our best, not only to those I love, like fam-ily and friends, not even to those I find it hard to like, but most important of all to those towards whom I am largely indifferent."

Later, he had been asked for an explanation of what he thought faith was exactly. In his neat hand he wrote an interpretation he hoped would stand the test of his time as a priest:

"Faith is the total acceptance of an unseen power superior to me; an in-visible and different order of beauty to which I must adjust if I wish to at-tain to the supreme good. Linked to this belief is also a total desire to communicate with faith."

His explanation had earned him a word of praise from the Dean, but more important, Seamus's progress was something to tell his mother, to reinforce her belief that all the sacrifices she continued to make to keep him in Clonliffe were worthwhile.

When Seamus seriously thought of the priesthood, money, never easy to come by in the Breslin family, was at a premium. Pennies were literally counted and recounted. Purchasing even a new pair of socks was a major decision: the old ones were first inspected to see if they could stand one more darning. The decision finally made that they should be replaced, his mother would sit at the kitchen table and count what she already owed local tradesmen. To ensure the family had three nourishing meals a day, Anne Breslin virtually stopped spending anything on herself. Yet she hid their poverty well. At Mass no one could tell how many hours she had spent mending clothes; and, no matter how worn, the family's shoes were always polished. She set great store by such matters, just as she did about her religion and telling the truth.

So, on the night when he had sat across from his mother at the kitchen table, as calmly as he could — though he was bursting to share the news with her that he had prayed for weeks and was finally convinced he had really been called — and said, "Mammy, I'd like to become a priest," she looked at him in silence. Her eyes had fixed intently on his, her strong, capable hands clasped, their fingernails chipped from endless scrubbing and scouring. Then she quietly asked, "Where would we get the money?"

He was shattered. His dreams and hopes gone; in all those weeks of prayer he had never thought of asking God if He would help provide. Seamus had just sat there, thinking: *Of course she's right. Where would we get the money?*

She suddenly rose to her feet and stood over him. She placed a hand on his shoulder, pressing firmly, as if she wanted to reinforce her words physically. The money, she said, would be found. Grown though he was, he impulsively hugged her, repeating endlessly, "Mammy, Mammy, thank you."

She had smiled down at him and said. "Don't forget God. Thank Him, too. You've been called. That's very special."

Events moved swiftly then. Seamus obtained one of the handful of scholarships to Clonliffe. It was worth eighty pounds a year for the first three years. By careful budgeting, his mother calculated, the bursary could be stretched to help cover his final years in the seminary. She would ensure, somehow, that the balance would come out of the family coffers. That settled, she took him to a clerical outfitter's, a shop where his father knew a salesman, who agreed to a discount. That night Seamus dressed for the family, first in his black serge suit and white shirt and black woolen tie. Then, as a climax, in his soutane and Roman collar.

"My God!" his father said. "He looks like a priest already."

*

Next day, Seamus arrived at the office of the seminary's doctor. The man was elderly, obese, and determined to explain the importance of the occasion.

"God may have called you, young man, but the Almighty has left it up to me to pass you."

He sat down behind his desk, adjusted his pince-nez, and drew a form toward him.

"Do you know about the impediments?"

Seamus was baffled. In his years of regular Church attendance, in his conversations with his parish priest, in his reading of religious books at no time had anyone mentioned "the impediments."

"The impediments," the physician repeated. "I've got to ask you about them. Illegitimacy. That apply? It's a bar. You can't be a priest if you're a bastard."

Seamus felt his face redden. "My parents have been married for —"

"Good. No illegitimacy impediment."

The doctor scribbled on the form.

"Any convictions?"

"Convictions?"

"Come, boy. You know, convictions for crime, particularly sexual."

Seamus shook his head rapidly.

The doctor made another notation. He suddenly looked up.

"You ever hit the bishop?"

"Sir?"

Seamus was astonished by the questions.

"Relax, young fella. I have to ask these questions. If you hit a bishop or even a priest, that is a bar. Surely you can see that?"

Seamus nodded, too stunned to speak.

The doctor told him to take off his clothes. Standing there, completely naked, the first time he had ever undressed before a stranger, he felt mounting panic. Why was the doctor peering so intently at his sexual organs?

"You can't be ordained unless you're a whole man. You've got to have all your sexual faculties. Eunuchs can't become priests."

The doctor stooped. He rose, walked to his desk, and made a further notation. Then he returned to walk slowly around Seamus.

"Move your left leg."

"Which way?"

"I don't care. Just move it."

Seamus did so.

"Move the other one."

Seamus repeated the action, moving his right leg back and forth.

"No wooden legs," said the doctor. "You can't be ordained if you've a wooden leg. It would mean you are not a complete person."

The doctor pointed toward a curtained alcove.

"Go in there and give me a specimen. Just pee in the pot."

Seamus could not pass a drop of urine. Beyond the curtain the doctor paced impatiently.

"Come on, come on, boy, bring me the specimen."

Seamus emerged with the empty jug.

The doctor sniffed. "You're the first one I've ever had who can't pee, but not being able to pass water on command is no impediment," pronounced the doctor.

He made a final notation on the form, signed it and addressed the envelope to the Dean of Clonliffe.

"Okay, young fella, God called you and I passed you. Good luck."

It has been exciting: learning to genuflect and venerate "in a priestly way"; accepting that he could smoke only at certain times, in all an hour a day, and then only in one of two specially designated "smoking sheds," their walls brownish-yellow from years of exhaled nicotine, their air reeking of stale tobacco; that he must rise at six o'clock every morning and must to go bed sometimes a full hour before dark, for it is light in these parts until 11:30 at night in high summer; that he must learn how to meditate silently and to examine his conscience; that he must never walk with his hands in his pockets, in case, as the Dean had put it on the first day, he might be tempted to let the Devil do his handiwork.

His life was governed by bells that punctuated a schedule directing him from chapel to classroom, from early morning prayers to Latin translation, then back to chapel before returning once more to the classroom. A routine of promptly hitting the pew kneelers and learning not to squirm on hard lecture-room benches. Somehow short breaks were fitted in for food and recreation, each signaled by a ring of the bell. In all, he once counted, the bell rang forty-three separate times throughout the day, each a sonorous tocsin. The noise emphasized that Clonliffe was a place of books and prayer.

He felt pleased with how much he had learned. He knew all the Days of

Deposition, the anniversaries of the deaths of saints. He had studied the *Depositum Fidei*, the sum of revealed truths given by Christ to the Church. He knew the history of Ember Days, days of fasting. He had analyzed the position of the Euchites and Quietists, heretical sects. He had read the Euchologion, the book that contains the rituals of the Eastern Orthodox Church, so similar in many ways to the Church of Rome. He had listened to lectures on Heaven, accepting it not only as a state but as a place of beatitude; a place where God imparts His glory to the blessed and clearly shows Himself to them. He had concluded that Hell is a place and state in which the devils and such human beings as die in enmity with God suffer eternal torment. He had come to grips with pastoral theology, the science of the care of souls, a mixture of dogmatic and ascetic theology and Canon Law. He understood the deeper meaning of the Pater Noster, the prayer Christ taught to His disciples; he had learned to use the liturgical name for the last three days of Holy Week, *Triduum sacrum*, and to examine the mystery of the Holy Trinity.

He knew the historical significance of the sacred vessels, among them the chalice, paten, and pyx. He learned about vestments and the meaning of the liturgical colors: white to be worn on Trinity Sunday, feasts of Our Lady, Corpus Christi, and the feasts of saints; red on Whitsunday and the feasts of martyrs and the Apostles; purple in the penitential seasons of Lent and Advent; black on Good Friday and in Masses for the dead; and green on ordinary occasions between Epiphany and Lent and between Trinity Sunday and Advent. He noted that when bishops celebrate pontifically, they take their vestments directly from the altar, but ordinary priests robe in the sacristy.

Through all this — and so much else — Seamus had come to comprehend the many, but all-important, roles a priest has to play. He is there to provide a sense of spiritual comfort to his flock; to be in constant communication with them; to convince them to accept that there is a time to live and a time to die; to act as a fulcrum between the Church and its congregation; to create a mutual trust between those who govern and those who are governed; to work, in every way, toward a purification of the religious sense of those he will be responsible for when he finally leaves Clonliffe.

But that is a long way ahead. He will need three more hard years to absorb all else he has to learn. For the moment, though, Seamus can take a pause on his road to ordination. His taxi has finally arrived. In the morning he will travel by train to Carlow to spend the summer weeks on his uncle's farm and once more drill the village choir for the *Quarant' Ore*.

He feels strong enough to avoid Brigid.

✝

The taxi was old, and in normal times would have been scrapped. But this was 1944 and any vehicle that qualified for a petrol allowance was pressed into service.

The cabman was middle-aged, a grumbler, torn like many Irishmen over his loyalties about the outcome of the war. In the past, when he had picked up Seamus, the man had sported a Nazi swastika in his lapel; the buttons were freely handed out by the German Embassy in Dublin. Now, the cabby wore a Union Jack emblem, and for good measure, a replica of an RAF insigne, a pair of flying wings sewn on his jacket sleeves.

When the taxi reached its destination, Seamus felt familiar emotions. After the vastness of Clonliffe, the house seemed tiny. It was hard, now, for him to believe so many lives had been lived behind its front door, with the brass letter box shining from a daily polishing by his mother. In a window was a plant, his Christmas gift to his mother. He reached a hand inside the box and pulled out a key on its string, the way he used to do as a child. He opened the door quietly, intent on surprise.

His mother was waiting. He put down the suitcase and she hugged him, as she always did when he came home. Behind her, framed in the kitchen door, he saw his father. Even in the gloom, Seamus sensed the raw, in-flamed, whiskey eyes measuring him. He greeted him politely.

Whenever they met nowadays, Kevin Breslin seemed to be searching for signs of decay in his son, as if seeking reassurance that Seamus was no more immortal than himself; to make it easier for his father to endure the damage drink had done to his once-healthy body.

But drink had not completely obliterated the timbre of Kevin Breslin's powerful baritone. Seamus had the same arresting voice. It was that of a born preacher, one of his tutors called it.

Abruptly, his father turned away, returning to the kitchen to sit by the range. Warm though the day was, he felt the cold.

Seamus followed his mother into the kitchen. The table was set, the meal about to be served. He should have known his mother would be waiting for the taxi to turn into the street. It was the same every time he returned from the seminary. As always, his mother immediately served a meal. She did the same for her daughters, all now married and living away from home. For her, food and affection were synonymous.

The kitchen was faintly pungent with anthracite smoke. Over the years the stove had deposited a sheen of black on the ceiling and walls and sifted coal dust into the mortar between the flagstones. The kitchen had always been the focal point of the house, where the family ate and received the occasional visitor, usually a relative or the parish priest. The front parlor was used only at Christmas and on feast days. The kitchen was cluttered. On top of the wireless an oil lamp with a bulbous base fought for space alongside a plaster figure of Mary and the Christ Child and a faded print of Kevin Breslin as a young man. There was barely room for the eight-day clock on the sideboard, its top crammed with framed pictures of the children, grinning into the camera until, as the years passed, they became self-conscious and solemn. There were no fewer than three holy pictures on the wall. Above the kitchen door was a crucifix.

Seamus described how the term had gone, how he hoped he had done well enough in the examinations, and how the next years were going to be the hardest. But that is how it should be; everything is carefully prepared to lead to ordination.

His mother perched on the edge of the chair. Seamus thought she had shrunk since he last saw her; her clothes almost enveloped her. Her slate-colored eyes were as alert as ever, but they were rimmed with more lines than he remembered, and he noticed she had an even smaller appetite. Once more, an old fear nagged him.

His father pushed away his plate, noisily cleared his throat, and lit a cigarette, using a jam-jar lid to flick his ashes into. He settled back, listening, catching his lower lip in his teeth. Finally he addressed his son on the war. Anne Breslin twisted her hands uneasily. Her husband drew so hard on his cigarette that his chest visibly expanded. Sitting in his chair, assuming a crouching, aggressive look, attacking Churchill and British policies, he continued to stare at Seamus. Seamus relaxed: this was safe ground. His mother begged his father not to talk about the war. Seamus noticed how weary her voice was. He was aware of his father's stare. He was off on a new tack. The government had just promised to supply electricity to every home in Ireland by the 1950s. It would mean a real bathroom and hot water in every home. He sat back, staring at the hairs on the back of his hand, the way he always did when he was about to plunge. Seamus waited, knowing there was nothing he could do.

The interrogation was measured and merciless. His father asked if he would disagree that clean bodies make for clean minds. Seamus was noncommittal. His father pounced. Seamus had promised himself to keep calm. Anne Breslin looked down at her hands, defeated.

The whiskey that had already indelibly marked his face now puffed it up, twisting his lips the way a stroke might. Nothing could now stop Kevin Breslin from pursuing his quarry.

"Clean bodies *do* make clean minds." He let the repeated words hang fire for a moment. "Fact is, makes it easier for a priest to tell a man to swear off beer and cigarettes. That's so, isn't it, boy?"

Seamus nodded, trying to relax by breathing slowly. But every muscle was taut.

His father touched his fingertips together in a cathedral of rectitude.

Seamus knew the tactic. His father would try to extract one admission after another. Priests used the same technique in the Inquisition. His father moved quickly, pushing the argument forward.

"You've no need to be sensitive! There's no room in the priesthood for delicate stomachs. You've got to be tough to do God's work. Hardened to the core to tell a man to give up the bottle and his fags. You going to be able to tell me that one day? When you've got your collar on and you're apart from the rest of us? You may have forty years of being a bishop's lap dog. Yes, Your Grace. No, Your Grace. But never fuck, Your Grace. Though they know about that, don't they? But never what the Bible says about he who is without sin."

Seamus remembered and said nothing. He prayed silently for God to save this frail and ruined old man he still could not stop himself from loving.

†

So his visit home had turned into a nightmare. For hour upon hour his father had sat in the kitchen, goading, determined to touch all the old sore places; venting his malice, using his primitive, guttural language to shock deliberately. *He wants to hurt,* thought Seamus; *that is the terrible thing: he wants to hurt me.*

In a sense, what was even worse was that throughout it all, his mother had sat and studied her lap. He could now see why: she had long ago made sure his father could no longer reach her; she had learned how to protect herself effectively from his flailing and lashing tongue. Her only comment on the whole horrendous business as Seamus left for the station was that his father was not himself on occasions. It had not been a plea, merely a statement. Nor had it diminished the nightmare.

His father had launched himself from some sort of springboard he nowadays carried around inside him, plunging into an even more bellicose sourness, suddenly displaying his dark gift, his inability ever to forget anything that he could later resurrect, a recalled moment to use as a weapon capable of verbally crushing or destroying the strongest. He had raised from the graveyard in his mind the story of the Failed Priest.

"What happened to him, boy? Remind me again, for my memory's not what it was."

The vehemence was suddenly no longer present; it had somehow been sucked back inside his wrecked body, momentarily replaced by a far more dangerous softness.

"What happened to the fella?"

Seamus had refused to be baited.

But his father had proceeded to show no avenue was too trivial for him to explore the sad tale of the Clonliffe graduate who had suddenly thrown away seven years of study to set up home with a widow, a parishioner. They had been forced by the scandal to flee the district, going north to Protestant Ulster, where nobody knew them. Later, children were born. But the priest was unhappy, wishing to legitimize his offspring, yet feeling unable to marry unless the Church blessed the union. He returned south to see the Archbishop of his old diocese and begged His Grace to arrange the matter.

Kevin Breslin had paused, waiting, knowing he was in full control: a scrawny-necked cat toying with its victim.

"Remember, boy, what you said happened then?"

Seamus had nodded miserably, wishing he had never, in the first place, told this story. He had been at Clonliffe only a short while, and the event was still recent, creating a deep impression on everyone. The case of the Failed Priest was still a seminary talking point when Seamus came home at the end of that semester; he had recounted it to his parents. His father had passed little comment. But he had clearly not forgotten.

"I'll tell you what happened, boy. I'll tell *you*."

Kevin Breslin had worked himself up, his nostrils flaring, enormous disbelief expressed as a loud clearing of the throat.

"I'll tell *you*. Our good Archbishop sent the papers to Rome. And the Pope fired them straight back. No dispensation! Remember what you said the Holy Father wrote? 'A priest should either be chaste or he should go to Hell.' Wasn't that it, boy? But he'd said it in Latin, hadn't he? What was that? *Outcastus outperinte.* Is that it, boy? Is that good Latin? I've forgotten. My memory's not what it was."

Whatever had motivated this — perhaps a morbid and often cruel prudery, the dreadful negative power of Kevin Breslin's built-in puritanism, in which breaches of sexual behavior were to be punished at all times — his victory over his son was complete.

†

The platform was filling and there was still no sign of Patrick.

From force of habit Seamus checked again a small card in his breast pocket. Its face was covered with a grid, each square containing a Latin word. There were several pencil ticks in the squares. Each one indicated that he was following the daily routine for all seminarians away from Clonliffe. So far today he had awakened at the prescribed hour, said his prayers, meditated, attended Mass, received Holy Communion, read passages from the Bible, recited the rosary, and examined his conscience. There were spaces for more prayers and meditation. In all he must spend a total of almost four hours every day in devotions. If he failed, he must place a cross against the relevant item. Ten crosses on the card could lead to expulsion. Seamus knew he could never cheat; he was on trust. But he was determined there would only be ticks on his card.

He put away the card and looked toward the station entrance. He saw him then, hefting his suitcase in one hand, and was surprised to see he was wearing a navy blue suit and a new cap. But Patrick was not alone. Clinging to his arm was a girl.

Seamus stood there, powerless to move. There seemed to be no air around him. The taste in his mouth was suddenly sour. Through a thick curtain he saw she was pretty, wearing a dress that seemed to be covered in flowers he had never seen growing in Ireland. They matched her hair.

Patrick put down his case and gently pulled her to him.

He saw them kiss. Oblivious of everything else, they stood nuzzled together. She pushed her face against his shoulder, a gesture somehow even more intimate than their kissing. Then she turned and walked quickly away, not once looking back, hurrying out of the station, disappearing into the unknowing crowd.

Patrick stared down the platform, his eyes searching.

Panic gripped Seamus. He must hide. He must hide and then emerge from someplace and pretend he had seen nothing. He must clear his mind of what he had witnessed by pretending it had never happened. He stood rooted, his heart hammering in his ears. There was nowhere to hide. Then it was too late. Patrick was smiling broadly, apologizing profusely and saying he had overslept but that it didn't matter because he had marked it down on his card. He did not mention the girl.

Nor did Seamus. Just as with his father, he realized how badly he wanted to preserve illusions.

They squeezed into a carriage containing a woman with a couple of children and some farmers and had only time to place their cases on the overhead rack before the train jerked out of the station, gathering speed, and left the city behind, heading out through the fields. Seamus felt trapped in this boxlike compartment. He blotted out the voices around him, staring through the window. There was scarcely a fence between the train and the horizon. Somehow this vast greensward, grazing ground for sheep, made him feel even more isolated. He was equally filled with despair about his father and Patrick. At Carlow, before they separated, Patrick arranged that Seamus would come for supper in a few days, adding that with five sisters it would be nice to have another man at the table. He reminded Seamus that one of them, Mary, had been in the choir last year.

Seamus pretended, but he couldn't recall her. Then he had had eyes only for Brigid.

Seamus bicycled one mile after another, eight in all, from his uncle's farm to the Gallagher house, and there was a glow in his cheeks that was not there in Dublin. What his uncle called seminary pallor had been wiped away by fresh air and sunny days: for weeks there had not been a cloud in the sky, a blessing for the harvest. Even now, with the day dying in an orange blaze through the hedgerows on either side of the lane, Seamus felt the warmth of the evening air.

He could not quite believe it was only five days since he arrived; it seemed as if he had never left. The old parish priest had welcomed him gently, his voice kind and understanding, but his words were more weary than Seamus remembered from last year, and interposed with the frequent stumbles and pauses of the aged.

When Brigid did not attend the choir rehearsal, the priest explained. A traveling salesman from Galway — though barely a hundred miles away the priest made it seem as remote as the Arctic — well, this traveler had swept Brigid off her feet, taking her back there to marry. He was a Protestant. In this closed country community, where no one married outside the faith, it would be a heavy burden for her mother to bear, having a daughter in a mixed marriage.

Seamus had been stunned; he still was. A marriage between a Catholic and a person of another religion, such as a Protestant, is legally binding. But unless dispensation has been obtained from the Pope, the union is invalid under Canon Law. It has been so since the Council of Elvira. Brigid, so true to her faith only a year ago, had not obtained permission and was now a heretic, to be denied the Blessed Sacrament. She was effectively a person who did not exist in the eyes of the Church.

Seamus had promised he would include her in his prayers. He wished he could do more.

Brigid's fate, if anything, reinforced his determination to cope with his own sexuality. Unlike Patrick, he was convinced that passions, however strong, would never rule his body.

In these past days, he had thought a great deal of what it was going to mean to be a consecrated celibate. It would involve an acceptance of responsibility, a dedication to the truth, and constant judgment; ensuring that the higher levels of his brain, where decisions are made, would always regulate and moderate the lower ones. In the seminary library, in one of the books Patrick had unearthed, he had read that the deeper parts of the brain were where sexual fantasies lurked.

Dusk approached as he pedaled up the Gallaghers' private road. The house was old, as many were in this part of the country, having stood for nearly a century, weathered and beaten by wind and storms raging in from the Atlantic winter.

He wheeled his bicycle around to the back; only strangers knocked on a front door in these parts.

The Gallaghers were farmers. Across the yard were the cow barns, from which came enough milk for a sizable portion of the county.

Seamus leaned his bicycle against a wall and knocked on the open kitchen door.

"Come in." The voice was liltingly beautiful. "Seamus, if you're coming in, come in."

CHAPTER 4

†

Always a Priest

Seamus stepped into the kitchen. It was perhaps twice the size of his mother's. In the middle of the room there was a wooden table with chairs for a dozen people. Along one wall were porcelain sinks, gleaming white, with long wooden draining boards, against the far wall a bigger range than he had ever seen, each burner occupied by a saucepan. From the ceiling beams hung haunches of bacon, curing; on side tables were bowls of eggs and fruit. All this he saw without taking his eyes off her.

"Well, you finally made it. You're welcome. I'm Mary."

She came forward, moving away from the range, wiping her fingers in her apron. When she smiled, her teeth were even and white.

He extended his hand. Her grip was cool.

"You look like you've seen a ghost." Mary smiled again. "Don't you remember? I was in the choir last year." There was the gentlest of teasing in her voice. "Next to Brigid."

"Oh, yes. Yes, Patrick told me." His face reddened. In the silence clocks ticked in light rhythm, one against the other: a mantel clock, a cuckoo clock above the sinks, and, glimpsed through a door leading from the kitchen, a grandfather clock. Neither the various chimes nor the chirp of the cuckoo were synchronized. Yet, he thought, their combined effect was not discordant but soothing.

Later, he would put on paper his impressions, not trusting his memory; taking particular care to record her words and his responses without embellishment, preserving all the finer details. The way she brushed a strand of hair from her forehead; her laugh, soft and throaty and used as a punctuation point; her eyes, which he would describe more than any other of her features. But he wouldn't be certain, if even now, in the kitchen, he was not searching for a need to justify himself and find expiation.

She looked at him levelly. "I can't come this year, though. Mammy died in the winter and I've got to run the house." She turned, indicating the kitchen, and through an open door the rooms beyond. "You must know how it is. Younger sisters all at school and a father who works all the hours God has given him."

He glanced behind him, through the kitchen door. It was the harvest season. Cycling here, he had noticed that the Gallagher pastures faced south and had already been cut for hay and winter silage.

"He misses Pat, you know. He'd never say so. But he misses him. It's difficult when you have a son who's been called."

He was suddenly reminded of a girl his sisters had played with at school. She, too, had always been self-assured and direct in what she said. He had, he remembered, been much too shy to speak to her. Mary seemed the same kind of girl. Her calmness was in direct contrast to the confusion he felt over a sudden overwhelming desire to impress her with some stunning remark, the kind he had never been able to make to that other girl.

"But I wish at times he was here. Mind you, I'd never tell Pat that. Nor must you. I wouldn't want him to feel guilty about anything. You understand, don't you?"

He could feel Mary's eyes on his face. She murmured something he could not understand. It must have been French. Patrick had told him she had spent a summer in Paris before the war. He suddenly wished he had not had such a conventional education — taking mathematics and Gaelic in preference to art and a European language.

"We all want him to be a priest. Mammy most of all. That was the last thing she said. 'Let our Pat be a priest.' She once gave him a holy card and he learned it overnight. It took me a month." She laughed.

"What did the words say?" He wished he hadn't asked the question. It made him sound such a seminarian.

She quoted: " 'To be in God's service is to live in the midst of every family, yet belong to none. To share all suffering. To hear all secrets. To heal all wounds. To teach and instruct. To pardon and console. To bless and be blessed forever. To be a priest.' " She laughed again. "I suppose that's why only a few get called. You have to be very exceptional. Pat is exceptional."

Seamus nodded, struggling to bring order to his mind. How could he have not remembered that terrible day when the Dean received a sudden telephone call and sent Patrick home? His mother had died shortly after the train left Dublin. Patrick had come back from the funeral wan-faced and withdrawn but composed. His grief lay hidden for a while, finally erupting some time later. When Patrick was discovered weeping uncontrollably in his room, the Dean sat with him for an entire afternoon, the door to the room closed. Afterward they emerged together and spent several more hours in the chapel, praying. Within a few days his friends and staff were saying how well Patrick demonstrated the innate resilience of man. He had wondered how he would react in similar circumstances, then quickly pushed the thought to the back of his mind, still not able to accept that his own mother might be seriously ill.

Mary was speaking about the eggs. He realized he had been staring at the bowls. She was saying he could take some to his uncle. Fresh eggs were a luxury in the war-rationed cities. He thanked her, still absorbed in her face. Her cheekbones were high, her eyebrows strong, slightly darker than her hair. Her nose was perfectly straight, her forehead rounded, wide, and deep. Her mouth was not only large, but had a clear and distinct shape, with corners that sloped upward. He had read that lips like hers denote a person who is sensual and emotional. But it was her eyes that dominated the face: elongated, with large areas of white on either side of the iris. She watched him carefully, no longer speaking. He could feel his blood racing and coursing through his body, a hot wash of excitement he had never before felt.

"Is something the matter?" The concern in her voice was genuine.

"Patrick. Is Patrick here?"

"He's helping with the milking."

Once more he felt a consuming urge to impress her. Like a peacock, he was desperate to display his feathers, to preen, to pay court, to do something to show her how he felt. Part of him, a losing part, realized he was taking leave of his senses, that he must not surrender his reason. It was okay for Errol Flynn suddenly to fall in love with Olivia de Havilland on the screen, but seminarians didn't behave like that. Yet standing there, he could not believe she did not sense how he felt; that Mary could not see his heart on his face.

"I'll go and give Patrick a hand. I do most of the milking at my uncle's. He says I'm faster than his cowman and cheaper too." Seamus half-turned, embarrassed over his boasting.

"You don't want to be getting that nice suit dirty over there."

He turned back to face her, a great blush pulsing like a tide across his face.

"Sit yourself down. You've had a long bike. Would you like something to drink?"

"Please. Thank you."

She smiled at him.

"Don't they teach you to say anything but 'please' and 'thank you' at Clonliffe? Patrick said you never stop talking!"

"You know Patrick, always paying a person a compliment."

He sat at the table, watching her pour milk from a pitcher.

"Take your jacket off. You must be hot in all that black. I couldn't imagine spending all my life in black. It must be worse for a nun."

She turned, smiling, bringing him the drink.

"I'm glad you are not a nun."

She burst out laughing. "You don't really think I'd do something like that, do you?"

Seamus draped his jacket over the back of the chair and sipped the milk. However hard he tried, his eyes could not leave her.

Seamus had no recollection of Patrick and the rest of the family arriving from milking, or what they had for supper, or even if he ate much at all. The meal, he was certain, was excellent. Mary had cooked it. Throughout the entire evening he was aware only of her: watching her bring the dishes to the table, first serving her father and then him, as a guest, leaving Patrick and her sisters to help themselves. She had asked him to say grace, a visitor's privilege, bowing her head with the others while he murmured a blessing. At the end of the meal, she made a fresh pot of tea for the men while she and her sisters cleared away.

He had no memory of what the others spoke to him about or what his responses were. But he remembered exactly the moment when she broke the drinking glass, slippery with suds from the sink. He had half-risen from his chair, eager to help her pick up the shards. She looked at him and quickly shook her head, asking lightly if they now trained a priest for housework. Then she laughed, taking any sting out of the words. But he still blushed, more conscious than ever of what had happened. He had fallen in love.

Seamus finally declared the fact to himself as he biked home. Into his mind came a new possibility, growing to probability and then certainty. He imagined any number of suitors making their way through the lanes, bringing her gifts, all of them knowing how to please her, how to be amusing and fascinating. They would all act quite differently from the way he had. Even Patrick had said he was quiet. How could he explain that while he was bursting to speak there was a reason why he was tongue-tied? In his black suit and tie and white shirt, he was conscious he had not cut a very inspiring figure. Next time he would dress differently, he promised himself, as he braked in his uncle's yard.

That was when he was overcome with new emotions. He felt almost physically ill, so strong was his guilt and feeling of betrayal: betraying his mother's scrimping, betraying the quiet optimism of his spiritual director that he could be a good priest one day; above all, betraying himself. This was the worst of all, the sickening sense of inner deceit. The words his director had offered before he left Clonliffe came into his mind. *Your vocation will be safe as long as you never abuse it.* They drifted mockingly before him as he undressed, folding his clothes and putting on his pajamas, then praying at his bedside. He stayed kneeling until all feeling had gone from his knees. Numb in the legs, he climbed into bed, but sleep would not come.

Now, with dawn breaking and the sounds of stirring in his uncle's bedroom, he was conscious of being bathed in perspiration; an all-over sweat; his scalp was damp. His fingers, probing inside his pajama top, came away soaked. His hand on a leg was wet; sweat so heavy on his forehead it ran down his temples. He tried to convince himself it was only a delayed reaction to his furious biking. He knew otherwise. Mary was the cause. He thought about her mouth and the unbearable sensation of kissing her. He could feel her skin on his. He could hear her last words to him, as soft and clear as if she were standing at the foot of his bed:

We'll see you again, soon.

He had made no attempt to touch her, or even to come close, as they said good night. She had accepted his thanks for supper with the hope that the meal had not been too heavy for him to sleep. Then she repeated the invitation to call again. The words had sounded casual. Yet in his bed he tried to drown them with silent Pater Nosters in Latin, remembering his spiritual director had said prayer is the only defense. Seamus finally closed his eyes as the incisive and persuasive voice of the priest floated into his consciousness.

†

The spiritual director was close to fifty. He sat in an armchair in his study, Seamus in another opposite him. Every student had to come here regularly to discuss problems and to receive guidance. The director's breadth of knowledge and understanding for all things human was a model of what a priest should be. It's strange, Seamus thought, the way I never noticed his height, well over six feet, or his weight, close to two hundred pounds. It was his voice, compelling and soft, rarely changing its cadence, which riveted, and never was this more evident than when, with the lightest of touches, the director mentioned celibacy. He reminded Seamus that at the Last Supper there were no women present. And when Christ said, "Come, follow Me," it was scripturally clear that the Apostles were expected to leave everything else behind; certainly they were not going to go forth and missionize the world with wives in tow. Matthew, that most accurate of reporters, recorded Jesus' exact words, which the director could quote from memory: *"And everyone that hath left house, or brethren, or sisters, or father, or mother, or wife, or children, or lands for my name's sake, shall receive a hundredfold."* Luke made it equally clear that Christ did not wish His priests to have any hesitation about the demands He makes of them — and again the director's voice intoned: "Son, give me your heart." Christ was clearly saying that at the core of every vocation is an essential emotional detachment in body and spirit possible only when there are no other ties. Picking his phrases with care, the director spoke of the celibate as a torchbearer for the eternal life. "You will come to accept that it is the detached celibate priest who best understands the commitment of what marriage is, because he is married to the Lord. Your soul lives in your body, and as long as you live you will have sexual impulses. It is for you to decide to let God help you to banish them."

†

Seamus awoke, bathed in sweat, trembling.

Mary was once more back in his mind.

The next days alternated between silent, anguished inner debate and mechanical actions. He shoveled down food but had no appetite; he conducted the choir by instinct. He gave wrong answers to questions or did not even appear to hear them, drawing peculiar looks from the parish priest and his uncle. His mood fluctuated from a burning calm to self-pity. He tried to reason with himself, and when he saw the flaw he became dis-

mayed and filled with despair. He wrote it all down. He constantly ran
through his mind her every word and gesture. He wondered what she was
doing at particular times of the day. Then the pain started in his chest,
making it hard to breathe. Was she with somebody else, bestowing her
favors on another boy? Once, to wash away the idea, he held his head
under the yard tap and let cold water soak his hair and face. He dried off in
the sun, biking to hold another choir practice for the *Quarant' Ore*. He invented a game to torture himself further. Each thrust on the pedal represented the emotional struggle tearing at him. A downward thrust of his
right leg meant he must think of his vocation. Engaging his left leg, the
heart side, was the time to defend his feelings for Mary.

Right foot down. A vocation is a gift, self-sacrifice a small return for
being called by God.

Left foot down. Human love is not to be condemned but developed and
treasured. This is why I feel new confidence, a heightened perception, and
an increased compassion.

Right. Not true. Where was compassion for Patrick at the railway station?

Left. That's different. Patrick isn't in love. Not like I am.

Right. The greatest love any man can have is the love Christ gave.

Left. But I love her.

Right. Still not too late. Those feelings can be cut off cleanly, clearly.

Left. I love her.

Right. I love Christ.

Left. We both love Jesus.

Right. But not in the same way.

Left. Yes.

Right. No.

By the time he reached the church he was bathed in perspiration once
more. Several members of the choir asked if he was unwell. Impulsively, he
said he was developing a summer influenza and would have to cancel practice and go home to bed. The choir watched silently as he climbed on his
bicycle. A mile down the road he dimly recalled their disbelieving looks at
his excuse. He was not on the road back to his uncle's farm, but cycling
toward the Gallagher homestead.

His mind was made up.

Half-broiled in his black suit, he arrived in the yard. He carefully knotted his tie and mopped his forehead.

He knocked on the closed kitchen door. He waited, then opened it and
hesitantly stepped inside. The kitchen was shady after the glare of the af-

74

ternoon sun. Only the ticking clocks broke the silence. The door leading to the front parlor was on its latch. He paused, not certain what to do. Then he rapped, but there was no response. His hand reached toward the latch and lifted it.

"Why, Seamus, where would you be going?"

He whirled, crimson in the face.

Mary was standing in the doorway, a basket of eggs on her arm. She walked to the table and put them down, then she looked quizzically at him and burst out laughing.

"Glory be! You should see your face. You look like somebody who's been caught with their hands in the till! But it's good to see you. You'll stay for tea, of course?"

He nodded, smiling foolishly, thinking: *I have met the person whom all the heavens intended for me. We will be able to satisfy each other's needs forever and ever and live happily for all our lives.*

Pedaling home in the darkness, he had a new game.

Left foot down. She loves me.

Right foot down. I love her.

Left. She loves me.

Right. I love her.

Seamus careened through the countryside.

He completed his prayers and peeled back the bedcovers in the dark, pushing his feet between the sheets, enjoying their coolness on his legs and back. He pulled the summer blanket up to his neck. He was not certain he had been fully asleep when the spiritual director surfaced in his mind.

He was consoling and understanding, reminding Seamus of that day shortly after Rome was liberated by the Allies, a cause of great rejoicing in Clonliffe, for it meant that the Holy Father and the Vatican were safe from stray bombing. That was the day the director also said that a good priest never judges anybody. People fail because they are people. That was all. Seamus must not think he has failed by accepting Mary's invitation to tea, by sitting opposite her at the table, watching her every movement and words. That, the voice in his head said, was not failure, but a test. The same kind of testing that allowed him to play games on his bicycle. Whether he survived depended entirely on his ability to pray.

Seamus could not sleep. Five full days and nights had passed since he had seen Mary. He had prayed, but it was of no avail; he felt as if God had left him in limbo. There were other times when he was almost euphoric, imbued with a new lease on life. Then his vocation scarcely came into his calculations. Nothing seemed to matter except making a deliberate effort to live for the moment.

He used logic, as if his love for Mary was a question set for an examination in advanced moral theology. Falling in love, he reasoned, is not an act of will or a conscious choice. It is immune to discipline. Willpower can only control the experience. He continued to reason as he worked the choir, walked the horse and cart to the barn, hefted the hay into the loft. Falling in love, he decided, was not a test the way the spiritual director used the word. It was nothing to do with extending his emotional boundaries to their limits. If anything, it was a collapse of them. Falling in love was also easy: he had proved that. He also discovered intellectual reasoning could not eliminate the deep dividing pain he felt.

On the sixth night he begged God to help him in a different way. He asked Him to understand — so that he could marry Mary.

He stopped, shocked. This is not the meaning of prayer. At Clonliffe he had been taught that it is rooted in the words of Christ: *My Father, if it be possible, let this chalice pass from me. Nevertheless, not as I will, but as thou wilt.*

Seamus resumed praying, saying he would leave himself in God's hands. For the first time in two exhausting weeks he slept deeply, without dreaming of his spiritual director or Mary.

The *Quarant' Ore* was four days away. The parish choir, he knew, was pitch-perfect. He also accepted this could be the last year he would direct them.

The crisis was over. He had straightened everything out through prayer. He had thought of and rejected the idea of writing a letter to his mother, explaining. In the end he decided he would tell her personally; sit in the kitchen with her and talk to her about his decision. She would undoubtedly be saddened and that would make him sad as well. But there was no other way. Better to do it now than live the rest of his life with resentment. He was certain his father would rant over the waste of money and roar about the scandal. But, he suspected, like most scandals this one would be confined and short-lived. Some priests, he had heard, wrestled all their lives with a woman problem. He could only be grateful that he had been spared that much.

Pedaling toward the Gallagher house for the first time in ten days, he was certain. He would leave Clonliffe, get a teaching post, and then ask Mary to marry him. He was positive he was right to discuss none of this with her before he had landed a job. She must on no account feel he relinquished the priesthood for her. But in his mind he was coming now as a suitor. He had used up his whole month's candy ration to buy her two bars of chocolate. When he cycled into the yard, Mary was waiting at the kitchen door. There was no smile, no welcome.

"Oh, Seamus, it's you."

"Who else?" He grinned.

"I thought you were the doctor."

He felt suddenly chilled.

"The doctor? Why, what's wrong?"

"It's Norma. She's ill. I think it's her appendix. Dad sent Patrick for the doctor hours ago."

She tried to conceal her yawning, saying she had been up most of the night with her sister. There was no warmth in her voice.

"Can I help in any way?" He saw her look and wished he had not asked.

"She needs medicine, not prayers." Her voice was sharp for the first time he could remember.

She walked quickly past him, to the corner of the yard, looking down the lane.

Seamus slowly wheeled his bicycle toward her, careful to place the machine between them. She leaned against the house gable and closed her eyes.

"I'm sorry, Mary. I really am." He tried to keep his voice normal.

She nodded, not opening her eyes.

He produced the chocolate bars. "These are for you. For all your fine cooking." He tried to smile.

"You shouldn't have bothered, really. I'd do the same for any friend of Pat's."

"Please, Mary. Please take them."

He almost thrust them into her hands.

"It was very thoughtful of you." She stared down the lane. "I'd ask you in, but with the doctor coming I can't."

He counted the number of times the cuckoo chirped in the kitchen before he made one last try. Would she be coming to the *Quarant' Ore?*

"Be there? God, don't ask me now. Anyway, I'm sure you don't need me there to appreciate what you've done. And you know what they say about a priest? About him going straight to Heaven because he's so good on earth." She smiled then, the way she had smiled on their very first meeting. "You're going to be a fine priest one day. Pat says so and I know so."

It was not indifference or cruelty he saw in her face, only honesty.

In the end, Mary came. He could see her standing beside her father and sisters from his position near the altar. She wore a new bonnet and looked more beautiful at this distance than ever.

Patrick sent word that Norma would be out of the hospital in a week and after Mass would Seamus join them for a meal. He politely refused.

He had seen the way forward. It would no doubt be lonely. It would be hard, certainly, but it was the only way.

The Dean surveyed the ordination class. Seamus thought: this is very much his style; lengthy pauses, almost great silences between the Archdeacon's carefully enunciated phrases. When he first had heard the Dean speak seven years before, he had been overawed by the man's mannerisms. Each gesture seemed to reinforce the Dean's claim to virtue. A man not troubled by so much as a knot in his conscience. A person who in every verifiable way knew he was doing and saying the right thing. On this morning the Archdeacon's pauses struck Seamus as theatrical, his cultivated speech and elaborate syntax hard to concentrate upon.

His mind turned, as it frequently did then, to his mother. She had finally told him she had a steadily progressing cancer. No further surgical intervention was possible. Nothing could change the inevitable outcome. His mother had never uttered a word of complaint about her pain, the regular spells in the hospital, and the attendant unpleasant procedures. Her faith, she had repeatedly said, would sustain her to the very end.

Her reaction helped him to cope. She had urged him to accept and he had, the notion that her fate was part of a constant rhythm of life; that death and rebirth form the keystone of their religious belief. Her impending death strengthened the bonds between them and she had spoken of her search for nirvana, a peaceful end of worldly desire and an acceptance of the illusory value of earthly struggle. On his visits home and to see her in the hospital, they were able to speak openly about death. She sometimes wondered if she had always behaved well enough to feel justified in hoping for eternal life. And he reminded her of what Saint Thomas Aquinas expounded: God's will is paramount, but He recognizes mortal weakness and gives grace to those who persevere, as she had, in wanting to be delivered from sin. Gradually, they came to accept her death by refusing to ignore it or deny its finality. He realized, too, that their attitude was based on an understanding of the nature of death that was far from complete. He tried to learn more. In the library of Clonliffe there were any number of theological books dealing with eternity. But there was not one that provided definite answers to facing death in a practical sense. He saw that if he were to be a good priest he must have a full insight into all the ramifications of dying. While his mother displayed an exceptional lack of emotional distress, very likely others he would encounter in his ministry would be unable to show such saintlike courage and calm. He would have to prepare himself to assist them, just as his mother had supported him by her example.

Her positive attitude helped in other ways. It strengthened his vocation, maturing him in a way he never before realized was possible. He became more compassionate toward his father. He accepted that his drinking was a safety valve to blot out what was happening. Death terrified his father; he showed all the signs of a man who believed he was condemned to endure beyond the grave the pains and uncertainties of this life. Seamus decided that the best way he could help was to turn a blind eye and continue to pray for his father's salvation.

Praying, he came to understand fully, was thinking about God and speaking with Him; it must always be done with great attention and devotion. When he prayed for his mother, he could see her clearly: shrunken now by her wasting illness, her hair grayer, the veins standing out more prominently on the backs of her hands. He asked God to comfort her. He did not beg for his mother's life to be prolonged, only that her pain be as little as possible, that her death agony when it came be short.

The doctors dated the onset of the malignancy from around the last time he returned from Carlow, two years ago, in 1945. That was the first summer "after Mary." He dated events, *Before Mary. After Mary.* It was another way to remind himself of his deepening maturity. Those past two years he had thought a great deal about his feelings for Mary and concluded that he had, after all, confused love with a feeling of love: that he allowed himself a brief spell of self-serving self-deception. He had come to see that for him, bound daily closer to the priesthood, true love must always be an act of will, which transcended ephemeral feelings. Genuine love required commitment and the exercise of wisdom.

A year of intensive work followed as he prepared for the diaconate. A deacon is second only to a priest. He is ordained to help celebrate Mass, to preach, and to baptise. Seamus had successfully rejected, to the satisfaction of his examiners, the Protestant argument that the original seven deacons were merely chosen to administer the alms of the Church. Displaying a command of the Scriptures that made even his spiritual director nod approvingly, Seamus had pointed out, with the same deadly accuracy his father once possessed, that they were chosen for higher work than merely handling charities. A year ago, having been questioned at length by the

Dean, Seamus was created a deacon, the final step toward the priesthood. In a week's time, he would be among the handful of men, seated on hard benches, listening to the Dean, who would be ordained.

One of them would not be Patrick.

†

Twice this past year, on trips into Dublin, he had seen Patrick with the girl. He finally took Patrick aside in the smoking shed, approaching the matter obliquely, saying everybody thinks being in love is unique, and this was understandable, because it was a gift from God; affection, after all, was at the core of human friendship; it designated warmth, tender feelings and emotions.

Patrick stared at him.

Seamus continued, saying there were various kinds of love: it was easy to love somebody who is physically attractive; to love a person whose personality is complementary to one's own; to love someone, not realizing it is infatuation. He paused, hoping for a response.

Patrick stood there, blowing one smoke ring after another, watching them spiral and dissipate.

Seamus plunged on. They both knew that some of those called to religious celibacy can fall in love. What was important was to be on the alert to resist even the first stirrings of such love; once its presence was discerned, it should be dealt with swiftly and the relationship causing it cleanly ended.

"You mean Helen?"

Patrick's use of her name jolted him. It gave the girl a new substance, making her that much more of a threat.

"I can't bear to see you destroy yourself." Seamus blurted out the words, wishing he did not sound so emotional.

Patrick pinched his cigarette between his fingers, slipped the butt into a pocket, and left the shed.

They had not spoken for weeks. One evening Patrick rapped on his door. He stood there in the familiar blue suit, raincoat over his arm.

"I'm leaving. I've told the Dean about Helen and I've been given marching orders. Out before supper. I want to say good-bye."

Walking with Patrick through the main hall, Seamus was conscious of a sense of irrevocable separation. Patrick said Mary was in Dublin, training to be a teacher, and he nodded, still not knowing what to say, when Patrick added his sister was dating a bank clerk.

"They're talking of getting married." Patrick laughed loudly, the sound echoing in the hall. "Maybe we'll make it a double wedding. You'll come, of course?"

"I'll see."

Patrick had not pressed. There was a sudden awkwardness between them. Without another word Patrick went out to the taxi, already loaded with his trunk.

†

The Dean was arguing that Christ taught that if there are excesses of the flesh, there must be those who will give up even the legitimate pleasures of the body. He looked piercingly into each face.

"If anyone of you feels a moment's doubt, the smallest of hesitations, then express them now. Just rise and leave the room. You will not be judged."

A further pause. Seamus sensed the sudden tension in the air. No one moved.

Without a word, the Dean walked away from the lectern and out of the room.

Seamus enjoyed the choreography of saying Mass and performing the rituals he had studied. All had one thing in common; to celebrate them, to learn to venerate properly, to be able to use every holy vessel at the right time and with the precise prescribed gesture, required endless practice.

Under the watchful stare of the Dean, the ordination class assembled in the sacristy attached to the seminary chapel. Surrounded by Clonliffe's precious church plate and some of its rarest of books, the robed deacons stood before benches, each one the precise height of a church altar. Before them were the chalices and pyxes they would need to practice celebrating Mass.

Beside Seamus was a tall deacon with flaming red hair and the longest nose of any seminarian in Clonliffe. In unison they both bowed to venerate and kiss the bench; until they became full-fledged priests, they would not be allowed to use a real altar.

The face of Seamus's companion hovered a good three inches above his section of the bench. Only his nose touched it.

The Dean was before them, glowering. He jabbed a finger. "Mister, why is your head at that angle?"

"It's my nose. It stops me kissing face-on!"

"Well, you can't say Mass with your head skewed! What do you propose?"

Seamus intervened. "He could come forward so that he rests his nose on the altar and kisses its edge." He demonstrated how it could be done.

The Dean stood back, watching carefully. He pointed to the redhead. "Now you do it."

Using Seamus's technique, the awkward deacon managed to kiss the altar full-face.

The Dean pronounced, "Not perfect, but nearly. I suppose God will accept it, having given you such a nose in the first place!"

Seamus noticed several things as he greeted his parents in the cavernous hall where seminarians received relatives. His mother was more wasted than ever. A few weeks ago the hospital had finally discharged her. No limit as such had been put on the time she had left to live, but she had calmly told him it could not be more than a year. He was, in a way, glad she was away from the place. The doctors and nurses had operated in a conspiracy of evasion, surrounding his mother with words and actions designed to suggest she was not mortally ill. She had finally told her senior doctor she had known the truth for some time. Even then he was reluctant to confirm the prognosis. Seamus had raised the matter with him, turning up at the hospital in his priestly garb to give further authority to his questions. The doctor spoke about white lies being kindly and the special responsibility of the medical profession to practice deceit because truth often produces distress. Seamus came away with the feeling that many doctors hid behind deliberate evasion because they did not know how to be properly candid with patients who were fatally ill.

Besides, in his mother's case there was no way of disguising reality. There was a stricken pallor about her face that spoke for itself. Cancer was destroying her before his very eyes.

Seamus sensed his father was close to being drunk. His hair was askew. He was wearing mismatching socks and a shoelace was undone. His inflamed eyes almost glowed in his perspiring face.

"How are you, Mammy?"

"No complaints. I'll be here for the ordination. Never you fear."

Seamus then took them to a corner of the vast hall, far away from the other family groups. He concentrated on his mother, seating her, placing himself beside her, as far from his father as possible. But his father was pleasant, almost jovial.

"You made it. You made it." He almost half-shouted. "Seven years. And in another week we'll be calling you Father. God bless you, boy. I'm real proud of you."

There were tears in his eyes.

Seamus was embarrassed and surprised. Since that summer night when the story of the Failed Priest had been dredged up, he had been careful to avoid any real discussion with his father about the priesthood, confining himself to generalizations: the work was hard but absorbing; there was talk of renovating part of the seminary and adding a new wing to cope with the anticipated influx of students in the next decade; some schools had as many as a score of final-year pupils eager to enter the priesthood. His father would listen and grunt, smoking furiously and saying there was plenty of work for them. England, he would roar, was in a state of moral decline; France was in the religious doldrums; the other great ally of the war, the United States, was turning into a cesspool. Once more the priests of Ireland would have to go forth and save the sinners. Just as he had been uncertain how to respond to those remarks, so Seamus had, until now, no clear idea where he stood in his father's estimation. His response was guarded. He leaned forward, keeping down his voice, hoping his father would take the hint.

"Thanks, Dad."

"Your daddy means it. We're all proud of you." His mother handed him a bar of chocolate.

For a fleeting moment Mary entered his head. Then she was gone. This was not the time for her to appear. She usually emerged in the small hours when sleep eluded him. No one knew she came — just as he was powerless to keep her away. He would tell himself there was no volition, that he had not cooperated. But he was not certain if he was really asleep at these times. Nor did he yet know her full role: the part of his brain, the one that handles sexual fantasies, had not been fully explored by him.

Kevin Breslin produced a packet of cigarettes from his pocket. "For you, boy. For the shed." His barking laugh turned heads.

Seamus felt a flush on his face.

When the visit ended, he led his mother out of the hall, her arm on his. His father trailed behind, staring at the paintings on the walls, saying they were valuable enough to pay the tuition fees for all the seminarians at Clonliffe.

Seamus turned and smiled. It was a safe and fixed response to a comment his father always made at the end of a visit.

*

At precisely five minutes to six on the morning of Sunday, June 1, 1947, Seamus awoke, totally alert, refreshed, and filled with an excitement he had never before felt on awakening in this room he had occupied for one thousand nine hundred and fifty-five days. He had just completed his last Retreat in Clonliffe. Retreats were not new to him; they formed part of his spiritual training. But the Retreat of these past few days had been different. It was the last one before ordination.

During it he had pondered on the truth of religion. He had examined his conscience more carefully than ever before. Under the supervision of his spiritual director he meditated on the end of Man and on the penalties of sin, so that he might flee with horror from it, the director had explained. Sometimes seated in a lecture hall with the entire ordination class, sometimes in the privacy of his room, he contemplated the full meaning of Jesus' life and death, reminding himself always that the Way of the Cross is not of this world. He spent almost a full day meditating upon the greatest of Christ's miracles, the strongest proof of His divinity, the Resurrection, reminding himself that all Christian truth, the very foundation of the Church itself, stems from total acceptance that Jesus arose from the dead. He let his mind dwell on the happiness of Heaven. Finally, before going to sleep every night he had, through lengthy praying, further united himself with God.

Climbing out of bed, he realized his pajamas were damp and clinging to him. During the night lightning and thunder rumbling overhead had briefly disturbed him. Perhaps the sudden spell of warm weather made him perspire. He could not believe it was another of those inexplicable night sweats, when he was half-awake and back in Carlow and suddenly feeling very lonely.

Entering the sacristy, Seamus received a shock.

The day he went into Retreat, Martin O'Keeffe, who had entered Clonliffe a year after him, was called to the office of the president of the college and dismissed on the spot. Three times in succession Martin had been late for Vespers. Seamus had urged him to appeal to the Archbishop of the Diocese. Nobody should have six years of their life ruined, he argued passionately, without another chance. He was convinced that Martin would be reinstated. The Archbishop listened in sympathetic silence to the crestfallen young deacon's pleas, then gently explained there was nothing he could do. Only the Pope in Rome could force the president to change a decision.

Seamus realized with a sudden chill that, with the Mass of Ordination about to start, the president could, if the whim took him, stride into the sacristy and order one of the deacons about to be ordained to remove his vestments and leave Clonliffe. The fate of Martin, coupled with the solemnity of the moment, made him dress with great care.

He took an oblong piece of cloth, the amice, touched it for the prescribed moment to his head, and dropped it over his shoulders before tucking it around his neck and tying it around his waist. As he did so, he murmured the traditional prayer: "Place, O Lord, on my head the helmet of salvation." He then donned an alb, a vestment of pure white linen that covered him from head to foot, reciting the words: "Make me white, O Lord, and cleanse me." Next he tied a white cincture around his waist. Now came the stole, a narrow vestment, which he draped around his neck and then crossed over his chest, fastening it in place with the ends of the cincture. It symbolized not only the suffering of Christ on the Cross, but also His obedience. He uttered another prayer: "Give me back, O Lord, the stole of immortality." He positioned the maniple so that it hung from his left arm below the elbow; pinning it in place, he reminded himself through another murmured prayer that, along with the cincture, the maniple symbolized Christ being bound by His captors in the Garden of Gethsemane. "Be it mine, O Lord, to bear the maniple of weeping and sorrow that I may receive with joy the reward of toil." Finally, he draped a chasuble over his right arm. Until actually ordained, he could not don this garment, which, more than any other, symbolized his calling: it depicted sacerdotal justice and the humility, charity, and peace that must henceforth govern his life. This, the principal vestment for celebrating Mass, a large mantle that would cover the body back and front and descend nearly to the knees, would shortly single him out forever as a man who had accepted that he would wear the yoke of Christ.

He was paired with his towering red-headed companion from all those months of practicing before make-believe altars. In all there were twelve pairs. Both the spiritual director and the Dean gave them a final inspection. Satisfied, they preceded the procession into the college chapel.

From their stalls, the choir chanted, the strong young voices rising and falling in perfect unison.

Seamus's eyes were fixed on the great altar and the figure of Christ on the Cross. He felt the blood pulsing through his head. He had fasted since the previous day. He remembered what his spiritual director had said.

"*Mortification of the flesh is a great means of not inciting us to become rebellious against God's law. By denying ourselves the lawful pleasures of sense, we are able to turn with greater freedom and earnestness to thoughts of God and virtue, making fasting one of the wings of prayer.*"

He saw the director standing on one side of the altar, the Dean on the other. These two men, so very different in character and approach, had brought him to this climactic moment. What did it mean for them, he briefly wondered, to launch a new batch of priests? Seamus knew what it was for him to be one of those priests. Into his mind came the word of the Apostle John, recounting what Christ said: *I have chosen you.*

The chanting stopped at the exact moment they reached the altar steps. He and the other deacons took the seats left vacant for them. It resumed as the Archbishop's procession appeared.

The High Mass, timed for the canonical hour of Terce, began its ritualistic progress. A sudden silence fell over the chapel. One by one the deacons rose and prostrated themselves on the marble floor below the Archbishop's throne. His Grace recited a litany.

The stone was cold against Seamus's face. He concentrated hard, remembering, too, what the spiritual director had cautioned about this moment.

"*You are meant to feel humiliated. You will be raised from the ground to a high dignity only by the mystery of prayer while the whole Church prays for God's grace to raise you to the priesthood. You must symbolically grovel in the dust, recognizing that God alone, not your brilliance, or anything else, can raise you. You will remember His words, 'You have not chosen me, but I have chosen you and ordained you.' Then, and only then, with those words in your head, will you be able to rise.*"

Seamus's turn had come. He felt dizzy but acutely alert. He waited before the Archbishop's throne, head bowed.

The Archbishop murmured a prayer, the Latin barely audible. Slowly, with infinite tenderness, he placed his hands gently on the head of Seamus. He left them in place for a moment. Then they were withdrawn.

Seamus stepped back and donned his chasuble.

He was now Father Breslin.

During the Mass he turned around time and again from the altar to run his eyes over his first congregation.

He had barely slept in the twenty-four hours since ordination, yet he showed no signs of fatigue. He had eaten little and sipped only water in this time. After being admitted to Holy Orders, he spent his last full day at Clonliffe. At mealtimes he sat with the staff at the High Table, a sign of his new status. In between he had cleared his bedroom, packed his suitcase for the last time, received his new chalice and vial of anointing oil, and had a brief discussion with the Archbishop about the future; there was plenty of pastoral work to be done in the diocese. Afterward, he prepared for his very first Mass.

He turned again to his favorite books, seeking the words that would confirm what he already knew, reminding himself that from now until he died he was, as a priest, at the core of the Christian mystery. It would be his job to elicit a loving response from all those he ministered to; the love he must offer could not, strictly speaking, be described but only repeated and retold from the Scriptures. He had been taught that the most rewarding way to express this love is through the Mass and the Blessed Sacrament.

He invited his family, all his relatives and friends, to share his celebration. There were probably close to five hundred persons present. In pride of place, in the front pew, were his mother and father and his sisters. Anne Breslin had saved for almost a full year for this occasion, putting aside a set sum each week so that the entire family would be fittingly dressed. Kevin Breslin wore a three-piece suit, his tie neatly knotted, his collar stud in place, his hair combed and sleeked down with hair oil. The girls had new dresses and hats. His mother had bought herself a gray two-piece costume and matching hat. Rouge put color into her cheeks. But no makeup could cover the deepening dark rings under her eyes or put blood back into her lips or hands, which trembled with the effort of holding the missal. She had moved a little closer to death in the past week. Yet, she was, he thought, the perfect example of Christ's victory over evil.

Father Breslin knew he must hide his grief. By not so much as a flicker must he show his mother his own pain. She would not wish this. Nor would he.

He had laid down a strict rule for his ordination breakfast. He would not pay for, or encourage, more than one round of drinks. Yet his father and a group of cronies were in a corner, tippling from a bottle of whiskey. They were already in a mellow mood.

His mother touched his hand. "He's so proud, son. He really is." Her voice was a pleading whisper. "He's waited years for this. And found the money, too, to pay for it. Let him have a sip or two. He'll not be a problem. Not today."

He looked down at her. There was a liveliness in her eyes he had not seen this past year; it was as if she was determined to prove the doctors wrong.

She had helped prepare this hotel banqueting suite, doing so with an eye for detail that he remembered from his youth, when she had organized Christmas and Easter festivities. There were printed place cards and individual menus. She had suggested the flowers and advised on the seating arrangements and asked the hotel to provide its best tableware.

No, he decided, he could not spoil it for her.

When guests sat down at the long central table for the meal, Kevin Breslin remained standing, glass in hand, rock-steady on his feet, looking down at his son, eyes brimming with tears.

"It sounds strange for your own dad to be saying this, but I'm real proud, son, to say, 'Welcome Father.' "

Then Kevin Breslin addressed the guests. "You know what they say? 'Once a priest . . .' "

In unison came a thunderous response: ". . . always a priest!"

That was the moment she chose to come. She was suddenly here, in his thoughts, reminding only him that she would never leave him. He might indeed be a priest until his dying breath, but to survive he would need her. Father Breslin told himself that was what Mary was saying.

CHAPTER 5

†

Illusions

S he thought he could never be a priest — not the way he was exploring her body with his tongue and fingers. Victoria began to laugh.

Art pulled away, puzzled, frowning, a sudden hardness around his jaw. He was nineteen years old, with bony features. Even in the darkness, in the front seat of his father's coupe, she could see his prominent forehead, cheekbones, and jaw. She had read it is what Chinese astrologers call a King Face, and with it goes a personality whose main characteristics are militancy, toughness, and persistence.

She laughed again, deliberately avoiding his mouth as he bent over her, hoping to will him into stopping.

"I could have your baby." At this moment she wanted the certainty of the words to make him stop. She also realized it was instinct that gave her a natural weapon — words to try to make him comprehend, to combat his physical superiority before her own passions took over. "If I get pregnant, you'll have to marry me. You'll have no money for flying school." She hoped the threat would work, this warning that he could place in her womb the seed to compromise his future. She had never used this tactic before, but until now she had not minded making love with Art. Now, part of her mind said it was wrong — in view of what she was about to embark upon. Yet another part said she did not wish to hurt Art. Victoria felt confused and torn. She kept her voice calm and her eyes averted from his face.

He smothered her mouth with his, then whispered urgently in her ear, saying she still had a week of freedom left and she should relax and enjoy.

Struggling to move, she begged to be taken home. He had not stopped trying to undress her since they had parked the car. Usually he was gentle, knowing this was how to arouse her; now he had a roughness about him she found off-putting. She wondered if this was in any way related to what she had told him; that in just seven days she would be gone from him forever. Is this why, she wondered again, the image of Art as a priest flashed through her mind? The priests she knew down at the parish church or who taught her religion at school had similar qualities about them: they were domineering and brooked no opposition; and sometimes she had caught them looking at women. She knew *that* look. It had been in Art's eyes ever since they drove to the park, a traditional trysting place for all young lovers in this small western Illinois town.

She had first been brought here two years ago by another boy, when she was fifteen years old. It was Labor Day, an end to a summer in which she attended seventeen bridal showers and eleven weddings, was a maid of honor at four of them. In those days there was always something about a wedding that made her realize that, apart from exploring herself, no one had touched her. Danny had been an usher at the Dinkler reception, a posh affair with champagne and vintage bourbon. She had at once been attracted to his lean, muscled body, gazing at him with unashamed interest. He had plied her with several glasses of wine and she was tipsy when they drove out to the park. After they watched the sun go down over the lake, he undressed her and they made love. She did not allow herself to admit any doubts about what she had done, not then. The guilt about her acquiescence came only when Danny never called. She felt soiled. She now knew that reaction had played a part in her decision — the one that continued now to make her resist Art.

Victoria sensed he was desperate to provoke a response, from his hands and words. His breath warmed her face.

"Listen to me, will you? Will you stop and listen?" She was ashamed of anger surfacing when she wanted to make a calm statement about a new lifelong commitment.

He lifted himself, looking down at her, asking if she had spoken like this to other boys.

She freed a hand and slapped him, hard, across the face, no longer concerned about her anger. "After Danny there's been no one except you."

Making love had never unleashed a craving for sex, the way it affected some of her girlfriends who were no longer virgins. She asked, again, to be taken home.

He sprawled over her, his hands moving to all places without her consent. Suddenly he was soft and gentle.

She knew he was holding her tightly to reassure her, just as she knew her defenses were collapsing. It was the speed of the collapse that surprised her. She wanted Art more than she ever had before, knowing that shortly he would never be able to touch her.

She was seventeen, with what the Chinese call a Jade Face. She had a fascination with the world of predictions, convinced that it was written in the stars what her life would be.

His hand left her breast to turn on the radio. The soft keyboard magic of Eddy Duchin filled the car. In spite of herself, she smiled. Only Art knew how Duchin affected her; there was something about his fluid rhythm. She could feel the moistness and then a new sensation as his finger entered her. She groaned.

"Please," he said, going deeper. She had always liked his use of the word, "please."

Why, she wondered, was she crying? She could feel other, old sensations. Her nipples tingled; a school of tiny fish seemed to be swimming inside her body, downward from where one of his hands touched her breast to where a finger of the other was lightly touching her vagina. She felt her entire body floating and her arms came around his back and pulled him down on her.

Into her mind — she would later insist she had not imagined it — came the image of the Mother Superior, coiffed and gowned, questioning in that ethereal voice of hers, the one that always made Victoria think of a handmaiden serving in one of the anterooms to Heaven, *Child, is it fun? Is it really fun?*

She felt sorry for Art. How could she begin to make him understand it was no longer her choice? That she really did not want to be part of a generation which the nun had once said failed to keep its promises? The Mother Superior had put it very clearly. *Don't live a half-life. Structure yours to have a real purpose.*

Victoria was suddenly scared again. Art was almost shouting in her ear, hard explicit words, interspersed with his demands that she tell him what she wanted him to do to her.

She had always known her passion had a way of taking over. But not like this. She pushed him, hard, in the chest. He came back, pinning her arms under his body, thrusting his thighs between hers, forcing open her strong legs. The leather of the car seat was cool on her buttocks, and her panties were down below her knees.

She felt his weight bearing down, rising and falling above her, as he labored to a climax.

After a while she spoke. "Can we go home, please?"

He nodded, at the same time doing something he had never done before. Art slid out of the car to dress himself in the darkness while she adjusted her clothes. She found his solicitude surprising and tender. Perhaps he already sensed her life would never be the same again when, in a week's time, she would enter a convent to become a nun.

†

Victoria's commitment to enter religious life had been there as long as she remembered. The first seeds may have been planted when, barely four years old, she paraded into her parents' bedroom, draped in a black cloth with a handkerchief on her head, announcing she was a nun. Her mother had called her cute. Her father was alive then, a fine, strapping man, always in robust health; because of this, his death came as all the greater shock. He left a widow and four girls — Victoria and three younger sisters. Her mother, when she recovered enough from her grief, continued her husband's practice of leading the family in saying the daily rosary. She had also encouraged her children not to be ostentatious about their faith, as were many families in this predominantly Catholic community. Rather, they must regard it as a gift from God and use their spirituality as an inner driving force.

When she was six years old, Victoria acquired a piece of old blanket, which she pinned to her hair in the semblance of a veil and habit. Then she would join the neighborhood boys, who used pieces of white paper pinned around their necks to imitate Roman collars. They would play Gas Company, a game in which they collected fuel bills throughout the neighborhood. There was keen competition for the roles of priests or nuns because they were the ones with the power to persuade the gas company not to turn off the supply if a family didn't have enough money to pay.

Hers was a working-class neighborhood: the men blue-collar workers, a mixture of Irish, Polish, and other mid-European nationalities. Their Catholic faith was staunch; their values simple: love of God, love of family, love of neighbor. Catholicism, like the air she breathed, was all around her.

It was both embracing and bracing, comforting and forgiving, demanding unswerving obedience and no challenge. When Sister Angela counseled about the dangers of necking, everyone in the class knew she was really warning that girls could get pregnant if they allowed boys to French kiss. This physiological miracle had stayed with Victoria well into her teens. When Father Bruce said at Mass one Sunday that Padre Pio regularly bled from his hands because he had inherited Christ's suffering for the world, everybody accepted it. When Brother Nicholas, one of the monk teachers at the high school, pronounced *The Catcher in the Rye* an obscene book, no one doubted he or she was doomed to Hell for reading it. News from the Pope in Rome was sacrosanct; if the Holy Father was reported as having a cold, people lit candles for his recovery. It was a world ruled by the penance of Hail Marys and Glory-be-to-the-Fathers. Nothing was too great a sin to be absolved. Sister Elizabeth, who taught religion to the graduating class, had stated as a fact that even murder can be absolved in the sanctuary of the confessional.

Confession had a powerful appeal for Victoria. It meant dressing up, putting on a hat, to stand in line, edging toward the box, remembering sins since the last time. The box itself was like a tomb. She sometimes imagined she was a pharaoh's daughter, buried alive for all time, or an assistant to Houdini, about to emerge in triumph on some celestial stage. These were the occasions when she did not have much to confess. But the routine was always the same: down on the cushioned kneeler, face against the fine mesh of the dividing screen. She knew her confessors on the other side of the screen by their odors. Father Bruce reeked of after-shave; there was a perpetual whiff of onions from Father Doyle; Father McDonald gave off an aroma of sweat and the peppermints he sucked while delivering absolution.

Between them they supervised a world where many of the prewar values had survived. The source of social stability remained the family. There was no teenage ethos as such: young people were still expected to ask their elders for permission to do many things: borrow the family car, stay out extra-late, sleep over at a friend's house. A counterculture, either as a word or a concept, did not exist: the thought of demonstrating against the government was too absurd to be considered. Equally, the work ethic was strong. It was a time when ambition and action combined. People continued to believe in themselves and in their country more than a decade after victory in World War Two. Then, unsuspected reserves of strength and emotion had been tapped to achieve it. They remained, in many ways, the driving forces in Victoria's neighborhood.

In this close-knit community, the priests and nuns were cast as people apart and enjoyed their positions of trust, admiration, and total power. They were figures to be turned to in times of trouble, the first to be invited to a wedding; they knew the right words to use for a christening party or funeral wake. Through them, God spoke; He was incarnate in their flesh and blood. They seemed to be aware of everything that went on: they knew what to do about a Catholic drunk, a Catholic wife-beater, a Catholic adulterer or adulteress. They used their power of prayer to heal them. Victoria believed she had regularly seen this work in a neighborhood where there were few Protestants and no blacks, where the houses were modest, each with its small backyard and basketball hoop. Out front were parked, for the most part, secondhand cars.

She walked along these streets to school for twelve years. She was taken that first morning by her mother to meet the Mother Superior, the elderly nun responsible for all the other sisters who would teach her. Victoria still remembered the impact Reverend Mother had had on her. She was covered from head to foot in heavy black serge robes. On that autumn day they were permeated by smells of another summer gone; in the creases of the cloth were traces of dust and tiny slivers of shriveled grass, as if the nun had spent her summer toiling in the fields. She did not appear to have any feet; her robes rose in perpendicular folds to her neck, where they were met by an equally imposing head covering, layers of white and black cloth. Victoria realized her strip of blanket was a poor substitute for the real thing.

It was Reverend Mother who first raised the possibility of Victoria's answering God's call. It had happened after early morning Mass on Memorial Day, when she was thirteen years old and the memory of her father's death was painfully fresh in her mind. She would kneel in the pew and remember the times when her dad was beside her, his powerful voice intoning the timeless Latin syllables.

Leaving the church, the nun fell into step with her, relaxed and smiling, not at all the way she was at school. Victoria found it surprisingly easy to answer her questions. No: she did not have any definite idea about what she was going to do after graduation. Yes: she did like religious class. Yes: she read her Bible every day. No: she never thought marriage should be the only aspiration for a girl. Then casually, as they went their separate ways, Reverend Mother posed the question: "Victoria, have you ever thought of becoming a nun?"

For most of that Memorial Day she had sat in her room and imagined the sort of life Reverend Mother led. Prayer, of course, must be at the center of it. But how easy was it to go to the bathroom in all those yards of starched linen and stiff serge? And what was it like to pray for strangers, people in China, someone you never knew by name? Nuns had to pray for everybody. Brother Nicholas said so. What was it like to work all day without wages, teaching an unruly class, running the altar-boy practices, cleaning the church? Did nuns eat different food to make them more holy? They couldn't drink alcohol, but they always seemed to have a good time at weddings. Victoria was certain of one thing. There was no secret underground passage linking the convent to the house where the priests lived. That was just one of those dirty Protestant stories. Anyway, she couldn't possibly, even in her wildest fantasies, connect sex with Reverend Mother.

Later she came to recognize there were other signposts along the way in her decision to enter holy life.

She began to read about the Church, trying to understand its present power through its past, discovering for a start, and to her utter astonishment, that between the death of Simon Peter the Apostle in A.D. 67 and the year 312 there were no fewer than thirty-one popes. Many of those first leaders had perished by garroting, crucifixion, strangulation, poisoning, beheading, or smothering. Some found no peace in the grave. Pope Formosus was dug up in 897, nine months after being put into the Roman soil, and his rotting corpse was robed in pontifical vestments and placed on a throne to stand trial before a religious court convened by his successor. While still warm enough to bleed, the corpse of Pope John XIV was skinned and hauled through the streets of Rome in 984.

Victoria avidly read on, about how the Emperor Constantine became a Christian and helped to ensure the Church's survival after its first three hundred years of internal peril from heterodoxy and the external threat of persecution; how this new policy of the Roman Empire toward Christianity, even if based on political expediency, transformed Western civilization; how by the end of the fourth century, Victoria discovered, her faith had become the official religion of the state under another emperor, Theodosius I, in 380 and the Church became an active participant in imperial politics. The Pope, the most important ecclesiastical personage in the entire world, headed a hierarchic Church with a centralized government and absolute authority. But behind the monolithic edifice was a world that no soap opera could begin to rival.

So shocked and excited was she by the story of Marozia that she read it by flashlight, late into the night, under her bedcovers. Marozia: the mother of one Pope, whom she conceived by another pontiff, the aunt of a third Pope, the grandmother of a fourth. Marozia: the woman who arranged the election of no fewer than nine popes in eight years in the turbulent tenth century; standing by while two were choked to death, one suffocated with a pillow, and four poisoned. Marozia: the greatest maker and unmaker of popes ... whose own fate remained unknown when Victoria's flashlight batteries ran out. She was forced to wait until dawn to read how two cowled monks had, on another dawn a thousand years earlier, arrived in Marozia's room with the telltale crimson-clothed cushion. They had locked the door and told Marozia there was no point in struggling. Then they placed the cushion over her face, steadily exerting pressure until all the life was smothered from the old woman. Another Pope John had ordered that this be done.

That morning Victoria had sat in religion class and wondered why Sister Elizabeth did not discuss women like Marozia, explaining why in spite of people like her, or perhaps because of them, the Church has survived. Instead, Sister Elizabeth dwelled upon the lives of other, more acceptable, women of influence in the pageant of Catholicism down the ages: Catherine of Siena, Teresa of Ávila. Yet, enthralled as she was by their struggles and triumphs, Victoria found these saints did not have the same appeal for her as did the murderous Marozia. And what of that mysterious nun, Sister Pasqualina, who looked after Pope Pius XII in Rome? Her position within the papal household had been dramatically borne home to Victoria by the episode involving the legendary secrets of Fátima, themselves held by Sister Elizabeth to be undisputed evidence of the power of the greatest of all women in the Catholic firmament — Our Lady. The Blessed Virgin chose to appear to three children near the village of Fátima in Portugal in 1917. Her appearance was accompanied by a miraculous change in the course of the sun, a wonder witnessed by hundreds. The children said Our Lady had told them three secrets, to be confided only to the Pope, each successive pontiff to be allowed to share them. Turn where she could, Victoria could not find a clue as to what the secrets were. Then one morning Sister Elizabeth said that the latest news from Rome was that Pope Pius had reread the predictions and fainted. He had been revived by Sister Pasqualina. The thought of a woman actually being allowed that close to the Holy Father was a potent one for Victoria. Perhaps she, too, could reach such a dizzy height if she entered religious life.

In many ways her final decision was reached by a familiar route: the influence of nun teachers on her young mind. They explained that "a call" could come only from God; those who received it were "special." Reverend

Mother had reduced it to an emotive sentence. *The stripping of yourself, the emptying of yourself, so that Christ can enter you with His fullness of being.*

Father Bruce, when she discussed her intentions with him, said that the formation of all those in religious life was solidly founded on three vows: poverty, chastity, and obedience. These, he said, were what made a vocation a state of perfection. She did not think the vows sounded very formidable. Poverty was probably just another word for frugal. Obedience was nothing new to her. Her mother instilled it early in all her children. She guessed that chastity meant giving up boys forever. That, too, need not be an insufferable problem.

Since Danny, she had made love on sixteen occasions with Art, every occasion code-marked in her diary. An arrow symbolized the act, piercing a tree or a tiny car to indicate whether it occurred in the park or on the seat of his father's Ford. Alongside the drawings were letters: T, G, N: terrific, good, nothing. There were only two Ts. Ten of the entries were accompanied by an N. There were gaps of weeks and even months between them; unlike some of her girlfriends, she had never felt a need to make out every week. Nor did she like to discuss her sexual experiences with them.

But, even so, she wondered if she would miss sex. Some of her friends said that she would, that she would never be able to cope. She replied that nuns had special instructions given to them when they embarked upon holy life. She had no idea if this were true, but she wanted to put an end to the probing. To try to confirm her words she sought proof through reading. But this time, unlike the history of the Church, there was almost nothing written about how priests and nuns remained chaste. There were vague references throughout the Old and New Testaments to the virtue of celibacy. Jeremiah and Ezekiel touched upon it. So did the canticles in the Song of Songs. The Apostles offered chastity as a model for all women who wished to follow Jesus. Saint Augustine tried to define it in his *Confessions.* But Victoria could find nothing to show her how to live that vow in a practical, day-to-day sense.

She began to watch the priests and nuns to see, if from their behavior, she could get some clues. Sister Elizabeth seemed to have an especially deep need to be loved, and expressed her own affection not only with words but with touch, putting her arm around a boy, hugging a girl, or even kissing, quickly, on the cheek a sister she had not seen for days. Brother Nicholas was incapable of uttering so much as a word of affection and shunned physical contact. Father Doyle never seemed happier than when on the sports field or at the pool, plunging into the activity with an energy visibly sexual. Father McDonald prowled the school corridors after class, looking for boys and girls locked in some furtive embrace. Father Bruce seemed to have less a need to be loved than to nurture it in others.

Victoria began to see that each one seemed to have personal guidelines allowing them to live with, and within, their vows. She was confident she would be able to do the same. It was reassuring to know that when the time came her faith, as always, would provide the answer.

From the very beginning, the nuns had taught her there were only two major religions in the Christian world, Catholic and "Others." Only Catholics went to her school. In the long summer vacations they played exclusively together and were expected to set higher behavioral standards than the "Others." Unlike Catholics, who were encouraged to attend church every day, the "Others" went only once a week, and then to a number of different churches, which, according to the teachings of Mother Church, were all the same anyway.

She increasingly became aware that no matter how the "Others" mocked Catholicism it contained for her a totally satisfying religious experience. Whether it was Mass, when the strong resolute masculine voices were a reminder that her faith was not for weaklings or doubters; or religious classes at school; or saying family prayers at home around the table in the kitchen, or discussions with friends; or chats with her nun teachers — she was certain that Catholicism contained all the world's truth she would ever need. Her religious world was a secure and all-embracing one. She could continue to confess her sins and be forgiven.

After her first sexual experience she had whispered her guilt over what she had let Danny do. On the other side of the grille Father Doyle asked her if she was genuinely repentant. She said she was. He asked her would she try not to do it again. She promised she would. He absolved her, murmuring the prescribed words of forgiveness. She said her Act of Contrition, their two voices praying in unison. He finished with his standard blessing for her to go in peace. She returned several times to confess similar indiscretions with Art. Father Doyle was always sympathetic, never keeping her more than a few minutes, satisfied to ask the standard questions and get her invariable response: she was sorry and would try not to repeat her sin. Father McDonald she disliked. She could always sense him sitting hunched on the other side of the grille, sucking one peppermint after another. It was not that he asked leading questions; he was not allowed to do so. It was his disconcerting habit of repeating everything she said, almost as if he wanted to savor the words and save them for some future use. She had finally told Art, who said that was probably how Father McDonald got his kicks. The thought of her confessions being a source of personal satisfaction to the priest had made her avoid going for weeks. In the end, by some discreet checking, she managed to ensure that only Father Doyle heard her admissions. Each time he had absolved her.

She believed this was what made her Church unique. It recognized and understood human failings. The "Others" could never claim that. A Church with such power and overwhelming authority was also one irresistibly attractive. She wanted to belong, not on the outside, but as an insider. The only way was to become a nun.

She finally told Reverend Mother at school. The arrangements were surprisingly easy and swift. There were several trips for Victoria to the Mother House, where she met another Mother Superior and a person called the Mistress of Postulants, whom everybody called just Mistress. They both spoke to her about Catholicism's roots in undying hope and promised they would devote repeated novenas for Victoria to join them. There was no pressure, there was no need to exert any. Vocations were booming; there was not a convent with a vacant place in this heyday of American Catholicism. A Catholic, John F. Kennedy, was being groomed for the White House, Catholics held high office in Washington and elsewhere, Catholic-owned periodicals had boosted circulation to unprecedented levels, a Catholic veto could close a pop concert, empty a cinema or give the thumbs-down to a play.

During the pre-admission interviews neither the Mother Superior nor the Mistress raised the question of whether Victoria was a virgin, or if she clearly understood what the commitment of chastity meant. Instead, the Mistress gave her a summary of the Rule of the Order. The guidelines would officially control her every movement and thought from the day she entered. There were twenty-five lines devoted to chastity. Victoria had yet to read them.

†

Her bedroom was small, and in many ways a contemporary social history of a typical young American girl. It was a time when the vogue in furnishings was to match. Victoria's dark-green chenille bedspread matched the curtains and carpet. The wallpaper design was composed of countless daffodils. The effect she wanted, of perpetual spring, was completed by the cream-painted woodwork. Tucked into her dressing-table mirror frame were snapshots: Victoria at a pajama party; she and her sisters at a birthday celebration for their mother; with her father shortly before he died; Art in his football uniform; Art and Victoria sitting on the front porch, drinking lemonade: that photograph had been taken by one of her sisters late in the evening. There was a dark shadow across Art's face. That was the night they first made love. A bulletin board above the mirror was festooned with pom-poms from a football game. Art had been on the winning team and presented them to her over dinner. That night, too, they made love. Below the paper tassels was a thumbtacked invitation to a friend's bridal shower, Victoria's high school schedule, half a dozen birthday and Christmas cards, including one from Art, and his valentine from last February, red imitation silk and gold letters, saying "I love you." There was a corsage of withered flowers, a reminder of the day she had been a cousin's bridesmaid. Art had come with her, gotten drunk, and nearly crashed the car on the way home. He was so shaken he did not even kiss her good night.

Neatly stacked in their stand were many of the pop hits of the day, albums featuring Frank Sinatra, Lester Lanin, Billy Vaughn, The Kingston Trio, Nat "King" Cole, and, of course, Elvis Presley and Bill Haley. Book shelves contained a fair selection of current best-sellers. Copies of Herman Wouk's *Marjorie Morningstar*, Morton Thompson's *Not as a Stranger*, and Robert Ruark's *Something of Value*, read, evaluated, and discussed at length with friends, now stood discarded. There were, however, three books in the collection constantly referred to, their pages well thumbed, corners neatly turned down to help her locate passages. One was *The Scrolls from the Dead Sea* by Edmund Wilson. The second was *Life Is Worth Living*, written by Victoria's favorite Catholic author, Archbishop Fulton J. Sheen. These books had helped her answer many questions, buttressing further the solace she found in all aspects of her faith.

Beside them was her copy of the Bible. Given her by her mother on the day she was confirmed, it had in the past year become essential reading. Time and again she plunged into the life of Jesus, trying to understand better the deeper message of the Gospels. Christ, she concluded, did not come to earth to *live*, He wanted to *die*, to sacrifice Himself for the sins of all others. His commitment on that first Good Friday was to ensure there would always be an Easter Sunday. Such selflessness had enthralled her, and fitted perfectly her own concept of why she wanted to be a nun.

In her diary for August 6, 1958, she wrote her leitmotiv. *"I want to save souls. To continue Christ's work. To give myself to the Lord, fully and completely, in a way I have never given myself to anybody before."*

Sister Elizabeth and some of the more intelligent of the "F.B.I.," foreign-born Irish, priests had all reminded Victoria that no evidence existed that Buddha's birth was foretold, or that of Confucius or Mohammed or Lao-Tzu. They had come into the world demanding to be believed. But throughout the Old Testament Christ was expected. From Genesis onward the Messianic currents had flowed down the centuries, leaving no room for doubt about that glorious moment when Mary received a sign she would conceive by the Holy Ghost and that when her time came she would deliver the Son of God in a stable.

For Victoria that image was powerful, as were all others that followed: of Christ strong, unshakable in His faith, filled with compassion, self-discipline, restraint, and self-mortification. She was eager to transfer to Christ all the love and devotion she would, in a marriage, give to an earthly husband. She had already envisaged her wedding in her diary. "I am to wed the Risen Christ and like Him walk humbly and poorly among his people. Among them, but not of them."

Though they had not said so, Victoria sensed her sisters, like many of her friends, now looked upon her differently. This year there would be three other local girls embarking on vocations. She did not know the way they felt, but Victoria inwardly enjoyed the respect and at times the adulation she received in deciding to be a nun. Within her circle, the notion a girl should aspire to become something other than a compliant housewife was not easy to grasp. Marriage remained the first goal in Victoria's set. She, though, liked the idea of being thought unconventional.

Victoria awakened early. She remained under the covers, enjoying the excitement. In a few hours she would enter religious life. Her eyes roamed over the room she knew she would probably never occupy again, remembering last night, the occasion of her final party. It had flowed through all the rooms upstairs and downstairs, and out into the yard. There were relatives, neighbors, classmates, even persons she hardly knew. Her mother said wistfully there were probably more people than even for Dad's funeral.

✝

Beneath some of the banter there was a sadness similar to that on the day they had buried her father. A number of people actually told her how much she would be missed and what a great sacrifice she was being called to make. There was no point in trying to convince them how wrong they were, not as they sipped lemonade and nibbled cookies. Why even begin to explain that while she was leaving their world, she was not leaving *the* world; that all she was doing was entering into a deeper relationship with

God? Why say anything except to thank them for their farewell gifts? She lost count of the times she murmured the words. There were dozens of gifts, expensive and beautiful, but not hers to keep. The Order had sent a list of what was "acceptable" to receive. Solid silver candlesticks, goblets, napkin holders, cutlery. Hand-polished glassware. Pure linen tablecloths and napkins. The Mistress of Postulants had written that Victoria could accept these, but on arrival at the Mother House she must hand them all over. It was Victoria's first practical experience of how, on one level, the vow of poverty was interpreted by the Order.

†

The gifts for the community covered the carpet of the bedroom. There were over a hundred items. In a small pile were the presents she could personally keep upon entering. There were a statue of Saint Joseph, a simply framed picture of Our Lady, a plastic shower cap, a knife, fork, and two spoons. And her Bible.

†

Victoria had stood in the living room, admiring an exquisitely formed candelabrum. The gifts she had received amounted to a trousseau any bride would find acceptable. As she turned the candelabrum in her hands, noting its hallmark stamped on the base, Sister Elizabeth appeared beside her. She squeezed Victoria's arm. Her voice was soft and reassuring. She took the candelabrum and gently led the way to Victoria's room. Sister Elizabeth closed the door behind them and placed the gift on the floor beside the other presents. Possessiveness, she explained, is one of the most ruinous elements in secular life. Soon Victoria would be free from this destructive force, to experience instead the consolation of a new life that would enrich her beyond all worldly goods. That, promised the nun, would give her an outward happiness and inner serenity she had never before experienced. They returned to the party where Victoria accepted more expensive gifts, aware that Sister Elizabeth's eyes remained upon her.

†

Still in bed, Victoria reached for her Bible, turning to the New Testament, to the words of her favorite Apostle, Luke, reading a sentence she knew by heart. *"No man putting his hand to the plough, and looking back, is fit for the kingdom of God."* This, she decided, was what the vow of poverty really meant. To look back was to covet possessions and in doing so lose any hope of acquiring the far greater treasure of Heaven. She was more anxious than ever to start her process of dispossession.

✝

Father Bruce had been among the first to arrive at the party. For a while he stood supportively beside her as she received the first of her gifts. He had doused his face, craggy-featured enough to be on Mount Rushmore, with after-shave. Father Bruce could have stepped out of De Mille's *Ten Commandments;* he always seemed to have descended from some perpetual height not even his priests could climb. As she began to receive her presents, Father Bruce murmured in her ear. Victoria smiled. She knew what he was driving at. But she allowed him, because he was Father Bruce, to say this to her. Still murmuring in her ear, he paraphrased the Bible. " 'The affectation of an elaborate headdress, the wearing of golden jewelry, or the donning of rich robes is not for you. Your adornment is rather the hidden character of the heart, expressed in the unfading beauty of a calm and gentle disposition. This is precious in God's eyes.' "

His true gift, she thought, what he would be remembered for was to always state the obvious at the right time. She was perfectly content to do what Saint Peter demanded. She knew there would be no more sunbathing in a skimpy swimsuit. No more putting on makeup or wearing a pretty dress, except, she had been told, for her marriage feast to Christ. No more making love to Art, to anybody. After her last confession, when she had admitted her resolve weakened under Art's caressing, Father Doyle surprised her. Instead of sending her out of the box with a blessing, he whispered to her through the grille, explaining that after she had entered, she would spontaneously know what was right and wrong. But she must see her new chastity as part of a package, a framework within which she could be secure to develop her service to others and find more time for prayer. He counseled it would be far from easy and she must have the humility to accept her mistakes. But in time she would find that the forces that had made her succumb to temptation would be directed toward new goals. He had spoken about no one being more welcome in God's eyes than the truly repentant sinner.

✝

It was time to get up. She stood for a moment among the gifts, staring at the dressing-table mirror. Her nightgown was of cotton flannel. She had worn it these past few nights to get used to the cloth. Flannel nightdresses were the only kind permitted by the Order. Victoria continued to stare at the mirror. Then, slowly and deliberately, she reached forward and plucked the photographs of Art from the frame. She tore them into pieces and dropped them into the wastebasket. Then she removed the pom-poms and the corsage. Next, the Christmas cards, not bothering to tear them, but letting them fall into the basket. Finally, she took down Art's valentine, which she shredded. It was her way of exorcising him. Even so, she could not forget the previous night.

†

The house was overflowing. More cars arrived out front and Victoria lost count of how many times she had carried gifts to her room. She returned from yet another trip when she stopped, suddenly tense, in the door of the living room. Art was there. He towered over most of the other guests. His back was to her, his head thrust forward, listening to a girl who lived a few doors away. She looked up at him adoringly. Victoria remembered she had always been there in the shadowy background, never seeking attention nor expecting it, so quiet that it was easy to forget she was around. Tonight, though, there was a difference about her — not just her pink dress, all bows and frills. She seemed more relaxed, more openly determined to hold Art in conversation. Victoria wondered why she felt a sudden pang of jealousy. Art turned, saw her, and smiled, cutting through the crowd to reach her, using his arms the way he swam to propel himself forward at speed. He wore a sports shirt and slacks. There was a bantering look in his eyes. He asked if she was still mad at him. She pretended not to understand. He rested his hand lightly on her arm, bent down, and whispered in her ear, reminding her. She saw Sister Elizabeth watching them. She removed Art's hand, determined to show the watching nun that his attention was not welcome, that he had no right to display an air of proprietorship. He laughed and asked why she was blushing. For a moment she felt resentment. She had not seen him since that night in the park. Nor had she invited him here tonight. Yet he was behaving as if she were still his, as if this were just an ordinary party, not her farewell from his world. Sister Elizabeth edged toward them. Victoria moved away from Art. He smiled, that sudden stiff smile of his she knew masked his inner fury. Father Bruce was at her elbow. He looked at Art steadily, his face more granitelike than ever. From his pocket Art produced a small package. He thrust it into her hand, and Father Bruce told her to open it. It was an expensive wristwatch. The priest said it was a fine gift. Ignoring him, Art addressed Victoria. The watch was to remind her of their time together. He abruptly turned and left, pausing only to take the blonde girl with him. She looked over her shoulder and smiled at Victoria. Sister Elizabeth, who materialized beside her, said, "A nice piece, my child, but you have a watch. I think it would be best to hand this in when you get to the convent." Victoria nodded. The watch, like Art, was no longer part of her world.

†

Bathed and wearing a simple black cotton dress and sandals, Victoria sat in her room, waiting. There were several hours to go. She wished the time would pass more quickly. She wondered whether she should write Art a letter, explaining she still wanted him as a friend. The restless surgings continued to create tension in her, putting her on edge.

†

When the party was over, Victoria and her sisters helped their mother to return the house to its neat-as-a-pin condition. On their way to bed, her mother paused in the doorway, staring at the spread of presents. "You got far more than I did when I married your dad."

"Mother, it's because they're for the community. It's people's way of showing their appreciation for all the Order means."

Her mother nodded, trying to understand. She pointed at the collection of silver and linen. "But what will the Order do with all this? Keep it? Sell it? Or what?"

Victoria smiled. "I don't know. But God will find a use for them."

Her mother kissed her on the forehead and without another word went to her room.

†

Victoria's mother turned to check that her three younger daughters were settled in the back of the car. Victoria sat in front, hands on her lap, hair neatly brushed, staring ahead. The girl who had left with Art was playing records on her porch. She gyrated slowly, in pelvic imitation of Presley. Farther down the road, a gang of boys were loading six-packs into a convertible. It was the last day of August and unbearably hot. They were off to the lake, Victoria guessed, and they'd also pick up burgers and French fries. On the way home they would probably stop and go bowling. Some of their parents, in sweatshirts and shorts, were mowing the little squares of grass in front of their houses. Her mother held her rosary beads, old and worn now, like her hands. The final ritual before they could depart was about to begin.

Victoria cleared her throat. In a strong voice she announced, "Saint Christopher, patron saint of travelers." From her mother and the backseat came a responsive chorus: "Guard and protect us on our journey." Her mother added: "Amen."

She checked the mirror. The two cars parked immediately behind had started their engines. They contained twelve of Victoria's closest relatives, aunts and uncles who insisted on escorting her into convent life. The gifts she was taking to the community filled the trunks of all three cars. In addition, in her mother's trunk, was Victoria's suitcase, stuffed with the clothes on the list the convent had provided.

"Did you pack everything?" Her mother had asked the question several times. "Yes, Mother, I checked everything."

"I wish you'd worn something a bit brighter than black. You are going to spend the rest of your life in black. I just wish you'd put on something with some color in it. I'd have liked that."

"I look good in black. You told me that. It makes me look slim, you said. Mother, don't you think we ought to be going?"

In convoy the three cars moved down the road. Victoria stared straight ahead, ignoring the neighbors' waves, wondering why she felt she suddenly wanted to cry.

The silence, deeper than any Victoria had known, enveloped her. She searched her mind for a comparison, seeking something apt from what she realized, with a strange feeling, she already thought of as the other world, the one inhabited by her family and friends. Just five hours into convent life, they had somehow started to recede in her mind; the total quiet obliterated them.

She began to undress. As instructed, she removed her shoes, positioning them as shown, beside the bed. Next, she unclasped her garters, releasing her new black stockings. She laid them carefully on the bed.

The professed sister who had escorted her here had cautioned she must take good care of everything. The nun, Victoria remembered, was controlled and calm, her face serene, with a beauty all its own. When she spoke, her voice was remote, as if living in this consecrated place gave her a special kind of energy, enough to maintain a distance from everybody and everything. In her words and gestures she conveyed the impression of carrying out the will of God. Victoria had promised herself she would strive to become as perfect.

She unhooked her cape. It was fastened at its pristine white collar and dropped without flare to her waistline. It was so designed, the nun had explained, to ensure custody of the hands. She had shown Victoria how to bend her elbows and clasp her fingers together beneath it. Henceforth, in public, whenever she was beyond the confines of the convent she must walk with her hands like this. When she had work to do or prayers to say, she could pin back the cape. The nun had demonstrated how it could be buttoned at the shoulder, but otherwise the cape must completely cover Victoria's hands until it became natural for them to be still. She placed the garment on the bed, beside the stockings. Victoria unbuttoned her dress. It was medieval-black, relieved only by cuffs as white as the cape's collar, with a featureless bodice cut to disguise any suggestion that she possessed breasts. She pulled it over her head, revealing a round-necked T-shirt, white cotton underpants, and a garter belt. These had all been ordered and paid for by her mother from a mail-order house specializing in clothes for nuns. She removed the T-shirt. Under it she had a bra that complied with the Order's specifications: black, without lace or fancy stitching. She unclasped the garter belt, placing it on top of her other clothes. The belt also was black, without frills. Victoria pulled on a cotton-flannel nightdress, covering herself to her ankles. She felt inside the nightie, undid her bra, and wriggled out of her panties, letting the garments fall inside her nightdress to her feet.

The nun had explained that was how she must always undress. The procedure was part of the Order's ritual. Victoria stooped and in one quick movement picked up the panties and bra and placed them with her other underwear in the top drawer of a wooden chest. She folded her dress and cape and stored them in the second drawer. The bottom one held her toilet articles. When she bent, Victoria was careful not to turn her back on the bed. Jesus — in His Passion on a carved crucifix — was lying on the pillow. The nun had shown Victoria how to place the cross, its top resting against the very center of the pillow, at an angle of forty-five degrees. The precise position was laid down in the Order's Holy Rule. While the crucifix was there, she must not sit on the bed. The nun's explanation had riveted her. "Our Lord is watching while you go about His work."

Before going to bed, Victoria must remove the crucifix and reverently place it on top of the chest. She was not ready for sleep yet. Her surroundings continued to fascinate her. Hemmed in by white cotton curtains on three sides, the enclosure was completed by one of the walls of the long barracklike room. The drapes were suspended from hooks in the ceiling and reached to precisely a quarter of an inch above the spotless and shining linoleum floor. On her way down the room, Victoria had counted: there were fifty identical pens. She shivered when the nun called them cells. She really was embarking upon a monastic life. All the saints, monks, friars, and hermits had lived in cells. She had an image of tortured-faced men struggling to ward off evil before reaching peace with God. But until the nun led her into the postulants' dormitory, Victoria had no idea women also occupied cells.

The nun had explained everything in the cell had its proper place. The iron bedstead *must* always be exactly two inches from the wall. The straight-backed chair *must* stand at the foot of the bed, six inches clear of it. Her shoes, thick-heeled and laced, the sort her grandmother wore, *must* be lined up on the left-hand side of the bed. The dresser scarf, a white strip of cloth, *must* be placed horizontally. Only one statue was permitted on top of the chest, which *must* always be two clear feet from the bed. A statue of Our Lady, pressed into Victoria's hand by her mother just before they said their final good-bye, *must* be kept in the bureau. She could take it out to look at it, or even change it for the statue of Saint Joseph. But only one item at a time *must* be displayed. Even her Bible *must* be kept in a drawer. Victoria's bed *must* be made in a certain way. The nun had demonstrated: untucking and then remaking the sheets, folding the corners diagonally, the way a nurse made a bed. She took unusual care to place the pillow exactly flat, with an equal amount of undersheet on either side. Once satisfied, she positioned the crucifix.

Victoria had noticed her movements: they were deft and economical. When she moved, she not so much walked as glided, only the soft swish of her habit indicating her passage. Standing at the foot of the bed, the nun eyed Victoria steadily. In the same gentle, distant voice, she delivered her final instructions. "Remember, you have been chosen for this life. But it is sometimes not easy, especially for parents, to understand God has called a daughter. You can help them, and please Him, by remembering that the best kind of advertising for what He wants of you is the 'show me' kind. You remember the saying, 'by their fruits you shall know them'? So let your family know you, in your new life, as someone who is glad to have been called. That you have been chosen to serve others. Remember what Jesus said: *'The harvest indeed is great but the laborers are few. Pray ye therefore the Lord of the harvest, and he send forth laborers into his harvest.'* You are now one of His laborers. You will learn here how to reap a harvest that is far more worthwhile than any other. So say good-bye to your family with that certainty. Be happy. For them. For God." The nun paused and indicated the crucifix. "And for Him." Without another word she turned and glided away.

Despite the nun's words and Victoria's determined efforts to follow the homily, the parting had not been easy.

✝

As she rejoined her family, everybody said how nice she looked in her postulant outfit. She took her mother by the arm, conscious that time was running out and soon they must say good-bye. They walked along the convent's path, past the chapel, and the seemingly endless red brick of the convent itself; roof below roof, eaves and narrow windows, all combining to give a totally enclosed feeling. Near the chapel Victoria held her mother's hands in hers. She chose her words carefully, insisting she was genuinely glad to be no longer her own person, free to do as she pleased, that when professed she could be sent by the Church to do whatever work was needed; that all she would do from now on would be based on selfless love, given without fear and offered in joy. There were tears in her mother's eyes.

The final act of parting was swift. A bell rang. The relatives of the nineteen other postulants admitted with Victoria were shown out by nuns. There was no time for clinging or last-minute appeals for daughters to change their minds.

The father of one girl tripped and lurched against a wall. His nun escorts stood scandalized. The man was close to being drunk. Victoria eyed the postulants. The man's daughter had the same dumpy figure, and in her eyes was a similar glazed look. Victoria wondered how they had managed to get that way. Then the massive convent door closed on the girl's father, Victoria's relatives, and the entire secular world.

The Mother Superior appeared, small and rotund with piercing gray-green eyes. Victoria suddenly thought she was far more forbidding than when they had met at her final pre-admission interview. Though reserved then, the nun was friendly. Now, she appeared distant, separated from the postulants by some invisible barrier. She remembered what Father Bruce and Sister Elizabeth had said about the Mother Superior: that she had a good degree in the classics; that her master's thesis had been on the first series of wars between Catholics and Protestants, ending in the Peace of Augsburg in 1555, giving Protestants the right to Church lands they had seized by arms and bloodshed and ending the old principle of the unique supremacy of Roman Catholicism; that the paper was now in the Secret Archives of the Vatican and the Mother Superior was the symbol of the Order's academic excellence; that she possessed, in Sister Elizabeth's opinion, a genuine Renaissance mind, but one that never lost sight of fundamental principles; that high on that list was obedience and humility; that in spite of all her duties she still found time to study silk-screening and the life of the bat. Victoria recalled, too, the words of the Mistress of Postulants. "When you come here, you must always remember that, in the spiritual sense, the Mother Superior is neither man nor woman. She is the Christ among us and as such is loved, obeyed, and looked up to by us all. You must always remember that."

The Mother Superior spoke. "You are welcome. We have all prayed for this day. That God, having called you, would give you the strength to answer that call. Your presence here shows He wishes you to be part of this congregation. To remain, you will need continuing strength and understanding."

She turned and looked across the entrance hall. As if by some invisible command a nun appeared from a room, carrying a pile of loose-leaf manuals. The Mother Superior turned back to the postulants. "Strength and understanding. Those are the most important qualities you will need. Strength to maintain your faith in God and what He wishes of you. Understanding why you must do certain things for Him. Always for Him." She smiled, giving her face a radiance that a moment before was not there.

"It is not easy to recognize you have been called. That you must know. But having answered, it is even harder to remain faithful to the call. To be a nun in this world is always difficult. The temptations to abandon your calling are many. And you should be warned, the life here is hard. It was never meant to be anything else. You will be tested to the limit, not in your faith, but in your ability to turn that faith into what God wishes from you. He, not you, will in the end decide if you have the capacity to perform His work. You are here because you heard the call. To live up to it you must listen every day." The Mother Superior waited, letting her words settle, her eyes scanning the group. She continued to outline the difficulties.

"In an age of increasing selfishness, you have been chosen to lead lives of sacrifice. There are some people who say it is a life against nature. You already know something of what is expected of you. Poverty, chastity, and obedience. You have been told, briefly, about these vows in our correspondence with you."

Victoria realized she had never read up on the vows. Thankfully, it appeared not to matter.

The Mother Superior spoke of the challenge of their new life. They were here because they were neither halfhearted in their religious determination or unsure of why they had been chosen. Equally, they must recognize they would live a life most women would find impossible. But they should not feel a need to apologize to themselves or anybody for the role for which they had been selected. Nobody would ask them for a reason if they married. They need not give, or seek, an explanation for their chastity. But just as a good marriage required working at, so did living a full celibate life, perhaps even more so, for it required disciplining nature's instincts and personal inclinations. They should realize that self-control was what distinguished a human from other species. In many ways, the ability to live naturally in a state of chastity was the apex of discipline. Some would find it a greater struggle than others. A few would undoubtedly discover the commitment too hard. They would not be judged but simply returned to the secular world. For those who remained, the celibate life would shape their views and values in a way they would find totally satisfying. Chastity demanded a renunciation of several things, but not of one's self. It was a gift before it was a choice or commitment. Only God had the power to choose who will receive such a gift. They had been chosen. They must not disappoint Him.

She turned to the nun standing beside her with the pile of books. Each one contained a mimeographed copy of the full Holy Rule of the Order. The pages listed every requirement to live in this cloistered world. Every day, she added, her voice pitched to reach no farther than the caped postulants, they would read and memorize a portion of the Rule. It would take them weeks. Once more she paused, surveying the group. The time, she continued, would be well spent, their discoveries standing them in good stead for the rest of their lives. The Rule would teach them how, as celibates, they could undertake tasks that married clergy in other denominations might find difficult to perform, unable or unwilling to take their families to areas of danger. But because they would not have husbands or children to consider, they could, when the time came, work in such places; with almost no worldly possessions they could travel quickly to where they were needed without having to be concerned at uprooting loved ones. Being celibate and impoverished, they could obey their call with undivided hearts.

The Mother Superior nodded to the nun, who began to hand out the books. The task completed, she left, with the same glide-walk Victoria was determined to acquire.

The Mother Superior continued. "Read and inwardly digest. Silence is a virtue to be used to recharge our spiritual batteries. You must always remember that. You cannot do God's work if you are being constantly distracted by other voices."

Her right hand, plump and white, appeared from beneath her scapular, and she made the sign of the cross over the postulants. She made it quickly. Then she glided away.

As if she had been standing in the wings waiting to make her entrance, thought Victoria, the Mistress of Postulants came forward. More than any other, she would be the one responsible for their religious formation. She welcomed them in a voice that was sharp and distinctive. "Tomorrow we start. You have just been told it will be hard. It will be harder than you can imagine."

The nature of a vocation, she continued, was not a job like teaching or nursing. It was "following Christ. That means saying 'yes' to the Way of the Cross. You must be prepared to strip and empty all the self in you so that Christ can be in you."

She reinforced what the Mother Superior had said. They should see their chastity as an adventure, just as others regard marriage. But marriages all too often failed because of the weakness of a husband. They would not ever face such a problem. Christ would never let them down. Only they could fail Him — and only then if they attempted to rationalize the very mystery of chastity. It must be accepted as something not to be explained; trying to rationalize a commitment to celibacy could only lead to failure, dissatisfaction, and a lack of fulfillment. She outlined the program for the rest of their day: evening Mass, supper, and then bed. Finally, she told them about the Great Silence.

✝

Victoria continued to stand at her bedside, staring at the crucifix on her pillow. She knew that beyond her curtained enclosure, in identical cells, were nineteen other girls who had undressed, put away their clothes, said their prayers, read their Bibles, and taken care not to touch their beds, each with its positioned crucifix. Yet there was not a sound. It was as if the Great Silence had somehow made the other postulants vanish. Victoria felt utterly alone. She gently lifted the crucifix from her pillow and placed it next to the statue of Saint Joseph. Then she turned back the covers and climbed into bed. At that moment two distinct sounds broke the Great Silence. From close by came intermittent snoring. She remembered the tipsy girl had a cell directly opposite hers. Farther up in the dormitory was the sound of whimpering. Then it stopped as suddenly as it had begun. Victoria closed her eyes and was asleep almost at once.

CHAPTER 6

†

Realities

Victoria began to prepare the essay on the question the Mistress had set. It was her last written task before going on the Retreat that marked the end of her nine months' postulancy. In ten days' time she would receive both her new name and the full habit of the Order.

Ahead lay seven more years of study. She knew much already. Canon Law, she realized, would continue to fascinate her. There was an all-embracing precision about its language which appealed to her orderly mind. Her only worry, never voiced but confided to the diary she continued to keep, was that the regulations were formulated by a male hierarchy that not only refused nuns a voice, but still effectively ranked women in religious life alongside children and idiots.

But a new Pope, the twenty-third to take the name of John, had been on the Throne of Saint Peter for a year. There was talk that he was planning a Second Vatican Council, when all the bishops would meet in Rome to examine the state of the Church. On the agenda, ran the whisper in the Mother House, would be a look at the role of the sisterhood. Already nuns outnumbered priests by almost three to one, but they remained the same silent, compliant majority they were when Pope Boniface VIII decreed in

1298 that all religious women must obey without question the commands of their clergy.

Just as Sister Elizabeth and Victoria's other nun teachers had regarded Father Bruce and his priests as superior, so did the Mother Superior and her charges look upon Father Lowell, the priest who lived in an apartment behind the convent chapel. For them he was invested with divine authority. Only he had the power to turn bread and wine into the Body and Blood of Jesus; only his hands could touch the flesh of Christ.

This was why before every Mass a postulant laid out a special set of hand-stitched towels in the sacristy where Father Lowell robed. In all ways he was an exalted figure; a tall sandy-haired man in his thirties, for whom nuns held open doors, laughed at his jokes, and bowed demurely when he entered a classroom or one of their parlors. If they were seated and talking, because it was an official period of Recreation, they would rise and stop in midsentence. Before he left one nun always asked for his blessing. They fell to their knees while Father Lowell raised a consecrated hand and asked the Spirit of God to descend. *In nomine Patris et Filii.*

Victoria thought his voice went all the way back to Moses. It was like this, she was certain, in all the convents of the one hundred and seventy-four orders in the United States. She had learned that only those in contemplative communities — in perpetual enclosure — are, strictly speaking, nuns. All others are what Canon Law terms sisters in Christ. The same law defined her Order as an active one: it provided teachers, nurses, prison visitors, social workers from its thirty-five thousand members. It ran houses for unmarried mothers, trained nuns to care for alcoholics, junkies, and the flotsam of city slums. Others had been sent to universities to become doctors, economists, and scientists. The teaching nuns spent their summers away from the classrooms, helping with handicapped children, ministering to grape-pickers, and assisting fellow sisters with an endless caseload of battered wives, pregnant schoolgirls, and the elderly who had been cast aside.

The Order is old, making it one of the aristocrats of the religious world, and the way its congregation lived had hardly changed in three hundred years. Victoria found the life confirmed her concept of what it would be like — an unceasing round of prayer, penance, and work.

Her day, she knew, would continue to be ruled by the canonical hours, which measure not the passage of time as does a clock, but the liturgical hours of the Divine Office: Lauds, the first paean of the early morning. Then Prime and its prayers. At nine A.M. the antiphons of Terce, a reminder of that moment when the Holy Spirit descended on the Apostles at Pentecost. Sext at midday, the sixth hour, to ponder passages of Scripture. None, at three o'clock, is the ninth hour, marking the moment when Christ died, a time for silent meditation. Vespers recalled that first gathering in the Temple of Jerusalem. Compline, at eight o'clock, is another period of intimate prayer. At nine o'clock, the Great Silence descended, never to be broken except in the gravest of emergencies: a fire or a nun discovered to have been taken seriously ill. Next morning Lauds resumed the timeless passage of being taught that chastity was not the only factor which singled out a nun from all other women: it was also the ability to accept, without demur, rules and strictures that are deliberately severe. Day and day out, within their ancient framework, she would continue to be instructed, initiated, shaped, and spiritually formed so that she would resemble in thought and deed all the nuns in the Mother House, and those scattered throughout the world.

Victoria had come to recognize when the Mistress sensed the slightest wavering in her charges. That was the moment she would stop whatever she was saying or doing. Then scissoring through the words, she would repeat the guiding principle of Jean-Baptiste de la Salle: *Now that you are sweetly dead to the world and the world dead in you, that is only part of the holocaust.* She frequently offered a recollection of her own days as a postulant: how she had washed her clothes in cold water with soda crystals that left her hands coarse and red and slept on a pallet of straw from which she rose at the dead of night to offer thanks to God for giving her the means to scourge herself for sins great and small; in Europe, she would add, there were many sisters who still followed such a regime, and were better for it. She had instilled in Victoria and the others that these past nine months had been a preparation for an irrevocable break with the past. Victoria accepted that to make it total and lasting there had to be severity; it was no more than the price she expected to pay. No visits home were allowed and her immediate family could see her only once a month, on a Sunday afternoon. All letters to her mother and sisters must first be read by the Mistress, who also censored all incoming mail. Art had written once. The Mistress flatly told her she had torn up the letter. Victoria briefly wondered what Art wrote. Now she could hardly remember what he looked like.

Once a week without fail, she had read aloud, with other postulants, the Mistress's favorite quotation from La Salle: *You must strip your heart of self, cut back hard on all the little shortcomings prompted by nature and the world.* The prospect of her individuality being excised did not daunt

Victoria. She now firmly believed she would continue to conform, to be the model of obedience, to be very exact in her religious beliefs. This was why she took particular care in preparing her essay. Its title was deceptively simple: "Describe the Vows of Religious Life as Defined by the Holy Rule of the Community." Six months ago, the word "community" to describe the Order would have sounded strange, but now she was completely at ease with the language and customs of convent life. Words like mortification and places like the Chapter of Faults were no longer alien. They formed an integral part of her life, just as bubble gum and soda fountains once had.

She knew the essay demanded a full understanding of the vows of poverty, obedience, and chastity. Poverty and obedience were clear-cut. She must relinquish all her worldly possessions in order to identify more closely with those who possess little. The Order provided for all her needs: food and lodging, clothes and shoes. When she was old, there would always be a bed in the Mother House infirmary. Obedience was giving up the right to determine her own path in life, so that she would be available for God to use as He wanted. These were simple unequivocal vows. Chastity appeared, on the surface, equally easy to grasp. She realized the vow was meant to help her consecrate her life more perfectly to God. She could understand why the Mistress had made her carefully copy out the essentials of chastity: *To abstain from any action, either internal or external, which is opposed to chastity. To practice continuous mortification of the mind and feelings. Taking care at all times to avoid exclusive or particular feelings for others and maintaining a sensible modesty in all things.*

That night, after writing the words, she awoke to find she had touched herself. She had been so scared at her need for genital gratification that she wondered if she was ill. She had spent extra hours kneeling in chapel before the fear went away and she was once again able to look upon her chastity as a way to consummate her love for God. Shortly afterward she experienced, while asleep, an orgasm. She prayed the experience away. Anxious to cleanse herself totally of those disturbing nocturnal moments, she had earned a thin smile of satisfaction from the Mistress with her succinct statement. *Our vow of chastity is a sacred undertaking to offer our soul to God. It means everyone can claim our love.* Later, in the solitude of her cell, she dared again to wonder how it was going to be possible to commit her body to forfeit sex for the rest of her life. She finally found the courage to discuss the matter with Sister Carmelita, the postulant who sat in the adjoining desk in class.

Carmelita, a tall, rangy girl from California, had a deadly gift for mimicry, especially when aping the Mistress's clipped Boston accent. *The Spirit abolishes the flesh in us. Anything physical must be avoided. Cross your legs and you're on the road to Hell.* Carmelita had stooped and pulled her cape about her, twisting her face into the taut look the Mistress adopted when dealing with a sensitive topic. *Now, Sister, remember the words of Saint John Chrysostom. "The pangs of celibacy are a little crucifixion." So hang in there, Sister.* Victoria had laughed then. But Carmelita was no longer here.

No one mentioned her after that morning when the Mistress had briefly announced her departure, adding that she had lost her struggle against pride and self-will. Those cryptic words officially closed the matter. Yet the reason Carmelita was suddenly ordered back into the secular world, deemed to have no vocation, continued to bother Victoria. It was not just the severity of the punishment that concerned her; it was her own role in the episode. If she had intervened, would matters have turned out differently? Instead, she had remained standing in the darkness by her bed on that cold December night, staring at her crucifix in its appointed place on the bureau, listening to Carmelita, aware of what she was doing.

✝

The dark, icy clamp of winter had come early, freezing the ground and frosting the convent windows; icicles drooped from eaves, giving the Mother House the semblance of a fairy-tale castle. Victoria wore a sweater beneath her flannel nightdress. Even then she felt cold, but this, she knew, was not the real reason she had awakened. She glanced at her watch. It was almost two in the morning. Other than the sound of the wind and the driving sleet, nothing broke the Great Silence. She closed her eyes, hoping sleep would swiftly reclaim her. The moaning sound, low, insistent, and suppressed, continued.

Victoria eased herself up on her elbow, listening hard, trying to identify from which cell the sound was coming. The Great Silence enveloped the dormitory. It was broken by another urgent moan. She snuggled back under the bedclothes. Perhaps one of the postulants was having a bad dream.

The moaning came again, longer now, more uncontrollable. Victoria, with a sudden feeling of shock, recognized the sound. She slid out of bed, wincing at the iciness of the linoleum against her bare feet. She hesitated, telling herself she could be wrong. She began to tiptoe out of her cell, trying to locate the source. The wind was gaining strength, whipping the sleet against the window panes. The moans were louder and more drawn out. Victoria realized they were coming from Carmelita's cell. She felt she should go back. This had nothing to do with her. She edged closer to the cell and looked in. Despite the cold, Carmelita had kicked back the bedding. Her nightdress was hoisted up around her waist. Her long legs were spread, a hand clamped across her mouth to muffle the sound. Victoria wanted to rush forward. *No, Carmelita, no. This is a mortal sin. You are committing a mortal sin. Stop it.* Instead, she turned and hurried back to her cell, her face burning. Victoria remembered the words of the Mother Superior on that first evening she had addressed the postulants. *A life against nature.*

Time and again, the theme had been taken up these past months by the Mistress. In one form or another she would remind them that religious life was hard, one of self-abnegation. Any weakness that became known would be proof, the Mistress had said, that God did not want that person. Victoria wondered, standing by her bed, staring toward Carmelita's cell, whether she should not go back and warn her of the terrible danger she faced. Carmelita surely could not have forgotten the lecture the Mistress had delivered. It had an uncompromising title: "Masturbatory Activity." It was, in every sense, the most revealing exposition of the past months, in a way made more so by the Mistress's matter-of-fact approach. She explained that masturbation came from two Latin words: *manus* and *turbatio*, hand and agitation, and was a mortal sin. Those who indulged in it endangered their spiritual growth. The Mistress permitted herself another recollection. When she entered the Order, though nobody dared speak of it, masturbation was held to be the cause of epilepsy, gonorrhea, weakness in the lungs, and depression. Now it was generally accepted by the Order's medical advisers that masturbation could still cause grave psychological problems by inducing guilt and fear. They must always have before them the thought that a healthy mind did not need unhealthy stimulation. She had spoken only for minutes on the subject. But the silence had lasted far longer. Afterward, Victoria had told Carmelita they could have been listening to a discourse on the life-style of the bats that fascinated Reverend Mother.

Standing in the darkness, numbed by the cold and at what she had discovered Carmelita doing, Victoria remembered the final words of the Mistress on the subject. *By the use of prayer personal temptation is reduced more and more and can be compensated for by proper sublimation. You were born with healthy minds. Only the Devil pollutes them. Do not let him. Dear sisters, I beg you all to remember the power of prayer to protect you.*

Victoria remembered how Carmelita had sat at her desk, listening intently, nodding from time to time, seeming completely in agreement with their teacher. Carmelita's moans were sharper and louder. Suddenly there was the sound of footsteps. Her gasp was joined by the voice of the Mistress, low and fierce. By the time the Mistress scuttled out of the dormitory, Victoria had crept back under the blankets, her eyes fixed intently on the crucifix on the bureau. Within hours, Carmelita had packed her trunk and been driven from the Mother House to the airport to collect a one-way ticket. Her family had arranged her flight home to California.

†

Her preparatory work for the essay on vows completed, Victoria began to write. She started with a quotation from Saint Augustine. "If you can say 'Enough' you are lost. Always increase, always progress, always go forward, stop not on the way, turn not back, turn not aside." Her second observation, penned in her neat hand, was from Saint Thomas Aquinas. "The religious pledge their entire life to the zealous pursuit of perfection."

Having established a framework within which she could discuss the theme set by the Mistress, she started to write steadily, assembling her arguments in a clear, concise manner. She began to expound the theological argument that distinguished between a mere promise and the totally binding commitment of vows. A vow is a deliberate promise made to God. She wrote that Saint Thomas's sacred undertaking was an act produced by the reason and ordered by the will, by which one person bound oneself to God to do something, or to abstain from doing something. She remembered what the Mistress had said. *A vow must be an act of reason, ordered by the will. A sister who takes it upon herself to make such a deliberate promise must have full knowledge of what she is doing, must give her full consent to it, and in no way must she be coerced. In short, there must be no element present of ignorance, fear, fraud, or force. A vow cannot be made to another person. Not even the Mother Superior, though she is the Christ among us, can accept your vow.* Victoria resumed writing. "This deliberate promise to God must be something which is good in itself. But even this is not enough. A vow must involve a choice. The choice between two good things."

She read back the passage. It would satisfy the Mistress. But she felt it needed an example that would strikingly clarify her argument. Victoria thumbed through her Bible to the words of Saint Paul, noted the reference, and resumed writing. "Marriage is a holy state, instituted by God. But Saint Paul says that the virginal state is better. Therefore, to vow oneself to that state, to choose between two good things, is meritorious and pleasing to God. This is a perfect example of the object of a vow."

She paused again. She recalled other words the Mistress delivered on the subject. *A vow must be possible to carry out. God does not expect you to promise the impossible. Nor can a vow be made for useless, petty, foolish, or unimportant matters unless the circumstances give them some semblance of moral good. For instance, you may vow never to go to a movie theater because it once showed bad films, even though now it shows only movies that would be approved by the Church. The act of going to the theater now is not sinful, but if you made a vow to stay away because it was once a place of temptation, that vow would be valid and acceptable to God. Remember the end in view in making a vow must always be God's glory.* She continued to compile her arguments, linking one thought with another, no longer surprised at how well she could manage this. It was one of the many changes that had taken place during her postulancy.

Physically, she looked the same. She was the tallest of all the postulants. Her uniform gave her a haunting paleness. Yet there was a glow to her skin that was not there before entering the Mother House. Without any cosmetics she could pass for a woman in her mid-twenties, rather than a girl yet to celebrate her eighteenth birthday. This appearance of physical aging had been accompanied by a mental maturing. She felt calmer and more responsible than she had ever done at home. She thought this to be so because she was free of all trivial decision-making, allowed to concentrate fully on important things such as learning to communicate properly with God, recognizing her imperfections, and correcting them.

She readily accepted things she once would have resisted. Many of the postulants found the discipline oppressive. Victoria reminded herself that, hard though it might be, unquestioning obedience was important in a community in which the Mother Superior was head of a hierarchical family. Like any strict mother's, her word was law. Until recently she had been entitled to a bow on being passed in a corridor and a full curtsy from everyone who entered her office. She convened a special council of the Mother House to announce she was relaxing such formality. But she remained authoritarian in other ways. She once asked two postulants to clear snow in the midst of a blizzard. When they hesitated, she sharply told them it was

Teresa of Ávila who ordered a nun to plant a cucumber sideways in the ground.

She was constantly on the lookout for any sign that a novice had forgotten the need for continual self-effacement. One girl caught glancing at her reflection in a polished brass plate was publicly reprimanded. Another discovered titivating her veil was told there was no room for such feminine vanities. A third postulant forgot herself so far that curves could be discerned beneath her dress. The Mother Superior assembled the postulants, lectured them on the virtue of being unattractive on earth, not only because attractiveness was a sexual lure, but also because to be unattractive showed they were saving themselves for eternal life. In eternity there are no men or women, said the Superior, only souls. Anxious to reinforce her point, she revealed she had not looked in a mirror since that day she became professed. She then reminded them how many rules had been relaxed. When she was a novice, it was forbidden to smell fragrant herbs, fruit, and flowers. Now, she permitted flowers in the parlors. When she had trained, she always sprinkled her food with a bitter flavoring to mortify her taste buds. That was no longer in the Rule, though she still did it out of choice. Life for a postulant was easy-going, she continued, because God willed it should be so. But they should not abuse His benevolence. She looked at the postulants and pronounced punishment. They would all spend an extra hour on their knees in chapel, praying for the help they needed, each one asking God to give it. She made the sign of the cross over them and glided away.

In her first month Victoria had discovered that tampons were barred. She was curious enough to ask the Mistress for an explanation. They had been alone and her superior was unexpectedly forthcoming. The doctors who advised the Order felt that tampons were physiologically unsuitable for virgins. They must use sanitary napkins. The Mistress further astonished Victoria by adding that when she had entered the Order after World War One, the custom was for each postulant to be given diapers, which were washed for reuse and when worn out replaced by new ones. Those were the days, the Mistress said nostalgically, when it was accepted that a girl entering holy life was without any sexual experience. For weeks afterward Victoria had a nagging fear that the Mistress knew about Art. Her doubts eased only when she read how the cult of virginity had survived.

She always had assumed that the Church introduced physical continence for women. Instead, she read, virginity was a pagan cult, flourishing centuries before Christ, reaching back into the darkness of prehistoric times, when totem gods demanded that untouched girls dance through the fields at dead of night to guarantee a good harvest. In pre-Caesarean Rome virgins guarded the sacred fire outside the Senate and were regularly whipped to death if caught in the arms of a soldier. In Babylon and Athens, in Thebes and Damascus, priestesses had to be virgins to exercise their supernatural power. To be a virgin was to be raised above all women and exalted in the eyes of all men. But in the two hundred years following the death of Jesus, religious virginity was seriously threatened. Throughout the Roman Empire celibate Christian girls were put to death. It was not until the fourth century that the concept found new favor. In Asia Minor, virgins banded together in communities. They spent their consecrated lives in prayer and spiritual counseling. Over the next eight hundred years, the cloistered life assumed a definite form: rigid laws, isolation, and, along with chastity, the vows of total poverty and obedience came into vogue. Then, for the second time, under the fury of the Reformation, holy virginity was almost extinguished. The Protestant Reformers Luther and Bullinger challenged automatically all the teachings of Rome. Chastity, cried Luther, was wicked, dangerous for the body and damaging to the mind. Bullinger thundered that a woman's role was to be only a wife and mother; to be a virgin was to deny her creator's intention. Celibacy was dismissed as no more than a mask for impotence and sterility. It was evil. It took centuries for the Church to reestablish the paramount claim of chastity.

Though Victoria was physically not a virgin, she felt in her new life a purity never there before. It allowed her to cope and to make sense of hundreds of rules and regulations that were a veritable Baedeker of convent life. They explained that chastity "should be angelic; that obedience should be prompt; that not a word or a single instant intervene between the order given and its accomplishment unless there is obvious sin in it." There were admonitions on how to show charity, compassion, unity, and above all, how to accept every "penance and correction as if it were coming from the very lips of your Heavenly Spouse, the Lord Jesus Christ."

She saw all this as part of the preparation, which would take her ever deeper into the disciplined routine of the Order, and she had been certain that Sister Martha would be among those to complete the journey. So she found it hard to believe that Martha was not seated a few feet away at her desk, her back straight, her marble-white face close to her work, not a muscle disturbing the fall of her cape, the first in the group to master the twin virtues of custody of the eyes and hands. Later she had acquired, shortly before Victoria managed to do so, the art of walking like a nun. It was Martha who had sat there so attentively when the Mistress of Postulants lectured on the meaning of interior silence, a required mental state that further distinguished a nun from other women. At its core was a total capability to banish the past, to excise memories, to remove any distracting echoes from the outside world. Victoria remembered how Martha asked how long it took to acquire such control. The Mistress had frowned and pondered before she finally answered. *It could be years: many, many years. But it is worth waiting for.* Martha had smiled and said she was convinced that, with God's help, she would find the patience to wait.

✝

Spring had brought color to the grounds. But the Mother House itself remained gripped in the pall of Lent; the prelude to Holy Week is the most solemn time of the year in the convent. For Victoria, the silence seemed, if anything, more profound and the piety more tangible. Father Lowell repeatedly reminded them this was the approach of Christ's supreme sacrifice. He offered a slogan to carry them through Lent. *Everything you do, you do for Jesus. Just as He did everything for you.* Victoria and Martha left the chapel after evening Mass and Martha stopped in midstride. She was shorter than Victoria, with delicate features and dark luminous eyes. They shone with excitement. "I'm leaving."

Victoria was too stunned to speak.

"I'm leaving. Tonight. I'm going out. To get married." She explained that for months, on Sunday visits, her sister had been smuggling in love letters from her boyfriend.

"To get married . . ." Victoria repeated. "But you have already promised to be married to Christ."

"That's what Reverend Mother said, Vicky. She wanted me to go with her and pray. I told her I've done all the praying. I just want Johnny."

Victoria looked at her, still stunned. "But, Sister . . ." She stopped, uncertain. Should she be calling Martha "Sister" now that she was about to reenter the outside world? She didn't know. Nor, she thought, pulling herself together, did it matter. "What time are you going?"

"Just before the Great Silence. They've asked my father to drive to the back door. It'll be dark then."

"But that's terrible. I mean, it's like you're doing something wrong. Not having a vocation isn't a crime . . ."

"They think it's the best way. Reverend Mother said this is the way they always do it."

Victoria decided she would be there to say good-bye. Martha vehemently shook her head.

"You must not come. You could get into trouble. You know what the Rule says about those going out? There must be no fuss and no good-byes. I guess it can be upsetting and unsettling."

Victoria was adamant. She would be there.

Shortly before nine o'clock Victoria hurried to the back door of the Mother House. She was too late; Martha's father was already driving away. She could not be certain, but she thought that Martha was weeping.

✝

Victoria reached the end of the first part of her essay, by succinctly defining the views of Saint Basil, who in the fourth century introduced the practice of lifelong vows. "The virgin, says Basil, is to be regarded as the bride of Christ and a chosen vessel dedicated to the Lord. If, therefore, she breaks her vow, she is to be punished as though convicted of adultery."

She remembered the shock when the Mistress ordered them to copy into their exercise books and then join her in reading aloud Basil's key contribution. *While we are in the world we are dead to God. We only rise to the life of God by dying to the world. This is the one great truth the worldly heart is so unwilling to receive. The natural heart is willing to do many things for God, if only it may be allowed to live. The one thing that God wants is that it should die. The natural heart cannot conceive how its death should be profitable to God because it cannot conceive how its life is hateful to Him.*

Five months later she decided to expand this concept. "Christ, when He came to this world, chose a life of suffering. We should do the same. We must try to purge away all thought of self. We should banish all self-interest. We should strive for nothingness. The way to achieve this is to remain faithful to the vows we take." She reread what she had written. *Purge away all thought of self ... banish all self-interest ... strive for nothingness.*

From the very outset Victoria realized her postulancy was a journey of self-discovery, designed both to test her faith and to give her superiors a chance to assess her suitability; that she was under scrutiny, which had started at five o'clock on her first full day in the convent — when the alarm bell broke, but did not end, the Great Silence.

✝

She sat bolt upright and saw, standing in the doorway of the dormitory, surveying its honeycomb of cells, the black-robed figure of the Mistress, lips pursed, eyes sweeping the area. Victoria leaped up, put on a black-and-white seersucker bathrobe, and went to the communal bathroom. Other postulants were doing the same, tying identical robes at their waists. Every nun in the Mother House, she would discover, wore the same style. It was part of the Order's continuous process of eliminating individuality. In complete silence they brushed their teeth and washed, the Mistress moving ceaselessly among them, ready to cut off with a warning finger any temptation to speak.

Victoria was the first to return to her cell. She removed the bathrobe, folded it, and placed it on the bed. Then from the bureau she removed the clothes so carefully placed there the night before, and in a reverse of the order in which she had undressed, clad herself in the postulant's garments — always careful to provide only the minimum exposure of her body to the crucifix.

Having put away her nightclothes and having made the bed exactly as she had been shown, with infinite gentleness she cradled the crucifix in her hands and placed it in position on the pillow. Only then did Victoria glance at her watch. She was within the time allotted: twenty minutes from awakening to the placement of the cross. She pulled back the curtains around her cell and stepped out into the dormitory. Other postulants were emerging uncertainly from behind white cotton hangings. These provided them with the only seclusion they could hope for, the semiprivacy of being heard but not seen.

Using her hands to issue a series of silent commands, the Mistress lined up the girls in pairs. From now on — at mealtimes, in chapel, in many of their duties around the Mother House — this would be how they would pair off. No postulant would be allowed to change her companion except at Recreation, when they could move freely around. From this moment, too, their chronological ages ceased and the only one they would be known by was their age in religious life, based on when they had been registered to enter the Order. Preceded by the Mistress, the procession filed out of the dormitory and down the main corridor to chapel. Victoria, conscious of a need to keep in step, again tried to imitate the effortless glide of the Mistress. She was still trying as she entered the chapel and genuflected to the altar, her body bending at the waist, her arms crossed beneath her cape.

By the end of her first day Victoria came to see the clear-cut stamp of her life as a postulant: her days would be divided among the classroom, the chapel, and domestic work. She would polish floors, wipe dishes, and lay tables between study and prayer. At the end of a demanding scholastic schedule, she would resume her chores: helping to serve supper, polishing more floors, or working in the laundry, before settling down to a further period of intensive study. Then a final visit to the chapel when she would sink to her knees, emulating the professed nuns: heads bowed, spines soldierly straight and feet turned back. A feeling of spiritual fulfillment had carried her through the demands of her seventeen-hour day.

Each one thereafter was almost identical. She believed this was deliberate, planned to encourage her to cope with a dawn-to-darkness struggle to master the minutiae that totally governed her mind and body. To further help this conditioning she developed the habit of writing down and committing to memory key passages from the lectures that flowed from the Mistress. The words charted her progress ever further into a world ruled by a discipline the like of which she had never remotely suspected existed.

It was November — nearly three months since Victoria had entered — and the realization that Christmas was little more than a month away had come to her when the Mistress delivered her lecture on temptation.

"None of you can receive Him if you yield to any one temptation. Let me be clear. I do not mean a temptation to commit a big sin. I am talking of the temptation to commit something small. Like not enjoying all your food. Like not putting enough effort into your domestic duties. Like complaining you are tired when you know you can continue to work longer. Small things. Little failures of duty. Tiny moments of self-indulgence. Thinking about candy when you should be thinking of God. Letting your minds wander, if only for a moment, into the past. Doing anything that compromises your promise to carry His Cross."

During the week before Christmas, the day after Carmelita left, the Mistress interjected into the curriculum an unscheduled talk on sin.

"You know, dear sisters, in your hearts you know this, that the more you try to serve God, the more you become aware of the pervasiveness of sin. The closer you are drawn to Him, the more you realize that things which did not seem like sins before are now serious ones. But remember, too: the greater the sense of your awareness of your sins, the greater is His love to take them away."

On an icy January morning, the Mistress had returned to the virtue of purification.

"It is the furnace, dear sisters, in which we all have to be cleansed. No one knows, except Him, how many times we must be cast into that furnace, before we emerge clean and worthy to serve Him. But however painful is the process, you must accept it gladly. You must see it as a sacrifice you thankfully offer to Him as a way of recognizing His suffering for you."

In February, with rain sheeting down the convent windows, the Mistress ended her discourse on willpower with these words:

"Whatever evil there is in your nature, it can be excised. It may be a long and bitter struggle, especially if that evil involves the flesh and blood. They are weak. But your will is stronger, if you allow it to be. You cannot win the fight alone. You can achieve victory only by praying as Our Lord prayed, allowing nothing to come between you and God. You will find, dear sisters, that the evil will then leave your body. This is a proven fact."

Before she gave out the theme of the essay on vows, the Mistress spoke about the dangers of satisfaction.

"My own prayer, dear sisters, for you is this. You will never, ever, allow yourself to be satisfied. For my part, while I have the power to do so, I will never allow you to be satisfied with any effort short of what you are capable of producing. I will encourage you to bear any trouble or pain if it brings the smallest advance in your spiritual growth. Indeed, I will continue to tell you that such travails are of no consequence if they stand between you and God. Your one aim is to be always with Him whom you love. Being with Him can give you joy beyond joy. You already have tasted that joy these past months. You can continue to do so if you stay true to your love, to your vows."

✝

Victoria paused in her writing, arranging her concluding thoughts on vows. She believed she had dealt fully with each one. Poverty she had identified as the first condition Jesus places upon those He singles out, quoting Christ's first beatitude. *Blessed are ye poor, for yours is the Kingdom of God.* Religious obedience, she concluded, is not submission by force; rather, it is a voluntary response to a moral pressure. Chastity liberates a person to show a greater love of God. Her style was detached and devoid of rhetoric. She knew this was the way the Mistress liked written work. She glanced at her watch. There were only minutes before the study period ended and the Great Silence descended. She wrote a concluding thought. "Vows do not dispense with our human responsibilities. They transform them. They are a religious act performed in faith and repentance. They are a sign that those who take them wish to receive the mercy of God." She put down her pen. She and the other postulants handed in their essays to the Mistress, who then marched them in complete silence to their cells. Tomorrow she would escort them to the Chapter of Faults.

In orderly file, paired as always, the postulants entered the study hall, hands clasped beneath their capes. On the index finger of each girl was a thick metal ring. Attached to it were nine separate strands of twisted steel wire; each piece was precisely three inches long. The strands were coiled and fit snugly into the palm of her left hand. They were cool against the skin.

This is the Discipline. It was the instrument each nun in the Order, from its inception in 1560, had used to punish herself for any breach of the Rule. The Discipline was fashioned by the same nuns who threaded rosary beads for their sisters in Christ.

Every two months, after supper, the study hall was turned into the Chapter of Faults. Before coming here the postulants had gone to the chapel, lit only by the vigil light at the altar, and silently examined their consciences. This was essential preparation for what was to follow. Victoria heard from a nearby pew a voice, low and breathy, murmuring: *"Mea culpa, mea culpa,"* the timeless words of self-accusation, a powerful reminder that no one is perfect in this world.

When they had assembled for the first time, the Mistress had warned them that under no account must they reveal any of the secrets of the Chapter of Faults. She explained that of all the rituals in their lives, none was more likely to be misunderstood by even those normally sympathetic to monasticism. She reminded them that the practice of religious penance would always hold an unhealthy interest for the uninitiated and they must do nothing to feed this craving for sensation. She spoke feelingly of how down the centuries the Order, like every other, had been harmed by revelations of what happened in the Chapter of Faults. Waspish novelists, from Boccaccio to Balzac, grew rich from their accounts of penance. Closer to hand, and more painful to contemplate, were unscrupulous books purported to have been written by former nuns; cruel attacks designed to fuel anti-Catholic feelings. A Montreal sister had made a fortune from her claims about the penance she had endured before escaping from a local convent. An Irish Poor Clare became wealthy from a similar account. Another Irish ex-nun had produced a book describing the harshness of her Order's penitential system. This dangerous trend had in recent years taken on a new guise. The Mistress spoke of the wicked abuse of vocation by the way "nuns" were portrayed in strip joints and in pulp fiction. Victoria had been amazed. In her diary she wrote: *How does she know all this?*

Victoria sank to her knees in her appointed place, bowed her head, and continued to meditate on her errors. She tried to remember every time she had failed to show humility, charity, compassion, understanding, sympathy, and tolerance toward other sisters, to recall those occasions when, however briefly, her mind had drifted during silent meditation; those moments in chapel when she had not concentrated totally on what Father Lowell was saying or doing; those times when she had caught herself thinking of trivial and unimportant matters, such as what record was in the top ten or what films were showing at the local cinemas.

There was only one way the Rule allowed for such lapses to be handled — through pain. This was why she held in her palm the traditional scourge of the Order. This was why, on each occasion she came here, into her mind returned the words of Saint Bernard of Clairvaux, the gaunt-faced abbot of the Cistercians. *Just as the Body of Christ was crushed, let us learn how to subdue our bodies.* He had advocated daily penance to discipline the imagination and memory and to excise all feelings remotely sexual.

Victoria knew that for some of the postulants a visit here was almost a relief; for them the anticipation of what would happen was the hardest to bear, being aware of the Discipline and its wicked tails stored in their bureaus, waiting to be brought out of its black cloth purse for this occasion.

Since the last Chapter of Faults, she asked herself, had she always prayed properly? Had she spoken out of turn? Had she displayed unseemly haste? Had she been silently resentful toward a superior? Spoken evasively? Displayed "a lack of regularity" — such as not getting out of bed promptly, failing to dress in the allotted time, or dawdling over some domestic chore?

She silently checked off the questions. She knew many of the faults need never be publicly confessed. The Mistress had explained that an edict from the Vatican specifically forbade any nun to publicize any "interior faults"; those errors no one but God must know about. This proviso dated back to the seventeenth century when the ruling Pope was scandalized to discover that Superiors regularly ordered their nuns to admit all their sins. This was a serious violation of confession, interfering with the role of priests, who were specially trained to act as conduits between private conscience and God. Instead, postulants now confined themselves to admitting "external faults"; any failing that their sisters could have noticed and that therefore lowered the state of community piety.

Before she was banished Carmelita had insisted to Victoria that the Chapter of Faults was correlated with sexuality, quoting Freud that pleasure and pain are opposite sides of the same coin. She had argued that all instruments of penance, instead of staving off sexual feeling, act as a substitute. A hair shirt, prickly on the skin, produced the very effect it was intended to subdue. The same applied to the chain girdles some nuns still favored, girding their loins with metal bands scored with tiny spikes. Or to the small wooden cross studded with the tips of nails and worn against the chest. Some sisters searched for dead hedgehogs, skinning them and placing their scaly hides against their own flesh. Carmelita had been full of such stories, remembered Victoria. No wonder she had not lasted.

Nevertheless, at the outset of the Chapter of Faults, each sister would be expected to review silently all those mistakes Victoria had carefully checked off in preparation for what the Rule defined as a subjection of the body to the spirit.

She was still working through her list when the Mother Superior entered. "We are here to seek to mortify ourselves by the power of the Holy Spirit. Remember the words of Saint Paul. *If ye through the Spirit do mortify the deeds of the body, ye shall live.* Otherwise there is no mortification." Her voice was toneless and remote. "The Spirit will enlighten you to see what requires mortification. But remember, too, what you have been taught."

Reverend Mother paused. The silence in the room stretched. Similarly, the Mistress had remained silent after she delivered her caution about the proper use of mortification.

Beware of excessive violence. That can defeat the very purpose of mortification. It can create the very passion mortification is designed to crush. There is no victory if mortification provides pleasure. Mortification is designed to destroy the inner will, to break it, to crush it, to bring about its death. When this is done, then those evil passions will no longer be able to survive. There will be no validity remaining in you, dear sisters, which can nourish them. But remember, in this matter of the Discipline, in the endurance of pain, you must be careful not to go beyond your own strength in the matter. You may think it is a question of pride to allow yourself excessive mortification. But what you are doing then is to nourish those very passions you wish to excise. Not only is it your flesh which requires to be mortified, it is also your minds. Your thoughts have to be put

to death, to be ground out of existence, so that your mind can be brought
into subjection to the service of Christ. Every act of mortification must be
an occasion of joyous thanksgiving.

She had spoken those words at the onset of Lent, a special time of penance. She had told them the cautionary tale of Saint Rose of Lima, who had
worn a headband of steel spikes on her shaven skull and carried a massive
wooden cross on a shoulder lacerated from self-torture. Throughout the
entire period of Lent she slept on a bed of rocks, sharpened with a hammer
and chisel, and on Good Friday spent the afternoon suspended on a cross.
An earlier penitent in Europe had been more extreme, carving the name of
Jesus on her left breast with a bread knife and branding the letters with a
lighted candle.

The Mother Superior addressed them again. "God cannot look with
favor on anybody who is not dying or dead to this world. He is constantly
watching those of us He has chosen to see whether we are really trying to
die to the world. Remember His words. *Mortify your members which are*
upon the earth. Let us now offer our bodies, souls, and spirits as living sacrifices to God, acceptable through Jesus Christ."

The Reverend Mother knelt and began to pray. Her lips moved, but no
sound came forth. She raised her eyes. "Let us begin."

There was a moment's hesitation. A nun kneeling beside Victoria rose to
her feet. She stood, head bowed in contrition. In a voice so faint and expressionless that the words were barely audible she uttered the opening
words of the next part of the ritual.

"I accuse myself to you, dear Mother, and to you all, my dear sisters . . ."

Victoria knew that when her turn came she would not mention she had
been almost raped in her dreams. Her attacker always came the same way,
edging around the curtains, dressed in a black sweater and pants. There
was nothing violent or unkind about him; that, and the authority he displayed, would stop her from screaming. She never saw his face because he
always whispered for her to lie facedown while he removed the case from
her pillow and pulled it over her head and shoulders, pinioning her arms.
He then would turn her over and she would continue to feel his every action. At the point where he lifted her nightdress she awoke, ending the
dream. She had been too frightened to mention it during confession, fearing Father Lowell might question whether she really could give her life to
God. She knew she would be heartbroken to be sent home and that could
happen if she admitted to anybody that the dream gave her relief.

In a rush of words, the nun begged forgiveness for being late for chapel and failing to polish the dining-room glassware properly. She returned to her kneeling position. Once more silence descended while they prayed that she would be forgiven.

Victoria rose to her feet. She clasped her hands even tighter under her cape, feeling the braided wire thongs against her skin. The Mistress had explained what she must think. *The sense of your sinfulness must make you contrite. You must think of what you are in the presence of God. You are nothing. You must seek to develop a voice of conscience. And then God will fill your nothingness with His glory.* Victoria spoke.

"I have committed the fault of displaying indifference toward a sister. . . ." She sensed that her voice sounded strange and disembodied. "I have been moody." She pressed the ring even harder against her skin, feeling the metal biting against a knuckle. "I have been oversensitive . . ." She fought down an urge to forge ahead, to bring to an end this catalogue of faults. But she knew she must not do so. That would be a further failure, the fault of impatience. To plunge on, without being fully aware of what she was saying, the Mistress had warned, would be self-defeating.

To rush, my dear sisters, is to give in to Satan. He is constantly trying to make you imperfect. Remember the words of Saint Peter. 'He that hath suffered in the flesh hath ceased from sin.' We must die to this world if we are to enter into the full power of the supernatural life.

". . . I have been thoughtless by excluding a sister from conversation during Recreation . . ." Victoria revealed other failings: that morning in the community bathroom when she had broken the Great Silence by asking if she could borrow toothpaste because her own had run out; the afternoon when, late for Vespers, she almost ran into chapel; that evening when she had suddenly closed a door too loudly. Since she last stood here, she realized she had committed so many breaches of the Rule. Worse — they were the same faults, repeated over and over. The Mistress's warning had been clear. *The smallest rules are the hardest to keep. Obedience is inseparable from faith.*

It was over: she stood for a moment longer, then slowly sank to her knees, her place taken by another postulant. Head bowed, hands clasped, Victoria concentrated on remembering, word for word, the encouragement the Mistress had said was due to all those who admit their failures. *Sorrow for sin is the next best thing to innocence. The more abundant your sorrow, the greater will be the sum of God's richest blessings. Remember His words. "They that sow in tears shall reap in joy."*

The Mother Superior's voice was suddenly firm and resolute. "You may now use the Discipline. Do so in the knowledge that it will advance your spiritual growth. I remind you again of the words of Saint Paul. *If ye through the spirit do mortify the deeds of the body, ye shall live.*"

Victoria unclasped her hands. As instructed, she firmly gripped the cat-of-nine-tails in her left hand, her eyes staring at the floor. Then she half-rose, kneeling on her left leg. With her right hand she carefully raised her dress, exposing the flesh of her right leg above her stocking top. She lifted her left hand almost to shoulder height, letting the braided wires hang free. Then in a swift downward motion, she lashed her thigh with the metal thongs. She repeated the action.

Soon the sound of the regular swishing of metal passing through the air and the distinctive sound of its impact against skin filled the room. There was not a whimper, nor a grimace of pain. Only a total concentration on the task in hand.

On a beautiful May Sunday, Victoria completed her seventh, and last, full day of the Retreat. She had spent the last week in complete silence, neither exchanging a word with the other postulants nor with anyone else in the Mother House. The Mistress's last instruction had been to pray and meditate from the moment she awoke until she returned to her bed. During meals she must continue her silent devotion. Victoria had found the experience exhilarating. The silence cleansed her mind of everything, bringing her closer to God than she had ever thought possible. On this Sunday evening she was beginning the final preparations to deepen further that relationship.

She stood in her cell behind the drawn curtains, staring at a pile of hairpins and rollers. During her absence at supper, a professed nun had placed them on the hard-back chair. Nearly nine months had passed since she paid any attention to her hair, apart from clipping it once a week, keeping it to the regulation length the Rule demanded. In preparation for her marriage feast, for that climactic moment when she would become a Bride of Christ, she must style it, trying to get her hair to resemble the fashionable way she once wore it.

She undressed, but did not fold away her postulant's dress and cape. She would never wear them again. After putting on her nightdress and bathrobe, she gathered up the curlers and went to the bathroom. Other postulants were already there, silently pinning up their hair. Victoria washed her hair and then wound it around the rollers, pinning them in place, frequently jabbing her skull in the process. From time to time she paused to look in the mirror temporarily mounted above the sink. As hard as she tried, her hair simply would not hold as it once did. Somehow she had lost the knack of winding it properly around the rollers. Suddenly the Mistress stood behind her, shook her head, and glided away. Moments later she returned with a bottle of setting lotion. She handed it to Victoria and broke the silence of the Retreat. "Use it, Sister. For God's sake, use it! Otherwise you will look a real mess!"

Without waiting for an answer, the Mistress left. At the doorway to the bathroom, she turned and addressed the postulants. "Tomorrow is the big day. So why not behave like brides? Don't look so solemn! Help each other. And you can talk, you know!" She smiled and was gone.

Returning to her cell, Victoria found her dress and cape had been removed. In their place was a white gown with a ruffled bodice and flounced skirt. It was on a plastic hanger. Over the back of the chair were draped a white silk slip, cotton panties, and seamed white stockings. On the floor where her granny shoes normally stood were a pair of white satin pumps. She recognized the garments and shoes. She had last worn them at her graduation. The Mistress had written her mother for them.

Beyond her curtained enclosure Victoria heard a sudden burst of giggling. She peeped out and laughed: some of the postulants were staging an impromptu fashion show. Their dresses had come from a special wardrobe next to the Mistress's office. In it were kept the convent's collection of garments and shoes, accumulated over the years, and worn by those who did not have any suitable clothes for their marriage feast. One wore a full-length ball-gown and teetered along on a pair of incredibly spindly stiletto heels similar to ones Victoria recalled her mother wearing. Another was draped in a lace dress, several sizes too big. She had a pair of pointy-toed shoes. A third girl was crowned by a white pillbox hat and veil.

Through her reading, Victoria had learned of the historical concept that on the morrow they would become Brides of Christ. It was more than a thousand years old, rising out of the time when the newly evolving Christianity was splitting itself from the parent body of Judaism. Almost as soon as Christianity had emerged from Palestine and began to spread throughout the Roman Empire, the birth of Jesus was presented as a divine incarnation and Mary was given special attributes: God could not have chosen an ordinary mother to bear His child, but required a virgin, blessed with the moral and physical gifts that would assure her being preferred above other women. From that developed the idea that a fitting reward for holy virginity is to take the Son of God as a husband. Religious literature is filled with the imagery of a virgin giving herself to Jesus. The Sisters of the

Visitation would exclaim on their marriage to Christ that they would "live, breathe, and pant" for their celestial spouse and cry out that they were ready to "let Him kiss me with the kiss of His Divine mouth." The Benedictines pray for these brides to "trim your lamps and go forth to meet your Bridegroom."

She looked at her mother and sisters anxiously. Behind stood her uncles and aunts. In all there were twenty of Victoria's relatives present for the clothing-ceremony Mass.

"Mother, how do I look?"

Her mother continued to stare. Finally, she nodded. "You look just fine. Just like you did on graduation."

Victoria's youngest sister chimed in. "You wearing the garter I sent you?" Victoria blushed. "Let me have it back. I want it for my own wedding day."

Her second sister peered at her. "Where did you get the makeup? I thought nuns didn't wear the stuff?"

Her third sister interrupted. "It's a wedding, remember. Just like any other wedding." She hesitated. "That's right, isn't it, Vicky? That's why you're wearing Art's earrings?"

She felt her face burning. His name evoked a past she thought was dead.

Her mother intervened. "She needs some jewelry to set off the dress." She kissed her quickly on the cheek. "You look really beautiful. A beautiful bride." She looked around her. The grounds were filled with postulant brides and their families. "The most beautiful bride of them all."

An uncle stepped forward, camera poised. Victoria shook her head, explaining that no photographs could be taken. "It's the Rule," she added, knowing they would not understand. Her uncle looked puzzled. "No pictures? And this is your wedding day?"

"I think we had better go in." Her mother came to the rescue. "We don't want to lose our places." Victoria watched her relatives walk toward the chapel. Then she went to the sacristy.

The sound of Bach's organ music, soft and restful, seemed to draw the procession into the chapel.

For the first time since entering, the postulants were not paired. They walked in single file, each carrying a spring posy and a Bible. Victoria was seventh in line. At the exact moment the first postulant crossed the threshold of the chapel, the organ music stopped. For a brief moment there was silence. Heads in the packed congregation turned and looked toward the door. Suddenly, the organ burst forth into the *Magnificat*, the hymn of Our Lady. The voices of the choir soared with the music. The sound reached a crescendo as the last bride took her place in the pews immediately in front of the sanctuary steps. Seated on a massive carved chair before the altar was the Bishop of the diocese. One by one the postulants rose and went forward to kneel before him. Watching them, Victoria told herself how eagerly she had waited for this moment; how this was the final proof that she wished to commit her life totally to God.

It was her turn. She put aside her bouquet and Bible and went to the Bishop. He looked down, peering intently into her face, as if seeking a final reassurance. She stared steadily back at him.

"My daughter, what do you wish?"

She repeated the words the Mistress had drilled into them. "The grace of God and the habit of this Holy Order."

The Bishop was not satisfied. The ritual demanded he should not be. Canon Law dictated the next question. "You are certain?"

"With all my heart."

The Bishop made the sign of the cross on her forehead, his spatulate thumb cool on the skin. He bent forward, whispering. "The Way of the Cross, my child, is not of this world. But your reward will be that much greater in His world."

She rose and walked out of the sanctuary. Waiting for her was a professed nun. She silently led Victoria to the sacristy, where the Mistress and several other professed nuns had gathered. There was an atmosphere of no-nonsense bustle. The Mistress told Victoria to undress as quickly as possible. For a moment she hesitated. It had taken her almost two hours to dress, arrange her hair, and put on her makeup, the cosmetics applied under the watchful eye of the Mistress; afterward she had gathered up the jars of creams, the powders, and the brushes and returned them to a storage cupboard in her office.

"Sister, hurry! There's no time to daydream!"

The words ended her reverie. She kicked off her satin shoes, pulled her dress over her head, and let it drop to the floor. A nun scooped it up and tossed it into a corner with other discarded dresses. She quickly peeled off her silk slip and rolled down her stockings. They joined the heap. In her bra and panties she was led to an adjoining room. It had a long table on which were stacked neat piles of black garments. Beyond the table the postulants who had preceded her were dressing. She thought how different they looked. But it was not just because they were wearing their new habits. With a sudden shock, she realized their hair had been hacked off.

The cutting of hair signified not only self-effacement but also a readiness to die to the world. So much of the imagery associated with a life of chastity has an association with death. Cutting off the hair was a part of mourning in ancient civilization. The Church has absorbed the custom as a means to help a woman eradicate her sensuality. Her eyes were riveted on the plain wooden chair in a corner of the room. A nun dressed in unrelieved black stood behind it. In her hand she held a pair of tailor's scissors. Around the legs of the chair was a mounting heap of blonde, auburn, and black locks.

The nun beckoned her to sit. She placed a cloth around Victoria's shoulders. Next, she grabbed a handful of hair at the nape of the neck and cut it, gathered another large tuft and sheared it off. In moments, Victoria's hair was gone forever; only jagged tufts sprouted from her scalp. The barber-nun removed the cloth. During the entire procedure she had not said a word. As Victoria rose from the chair, stunned by the sheer speed with which she had been shorn, the nun was already motioning forward the next postulant.

The Mistress escorted Victoria to the table. She pointed to a pile of clothes, and hurried back to watch the nun shear another bride. Victoria took the new black garter belt from the top of the pile and slipped it around her waist. Next she put on the black stockings, then a black slip that reached to her ankles. She picked up the habit — for which she had been measured weeks ago and which had been made by the Order's seam-stresses — and shook out the folds, holding the heavy black serge garment before her, admiring its cut. It had a lace bodice overlaid with a series of pleats at the front. The back was gathered so that the cloth fell gracefully from her shoulders to the ground. The Mistress had explained the habit was modeled on the mourning dress of high-born French widows in the Middle Ages. Victoria donned the garment, her strong young limbs disappearing under the folds of black cloth. She moved a few steps, testing how she could walk in this outfit, far heavier than any of her old winter coats. Victoria put on the headpiece of stiffened cloth with two veils, which distinguishes the Order's nuns from all others. She fastened the chin strap. The shorter white veil hid her forehead. She pulled down the longer black veil made of fine-mesh nylon so that it completely covered her face. She put on her old shoes, glad that they were invisible beneath the folds of her new habit.

Fifteen minutes after the first postulant had entered this room the last one was fully dressed in her new habit. Once more they formed a procession and reentered the chapel, to be greeted by a peal of triumph from the organ. The music stopped as they resumed their places. A tomblike silence filled the chapel. The first postulant rose and, skirt swishing, walked into the sanctuary. This time she stood, not knelt, before the Bishop. In their stalls the choir softly chanted the words that for centuries had accompanied this moment of consecration for all the sisters of the community, when they become Brides of Christ.

> *Save Thy handmaiden, O Lord,*
> *For in Thee is her hope.*
> *Let her be good and humble.*
> *Let her be exalted by obedience.*
> *Let her be found in peace.*
> *Let her be content in prayer.*
> *Lastly, O Lord, we beg Thee to*
> *receive gracefully her offering.*

Victoria prayed.

Another one rose, stood before the Bishop, and returned. Then the next.

Each postulant had been given an option of choosing one of three new names by which she would in future be known. The Rule specified there must be a suitable male name to accompany the choice. The Reverend Mother had approved Victoria's wish to use her dead father's Christian name. She had chosen for her other name Sarah, the wife of Abraham.

It was her turn to stand before the Bishop.

"Receive, Sister Sarah John, the veil of Holy Religion."

She turned and walked from the sanctuary back to her pew, head erect, eyes shining. She joined in singing the evocative *Regnum Mundi*.

> *I have despised the Kingdom of the*
> *World and all worldly happiness,*
> *For the sake of My Lord Jesus Christ,*
> *Whom I have seen, whom I have loved,*
> *In whom I have believed, and in whom*
> *I am delighted.*

At last, she told herself, she was really a nun, committed to a life of obedience, poverty, and chastity; that He, having chosen her for a life of eternal celibacy, had freed her from all earthly cares and obstacles that might impede her search for perfection in religion.

Then, in sudden panic, she touched her earlobes. She had forgotten to remove Art's earrings.

CHAPTER 7

†

Encounters

Before walking to the lectern, Father Philippe ran over in his mind the key points of his lecture. How did the Virgin Mary become blessed among women? How had she avoided the ancient Hebrew ritual of the bitter water? What are the historical facts that led to *hyperdulia*, the ecclesiastical designation for the unique veneration of the Madonna? He mentally underscored the words that would allow him to evoke life two thousand years ago in Nazareth, the tiny village in a narrow Galilee gorge, some twelve hundred feet above sea level, accepted by all Christians as the hometown of Jesus.

And what about the pendant for Blanche Watts?

There were several weeks to go before his planned pilgrimage to Galilee, yet he felt he knew, through reading, its people and their culture as well as he did those of his parishioners, with their modular homes designed to look traditional, the glass and steel buildings along the interstate where they worked and the bayous where they fished and hunted. Their warm response to his mission had convinced him he was not just smitten with the romance of being a priest. He was certain he belonged in the rural South, as sure as he was that spring is the time when his neighbors prepare for another year of living; that high summer is punctuated by the whir of mowers and complaints about the bugs; fall is when the last of the summer folk are replaced by hunters. It was as comfortably repetitive as the Church calendar. That was why he liked it. That was why he wondered about the pendant.

Parishioners remarked about how well he chose and wrapped a gift; expertly forming bows and twirls from ribbon, picking just the right words to suit the occasion. From Persius to Pepys, Father Philippe seemed to know all the quotations. They accepted that this was as much a part of his style as were his formidable knowledge of Scripture, his elegant off-duty clothes, his gourmet cooking. In this area of vast mysterious swamps, woodlands, swirling rivers, and sluggish bayous, food is usually cooked simply, but he would skillfully create European cuisine and had an unerring ability to select good wine. His congregation insisted these attributes were to be expected in a priest with such a fine education, impeccable manners, and polished accent. No one asked about his past. Expansive though he was, Father Philippe discouraged such questions. Nobody pushed. It was that sort of a community.

He knew he was physically attractive. His dark hair shone, his hands were soft, with carefully manicured nails. He had a winsome little-boy quality that often aroused the mothering instinct in women — something it had never done in his own mother. She formed part of the dossier kept in the diocesan chancellery. There, some of the priests remained openly critical of him. Chiefly, they were the collectors of paper. They judged a priest's worth or rating as a troublemaker by the thickness of his file. His was already fat. From their urban citadel they still made discreet telephone calls to fill in the gaps, seeing if the damning words on record could be embellished. What hurt was that he had always tried to show them he had risen above the recent past.

He knew they thought he was too aggressive in his preaching; that he failed to maintain something they reluctantly conceded was indefinable — a proper distance between a priest and his parishioners. The most frequently voiced complaint was about his winning ways with women. The chancellery staff disapproved of the way he joked and joshed with them, especially the youngest and prettiest; the way he gripped a woman's elbow when he ushered her out of the rectory; the way he stood in the door, grasping her hands, reluctant to end the intimacy and resume his business. They didn't like the way he sometimes gave a woman a little gift to mark her birthday or an anniversary. Priests do not behave like this. He rejected such criticism, accepting that women gravitated toward him. Enjoying their company was compensation for all those barren years when his mother had rationed affection. Why should he tell anyone that the energy and ambition which drove him now were derived from the same emotions that first took him away from home? Why should he open that cupboard when he knew only too well the pain and misery stored there? After all he had gone through, the only thing that made sense was Jesus Christ. He had entered the priesthood believing He was the only salvation of mankind. He had left his last seminary knowing it.

From the beginning women in the parish had come to him. They discussed their infidelities; the drug scenes their children were involved in; the sheer boredom of their lives. He had nodded sympathetically as they apportioned blame. It was always somebody else's fault, usually the husband's: he drank too much; his sex drive was gone; he was mean with money; he was violent. He had tried to help, giving advice that did not always follow Canon Law, even recommending divorce when a marriage was irrevocably doomed, aware of the disapproval of the diocesan bureaucrats.

It was not because of them that the pendant, in a box in his soutane pocket, bothered him. It had caught his eye amid the jeweler's trays of paste necklaces, cheap bracelets, and the rings boys gave their girls before being drafted for Vietnam. That part of his mind, governed by the caution of a born survivor, told him that a priest did not give expensive jewelry to a girl he barely knew and especially one about to become a bride. The part that controlled his emotions and impulses urged him to ignore convention. No one in the hall knew his dilemma. He wondered how they would react if he prefaced his lecture by asking them to vote: *Do I or do I not give Blanche Watts the pendant?*

The chancellor's watchdogs would undoubtedly pounce. They would not bother with motive. It would be enough for them to believe he was a profligate. His mother had warned him this would be his fate. She had been going through one of her bouts of manic-depression at the time. It was not her threat that frightened him, but the idea that he could inherit her illness.

If he had not become a priest, he would have taken up medicine, believing he could have found a niche in psychoanalysis. Duty in the confessional is very similar, requiring the same observation of human functioning and behavior. A confessor, like a psychiatrist, is skilled in understanding; both are products of intensive study and training that make them unusually sensitive to others. In his final year at seminary he had mapped out a project to evaluate the psychological makeup of Old Testament prophets and the people contained in the Gospels. He decided Jesus could be labeled clinically obsessive in some of His behavior. He concluded, too, that in presenting Christ as compassionate, gentle, and loving — someone who touched people physically, psychologically, and spiritually — the Apostles had accepted as a fact His sexuality — not genitally, but in an affective way. Affectiveness — gentleness and tenderness — is a basic part of sexuality; those very qualities elevate sexuality to a level where it is not a sin but an integrated part of human life. He had offered this idea to his spiritual director, but was warned that even at this late stage, months from ordination, he could be dismissed for daring to think such heresy. Crestfallen, he returned to safer ground, concluding that Herod had all the traits of a severely disturbed personality.

As he approached the lectern, he could see Simone wedged in the front pew. Even if she had not been unusually pretty, her clothes singled her out in the conservatively dressed audience. She was wearing a floral skirt and plain white blouse that showed off her deep tan. Her chestnut hair fell naturally around her face. Even in repose, hands clasped in her lap, there was something about her, he thought; more than mere beauty, it was a quality that could best be described as presence. She accepted her looks as she accepted everything else: a secure home, a good job, an engagement ring on her finger. He knew it had all happened as naturally as it was for her regularly to change her hairstyle. She was twenty-two years old, with a love for the Church and a fascination with Scripture. For the past year she had taught Sunday school at Sacred Heart, where she was also a lector. A week ago he had met her and her father in the street and enquired about Brad. She had hesitated. Her father had explained that though she wore Brad's ring and pin she was no longer certain she wanted to marry when he returned from overseas. Next day he had sent her a note inviting her to the lecture, signing it: "Very affectionately, Philippe."

Many members were decked out in their Sunday finery. Leaning on the lectern, he assumed what Father Brannigan had half-mockingly called "the imposing look," the one to adopt when facing an audience — never forgetting that public speaking hinged on taking command from the very first moment. He stared at Simone and thought how well the pendant would look around her neck.

In Pulpit Class at his last seminary he had improvised on Father Brannigan's rules. When it had been his turn to stand at the podium, he had developed the trick of fantasizing that one of the seminarians was a girl. He would concentrate hard and imagine what it must be like to go with a woman. At the seminary they had a code for it: G.L. — getting laid.

Jay had gone G.L. one memorable weekend, driving to a motel on an interstate. There he had buried himself in the plump arms and creased thighs of a hooker. He had saved almost six months' allowance from his parents to pay for it. Jay and the girl had never left the room, ordering up six-packs, steaks, and fries for breakfast, lunch, and dinner. When he returned, he had been pale and had a fresh outbreak of acne on his face, clear proof how G.L. could affect a person. He had barely begun to describe his experience before an outraged Father Brannigan drove him and his trunks to the railroad station. The last Father Philippe had heard, Jay was a lingerie salesman in Memphis.

More thought-provoking was that Father Brannigan — who always began Pulpit Class with the entreaty *O most precious blood of Jesus, oozing from every pore, grant us the grace to love Thee more and more* — had one day driven out of the seminary dressed in a black mohair suit, white shirt, and black tie. At the Houston airport he had purchased a one-way ticket to San Francisco, where he moved in with a set designer fortuitously named Mark. When the shock subsided, everyone remembered Father Brannigan had never done things by halves.

Father Philippe began his lecture with a question. How many of the Apostles actually mention Mary by name as the Mother of Jesus? He waited, allowing his words to sink in. While the four canonical Gospels speak of her, two add that she had tried to dissuade her Son from His mission because she was certain He was mad. *Shock them,* Father Brannigan had recommended. *Biff them in the gut. Take their breath away. That's how all the great orators perform. John Kennedy had gone to Berlin and said he was a Berliner. A perfect example of audience identification.* (Father Brannigan was fond of using the terminology of the advertising world.) *Don't be wishy-washy, just hit them like the Marines did at Guadalcanal.* (He also liked war movies.)

He began to explore the radically different genealogies of Mary and Joseph in the Gospels of Matthew and Luke. He reminded them that the couple was born into a clearly defined society at a definite point in history. The basic sources for what their life was like are the Gospels: the four canonical ones, and also, with reservations, the Apocryphal versions. Father Philippe said the Church had always recognized that the only way to understand the development of Christianity was never to lose sight of all available evidence. But the Church does not teach that the Gospels must be taken as literal truth. They were written at least fifty years after the death of Jesus and united the hazy personal recollections of the disciples with the earliest Christological speculations of the primitive Judeo-Christian community. But the Gospels remain the set of documents that people use to interpret the reality of New Testament philosophy.

Formgeschichte!

He hurled the word into the hall, pronouncing it impeccably, pleased at the startle it created. He repeated the word, this time explaining that it means "form history," a name coined by German scholars who held the view that the Gospels contain myths and doctrines expressed as being true. This, they should realize, was a familiar practice in the flowering stage of Christianity when religious fervor demanded a dramatic interpretation and the facts were of secondary importance. He returned to the family trees of Mary and Joseph, aware that Simone was smiling.

Never rush, Father Brannigan had admonished. *You're not in a race. The story you tell has been around a long time. It's how you tell it that counts.* They must still miss Father Brannigan; there could never be a better teacher in the art of preaching the Scriptures.

"Mary and Joseph." He spread his hands as though balancing the biblical couple in his palms. He clasped his hands. "Matthew and Luke. Between them, they offer a perfect example of distinguishing between historical fact and apocryphal truth."

Matthew, he continued, was content to trace the ancestry of Jesus back to Abraham. He began to quote, his voice suddenly rising and falling in parody of an auctioneer. *"Abraham begot Isaac and Isaac begot Jacob. And Jacob begot Judas and his brethren. And Judas begot Phares and Zara of Thamar."*

He made no mistake in reciting the first sixteen verses of the Gospel. A burst of applause greeted his performance. He cut it off with a swift wave.

"Luke takes the family tree of Jesus all the way back to Adam. They didn't have the advantage of an IBM computer to check all that begetting." He had learned the importance of timing. Now was the moment to lighten the mood. "But they sure begot it wrong!" The sudden twang in his voice was a perfect imitation of Presley. It brought a burst of laughter.

He raised his hands the way he had seen Pope Paul VI do it on television, after he confirmed from his balcony that there was going to be a second session of Vatican Two. Father Philippe was serious as he went for his first point. He asked them to consider the ancestors of Jesus from that point in the Old Testament which Matthew and Luke agreed upon: the emergence of David.

"But look what we have. Different names and figures. Luke lists forty-one persons, many of them not in Matthew's list. He can only give us twenty-seven. There is a difference of fourteen generations." He allowed the silence to stretch, knowing he had captured them — knowing he would. He reminded them that a generation averaged twenty-five to thirty years. That left a gap of some four centuries between the ages of Mary and Joseph.

The problem, he explained, had been neatly solved and historical truth blatantly rearranged. Joseph was said to be the eldest brother of Mary's mother. Born and raised in Bethlehem, he went to Nazareth to marry his young niece. "If age did not worry them, neither did it matter when the facts were rearranged!" He let the laughter subside before confiding he had always found a problem accepting the claims of hagiographers. He did not tell them that first and foremost had been the inventions of his mother.

✝

Holy Mary, Mother of Jesus! The sudden speed and fury of the words were always in striking contrast to his mother's slow, sad movements. She used them when everyone's plate was not cleared, a pair of shoes required mending, or a new dress was needed for one of the girls.

In his first years, Philippe mostly wore hand-me-downs. Donnie was tall and already broad by the age of twelve. Philippe, seven years younger, looked like a clown in his brother's baggy trousers and floppy shirts. He had been almost eleven before his mother bought him a suit, for the inaugural Mass of the new parish priest. For years she had refused to go to Mass or allow her family to attend, on the grounds that the old parish priest was too soft on sins of the flesh. He died in his sleep after returning from a vacation. She had heard his replacement would be tougher, wise to the vices of the world. At the Mass the new man had taken as his text First Corinthians 6:18 — "Fly fornication."

From then on, every Saturday she would march the family off to confession, afterward demanding to know how many Our Fathers and Hail Marys were doled out. At the end of the count, she would always say: "Holy Mary, Mother of Jesus." And so, by repetition, Our Lady became fixed in Philippe's mind. She was a central part of a world his mother always spoke about with an intimacy he found baffling; Heaven and Hell were places over the horizon. "Purgatory" and "plenary indulgence" were other words he came to know equally well.

He was twelve when he heard two more: "premature ejaculation." His mother shouted them at his father. Philippe should have been asleep, but even at night, the heat and humidity of high summer permeated the house. Bathed in sweat, he listened to her sudden outburst. Though the words had no meaning for him, he had heard the anger in her voice, with its built-in hurt that for years she had used on his father. She had stormed from their bedroom to the kitchen, running taps, washing dishes, and making a racket as if it were the middle of the day. When he asked Irene what the words meant, his older sister demanded to know where he heard them. He told her; she looked shocked and made him promise he would never mention the incident to anyone. She was fifteen at the time. Three years later, she had married. By then her future husband had explained their meaning to Philippe.

At a cookout Irene and her new husband gave, Donnie had slipped away with a girl, sneaking into the backseat of the family Chevy. Philippe crouched by the trunk and listened to the thrashing and moaning from the backseat. Then came a sudden mocking voice saying his brother couldn't satisfy a corpse. The girl pushed open the doors and flounced away. When Donnie emerged, he had the same hangdog look their father perpetually wore. Philippe walked the five blocks to the church and prayed for his father and brother, asking God to help them, as He was helping him.

He still did not fully understand why he had decided to become a priest. Sometimes he thought it was because he would be the first one in the family. Other times he wondered if it was because his mother respected their parish priest and that he badly wanted her love. Whatever the motive, his decision was welcomed by the nuns of the Holy Cross, where he attended school. Sister Mildred had set a term paper for the Scripture class. "Why do you believe Jesus Christ is God?" His answer was read aloud before all the staff and pupils: "I believe Jesus Christ is God because I speak to Him every morning and evening in my prayers and I know He is God ever since I could read the Bible. I don't ever remember not believing Jesus is God, and not accepting He is my best buddy, even though I am not always His. But I want to try and be His best pal always."

Sister Mildred called at his house that evening and had a long talk with his parents. He had stood outside the door listening: his father said little; from time to time his mother interjected questions about how much it would cost. The nun had brushed that aside, insisting God would provide,

saying repeatedly that a seminary was the right place for Philippe, reminding his parents that their faith was rooted in hope, and there could be
no doubt that God hoped their son would be allowed to answer His call.
The final verdict came from his mother. Holy Mary, Mother of Jesus — so
be it. But for once, there was no anger in the words.

After several meetings with the parish priest and Sister Mildred, Philippe selected a seminary he would enter when he would be exactly seventeen and a half. He had yet to kiss or even date a girl.

A year after entering, he learned that to control her mood swings his
mother was on lithium and Valium. On visits home he never knew how he
would find her. She could plunge from extreme elation to profound depression, so severe that she refused to attend Mass. He remembered one
New Year's Day when his mother raced from one thought to another,
talking volubly, even incoherently, as she crossed over some frontier in her
brain. Throughout the following summer she moved in and out of despair.
She would refuse to speak, except to insist she was being punished for
something she could not discuss. Philippe's father finally told him that the
doctor diagnosed her condition as manic-depressive psychosis. He hugged
his father, the way he did as a child. Together they knelt on the kitchen
floor and prayed for her to get well. Their entreaties were interrupted
when she stood in the doorway, repeating, "*Holy Mary, Mother of Jesus.*"

There were other expressions at the seminary. Holy shit! Holy damn!
Holy hell! Philippe learned to use them as adjectives, nouns, and impera-
tives, aware he was being profane, but so were all the other seminarians.
Besides, weekly confession wiped the slate clean. By his third year he
found an uneasy dishonesty about much of the life within seminary walls.
He was increasingly aware that the seminary was pervaded with its own
kind of sexuality. It was there in the chicken fights, horse and rider, charg-
ing each other around the gymnasium. He once felt a hand stroking his
crotch during a struggle. He recognized there was no way of avoiding sexuality. It was there in the way a seminarian suddenly put an arm around his
shoulders. It was there when he swam and someone dove underneath and
grabbed at his trunks. It was there in the shower room when several boys,
soaped all over, wrestled with each other, ending in a heap on the floor. It
was there at night, in the movement of the bedclothes.

He finally began to think he should accept the grabbing and close contact. The idea at first scared him. But it would not go away; there was
something exciting about it. He began to wonder if it was possible to make

out a theological case that Christian love and sexuality are not incompatible; that far from being sinful, sexual feelings are an important dimension of a total person and therefore make for a better priest. Like his mother, he began to search for support in religion. In Paul's Letter to the Ephesians, he found the Apostle took a positive position. *For no man ever hated his own flesh; but nourisheth it and cherisheth it, as also Christ doth the church: Because we are members of His body, of His flesh, and of His bones. For this cause shall a man leave his father and mother, and shall cleave to his wife, and they shall be two in flesh. This is a great sacrament; but I speak in Christ and the church.*

Clearly, he concluded, Paul believed that a sexual relationship was an appropriate analogy to describe Christ's closeness to His followers; Paul was also saying that making love was analogous to the relationship between Jesus and the Church. Fired by his own quest for answers, he further interpreted Paul's words. The Apostle would not have used a sexual analogy if he had thought it degrading. Paul was concerned only with explaining his loving understanding of Christ. In choosing to use the sexual union as an example, he was taking a positive attitude toward sexuality, arguing it is symbolic of love. In this context, sex could be seen as sacramental, a sign of Christ's lasting love. Remembering from where the parish priest had chosen his text on the dangers of sex, he turned to Paul's first Letter to the Corinthians. The Apostle had indeed cautioned the licentious population of Corinth about their ways. But on closer reading, he made other discoveries. Paul clearly stated that he did not favor sexual abstinence in marriage; his only wish was for sexual fulfillment to be balanced against a life full of prayer. In verse twenty-five of chapter seven, Paul advanced an argument that he found electrifying: *Now concerning virgins, I have no commandments of the Lord; but I give counsel, as having obtained mercy of the Lord, to be faithful.*

Philippe copied the words into his notebook. Then he blocked out in capital letters that Paul was saying celibacy is a condition Jesus did not teach. He underlined the words. It was then that he began to ponder how the Blessed Virgin could be fitted into this exciting and, for him, totally new and revealing interpretation.

✝

Father Philippe was at the midpoint of his lecture. He had explained the role of angels as divine messengers from the time of the star worshipers of Assyria, adding that for the ancients they were guardians of the air, water, and all vegetation; guiding souls into bodies and, after death, escorting them to Paradise or Hell. He had led his audience, captivated, to that moment when Mary had come face to face with the Archangel Gabriel, who announced she had been chosen to bear God's child. He explained that Mary, understandably perturbed for several days after Gabriel's visit, confided the extraordinary event to her elderly cousin, Elizabeth, who was also with child — later to be known as John the Baptist. He paused, eyes searching the hall, settling briefly on one rapt face after another, remembering another injunction of Father Brannigan. *Build them up. Just keep them waiting. Never fails.*

He related that among the Jews at that time marriage was taken very seriously. It was a firm contract, so binding that if a woman's intended husband died before they wed she was entitled to the full legal protection of widowhood. Rabbinical teaching was equally strict on other matters. Preparations for a wedding could take up to a year while the rabbi checked that the couple were aware of all their obligations and duties to their faith. During that time sexual relations were strictly forbidden. He described how adultery was punished by an ordeal known as the curse of the bitter water.

A women suspected of being unfaithful was led before her rabbi, who poured consecrated water into a bowl to which was added powder. If she sipped and died, she was guilty. If she drank and survived, she was innocent. Since Mary was formally promised to Joseph, she should have been subjected to the test. Father Philippe quoted the nineteenth verse of Matthew's Gospel. *"Being a just man, and not willing publicly to expose her, he was minded to put her away privately."* Joseph didn't renege on his promise to marry Mary because an angel appeared to him and explained she was still pure. She was, said that angel, expecting God's child. Therefore there was no question of putting her through the test of the bitter water."

Walter, he remembered, had raised the question of what would have happened if there had been a similar ordeal for men and they had both lived at that time.

†

Philippe was certain of one thing. The seminary was suddenly too close to home. His mother started to telephone there, speaking to anybody who would listen. Her mind was becoming a gray area, reality was obscured. He tried to take as many of the calls as possible, listening while his mother rambled on about secrets in the Bible only she knew. Finally the administrator said it must stop.

That was the day Philippe made two calls of his own. The first was to Sister Mildred to explain what was happening and what he wished to do. She called back in the afternoon saying he could telephone another seminary. It was arranged he would enter there in the fall of 1962. It was the greatest distance he could put between himself and his mother. Philippe feared that his wit and energy, his constant flow of ideas, his own Scriptural discoveries, were no more than a precursor to becoming like her.

The new seminary was identical to the old. There was the same routine, the same sexual horseplay, the same petty cruelties, the same periods of stifling boredom. To fill these he read anything and everything. He would gut a book in a few hours; he had calculated he could consume everything worth reading in the library by the time he was ordained.

Bookshops, particularly an old, scholarly one, became a stalking ground. One day, Philippe found Schopenhauer and Comfort wedged between an early street guide to the town and an account of De Soto's expedition down the Mississippi. Schopenhauer's *The World as Will and Idea* was in mint condition. Comfort's *Sex in Society* was dog-eared. Philippe bought them for a couple of dollars and was coming out of the shop when a fellow seminarian strolled by. Philippe had seen him before but they had never spoken. He decided to take the initiative.

"You read Schopenhauer?"

"Yeah."

"Good?"

"Depends what you want."

"How about Comfort?"

"Depends if you want comforting." Walter had a soft voice for so big a man.

They laughed together and walked back to the seminary, discussing the two authors. Walter asked why Philippe was reading about sex.

"To see if I'm normal."

"What's normal?"

They laughed again. As simply as that it had begun.

Schopenhauer and Comfort had been the starting point; Walter would be Philippe's answer to his need for a deep and lasting friendship, his desire to share permanent emotions, to have someone fill the void his mother could not. On that November afternoon Philippe was as hungry for love as

Walter to provide it. By the time they reached the seminary, Walter had expressed the view that Schopenhauer was right about sexual impulse: it is the strongest and most powerful of motives. He took the book from Philippe and opened its pages, immediately finding what he wanted.

" 'The sexual impulse is the ultimate goal of all human effort, interrupts the most serious occupations every hour, sometimes embarrasses for a while even the greatest mind, does not hesitate to intrude with its rash interfering with the negotiations of statesmen and the understanding of men of learning, knows how to slip its love letters and locks of hair even into ministerial portfolios and philosophical manuscripts.' " Walter looked at Philippe and quickly squeezed his arm before continuing. " 'It breaks the firmest bonds, demands the sacrifice sometimes of life and health, sometimes of wealth, rank and happiness, nay, robs those who are otherwise honest of all conscience, makes those who have hitherto been faithful, traitors.' "

Walter snapped shut the book and thrust it at Philippe. "What Schopenhauer is really saying is that love is more important than anything and is therefore quite worthy of the profound seriousness with which every one pursues it. Always bear that in mind when you read Comfort. He tends to overrationalize. But he's right about one thing. There's been a failure of social education as far as sex goes. Especially in the Church. Too much emphasis on moral prohibition."

It took Philippe a couple of days to read both books. He was intrigued by Comfort's view that there is no evidence to support the Church's claim that celibacy could be directly linked to increased creativity; while it may be true that the tension of abstinence or of ungratified desire could be productively channeled into work, there was no acceptable evidence to relate continence with a capacity to work *harder*.

The following Saturday, they spent two hours in the bookshop. Philippe had waited inside the door until Walter arrived. The place, as usual, was empty as Walter led the way to the back of the shop, to a little L-shaped passageway that ended in a cul-de-sac filled with religious books. There were titles not just on every aspect of Christianity but also on Hinduism, the oldest of mankind's great religions, flourishing a full three thousand years before Christ walked the earth. There were accounts of the life of Brahman priests, volumes detailing the findings of Vedic study, as well as interpretations of the Torah.

"My private library," said Walter. "I found it a year ago. I crib all my answers for term papers here. You're welcome to use it."

"Thanks."

"Don't mention it. I like you."

They conversed sitting on the floor, facing each other, knees bent and touching. From time to time Walter scrambled to his feet to locate a book and confirm some particular point; as he rose, he rested a hand on Philippe's shoulder. It seemed the most natural thing to do. He commented that Comfort was right when he said all human relationships were sexual in the widest sense of the word, but wrong to say that homosexuality is automatically unhealthy. There could be healthy and unhealthy homosexual relationships. The problem was that most people, including the Church, didn't understand the role of homosexuality in a culture.

"Why not use a different word?" Philippe had suggested.

"But that would be dodging the question that healthy relationships can be homosexual."

Walter had not pressed his point, just sat there silently looking at Philippe. Before they left separately, Walter had reached across and gently run his hand over Philippe's face. They had been coming to the shop for about a month when Walter had placed a hand on his thigh. Philippe quickly removed it. Walter had not touched him below the waist again.

It was Walter who reminded Philippe that Scott Fitzgerald wrote: "A person's temperament is constantly making him do things he can never repair."

"Fitzgerald was talking about a writer, not a budding priest."

"Touché. But do you regret anything between us?"

Philippe shook his head. In all truth, he said, he had never been happier. He could not believe how swiftly the months had passed. It became a routine to come to their hideaway and sit close together. During the semesters they hardly missed a Saturday. On vacation Philippe found his impatience mounting toward the end of his time at home, not just because he wanted to escape from his mother's delusions, but because of a desire to return to this confined space where Walter and he had explored so many ideas. It had taken weeks before he became comfortable with having Walter hold his hand and stroke his face. One Saturday a year later, in the fall of 1963, they had sat in silence mourning the news from Dallas, not able to accept that Kennedy was dead. That afternoon, Walter had reached over and gently kissed Philippe on the mouth. He accepted their sexual relationship. In one way, loving Walter was like loving someone in a dream, as if nothing that happened between them could affect their future. Walter never asked him to go farther than he was prepared to go.

In the seminary they kept a distance, instinctively knowing this was the way to survive, to keep their relationship flourishing, allowing it to come to life only in the womblike cavern of books. Philippe attacked his studies with a new zest: his marks in moral theology were second only to Walter's; his altar practices were graded as exemplary; several of his sermons had been preached by tutors in the seminary chapel. Life was perfect.

It was Walter who raised a doubt. "The Snot is getting curious. He gave me a funny look today. You know, the one they call his 'homo-mind' look. Real creepy." The Snot was the prefect of discipline.

Philippe reached over and squeezed Walter's hand. "He doesn't know about this place. He wouldn't know what a bookshop looks like."

They spent the remainder of the afternoon exploring the possibility that man is neither heterosexual nor homosexual but plurisexual. Walter rummaged through the shelves and located a copy of Kinsey. Heads together, they analyzed how Kinsey defined homosexuality. Walter asked why homosexual feelings should stand in the way of self-acceptance; no one should be made to feel he was going to be a bad priest because he was a homosexual. The Church was full of hard-working homosexuals, healthy in every way, and this fact should be recognized and accepted. Philippe had suggested they write a letter to their congressman urging him to raise the matter in Washington — knowing they never would.

One Saturday, they sat side by side on the floor, talking quietly about the difficulty of accepting the virginity of Mary solely on the historical reporting in the Gospels. Walter felt the problem was not whether Matthew and Luke were accurate; it was that the entire question must be seen in a wider context. Nobody would have been interested in the details of Jesus' conception had He not risen from the dead.

"If Christ had not dramatically rolled back the stone and walked out of His tomb, there would be no Church," agreed Philippe.

"The problem is that if the Church continues to look upon Mary's virginity as a historical fact, it will go on getting attacked," insisted Walter. "I wish one day a Pope would say, 'Okay, let's look at it this way.' "

He wanted a pontiff who would see that it was not important whether or not Mary was a virgin, what was important was that she represented the perfection of the chaste life. Everything she did was directed toward the will of God. Philippe developed the notion, saying that at the core of Mary's response to the Archangel Gabriel was the totality of her religious belief, her fidelity to God. Her faith, not her virginity, was important.

Walter had an idea. "We should start a movement to drop 'Virgin Mary.'

Just call her 'Holy Mary.' " He impulsively kissed Philippe. "Man, just think of it. If we pulled it off and they ask us where we thought of the idea, we'll just say, sitting on the floor! But we gotta get out of this seminary first."

"You're on your way, Mister. Both of you! Get to your feet!"

The Snot was standing over them. By nightfall they had both been expelled without having had a chance to say good-bye to each other.

✝

He moved to his next point, without breaking the fluency of his argument, buttering the closing stages of his lecture with the reminder that allowing a person to be spawned by a deity was neither unusual nor as ingenious as the Gospels proclaim. Perseus, hero of all the Greeks, was fathered by Zeus. Mars produced Romulus. Aristotle, Alexander the Great, and the Emperor Augustus, who ruled when Mary conceived, were all said to be of divine origin. Buddha the Enlightened was conceived by a god who appeared in the form of a cloud. Centuries later, Montezuma, the emperor of Mexico at the time of the Spanish conquest, was worshiped as the son of Tlaloc, the Aztec god of rain. He had acquired all this knowledge as a result of those Saturdays spent with Walter. He had tried to contact him once, calling his home from a pay phone, but Walter's father said his son had gone to South America. There was no point in calling again.

Father Philippe explained that the birth of Krishna the Redeemer was remarkably similar to that of Jesus; there was the same angelic announcement to his mother, a similar adoration of the shepherds, and an almost identical persecution by the rajahs, who ordered the execution of every male child in their domains on the night of Krishna's nativity.

"The story of Mary has survived in one form or another for one single and inescapable reason." In a resonant voice, he quoted the words of Saint Thomas Aquinas on the subject, the ones that have sustained the Church since they were written: *Miraculorum Dei quaedam sunt de quibus est fides sicut miraculum virgine partus ... et ideo Dominus voluit ista occultiora esse, ut fides eorum magis meritoria esset.* (Among the miracles of God, some are articles of faith, like the miracle of the Virgin Birth. And, precisely because the Lord wished them to remain incomprehensible in order that faith in them be the more worthy.)

"He was talking about an article of faith. We are still talking about one. That is what the Virgin Birth is."

✝

The period after being expelled had been traumatic. Life at home re-volved around his mother. She required increasing medication. She could have lengthy lucid spells, filling her with energy and good thoughts, then swiftly plunge into despair, wailing she was possessed by demons. Once more Sister Mildred intervened. She persuaded the Bishop to give him a final chance at yet another seminary.

It was no different from the others, except for the food. Bells governed his life; sensuality was all the more potent because everybody tiptoed around it, and so did he, sublimating in a frenzy of work; the endless grind of class; the sudden departure of a student, gone as if he had never existed. It had all been the same at the previous institutes. But the food at this one was not just badly cooked, it seemed to be tainted before it ever reached the kitchen. He managed to eat as little as possible, existing mainly on cheese, crackers, and coffee. He lost weight and became nervous and irritable, con-vinced again that the ills of his mother were about to descend on him. He began spending all his free time in the chapel, praying, asking God to im-prove the supplies. He finally called the Health Department. An inspector was promptly sent. He impounded twenty pounds of bad meat and recom-mended the seminary president give Philippe a reward for his vigilance. Instead, the president ordered Philippe's immediate expulsion.

He realized he was on his own cliff edge and he must find the strength to move back. He was almost twenty-six and had spent the past nine years in trying to become a priest. Hour after hour he went over his arguments in a shabby motel room. Each time he reached for the telephone a new thought entered his head and was fitted into his defense. On the third day, he called the Bishop's office and was put on hold by a secretary, a man with an anon-ymous voice, before the Bishop came on the line.

"Yes? What do you want from me?" The words accentuated the gap be-tween them, one created by rank and class, reinforced by the Bishop's au-thority.

"Your Grace, I want another chance. To explain."

"What is there to explain?" The voice kept him at a distance.

He began again. "Your Grace, I want to be a priest. I know Jesus Christ is in me. I want to serve Him."

"Did you think you were serving Him by trying to get a seminary closed?"

He had to be honest. There was no other way.

"They found tainted meat, Your Grace."

"Then perhaps God intended you to be a health inspector."

The Bishop was wrecking his thoroughly crafted text; unable to defend himself, he found tears glazing his eyes.

"I'm sorry, Your Grace. I thought you would give me another chance."

"Why? Why should I?"

"I want to serve Christ. I want to be useful to Him." It was, he knew, the absolute truth. He would be willing at that moment to have the words carved as his epitaph.

"You have still not told me why you did it."

Philippe was aware of the Bishop's technique: going forward one pace at a time, grinding each point to dust before moving on, not trying to exact some tribute of revenge or humiliation, but testing if there were to be a future. Philippe had a sudden hope. They spoke for almost an hour more, the Bishop questioning him closely, saying the ammunition against him was there in the file. Finally, the questions ceased.

"The nub of the problem is this. Can you be trusted not to do it again?"

Philippe did not hesitate. "God will give me the strength to serve Him properly, if you give me the chance."

"Very well. You shall have your chance."

The parish ran between two state highways. The church had walls of gray stucco, grooved with lines to make it look like granite. Inside, it was narrow and lofty, bathed in diffuse hues from the stained-glass windows behind the altar. The air was redolent of burned incense and the varnish of the pews. He quickly came to love the place as much as he loved and respected Father Franciscus. From the very first day he allowed Philippe to call him Frank, while at the same time he established their situation. "Okay, you got drafted here. I didn't ask for you. You didn't ask for me. They told me the score. You flunk here and you're out. O-U-T." He had a western twang when he spoke English, although his native tongue was Italian. There was an extraordinary briskness about Frank. Whether it was distributing communion with Philippe as his server, or conducting a baptism, wedding, or burial, he always gave the impression of frenetic activity. He said it was his version of the sexual compulsions of middle age. But, in fact, the passions of the body were quiet in Frank, who was a genuinely holy man. Long ago he had understood his choices, what the Church needed from him, who Christ was and what he wanted to give Him. He wanted to teach Philippe about prayer, about giving and receiving love, and understanding and believing. Sometimes, because Philippe was a deacon, Frank let him preach, afterward analyzing the sermon over a meal. He would say that what a man thinks is less than what he knows; what he knows is less than what he loves; what he loves is less than what there is to give. Sometimes he would smile, that brisk smile that was a part of his character, and add that a man is wrong to see himself as less than he is.

A year later Philippe was ordained. At his first Mass he preached on the meaning of *hyperdulia.*

†

He told them that until the Council of Ephesus, Mary had no special place in the Church. The Council had granted Mary the status of Mother of God, because she "after the flesh bore the Word from God, who had become flesh." It was undoubtedly the most important definition of faith promulgated by the Fathers at Ephesus. It came at a time when several popes had slowly begun to move toward an explicit statement of papal primatial authority. They were preparing the groundwork for Rome's assertion of its claim as the *prima sedes* of Christianity, a move begun during the pontificate of Damasus I (366–384) and reinforced from the outset of the reign of Leo I. Using all his skills as orator, theologian, administrator, and saint, Leo defended the rights of the Roman see, advancing as one of his main arguments the continuity and identity that existed between Saint Peter and himself. He had been pontiff for eleven tumultuous years of barbarian invasions and renewed Church disputes when the elevation of Mary assumed vital importance.

The greatest of all the barbarians, Attila the Hun, was ready to sweep the Church into the Tiber. Having heard that Mary had been raised to be the Mother of God, he hesitated. In the oppressive summer heat of the year 452, he agreed to meet with Pope Leo on the muddy banks of the River Po in northern Italy. The papal entourage arrived to find Attila camped out with a vast army. Leo had two hundred monks, equipped only with their psalm books. While they chanted in the background, Leo explained to Attila the terrible fate he would suffer if he made any move that would harm the Mother of God. While the precise words have escaped record, Attila, the son of Mundzuk, who could trace his lineage back to Schongar, ruler of the air, had listened as Leo told him that he too could claim a divine lineage. His empire was even greater than that of Attila's and not of this world, but part of the invisible and supernatural one where salvation came through Christ's Church; one able to claim the Mother of God as its own, and invest in her special powers of redemption. Leo would pray for Mary to redeem Attila if he turned back. Attila broke camp that night and marched home, his thundered promise echoing in Leo's ear: *I will leave the Mother of God in peace.* One year later he was slain and his last reported words were to ask Mary, "the great goddess of Rome," to ensure his redemption.

In the decades that followed, theologians of the Church were urged by successive popes to study every verse of the Old Testament and any reference, however vague, be examined to provide evidence of the virtue of Mary.

Father Philippe paused, recalling the quotations he would now need. He reminded his audience that Mary was subsequently deemed to be the spiritual Eden on the grounds that in chapter two of Genesis are the words *Yahweh God planted a garden in Eden which is in the east, and there he put the man he had fashioned.* She was Noah's Ark, for in giving birth to Jesus, she saved all humanity from eternal damnation. She was Jacob's ladder, because through her God descended to earth. She was the flaming bush Moses saw on Mount Horeb, which burned without being consumed, as Mary gave birth without impairing her virginity. Mary was Aaron's rod, which produced shoots without rooting, as she conceived without the seed of man. All these and many other allusions had been triumphantly reconfirmed in 1546 at the Council of Trent with the proclamation that Mary had been forever without sin.

He paused, preparing them for the next point. The Immaculate Conception, he continued, had been a matter of conflict from the thirteenth century. The Franciscans supported it; the Dominicans rejected it. Trent had ended such divisions. Successive popes set about reinforcing the Council's exclusion of Mary from all original sin, even if this implied a divine conception on the part of her own mother, Anne. Another pause. Not a sound could be heard. They were his, as he knew they would be, just as he also knew they would remain totally attentive as he led them through the ramifications of the Papal Bull of Sixtus IV in 1476. It had been promulgated in part to reject opposition from Protestants and some Catholic modernists to Mary's total absence of all sin, even the tiniest venial one. Father Philippe said this doctrine was made an absolute article of faith by Pope Pius IX in 1854. Another pause, longer. "We are taught with what can only be seen as divine good fortune that striking confirmation of this article came through a shepherd girl, Bernadette, in February eighteen fifty-eight. The Madonna appeared to her and said 'I am the Immaculate Conception.' "

He stifled the start of applause.

"What Mary should have said was, 'I am immaculately conceived.'"

Once more the silence was total. He had expected no less. He waited a moment before adding how the glorification of Mary continued when Pope Pius XII, in 1950, declared yet another article of faith — the dogma that the Madonna, after her death, ascended into heaven, body and soul. Finally, five years ago, Pope Paul VI had exercised his authority to proclaim Mary *Mater Ecclesiae*, elevating her to the very pinnacle of the Church, alongside her Son and His Father.

A wave of applause swept the hall. He let it roll on, before waving them to be silent. "It is my contention that the only way properly to understand Mary's virginity is to see it in the context of prayer, faith, and holiness. Mary teaches us what prayer is, how to pray, to realize that our very faith is irrevocably linked to that power to pray. It has nothing to do with whether she was a virgin or not."

He noticed Simone was looked at him carefully.

"If it helps to believe that Mary was a virgin, that's fine. But it is not important. I think she should primarily be looked upon as holy. I believe that the essence of virginity is unison with God. Mary is the perfect example of life given to the service of Our Father. Virginity today does not mean the same as it did at the time of Mary. Nor does it gain value by being defined in biological terms. Like marriage, it is only because of the role it plays in the life of a particular person. I look at you and wonder if you are virgins in the sense I mean."

There were murmurs of surprise. Simone was smiling. "You may look at me and wonder if I am a virgin in the sense I mean! But our physical state is not the issue. The important thing is to recognize that virginity is meaningful only if it is part of a definite system of values. Just as with Mary, so it is with us. It is our interior selves, not our physical condition, which matters. I believe it can be summarized in two words: Holy Mary!"

He stepped back from the lectern. *Walter, wherever you are, I tried. I really did.*

With the moon rising over the starboard wing, the plane cruised toward Dallas. Daniel Watts, the bride's father, had sent Father Philippe a first-class round-trip ticket. They had never met and had spoken only twice on the telephone. The first occasion was when he was Frank's deacon. Mr. Watts had called the rectory to inquire about the times of Sunday Mass. Frank was out on a sick call, and when Mr. Watts learned Philippe was Frank's assistant, he had wished him luck. Later, Frank told him that Mr.

Watts was powerful, a good man to have on your side. The second time he wanted to know about local fishing. Father Philippe was surprised at the question but replied that the fishing was as good as always. Mr. Watts inquired how he was liking parish work. He told him he had never been happier. In spite of the brief encounters he had at first thought the wedding invitation was a mistake, but his name was in the appropriate space on the card. With it came the ticket and a slip informing him that a room had been reserved at the Fairmont Hotel — all expenses to be charged to Mr. Watts's account. He wondered what would have happened if he had sent back a polite note of refusal. He decided it would be irrational and ridiculous. He had called to thank Mr. Watts for his generosity and spoken to Blanche. She said how glad she was he was coming. He had asked about her future husband, and she replied that her fiancé was a wealthy banker. She had added that there would be a number of people at the reception who would be simply dying to talk to him.

He wondered what his fellow passengers would think of him, sipping champagne and nibbling oysters stuffed with shrimp and caviar, if they knew he was a priest. He had chosen to travel in a smartly cut blue suit. In his case were two more outfits; buried beneath them were his Roman collar, Bible, and black shirt and trousers. He did not expect he would need them, but he saw himself like a police officer, never going anywhere without his badge and gun. The clothes, like his luggage, were gifts from a haberdasher, a parishioner. Every six months he provided Father Philippe with a thousand dollars' worth of clothes. He called it his insurance policy to heaven.

In Father Philippe's pocket was the pendant. He still could not decide whether to give it to Blanche or not.

CHAPTER 8

†

Proposals

T he blaring trumpets swung into "The Age of Aquarius." For the
moment she was content to cling in his arms. Shiny buttons were
pinned to the front of her dress. Over the left breast one urged, "Make
Love, Not War." Beside it, in purple lettering, was "Had Any Lately?"
and on a shocking yellow background, "God is on a Trip." Among the few
questions she had asked Father Philippe was his age. He told her he was
almost thirty. She squinted her eyes and said she liked older men.

In their first minutes together she had said her name was Lauralene, but
everybody called her Lolo. She was nineteen years old and knew Blanche
from school, where they both studied business administration. The two
friends had worked together in the Poor People's Campaign in 1968. Their
efforts had made no difference. Nixon had won by a landslide. Lolo insisted the President was devious; he was even changing the flowerbeds
outside the Oval Office, bringing in his own gardeners from California.
Sometimes Father Philippe found it hard to keep track of her conversation,
yet being with Lolo had also made him feel as if the clamps bolted on his
senses had been pried loose.

†

He had been picked up at the airport by limousine and driven to the Fairmont. His room was twice the size of his entire living space at the rectory. There was a split of champagne and a bowl of fruit on a table, compliments of Mr. Watts. Father Philippe had swum in the hotel pool and breakfasted in its Pyramid Restaurant before visiting the shops in the lobby. He had decided the pendant was unsuitable. In the Neiman-Marcus boutique he bought two napkin holders, which he had engraved with the initials *B* and *G*, Blanche and Greg, bride and groom. He liked that. He charged the gift to his American Express Card, knowing he had expended almost a quarter of his monthly salary. On a card he wrote: " 'We are one, after all, you and I. Together we suffer, together exist. And forever remember each other.' When Teilhard de Chardin wrote that, he was thinking of you. Affectionately, Father Philippe."

Dressed in a tan lightweight suit, he went to the wedding, the package in one pocket. Impulsively, he slipped the box with the pendant into another. An usher directed him to a pew on the bride's side of the church. Standing there, surrounded by couples, he was reminded of what Frank had once said. A priest stood out because he was set apart. He must always remember that he was part of a higher life and a nobler love. That was why he must remain detached. That was the only way to spare himself a great many crosses. That was Christ's way.

After the Nuptial Mass he returned to the Fairmont, where a banqueting room had been reserved for the reception. Despite its size, it seemed barely big enough to accommodate the large number of guests. There was a pointless ostentation that almost vulgarized the occasion. He placed his gift on a table already piled high with presents. Blanche turned out to be what he expected and Greg looked like a banker. The couple greeted him quickly, moving him on up the reception line. Mr. Watts's welcome was warm and genuine and included an explanation of why Father Philippe was present. He made it a rule always to have a priest at any function; it was a way of reminding them how much he admired their strength; it could not be easy nowadays to live up to the ideal that priests must not be like other men. Mr. Watts released him with the injunction to have a good time, and he had drifted over to one of the bars. Ordering champagne, he asked the barman if he knew what Chesterton said when he had been converted to Catholicism.

"No, sir, I don't."

"He said it was to get rid of his sins."

The barman looked at him carefully. Lolo, standing next to Father Philippe, turned and said no one should want to be rid of all their sins. His first reaction was to wonder if beautiful girls were aware of the effect they created when bestowing favors. She had taken him by the arm to the buffet, where she filled their plates before leading him to a table. He sat beside her, sipping more champagne and, between mouthfuls, murmured he was a priest. His words made no impact. Lolo passed over them as though priests were a routine fixture in her life. Later, after they had eaten and toasted the speeches, the band boomed into life and she had led him onto the dance floor. There he felt a sense of panic. It was not that he hadn't danced for thirteen years — the last time was at his sister's wedding and then only to move awkwardly around the living-room floor with a cousin in his arms. It wasn't that his legs felt numb and he moved them consciously, his own puppeteer. It was the proximity of Lolo that unnerved him.

✝

He felt the heat of her young body and there was an uncontrolled excitement about her. He was relieved that the dance floor was crowded. Couples shuffled where they stood. Conversation was impossible. The psychedelic lighting increased his feeling of unreality. It pulsed across the room, everything seeming to go in out and out of focus. But the combination of light and music and Lolo's obvious enjoyment had its effect.

When the band stopped for a break, she motioned to a waiter to give them a bottle of champagne and two glasses. She led him to one of the couches along the wall, talking all the time. She had been to Woodstock, one of four hundred thousand who attended the festival. When she asked him if he liked acid rock, he felt almost middle-aged. Suddenly, she switched to the murder in Los Angeles of actress Sharon Tate. Had he heard that Charles Manson might be crazy, but was also a bedroom jock? Father Philippe said he had not been following the case.

The band began a new piece and he wondered what decibel level they'd reached. Walter had once said he hated rock bands; they always sound like an iron foundry. She reached across and kissed him before he realized what happened. She said she liked him. He replied that he liked her, too. Lolo said she was glad and poured champagne. He searched unsuccessfully for a less dangerous conversational gambit. Suddenly, she was on her feet, saying she was bored, running her tongue over her lips. He was aware that she was challenging him.

"Let's go someplace."

He suddenly felt awkward. "We just can't walk out."

"Who'd notice? Half of Texas is here. They wouldn't miss us."

He still hesitated. "Where would we go?"

"Your place."

The color rose in his face. "We can't do that."

"Then mine. I'm over at the Holiday Inn."

He had assumed she lived in the city. She explained she had recently moved away and Blanche had booked her a room. She smiled and he looked away.

"You're not scared, are you?"

"Scared? Why? I'm just surprised, that's all." He hoped his voice was steady.

She said something which he could not make out above the blare of "The Yellow Rose of Texas." Lolo took his hand and he allowed her to lead him toward the exit.

Her room was on the seventh floor. As they stepped from the elevator, she paused. He wondered if she had changed her mind. He couldn't tell if he was relieved or not.

"A bucket," she sang out. "I see a bucket."

Lolo handed him the bottle of champagne she had triumphantly purloined from the reception. She hurried to a service cart parked nearby, removed the ice bucket, took the bottle from him, and planted it in the ice. Then bearing it aloft like a trophy, she led him back down the corridor, halting outside a door.

"You strong enough to carry me over the threshold?"

"Sure."

She opened the door and put down the bucket. He picked her up, carrying her into the room, his hand under her knees, her arms around his neck. Lolo giggled as she gave him a love bite on the neck.

"Don't do that." He lowered her to the floor, his voice sharp, thinking what any of his parishioners would say if they saw the mark.

Lolo said she would like to eat him.

He went back to the corridor for the bucket, remembering another piece of advice from Frank. *None of us have absolute control over our physical and emotional feelings. But we do have control over the consequences they bring. We must not kid ourselves that we don't know where they can lead. We know that it is also foolish to run from them. That's just putting off the day when we must see if we have the strength to cope with temptation. That comes to all of us sooner or later. When it does, we must know we cannot give way. Being celibate is showing our ability to control our desires. That doesn't mean we have to play at being angels. We just need to be humble about thinking it is ever going to be easy.*

Philippe stood in the doorway. The room was as large as his own, with a long window along one wall; it was sealed. Below, set into the wall, was an air conditioner. On either side of the window were lined drapes made of a green fabric. Lolo was drawing them. He put the champagne on the table, watching her turn down one of the two double beds. She told him to open the bottle.

"We need glasses."

"Try the bathroom."

He walked past the bed, its headboard designed as a shelf to hold a telephone, a room-service menu, and a card bearing the words "Please be a Watt Watcher."

She sat on the edge of the bed, watching him as he filled the glasses and put the bottle back into the ice. Then he rose and gave her one. She motioned for him to sit beside her.

He started to speak, wanting to explain how he felt scared to be in violation of one of his vows, but she shushed him into silence, touching her glass against his. The sound was flat, plastic clinking against plastic. She rose to her feet and began to undress. He watched as she refilled her glass, clad only in her bra and panties. She asked him if he liked her. He said he did, very much. She told him to take his clothes off.

Later he would have no clear recollection of undressing, or if she helped him. There was just a swirl of blood racing through his body, rising to his head, pounding in his ears, catching in his throat. All the years of fantasy and frustration, of wondering what it would be like, swept over him. One moment she was under him, the next on top. Her body was hot and damp against his as she moved and begged, moaning over and over again for him to take her.

That was the moment the sweat began to pour from him and he knew he could not, *cannot* make love. He tried to pretend, crying out he wanted her, too; that she had the most beautiful body he had ever seen. The more he did this, the faster this awful deadness spread over him. She continued to urge him with her own moans and words. Yet the more she pleaded and the more urgent grew her demands, the greater was his sense of impotence. A feeling of panic choked him. *Why can't I make it happen?* He realized he was pounding the mattress with his fists in frustration.

She suddenly pushed her hands against his shoulders and slid away, her body soaked with his sweat. She began to cry. His panic drained to dejection. He buried his head in a pillow, wishing he could die. Through her sobbing he could hear words. Why did he not find her attractive? Why did he come if he didn't want her? Didn't he understand that she had asked him here because she wanted him? Why had he come? He lay there, feeling miserable.

She continued to rail at him, standing by the table with the champagne bottle in her hand.

"I told you. I'm a priest."

Her next words shocked him. "What the fuck's that gotta do with it? You think priests don't fuck? Well, they do. Women, men, and probably dogs for all I know? But you. You can't do anything!"

He half-rose on the bed, turning so that he shielded himself from her. He knew what he wanted to say. *Look, you are the first girl I've ever been this close to, ever. Give me time. Let's talk about it. Don't rush me. It's not your fault. I think all those years in seminary killed everything I am as a man. But you've given me a chance. Please give me time. It'll be okay. I just need time.* The words would not come.

"Get out. Just get out. Just get out of here now."

He began to dress, avoiding her eyes, realizing she was staring at him, knowing he should reach out and try to console her. His hands continued only to button, zip, knot, and tie. She dropped the bottle into the ice bucket, then she threw herself on the bed, spread-eagled on her belly, clutching at the sheet with both hands. She sobbed louder than before.

Father Philippe turned and walked to the door. He paused, feeling for the little package in his pocket. He returned to the bed and placed it on the headboard shelf, opening the box to display the pendant. He let himself out of the room. Even in the air-conditioned corridor he was sweating.

Father Philippe opened the door of the vestibule. The church was empty; not a hint, not so much as a trace of confetti or a flower, remained from the Watts wedding. He walked down the middle aisle, past the pew he had occupied. He was still bathed in sweat, making him shiver in the cool air of this lofty shaded place. Above the altar, where Blanche and Gary had knelt and made their sacred vows, suspended from a heavy chain dropping from the dome, was a larger-than-life Christ on a Byzantine cross. Behind Him, traced into the leaded central window, was Our Lady, arms extended toward her son. In adjoining windows were depictions of the twelve Apostles. At the latched altar gates he paused, genuflecting deeply.

He rose and looked about him. A cassocked figure emerged through a side door, asking if he could be of help.

"I want you to hear my confession." The priest led him to one of the confessionals off the central nave. Father Philippe closed the door behind him.

"Bless me, Father, for I have sinned. My last confession was a week ago, but today I . . ." He stopped.

"I have time. Take it slowly."

"I'm in big trouble."

"That is why you have come. Just start where you want."

"I don't know where."

"Wherever you like."

Father Philippe wished the priest would stop trying to be encouraging. "I would like to . . ."

"Just to talk? That's fine. You go ahead. I'm here to listen."

He shifted on his knees. He could hear the priest breathing.

"Is it a mortal sin?"

"I'm a priest. And I've been to bed with a woman."

In the silence, the confessor's breathing became irregular.

"Maybe you ought to state your sin."

Philippe did so, describing exactly what happened. There was another silence when he finished. He remained kneeling, his face buried in his hands, remembering that morning when the Bishop made him a priest and how afterward his superior had told him, as they unrobed in the sacristy, that penance is a wonderful sacrament and he must never fail to use it to ensure he could return to a state of grace.

"Was there volition?"

"I wish to confess it."

"Of course."

"And I wish to place before God my sin of rejection."

"Rejection?" The voice couldn't contain its surprise. "Who have you rejected and how?"

"God. His Son. Our Lady. All of them."

"Aren't you being too hard on yourself? You were genuinely tempted. That's possible, isn't it? You'd drunk quite a bit. The volition would not have been clear to you, would it?"

Father Philippe realized the confessor was trying to minimize what he was saying. He just wished he would accept it. "But I feel as if I have rejected them."

"Of course you do. That's natural. But it is, after all, your *feeling*. Like being depressed is a feeling. But God doesn't say depression is a sin. Does He?"

"No."

"Exactly. You really must not be so hard on yourself. Try not to be."

Father Philippe dropped his face into his hands once more, feeling the sweat under his arms. Can't the voice on the other side of this stifling box understand? *I feel dirty.*

"Father." The voice was coaxing and gentle. "You are truly repentant, aren't you? For all you have done? For even those sins you may not have remembered?"

"Yes." He wanted to get it over with.

"Then we shall make an Act of Contrition. Are you ready?"

"Yes."

"O my God —"

"O my God, I am truly sorry for having offended Thee . . ."

He received his penance.

"Go in peace, Father."

Father Philippe unlatched the door and left the confessional.

He was still sweating.

It was early evening. He had showered and dressed in his priest's suit, relieved that the love bite was below his Roman collar. He sat at the desk in his room, writing a thank-you note to Mr. Watts, clock-watching — waiting for the time he could check out and take the bus to the airport. He had rebooked on an evening flight that would see him in the rectory before midnight.

Walking back from the church and in the shower, he had tried to fathom his behavior. It was like pulling a newly formed scab from a wound, an exercise of pointless pain. There was no excuse. He had allowed himself to ignore what Frank called a basic rule. *The more passionate a celibate feels for another person, the greater is his or her doubt about loving God the way He should be loved. The conflict will always come down to one between God or another person. In a way that is what our love is all about. When we celibates love, we are no different from anybody else. We want to see a return for our love. Now that's easier to get when we love another person. It is there in that person's words and gestures. But with God we find it harder. God doesn't go around holding our hands, not in the literal sense anyway. But we can reach Him through prayer, and He will enter our hearts and reassure us of our vocation.*

The knock on the door startled him. When he opened it, Lolo was standing there, holding the pendant box.

"Hi."

"Hi."

"You going to work?" She indicated his clothes.

"Not at once. I'm going home."

"I thought you might take me to dinner."

"I'm sorry. I don't think I would be much fun."

"Take a later flight."

"I'm sorry."

"You're not really."

He said nothing.

"You going to ask me in?"

"I don't think that would be a good idea."

She squinted at him. "You don't understand, do you?"

"I think I do."

"Father," she said pleasantly, acknowledging his position for the first time. "Father, go fuck yourself. And use this."

She thrust the box at him and without another word turned away and walked down the corridor. He opened the box. Inside, where the pendant had been, was one of her buttons. *Had Any Lately?*

"Not only is there no God, but try getting a plumber on Sunday." Woody Allen's one-liner on the comedy hour coming over his El Al headset was the only memorable moment on the long flight to Tel Aviv. After his return from Dallas he had immersed himself in the comfortable and demanding routine of parish life. He took care to hide the bite mark until the bruise faded. He had been surprised to receive a note from the chancellor saying his lecture to the women of the Sodality of Our Lady had been well received; he should repeat the talk to other Catholic groups. He had given his views, when asked, on a number of issues plaguing the community and the national psyche. He agreed with those parishioners who saw danger in the way conglomerates were becoming virtual sovereign states. He supported a Moratorium Day, joining a procession of men and women wearing black armbands and carrying placards and candles to protest the Administration's involvement in Vietnam. That same night, he watched on television a quarter of a million protesters clog Washington while President Nixon viewed a football game on ABC. Later, on a talk

show, a guest quoted the latest witticism. "God isn't dead — He just doesn't want to get involved."

The following Sunday he dropped in to watch Simone teach. She had a clear style, making her points with a simplicity he admired. He liked, too, the way she had not interrupted her class when he arrived, merely motioning him to the back and continuing with her account of how Pope Gregory VII had laid down no fewer than twenty-seven principles to establish his superiority and that of future pontiffs over all other European monarchs; the Pope can be judged by no one. That was in 1073. He had sat there listening to Simone, thinking how eight hundred and ninety-seven years later the sixth man to call himself Pope Paul presides over a Church at a time when religion itself is no longer assured of automatic respect. Walking Simone to her car, he said it was only a matter of time before the effects of the moral and ideological schisms developing in Rome would be felt here. There was no way, he insisted, that the hard-liners could turn back the clock. What was needed was for the Pope to show a firmer hand. It was not enough for Paul to have removed the notorious Index of Prohibited Books, which had barred the works of Voltaire and Victor Hugo from being read by any Catholic; or to have allowed Mass to be celebrated in as many languages as there were people to speak them; or that he continued to warn the rich nations they must share their wealth with impoverished countries or risk the judgment of God and the wrath of the poor. That, he told Simone, was good — but not enough. The Pope needed to end the die-hard opposition to the recommendations of the Second Vatican Council. He told Simone that on his way back from Israel he would visit Rome and try to judge for himself what was happening to implement those recommendations.

He had managed to put that encounter with Lolo into the context of an aberration, convincing himself that he had momentarily taken leave of his senses; that his behavior then was out of character, even as he had now come to see were all those Saturday afternoons spent with Walter. Every night he prayed for there to be no repetition. Frank was right. Each celibate had to face and overcome temptation. There was no other way.

He was disturbed that there had been no guidance on how to handle the deepening crisis over chastity that was particularly affecting the American Church. In the past year almost 4 percent of all its priests had left — nearly four times as many as in the previous ten years. Many had done so because they no longer felt able to subscribe to the vow of celibacy. In a comment on the matter, the chancellor circulated a reminder to the diocesan priests; "Through prayer we can always find the correct solution. Through prayer we will always find the appropriate truth of how the Father, Son, and Holy Spirit wishes us to behave. Through prayer we know we can love them and our neighbors in a proper way, one which will always allow for a faithful concept of our calling."

Father Philippe had thought that typically the chancellor had dodged, or perhaps was unaware of, the central question. More than the alpha and omega of a celibate life was under scrutiny. There had begun a process outside the Church of integrating psychological concepts with theological dogma to see whether sexuality and celibacy need not be enemies for those wishing to live within the Body of Christ. So far there were many questions and few answers. Could celibacy be compatible with human intimacy? How far could that intimacy properly go? How far did culture have a part to play in redefining celibacy? Where did humanism fit into a rethinking of the traditional understanding of sexuality?

As the plane landed in Tel Aviv, he remembered Walter had predicted such questions would be asked, and had proffered a piece of advice. *Go back to our roots for the answers. As good a place as any to start is the Holy Land. Walk in the footsteps of the prophets and the Apostles. Form your own opinions. That's better than any book. Besides, there's isn't a book written yet on what we want to know.* That had been on the Saturday before the Snot discovered them.

The Snot had died six months ago. But Father Philippe still had no idea of Walter's whereabouts. He knew it would be dishonest to pretend he did not miss him. Sometimes he wondered what part Walter's influence had played on that hot afternoon in Dallas. He also pondered if, without it, he would have behaved differently with Lolo.

Clearing formalities under the scrutiny of customs agents and the watchful stare of soldiers, he wondered how many of them realized their presence was striking proof that miracles do happen; that they were here because of the biblical prophecy of returning to the Promised Land. He asked the question and received no reply from the official who tipped out his bag, going through his books, Bible and missal, and turning over in her hand his gleaming white Roman collar before feeling through the pockets of his priest's suit, which was stowed at the bottom of the bag. She said anyone who arrived in Israel with one suitcase automatically aroused suspicion. He explained that being a priest, he traveled light. She stared at him bleakly, saying that terrorists nowadays used all sorts of disguise. It was his first reminder that this was a land under siege.

That had been ten days ago, and he had still not become used to the rudeness, the sharp Hebrew words, the jostling, the indifference to polite requests. The food was often inedible, the wines sickly sweet, the beer weak and tepid. The humidity was draining. His cotton shirt and slacks, cool for the South, clung to him in the heat of the Middle East. At night his sheets felt like thick blankets. Yet he would not have missed the pilgrimage. There was that unforgettable moment he climbed the hills of Jerusalem, appreciating the truth of the repeated phrase in the Bible: *Going up to Jerusalem.* It was both a physical and religious experience. Everywhere he turned, he realized history was not just something he had been absorbing from books in preparation for this trip. It was here. In that first view of Jerusalem itself, a white and terra-cotta city on twin hillsides, with the Church of the Holy Sepulchre and all the other domes of worship giving a strangely futurist look to the place. He walked through the Old City, marveling that Jesus and his Apostles had trod the same cobbles beneath the shadow of Solomon's walls. He went to the Mount of Olives and stared from its summit at the wilderness. Out there a man, Christ, had stayed for forty days, living on locusts and wild honey.

Getting used to the heat, which relentlessly removed moisture from his body, he went to Nazareth, discovering that where Jesus grew up had changed little in two thousand years. On a postcard to Frank he described the houses as tiny, formed from cubes of stone and mud covered with white plaster, devoid of windows, with flat roofs of reeds and olive branches covered with a mixture of earth and stone baked hard in the sun. To Simone, he sent another card, saying that just as in the days of Mary, the men were idle while the women fetched water, dried carobs, figs, and grapes, worked in communal courtyards, each open space equipped with its clay oven. He ended with the words: "I wish I could show you all this. Very affectionately, Philippe."

He traveled into the depths of the land once called Judea, to Bethlehem, and stood at the mouth of the cave where Jesus was born, encased these past sixteen hundred years in the Basilica of the Holy Nativity, constructed by the Emperor Constantine when he embraced Christianity. Here he sought answers to questions he had asked himself for years. Had Joseph hurried from this spot when Mary was seized by labor pains, seeking a midwife? Did that midwife, bearing the historic name of Salome, express understandable amazement that even at the moment of giving birth

Mary preserved her virginity? Had the shepherds sat on the hills behind the cave, watching over their flocks by night and telling stories? And had, as the Apostle Luke reports, an angel appeared, followed swiftly by a troop of the heavenly Host who praised God and expressed glory to God in the highest and peace and goodwill to all men on earth? He accepted that it happened. But had it occurred, *then?* The tale of the shepherds had nagged him through his seminary studies. Now, at last, here where the story began, he could satisfy himself on the issue. He asked, and was told, that during the winter the temperature in the hills around Bethlehem falls to well below feezing and the rainy season lasts into March. Animals are not left outside. Therefore how could those shepherds have been watching over their sheep on the night Mary gave birth?

In the records in Bethlehem's library, he discovered that once the birth of Jesus was widely accepted as falling on a day between March 28 and May 29. Then in the wake of the introduction of celibacy into the Church, which began the process of Mariology, the birth date was recalculated. Leo the Great — he who had confronted Attila on the banks of the River Po — became convinced that Jesus had lived for thirty-three years. That meant he had spent over thirty-two years living on earth, passing the remaining months in the womb of Mary. Working backward from the date Leo gave for Christ's death, April 6, his theologians calculated that the Nativity fell on January 6, the Day of Epiphany in the Western Church. Leo was not satisfied. He wanted and obtained a further revision, one that placed the birth of Jesus on December 25. That was the day the ancient cult of *Sol Invictus* celebrated the annual ascendance of the astrological sign of the virgin over the horizon. It symbolized the powerful goddess giving birth to her son-god, the most awesome of the pagan deities in the entire Mediterranean basin. The virgin was the bearer — through the god's mythical person — of all good things: the end of winter, the sowing of crops, the harvest. Through his skillful manipulation, Leo the Great managed to have the attributes of the sun-god imbued in Jesus and those of the pagan virgin assumed by the Madonna. A simple change of a birthday thus helped to ensure the ultimate triumph of Christianity. Fifteen centuries later, Father Philippe not only marveled at Leo's sleight of hand but wondered what else had been changed.

Back in Jerusalem, the Jewish quarter was as quiet as he imagined the Day of Judgment would be. It was Shabbat, the Jewish Sabbath, when hardly a car moves and traffic lights blink on empty streets and shuttered shops. It reminded him of Sundays at his seminaries when he used to think God had come and gone, taking His chosen with Him and leaving Philippe to fend for himself. On this Saturday, he sat in his hotel room and contemplated a subject he realized had never been out of his mind. He tried to formulate thoughts on celibacy that had come to him in this ancient land, with its abrasive people and their customs and rituals, established long before Jesus walked among them.

He worked as he did when a seminarian, concentrating on assembling all the information of the past two weeks, laying it all on his bed and the floor, moving the material around so that it was easier to follow, in chronological order. He then divided it up under separate headings. It took him most of the morning.

In the lunch hour, he took another walk to the Via Dolorosa, the road by which the Crusaders said Christ entered the city on Palm Sunday and along which He later dragged His Cross to Calvary. Beyond, in the Arab sector, the streets were crowded, the shops open, the air filled with the sickly smell from butchers' trays of sheep heads, the dark eyes open, the blood dripping on displays of olive-wood crosses, trays of confectionery, mounds of Stars of David, baskets of fruits. He had been warned not to buy from the street vendors for fear of amoebic dysentery. He crossed Christ's Street of Sorrows and was back in the virtual solitude of the Jewish sector. He knew where he wanted to go. He had been there before, and it drew him back like a magnet. In a narrow side street was an Israeli checkpoint. He was silently frisked and motioned through. Beyond was the Wailing Wall, reached by a descending flight of steps carved into the limestone. This was the world of Herod and Caiaphas, his High Priest; of the Pharisees and the Sadducees, those hereditary priests whose lineage went all the way back to the Maccabees.

Centuries before the New Testament, the Pentateuch was the only gospel spoken of here. What concerned him was that central to it, written in the reign of Solomon, in the tenth century before Christ, was a clear-cut statement on sexuality. While the old belief is opposed to sexual excess, it approves of sexuality itself — even for priests.

Back in his hotel room, he read Genesis and the second account of the Creation. *Yahweh God said, "It is not good that the man should be alone. I will make him a helpmate."*

He could formulate his first point. "God does not want man to be lonely. That is why He created woman, a sexually different person. In the Genesis account, sexuality is not primarily associated with propagation. It is shown as a gift from God to man, so that man would not be lonely. A woman is God's way of showing His creative solution to end that loneliness. Sexuality was given to that first man in Paradise because God wished him to possess it. From the very outset, God is saying that man must associate sexuality with the fellowship of his contact with woman."

It took him longer to make the next point, based on the Old Testament's Song of Songs, an anthology of lyrical love poems, most certainly the work of several priest-authors.

At his seminaries and later with Frank, he had immersed himself in this celebrative literature, attracted in part by the mystical beauty of the relationship between two lovers, drawn too by the explicit images of physical copulation and the way they suggest the sacredness of lovemaking. Frank had said the Song represented the Church's recognition of marriage as a sacrament.

Every night before going to bed in Israel, he read a portion of the Song. The words remained as clearly appreciative of sexuality as always. But now he saw them in a different light. There is a distinct theology of sexuality behind the poems. Each stanza, in its overtones of sensuality, passion and eroticism, speaks of the beauty of the physical relationship. The priests who wrote the stanzas were familiar with sexual experience and enjoyed it. Father Philippe felt there was no other way they could have conveyed such excitement unless it had been based on firsthand knowledge. Throughout the Song is the explicit message that physical love and spiritual giving are closely related. But the insights go deeper. The Song makes it clear that at times words — spiritual giving — are not enough to express love fully. There is a need for physical contact. The poems do not endorse promiscuity; they are devoted to exalting a one-to-one relationship that is permanent. There is not a word, as far as he could discover, that precludes the successors of those who wrote them from enjoying the same physical intimacy that runs through their poems.

It was late afternoon when he finished his notes. He was filled with an urge to explore further the city where Jesus had set the foundations for all the later clashes between Church and State. At the end of the Old City walls he walked into the Kidron Valley, beyond which is the Mount of Olives. The evening sun was hot on his skin. His destination was one of two churches, both clearly marked on his map. The first, of black stone, was erected eighteen hundred years earlier, to mark the spot where Mary is traditionally held to have been assumed into Heaven. It was locked. Farther along, on the right-hand side of the road where Jesus Himself often walked, was a more magnificent church, set in a vast garden of ancient, gnarled olive trees. This is the Garden of Gethsemane. He had acquired enough Hebrew to know its pronunciation as *gath shamené*, the olive press. Here in a cave where olives were stored for the winter, Christ and His disciples sheltered before entering Jerusalem on that Passover which the miracle of His Resurrection would turn forever into Easter for all Christians. The cave was now looked after by Franciscans. He could see the monks walking among the trees, saying the Divine Office.

He had a sudden longing for home: to say Mass again, to administer the Holy Eucharist, to see Simone. He had thought about her a lot these past two weeks: after that first postcard from Nazareth he had sent her six more, and two letters as well. All contained vivid descriptions of his impressions of the Holy Land. He had frequently said to himself that was all they must contain. But in his diary he had admitted she made a powerful impression on him. He had tried to reassure himself. *I am not worried, I can handle myself. It's just nice to write to her.*

He sat and stared at the monks, trying to imagine that evening when Jesus walked out of the cave, followed by John, James, and Peter. Legend has it that Christ was trembling and miserable, with a fear he explained to the Apostles. *My soul is sorrowful to the point of death. Wait here and keep awake.* Peter described how Jesus staggered farther into the garden, His hands groping for support from one olive bough to another. Finally, He fell exhausted to the ground and Mark heard Jesus cry out: *Father! Everything is possible for you. Take this cup away from me. But let it be as you, not I, would have it.* Luke had watched Christ, prostrate on the earth. *His sweat fell to the ground like great drops of blood.*

In that psychological study of great biblical figures in his final year at seminary, he had come across an acceptable medical explanation for what Luke observed. Jesus could have experienced an attack of hematohidrosis, acute dilation of the subcutaneous capillaries, the effect of excessively high blood pressure produced by violent emotions. In a typical attack the blood flows into the pores, causing edema. In the most extreme cases it can actually make its way through the pores onto the skin. It is frequently seen in highly sensitive persons experiencing hysteria. Aristotle and Galen were known to suffer from the malady. Historically, it is more prevalent in men than women; it is sometimes associated with stress resulting from sexual problems. He had questioned his tutors whether this passage showed a weakness in the Son of God and why it did not appear in any Catholic codex. He had been given no satisfactory answer, merely fobbed off with the dogma: he must believe without challenging. There is so much, he realized, that has not been explained.

After dinner, he resumed making his notes on celibacy. Over the years, the Gospel he had marked most was Matthew's. There were scores of ticks and numbers alongside the verses, which corresponded to those in a thick notebook containing his own thoughts on their meaning. Until now, he had felt there was relatively little in any of the Gospels regarding celibacy. He was positive he had been wrong. Those earlier thoughts he had had in seminary, about Jesus being sexual in an affective way, were reinforced. When Matthew deals with sexuality, its role is often dramatically demonstrated through Jesus. He noted: "Matthew is certainly saying that Christ is like everyone except He is without sin. From that it can be derived that sexuality is not sinful but part of being a total human being. Question: is it possible to accept Jesus' humanity without taking into account His sexuality? Answer: almost certainly not. Matthew demonstrates that feelings of affection, warmth, and compassion are to be found in Jesus."

He was convinced of one overriding conclusion: abstaining from sex did not place a person, in the sense of meaningful Christian values, on a higher plane. This thought was still uppermost when he flew from Tel Aviv to Rome.

The Pope was small, he said, lowering his fork and bringing his hand a little above the candles on the table, indicating height. He estimated Paul VI was about five feet five inches tall, with a sad, wizened face. He had been told the pontiff's regalia weighed forty pounds, much of it gold. The chain and cross around his neck were claimed to have a value of two hundred thousand dollars. When Pope Paul died — and already in Rome they were speaking of the day — the priceless gold ring he wore, symbolizing he was the direct descendant of Peter the Fisherman, would be melted down inside the Vatican. Later, when a new pontiff was elected, the precious ore would be reformed into a new ring. The same metal had been reconstituted for almost five hundred years. At the moment, it was on the bony index finger of a man christened Giovanni Battista Montini, now known as Bishop of Rome, Vicar of Jesus Christ, Successor to the Prince of the Apostles, Supreme Pontiff of the Universal Church, Patriarch of the West, Primate of Italy, Archbishop and Metropolitan of the Roman Province, Sovereign of the State of Vatican City, Servant of the Servants of God, His Holiness, Holy Father.

The Pope was not just physically small, Father Philippe went on, he was also mentally shrunken. The abiding impression of his stay in Rome was one of a pontiff shying away from the opportunities the Second Vatican Council had provided to set the Church on an exciting course toward the next century, into the third millennium since Christ. He paused, eyeing Simone, aware that the maître d' was watching them. He had hardly taken his eyes off the corner table that Simone had reserved and to which he had led them with the same stately gait in which he brought his family down the aisle every Sunday to receive Holy Communion at Sacred Heart.

The waiter had kissed Simone's hand, murmuring in French how well she looked and asking how her father was. When he greeted Father Philippe, his face was suavely blank. After they were seated, he retreated, and Simone explained she taught his children eighth-grade catechism. She laughed, unselfconsciously, the way she had when he had called her a few hours earlier and asked her to dinner, saying he wanted to tell her all about his trip. He knew before he heard her voice that he really wanted to see her. He had sent her postcards from the Vatican post office in St. Peter's Square, describing his impressions but also writing: "If I had the money, I'd send you a ticket to come here. This is the most romantic place in the world. Rome is full of lonely priests and nuns. It should only be filled with lovers." When he called, she thanked him for the cards, and he said he hoped he had not embarrassed her. She simply said no, as if there was no reason for him to feel otherwise.

The restaurant was twenty minutes' drive out of town, authentically French in furnishings and food. Her father had told her this when he'd brought Brad and her here to celebrate their engagement. Father Philippe felt a sudden pang of jealousy he realized was irrational. Glancing at her hand, he noticed the ring was missing. He'd asked her, and she said quickly, as if it were a topic not to be pursued, that she and Brad were no longer engaged. He thought again how hope can be raised by a few words.

"Now, Father Philippe, I want you to tell me everything. About Rome, about Israel. About everything."

He smiled and said only if she would stop calling him Father. He was surprised how long she had hesitated. She was suddenly serious.

"In our family, we were brought up to show respect. 'A priest is always a priest,' my dad says. It's hard to forget that."

"Try. Calling me Philippe doesn't actually change anything." He would not be able to remember exactly his feelings at this moment, but he was certain he had moved the conversation to a new level.

"All right. Philippe. But only between us. You're still 'Father' in front of everyone else."

The maître d' returned and suggested cocktails. She ordered kir for them both, in fluent French. Then she asked him about the Pope.

He spoke with quiet conviction, explaining how, as he stood in St. Peter's Square, he had been struck by the distinct shift of emphasis in the Pope's attitude to a familiar subject: celibacy in the priesthood. His position had hardened. To even suggest optional celibacy now appeared to him a dangerous novelty that could lead to the dismantling of the Church. The reedy voice echoing over the square's loudspeaker system had said that a priest is the crucial link between God and man, and man and God. From his pocket Father Philippe produced the notes he made at the time and read: " 'The Pope says the chain must be perfectly forged for man to climb toward Heaven. The weakest and strongest link is the one upon which the strain is greatest — the priesthood. But a priest must continue to represent stability in an unstable world, fidelity in an unfaithful world, the supernatural in a natural world, the bringer of immortality and eternity in a temporal and transient world.' " He put down the paper.

The waiter returned and listed the house specialties, addressing Simone. Father Philippe studied her. Later he would write down what he now felt. *I know what was happening. I was discovering a simple fact of life. In spite of everything, I am still able to fall in love.* He watched her discuss the menu. Illogically, he wished the man would go away so that he could reclaim her undivided attention.

Her hair was in bangs and she wore a peasant blouse and full skirt. Her legs, as usual, were bare. The waiter finally bowed and retreated. Her ordering, Father Philippe thought, was part of a wider revolution, a sign that the delicate balance between the sexes had altered, probably for all time. He still found it a shock that in the period between his entering and leaving seminary, women had moved into jobs always considered masculine: there were now women miners, truckers, ditchdiggers, and Secret Service agents. He was certain it would only be a matter of time before there were women priests. Sex had become a prime issue in the Church. Every word of Pope Paul's seventy-five-hundred-word encyclical, *Humanae Vitae*, was being hotly debated. It had infuriated millions of American Catholics. While he was abroad, a poll conducted by Jesuits showed that 70 percent of Catholic students at the University of San Francisco approved of birth control; another survey revealed the priesthood itself was divided on the issue. The majority of those over fifty favored the encyclical; below forty, there was overwhelming clerical opposition. Young priests had organized sit-ins at diocesan meetings and walkouts at church services. Bishops had suspended protesting priests or banished them to Retreats. But the revolt continued.

Simone wanted him to run a seminar on the changing face of Catholicism. She would call it "A Life in the Spirit." Just as she had intrigued him with her knowledge when they had first spoken, she did so again. She urged him to demonstrate that the Pope's office should be one of ministry, not of domination; he is there to serve, not to control; his prime concern should be with human feelings, not the institution of the church. Philippe could begin by explaining why there could be a case for optional celibacy.

He nodded, aware of the perversity of the situation. There and then, he thought, was the moment he stopped deceiving himself. Again he asked her about Brad. She shrugged, saying she was uncertain about getting married. Brad told her if she did not want to be engaged, she should stop wearing his ring. She had removed it.

"He's obviously very much in love with you?"

"I suppose so."

"Of course he is! He'd be crazy not to be!"

She made no response, sitting perfectly still, her eyes on him.

"Do you love him?"

"I don't know."

"That means you probably don't."

"Probably."

"Is this embarrassing?"

"No."

"I don't want to embarrass you."

"You're not. Honest."

"The thing is, you see, I think I've been in love with you for weeks." Finally, she answered. "I know."

Simone reached across the table and held his hand.

The seminar was a success. It formed part of a life within a life for them both. Twice a week up to thirty young people, either married or engaged, gathered in Simone's newly rented apartment. They sat on the long couch before the TV set, or on the floor. He would perch on a window ledge, in his priest's suit and Roman collar. She always addressed him as Father Philippe. His lectures covered every reason for reform in the Church. At first he was cautious, fearing one of them might report him to his superiors. Simone reassured him. She had chosen carefully: they were intelligent and well-informed Catholics concerned only with getting a better insight on the complex issues facing the Church and challenging their faith. He had relaxed and argued that the full promise of the Second Vatican Council was being sabotaged by powerful voices in the College of Cardinals, who were opposed to collegiality and a greater involvement by the laity in Church affairs. He attacked *Humanae Vitae* and expressed the fear that Pope Paul was failing as a teacher. They questioned him for hours.

Later, he would always leave with them, bidding a formal good night to Simone. He would drive away and then park his car in a side street and slip back to the apartment by the service elevator. She would always have a glass of chilled kir waiting. Simone had begun renting the apartment while he was in Israel, after receiving his postcards. Even then, she told him, she knew what was going to happen. In that first week they just talked. But on the Monday night of the second week she said quietly, as if she did not wish to frighten him away, that she wanted him to make love to her.

He felt the fire on his face and the sudden dampness of his body. She looked steadily at him as she declared herself. She had never asked a man to make love to her before, because she had never wanted to; until now there was nobody she wanted to give herself to.

He told her about Lolo and Walter. She assured him it would be all right this time. As she led him to the bedroom, he suddenly felt like a schoolboy and not a grown man. She carefully pulled off her blue sweater and then stepped out of her skirt and placed it over the back of a chair. Clad only in her panties, she guided him to the bed. He could smell her body, which was without perfume, its aroma only that of clean womanliness. His eyes watched her, mesmerized.

"Is the way I am behaving so terrible?" she asked him.

"No. Oh, no," he said softly.

She moved backward, slowly helping him to undress. His shirt came off, his Roman collar coming with it, then his pants. Lying flat on the bed, she removed her panties and pulled him toward her. He told her how beautiful she was; so beautiful he could cry. She told him tenderly not to cry. As she spoke, she helped him remove his shorts. Naked, he felt neither awkward nor embarrassed. The sweating had stopped. Suddenly, he wanted to make love and enjoy it, and he did. There was one short moment of resistance as he entered her, but it passed and was replaced by exquisite pleasure as she arched her back in time to his rhythm.

Since then, they had made love every day, some days as often as three or four times. He would hurry from the confessional to the apartment at the lunch hour. He would visit before saying early Mass, returning when his duties were over. On evenings when there was no seminar, they drove to a neighboring town to see a movie. Then they would return and he would cook her a meal, serving it with flourish, uncorking the wine and sampling it as if he were a sommelier and not a priest. They made love on the couch, on the floor, but mostly on the bed. They experimented and came to know how to arouse each other, discovering the many joys of sex.

After three weeks, he continued to resist her pleas to sleep over. He explained that his fellow priests would become suspicious. He could not tell her that while he enjoyed her body, he preferred his own bed, or that he often now rose from it in the small hours and crept down to the darkened church. There he would plead, often for an hour or more, to be forgiven.

Father Philippe gave the man penance and absolution and released him from the confessional. He wondered again if his absolution was valid since he was no longer in the state of grace. He had not been to confession since first making love to Simone. Sitting on the hard bench in the confining blackness, he pondered: *What do I do?* The diary in the breast pocket of the shirt he wore beneath his cassock was filled with tortured imagery. He had written that he felt he was adrift on a river in flood, being carried toward a waterfall and certain death, or in a rocket hurtling out of control through space. In these fantasies there was no escape. At other times, he wrote that he no longer wanted to flee from himself, from his feelings, as he had done all his life. *The marvelous thing about my love for her is that it is spontaneous. When I touch her, I know I am alive. I need that affirmation. Existentialists say that we have to commit suicide to show we have lived in the first place. I don't believe that anymore. When Simone holds me, I am affirming that I am alive. She has shown me the easiest thing in the world is to be what you are, how to love.*

In the confessional, he experienced old doubts. He began to pray, silently, hoping once more to find an answer. *Dear God, what can I do?* He asked, was it true what Frank had said: that love can be a curse as well as a gift if it destroys what God intended? He continued to pray, his mind to drift, as new hopes and visions surfaced. His love for her was genuine, a clear indication he was not meant to be a priest. His vocation must be set aside in favor of Simone. He could still serve Christ in some other capacity.

He heard footsteps. He placed an eye against the small hole in the side of the box to see if there were supplicants waiting. Through the tiny slit of light he looked into the church. Simone was in a pew on the far side of the nave. He left the confessional, pausing quickly to genuflect before the altar, and walked past the statue of Our Lady, draped in folds of white and blue.

She was smiling down, palms turned outward to the world. The sculptor had given her eyes that were both unflinching and compassionate. He knelt beside Simone. She looked at him and he would always remember her smile. He would remember, too, her whispered words: "It's going to be okay. We love each other. I want us to get married."

They had gotten into the habit of giving each other little gifts: paperbacks, a handkerchief with his initials on it, a key ring formed in the shape of an *S*. One day she surprised him when he arrived at the apartment. He had come straight from a funeral and there was a trace of incense on his cassock. She led him into the bedroom. Laid out on the bed were a new shirt, tie, and trousers.

"What's this? You come into a fortune?"

"You're going calling," she told him matter-of-factly. "My parents have invited us for dinner. I thought you'd feel more comfortable in these."

He kissed her and asked how much time they had.

She smiled. "Enough."

Afterward, when she had hung his soutane in a closet, they showered, soaping each other, washing away the last traces of lovemaking. They dressed slowly, eyes constantly on each other.

"I've told them," she said as they left the apartment.

"What did they say?"

"It's going to be fine. I've told them we love each other."

She pressed the elevator button and kissed him, pulling away only when the door opened. It was one of the games they played, seeing what intimacies they could risk in public without being discovered. Dining out, she would kick her shoe off to stroke his leg with her toes, or he might reach across the table and quietly place a hand on her breast. She told him her love could not be imprisoned; it would wriggle free of any bonds. She loved him freely, and knew she would grow to love him more. Driving to her parents' home, he remembered how well she expressed her feelings: *Being in love with you, I've learned more about myself than I ever thought possible. How to trust. How to give. How to realize that love is faith and it needs to be strong.*

He wished he could put it so succinctly, just as he wanted to stop feeling he was on that river heading for the waterfall, powerless to save himself.

Father Philippe thought Simone was like her father. Until then he had always believed the old adage held true: "Before you marry the girl, look at the mother." But Simone had her father's eyes and voice, his directness and smile. Judge Dupois led him to the back terrace as Simone and her sisters helped their mother in the kitchen. The judge sat on a rocker opposite Father Philippe.

"Simone says you want to marry?"

"Yes."

"You realize, of course, what that means, for you and for us?"

"I do."

"How will you live?"

"I'll get work."

"What can an ex-priest do?" His questions were polite but firmly framed.

"I'll try anything."

"Trying is one thing, succeeding is another. What qualification do you have, Father?"

"Call me Philippe. I guess we had both better get used to the idea."

"Okay. Have you any money?"

"Only what I've saved out of my salary."

"Where will you live?"

"I'll move in with Simone."

Judge Dupois rocked back and forth, his eyes fixed on him.

"How long have you been a priest?"

Father Philippe told him.

"And before that, years of study. A long time. A lot to give up. Are you certain?"

"I love her."

"Love is not always enough."

"It's all that matters."

"Maybe now, yes. But what about later? You know how the Church feels about priests who take off with parishioners. Unless you get a dispensation, you'll not be able to marry my daughter in the Church. I've always wanted my girls to have that blessing."

Simone joined them. "Papa! We love each other. That's all that matters."

Father Philippe looked at her. Her use of the word "Papa" made her seem suddenly young in his eyes. He felt strangely uneasy, wondering what her father would say if he knew the truth about their relationship. Walter had once said that all fathers have a deep-rooted complex about their daughters. They had been talking about Freud's views on sexuality at the time and Walter remarked that Oedipus was much maligned: it was really fathers who mixed up their daughters, not mothers their sons.

"I can wait for dispensation before we marry."

"Philippe, no! Why should we wait? We love each other."

Judge Dupois looked at them both. "What about Brad?"

"Papa, I've written to him. He'll have to understand. It would never have worked." Her father nodded, then said something Father Philippe would never forget. It was not a phrase he had heard before: "Simone is under your protection from now on. Always try and remember that."

"Yes, sir. I will."

Being in love, insisted Frank, was one thing, but had he thought through all the implications? Could he really mean to give up fourteen years of a vocation to marry a girl he had known well for only six weeks? Why not wait? Go away for a few months. Something could be worked out with the Bishop. They could work together again and talk things over, as they used to do. Then, if he really felt he wanted to marry, Frank would do everything to help.

Father Philippe held the cassette recorder close to the telephone. He had asked permission to record the conversation, and Frank had said he would do anything if it would help him to see things more clearly.

"You make it all sound so easy, Frank."

"No. You're the one who makes it sound easy. Turning your back on all you've struggled for, just like that. Where's all the discipline that kept you going? What's happening to you?"

"I've told you, Frank. I'm in love."

Frank was silent. Father Philippe could imagine him seated at his office desk in the rectory, surrounded by papers of all kinds. Frank was the untidiest man he knew. He was also the only priest he had ever been close to. Even so, he had put off calling him until now, just two days before the wedding. Frank began again. His personal history had no doubt played a big part in what had happened. His unhappy home, the rejection of his mother, the battles at his seminaries. It had been struggle and rejection at every turn. He had come through more than probably any other young priest in the diocese had faced. Why not see what was happening as another test of his faith?

"It's not, Frank. It really isn't."

"How do you know? How do you know that God doesn't mean this to be something that can bring you even closer to Him?"

"I'll still be close to Him when I get married, Frank. Don't *you* see that?"

"It won't be the same. It can't be. You have a vocation. You're one of the best preachers I know. I hear great things about your ministry. They love you. Are you going to walk out on all that? All those people who need you? And you think you're alone in your dilemma? Listen. For years I have wondered at times about my celibacy. Is it really worth all the struggle? The loneliness? The hassle of doing everything myself? Going to the Laundromat, shopping. Of not having someone to talk to. Then I stop being negative. It's not a question of being married. That's not it at all. I come back to what my celibacy is. Something positive. I didn't choose it. It chose me, part of the package we call a vocation. When I see it like that, my doubts go away. I know God wants me. He really does. That's why I don't mind working all the hours He gave me, and some more. Doing the house-work, making the bed, making sure I eat. It's no sweat because God wants me. I know that He wants you too. He really does. Are you going to say no to God? Are you going to turn your back on all those values that He first saw in you? Are you?"

Father Philippe was silent. He could see the tape revolving in the re-corder.

"Frank . . ."

"Yes?"

"I'm sorry, Frank."

"Come and see me. Come and spend a few days?"

"No, Frank. It won't help."

"Let me talk to the young lady. At least let me do that?"

"Why, Frank?"

"Why? Dammit, does she know what she is asking of you? Does she understand that you just can't say to a priest that you love him and he's got to give up everything else for you? Does she understand that?"

"We've talked, Frank, believe me. We've talked. She's a fine person. We pray together."

"What do you pray for? That's the question. What do you pray *for?*"

"Frank, I'm sorry, I really am. I don't want to hurt you."

"It's not me you're hurting. It's yourself. You need help. If I can't give it to you, go and talk to somebody. The priesthood is not just a part of your life to be picked up and put down. It is your *whole* life. You eat and breathe it. And celibacy is a part of it. That doesn't mean it isn't something you don't have to work at. You've got to do that every day. Every single hour you've got to remember that your vow is really a declaration made before God and the Church for life. That's what it's all about."

"That's the ideal, Frank."

"I'd prefer to call it the reality. Let me talk to her. If she's a good Catholic girl she'll not make you do this."

"You'd rather I'd stay and be unhappy?"

"No. I'd rather you stay. And be happy. Period. Listen, you think you're the first priest to fall in love? It happens all the time. But falling in love is one thing. Being able to handle it is the real test. You *can* handle it. You've got to see that."

"Thanks, Frank. You've been terrific."

"You've made up your mind?"

"I guess so."

"I guess you probably had it all figured out before you called. You just wanted my rubber stamp. To say it's okay to throw it all away. Everything God gave you. The Church gave you. Give it all up. I guess that's what you're doing."

"That's not so, Frank. It really isn't."

"Well . . . I can't convince you, can I?"

"It's not you, Frank. It's me."

"Good luck, Father Philippe. I'll pray for you."

"So long, Frank. And thanks."

It was Walter who had said sadness always thickens the voice. Damn Walter.

The Bishop's office was modern and expensively appointed. The Bishop and the chancellor were seated beneath a portrait of Pope Paul. They questioned him in turn, to establish that he had come to his decision only after prayer, that he had not been coerced, that he was leaving on his own volition. The chancellor stared bleakly at Father Philippe. He said it was customary for a priest who resigned to move out of the area. He assumed he would do so.

"No, monsignor. I intend to remain in the parish."

The Bishop urged him to think of the effect this would have on his former parishioners. "And think of the girl and her family. Start elsewhere. You owe us all that much."

"I don't see it like that, Your Grace."

The Bishop sighed.

The chancellor motioned him to a side table. On it was a single sheet of paper. Printed across the top were the words *Request for Dispensation from Holy Orders.*

"Sign where your name is."

Father Philippe did as the chancellor commanded. He turned and faced his superiors.

"Is that it? What happens now?"

"Go back to the rectory and remove your belongings before nightfall."

The Bishop rose to his feet and addressed Father Philippe.

"You are not yet dispensed. You are only suspended from your priestly functions. You cannot say Mass or hear confession, nor can you receive the Holy Eucharist. But you are still a priest and will remain so until Rome releases you."

In the darkness, disembodied voices spoke to Father Philippe again like the whispers of madness. Simone had turned over in her sleep and lay with her back to him, legs outstretched long and bare to the thigh. He continued to stare at the ceiling listening to the voices in his head. There were always the same two. One was uncompromising. The other was pleading.

They had started to fight for his attention on his wedding night, offering him two very different explanations for his failure to make love to Simone. The pleading voice suggested he was emotionally and physically exhausted by the sheer speed of events. He had completed moving out of the rectory only hours before the wedding ceremony in the Dupois living room. His mother had come and offered her congratulations. She had not stayed long, abruptly asking his father to drive them back home. The other voice said he failed to consummate the marriage because of guilt over what he had done. He was condemned to live on the border of disintegration. The more he realized the enormity of betraying his vocation and, in the end, God, the greater was his guilt. It would possess and control him, driving him to reject Simone. The guilt had grown from that first disastrous night of unbearable failure.

Now, two hundred and thirty-four nights later, he realized how complete the destruction had been. For months he had taken tranquilizers, which made it even harder to ford the blurry chasm that separated him from Simone and the life he led. He hated the ladies' hair salon, the only place he had found work. He had been taken on because the owner said an ex-priest could attract business. *You're a bit of a celebrity, Father. All those you once confessed will want to go on sharing their secrets with you.* He was paid a minimum wage, standing for hours, shampooing their hair, and hearing about their lives. At first he thought it would be like listening to them as a priest. And indeed many of them still called him Father. But they didn't want his advice anymore. They would speak to anyone who listened. The doctor had said he must keep himself busy. He shouldn't take himself so seriously. Simone came to the first consultation. Afterward she said, "It's going to be fine. I love you." She said it all the time. It made no difference.

"Oh, God, please help me." He whispered the words, reaching for the pill bottles on the night table. He couldn't see which was Valium and which was Thorazine. He was prescribed ten milligrams of one and thirty milligrams of the other at night. Simone counted them out before she went to sleep. He looked at his watch. It was too late to take more medication. He would have to lie there, awake. It was going to be another awful day, stretching empty and hot, a tunnel through which he must drag himself before he could return here, to this bed, for another torturous night, lying beside a woman he knew he was destroying.

†

From the outset he had competed with her — and won. He was a better cook and a more imaginative housekeeper. The more she had tried to please him, the more he had been goaded on by that commanding voice to destroy her confidence in herself as a woman. It made no difference that the other voice, pleading and patient, would try to appeal to his good nature; to say that what he was doing was deeply hurtful for them both; that he must not give way to a fear of breaking down; that he should not see his future as being one of unknown chaos. Above all, he must not lament his decision to leave Holy Orders. Simone was there to offer him other compensations.

In the second month of married life his body began to be covered with a painful rash. It spread from his scrotum over his trunk and arms, red and unsightly. The more he scratched and drew blood, the worse it became. The doctor had increased his dosage of tranquilizers and had prescribed antihistamine tablets. He also said he must stop making love. Simone had nodded, biting her lip. He had seen the tears in her eyes and it made him angry. Didn't she understand what he was going through? And the voice, when he could not sleep, had answered. *Of course she doesn't understand. She can't because she has never given up what you have. She is just a woman.*

On his visits to the doctor or to the shopping mall, or going to and from work, he always made detours that took him past Sacred Heart. He would sometimes stand across the street, staring at the church, knowing what was going on inside and wishing to partake. But for some reason he could not understand, he had never gone inside. When they recovered from their shock, most of his former parishioners had been distantly polite. But a hard core remained implacably hostile, crossing the street when he approached or ignoring him in the market. Priests were clearly embarrassed when they met him. Invariably, they had time for little more than a few words before saying they were already late. His search for religious satisfaction had become a mishmash of reading the Bible and watching the preachers on Sunday morning television.

By then their attempts at lovemaking were accompanied by unbearable tension. The act itself would be consummated before she reached orgasm. He would mumble an apology and Simone said he mustn't worry. Next time it would be fine. It never was.

†

Staring at the ceiling, he counted again. They had not made love for forty-seven days. He knew because Simone was keeping count. A few mornings ago he had found her putting a tiny check mark on the calendar in the kitchen. He asked her, and she blushed and said she was keeping track of her period. While she dressed for work, he'd counted the checks. The total added up to the number of days since they had last made love. He had gone to work that morning filled with new guilt. Why should he no longer experience the joys of sex and celebrate the mystery of creation? He did not know. All he felt was a sense of overpowering guilt.

He stared toward the window. He could make out the furniture in the dawn light. The room was filled with his belongings: cases of clothes and boxes of books. Beyond, in the living room, it was the same. The furniture had been rearranged, brought closer together, to make room for his possessions. Simone had not complained. But the voice had told him she was secretly resentful. *She doesn't understand that a priest needs room for all his stuff. You notice how she doesn't throw away her things to make room for yours?*

Lying on the bed, he recalled what Rousseau said two hundred years ago. The words had made such an impact on him when he'd first read them that he promptly copied them into his notebook. They returned to him now, prodded into consciousness by that voice insistent on bringing up the past. *Man is born free and everywhere he is in chains. One thinks himself the master of others, and still remains a greater slave than they. How did this change come about? I do not know.*

The words swirled through his mind. He knew something was beginning to jell inside him. As he silently repeated the words, the thought became more rounded and firmer. His decision was growing, turning to resolve. He wondered why Simone didn't hear him. On the edge of his brain that second voice was pleading with him to try once more. *Remember, she loves you. She really does.* The first voice drowned out the words. *It is possible to get out of a trap. But to do so requires an admission of being imprisoned. Say it. Admit that the trap is your emotional structure, the fiber of your character. Say it. And then you can begin to find a way out.* He looked at Simone and spoke silently and directly at the sleeping form. *You don't understand. I can't go on. It hurts too much. I know now what I must do. Please don't be angry. It's not that I don't love you. But that's not enough, loving you. I don't want to be hurt anymore. Don't ask me to explain. I don't know if I'm doing the right thing. But I have no other choice, don't you see?* He could not remember when he had been so calm. *You must leave. Save yourself, otherwise you will be smothered to death by your guilt. The trap is comfortable, but it is still a trap. Stop trying to stay away from the exit. It is clearly visible now. Go through it. Leave her to sleep. She is happy here. Outside there is living life. Go and live it.*

He rose from the bed and tiptoed to the kitchen. He dialed Frank's number. They spoke for a short time. Afterward, he held the receiver against his chest, his arms folded over it. He began to cry. Finally, he put the telephone back in its cradle.

CHAPTER 9

†

A State of Perfection

A robed figure insistently shook her from her sleep. Once Clare was fully awake, the other nun left the bedroom as silently as she had entered. It was ten minutes to midnight. Clare rubbed her eyes. In her full-length nightdress, she slid out of bed and doused her face with cold water from the hand-basin and dressed for the death vigil. The stained floor-boards were warm under her feet because of pipes running beneath to radiators. Central heating was one of the many innovations introduced in the aftermath of the Second Vatican Council. Others included the abolition of flagellation at the Chapter of Faults and the freedom to modify habits. But the permanence of other aspects of religious life still had an abiding appeal to her after seven years in the sisterhood. One was the ritual surrounding an impending death in the community.

In many ways, Clare fitted into the Church's ideal of a contemporary nun. She was well educated, with a knowledge rising from a bedrock of traditional belief. Her prayer life was exemplary, as was her grasp of Canon Law, moral theology, and philosophy. She had encountered few problems in adjusting to the new religious world that the Council had envisaged, finding time to attend all the regular workshops and community discussions that had followed its deliberations. But her voice had been one for moderation, consistently suggesting that the independence, freedom, and liberty the Council had indicated were possible for the sisterhood must be handled sensibly. She had stated her position, as she did everything else, with a minimum of fuss.

She ascribed her successful integration into the community to her ability to strike the difficult balance between obedience and servility. She was not afraid to ask a question, but did not do so, like some of her sisters, in the spirit of newfound bravado that the Council had engendered. She thought that was childish and defeated the main purpose of community life, a drawing together under the common umbrella of prayer.

Within the Mother House the broad pattern of life continued as it had for centuries: academic work, manual laboring, prayer, and meditation. Any changes in that hallowed routine had been carefully evaluated. Reverend Mother had spoken of a need to remember tradition, repeating time and again that change must be evaluated in a historical context. This particular warning had preceded the first of many discussions on what length the Order's skirts should now be. The Council had left that to the sisterhood. Each Order could decide how far to raise their hems, providing it was no higher than mid-calf. There had been shock and consternation over a report that some American sisters had hoisted theirs to the knee.

Clare had little patience with the general behavior of many nuns across the Atlantic. They had become openly resentful of their priests. Here, she was glad to see, the convent's chaplain was treated with reverence. She was among those who served him a traditional Irish breakfast after early Mass; or on other occasions freshly baked cakes and tea from a silver service. Only Reverend Mother, her Deputy, and the Superior General of the Order were entitled to converse with him freely; all others must wait to be spoken to. Yet in America nuns were campaigning to be ordained. Each time the subject was raised, Reverend Mother shook her coifed head disbelievingly.

During discussions, Clare tried to excuse the behavior of those American nuns by suggesting they were only overreacting to their newfound freedom. Within memory was a time when nuns traveled only at night, in cars with drawn blinds, ate off bare wooden tables, or walked through chilly corridors. Those days, said Reverend Mother firmly, had been hard but they helped a nun to know her identity. A nun had asked how being cold could make someone pray better. The Superior had stared at her. Then, in a frigid voice, the one she had once used when doling out penance at the Chapter of Faults, she replied: *God through prayer should warm you. If He does not, Sister, you should consider whether or not you have the necessary spiritual voltage to pray properly.* Reverend Mother had abruptly risen to her feet, given a benediction with quick, stabbing motions of the hand, and glided out of the community room, her back perfectly straight, supported by her anger. Yet she had been the first to approve the proposal that each nun could decorate her own room as she chose.

Clare had adorned the plain white walls of hers with scenic posters of Ireland and quotations from the Bible Scotch-taped in place, each excerpt printed in her bold hand on drawing paper. On the shelf over the radiator were photographs of her parents and sisters. The most recent one showed her father in a wheelchair. Grave though his illness was, she had learned to cope. The possibility of her father's dying was not something she even thought about. But she was uncertain how she would face the death vigil. She only hoped Sister Cora would not die during her watch at the old nun's bedside in the infirmary near the chapel.

Twenty-four nuns had been chosen by the Superior for the task. She had assembled them in her office and explained how for once they would not measure time by the tolling of the great iron bell in the chapel campanile, but by their watches. Each would sit for six hours at the bedside. Then Reverend Mother had somberly reminded them that Sister Cora was a special case. Many years ago, she had been Mistress of Novices, strong in her faith, a sister whom a bishop visiting in the thirties had commended as a living example of what a nun should be. He had spoken of Sister Cora's love of God as being unhampered by theological arguments. Afterward, she had gone to work in South America. Reverend Mother had stared at the nuns grouped before her. In a hushed voice she explained: "Our beloved Sister has lost her faith. She has a fearful reluctance to accept that her time has come, that Our Lord is calling her home. She fights a struggle she cannot win, refusing to surrender to the sleep which comes to us all. She will tell you she no longer believes in God or His Church. That is her fear speaking. It will be your duty to try and help her regain her faith. You must show our dear Sister, by your own belief, that death is not to be feared. The love and companionship you can offer will help her to be composed to meet her end on earth. Do not, above all, withdraw the hope of eternal life. Whatever she says, you must try and remove the bitterness of her dying from her. Make her again aware of the glory of the Resurrection. Convince our dear Sister that death is the start of a new and glorious journey for her."

Clare made her bed, covering the sheets with a gold coverlet that matched the curtains and the paint on the back of the door. She had read that gold and white were a restful combination. Space in the room had been cleverly maximized to allow for a desk, a wardrobe, and a cupboard to hold her underwear and toiletries. Her lace-up shoes fitted under the bed. A bookshelf contained several interpretative lives of Jesus and the Scriptures. There was also a well-thumbed copy of Cardinal Suenens's *Nun in the World* and a paperback edition of the documents of the Second Vatican Council.

The community was equally divided on the contents of both books. Reverend Mother was steadfast in observing the letter of the documents, but had calmly defended the Cardinal's right to advocate change that went far beyond what the Council had recommended. Her Deputy had said the Pope should dismiss His Eminence for publishing such revolutionary ideas — whether they could remove their veils in public, wear makeup, panty hose, and fashionable shoes. If nuns wanted to dress like that, they should leave. The Deputy had looked aggressively around the community room. In the embarrassed silence Reverend Mother surprised Clare by gently asking what Freud would have made of a patriarchal Church that continued to call itself *Holy Mother Church*. Everyone except the Deputy laughed.

Clare switched off the bedroom light and walked through the dimly lit corridors of this large rambling edifice; red-bricked and forbidding on the exterior, it was remarkable throughout its unfurnished interior for an abundance of religious statues. In her last week as a postulant, Clare had counted them as a punishment from the Deputy, who had caught her running down a corridor. There were seventeen Baby Jesuses in the arms of His mother, nineteen Blessed Virgins, and forty-one separate replicas of Christ on the Cross. There were also statues of Saint Joseph and other saints. Throughout the corridors and guarding the staircases there were almost a hundred monuments. The walls were covered with an even greater number of religious paintings.

A former nun, one of those who abandoned her calling in the wake of the Council, had recently written to a newspaper suggesting the Order should sell its art collection to help feed the poor in the Third World. The letter upset Clare because it clearly gave the impression the convent was a treasure trove of useless wealth. In fact, there was barely enough money to keep the building heated and to feed the women who lived within its walls. It had been built in the time when women often had no choice about becoming nuns. Then, rulers of small European kingdoms avoided unsuitable political alliances by forcing daughters of matrimonial age into religious life. One German duke committed all nine of his girls to enforced celibacy. They entered with considerable dowries, large enough for them to create their own orders. Convent incarcerations also once provided the solution for another problem — the political woman activist. Russia's Peter the Great had his sister, Sophia, placed in a community beside the Kremlin. To induce proper terror in her, he arranged every day to have a freshly disemboweled corpse suspended outside her barred window.

The windows set into the corridors Clare walked had never been barred. But through them generations of nuns had watched history sweep past: the Great Famine, the Fenian Rebellion, the foundation of Sinn Fein, the bloody conflict of the Easter Rising in 1916. On that day sixty-one years ago, Clare realized, Sister Cora was her own age when British soldiers came to search the convent looking for Irish rebels. Sister Cora had met them at the front door. She had asked all those who were Catholic to raise their hands. Some of the troops did. She had lectured them on the mortal sin they had already committed by carrying weapons onto consecrated ground. The shamefaced soldiers had wheeled their horses around and galloped down the driveway. She had returned to the chapel and knelt beside the two terrified young boys who had sought sanctuary. Later, she accompanied them to the docks where they boarded a mail boat to America. Before they left, she made them place their rifles in the convent furnace.

Clare walked past the parlors, different in size, but uniformly furnished. In each, there were comfortable chairs for visitors and hard-backed ones for the nuns; the space between callers and a sister was formalized by a separating table. For the past week, while Sister Cora was dying, the parlors had remained closed.

During that time Clare had increasingly felt the presence of death as something tangible. At mealtimes, everyone was careful not to make a clatter with her knife, fork, or spoon. Clearing away and washing up were conducted with whispered speed. At Recreation no one switched on the phonograph. It was a gift from a relative of Sister Cora. The Deputy had covered the stack of records with a purple cloth, hiding the bright laminated covers depicting Irish fiddlers and reel dancers and Johnnie Ray: *Live at the London Palladium.* The small collection also included Gregorian chant and a Welsh choir singing hymns. As instructed, tradesmen left their deliveries outside, instead of carrying them into the cold-storage rooms below ground. Buried under the weight of the sacks and boxes, the nuns on kitchen duty brought in the supplies. Impending death had made the community draw away from the outside world into a self-imposed emotional isolation, so that each of its members could remind herself of the positive aspect of dying: it was merely a stepping-stone to an eternal and glorious life.

Apart from the doctor, no visitors were admitted through the massive front door. He had seen Reverend Mother in her office. Shortly afterward, Dominic, the handyman, went to the graveyard beyond the main house with the Superior and agreed upon a burial plot. By tradition, he would start to dig the grave immediately after the campanile bell began its sonorous toll. That would also be the signal for Sister Dualta to go to her workshop and begin to carve in stone the figure 93. It was the number assigned to Sister Cora when she was registered as a postulant in the reign of King Edward VII.

Since Reverend Mother had announced the death watch, Clare had been thinking of ways she might help Sister Cora to see that only acceptance of death could give her peace of mind. Walking through the silent corridors, she continued to frame her arguments. They were based on common sense and a natural instinct for what is right; her father had the same quality. She decided she would remind Sister Cora that death is the only predictable event in life and that only by believing in the life hereafter would it be possible for her to make sense of her life so far. Her route to the infirmary took her past the chapel where the nuns assembled for prayers seven times each day. She pulled open its door. Inside, it was dark except for the vigil light burning at the altar and the shaded lamp that illuminated the statue of Our Lady. Clare came here often, outside appointed times, to kneel and pray for her father; to ask God to give him courage and spiritual strength. She knew her father was not pretending when he told her as she entered religious life that he was proud to give a daughter to God.

The bond between them was close. Growing up, she was the one who had always accompanied him to daily Mass; she was still the one to whom he turned to discuss religious questions. She had often thought he would have made a fine priest, and a handsome one too, with his shock of dark hair and his spare frame — an athlete's body, she used to think, before his crippling illness misshaped it. His presence seemed, as it often did nowadays, to slip into the pew beside her as she quickly knelt and said a prayer for Sister Cora. She hurried from the chapel, the swish of her habit the only noise to break the silence. There was a junction in the corridor. To her right a passage led to the kitchen and laundry. Clare had often marveled at the contentment of those who dedicated their lives to Christ by stirring pots and folding sheets. They accepted without question that this was what God intended for them. In spite of her own serenity, she knew she had an ambition to serve Him on a higher level, to have her intellectual capacity fully extended.

Clare was no feminist. She worried about the radicalism manifesting itself throughout the sisterhood. She did not think it mattered either way that men — the Canon lawyers in the Sacred Congregation for Religious and Secular Institutes in Rome — must approve any constitutional change in the Order's Rule, and therefore her life. That it was they who decided when she should get up in the morning, when she would eat, and what she would wear. These were small matters to her. Nor did she yearn, as some did, for a return to the days when women in religious life wielded tremendous influence, both within their convents and in the world beyond. In the Middle Ages, nuns had been consulted by the kings and queens of Europe on many matters of ecclesiastical influence. But the Council of Trent stripped them of such power and ordered all nuns to remain in their enclosures. Even now, the Rule of Enclosure remained strict. Clare knew that if she was to leave the Mother House without permission from the Superior she would face exclaustration — expulsion from the Order. Yet, she hoped that one day soon, with the blessing of Reverend Mother, she would join that select band of sisters who left every morning to receive the finest education the Order could provide so that they could become senior teachers in one of the community's schools. A chance to improve herself further and use her knowledge to improve others would put a seal on a life-style Clare saw as already close to perfection.

Long before she formalized her commitment in the Mass of Solemn Profession, she was comfortable with her vows. Clare had never experienced a problem over her sexuality. She was aware of her body, but its sexual function had no part in her life. Fantasies and self-stimulation were simply beyond her imagination. It was not merely a question of self-control, but a total belief that forsaking marriage and the possibility of motherhood were more than compensated for by the realization that she was living as God ordained she should. She doubted that anyone, except her father, would understand how content she was to devote all her affection to God and, through Him, to love the world. Understanding why she must be obedient made it easy to accept the pattern of her life. It began and ended each day with the call, "Praise be to Jesus Christ." They were the first words she spoke on awakening, the last before going to sleep. In between the exaltations, she taught juniors at the school within the grounds, helped to supervise their games, and corrected their homework. Moreover, she had her responsibilities within the community, taking her share of dining-room duties, polishing silver, sweeping, and dusting. It was an exacting timetable.

She took the left fork and climbed the stairs. The profound silence continued to envelop her. Years ago the Mistress of Postulants described the hush: *The stillness you will find here is like that in the perfect marriage — the one between you and Jesus.* At the top of the stairs was an unmarked door. It led to Reverend Mother's office. Clare was certain that, through the Superior, God had chosen her, Clare, for the loneliest part of the death vigil, to see if she had the ability to support Sister Cora in her agony. The period from midnight to dawn, Reverend Mother had warned, is an especially lonely and difficult time for both the patient and the sister at her bedside. Outside Sister Cora's room the Table for the Dead was already in place, its top covered by a white cloth. On it stood two white candles in solid silver holders, a bowl of holy water, and a vial of anointing chrism. There was also a crucifix and a small vase of flowers from the convent garden. The other nun on duty rose from her chair and whispered, "She's still worried that she's not ready. She's back at the 'why me' stage." The infirmary was the only place where it was permitted to break the Great Silence.

Clare looked at the frail figure in the bed. She recalled the familiar maxim of the Mistress: *There is no heroism in religious life.* She remembered, too, the wisdom of her father: *Everybody bargains with God.* He had said it after he came out of the hospital, after tests to establish the course his own illness would take. He was in a ward where several of the patients prayed, promising to be good Catholics in exchange for an extension of their lives. One man, a father of several small children, had asked God to allow him to live until they left school. Later, he extended his prayers and implored God to spare him until they were married. Her father had smiled and said the man was probably now praying to live until he was a grandfather. *It's not like playing cards. You can't deal with God.*

The nun left and Clare sat down on the chair, taking stock of the room. It was painted white from skirting board to ceiling. There were no curtains on the window. The floor was covered with gray linoleum. Apart from the bed and chair, the only furnishings were several small tables. On each one was a lighted candle. There was a box of unlit candles on the floor beside the chair.

"Have you ever seen anyone die?" The voice was barely audible.

Clare waited a few moments before replying, aware of the luminous eyes set deep in their sockets. They continued to watch her.

"No, Sister Cora. I have not seen anybody die."

"I've seen a lot of death. You do in South America. I was in one of our schools out there."

She paused, lost in some secret reverie, her eyes never leaving Clare.

"Have you traveled?"

"No, Sister Cora. But maybe if God wills it . . ."

She hunted for words to build, in the short time available, a proper rapport. Instinctively, she knew she must achieve more than a superficial connection.

"I'm full of cancer."

"I know." Clare thought: *If I can get her to talk, it may become easier for her.*

"They told me when it was too late."

Clare was aware of the smell and the stuffiness of the room.

"They didn't give me time to prepare for death. Everybody needs time."

"In that sense, there is never time. But God understands that. Would you like me to read to you?"

There was a Bible on the table nearest the bed.

"No, hold my hand."

Clare did so.

"I had warm hands like yours once. You feel how cold they are now?"

"Would you like a hot-water bottle?"

"You can't help me. Nobody can help me except God, and I'm not certain about Him now."

"If you stop believing now, it will all have been wasted."

"Have you always believed?"

"Yes. Always." And Clare began to tell her.

✝

When she was six years old, a favorite uncle asked Clare what she wanted to be when she grew up. She replied without hesitation — to be a good Catholic. She was puzzled when he laughed and repeated the answer to the rest of the family: her father and mother and six sisters. As she grew up, this ambition never wavered. Her Catholicism was handed down to her as a birthright, instilled by her parents as the only practical way to live, because among other things it would help her practice self-reliance. Her mother was self-sufficient, out of necessity and belief. Home-grown vegetables and homemade bread were cheaper and more nutritious than those from the local store. Her mother bought only what was necessary. The concept of a consumer society had still to reach the Dublin suburb where they lived. Buying something because the media advertised it or running up credit was anathema. It was a neighborhood where people tried to live within their means, not beyond their dreams. Work was not only a necessity, but a virtue: to be without it was close to committing a sin.

Her father was employed on the production staff of a national newspaper: away five nights a week, back with the early dawn bus, sleeping until lunch, then another night of supervising the presses. His had been a painstaking rung-by-rung achievement, and he was determined his daughters would have a better life. He had put aside enough money to educate them privately. Her mother was busy from morning to night, working for the pleasure of the children. It was a loving, caring home, and Clare's childhood was a happy one, with summer trips to the beach or the countryside and her father pointing out the sand crabs or the different foliage in the hedges and the variety of life in ponds and ditches. On hot days ants would march up to the kitchen door in columns and her mother would repel them with a kettle of boiling water. In winter it would rain for days, and after homework was completed, there were books to read. Father Dolan, the parish priest, kept a careful check on what was or was not proscribed by the Church. James Joyce remained banned.

When the girls were old enough, they learned to darn and patch, sew new collars and cuffs on their father's shirts or their school uniforms. Their mother always said there was no point in buying new when old would do. On Fridays, they ate fish. There were no sweets during Lent, but hot-cross buns on Good Friday. After Mass on Easter Sunday, chocolate eggs were distributed, an identical one for each child. There were no favorites in the family. Her parents loved them all equally, showing the same quiet pride over each daughter's school reports, First Communions, popularity among the neighbors. Clare grew up wth an acceptance that when she left school, she would work for a while, meet a boy, go steady, accept his proposal of marriage, settle down close to home, and raise her own family. Her husband would have the same strong religious beliefs as her father. There would be a picture of the Sacred Heart on the living-room wall identical to the one at home; the same ritual of saying the rosary before going to bed; the same strict observance of Mass on Sunday and on every feast day. It was the story of Clare's mother. It was still the expectation of thousands of Irish girls in the 1960s.

Nuns fitted naturally into the landscape. Clare's first impression of a nun was of a person who gave herself to God; who always knelt longer at Mass, and even when walking, had her hands clasped as if in prayer. Nuns were persons who seemed to have no legs, who dressed in black to the ground and moved with no visible means of support. She was too young to wonder why God wanted them to wear black; in any case it would have been incomprehensible to a nine-year-old that black symbolized a nun's commitment to die to the world. Later, in sixth grade, she imagined them in their community room in the convent, seated at a long table, each one with a perfectly aligned plate and a white napkin, just as the nuns had sat in *The Bells of St. Mary's*. Sister Imelda could easily have played opposite Bing Crosby with her strikingly beautiful face and a voice that soared above all the others at morning prayers. It was she who explained that her habit was an outward sign of renunciation of self, mentioning it casually during religious instruction. The words planted a seed.

By the age of seventeen, Clare knew boys looked at her, walking her home from school, as aware as she was that she was well developed, that she never had spots, a weight problem, or any of the adolescent difficulties the teenage magazines write about. She had been one of the Three Wise Men in *The Nativity*, the Christmas play that Sister Imelda produced one year. Afterward, the nun said, in her no-nonsense way, Clare must think about her future. With her interest in Scripture, her consistently good marks in English, history, and geography, there were definite openings. Those words nurtured the seed.

At school, the teaching was a mixture of tradition — the Irish language and religion figured prominently in the curriculum — with a forward look into a brave new world: science ruled alongside Latin; technology competed with declensions. During break, there were copies of the *Eagle* to swap. The Christian-educational comic featured a colored cartoon of the journeys of Saint Paul. It was a short step for Clare to more serious Bible study. She began to talk to Sister Imelda about the Scriptures, marveling at the way the nun was never stumped for an answer, making Saint Paul's adventures sound even more exciting than the *Eagle* did. On Sundays, Clare listened carefully to Father Dolan's sermons. The Christ he preached about was someone who demanded the very highest standards from all those who wanted to accept His invitation: Follow me. On her eighteenth birthday Clare realized she had come to a crossroads and chosen her path. Sister Imelda was the first to be told outside the family. She was her usual forthright self. "Are you certain?"

Clare nodded. "Yes, I know. I want to be a nun. I want to be like you."

The nun was insistent. "You must not use me as your model. God would not want that. The start and end of a vocation is following Christ. Only Him. He is your model. No one else. And that means you must be ready to say *yes* to the Way of the Cross. No one else must come between you and Jesus."

The nun had other questions.

"What about your family? Your father is sick. It will not be easy for your mother to manage. You'll have no money to give her. You'll have nothing except the clothes you stand in. How do your parents feel?"

A few weeks before, the doctors finally diagnosed her father's illness as incurable. He took the news stoically. Her parents seemed, if anything, to draw closer together.

"My father says he always knew I would be a nun. He even quoted what God said to Jeremiah."

"What was that?" Sister Imelda smiled. "Can you remember? If you're going to be a nun, you'll have to be able to quote the Bible accurately."

"I think so. *'Before I formed thee in the bowels of thy mother I knew thee; and before thou camest forth out of the womb I sanctified thee.'*"

"But remember, too, what Jeremiah said to God. *'Behold, I cannot speak, for I am a child.'*"

"I'm eighteen, Sister. Girls get married at eighteen."

The nun explained that renunciation also meant visits home would be strictly curtailed. There would be no more going to the cinema, or rocking to the music of the Rolling Stones. Even her books — which included Amis's *Lucky Jim* and Kerouac's *On the Road* — would have to be given up. Could she really do all this?

"Yes. I am certain."

"I think you are." Sister Imelda nodded. "I think God is calling you."

Now, seven years later, He had brought Clare to this deathbed.

She came to believe that Sister Cora's attitude toward her death was desperately dependent on how well her mind could be diverted.

"Would you like me to read to you?"

The old nun stared at her. "Isaiah. Thirty-eight, twelve." The words rattled in her throat. "Can you find it?"

"I think we both learned it in the novitiate. Reverend Mother said it used to hang on the wall outside the door."

"She's wrong. It was above the door. I put it there myself." For a moment, Sister Cora's eyes were no longer gray and remote. "Nineteen

twenty-eight, the year they made me Mistress of Novices. I had it put up."
She stared at Clare. "Do you remember the words?"

"I think so."

Clare was suddenly glad the old nun couldn't see her tears. She began to
recite. *"My generation is at an end, and it is rolled away from me, as a
shepherd's tent. My life is cut off, as by a weaver: whilst I was yet but
beginning, he cut me off: from morning even to night thou wilt make an
end of me.'"*

She watched Sister Cora's hands compose and recompose themselves.
"My mother taught me that."

"They are beautiful words, Sister Cora."

The silence in the room was broken by the old nun's croaked question.
"What time is it?"

"Four o'clock."

Clare sensed the elemental fear grasping Sister Cora.

"My mother died at this hour. Four in the morning, with no one with
her. No one. Not the priest. Nor my brothers. Nobody." She struggled up
from her pillow. "I was a postulant, several months in. They wouldn't let
me go home. They said ... I should ... be glad. Sacrifice. They kept saying, sacrifice ..."

Clare cradled her, letting her whimper. She felt she had a very old child
in her arms.

"I don't want to die."

Clare rocked her gently, listening to the little wailing cries and thinking
she had never realized how painful it was to let go of life.

Holding Sister Cora, she began to recount a story her father once told
her, shortly before she said she wanted to enter religious life. The paper he
brought home from work that morning was full of a boating tragedy: two
children were drowned while their father had gone to England to find
work. Her first reaction was of the terrible shock it would be for the father
to be away at such a time. He then told her the story.

"Once there lived a man whose sons died while he was away on a journey. In spite of his wife's own grief and a need to be comforted, she decided
not to break the news to her husband on his return home until he had
bathed and eaten. Over dinner he asked several times where his sons were.
She always gave the same answer. He would see them presently. At the
end of the meal she had taken him by the hands and said she wanted his
help over a very important matter. It concerned two precious stones. They
had been given on the strict understanding that their owner could take

them back at any time. Was that fair? He had pondered the matter before deciding. It was fair. His wife then led him to the room where the boys were laid out for burial and said that God had asked for His precious stones back."

Clare murmured, "You see, God wants us all back at some time. We should be glad to go, to renounce this life for a far better one."

She opened the Bible in an effort to comfort Sister Cora and read on while the first trace of daylight penetrated the long night watch. A few minutes before six o'clock, the aged nun suddenly stretched out a hand. Her lips moved, but there was no sound, just a terrible rattling in her throat and a sweet sickly smell from her mouth. For a moment, there was a look of puzzlement and despair in her eyes. Then it was gone and she folded her hands in prayer. She was smiling as she died.

Clare dropped to her knees and prayed. Then she rose and fetched the Table for the Dead, carrying it to the side of the bed. Using one of the already burning candles, she lit the two candles on the table. Next, she placed the crucifix in Sister Cora's hands, folding her fingers around the cross. Finally, she closed the old nun's eyes, using a thumb gently to press shut the lids. Then, Clare fell once more to her knees and resumed praying until Reverend Mother, accompanied by the priest, arrived to take over.

After the undertakers completed their work and placed the body in a plain white-deal coffin, lined with white cloth, it was wheeled on a dolly into the chapel. Members of the death vigil escorted it to the altar. The priest received the remains. Candles were lit and positioned around the coffin. The priest recited prayers for the soul of the dead sister before he left. Only the nuns remained, kneeling in silent vigil on either side of the coffin.

While Clare slept, the Superior informed first the community and then the Archbishop's office of the death. Next, the Papal Nuncio's office was told. A secretary would include it in the next report to the Vatican. In a Curia office, a priest-clerk would record the passing of Sister Cora in the Ledger for the Dead.

That evening the chapel was crowded. Every member of the Mother House was present except those too ill to be brought down from the infirmary. Sisters had come from other houses in the diocese. Row upon row of black-robed figures knelt in the carved stalls. The funeral music hung like a pall in the air. During the day the casket had remained open, exposing Sister Cora in her full habit, dressed exactly as she had been on the day she took her vows. Her face had a rested appearance, and her hands clasped a rosary, its wooden crucifix facing upward. Nuns knelt beside the coffin, often placing a posy among the many other tributes on the chapel floor around the bier.

Clare arrived late in the afternoon, crouching beside the casket, thinking how the flames from the candles gave Sister Cora's face a rosy glow. Early in the evening the dead nun's relatives, escorted by Reverend Mother, paid their respects before leaving again. Afterward, Dominic prayed with Sister Dualta before they replaced the casket lid and tightened the nuts. Everyone then left the chapel, leaving Sister Cora's body for another day in His presence.

The Requiem Mass was on the third day. Once more, the chapel was crowded. The Archbishop sent a representative. The Nuncio's letter of condolence mentioned that in this time of grief they must remember that the Church does not weep for death; it is merely the narrow gate that leads to everlasting life. The theme was central to the Mass, in the homilies and the voices rising and falling in supple harmony. Afterward, Dominic and the men from the funeral home carried the coffin to the graveyard. The nuns followed in procession, paired in seniority, heads upright, eyes shiny. A little distance behind walked the visitors. The only sound was the crunching of feet on gravel and the mournful tolling of the campanile bell. The community formed a loose circle around the head of the grave. As the coffin was slowly lowered into the earth, the nuns chanted the final dirge: *All things are alive in the sight of their King.*

Reverend Mother escorted the visitors from the graveyard. Then she returned to stand at the foot of the grave while Dominic filled it, mounding it into shape with the back of his shovel, striking the earth in time to the tolling. Sister Dualta stepped forward and placed the stone she had carved at the head of the grave. When she stepped back, the sound of the bell stopped. It was over.

Walking out of the graveyard, Clare noticed again the grave near the footpath. The stone at its head had tilted with the subsidence of the soil. But she could still make out the figures: 136. It was now her number, given to her on the day she was admitted, handed on from that sister buried there, a nun she had never known. When she died, or for any reason left the Order, the number would be assigned to a postulant. It was another of the timeless things about the religious life that so appealed.

After supper she returned to the chapel. Kneeling in prayer again, she felt the peace and stillness. The tiny living flame of the vigil lamp was visible proof of His presence. She could feel Him all around her, as once more she asked: *Dear Lord, if I am worthy of Your trust, please tell Mother.*

CHAPTER 10

†

An Attitude of Mind

Clare knew she was going to a wedding by Dominic's behavior. He was like this only when he drove the Mother House choir to sing at a Nuptial Mass. The Order rented out the choir for these occasions; it helped pay the community's housekeeping bills. Normally, Dominic drove the aged convent bus like a hearse when he transferred nuns from the Mother House to one of the outer houses or to the airport, as they departed for mission stations in Africa and Asia, knowing he might never see those sisters again. They could be away for as long as twenty years. Then, he wore blue overalls and was morose. Today, he was dressed in a green tweed three-piece suit with a rose in his buttonhole, plucked from one of the flower beds. He handled the bus like a racing car, crashing the gears, jumping the traffic lights, whistling and singing and bellowing happily at the startled looks from passersby as the bus roared on. Its twenty-six passengers sat bolt upright, knees braced against the seats in front. Clare was certain he had already taken more than his share of nips from the flask in his breast pocket. Not even the protests of the Deputy Superior, seated immediately behind him, could slow Dominic's speed. Bent over the steering wheel, he shouted over his shoulder at her.

"Don't be worrying, Mother. God is with us."

He burst into another song.

The songs were a reminder to Clare of how fashions in music, like everything else, had altered in the time she had been in. She had entered when the Beatles were on the charts. Now nostalgia was in vogue and once again Burt Bacharach did not mind raindrops falling on his head. Other changes were visible around her. Just as in the sisterhood, hems in the secular world had changed, the mini-skirt replaced by calf-length; the bra industry had plunged into a recession peculiarly its own, as millions of women abandoned that particular form of uplift. There was a report in the morning paper that an Irish bishop still wanted *Portnoy's Complaint* banned. There was no longer a Church index of proscribed books, though the Irish hierarchy still managed to persuade the government to ban *Playboy*.

Her father had said that approach treated only the symptoms but didn't cure the problem. "Denying access creates a greater demand. Let people judge. Let them read and make up their own minds. They will soon see that dirt is dirt, no matter how glossily packaged."

Though he never mentioned it, she knew he missed work. Ill health had finally forced him into early retirement, his only comment being that he was glad he had been able to educate his children before it happened. As the bus cleared the last of the city traffic lights and headed into the countryside, she thought of him on the bed in the downstairs room her mother had converted for the purpose. His wasted legs could no longer carry him upstairs. He would be propped up on pillows, combing the newspapers. This morning, they gave space to the aftermath of the collapse of Rolls-Royce, the dismaying spread of venereal disease, and the discovery that one of America's largest soup manufacturers had been marketing canned botulism. There had been another homosexual march in New York, another student riot in Paris, another demonstration at the Berlin Wall. The Church was once more in the news; nowadays, it seemed to Clare, it was rarely out of the headlines. The latest crop of reports dealt with the closure of parochial schools in the United States; in all, one thousand four hundred had done so since she joined the Order. Many convents and seminaries in Europe were reporting a definite fall in vocations. An editorial asked: "Where are tomorrow's priests and nuns?"

She wondered, again, why Pope Paul did not rally the Church, instead of further dividing it by his own obvious indecision in so many areas. She was certain he was failing because he tried to reconcile every point of view. He looked benignly on Castro's Cuba and turned a blind eye to the decimation of Lithuanian Catholics by the Russians. He had aroused wrath by his vision of "a people's Church," where everyone would have an equal voice. He had failed to be resolute about those sisters who wanted to be ordained, those priests who desired to marry, those bishops who wanted to have the status of regional pope, those theologians who wished to rewrite doctrine, those Marxists of liberation theology, and the homosexuals of Catholic Gay Liberation who demanded change for reasons that Clare had never quite grasped. All she knew was that the Pope had apparently failed to recognize how deeply the divisions ran. His awareness had gone no further than his latest pronouncement from his balcony: "The smoke of Satan has entered the Church and is around the altar." When she saw the news clip on television, she had wondered what he could be saying. As the bus sped through the countryside, she also thought again of how, in these past weeks since the death of Sister Cora, change had entered her.

✝

She could pinpoint its onset from that evening in March. It was after Compline and before the Great Silence, the time assigned each day for Silent Meditation. Then, each member of the community rededicated herself to God, choosing a text from Scripture to ponder on. She had selected the words of the Apostle John: *If the world hates you, remember that it hated me before you. If you belonged to the world, the world would love you as its own; but because you do not belong to the world, because my choice withdrew you from the world, therefore the world hates you.*

She had picked the text for the very reason that it required total concentration to meditate upon the fuller meaning of John's words. Of all the disciples', she had found his words demanded the most attention but were the most rewarding. It had been John who showed her, in her novitiate, how to gain new insights into the meaning and the purpose of her life and how it should relate to others. Through him, she had come to see the Bible as one of the greatest gifts God had given to the world, with its revelations about human redemption. John's words — spare and unyielding, the way she liked to think the Apostle himself was — thrilled her with their unfolding of a divine plan to save mankind. The evangelism of John had always held a strong appeal for her. He ignored Christ's birth, genealogy, youth, baptism, temptation, transfiguration, and ascension to concentrate on Jesus as the Saviour of a sin-cursed and lost mankind. The glorious message of John is that everyone can be restored to a state of grace through belief.

Yet, as she knelt in her stall in chapel, the text that seemed such an inspired choice had the opposite effect. She began to reject the words. Why would the world hate her because she had chosen to follow Christ? John made the decision sound so selective. In a way the kind of behavior he was describing has an inverted possessiveness. It is directed inward, not outward. Yet Jesus wanted those who followed Him to love the world, not to have the world hate them. She realized she had lost her concentration totally at this point. She felt tired and on edge. For the remainder of Silent Meditation she knelt there, not thinking of anything.

That night when the campanile bell rang three times — one sonorous clang for each member of the Holy Trinity — she found it difficult to sleep, lying awake until well past midnight, her mind restless and flitting. She thought of her mother and father and whether — though they had never mentioned it — they might in their reduced circumstances have welcomed any financial support she could have provided if she were in a job instead of religious life. She wondered what type of work she would have chosen. Most likely she would have followed her classmates into one of the banks, or the civil service, before getting married. Many had gone on working afterward, delaying having families. Until recently she had had only a vague idea of how this was possible. Then, on a parlor visit, a cousin had worn a pretty, close-fitting hat, reminding her of one of those Dutch caps in a Renaissance painting. Her relative had laughed and whispered that a Dutch cap is a contraceptive. Clare had looked blank until her cousin explained that this was how many women managed when the only family planning allowed by the Church was the rhythm method.

Next morning, the new electric alarm — another Vatican Council innovation — dragged her awake. This had replaced the campanile bell as the community timekeeper. The great bell in the tower was rung only to herald the Great Silence and on Sundays and feast days. Dressing, she felt heavy, as if she were drugged. For the first time in years she was almost late for chapel.

A few days later she again tried to meditate on John's words, reminding herself that they were a powerful reminder of divine inspiration. Then once more she found herself asking the question, what is wrong in wanting someone to love me and for me to love that person in return?

At the end of her weekly visit to the confessional she put the question to the priest. She knelt, one hand entwined in her rosary, the other caressing the crucifix suspended from the beads, and hesitantly explained her feelings. He whispered to her, his voice so low that she could hardly hear the words: the Gospel spoke of loving her neighbor as herself. He asked her to ponder the greater meaning of love: that loving everyone is the same as loving one person. Because she had never thought of him as someone who read widely, he surprised her by quoting Kierkegaard, that everyone is one's neighbor and that if it were not a duty to love them there would be no concept of neighbor at all; that only by loving all her neighbors equally is the selfishness of preferential love rooted out and the equality of the eternal safeguarded. "You must pray, Sister. Ask God to lift this heaviness. He will deliver you."

She prayed and in a way had been delivered. The lethargy lifted. Yet something remained. She could not define it, but it was there, a vague, unsettling feeling that woke her in the night, reminding her of words the Mistress said when she first lectured on preparation. "You will symbolically put your flesh to death, so that your love becomes absolutely focused on God's will." There had been that moment during Recreation when the Mistress synthesized her life: "You are being prepared to wait on God. To serve Him and His Son here on earth."

Clare knew she wanted nothing more. Yet this troubling feeling persisted. What was so unsettling was that she could think of no reason for it.

✝

Dominic parked the bus in a lane fringed by dog-roses and bluebells, wildflowers, with a delicate fragrance many cultivated ones do not have. She had not forgotten the lessons her father taught her about nature. For a moment, while the choir assembled, Clare stood in the shade of the chestnuts around the church, staring into the green canopy above, supported by dark ropes of branches crossing and crisscrossing. It was so peaceful, yet once more she felt a stirring of restlessness.

The newspaper she had left on the bus had carried a report that in America the latest fad was for couples to write their own marriage vows. A common pledge had struck her as deceptively simple. *I will love you as long as I can help you to grow in love.* Here was a promise, accepted by the Church, which narrowed love to an explicit guarantee: a couple would journey together through life only so long as they both felt able to contribute to their mutual development. Conversely, they seemed to be saying that without a continuous growing of love, the relationship became stagnant. The onus of living up to such a promise was, she thought, awesome. Was it possible to reach a stage where there was no more love to give? But then, why should love founder and fade at this point, as the vow seemed to imply? The questions bothered her because she could not really recall anything that would help her to answer them. She also realized that it might be unrealistic to expect to grow a little more each day in her love for Him. Might she end up like the Deputy, a woman whose prayer life seemed to have soured, who even on a superficial level seemed genuinely afraid of any meaningful relationship with anyone else? Was this what happened when someone reached the apex of love in religious life? Did it mean, as the Deputy's behavior suggested, that loving was a doomed process, drained of energy, replaced by the emptiness of a chore? Was this why she felt restless? Was this born out of a fear that she, too, might reach a point of loving Him beyond which she could not go?

The church was filled to capacity. The glimmer of the altar candles paled in the bright sunlight. The sanctuary was banked with flowers. The choir filled two stalls to the left of the altar; in the background, the organist played Bach. Clare thought the setting was perfect. The music stopped and the choir united in psalmody. As the singing faded, the organ began the wedding march, the chords swelling as the bridal party entered the nave, the sun catching the dazzling white of the bride and the gauzy pink of her bridesmaids.

Suddenly, Clare wanted to cry. She could feel the tears forming and blinked her eyes rapidly. She felt faint. She tried to concentrate on something; her eyes darted from the candles, to the crucifix above the altar, to the sanctuary lamp, to the priest. She gripped the ledge of the stall to steady herself. *I must not, I must not faint.* In the last weeks of the novitiate a girl had suddenly slumped to the floor during a lecture on self-control. She was revived by the Deputy splashing a glass of water in her face and sternly reminding: "Fainting is for people who indulge themselves." She forced herself to remember.

Loving Him requires special self-control. It has nothing to do with satisfying any physical or emotional needs. When you entered this life, you made a contract with Our Master to forgo such feelings. The love we acquire here has nothing to do with sexual gratification. This is why we distance ourselves from each other. We do not need physical contact or exclusive friendships because we have Him. In our marriage to Him, He does not need such contact. The love we acquire for Him demands a greater challenge than that of any marriage. It is the greatest challenge of life itself. It demands sacrifice, understanding and, if need be, pain to remind each one of us that He suffered for us. To be denied on earth is to love in Christ. The freedom of earthly love is the trivialization of our love for Him.

The dizzy feeling passed. Staring at the bride, Clare thought: *I accept this is not for me.*

*

Two days had passed since Dominic drove them back to the Mother House. Sister Imelda was waiting for her in a parlor. Clare was delighted and surprised to see her old teacher, whom she had not seen since her Clothing. Without a word, Sister Imelda closed the door and leaned against it. She looked steadily at Clare.

"How are you?"

"Great, of course. Why shouldn't I be?" She staved off a sudden feeling of panic, quickly praying under her breath. *Holy Mary, help me to stay calm.* "I'm fine, really."

"I heard you nearly fainted at the wedding."

"What? Who told you that?"

Sister Imelda smiled. "Don't worry, it wasn't Deputy Mother."

"If it had been her, I would have heard about it by now."

The shrill sound of the electric bell announced the start of free time.

"She's tough, Clare. But that's what the job calls for. She was Novice Mistress when I was here. We used to call her 'God's Warden,' behind her back, of course. No. It wasn't her. It was a guest. She mentioned a nun had started to sway as the bride came up the aisle. The description could only fit you. She thought you were going to fall. What happened?"

Clare gave a little shrug. Her father did that when he wanted a subject dropped.

"It was nothing. Probably I was a bit light-headed from the journey. You know the way Dominic drives to weddings."

"I do. But it's never happened before, has it? And you've been to a lot of weddings." Sister Imelda paused. Her silence was a little alarming.

Clare forced a smile. "It was nothing, really. Anyway, I'm fine now."

Sister Imelda moved away from the door and gently put her hands on her shoulders. "Would you like to talk about it, Clare? I just want to help."

"I know."

Apart from her family, no one had called her Clare in years. She felt the undertow of sudden emotion and knew she must resist the urge to cry. A slight flush warmed the cool beauty of Sister Imelda's face, hinting that she too, for all her skill in controlling feelings, was touched by the moment.

"This is just between you and me. If I can help, don't push me away."

Sister Imelda led her to one of the chairs and sat opposite her, studying her face. After a while she again started to speak.

"We all have to go through this, Clare. It's part of celibate living. What you are experiencing is very natural."

"Natural? How do you know? How do you know what I am feeling?" She wished she did not sound so defensive.

Clare felt, as she had so often at school, that she was being pulled by some magnetic force to tell Sister Imelda everything: her doubts, her fears, her struggles. *Everything.* Late afternoon sunlight filtered through a high gabled window into the parlor, giving the dark wood a new richness. It made her think of a waiting room to Purgatory, dark and heavy.

Sister Imelda spoke. "I don't know for certain. But I can guess. What we must do is try to find a proper place for our feelings within the framework of our sacred vows."

Clare finally allowed the pulling and twisting of the past weeks to come to the surface. Something had gone wrong. She felt at times as if she were heading down a religious cul-de-sac, as far as obedience went. She could not accept that the cross is only suffering; that to follow Him means endless pain and being emotionally racked. Surely the emphasis should be that the cross is hope? She stumbled into silence, uncertain how to continue and unwilling to do so.

Sister Imelda spoke frankly. She explained that sexuality and spirituality can live in the same body. Developing one did not mean denying the other. Both were powerful driving forces. It was not a matter of having to choose one and pretend the other did not exist, but integrating them into the commitment to chastity. She posed a question. Could Clare think who once said that holiness and sexuality were not incompatible? Clare shook her head.

"Reverend Mother. At the time I was in the novitiate, she was Deputy, and when she lectured on self-control, she always ended with the words: *Holiness and sexuality are not incompatible.* Then she would give a warning shot with her eyes and add: *But remember, we need self-control to place them in proper context. Only you and God know where that is.* That was well before Vatican Two."

Clare smiled. The behavior of Reverend Mother continued to astonish her.

"To live 'in Christ' does not mean you have to deny being a woman. What it means is that you must have a proper awareness of the dangers. We both know what they are. We have known from the day God called us that we didn't expect to live like the Corinthians. But I don't think anybody expects you not to be troubled from time to time."

Clare was aware of the complex feelings this simple statement produced in her. She had been shocked when two novices were discovered in the forbidden "particular friendship," known as "p.f." Holy Rule was explicit on the matter. *Do not engage in any physical familiarities with others, nor let them with you. Such behavior is dangerous to the very spirit of community life. Do not be tempted even to begin to be engaged in conversation that can lead to intimacies of any kind.* The pair were discovered in a larder by the Mistress. They were packed and gone from the Mother House before midnight. Clare had listened to the more knowledgeable girls explain what caused this swift consignment back to the outside world. It was the first time she had heard the word *lesbian*.

That evening Reverend Mother had assembled the novices and spoken calmly, saying that to live in chastity was never easy.

"It does not mean living without a heart. But it does mean remembering there is a great deal of truth in the words 'when you go in twos, Satan makes a third.' But, remember, too, what Saint Augustine said: 'No one protects the virginal blessing except God who bestowed it and God is love.' Therefore, the protector of our chastity is the love we practice here — selfless and inclusive, designed to reach all mankind."

Clare explained it was this concept with which she was now having difficulty.

"I don't know what is happening. I don't know why I feel like this. All I know is that I keep thinking if I feel like this, I can't be loving God in the way He wants."

"You're being too hard on yourself. Everybody has felt like this, from Reverend Mother down. It's part of what makes a good nun, having to go through this. But the important thing to remember is that you go *through* this. You don't *stay* with it. What matters is not that you have these feelings, but that in spite of them, you have never stopped loving God. That's what's important. Everything else will fall into place as long as you don't lose sight of that."

"I wish I had your confidence."

"You haven't lost your confidence. You've just buried it for the moment under all this soul-searching."

Clare laughed. She had not felt so calm and secure for months. She felt able to put the question she had been unable to ask until now.

"Why do I feel so lonely? I used to sleep so well. I used to feel so confident about what love is, where I was going, what the Church represents, where the challenges and promises are. Now I wonder. I wake up feeling so alone."

Sister Imelda looked at her thoughtfully.

"Clare, the very fact that you can even identify what bothers you is a sign that you are coping. We have all woken up feeling alone. Just because we were told to distinguish between aloneness and loneliness does not make it any easier. We have all got to find our own way forward."

"But, how? *How?* Sometimes, like at the wedding, I just want to love some person and have that person love me." Clare's voice was small and muffled.

"As I keep saying, that's a natural emotion. But we have both learned that we must strip ourselves of such feelings because that is what God wants of us."

"That's what I want to do."

"And you will. You have, and you will. Clare, you will. I promise you. Reverend Mother tells me you have more than lived up to her expectations. There are high hopes for you."

She knew the other nun was watching her carefully. Clare smiled. She really believed everything was going to be all right.

Once more, Lent empurpled the convent. Statues and paintings were draped in violet cloth while personal sacrifices were silently made on knees in chapel. Clare gave up all other reading for the Bible. Hour after hour, she pored over the thirty-nine books of the Old Testament and the twenty-seven of the New. For hours she had silently meditated on various passages that state temptation is essential to test the strength of commitment. A great peace filled her. She felt renewed.

Clare stood at the foot of the main staircase and gripped the two wooden shapes that resembled butter paddles. She clapped them together, creating a sharp report, like a hunter's rifle. Throughout Holy Week, the clappers marked the passage of time. Both the electric alarm and the campanile bell had been silent because the Rule decreed they were symbolic of joy and unsuitable in this period of mourning.

The days preceding Easter, more than any time in the year, reminded her of the true purpose of her life: prayer and meditation. There had been vigils in chapel to mark Christ's agony in the Garden of Gethsemane and the Passion of Good Friday. During this time, there were no Recreation periods and talking was restricted to essential commands in the infirmary. Meals were cooked and served in complete silence; all domestic duties were performed in the same way. It was as if the entire community had been struck dumb. Only at chapel was its collective voice heard, when the choir led the community through the liturgies, the lamenting psalms and chants.

On Good Friday, just as Jesus died, so the convent seemed completely to die. Corridors were empty, the community room deserted. The silence had a life of its own: watchful and enveloping like death itself over everything and everyone. Inside the chapel row after row of motionless bodies were precisely separated as if they had been positioned by a straightedge, so many inches between each inert figure. Throughout the Good Friday watch a wooden cross lay before the altar. No member of the community, not even the newest postulant, needed to be reminded of why they were assembled. For hour upon hour, they considered His agony, symbolized by the empty tabernacle. The Host had been removed and its doors left asunder, as a mute reminder of the violation He endured.

Kneeling, her face buried deep into her hands, Clare meditated upon the Last Supper, remembering John's description of how, before the meal, Jesus fetched water to wash the feet of the Apostles. She pondered upon that electrifying exchange between Jesus and Simon Peter when the disciple tried to protest.

"Lord, dost Thou wash my feet?"

"What I do, thou knowest not now, but thou shalt know hereafter."

"Thou shalt never wash my feet."

"If I do wash thee not, thou shalt have no part with me."

"Lord, not only my feet, but also my hands and my head."

"He that is washed needeth not but to wash his feet, but is clean wholly; and you are clean, but not all."

The conversation had a hermeneutical significance for her: Peter resisting, then almost childishly eager to be bathed; Jesus, sad and measured, knowing what is to happen to Him. The symbolism reminded her of the importance of remaining unswerving in faith, and in a wider sense, of her commitment to her vows. Encompassed in the Last Supper is the spirit of poverty, obedience, and chastity.

Holy Saturday stretched from the first crack of the clappers, and was spent kneeling in chapel, waiting for hope, just as on that First Saturday after the crucifixion, the Apostles waited for a similar sense of purpose to enter their lives. Through prayer she dwelled upon her sacred vows, reminding herself of their theological roots, which extend all the way back to Jerusalem. This was the time when she once more thought deeply about her consecration to God. While she was glad that the Vatican Council had dispensed with the symbolism of her being a Bride of Christ — recognizing, at last, that this very masculine attitude was unacceptable to the modern sisterhood — she nevertheless felt, kneeling before the cross at the altar, that her responses of grief and sadness for His death were essentially no different from what a widow feels on losing a husband. Caught up in the moment, she saw her sorrowing as the logical extension to the courtship, engagement, and marriage she had experienced with Him. Then, gradually as the long day drew to a close, her mood lightened. She reminded herself: *He is the Resurrection. This is all that matters.*

Then, at last, the miracle of Easter Sunday: the Host returned to its rightful sanctuary, the altar clothed in fresh white linen, the Paschal candle relit, its steady flame illuminating the picture of the Resurrection carved into the wax. Renewal and joy were heralded in words and song as the choir swept the community along through the Gloria.

Yet as Clare watched the priest celebrate Mass, thoughts, new and disturbing, flickered through her mind. A year ago, she would have been shocked to discover she could think them. But, waiting to go to the altar rail to receive His Body, she wondered again how Christ, who always stressed the role of women, would feel about the way the power of the Church remains firmly clasped by men. The Vatican Council, the Pope said, acted in His name, and the Council had come out clearly in favor of a great role for women in the Church. But male domination remained paramount.

Women, whatever the Vatican said, had a subordinate role. Even the devotion to Our Lady is designed to remind nuns of their duty to be meek and compliant. She wondered, again, whether such thoughts were a precursor to the return of her restlessness. She was glad when it was her turn to go forward to receive Communion. The act of dissolving a sliver of unleavened bread on her tongue removed everything else from her mind.

Clare made her way to Reverend Mother's office. She knocked and counted to five under her breath. The habit went back to her days as a postulant when the Mistress warned that Reverend Mother must never be surprised. Clare opened the door and entered. She waited for permission to advance.

"*Benedicite.*" Reverend Mother's voice was modulated and controlled. "*Dominus.*"

"Come in. Sit down, Sister Mary Luke."

Clare raised her eyes. Walking across the room she was reminded again of how the crucifix on the wall behind Reverend Mother somehow heightened the impression that she was more than a woman, well into middle age, who for a quarter of a century had carried more responsibility than many corporation directors. Only the lines around her eyes suggested the demands of combining the role of spiritual leader with a wide range of administrative duties.

As usual, she was seated bolt upright on the hard wooden chair behind the desk. Its surface was covered with papers. On each visit to this office, Clare had been confronted by piles of bills, receipts, invoices and reports; the mound of paper never seemed to diminish. Yet there had been a significant change in Reverend Mother's appearance. She was one of the first to adopt the modified habit and veil.

✝

Reverend Mother had attended all the discussions on modification, held in the community room, seating herself among other nuns, novices, and postulants, listening carefully to the excited comments about the various sketches produced by the Order's domestic science and art teachers. These seminars spread over weeks. Drawings were scathingly criticized, discarded, or sent back for redesigning. Some suggestions involved no more than lopping off a few inches from existing habits and shortening veils. Others would not have disgraced a high-fashion house with their sculpted bodices, pleated skirts, tucked-in waists, and ruffled sleeves and collars. Designs that passed the drawing stage were made up, stitched together by the seamstress-nuns. Other sisters took turns modeling. These prototype habits drew even more intense discussion; the model-nuns spent hours walking back and forth before the crowded community room, and nun after nun rose to her feet, to deliver a verdict or ask a question.

"How can I cook in such a fancy dress?" This came from the sister in charge of the kitchen.

"How would I manage in a thing like that? It's not much bigger than a duster." This came from a stout nun, convulsed at the sight of a close-fitting design.

"I can't possibly wear that. I'd look like a brother!" This from a junior professed, pointing to a habit cut on the style of a monk's robe.

The models swept in and out with increasing aplomb, pirouetting and turning in gentle parody of the way professional mannequins move. The cheers and laughter at times were deafening.

It was left to the Deputy to dampen the mood. A young nun swirled into the room in an elegant creation: white lace collar and cuffs, a scalloped blouse-top and a straight skirt. As she spun around, the line of her panties was clearly visible. The Deputy rose to her feet, a short, stocky figure in a full-length habit that fell around her in tentlike folds. She was trembling with fury.

"Sisters, how could anyone go to chapel in that? How could we be close to God when we would be dressed to tempt the Devil? Sisters, I veto this on the grounds of immodesty!"

Reverend Mother sat there saying nothing. Next day she appeared at Mass in a perfectly tailored habit, its skirt exactly two inches below the knee, her legs covered in black panty hose, her veil shortened and neatly clipped to the back of her head, the exposed hair neatly brushed off her forehead. It was a sign for the community to stop debating. The Superior's modified habit was the acceptable option.

✝

As she approached the desk, Clare reflected that this had been typical of Reverend Mother; she preferred to lead by practical example, rather than by endless discussion. The Superior motioned for her to sit down on a straight-backed wooden chair at a corner of the desk and reached a hand into the paperwork and located what she wanted. She held the sheet at a distance, her reading glasses at the tip of her nose. Clare knew that in recent years several nuns had sat in this chair, explaining to Reverend Mother why they were leaving religious life. She suspected they were the ones who had never been able to come to terms with the changes the Vatican Council continued to bring.

Almost every month there were new instructions from Rome on the way a certain document should be interpreted. The Sacred Congregation for the Religious had recently allowed the community to speak during supper, but during breakfast and lunch, nuns must still maintain the silence of centuries, using precisely defined gestures: for the salt and pepper, a pinch of the fingers; for the bread, a cutting motion; for the water pitcher, a pouring gesture. Another paper from Rome announced the abolition of many Latin prayers. A further edict revised the form of the Divine Office itself; some prayers were dropped. The bowing that had accompanied the Confiteor since the inception of the Order was abandoned. There was guidance on newly appointed pocket money — fares for those nuns who taught in the Order's schools and who did not journey there in Dominic's bus. Gone were the days when the city's busmen automatically allowed them to travel free of charge. In the liberating atmosphere of post-Council, some sisters found the idea of being doled out bus money too demeaning and left. Clare had no strong feelings on the matter; she thought it was unimportant, either way, in the context of a more significant reason for leaving. Nuns were increasingly aware of their biological function. Almost all who resigned their vocation were between the ages of twenty-eight and thirty-eight, a time when they could marry and still bear children. Many, she had heard, married priests who had also abandoned their calling.

Reverend Mother lowered the paper.

"You have done well, Sister Mary Luke. I believe the time has come when we must make fuller use of you."

Clare felt her heart begin to race. She willed herself to sit perfectly still. The Superior's voice was decisive.

"There is a place at Catholic College. You will fill it. You will get a further grounding in theology and Scripture. I am sure you will do well, because God has given you a special gift, a brain able to understand His words better than many. You have a future in His work."

She rose to her feet. Clare bowed her head for the blessing. After leaving the office, she went to the chapel and knelt. Her prayer was short and heartfelt. *Thank you, Lord, for choosing me.*

The lecture that set the community agog was given on the first Thursday after Easter. Reverend Mother had arranged for a clinical psychologist, a nun from another Order, to address them. When the notice appeared in the community room, there were murmurs from some of the middle-aged nuns. The Deputy had stared in glazed disbelief and walked away. In block letters the announcement proclaimed: CHASTITY — A REASSESSMENT.

The reaction to the lecture illustrated perfectly the continuing polarization within the community. The older nuns, led by the Superior, had responded with equanimity to all the changes in their life-style. Perhaps it was because of their age, Clare had mused, that they saw no threat in the new proposals. Opposition had come from among the middle-aged, led by the Deputy. They challenged every liberalizing word and disputed every relaxation of the Rule. They pointed to the irony that those orders which had set the pace in change, especially in the United States, had suffered the greatest losses. Change, they argued, had actually driven out from religious life those who would otherwise have stayed.

At each meeting to discuss a proposal to abolish or alter something, they brought up statistics to support their demands for less, not more, freedom. A hundred Italian Daughters of Saint Paul were the latest to resign in protest at a change in their habit. The Glenmary Sisters were in disarray over proposals to revise their Rule. The Sisters of the Immaculate Heart of

Mary were racked with uncertainty over plans to rearrange their daily routine. There was not an Order, they claimed, which was not fearful of the future that would follow change. Those below the age of thirty-five countered that even greater numbers were leaving because the promises of the Vatican Council were not being implemented. They argued that Rome and the councils who ran the orders were being obstructive. At the last meeting they had produced figures that showed the Holy Cross Order had lost hundreds of its younger members and the Sisters of Charity had suffered a similar fate. On that occasion, the community room rang with charge and countercharge and tempers came close to fraying.

Clare had kept her own counsel. But increasingly she feared that in spite of Reverend Mother's leadership, the community was bound at the Deputy's level of middle age. She was an effective cork to bottle up the cultural leap that many of the younger nuns wanted to make. Yet Clare would not go as far as some of them in wishing to abolish what they saw as the intransigent and outmoded state of much of religious life. Equally, she realized that by going to one of the most prestigious Catholic colleges in Ireland, she would grow away from the life she had led these past years. She would no longer be contained within the walls and grounds of the Mother House, but exposed to all kinds of new and exciting stimuli. That was why, among other reasons, Clare was eager to hear the lecture.

The psychologist was in her forties, dressed in a dark gray suit and a back-of-the-head veil. Above her eyebrows was an indentation, a reminder that until recently she had worn a constricting headband beneath a wimple. She invited anyone to make notes. The hall was crowded.

She began with a quotation from Graham Greene: "The Church knows all about rules. But it does not know what goes on in a single human head."

Clare jotted down the reference. The lecturer said that abandoning her habit was not an emotional experience.

"It has always been claimed our habits state that we have been called. More than a priest's garb, they single us out as belonging to Christ. That is an idea perpetuated by men, the popes and the cardinals who down the centuries have ruled our lives. Remember what Saint Ignatius said: 'No man should look into the eyes of a woman in a habit.' But what about a religious woman? What happens if she wants to look into the eyes of a man? No saint has ever laid down a rule about that. When the saint said those words, he was laying down a rule to imprison us.

"Many of us here can remember our investiture. Those were the days when we wore wedding dresses and each of us had our wedding cake complete with fancy icing. But we were also shorn, and draped in black. Have you ever thought of the contradiction of brides becoming widows within the space of the same Mass — and yet having to continually accept, as we all do, and it is right and proper that we should, that He lives? Those customs were designed, I repeat, by men. They have nothing at all to do with Our Lord. Only a man could continue to approve of the psychological trauma that the Poor Clares still endure at the time of their Clothing. On that day each novice must stand before a skeleton, who represents Sister Death. What possible motive can there be for such an outlandish practice, except to reinforce the idea that we die in our bodies when taking our vows? As a doctor, I can tell you that is dangerous. It can cause permanent psychological harm and distort our view of religious life. As a nun, I find that unacceptable. As a woman, I say it is disgusting."

There was murmured agreement from the audience, and she made her second point about religious garb.

"It was originally designed to make it easier for us to forget we are women. We all look the same in habits because they formed an integral part, until Vatican Two, of the concept that upon entering religious life, we must renounce every thought about our sexuality. We are never told how this is to be done. The reason for that is clear. There is no way it can be achieved. For centuries, it has been simply assumed, almost as an act of blind faith, that we find it easier to cope with chastity than men do with their celibacy. This is an arrogance once more perpetuated by men, based in part on the premise that if we are shrouded in habits it will stifle all our emotional feelings."

In the silence that followed, Clare made a further note: *Ten years ago she would have been thrown out of here. Fifty years ago she would have been excommunicated. A hundred years ago she would have been imprisoned for heresy. Four hundred years ago she would have been burned at the stake. She is the most exciting speaker I have ever heard.*

The psychologist swiftly placed chastity in its historical role by citing Saint Ambrose: "A virgin is purity's immolation, the victim of chastity."

"The word 'victim' expresses clearly what I object to. Our chastity, as such, is indeed important. It separates us from all other women. But we should not allow ourselves to be seen as victims. Chastity is a grace, not a penance. It is a virtue, not a sacrifice. But, above all, it is a voluntary condition, not something we must be coerced into by clothes and rules designed to exclude our femininity."

A burst of applause greeted the words. Seated beside the Superior, the Deputy looked askance.

"Celibate bodies are still feminine bodies. We get periods. We go through menopause. And we are all capable of sexual drive, which can bring us into direct conflict with our vow of chastity. Yet most orders prefer not even to consider such a possibility, let alone allow it to be discussed openly as we are doing here."

She paused and smiled at Reverend Mother, sitting as erect as always, knees together, hands folded in her lap.

"Built into every Holy Rule is the warning that anything physical is taboo. There are good reasons for that. Community living does demand certain restrictions. We all know about p.f.'s and the dangers they can bring. But that does not mean that friendship is not possible. It is a matter of balance. There is nothing wrong in two nuns walking together. Indeed, it is clinically healthy to have contact, provided it does not get in the way of our relationship with God."

She looked again at Reverend Mother.

"I am sure there are some of us who remember the days when a Superior said it was somehow ungodly to cross our legs in case it broke the vow of chastity!"

In the roar of laughter, Clare noted: *Reverend Mother seems delighted. She must have been very attractive when she was young. How did she manage? She couldn't do what Saint Benedict did to suppress his passion — throwing himself into a nettle bed.*

"What the Church must understand is that, in or out of our habits, we are all still women. And the more feminine we are, the better we can serve our Order and Our Lord. God doesn't want people who are dried out in their feelings. That sort of people have no love to give. And that is what chastity is all about — giving love in its purest form."

She looked challengingly at her audience.

"Suppression breeds fanaticism. Following Him takes on a dangerous distortion when sublimation leads to a misuse of power. No one who has never come to terms with one's own emotions should have power over other people's."

Clare noted the Deputy's response: *She looks as if she could spit.*

The speaker developed another theme. Physical virginity is no longer an essential requirement for admission to religious life because many orders now recognize that the act of consecration ensures spiritual virginity.

"Our chastity begins and ends with our hearts. What we must do is to place our sexual feelings into the framework of love."

She said there is an urgent need for every religious woman to face certain questions. Does she accept that the sexual drive is the most powerful single force in nature? Does she accept that it can be destructive unless handled properly? Does she accept that to forgo sexuality is a constant struggle? Does she accept that to deny the struggle is to deny the right to live?

"If you can honestly answer 'yes' to these questions, you have done rather better than Saint Thomas Aquinas. In his *Summa Theologica* he said the only way to cope with chastity is to steep yourself in a hot bath. That view prevails today. There is a mistaken idea that everybody can discipline themselves to withstand natural inclination. The theory is if we say 'go away' it will go away. Saints may be able to do so. But that is what makes them different from the rest of us. For us, if we are honest, it is a daily battle, perhaps even a struggle for every hour and even every minute we are awake. Unlike any other emotion, sexuality can surface at any time. A pretty painting. A scenic view. A passage in a book. Words and pictures. These are some of the potent forces which play upon our imagination and arouse our feelings."

She reminded them that systematic theology argued chastity was not a blind frustration of bodily desires but required discipline. She pierced them with her eyes.

"That is perfect — for the textbooks. Paul Tillich has translated chastity as the full revelation of human potential. There is only one thing missing. A sense of reality. How realistic is it to try and wrap up celibacy as he does? We all have a different potential. What is missing in his definition is reality. What is the reality of coping, not just on a physical plane, but on a psychological level?"

She had more questions. Are there any lessons to be learned from the world outside? From the widowed? From the divorced? From all those forcibly separated from loved ones?

Clare flexed her fingers; they were cramped from writing. She was glad she had brought a clean exercise book. As it was, the pages were more than half full of her notes. The psychologist moved on, reminding them that chastity was a binding of their lives to Christ. But, just as in any relationship, that which they had with Him is not one monumental single struggle to achieve closeness, but a continuing series of efforts. She said that a life of chastity involves a problem no theological text can teach them how to handle: risk.

"There is the risk of unhappiness. There is the risk of suffering. And there is the greatest risk of all. That, at the very end, you will not be able to accept it. That all the struggles mean nothing because you may still fail before the finishing post."

The nun paused. Clare sensed the sudden tension in the room.

"Each one of us here, if we are honest, if we stop and think, knows how high are the stakes. On the one hand, we are seeking human fulfillment in His name. On the other, we can be staring into the face of failure."

She reminded them that religious life is based on the concept that satisfaction comes from determination, that internal resources are always strong enough to grapple successfully with external forces.

"That is almost certainly not true in chastity. There are no guarantees that we will not fail our vow. Yet that knowledge is the best guarantee of all. Be aware of your desires. To deny them is never a good thing. They must be faced. What is temptation for one of us is not for another. But how do you achieve what you want — living in Christ and living with your body?"

She returned to an earlier point in her lecture: human relations are the key. She then took a sheet of paper from her pocket.

"Let me read you a letter. It's from a Sister who has until recently never doubted she can cope. This is what she writes: 'It hit me last Christmas, a time when all families are together. I have my family, of course, the community. But I still felt alone. I got up alone. I ate in silence. I opened my presents in silence. I prayed alone. And I ended the day going to bed alone. I would give anything to take away this feeling of being alone. . . .' "

Clare found her hand was shaking as she wrote her final note: *It could be me. That's exactly how I feel.*

The Deputy Superior's office was on the ground floor, close to the chapel. It was small and its walls were lined with dark wooden shelves filled with leather books, the ledgers of the Mother House, bound balance sheets. Standing inside the door, waiting for the command to approach, Clare wondered how a room could take on a person's personality. This one was stuffy and imbued with the Deputy's own sense of permanent disapproval. She sat behind her desk, the cross on its heavy chain dangling below the desk top.

"Come forward and sit down, Sister Mary Luke." Her voice was cold and impersonal.

"Thank you, Mother." Clare walked to the chair, identical in shape and position to the one in Reverend Mother's office. The symmetry of convent life, she had often thought, knows no limits. Table settings and altar candles, kitchen pots and boxes of communion wafers: everything was aligned.

"You start at college next week."

"Oh, Mother! I'm so excited." Clare could not contain her joy. "Oh, thank you, Mother."

"You have nothing to thank me for. You might as well know that I did not approve of you going on to further study. In my view you would have been better used elsewhere."

The silence stretched endlessly. Then she spoke again.

"There is work for you here." The Deputy's stare forced Clare to lower her eyes. Canyons of ledgers seemed to be drawing close to her. She felt a crushing in the chest.

"But, Mother . . . I have always wanted to teach . . ."

"What we want and what God thinks is best are not always the same. Surely you know that?"

"Yes, of course, Mother." She could sense the bulky figure behind the desk, closing and opening her hands, making and breaking fists. It was a motion the Deputy used when she tried to control her anger.

The movement helped Clare to decide. She raised her head.

"Mother, I believe God wants me to be a teacher."

The Deputy broke another silence. "Very well. I am glad you are so certain what God wants of you. But may I remind you what I expect from you?" Her voice was even more chilled. "You are going into the outside world to learn. The Order is paying for you to have this privilege. I need hardly remind you of the cost."

Clare tried to keep her voice steady.

"I know, Mother, that it's expensive."

"It is not just the cost I am talking about, Sister, as you know full well. I'm speaking of the Rule. Just because you are among seculars you must not think you can behave as they do. Do you understand?"

"Mother, I'm not certain —"

"Then I will tell you precisely, Sister! You will limit your contact with them to the minimum. To the absolute minimum. You will not start a conversation. If they engage you in one, do not prolong it. You will confine any discussion to work. You will discuss absolutely nothing else. You will remember at all times that you are there to study and not fritter away your time. Do you understand now?"

"Yes, Mother."

"Very well."

The Deputy opened a drawer and took out a red money box, which she unlocked and opened. She carefully counted out a number of coins and some notes, then passed them across to Clare.

"This is your bus fare and lunch money for one week. Every Sunday evening, before Compline, you will come here and receive your allowance for the next week. If for any reason you have to miss college, then you will bring the unused money back here. You will not use it to buy sweets or anything else. Is that clear?"

"Yes, Mother. It's perfectly clear."

Clare thought: *Why does she treat me like a child? I'm twenty-six years old.*

The Deputy was reluctant to end the interview.

"I could not help noticing how approving you seemed of that dreadful woman's lecture. I cannot imagine what she thinks she is doing in religious life. It was disgusting. And I think it is disgusting for anyone to even think she represents what our life is all about. If it's still in your mind, Sister Mary Luke, put such rubbish out of it. Every word of it."

Clare stared at her, horrified. Could this still be the voice of the Church? In spite of everything, was this how little religious life had progressed?

"Thank you, Mother. I'll remember what you have said."

The Deputy glared at her. "You do that, Sister, you do that. And do it with humility. That's what you need, humility."

"I will try, Mother. I will try to be more humble."

"Do that."

Seated in the tiered lecture hall, Clare listened to the monsignor building his argument that the Apostle John's authorship of the Book of Revelation is supported by the independent evidence of Justin Martyr, Irenaeus, Tertullian, and others. The discourse not only covered familiar ground but the lecturer's dusty-dry delivery was her first disappointment of the morning. She felt her concentration fading.

Outside the convent she had caught a bus crowded with rush-hour commuters, elbowing their way on and off at stops. She had instinctively tried to stand aside, remembering the lessons on self-effacement she had been given in her postulancy. Nobody had taken any notice, let alone thanked her for such courtesy.

Until the monsignor, she had found her lectures stimulating. A theologian had spent an hour discussing the Creation from the position of how it effectively destroys the argument for evolution: the choice is either to believe God's revelation or man's theorizing and the inherent weakness of the latter is that evolution merely drives the idea of the origin of man back into oblivion but does not provide the original source from which he sprang. Another tutor had devoted his time to discussing the three stages of death:

physical, spiritual, and eternal, and how all are linked by the Resurrection. A third had concentrated upon the significant unnamed women of Scripture: John's adultress and the elect lady; the great harlot of Revelation; Matthew's woman with seven husbands; all are among those, he said, who symbolize punishment and repentance, divine wrath and forgiveness. She filled page after page, excited and stimulated by what she heard.

With a start, she realized the monsignor's lecture on Revelation was over. He asked the class to write an essay on the position of the Preterist Method of interpreting the Gospel in conjunction with the Continuous Historical Method.

She sat, frantically writing, wishing she had paid more attention.

"It's okay. You can borrow my notes."

Clare looked up, startled. Standing over her was a tall, spare-framed man, wearing a white shirt and black tie and trousers. Stuffed into the pockets of his sports jacket were papers, and he had a pile of books in his hands. He looked at her quizzically.

"Anyway, it's no sweat. The monsignor will give the same lecture in one form or another right through the whole term. He's hooked on Revelation. He drags it into everything."

"I see." She thought: *Do not encourage this. Do not get involved. Remember the Rule. Remember Deputy Mother. She could have sent him to test you.*

"You're not one of those nuns who spend their time sitting in an empty classroom during lunch, are you?"

"What?" She started to pack her briefcase. "Sorry, I wasn't listening." She wished she didn't sound so distracted.

"We get a lot of sisters here who don't eat. They just sit in class waiting for the break to end."

She knew he was staring at her.

"You can always tell them. They're the ones who wear full habits to try to hide their thinness. Nobody's fooled, of course. We all know convents are a breeding ground for anorexics."

"Really? Do they teach you that here?" Her voice was edgy, but she suddenly didn't care.

"Sorry. I didn't mean to offend you."

"You didn't. It's just that I dislike —"

"— people who invite you to lunch and never take you!"

She felt herself shrinking away, wondering how she could escape.

"Tom, are you coming?" The voice came from a group going through the door.

He addressed her again. "Would you like me to show you where the restaurant is? I'm Tom, by the way."

She knew he was trying to reassure her with his smile.

"It's okay if you don't want to come. It was stupid of me to say what I did."

"No. I'd like to come." She hoped her voice sounded nonchalant. She rose to her feet and closed her briefcase.

Tom stepped back, smiling gently. The group in the doorway had gone.

"The first day's always the worst. After a week or so you'll get used to it."

"How long have you been here?" she asked, thinking: *Stop this. You must stop this now.*

"A year. I'm coming up to my diaconate."

"Oh." She wished she didn't have this urge to know more.

"What's your name?"

"Sister."

Tom laughed. "Not what they all call you. Your real name?"

"I'm not sure if —"

"Of course you can! What do you think Vatican Two was all about?"

"Certainly not about nuns giving their names to anybody who asks." She hoped her smile took the sting out of the words.

Tom looked serious. "I know about the Rule. Here we try and put that aside. But nobody's going to push you. If you want to be 'Sister,' that's okay. Only you'll miss a lot, and that would be a shame."

For a moment, she felt petrified, knowing and unable to help herself; she was staring at him, at the texture of his male skin, at the small nick on his chin, at his thick eyebrows, his nose, his eyes, at the way his lips curved when he smiled. She was shocked to find herself in such proximity to his alien masculine world.

"My name is Clare."

"And you'll be a poor starving Clare if you don't get something to eat!"

He led the way out of the lecture room. She was glad he could not see her face crimsoning, or detect the panic he had created in her. She had come here determined to attain intellectual excellence. Yet suddenly, emotions and passions that had troubled her for months became sharply focused on the back of this tall man striding ahead of her.

With easy assurance Tom led her into the restaurant, through the wall of noise, to a table. He dumped his books on a chair and held another out for her. No man, she thought, had ever treated her like this.

Clare felt both stunned by his warmth and dismayed at her response.

CHAPTER 11

†

Recollections

S he was totally naked, kneeling in the sand, legs slightly apart, one hand casually dropped between her thighs, the other reaching for her long blonde hair streaming in the wind. Andrew forced himself to concentrate, knowing he must let the memories surface as smoothly and automatically as the steady beating of his heart. They came to him in fragments, like pieces of broken cloud driven before the wind. In them, time was melded, some details obscured, others highlighted. Long ago, he realized his subconscious was highly selective. He wondered if this was how he coped with his introspection, why he was able to come close to melancholia and enjoy the experience. He continued reviewing his life, seeking from his twenty-four years a lesson learned, an experience undergone, pain and pleasure, denials and desires. They all floated into his consciousness as he sifted the past to help him decide the future.

He used his diary to note the date of this exercise: *Sunday, August 8, 1982;* and to identify the hour and the place: between eight o'clock and closing time in a public house in one of the villages in the counties around London. In this respect he was like his father, whose stockbroker's grasp for detail had given him a flourishing business. Yet it was one of the sadnesses of Andrew's life that increasingly they had moved farther apart in the one area he never wished there to be conflict: religion. His father was a staunch Protestant, as devout in his faith as his mother was to her Catholicism. This had made it that much harder for Andrew to decide. He concentrated on trying to make the recollections coalesce, to bond them together like molecules so that they created their own permanent matter in his mind, each memory slotted into place, each given its importance: Jane and his family; school; university and the army.

Andrew noticed, abstractedly, that her breasts were as deeply tanned as the rest of her body. They reminded him of Jane's. He continued to stare at the girl on the Pirelli calender, at the way she tilted back her head, had her eyes closed and her mouth slightly open. This, too, was reminiscent of Jane. The nude seemed to have arrived on this deserted beach in some mysterious way. There were no footprints in the sand, no horizon, nothing to distract his attention from this unknown girl who reminded him so much of the woman he loved, who said she loved him, yet could not understand why he felt as he did about God, his religion, his wanting to serve the Church in some capacity. In this respect Jane was like his father.

His reverie was interrupted by sudden laughter from another part of the snuggery. They were in civvies but he recognized them by their haircuts, the cavalry twill trousers and the leather patches on the tweed jackets. It was the off-duty uniform of Sandhurst cadets, as distinctive as the shine on their shoes and the way they ordered pink gins. Tradition dies hard in the army. That was one of the reasons he didn't want to remain part of it. More than any other of his objections, this was the one his father had not understood. Tradition was one of the most important elements in his life.

The calender hung above the bar. Legend had it that Oliver Cromwell stayed here on his way to purge Ireland. It was not true, of course: he had marched northward by a different route. Andrew had often thought how much useless information he had had to prove or disprove to obtain his history degree. He knew his father was, nevertheless, disappointed that he had not obtained a First. He had put it in his usual indirect manner. This was accompanied by the interrogative smile, which somehow suggested not so much a criticism of a provincial university's academic standards, but surprise that anyone who had gone to what his father insisted was still one of England's finest public schools should not have automatically acquired a First Class degree.

His mother had wished him to go to Ampleforth, Britain's leading Catholic school. His Eminence the Primate of All England and Wales had once been there. When Andrew was old enough to understand such important matters, his mother quietly explained that she knew the Cardinal personally; he still remembered her sigh when she spoke of his monkish good manners and his beautiful voice. She had always liked her priests to be well groomed. Nowadays, when she spoke about His Eminence in front of his father, it invariably evoked a polite little smile. Nothing was said; the smile expressed it all. That, Andrew reflected, was like so much of his parents' marriage. Their relationship was far more complex than it appeared. He wondered, too, what part that had played in the indecision he now faced.

†

When Andrew was seven years old and about to enter preparatory school, his mother explained that being a Catholic is an attitude, not an act. It was an extension of an idea she had gently pressed upon all her children from the day they were old enough to understand. Catholicism, in this part of the country, is a minority religion, its places of worship hopelessly outnumbered by the square Norman and Gothic structures of the Church of England. His mother had a collective label for them: *The Tory Party at prayer*. She used it as the ultimate weapon to silence his father when he went too far probing old wounds: the role of the Pope in World War Two, Church finances, and, in his father's favorite jibe, *All those mysteries the Vatican keeps under lock and key, no doubt for very good reasons*. Over the years "mysteries" had come to include the death of the first Pope John Paul after only thirty-three days, and the election of his Polish successor, whose name his father always managed to mispronounce — somehow implying in doing so that Karol Wojtyła would never have become Archbishop of Canterbury, with its tradition of appointing prelates with names rooted in yeoman England. Then his mother would sigh, and, choosing her moment very carefully, interject with just the faintest of undertones: *Dear, you really sound like the Tory Party at prayer*. It was another round in the shadow-boxing at which they were expert: verbal punches meant to score points, not scar. It was one reason the marriage had survived: both understood the rules of engagement. Andrew had eagerly absorbed these adult lessons in lifemanship.

He liked his prep school, not so much because of a total absence of religious bias, but for its uniform: battleship gray, with red piping around the jacket and stocking tops and a red cap worn squarely on the head, like a priest's biretta. For the first time, he was conscious of a liking to dress up. It was the one reason he looked forward to going to his father's old public school. It had one of the most distinctive uniforms in Britain.

Uniforms, said Father Patrick, in his custom-made clerical suit ordered from the Pope's tailor in Rome, made a person stand out. Every Thursday afternoon, except during Holy Week, the parish priest took tea with Andrew's mother. During Lent he refused sugar and her home-baked cakes. Father Patrick had a shock of hair, almost as white as his collar, and fingernails bitten to the quick. His every word and gesture contained its own sense of drama; the most trivial incident retold with a sense of urgency, gushing from the priest in a soft lisping outpour. Andrew's father had frequently said that Father Patrick should have been an actor, that he could have made a decent living on the stage, particularly with those eyes of his: brown and staring fixedly; passionate and unsettling. A convert's eyes, Andrew's father called them. *There's no one worse than a convert,* he would conclude; *they are always trying to make up for lost time.*

When he was small, Andrew used to sit on Father Patrick's knee to be bounced up and down while the priest nibbled crustless sandwiches of cucumber and cress and sipped from a bone-china teacup. When he was older, he sat at the priest's feet, marveling at the buckles on his shoes. Before leaving, Father Patrick would stoop down and unfailingly ask Andrew how he was coming along with his catechism and remind him to say his prayers every night, otherwise God would be sad and perhaps even angry. In Andrew's impressionable mind, the Almighty took on a definite shape. He was a being not only capable of sorrow and rage, but one who knew how to exact all sorts of punishment: Our Fathers and Hail Marys were penances He had appointed Father Patrick to administer. It was Andrew's first realization of the importance of a priest.

One night, as his mother tucked him in, he murmured sleepily to her that when he grew up, he would like to have Father Patrick's job. His mother bent over him and whispered words that, from time to time, would surface in his mind: *Darling, if that's what God decides I will be very happy.* She had kissed him on the forehead and asked God to keep him safe. She had recounted the incident to Father Patrick, who patted Andrew on the head and said it would be wonderful if he were to receive a call from God. Andrew sat there for the rest of the afternoon wondering how God would do this. More than likely, he decided, He would use the telephone; God would be too busy to write. That was what Father Patrick must have meant by a call. The telephone would ring in the hall and either his mother or father would answer it, and they would stand there, awed, and call out: *Andrew, it's for you — God is calling.* It seemed the most natural explanation to a young boy.

Father Patrick was the only person, who could literally drive Andrew's

father out of his favorite chair in the drawing room. On Thursday afternoons, his father would not return to the office after lunch, but sat in the
chair reading, giving the impression of a man with all the time in the world
on hand. But the moment Father Patrick's car arrived, he rose from his
chair, saying to Andrew's mother that he had work to do, a new stock issue
to be evaluated, and he would stride to his study and remain closeted there
until the priest's car had driven away. Only then would he emerge and
prepare for the cocktail hour.

This was another of the little ceremonies that punctuated the lives of
Andrew's parents. His father went upstairs to change into an old sweater
and slacks, then back down to the drawing room, where he poured drinks: a
double gin for himself, a smaller one for his wife, a lemonade for Andrew
and any of the other children who happened to be at home. On Thursdays,
his father would reoccupy his chair and listen to a recounting of Father
Patrick's latest problems with the parish funds, with the bell-ringers, with
the grave-diggers, with the sacristan.

Andrew always sat without stirring, perched on the arm of his mother's
chair, as she faithfully reported the entire conversation, in a tone full of authority and quiet understanding, very similar to the one Father Patrick
used. His father invariably interrupted. *Now what is it he wants? How
much this time? You know I'll do what I can, but how much?*

On Sundays, when Andrew's mother took the children to Mass, she
often placed a sealed envelope on the collection plate. It would contain a
check made out to the parish church account and drawn on his father's account at the same bank.

God and mammon under the same roof, his father would say. *Just
like your Church.* This time, his mother would ignore the bell for a new
round.

By the time he was ready to go away to public school, Andrew had
learned how to define his family's position in local society; one firmly an-
chored in the professional upper middle-class, where everything is under-
stated and patriotism goes without saying. His mother occasionally gave
small dinner parties and the guests were studiously chosen to celebrate a
mutual affection and self-esteem. The mere possession of money, particularly through Trade, was not a guarantee of a place at the table. His father
and mother were extremely careful never, by so much as a gesture, to emphasize their own wealth and social position. His father spoke with certainty of the coming of a new Elizabethan age of British supremacy; in the
meantime he enjoyed sitting with Andrew to watch another rerun on television. On these occasions, he would frequently add an injunction. *Re-*

member what people sacrificed to keep us free. He was not, he would add, anti-German or even anti-Japanese; he was just pro-British. The only time Andrew had seen him close to becoming angry was when his mother said that jingoism was at the root of all wars. His father, visibly containing himself, replied: *But patriotism won for England.* His mother had colored and said no more. The meal ended in embarrassed silence.

Each parent had clearly defined responsibilities. Andrew's father supervised homework and acted as a liaison with school. He wrote the occasional sick notes and asked the questions at the parent-teacher meetings. He handed out pocket money and checked how it was spent. His mother instilled the ideal that children do not speak out of turn, they carry the shopping from the supermarket to the car on Saturdays, save their pocket money to buy Christmas presents, help the elderly to cross the road, and never, ever, discuss family matters outside the home. Honor and respect for their parents were more than taught: they were embedded in the bone marrow of each growing child. She was in charge of religion. Offering herself as an example, she made sure the children never forgot they were Catholics. Their lives followed the pattern of the Church calendar: Mass every Sunday; Lent, a time of renouncing, of giving up sweets, television, or going to the cinema, of being encouraged to go more than once a week to church and to recite the rosary every evening. It was all done with the minimum of fuss, but the ancient names and rituals reached far into Andrew's developing mind and stayed there. Early on, his faith started to burn as steadily as altar candles. In every sense, it was a good home, and one where Andrew's religious outlook began to flourish. When he understood the Act of Contrition, he began to fret over the fate of non-Catholic friends. Father Patrick had made it clear that outside the Church there was no salvation. The thought, for Andrew, of his neighborhood pals being consigned to Hell merely because they were not Catholic was an unsettling one. He offered to teach especially close friends the Act of Contrition because Father Patrick had also said that, if it was made even by a non-Catholic at the moment of dying, the repentance would miraculously wipe away all past sins. Andrew saw this as one of the many benefits of Catholicism: it offered hope to everyone.

It was his mother who explained to him that her family was *old Catholic*, in the same way people were described by her as being *old rich*, like his father's family. His maternal great-grandparents crossed to England after the Great Famine swept Ireland in the 1840s. They had money enough to establish themselves on the fringes of Victorian society, suppressing their effusive Irishness for a low-key English profile. By the time Andrew's parents married, ethnic identity had been reduced to his father's solemn promise that all the children would be raised as Catholic and encouraged to remain loyal to the true Church.

The family tree on his father's side went back four centuries, to the days of the Stuart kings; one ancestor went with Cromwell to brutalize Catholic Ireland, another fought at Culloden. Since then, in time of war, it had given officers and gentlemen to serve king and country, and women to act as nurses in field hospitals in the Crimea and Gallipoli, and aboard the hospital ships of World War Two and Korea. Its sons and daughters continued to stock the Church of England with vicars and rectors, and provided wives for Anglican clergymen. Some, like Andrew's father, had reached the upper echelons of the professions: the law, medicine, merchant banking, underwriting at Lloyd's. None, his father had told Andrew with quiet satisfaction, had ever gone into Trade. When they met at family weddings and funerals, his father's relatives sang lusty Protestant hymns and recited prayers. Andrew noticed his mother never joined them. He was twelve when she explained that each time she took the children to a Protestant church, she needed Father Patrick's permission, always granted, but only on condition that none of them participated in the worship and prayer. Since then, he had always thought of Protestant churches as lacking something. Father Patrick had identified it. *Only we Catholics have enough faith to accept transubstantiation. That's why we keep Jesus' Body in the tabernacle at the altar at all times. It is to remind us that He is in the church and His Presence is always there for us.* He pointed out more differences. Other faiths do not always insist upon a red light burning on the altar as a further reminder Jesus is there. Nor do they always use incense and bells to signify reverence. Often the cross on a Protestant altar is empty, as though the agony of His suffering is an embarrassment. Protestants have changed the Our Father and interpret the Bible differently. By doing so, they do not obtain the full value of God's word; they are denied the complete understanding of the true basis of faith on whose living experience the Church is founded. Only to Catholics, insisted Father Patrick, does God reveal Himself totally.

†

The bar was crowded and noisy and Andrew's memories came agonizingly slowly, jumbled together, not always easy for him to sift and understand.

✝

The day before he entered his Protestant public school, Father Patrick called at the house and spoke about the need to remember that while Andrew's own thoughts and feelings could not always be relied upon, the Church is the source of all faith. *God bless you, my boy,* the old priest ended, *God bless you and may you come back to us safe in your faith.*

His years at home had given him a good grounding in many things, but at school he realized they had been memorable for a total absence of any form of sexual discussion. He had never heard his mother or father express a single sexual thought or seen either of them naked or heard any sounds coming from their bedroom. It had never occurred to him to wonder whether they did make love. At school such matters were openly discussed among pupils. The sexual lives of elders were bandied about with a frankness that Andrew found both shocking and exciting. Boys went out of their way to catch a glimpse of matron or one of the domestic staff bending or reaching up, revealing a glimpse of a petticoat. These sightings fostered further speculation about the sexual behavior of that particular member of staff. On visiting days, the potential of older sisters and the younger-looking mothers was also coolly considered. All forms of sexuality aroused deep interest among schoolmates, and Andrew's initial confusion and uncertainty gave way to stimulation; his feelings of misgivings disappeared as he began to feel a need to release the stirrings in his body. He was almost eighteen years old and a virgin.

At school the emphasis had been that nothing must get between him and experience. He had been encouraged to place a high value on self-reliance, to recognize that while there is a time and place for critical analysis and discussion, there must first be a proper bedrock of self-awareness. He had been schooled in the process of *how* to acquire knowledge; how, for instance, scientific truth and poetic truth did not need to be pursued along separate paths, but could be approached on a common front. His English tutor had summarized the search for truth by quoting Pasternak: *Facts do not exist until man has put into them something of his own.*

He used the maxim to explore his religion, to see that Catholicism offered him the precious gift of certitude. He enjoyed discovering the ancient truth of his faith and the reassurance of its fundamental ideals, along with the clear-cut way it distinguished between good and evil, not relatively but absolutely. No other institution in history, he believed, puts such emphasis on continuity and authority as does the Church, and the tone of its voice, the

comforting institutional cadence, was steadfast down through the centuries. No other church could say that; this was what made the security of
being a Catholic so indissoluble.

His five years at school, he now saw, provided him not only with the
foundation of an excellent education, but also enhanced his belief that
Catholicism was the only faith by which he could really live. It was realistic in its understanding of the human predicament while never losing its
optimism; its concept of original sin and salvation was an honest acceptance of human imperfection coupled with a belief in rehabilitation
through the grace of God. In the Church, the redemption of entire communities, even the whole world, was seen as possible. And, since death did not
end matters, indeed quite the opposite, there was a victory about Catholicism that no mundane evil could defeat.

His faith, he came to see, made sense of history because it went beyond
history: faith was the only way to understand the endless struggle of the
human spirit and the continuous frustration of its hopes. Faith was the answer to those who argue, that, after six thousand years of civilization, man
is as far as ever from creating a perfect human society. By using faith as a
measurement, the failure of history not only becomes intelligible; it is essential and to be expected. He had spent a great deal of time cogitating
upon the teaching of Niebuhr: *The most obvious meaning of history is that
every nation, culture, and civilization brings destruction to itself by ex-
ceeding the bounds which God has set upon all human enterprises.* By the
time he was seventeen, and history had become his main interest, he fully
believed Catholicism reckoned realistically with the subject because it was
a faith, more than any other, which gave meaning and purpose to living in
this world.

✝

Raised, clipped voices interrupted his reverie. The Sandhurst cadets
were arranging themselves before the bar for a photograph but could not
persuade the barman to take it. Andrew wanted the noise to abate so that
he could concentrate on sorting out his past. He offered his services to the
cadet holding the camera. Focusing, Andrew stepped back a pace to include all of them — from close-cropped heads to polished shoes — with
enough of the bar in the background to give the photograph a perspective.
He held them in frozen cheer for a moment, then snapped the shutter.
Smiling now, he waved them back into position and rewound the camera.
He knelt on one knee and tilted the lens up, filling the viewfinder with only

the tops of their heads and centered on the Pirelli girl. As he pressed the button, he remembered how he felt in his last term at school, when as captain of the house he had smuggled nude photographs into his room.

†

Andrew was astonished that he had actually done what months before he would have rejected as incredible and wildly shocking. He briefly wondered if this was a sign of his declining morals. Then he reminded himself he still attended Mass regularly. Besides, scores of boys he knew regularly did what he had done.

He reached his room and closed the door, feeling mounting excitement. He was finally alone. As captain of the house, he had a nicely furnished room, with a comfortable chair and a bed, a desk, shelves filled with books, and a closet. He had a washbasin and carpet on the floor. No one, not even the housemaster, would enter uninvited. He put his squash racquet in its plastic cover on the bed and removed his clothes. Then he washed his hands and dried them. He unzipped the racquet cover, and removed the small flat package he had hidden there. He placed it on the bedside table, slipped the racquet and cover under his bed, and slid between the sheets. Outside, dusk gathered.

The photographs were all of the same naked girl. She was big and tanned, with heavy black hair hanging over one shoulder in a thick braid. She had the look of a well-bred, carefully groomed animal in the peak of condition.

In the first photograph she faced the camera, cupping her breasts, her legs apart, her pubis visible. Andrew raised his knees under the blankets, forming a slope on which he could display the prints. In the second, the girl was tilted back on her buttocks, the photographer placing his camera between her thighs, so that her vagina was the focus of the composition. Andrew felt himself becoming aroused. In the third, she used her fingers to fondle her clitoris. He reached under the blanket and began to touch himself, something he had never done before. In a fourth picture she was kneeling, her back to the camera, peering at the photographer through her legs. He took his hand away, thinking: *This is just awful, just awful.* He pulled his hand from under the blanket and gathered up the photographs and put them back in their wrapping. He jumped out of bed and placed them behind a row of books. Then he climbed back between the sheets feeling tired and guilty at how far he had gone. He was still undecided whether to admit his action at his next visit to confession, when sleep claimed him.

240

†

The barman shouted for last orders. Andrew edged himself through the throng, now remembering another night in another bar when he had told Jane about the photographs. She'd laughed and said, teasingly, he shouldn't be such a prude, that there was nothing wrong in achieving solitary fulfillment. She had quoted a Kinsey statistic, that more than half the American student population masturbated, adding without pause that she regularly took care of herself.

Until then, he had always thought of masturbation as sinful. She had laughed and this time, quoted Wilhelm Reich, the Austrian psychoanalyst, who had argued that the Church, more than any other organization, was guilty of perpetuating dangerous nonsense about sex. In promoting anti-sexual moralism among the young at its schools and colleges, the Church continued to produce people who could not obtain sexual satisfaction in their own lives, and who opposed almost any sexual freedom in the world around them. With a passion that had taken him aback, she launched a fierce attack on the Church's traditional view that sex, except for procreation, is something wicked, rejecting this as a convenient argument of the celibates who manage its affairs. God-fixation, she said witheringly, and its association with bodily perfection and purity of the soul, was mostly found in people who had never achieved sexual satisfaction.

He had not been able to think of an argument in rebuttal, and had listened, fascinated, as she expounded Reich's theory that sexual pleasure is positively healthy, not only banishing neurotic numbness about sex, but putting a person more in contact with his body, his needs, his drives — and the requirements of others.

She had then looked at him and said: "Take me to bed. It'll be good." He had and it was.

Standing at the bar, he remembered how she had introduced him to the writings of Kerouac, Burroughs, and Ginsberg and made him read Reich and Karen Horney, another controversial psychoanalyst. Jane argued that the Church cleverly used Freud to support its argument that sexual abstinence, especially among the young, is necessary in the interest of social and cultural achievement. She encouraged him to accept Reich's rebuttal of Freud. Even now, in the crowded snuggery, the memory was vivid of her voice, slightly breathy, the way it always was when she read. "Listen to this," she said, plunging into Reich. "The fact is, as all modern sexologists accept, that all adolescents masturbate. That alone disposes of Freud's argument."

She had sat back and said that Reich had been the trigger which awakened society from a sleep of centuries, held somnolent by the Church, which at last was beginning to lose control over people's minds and bodies.

Jane had surprised him many times in those first few months together. Before meeting her, he had never thought it possible to have a totally open sexual relationship where anything could be discussed. She had shown him how to be free about everything, with their bodies as well as their words. She taught him more about love than anyone else; how to make it, how to express it, how to recognize it. She was not merely sexy, but used each sexual episode to initiate him into another sensual mystery. Afterward, she would discuss the experience openly, oblivious even of who was listening or where she was. Though she was a Catholic, she regarded her faith, when it came to sexual freedom, as tyrannical and an invasion of her privacy. She insisted the Pope could not be infallible on such matters as birth control and abortion.

He had been, he now saw, too preoccupied with the sheer joy of possessing her to make an issue of her views on religion. Perversely, it was their common faith, however differently they interpreted it, which attracted him. Within an hour of their first meeting, he had asked outright: "Are you a Catholic?" When she nodded and smiled, he relaxed. By the time he began to explore with her her own Catholic girlhood guilt feelings about sexual pleasure he had been able to listen without feeling uncomfortable.

She was taking a degree in psychology and English literature and was, for a while, captivated by D. H. Lawrence's *Lady Chatterley's Lover*. They had sat in pubs all over town and later, when they closed, in all-night cafés, and still later, in their bed; he listening while she analyzed the symbolism in the story of the frustrated wife of an impotent aristocrat who fell into bed with her gamekeeper, bore his child, and endured the loss of her place in society. Like Lawrence, Jane scorned society's warning against infidelity. Lawrence, she asserted, was concerned to end unhealthy sexual puritanism. It was in a student bar, as crowded as this snuggery, that she suddenly shouted out: *Lawrence is only trying to put an end to our terror of our bodies.* People staring at her, running her fingers through her hair, bleached by the summer sun, her nipples pressed against her cotton blouse. A little tipsy, she had stood up and addressed the bar in a commanding voice. *Lawrence is saying that for too long we have not had a proper reverence for sex and our bodies. We do it, but we don't enjoy the former, and are ashamed of the latter. That's why he created Lady Chatterley, so that we can all know what pleasure is. There's nothing wrong with enjoying sex. Nothing at all.* Fellow students cheered and winked at Andrew as he led her from the bar. That night their lovemaking had been urgent, intense, and quickly consummated.

From the very beginning, he was a Trilby to her sexual Svengali, content to exist in a state of perpetual sated euphoria; their lovemaking so potent that he believed it would never change. In a way, this was why he welcomed the pain he now felt.

The Sandhurst cadets had moved to a corner and were standing arms around one another's shoulders, crooning. Jane enjoyed pubs as much as anything for their singing, content to spend an evening seated near the piano, a glass of beer before her, joining in to belt out one song after another as if she were a street vendor's daughter, not the eldest child of a prominent stockbroker. As the night wore on, she would persuade the pianist to play songs that spoke of the forlorn sadness of love ending and of arms locked in last good-byes; he would watch her and suddenly begin to sense it could never last with Jane, not because of her, but because of him.

Her response to his question: *You really do love me, don't you?* could barely stifle his doubts. He wanted her constant reassurance, and when she provided it, he would still experience an inner anguish: *She has said this before, can she mean it now?* She told him there had been other men and he probed for details, saying there must be no secrets between them. He tried to convince himself that once he knew all of her past, it could be excised from his mind. It was, of course, impossible: he would often look at her and imagine other men enjoying the feel of her skin against theirs, the taste of her lips, the sound of her words. And, only too well, he remembered that night when, lying beside her in the darkness, he began to question her again about her past. Her hand tightened on his. *You really should stop this. Just because I've been honest with you, it doesn't mean you have to go on grilling and judging me. I'm tired of it. My past is mine and nothing to do with you. My body was mine to give then, and I wanted to give it, as I am happy to give it to you. But you don't own me and I don't owe you anything. You'll either have to live with your jealousy or we can't go on. I mean that.*

He had held her close and whispered. *You really do love me, don't you?* She said she did over and over again as they made love, and for the moment he had believed her, totally.

Returning to his seat, holding his beer close to his chest to avoid spilling it, he knew it would be easy to say he always expected to end up alone in a crowded pub on a Sunday night; that every step he had taken was intended to bring him to this point in his life, when he must make decisions; that all that happened to him was part of a grand design. Even his experience in Hong Kong and the fact that he could still savor the guilt it induced, fitted.

†

That he would get no pleasure from what was about to happen was important, Andrew decided, as he walked with Tim through Kowloon. He continued to explain to his cousin why he disliked Australia. "It's impossible to find a church that's open when you want it. It's rather like their drinking hours. Religion is crammed into a few hours each day. A funny place."

He looked at Tim and wondered why he couldn't be like him, relaxed and happy, instead of loathing what he had agreed to do.

His father had paid for the trip, a gift for leaving school with four A-levels and seven O-levels, good enough to get into any university. Several immediately offered him a place. He accepted an offer from the army to pay for his university education, in return for a promise then to go on to Sandhurst for a short-service commission. Before entering the university he would travel, spending six months in Australia and the Far East. Family connections and contacts had been mobilized to provide a series of havens in Sydney and Perth, where his father had business friends; in Samoa, a cousin was in banking; in Manila, an uncle was a lawyer; in Hong Kong, Tim was a ship-broker.

Andrew had thought Tim a model of rectitude until he suggested a visit to Madame Kwok's. After dinner, Tim's chauffeur had driven them to the Golden Ferry Terminal and they crossed the well-protected harbor to Kowloon. The entrance to Madame Kwok's was brightly painted and festooned with bamboo-framed photographs of the occupants. Andrew counted a dozen ladies of indeterminate age and nationality, united in a common nakedness and tawdriness. Tim led the way down a staircase. At the bottom was a door painted orange with a spy-hole in the center. Tim knocked and an old woman opened the door. She had scars above her eyebrows and chin and a squint in one eye. The air was redolent with the aroma of joss sticks. Madame Kwok pointed to Andrew. "He first time. Pay membership." Tim pulled out his wallet and counted out Hong Kong dollar bills. Madame Kwok recounted them before slipping the money into her kimono. She motioned them to a couch, addressing Tim again. "He must buy drink. All new member buy drink." Tim handed over more money. They sat down and Madame Kwok shuffled to the bar returning with two open bottles of beer and glasses. She poured the drinks, continuing to address only Tim. The house had a new attraction, Korean and barely out of school. Would Tim like her? He wanted his usual girl, Susie. He indicated Andrew, lapsing into the crone's pidgin language: "New girl for him." He handed over more money.

Madame Kwok carefully counted and looked at Tim sharply. "New girl cost muchee more. New girl always cost muchee more, Tim-san." Her tone was reproachful, as if Tim should not need to be told. "Ten dollar more."

It was like buying cattle, thought Andrew, watching as Tim gave her a further bill and Madame Kwok shambled from the room. His beer tasted warm and flat. There was the sound of giggling in the corridor. It stirred a memory of Father Patrick warning him about the perils of travel: alcohol and loose women. He wondered if he could leave now without offending Tim. Madame Kwok returned with two girls and Tim approached the taller, older one of the pair. The second girl, wearing a blouse and skirt, stood smiling, eyes averted, beside Madame Kwok. "Girls like drink," pronounced the old woman. Tim ignored her. "You like drink now — or later, Susie?" Susie smiled. Andrew noticed her teeth were as white as her linen suit, cut Western-style, like her hair, falling black and shiny to her shoulders.

"Whatever Tim-san likes."

"Tim-san likes drinkee later." He grinned at Andrew and took Susie's hand.

Madame Kwok pushed the other girl toward Andrew. "This Miki. Very fine girl."

Miki stood before Andrew, so close that he could smell the fragrance of her perfume.

"Do you speak English?"

She giggled.

"Koreans all speak English," interrupted Susie. "Americans teach them all fuckee-fuckee words."

Tim laughed. "Not as many as I taught you, Susie." He slid his hand inside her blouse.

"You teach good fuckee words." Susie laid her head against his shoulder, allowing one hand to brush across the front of his trousers.

Andrew was shocked at the display. He looked at Miki and asked how old she was.

"For Christ's sake, Andrew, you're only going to screw her, not marry her!"

Susie guided Tim out of the room, whispering in his ear.

Andrew turned and faced Miki. "You like a drink?"

"You like me drink?" She giggled and sat beside him, placing a hand on his thigh. "Or maybe you like make love first?"

Suddenly he wanted it over with. He wanted to end this business, not because of a physical need — he felt even less excited than he did when staring at the photographs in his room at school. He was appalled he had allowed himself to come this far. Miki rose to her feet, holding his hand. He felt powerless to resist. The room was at the end of the corridor. Miki closed the door behind them and gently pushed him onto the bed. She poured water from a pitcher into a bowl and washed her hands. Smiling at Andrew, she started to undress, unbuttoning and removing her blouse to reveal her small firm breasts, her eyes fixed on him. Andrew looked away as she wiggled out of the skirt and stood before him naked, smiling and waiting. He struggled to his feet and plunged past the girl into the corridor. Madame Kwok was standing there. Behind her were two men, watchful, muscled, arms swinging loosely. Miki was standing at the bedroom door, naked, finger in her mouth, looking more vulnerable and childlike than ever. Andrew fished in his pocket, handed Madame Kwok a wad of dollars, pulled open the door, and ran up the stairs.

†

The barman moved among the tables collecting empties. There was an air of stifled anger about him, as if what he did was beneath him, that he was really cut out for a greater role in life. A new wave of memories rolled in. The barman's attitude reminded Andrew of Rose: she often displayed a similar hostility toward people.

†

At nineteen he was older than most of the entering students and his public school had given him an assurance and poise that six months in the Far East had enhanced. Socially and intellectually, he felt at least level with everybody on the campus. He saw himself as more mature, and listening to those first student conversations, he was certain he was more widely traveled. Within his first weeks, he made a sizable circle of friends, and one evening Rose drifted into his group. He had been recounting his experience at Madame Kwok's, giving it a veneer it never possessed, presenting his visit to the brothel as a slice of living social history, with himself cast in the role of sociologist. Rose sat transfixed. Finally, she asked him if he had not been frightened. He didn't understand and she explained.

"You know, frightened of catching something?" Her flat Midland vowels gave the words an aggressive edge. He smiled and shook his head. Afterward, they strolled back to the halls of residence and discovered they lived in the same building; her room was on the floor below his.

It took three more days before she invited him to her room. She asked him to tell her what really happened at Madame Kwok's and when he did, she looked at him with a triumphant little smile. She reached for him and pulled him to her. After kissing for a while, she began taking off her clothes.

They regularly made love for a whole year, sometimes in his room, more often in hers. But when they were not in bed, she seemed bored with him. Gradually, he became aware that she was seeing other men. At first, he said nothing, but finally the knowledge became too great to bear and he confronted her. She admitted she had slept with several other students during the time they had been together. The admission upset him, and she said he was being naive and that part of the fun of being at university was to be sexually adventurous and she had no intention of keeping herself exclusively for him. He began to imagine her wrapping herself around the bodies of other men, and what troubled him most was that he actually began to enjoy the fantasies. But the relationship with Rose faded; later he recognized it had naturally run its course.

†

Now, after all this time, he could barely recall what she looked like. Nor could he remember with any real clarity the girls he bedded after her. They were just names in his address book. Jane had effectively blotted them out.

†

He had been returning from delivering an essay to his tutor when he saw her for the first time, standing by the notice-board outside the cafeteria. It was festooned with items for sale, rent or exchange: mopeds, cars, apartments, skis, books; the endless trade of campus life. She said she was looking for a bicycle. He carefully scanned the board. There was none offered. He introduced himself, saying he had a car and would be happy to drive her anywhere. She had looked at him and laughed. He noticed she had perfect teeth and a dimple in her left cheek. Her eyes were the darkest of blue, almost black, in vivid contrast to her fair eyebrows and hair. He asked her name. She looked at him, hesitating. "Jane." She gave the board another look.

"How about going for a coffee?"

She shook her head. "Sorry. I never touch coffee or tea." She started to walk away.

He called out, "How about beer?"

She turned, looking at him. "Beer's fine."

"How about tonight?"

"Sure, pick me up at seven."

She gave him her address.

One of the first things Jane had said was that she could not stand people who weren't able to hold their drink. She surprised him that first night by the amount she consumed, matching him pint for pint, and insisting on paying her share. After driving her home, he parked outside her flat. She turned to him.

"Andrew, I think we should both understand something."

He tried to sound nonchalant. "You're married. Your husband's a millionaire indulging a whim to put you through university. If you flunk he'll buy the place for you. The story of my life — filled with beautiful women having rich husbands."

"Be serious."

"I am, believe me, I am. You've got that married look all over you." He was determined to be flippant.

"Please, listen. If what I think is going to happen, does happen, I want you to understand certain things."

"Like what?"

"Like not prolonging something beyond its natural span."

"That sounds a trifle premeditated."

"Maybe. But it's better to be honest. I'd like to go to bed with you. I suspect you'd like to go to bed with me. But if it doesn't work for me, I don't want to go on. Sex is very important to me. I enjoy it. That's the way I am. If I'm not satisfied I don't want you to feel bad, just accept that my needs are different. It's the way I am."

†

He felt the tears sting his eyes. It was the way she was, and probably still is.

248

✝

From the beginning, their sex life had been harmonious. She led him from the car to her apartment and directly to the bedroom, closing the curtains and lighting candles. Then she went to the bathroom, telling him to undress. He sat naked on the double bed, wondering which side she slept on and tried not to think who had previously occupied the other side. She stood in the doorway, her body even darker in the candlelight. She walked across to him, bent over and asked him to kiss her breasts. Then she gently guided his head down to her stomach, all the time softly telling him what she felt. She placed his head between her legs and groaned that this was what she enjoyed most of all. Afterward, she lent him one of her collection of Henry Miller books, and he saw she had underscored the descriptions of cunnilingus. Night after night, they expended their passions on her bed.

Six weeks to the day after they met, Andrew vacated his room on the campus and moved in with Jane. It took several car journeys to bring all his books and sports gear. The flat was overflowing, but she didn't mind. A month later, he came back from a tutorial to find her in the throes of packing. She paused long enough to tell him they were moving to a new apartment. She had spotted it on the notice-board only that lunch hour and rushed off to take over the lease from the departing students.

"It's perfect," insisted Jane. "Twice the size of this place. And, guess what?"

"Surprise me again."

"They're throwing in a bike."

The new apartment covered the entire ground floor of what had been a Victorian merchant's mansion. The red-brick building still had its original entrance pillars and massive front door. It took them a week to clean the place and six months to give it the stamp of their own personalities, each week adding an item bought at an auction or junk shop: a table for Andrew's side of the bed, on which he kept his radio, given to him by his mother one Christmas. They argued over the Edwardian chair. He thought it too expensive, she insisted it was a bargain and outbid several other students. Afterward, she smiled with satisfaction when the auctioneer's clerk told her she would have paid three times as much for the same chair in a store. They were, they discovered, in a working-class neighborhood of narrow streets, back-to-back housing, small factories, fruit and vegetable markets, warehouses, and cafés. It was a tightly packed community of friendly neighbors and obliging tradespeople, full of advice about the cheapest place to get curtains cleaned, who would come and shampoo the bedroom carpet. They worked late into the night and on weekends, refurbishing the apartment, and it took on a sparkle that pleased them both. They divided the household chores equally, shopping, cooking and washing up together; he vacuumed the floors while she made the bed and cleaned the windows once a week. Each had a good eye for a bargain and they rarely argued over an acquisition. He had registered his objection to the painting of the Forth Bridge hanging over the bed, but she insisted it had character, winning the day, just as she refused his suggestion they make a leg for the bed to replace the pile of textbooks that propped it up.

She had looked at him and assumed a quoting tone. "To screw on a bed of learning is to make intelligent use of pleasure and time."

He asked who had said that.

She teased. "Guess? How about Henry Miller?"

He looked at her suspiciously. "It sounds more like Norman Mailer."

She burst out laughing and said she made up the quotation on the spur of the moment. He chased her around the bedroom, caught her, and threw her on the bed, and they made love.

The bedroom was the focal point of their lives in the apartment. Not only did they consummate their relationship every day in its bed, but they frequently ate there, propping pillows against the wall, with plates of buttered toast and mugs of warm milk. On Sundays, after reading *The Observer*, they studied in bed, scattering their books on its surface. After a few weeks she found a pair of square Indian brass trays which became ideal writing tables while in bed.

At first he secretly counted the weeks they were together, then the months. After a year, he finally stopped, believing it would go on forever. Their families knew of their liaison, and if they did not openly approve of their living arrangements, neither did they raise any objections. They went on a holiday together, to France and Italy, returning to the apartment, ready for a new term, displaying mementos from their vacation: posters, seashells, and figurines for the mantel and alcove shelves. Every day, he thought, the place took on a deeper feeling of permanence.

The letter changed everything. It came in an envelope officially franked with a Whitehall postmark. It was waiting when he returned from a tutorial on the meaning of integrity in history. He had argued his points well, about the unreality of Macaulay's romanticized attitude toward integrity and the way Communism bends it to create a visible and disciplined front. She had handed him the envelope as soon as he walked in. Then, without a word, she turned and went to the bedroom, closing the door behind her. He read the letter quickly, then more slowly. There was no doubt. At the end of this term, his last, the army wanted him to report to Sandhurst.

†

Andrew saw the barman look up, irritated, staring at the snuggery door. The cadets had returned, one of them calling loudly. "Cigarettes, old boy. Out of cigarettes." They propped themselves against the bar, plonking coins on the counter.

The barman said he was closed.

"That's all right, old boy. We won't tell anybody." The cadet's voice was slurred.

"Sorry. It's after hours."

The tallest of the cadets leaned across the bar, his voice aggressive. "Barman, we've asked for cigarettes. There's no law against selling cigarettes outside licensing hours. Now make up your mind. Sell them to us, or send for your boss. Don't just stand there, do something. Move, man! Move."

Andrew was on his feet and walking to the bar. He tapped the tall cadet on the shoulder. "Stop throwing your weight around, soldier."

The cadet turned and stared at him. "Who asked you to butt in, old chap?"

Andrew looked at him carefully. "I'm not your 'old chap.' And nobody asked me to butt in. But just stop throwing your weight around. All right?"

Another cadet spoke. "You can't talk to officers and gentlemen —"

"Then behave like officers and gentlemen." Andrew turned to the barman. "Can they have cigarettes?"

"Sure. They've only got to be polite."

Andrew addressed the tall cadet. "I believe that's clear." Then he turned and walked back to his seat, remembering.

†

The night before he left the university, they had gone out and gotten slightly drunk and he was filled with a gnawing despair that he tried to hide. That night in bed he asked her to marry him. She looked at him thoughtfully and replied, in the gentlest of voices, that she didn't want to marry anyone just yet. He pushed, saying he would wait until she finished her studies; they could marry then. She had said nothing. He again pushed.

Could he hope that she would let him propose to her when she felt ready? She laughed and said he sounded positively Victorian. He would not let go, saying he really meant it. She switched on her bedside light and sat up in bed, hugging her knees.

"Andy, you're going to be away for quite a while. I'm still young. I said at the beginning I didn't want there to be any misunderstanding. I need a man around me. I just wish it could go on being you."

He asked, the words burning in his throat:

"What are you saying?"

She patted his face. "Only not to be so pushy. Let's just wait and see."

Next morning he left at dawn. The memory of their parting depressed him. Jane had been cool and almost distant. He had offered to call her as soon as he arrived at Sandhurst and she said he could try but she might not be in. He'd finally reached her at midnight and she said she had just come in from visiting friends and was too tired to talk.

When he got home, even before he broke the news to his parents that he was resigning his army commission and leaving Sandhurst, his mother asked him about Jane. He told her she had gone to Latin America, back-packing for the summer.

He then said he was leaving the army.

"You're doing what?" His father seemed unable to believe it.

"I'm getting out. I can't stand all the pointless rigmarole."

In the end it was his mother who broke the stunned silence. "But, my dear, what will you do?"

His father interrupted. "None of our family have ever bought them-selves out of anywhere."

"I'm sorry, Dad. I guess there has always to be a first."

"Sorry! It's not a damned matter of being sorry, you know! The army's paid for your degree. Surely you owe it something?"

"Lots of students change their minds. The army accepts it's a high-risk business, investing in education."

"Oh, really?" His father poured himself another double gin. Fortified, he returned to the issue. "You just can't resign after three weeks. Good God, people have been shot for less in war."

"A long time ago, dear." His mother tried to be placatory. "Nobody's going to shoot Andrew because he wants to give up the army."

His father searched for a culprit. "It's Jane, isn't it? She's behind this?"

"No, Dad. She's not. She doesn't even know."

"Jane's in Mexico, dear," said his mother.

"Mexico? Good God, whatever for?"

Andrew didn't know.

Before leaving, she had sent him a short note with her itinerary. Beside each date were a hotel address and a telephone number. At the bottom of the note she had scrawled. "Call me if you like."

He called her twice, in Mexico City and Panama City, person-to-person, and each time the flat voice of the operator said she was not available. On the third occasion, he had spoken to the hotel receptionist in Caracas, who had promised to leave a message to say he telephoned.

"I suppose you're going to join her?" His father poured a third drink.

"No. When I leave the army, I'm going to do some voluntary work."

"Voluntary work? Good God, what on earth have you in mind?" His father stared at him in disbelief.

"Well, something in the Third World. Working with the poor. I'm sure Father Patrick will know of something."

There was another lengthy silence. "I'm not against charity. Far from it. But do you think it is the best use of your years at university to bury yourself in some desert or jungle? Do you really?"

"Albert Schweitzer did, dear."

"Andrew is not Schweitzer. I think even he will accept that."

"It won't be forever, Dad. Lots of young men do it."

His mother made her final point. "Only the other day, the Pope said more are needed to help." She looked at Andrew. "I think that's a very selfless idea, giving yourself to the service of Christ."

✝

Andrew watched the cadets leave. The barman walked over to the table. "Snotty bastards."

"It's the system. It makes them like that."

The barman shrugged. "Time the system was changed."

"Yes."

"I hated the army. Two years on the Rhine. Best thing was the beer." He looked at the watch. "Like another pint?"

"Thanks."

The barman walked back to the bar and began to draw Andrew's beer.

Later, after he had spoken to his mother, who then sent for Father Patrick, who in turn had listened carefully before arranging for him to see the

Bishop, who asked searching questions before coming to a decision — later Andrew would understand what happened to him as he watched the barman.

But, for the moment, all he felt was something so unusual that he asked the barman for something on which he could write. The man brought him an old menu with his beer. On the back of the menu Andrew scribbled rapidly.

10.40 p.m. Sunday. A thumping feeling in my chest. My heart beating furiously. In my head a sudden refrain. God wants me. God wants me to become a priest. I've found Him. He wants me to become a priest. Very strong feeling. Very positive. Very clear. I've been called.

Clutching the menu, he rose to his feet and hurried from the snuggery, ignoring the barman calling him back to drink his beer.

CHAPTER 12

†

Discoveries

T he rectory Father Patrick shared with a curate stood on the church grounds. The widowed middle-aged housekeeper who lived in a self-contained flat at the back opened the front door to Andrew and his mother. He was struck again by the faint but unmistakable aroma of burned incense and candle wax. For the past six weeks the cloying odor had greeted him as he arrived to answer questions, fill in forms, bring character references, and once to collect a sealed letter to take with him to the Bishop's palace. The room was filled with overstuffed furniture: a settee and three armchairs, their covers green and faded like the curtains. There was a large glass-faced bookcase, its shelves filled with titles like *The Religious Experience, The Individual and His Religion,* and *The Two Sources of Morality and Religion.* On a sideboard were copies of *The Journal for the Scientific Study of Religion, The Universe,* and *The Tablet.* On a coffee table a tray was set with cups, sugarbowl, and a creamer. There were two standard lamps, their shades matching the lime-colored carpet and wallpaper. In a corner was a rolltop desk, closed.

Andrew wore a sweatshirt, jeans, and jogging shoes. He had, in all honesty, never expected that the process of deciding if he was suitable to become a priest would be so thorough. *It's worse than positive vetting in Whitehall,* his father said after the interviews had gone on for a month. *Barmy, if you ask me. All this checking up just to wear a dog collar for the rest of your life. What do they want a character reference for? What good's that? Nobody's going to write a bad reference, even your Bishop should know that!*

†

The Bishop hemmed and hawed, cleared his throat and peered over his glasses, hesitant and distant.

"You had this . . . feeling? Something had . . . happened to you? This feeling of wanting to become a priest? You are certain that is what you felt? You can't be certain, can you? But we . . . we have to be. Can you tell me again, exactly . . . what you think you felt? Perhaps, your surroundings might have played a part? Tell me exactly . . . what were you doing and thinking when you had this . . . this feeling?"

He leaned back in his chair and carefully inspected Andrew. Over the credenza along one wall hung a life-size color photograph of the Bishop greeting the Pope. Behind the desk, in a massive carved gilt frame, was a painting of Our Lady, signed by the artist. The questions about what happened in the pub had been pressed.

"Why did you write it down? Is that what you normally do . . . write things down? Do you . . . perhaps fear that you cannot remember exactly? How can you be certain that what you wrote down is what you felt? Have you ever had a similar experience?"

The Bishop's stubby fingers stuffed flakes of tobacco into his pipe. Father Patrick had warned that the smoke from the pipe was a sign of his feelings. When it rose steadily, His Grace was prepared to accept something. When it escaped in rapid bursts, he was not. He drew the flame into the bowl, sucking noisily, and the smoke rose in an uncertain spiral, wreathing his cropped gray hair.

"Tell me once more . . . everything. What you were doing and thinking about when you had this . . . what do you call it — ?"

Andrew answered. "I suppose some kind of supernatural experience. I don't really know what to call it."

The smoke from the Bishop's pipe spread, filling the air between them with a pungent smell.

"Perhaps not supernatural. No . . . certainly not that. That would never do. But . . . interesting. Take me over it again, step by step."

Andrew did.

A week later came another summons to the Bishop's palace. This time he was shown into a small room, bare of furnishings except for two armchairs, a strip of carpet between them, and a photograph of the Pope on the wall.

The monsignor was middle-aged, bespectacled, and portly. He explained he was also a medical psychologist. His eyes were bloodshot and he needed a haircut — overworked, Andrew supposed. He invited Andrew to sit down. He mustn't look upon this as an interview but merely an informal chat; just another step in the process of deciding his suitability for the priesthood. His voice was soft and devoid of any pressure, as he began where the Bishop ended.

"Now, Andrew, let me tell you that I'm not unconnected with the sort of experience you describe. Quite the opposite. But my problem is to try and make linkage. To put what you say happened into the framework of a vocation. So let's go right back to the beginning."

He had listened, attentively, without interruption, while Andrew once more described the incident. Then came the first questions.

"Do you think you could be striving too hard. Andrew, to connect what happened with a wish to be a priest? It's quite common, you know. And there's nothing wrong, as such, with it. Everybody has to have a motive, don't you agree? All I'm wondering, and really it isn't any more than that, is whether you've placed what happened into a rather dramatic framework. It happens to lots of people. They undergo something and say that it is responsible for something else. But the linkage isn't always there. That's the problem."

Andrew watched the monsignor clasp his hands, as if to restrain himself from saying any more. He answered as emphatically as he could.

"It really did happen the way I said. Although I know that the mind can play all sorts of tricks."

The monsignor nodded. "Quite right, Andrew. But you don't seem to have left anything out." He was smiling and reassuring. "I have seen your medical history. Nothing to worry us there. You're fit as a fiddle."

Andrew sensed he had come through another test, yet the monsignor continued to watch him carefully. Andrew met his gaze. Nevertheless, the monsignor's next words surprised him.

"I see history is your subject. I must say, your thesis on the correlation between faith and historical truth is intriguing."

Father Patrick had asked to read it, but had not even hinted he had passed it to the monsignor, who began to ask probing questions about Andrew's views on Nietzsche's contrasting of the Apollonian kind of religious belief with the Dionysian ecstasy and excitement. He wondered whether

Andrew could see that very often a specific religious experience could be based upon mental conflict and a feeling of inadequacy.

"It's a bit like falling in love. Remember how Faust, before he meets Gretchen, and Romeo, before he encounters Juliet, are both filled with discontent? Love for them is not a crisis but the way out of a crisis, caused by discontent."

He did not argue a case but simply stated what he knew. Andrew sensed that beneath his gentleness was a toughness, which could be unbending and uncompromising. In another time, he could have been a warlock initiating a neophyte into a secret rite. His questions, often oblique on the surface, had a pattern. Each one was carefully placed in counterpoint to a previous one, the overall method designed to verify Andrew's responses and motivation.

"There is respectable evidence, Andrew, that sudden religious experiences often happen at a time when a person's personal life is disturbed. They frequently occur after a bereavement or when a relationship breaks down. We don't exactly know what causes this phenomenon, but it is definitely associated with an upset in the normal living pattern."

He paused to give Andrew time to consider.

"I don't really think that applies to me. I've never felt a need to use religion as a substitute."

The monsignor raised the question of religious experiences emerging from intellectual reasons.

"It's really far more common than most people believe. You'd be surprised how many rationalists suddenly have what you could call a blinding flash. Something hits them and they say it's God. Many people have sat where you are now and insisted they have undergone a religious experience and want to throw out the window all their previous intellectualism. It's very dramatic. They believe something special has happened to them. It may well have, but it is not the basis for entering the priesthood."

He peered at Andrew and asked if he thought it possible to classify his religious experience in the snuggery in a similar way.

Andrew said he did not think so, remembering how Jane had introduced him to the writings of Wilhelm Reich. He paraphrased Reich to the monsignor, saying he was certain his experience had nothing to do with trying to find a creative solution to his life.

The priest-doctor asked Andrew to accept there are only two ways in which it is possible to eliminate anger, fear, despair, and other undesirable feelings.

"One is to oppose them with an even more powerful opposite affection, an example being turning the other cheek. The other is to give up the struggle, so that you don't care anymore. That part of the brain which deals with emotions goes on strike, creating a feeling of apathy."

He paused, measuring his words, his eyes never leaving Andrew's face. "There is ample proof that when this kind of exhaustion takes place, happily often only temporary, people undergo a sudden religious experience."

Andrew quietly rejected that possibility.

The monsignor probed into his relationship with his family, his life at school and the university, and gradually focused on his affair with Jane. Saint Augustine, he murmured, prior to entering the priesthood, had been pressed by his mother to give up his mistress. Had Andrew's parents opposed his relationship with Jane?

Andrew had answered unhesitatingly. "No, not at all. They were very good about it."

The questions resumed, elegantly and leisurely prefaced, with a reminder that Pascal was hopelessly in love with a woman until, said R. H. Thouless, he was drawn to the celibate life by what is now seen as a highly emotional conversion. Saint Catherine of Genoa and Madame Guyon had both been insecure in their relationships with men before they claimed mystical experiences had led them to the Church.

"Man's extremity, you could say, is God's opportunity. The question is: do you think your experience is in any way a response to Jane?"

Andrew finally admitted to the physical emphasis she had set on their relationship.

The monsignor silently considered this before asking if Andrew now felt a sense of guilt about his sex life with Jane.

Andrew smiled. "Jane gave me Horney to read, so I know how to answer that one."

Dr. Karen Horney demonstrated that the greatest number of sudden religious experiences occur between the ages of twelve and twenty-five, a span when the stress of adolescence is at its peak.

"Do you think you could be one of her statistics?"

Andrew replied that, truthfully, he did not know.

"What exactly does that mean?"

"Well, I still love her. But it's different now. I don't feel possessive anymore. I know she is part of something that has gone."

"How can you be so sure?"

"I see her from a different perspective. I've thought about it. I've probably thought of nothing else. But I still have this overwhelming conviction that I have a vocation."

The monsignor pondered.

"You really mean that? In my experience, there's always an element of the repenting sinner about so many of those who have a sudden religious experience. The attitude that they're going to give up something for God. It's very human. The danger is that they actually want everybody else to give up what they're giving up. Are you familiar with the story of Saint Bernard?"

Andrew shook his head and the priest explained that the fervor of the saint's religiosity had been so overpowering that when he preached, mothers had hidden their sons and wives their husbands, in case they were lured away into newfound celibacy.

"He broke up so many homes that the abandoned women formed themselves into a sort of nunnery." He smiled. "I'm not suggesting you're another Saint Bernard or that Jane will go into a convent. All I'm trying to explore is your emotional responses. It's a difficult life being a priest, probably more so today than ever before. And it's expensive to train someone and then lose them afterward. We try to be certain, as far as possible, from the outset."

The monsignor probed him about his attitude toward guilt, anxiety, and suggestibility and what created emotional turmoil in him. Andrew explained about his visit to Madame Kwok's and the sadness he felt that his father did not embrace the Catholic Church.

The priest spoke about Horace Walpole's detachment from religion, before returning to the central theme of the discussion, this time musing whether Arthur Koestler, daily awaiting death in a Spanish prison during the Civil War, was right to believe that he underwent a religious experience.

"And what do you make of Tolstoy's experience? His call to God being preceded by suicidal impulses and other trauma. How do you see that?"

Andrew responded by saying he had no reason to doubt the validity of Koestler's claims and that while Tolstoy's conversion to Christianity was highly unorthodox, nevertheless it had been strong enough to allow him to embrace the life of Russian peasants as a lasting cause.

The monsignor put a final question: "If you are accepted, are you prepared also to accept that old ties, where they exist, must be severed? That, in effect, you must pass a sentence of death upon everything which is of this life? Can you do that?"

Andrew had replied: "I can't be certain. That would be arrogant. But I will try with all my power because I really feel God has asked me to serve Him."

A few days later, he was summoned again to see Father Patrick. The questions were direct. What did God mean to him? How did he see the Christian humanism of the Holy Father? Did he agree that the celestial manifestations of faith were evidence of a growing presence of God in the world? What did he say to the argument that respecting truth meant respecting and fearing God. Did he accept that infallibility was a truth of last resort, the ultimate deterrent to error? Could he recognize that conception, birth, marriage, procreation, and death were all contingent upon one another, impossible to isolate, and that to deny the sacred quality of one would mean the same for all? What role did he think the Church had to play in political commitment? How did he see the real perspective of Jesus' mission, and how would he interpret it?

Andrew had discussed the questions from the standpoint that this was the age of perplexity, that many religions and theologies offered different ways to escape from the real necessity of thinking about the meaning of life and how it should be lived. The Pope's humanism was uncompromising; his affirmation of Mariology was a restatement of a fundamental truth of the Church; infallibility was in danger of being excluded by the manipulation of faith; birth, marriage, procreation, and death were given a vicarious glamour, which in itself was symbolic of the untidiness of living. The message of Jesus was as true as ever: Baal was alive and well and the Church must use every means, political and spiritual, to combat these influences.

He had concluded: "The mission of Jesus is to end the dilemma of all those who do not know how to live. By the time we think we do, we are well on the way to the grave. The words of Jesus are not interpretation of 'a truth.' They are *the* truth. They are not to be thrown away when we think we have achieved some goal. They are our goal. We should try and live by them, just as Jesus lived by His words."

Father Patrick had stared, silently and fixedly, at Andrew for a long, long moment. At last he had spoken, his voice devoid of any theatrics.

"My boy, this is quite remarkable. Please go home and write it down for me."

✝

There were further sessions, more intricate questions, and now this meeting. Andrew's mother turned toward the door as Father Patrick walked in, holding a coffeepot.

"Make yourselves comfortable. We've lots to talk about."

Carefully putting down the pot, he went to the desk and raised its roll-top. It was stuffed with papers. The old priest started to riffle through them, calling over his shoulder:

"Be patient! Drink your coffee! I have news."

He finally turned, two pieces of paper in his hand, waving them dramatically at Andrew and his mother.

"My Lord Bishop has written. And His Eminence."

He pulled down the rolltop and walked stiff-legged from the desk, reading to himself. He stopped before the couch and tapped the letters almost with reverence.

The Bishop and the Cardinal had written to say that Andrew had secured a place at the Gregorian University in Rome, one of the most prestigious in the Catholic world.

"Is it settled, then?" His mother wanted to be quite certain. "Nothing can go wrong?"

"Nothing at all, from this end."

"There'll be no problems." She spoke quietly. "My husband, deep down, is quite pleased that Andrew has finally made up his mind on a career."

"I'm glad." The priest smiled at her, his eyes fixed on Andrew, watching his every reaction. Then: "I still have a few questions of my own."

Some invisible fist buried itself in Andrew's stomach; the unexpected always produced this feeling.

"Yes, Father."

Father Patrick scanned one of the letters.

"My Lord Bishop is still concerned about the validity of your experience in the bar, my boy. His Grace feels, and I must agree with him, that no one who is totally honest with himself can ever pinpoint the exact moment he experiences the call to God. No one is given a vocation in a moment. I think you should see what happened as the final extension of a growing awareness of what you want to do."

Andrew's mother interjected: "I think Father's right, dear."

"Maybe, but that was the moment I really felt I needed to serve Him." Andrew plunged on. "I'm quite sure that what I felt I wrote down. It was a very clear feeling. God called me."

Father Patrick raised a hand dramatically.

"But, my boy, you've clearly been thinking of this all your life. It isn't something sudden. It's been there all the time." His eyes stared unblinkingly. "Creation in a sense is vocation's first moment. God leads us into the world. He chooses our path in life. If you see it like this, what happened in the bar can take on a proper perspective."

"I understand what you're saying, but I can't find a logical way to fit it into my experience."

Father Patrick's voice quickened. "I don't think it serves any useful purpose to say your whole life from now on is going to be based on some blinding revelation in a pub."

"Why not, Father? It's what I think did happen."

The priest sighed. "In recommending you, His Grace, and I suspect His Eminence would concur, would like to think that there is a more solid foundation to your vocation. It's always better to know, my boy, that God's been there from the outset, steadily nudging you along. That's the way the Church likes to see its priests. Just because Saul was transformed into Paul does not mean we all need such psychodrama. I'm sure you can see that."

Following him into the study, Andrew was reminded how the furnishings complemented his father: they had the same solid, dependable look, built for comfort rather than elegance. There were two leather armchairs before the large partner's desk and a high-back swivel chair behind it, its headrest shiny from years of constant rubbing. The drapes on the French doors were dark brown velvet. His father drew them, shutting out the night, moving laboriously, a tall, heavy man, even bulkier in his fisherman's knit sweater and baggy slacks. He lumbered over the dark pile of the carpet in slippers, stooped by age, yet still tall enough to be able, when he wanted, to reach books on the top shelves of his library.

On either side of the French doors the wall was covered with the memorabilia of his father's life. There was a faded print of him as a child in the arms of his nanny. Beside this was a group photograph of his school's cricket first eleven of 1936; his father, unmistakable in the front row, staring solemnly into the camera, bat between his knees. He had been a fine player and Andrew had acquired his skill. There was a formal portrait of him, dressed in mortarboard and gown. Above was a picture taken when he was commissioned into his regiment, stiffly erect, a swagger stick under his arm, captain's pips on his epaulettes. He had commanded an artillery unit in North Africa, Italy, and across the Rhine, collecting a Military Cross and bar for valor under fire in 1944.

Fixed to the wall among the photographs were trophies: stuffed pike and perch in display cases, and a shotgun, its hammer long removed. Beneath was a framed inscription: *1937: Bagged 280 pairs of grouse and 127 pairs of pheasant.*

His father stood beside a table crammed with bottles of vintage whiskeys, wines, and liqueurs.

"What'll it be?"

Andrew asked for port.

"Pack a bottle or two to take with you. You can't buy this stuff in Rome."

"Thanks, Dad."

His father poured the drinks, handed one to Andrew, and motioned for him to sit down opposite him. He began:

"Long ago I learned that attempts to change the opinions of others are older than recorded history, going back, I suppose, to the development of speech. Well, I'm not going to make a speech."

"Dad, I know it isn't easy for you."

"It isn't." He sipped his gin. "It isn't and it hasn't been. I still think this is a fad."

"Dad! I don't think it's going to be —"

"No, no. Let me finish. I said no speeches. But at least let me have no interruption. I thought at the beginning it was a fad. I still think so. Nothing you have said or done can convince me otherwise. I'm personally very sad about that. In a way I wish I could be convinced that you know what you are doing."

"I do, Dad. I really do!"

"You think you do. That's the problem. That's what's so especially sad about you going off like this —"

"Dad —!"

"Please, Andrew. Let me finish. I've tried, but I can't really buy this idea about giving a son to God, this business that your mother and Father Patrick keep on about. That's their Irish Catholicism poking through . . ."

At the university he had gone with Jane to listen to an experimental psychologist lecture on attitude changes. There had been a lot of talk about unconscious mental mechanisms, responses to frustration, and reactions to adversity. He had thought then, as he did now, that neither Freud nor anyone else could have made headway with his father. He was as formed in his ways as the Arapesh tribesmen of New Guinea or the Zuñi in the pueblos of New Mexico. His life was centered on ceremony and tradition, prosperity and social acceptance. In any study of the typical Englishman, he would assuredly qualify for a place.

264

Andrew tried again. "Rome's not the end of the world, Dad."

"It's the end of my world, Andrew." His father pointed vaguely toward the desk and high-back chair. "I always had in mind these would be yours one day. It would have made me very proud to see you come into the business." He shifted in his chair, silent and brooding. "To marry and have a family."

"Dad, I know it's hard to see, but God has a definite plan for each one of us. He wanted you to become a broker . . ."

"I do wish you'd try not to sound like Father Patrick! This whole idea of some divine planning authority is just too Catholic for me. It really is. I'm afraid I can't take on board the idea of God being up there with a list, ticking off what He wants you all to be. Really, Andrew that's a bit much. It's the sort of guff Father Patrick falls back on when he's got nothing new to say on Sundays."

Andrew had once discussed with Jane his father's religious attitude. She had offered one of her immediate judgments. *His prejudices go with his authoritarianism. The older he gets the more prejudiced he'll become.*

In a way, he thought it was true. His father saw issues in terms of black or white. Catholicism was very much in the black. Andrew sat staring at his glass, thinking: *He's hurting. I'm hurting him. But I can't turn back, not now.*

"Dad, nobody's talked me into this. Quite the opposite. They checked me out very carefully."

"I'm sure. It can't be every day they get a priest from a mixed marriage. I bet someone was a little worried that you could still have a touch of good old Protestant England in your genes."

Andrew knew he regarded the Reformation as sharing equal importance with the French and Russian revolutions. A large part of his father saw his Protestant faith as a kind of armor against all sorts of external pressures. And, just as he abhorred Communism for its ideological effectiveness, so he suspected Catholicism for similar reasons. He believed both systems operated, for very different ends, with a curious similarity; both ruled through carefully structured hierarchies; each used confession to create a binding effect upon its people; there was an identical demand for regular attendance — one at Church, the other at party meetings.

"Don't try and tell me it's no different from doing another university course. The priesthood . . ." His voice trembled slightly. "Where do you expect to end? There's only one Pope and a handful of cardinals. Pretty limited chance of getting promoted from the ranks, if you follow my meaning. You'll probably begin and end as a foot soldier."

265

His father downed his drink and poured himself another. He indicated Andrew's glass. Andrew nodded and his father refilled it, smiling thinly.

"You'll get used to having drinks poured for you. Look at Father Patrick. Your mother has waited on him hand and foot for years. Can't think why, unless she hopes it will give her a pass to Heaven."

"Dad! Please don't go on like this. It really doesn't help, you know."

"It's purging. My version of your confession. You're off in a couple of days and I want you to know how I feel. You think I won't miss you? You think it's easy to accept that I'll never get to meet your wife or hold your children?" His voice was suddenly husky. "You think that's easy, Andrew? You'll never know the pain I feel now. You've chosen a life that excludes my hopes. But I can still feel. I'm sorry, but I do."

Andrew blinked back the wetness in his eyes.

"Have you told Jane?"

"Not yet. I missed her in Caracas. I've booked a call to her in Bogotá."

They continued to sit in silence.

"It wouldn't have worked, you know. You and her. She's much too independent. But she's going to miss you. We're all going to miss you."

"I'm only a couple of hours away by plane." Andrew tried to sound reassuring.

His father stared at him. It was a trick of his, not answering when he didn't want to, as if he had been suddenly struck dumb. Finally, he spoke.

"It's not the same, Andrew. Can't you see that? Going off to be a priest is not like joining the army or going abroad to work. It's supposed to be forever." He stared moodily at the trophies on the wall. "Do you really know what you're giving up? Not just a chance to make a real go of things in this world, but a lot more." He turned back and stared at Andrew.

"Listen, you're twenty-four. For the last three years you've been living with Jane. Your mother and I weren't exactly wild at the idea, but we said this is the age we live in. You've had a full relationship with Jane. How do you think you're going to cope with the rest of your life? Have you really thought of that? Wouldn't you think it is the sort of matter Father Patrick would talk to you about? Though I bet he didn't."

His father had never before discussed any aspect of sexuality with him.

"You're wrong, Dad. He spent a whole morning explaining that the call to Christ does not magically negate a person's sexuality. Father Patrick said that the temptation can be even greater than before the commitment."

"Without wishing to lower the level of this conversation, I think both of us are aware of the regularity with which priests fall by the wayside. But that's not the point. My point is that just because the Pope says you have to become celibate, you don't become a celibate."

"That's absolutely right. But it isn't the Pope who says I have to be celibate. It's my choice. That's the difference. I make the choice voluntarily. Because I want to."

Andrew paused, remembering Father Patrick explaining how insistent Pope John Paul is over the matter of sexuality and the priesthood. *He has no patience with the old teachings that the body is merely a housing for the soul. John Paul says the body has its own special importance and all its functions, especially those in the sexual area, are part of God's plan. For a priest that involves recognizing there can be no half measures on the issue. Celibacy is total. To fulfill his function, a priest must undertake sacrifice, complete and unconditional. Just as marriage is a gift of the spirit, demanding its own dedication and devotion, so celibacy demands a similar response. For those who accept it, it does not infringe on our humanity. It is a reminder that we are ready to follow Him. That is the eschatological reality. Have that clearly in your mind, my boy, and all else will fall into place.*

"Dad, the Church doesn't want supermen. It wants men to understand what the struggle is all about, yet have the strength to face and overcome it. Men who recognize why they must be free from personal commitment, and who see celibacy not as some sort of restriction but as a wider freedom."

His father remained still and expressionless. His hands gripped his glass tightly.

"You would make a fine lawyer, Andrew."

Andrew smiled. "But, Dad, I could still be a lawyer. The Church has trained lots of canon lawyers . . ."

His father looked weary and defeated.

"It won't be the same, Andrew. It won't be the same at all. We both know that."

A knock on the door ended another painful silence. Andrew's mother said his call to Bogotá was on the line. He strode rapidly from the room.

"Hello, Jane."

"Andy? How are you?"

"Fine. I tried to call you in Caracas. They said you'd left for the airport."

"The place was awful. Full of bugs and lecherous men."

The telephone was in an alcove in the hall, with a bench and ledge; beside it was a pad and pencil. Andrew jotted down: *J. had bad time getting to Bogotá.*

"I miss you, Jane."

"I'm okay."

He tried to translate the hesitation.

"Are you alone?"

"Of course, silly. In my room, lying on the bed. You dragged me from the shower."

He tried to imagine her, six thousand miles away, to put flesh to the voice. There was static on the line.

"Jane?"

"I can still hear you."

"Jane. I've got something to tell you."

There was silence.

"Jane, can you hear me?"

"Yes."

This time the hesitation was more definite.

"Jane, I'm going to be a priest."

The only sound was a faint crackle on the line.

"Is that why you called?" Her voice was cool.

"I wanted you to know."

"I already did. Giles dropped me a card a week ago."

Giles worked in the university administration office. He would have known after the Bishop's secretary wrote asking for information.

"I'm sorry I didn't write."

"That's all right, Andy. I suppose it has been very hectic for you, getting everything fixed up."

"Rather, yes."

"Yes, well. I must say it is a surprise."

"But you do understand?"

"Understand? That's a funny word. What is there to understand? I mean, you've made your decision. What more is there to say?"

"Will you come to Rome to see me?"

"To see you? I don't quite see that."

"Jane. I still love you. Don't you understand that? It's just, well . . ."

He closed his eyes.

"I'm sure you've thought things through very carefully, Andy, I'm sure you have."

The formality of her words hammered in his head.

"Jane . . .?"

"Yes?"

"I'm sorry."

"What for? About us? There's no need to be. Not at all. You'll be a terrific priest. You really will."

"I miss you, Jane."

"Please don't say that. Please don't." She laughed. "You're lucky in a
way, having settled your future. Giles wrote that more grads than ever
have no work."

"What about you?"

"Oh, I'll be okay. Remember, I'm a survivor. I'll manage."

"Come and see me in Rome. Please."

The silence stretched. He wrote: *Rome + 2.*

"I'm not sure. I don't think it would be a good idea. It could be very unsettling. Remember what Milton said?"

He remembered the night they had sat in bed and read Milton. *Of man's
first disobedience, and the fruit/Of that forbidden tree . . .*

"I still want you to come."

"We'll see, Andy. Listen. This must be costing your father a fortune.
Why don't you drop me a line when you've settled in? Tell me what a seminary is like."

"Will you write back?"

"Sure. I always answer letters. Have you forgotten?"

He had not. Every Sunday afternoon, without fail, she would answer all
her correspondence, writing to her mother and friends, long, detailed accounts of what she called her week's adventures, enclosing snippets from
newspapers and magazines that might amuse or interest them.

"Jane."

"Yes?"

"I love you."

"I'm glad, Andy. I really am glad for you. I know you won't believe this,
but when I got Giles's card I went into a church in Caracas and said a
prayer for you."

"Oh, Jane. I feel awful. I just wish . . ."

"Andy, I think we should hang up now. I really do."

"Jane . . ."

"Take care, Andy. I'll be thinking of you. I really will."

He heard the click of her receiver being replaced and felt the tears on his
cheeks.

*

The traffic was heavy as they left London, heading north on the motorway to Luton Airport.

Andrew sat in the back of the Bentley, watching his father grip the wheel tightly, easing the car past another truck, constantly checking the mirror, staying exactly at the speed limit. His mother was huddled in the passenger seat, a light autumn coat over her dress and a hat on her head. His father looked at him in the mirror.

"Will they let you out for Christmas?"

"I don't know, Dad."

"You make it sound as if Andrew's going into prison, dear. Father Patrick showed me pictures of the university. It's a lovely place." His mother's voice was brave.

After checking in, they strolled to the bar, his father once more drifting toward sharpness, complaining about the poor service. His mother sat in forlorn dignity. Andrew felt close to tears for them both. Each, in their own way, seemed lost. He was relieved when the flight was called. His mother clutched Andrew by the arm and looked suddenly broken.

"Andrew, you really can come home anytime. I'll keep your room for you. And write, won't you?"

"Of course, Mother." He bent down and kissed her on the cheek.

His father continued to stare woodenly at the line filing past passport control.

"Good-bye, Dad." Andrew thrust out a hand.

"Good-bye, Andrew." His father's grip was still strong for a man of his age.

"Here." From a breast pocket he produced a sealed envelope. "Read it on the plane."

Without another word, he took Andrew's mother by the arm and led her toward the exit.

My Dear Andrew,

The experiences of a long life have convinced me that nothing ever happens without a reason. Having said that, I must tell you frankly, that I can see no good reason for what you are doing. With pride and joy I watched you grow up, daring to hope, in my image. When I watched you develop, I thought you were the perfect answer to those who say that life is a pointless distintegrating process; that we grow old to no purpose. You were my purpose. For me, watching you grow was a great creative process, like the coming of spring. You were my summer, but never my autumn.

When I saw you go off to school and then university, I thought of you in terms of destiny repeating itself. And I remembered then, as I do now, the words of Apollinaire, "Shadow into the sun, signature of my light, holder of sorrows, a god that conquers."

Andrew felt a lump in his throat. The plane was banking, the sun on one wing, then banking again over the sea. He turned back to the letter.

I had the unshakable conviction that you would never do anything that would cause me disappointment. That is why it distresses me so to write what I must now put on record between us. I protest most strongly at what you are doing. I believe that the purpose of your education is not to do what you are bent upon. I say that not with blind indignation but as a reasoned fact. I would not be a father to you if I did not ask, even now, that you ponder the pain and anguish your actions cause. You have been fired by notions which are frankly absurd. In many ways I blame Father Patrick for encouraging what seems to me to come very close to emotional hysteria. He would have impressed me far more if he had said to you to wait a year and then see. But no: he has bundled you off to Rome with indecent haste. The doubtful wisdom of that will become clearer in time.

I can say no more, because there is no more to be said. I love you, my son, even in my grievous disappointment.

Your father.

His room was on the top floor of the seminary, providing a breathtaking vista of the Roman skyline: terra-cotta–tiled roofing on baroque buildings and the domes of some of the city's five hundred churches. He stood at the window, absorbing and sifting in his mind his impressions of this part of the city. The overriding one was of noise: traffic and bells. He had been almost deafened by their ringing, pealing in mysterious discord, marking the canonical hours and calling the faithful to Mass. This must be why everybody shouted: outside wonderfully tall doorways, from balconies and windows, in alleyways. Then there was the tactility: people seemed continually to touch and embrace. He noticed the architecture: some buildings were old when Nero ruled. Walls were irregular, windows narrow — many chockful of flowers — balconies iron-railed and projecting over cobbled, narrow, tortuous streets. Only with dusk did the noise temporarily ease.

He surveyed the room once more. The impression remained: it could be a prison cell. The walls were a dingy white, the floorboards were scarred, and the furniture had the look of battered misuse. There were a closet, a desk, a chair, and shelves above the bed, itself narrow, its mattress lumpy, the springs sagging slightly. He wondered how many seminarians had tossed and turned here before him. While unpacking he made his first decision: as soon as possible he would replace the mattress.

Andrew removed the radio he had wrapped in several shirts and placed it on the floor beside his bed, continuing to unpack, and remembering the day he and Jane had bought a table for it. He Scotch-taped her photograph to an otherwise empty notice-board fixed to a wall. It was a Polaroid snapshot and the color had faded, giving her face a wan look. He turned on the radio, trying to locate an English-language station. All he could find was an endless Italian babble. He looked at his watch. It would be nine o'clock in England. His mother and father would be settling down to watch the news, each with their after-dinner liquors, sitting side by side on the sofa, occasionally murmuring what a dreadful place the world had become. Lima was five hours behind Rome. Jane, if she had stuck to her timetable, would be heading for the airport to catch her flight back to London. She would be tanned —

There was a knock on the door. A soutaned priest stood there. He introduced himself as Andrew's spiritual director.

"Just popped along to see how you're settling in. May I come in?"

"Of course." Andrew stood aside.

The director nodded approvingly. "It takes some people a week to get sorted out. It looks like you've been here for ages."

He walked over to the books Andrew had placed on one of the shelves.

"An interesting selection. Sheen's a bit simplistic, don't you think?" He indicated *Life of Christ.* "I'm not sure he's got it absolutely right about Christ's attitude toward property."

Beyond the open window, the night sounds of the city were gaining strength: a renewed blare of scooters and car horns, the clamor of radios and television sets, street calls, raucous and repetitive, a narcotic mish mash funneling through. The director closed the window.

He noticed Jane's photograph. "Your sister?"

"A friend. We were at university together."

"A pretty girl." He continued to study the picture. "I always encourage friendships with the opposite sex. It's a healthy way to remind ourselves about resilience."

He turned and faced Andrew.

"John Paul's vocation came late in life. He had girlfriends and knew all about the normal emotional relationships that any virile young man faces. But when he recognized his vocation, he embraced celibacy. I've always thought that because he has had such a full life before entering the priesthood, it has made it that much easier for him to stay in touch."

Andrew wondered, briefly, what Jane would make of this priest. Would he be someone she could easily place in the Jungian matrix she used to evaluate people? Perhaps she would find him too cool and casual in manner to be easily pinned down. Toward the end of their last year together he had sometimes questioned if personalities easily fitted her textbook definitions, and she smiled and, with just a hint of malice, said history was making his mind too rigid.

The director sat on the chair, his hands on his knees.

"Andrew, these first weeks are going to be tough. For you. For us. But there's one area where, from the outset, neither you nor we can afford to fail, and that is over the question of celibacy. There are no 'ifs' or 'buts.' The Pope has made it clear to each of us that he will enforce it with all the sacramental intransigence at his command. And he's right to do so."

Andrew suspected the priest had already delivered, or was about to deliver, his homily personally to each of the twenty-five new students who had arrived throughout the day. Jane, he decided, would like the director, because of the way he had chosen to set out the position, instead of collectively addressing the new intake the way they had in the army, with a pipsqueak of an officer rattling off the dos and don'ts of military life. He disliked that sort of blind regimentation as much as Jane, who had once called it an example of society in pursuit of the predictable.

The director walked back to the window, peering down into the courtyard. He turned and leaned against the ledge.

"This place has seen a lot of changes and a lot of popes come and go. But one thing that has not changed is the rule of celibacy. Obeying it totally is the only way for us to have the proper stability, certitude, and concentration in our lives. I always say our celibacy is a blazing symbol, plain for everyone to see, telling the world that our Church has not lost its way. That the standard of conduct and self-sacrifice we expect from our priests is not going to be lowered. That is the salient truth of Catholic sociology. I want you always to remember it. Our celibacy is a fixed point in an increasingly unstable world."

The director returned to the chair. He half-smiled, the way Father Pat-

273

rick did, as much with the eyes as with the lips, the brown of the pupils becoming darker under the short-cropped hair. He probably can't smile in any other way, Andrew thought; it's a priest's smile.

"The one thing I try to get across from the very start is that celibacy is the one value which sets us apart from all other Christian religions. Here, you will be encouraged to debate everything. Liberation theology, moral theology, philosophy, objective values, and what Socrates should have said to Thrasymachus. The elements of ethics, rationalism, and empiricism. You'll have them for breakfast, lunch, and dinner. Here, you go to the limit with God, free will, and determinism.

"You'll get a dozen different interpretations for any point, and it's right you should because we want you to have the broadest possible spectrum. I need not remind you that our faith is a practical one, designed to offer the greatest number of people the best possible opportunity for salvation. Remember what Matthew said about the narrow gate which leads to Eternity? In a sense we are the gatekeepers. And the only way we can keep the gate open for millions of others is to show them that we will not fail them. That's why we don't debate celibacy here: we know it works. It goes with being a good gatekeeper."

The priest stood in front of Jane's photograph. After a while he turned and waved a hand to embrace the building that had been used for the preparation of priests for centuries.

"All this exists for no other purpose than to remind each of us that we are here as an act of voluntary renunciation. Sets us apart as God's chosen. Giving up small earthly pleasures is not hard when you see it like that."

He half-smiled again and left.

Alone once more, Andrew opened his diary and began to write down the priest's words and mannerisms.

Over the following weeks, his diary entries formed a careful record of his transition into religious life. They were written up every night before he went to bed, with the patch of sky black beyond his window and the seminary gripped in the silence of a vault. He made no pretense at style. Instead, he concentrated on simply recording what he saw, thought, and felt during the day. On that first night, after he recorded the director's visit, Andrew added a postscript. "This is going to be a story of personal discovery. In a way it is a mystery story, trying to explain the romantic ambiguity and the reality of what it means to try to become a priest in the 1980s."

The early entries described his exploration of the vast building that was

274

now his home, its foundations laid when the popes were in exile in Avignon. For centuries, with brief interruptions — during World War Two it served as a hospital — little had disturbed the monastic calm of its chapels, libraries, study rooms, refectory, and the majestic Corridor of the Cardinals, its walls lined with portraits of the seminary's cardinal-protectors, all of whom held high office in the Church, some eventually becoming popes. At the end of the corridor was the rector's office. From here he ruled over the lives of the students.

The building, for all its size and brooding presence, provoked the comment: "I expected it to be much holier than it is; much more Christian instead of a cross between a residence hall and a barrack-room." He had been equally candid about his fellow seminarians. "Some are straight from school and rather provincial in their outlook. This is the first time most of them have been away from home, and it shows. I don't feel I have anything in common with them."

He felt uncomfortable with their sanctimoniousness; the way they fawned on some of their tutors and always seemed to spend hours on their knees in the main chapel, alternately bowing their heads or staring at the massive portrait of the martyrs behind the altar, or turning up the whites of their eyes and almost swaying in rapture at the fresco of the Assumption covering the entire ceiling. At mealtimes, they talked endlessly about how the Pope should solve the continuing crisis in Catholic theology. "An interesting question raised at lunch. How is it possible for the Church to accept much of Vatican Two when Christ made it quite clear His kingdom is not of this world?" And: "Over dinner everyone involved in a lively discussion on why there were no women Apostles. I mentioned that Luke lists a group of women, standing behind the Apostles, assisting in Jesus' ministry. That led to a wider discussion on the Pope's view that being a housewife is not a humiliation but a consecration. It strikes me as rather amusing to have such intense discussion without a woman present."

Andrew was enrolled in the pontifical Gregorian University, the most influential seat of Catholic higher learning. Founded by the father of the Jesuits, Saint Ignatius of Loyola, in 1551, the university had seen no fewer than sixteen of its students acclaimed Pope, almost a thousand become cardinals, and close to ten thousand go on to wear the miters of archbishops and bishops. Nine former graduates had eventually been canonized.

"Everybody calls it "The Greg." It's a few minutes from the seminary. It's built to last, and, like the Vatican, massively ugly. There are three thousand students, literally from all over the world. I had a Kenyan on one side and a Thai on the other. There are nuns, too. Only some of the tutors dress in clerical garb. Most of them just have crosses in their lapels. Those who do dress formally stand out. The Scots because of their fancy cassocks and red sashes. The Americans with blue braid on their soutanes. In spite of what the Pope says, many of the students are very casually dressed, lots of Levi's and open necks. The exception are the Germans. They all turn up in crimson cassocks and round hats. An Italian told me they call them *gambari*, crayfish. I was astonished to see how many students walk around openly with books by Küng, Schillebeeckx, and other forbidden theologians. All lessons are in Latin or Italian."

He recorded other discoveries. The university was one of thirty institutions in Rome where priests trained; it had, however, an international prestige and intellectual standard none of the others could equal. The Gregorian Centre for Marxist Studies was rated among the best in the world. Its Bible Institute regularly sent graduates to the Hebrew University in Jerusalem for further scriptural research. Its department for the study of non-Christian religions was unrivaled. The faculty's professors included the world's leading authorities on philosophy, metaphysics, Nicomachean ethics, monadology, pure reason. There were academics on the campus who spent their lives considering the words of Saint Thomas Aquinas, the meditations of Descartes, and Locke's essay on human understanding.

Andrew learned his tutors regularly traveled to scholarly conferences or to supervise a variety of religio-scientific projects. They spent their vacations in the deserts of the Middle East, searching for further evidence of the life and times of Jesus, or traveled deep into the Soviet bloc to make further contact with Communist scholars and leaders of the Russian Orthodox Church. They had gone in search of Noah's ark in Turkey, and traveled to Portugal to ponder anew the miracle of Fátima. They had flown to Canada and the United States to see for themselves the stress on the Church within the North American continent. They regularly visited Central and South America to debate with the exponents of liberation theology. They turned up in the bush of southern Africa and the jungles of Asia seeking answers to complex questions of faith. When they returned to Rome, their discoveries were often of sufficient importance for a faculty member to be called to the Vatican to brief a member of the Secretariat of State, or even on occasion, the Pope.

In his second week at the university Andrew made a judgment. "The

Greg is, in religious terms, mainstream liberal. But everybody says that the Pope is tightening the reins and his influence is very clear."

His first encounter with papal thinking was the lecture dealing with the concept that violence was the antithesis of truth and love, a favorite theme of Pope John Paul. The lecturer emphasized the pontiff's belief that the anti-truth was as great an enemy as the anti-Christ, and that there was a direct connection between violence and verbal or written distortion. He offered Lebanon and Northern Ireland as examples, saying that in both places violence had been allowed to establish its own immoral authority because of anti-truth. He asked the class to write an essay based on the Pope's message for the World Day of Peace in 1979. In it, the Pope had identified an inherent danger. "The idea is spreading that the individual, and humanity as a whole, achieves progress primarily through violent struggle. Violence flourishes and needs lies."

That afternoon, back in his room — equipped now with a new mattress purchased from his monthly allowance from home — Andrew fashioned his arguments. He worked slowly, frequently consulting a dictionary to check the precise meaning of a word in Italian. He devoted a portion of every day to improving his fluency in the language. After a month, he was surprised how much progress he had made.

He began by quoting the Pope. *Murder must be called by its proper name. Murder is murder. Political and ideological ideas do not change its nature. On the contrary, they are degraded by it.*

He then launched on a coolly reasoned assessment of the role the Church could play in bringing peace to Belfast and Beirut, arguing that the priesthood should raise its collective voice to make clear that to relinquish violence did not mean having to remain silent against injustice; that truth demanded any form of injustice, especially in religion, must be challenged without fear of the consequences. His essay was one the lecturer chose to criticize before the class. He said Andrew's views were far too absolute and failed to take into account that very often direct challenge can be self-defeating. He reminded them of another papal pronouncement: *Injustice must never be exposed in a way which can provoke further violence.*

Part of his general studies were directed to understanding why the Church is the only religious body that engages in global diplomatic relations in an age when religion and the state are supposedly diverging; he began to grasp that under the present Pope ecclesiastical diplomacy is now more active than probably ever before in its four-hundred-year-old history.

His letters home reflected the developing pattern of his life; descriptions of Rome interspersed with references to the struggle between Man and God, where the created challenged their Creator. The daily rituals of the Romans, their endless visits to espresso bars and siestas, came between thoughts about secularization being the dogma of defiance. On one page he wrote about the outrageously poor public services, on the next he devoted space to arguing that desacralization paves the way for dehumanization. He recounted how his professors discussed such abstract ideas as how to resist evil with good; Catholicism as a faith of choice; God as love; why the entire mystery of Jesus is summed up in two words, gentleness and humility. Throughout his letters a number of themes recurred: the meaning of life; the total authority of Christ; the need for personal faith; the benefit of silent meditation. He allowed himself to be carried along by the undertow of Catholic mysticism, analyzing why Catholicism must fight structuralism because it was not only a dangerous moral relativism but was also a way of circumscribing the truth. He described how his priest-tutors regularly warned about Satan. "We were told again today that he is never more deadly than when he waits for those of us traveling the road into religious life. This is the time we need all our pure faith to fight him off. Our lecture was all about pride of error and how the smallest lapse in humility opens the door to Satan."

As the weeks passed, his observations become more acute. He began to see that theology generated its own special kind of emotionalism; that it could indeed, as the great Reformer Philipp Melanchthon observed, possess a man like a disease: *rabies theologorum*. In the eyes of his tutors, its victims now included Hans Küng, Jacques-Marie Pohier, and Edward Schillebeeckx. In another letter home, he confided that the more he read the more he saw that whether a theologian remained within the religious pale or became an outcast, accused of error and dangerous affirmations, depended on how well he managed to combine intellectual audacity with modesty and temperateness.

His professor of theology, who from time to time personally advised the Pope, encouraged Andrew to judge for himself the extent of the errors committed to see how far some thinkers had moved from the highly rational and theoretical theology of the Church. For a week, he read far into the night about Schillebeeckx's distinctive doctrine in which existentialism, phenomenology, and philosophical inspiration blend together. Intellectually, Andrew saw its attractions. The following Monday he sat in class, spellbound, as the professor quietly attacked the theologian's arguments. He pointed out how far modernists like Schillebeeckx departed from the theological essentials Thomas Aquinas insisted upon by their refusal to make a complete submission of mind and heart to divine revelation. Instead, the professor concluded, they had launched a bitter assault on the Church's interpretation of the Gospels and on Saint John in particular, the Apostle who most emphatically pressed the divinity of Jesus. In doing so, they had challenged the sacred authority of the Pope. The professor paced before the class, a slight figure with wispy hair and nervous darting eyes, quoting Schillebeeckx's words: " 'I do not deny that Jesus is God, but want to assert that He is also man, something that has been overlooked. It is precisely as man that He is important to us. But when you say that you are suspect.' "

The professor paused, his eyes glinting. Then he asked them to write an essay explaining why the Dutch theologian was right to feel he was under suspicion. Andrew spent the next week in further reading before he was ready to distill his argument. His style, for all the languid ease of the Italian language, was crisp and precise as he argued that Schillebeeckx grounded his argument solely in systematic theology and took little account of traditional Catholic doctrine, and in particular, left no room for the role of the magisterium, the very heart of that doctrine. The scholar, he reasoned, for all his intellectual brilliance, in the end argued a flawed case because he was bent on presenting an irresponsible dilution and simplification, bordering at times on a heretical one-sidedness that took no account of the thought-through and time-tested teaching of the early Fathers of the Church. He ended his paper with a resounding judgment: "The modernists seem to be proposing we each become our own Christologist and, ignoring the fundamentals of revelation, around which our faith revolves, allow Christ to become what we might wish Him to be."

Trained to think for himself by his tutors at school and university and influenced by Jane's fascination with psychological development, Andrew began to structure on paper rules for living within the framework of his new commitment to celibacy. He pursued his research among the miles of library shelves at the Greg, and found there was surprisingly little published on the issue; what there was seemed academic.

One of his talents, developed at the university, was an ability to take disparate information and reform it so that it assumed a far more cohesive meaning. In his short time at Sandhurst his commanding officer had said this methodology — the skill to combine sketchy data with informed conjecture and firmly fix it in the middle range of probability — made him highly suitable for intelligence work. The prospect of spending his life in the world of subversion was an early reason for his leaving the army.

Andrew began to apply techniques that might have served the intelligence community to form practical guidelines for taking account of his sexuality and the demands of celibacy. He realized that his time in Rome, living in an all-male community, had already had a profound effect on his emotional life.

He was more aware of women. He discovered some of the younger ones stared at him, and he stared back, forcing them to lower their gaze. He enjoyed the satisfaction this gave him. Sometimes he sat in sidewalk cafés, sipping a beer, watching them go by, often thinking that a passing girl resembled Jane. Either it was the way the stranger styled her hair, or the look of her mouth or her nose, or her coloring. But none was as beautiful.

Jane's voice remained a living reality in his mind. He could recall entire conversations between them. At first it was a game; now it was a serious business. He would suddenly stop what he was doing and concentrate on a discussion they had had. The rules he invented insisted he set the scene with total accuracy and that he remember exactly what she wore and how the conversation had gone. Almost always his flashback ended with them making love.

He wrote her a long letter about these experiences. She responded with a short friendly note, suggesting he should read Schonfeld's *Normal Sexuality in Adolescence.* He had been slightly hurt by her response and had not mentioned his fantasies again, though he wrote to her regularly.

Andrew continued to probe his inner feelings, trying to place them within the framework of what he read and felt. He began to understand that self-control was the high ground between self-destruction and self-repression. In the university's medical library, he discovered the writings of the American psychologist Nathaniel Branden, and came to accept that a positive way to handle both his sexuality and his celibacy was neither to repress his feelings nor allow them to make him act impulsively. He must always try to identify his emotions calmly and to justify them without feeling fear and guilt.

He made a diary entry: "What is love? It is to give everything to another person — complete generosity. Is the only true love, the love of God? Do all other loves fade into pale insignificance when compared to the love of God? If a man is to give himself he must first possess himself completely; that is, to be in complete possession of his inner being, completely open and available."

One evening, having brooded over the past, around midnight he tiptoed down the main staircase to the pay phone near the massive front door; he resisted the impulse to call her, thinking how he wanted to be a *gatekeeper*. Then he climbed back up the stairs, feeling better, glad that the irritable, depressed feeling which had filled him for most of the day had lifted. Reaching the Corridor of the Cardinals, Andrew paused to stand and stare before each of the framed portraits. How many of these eminent men, he wondered, had led secret, passionate lives, subject to awful moods and enraged by trifles, which a year ago, when he shared a bed with Jane, would never have troubled him?

He fell asleep thinking of that passage in Isaiah about the man singled out by God whom God keeps in obscurity. Is this why he was here? Suddenly he awakened, grinding his teeth and sweating. Jane had been here, standing at the foot of the bed, staring at him. She said his name, over and over again, the way she used to when they made love, *Andy, Andy, oh Andy.* He stumbled out of bed and went to the window. Dawn was breaking. He turned and shook his head and slumped back on his bed, wondering about the mysterious and powerful forces that had once more broken his sleep.

He knew he must develop a new way of loving. But how? How, he wondered, would he handle these sudden bouts of intense anxiety and dissatisfaction? Why did he feel so intolerant of others? Above all, how could he, a committed witness to Christ, live with the strong sexual emotions that gripped him?

The saints of old had been able to go into the deserts, having nothing except the wild animals to tempt them. But here in Rome, temptation was at every turn.

Every day, there were questions to face. Was it psychologically healthy for him to be so focused on her? Was there some meeting place in which both his sensuality and spirituality could rest easy? Perhaps, after all, accepting celibacy was a slow process, not something to be achieved in a few months, but requiring years of practice, maturing in him as wine ages in a cask?

This particular thought had come as he listened to an interminable discussion about what Pope John Paul had meant by saying that contemplation purifies. There was a lot of hyperbole about the risk of *interior pollution* and *the contract of faith,* and could contemplation eventually lead to total redemption and alienation from every form of sin. Andrew suddenly excused himself and went to his room. He felt tired. For the past few nights he had wandered alone through the streets of the neighborhood.

Then he'd sat in his room staring out the window. He felt groggy in class. Tonight he was determined to retire early. But first he made a further entry in his diary. "In spite of all the work, which often leaves me mentally exhausted, I feel alone. This is when I have to face myself and ask questions. Do I really understand I am always going to be alone, until I die; and that from now on, I have to be as a stranger even to those who love me?"

He stopped writing and stood at his window, listening to the anonymous radio, looking at the moon and stars, wishing he had a telescope so that he could feel closer to the immensity of space. Staring into the night sky, he felt his outer senses drifting into a strange dreaminess. Jane floated before him once more, naked, her hand beckoning him. Then she was gone.

Andrew returned to his desk, shivering, reminded of what his spiritual director said at their last meeting: *Each one of us from time to time experiences a moment when we judge ourselves capable of coming close to being like Saint Jerome, out in his cave in the desert, gazing into the night sky, imagining that the grace of God is descending. These are the moments when we are happy to be impaled by the spirit of the Church and accept the limitations she asks of us. But there are also those moments when our souls have the makings of a Torquemada. These are the times when we no longer clearly feel the spiritual superiority God has seen in us. Those are the times dark thoughts enter our minds. Don't run from them. That's what the Devil wants. They must be faced. They are our old enemies, the Devil and the flesh. See them for what they are: temptation. Face them squarely and without fear.*

He remembered the searching eyes of the director, murmuring that he was filled with understanding about the hot blood of strong young men. And the priest said again, softly, his voice filled with certainty. *Andrew, God doesn't think you are a superman. He just believes you can do what He wants. So do I.*

He left the director's study, his mind filled with pride at his sacred calling. The feeling was there now, as he wrote another long letter to Jane, filled with incidents of Roman life. He had been in Trastevere, the raffish night district on the right bank of the Tiber, when two white-uniformed policemen tried to apprehend a purse-snatcher on a motorcycle. His machine skidded out of control and his body had been hurled, broken, into one of the outdoor restaurants around the Church of Santa Maria. It had all been over in moments. "Nobody has been unduly perturbed. He was just another thief. Terrible, I know, but that is how Romans look on things. When you come here I'll show you how to carry your purse properly."

All his letters to Jane contained suggestions that she should visit him. Suddenly he felt smothered. He returned to the window. Staring out into the darkness, into the tranquillity of the sleeping city, he felt again that first love he had felt for Jane. Once more he saw her naked body, and all his soul reached out for her and he groaned aloud, begging her to understand why he must now love her only with a sweetness that renounced all carnal thoughts. For the first time since he stepped off the plane, clutching his father's letter, Andrew felt tears running down his cheeks.

Two days later, the Greg was agog. A Spanish Jesuit had privately published a booklet on the spiritual and moral travails he had faced. He admitted to masturbating to cope with his bodily demands, but argued this was not a breach of his vow of celibacy. No one could recall a precedent for not only a priest, but a Jesuit, making such a public admission. Copies of the booklet circulated like wildfire.

That night, Andrew wrote the following: "The Church expects many things. Because I am a very passionate person and because there are times when I do want sexual satisfaction, there is no doubt my faith will fail me. I have this feeling that there is a good chance I could fail because I am a sinner and because I am a man."

Somewhere a clock struck the hour.

What would she be doing now? Surely she would be home. Andrew was halfway down the great staircase, dark and deserted at this hour, before he realized what he was going to do. He stopped before the phone and began to feed coins into its slot. When he had inserted the required number, he began to dial the number they once had shared. There was a delay before he heard the ringing.

A man answered.

Andrew almost slammed the receiver back into the cradle. By the time he returned to his room his eyes were filled with tears. Then, through his desperation, he began to reason. Why had he felt so angry and jealous? That other voice, if she chose, could be a husband to her, could give her his name, a home, a child — things he could no longer offer her. It was perfectly natural she should find someone else. Why should she remain beautiful and alone?

This, he reminded himself, is what renunciation is all about; it was a sign of his spiritual maturing to show such selfless love. He wished he could tell her.

The next day he felt a great peace as he went about the chapel duties each seminarian must perform.

Each morning in the seminary began like any other. He went to chapel for Mass, the faces around him pale and puffed with sleep. The more openly pious pressed their hands tightly together. This morning, though, he did not feel irritated — as he usually did — with their fervor, the way they prayed too loudly, exaggerated their responses, gazed continually at the chalice in the priest's hands as he consecrated the wine and lifted up the Host. This was the way they were and he accepted it.

The last lecture of the morning was a discourse on Gnosticism. Andrew was enthralled that the professor at the podium was one of those who had evaluated the Gospel of Thomas, discovered only in 1945, part of a collection of thirteen volumes of Gnostic papyri unearthed far up in the Nile delta.

He walked back to the seminary, his mind filled with how the Church had survived because it had the strength and skill of men ready to safeguard and hallow its symbols.

A letter from Jane swept such thoughts from his mind. She was coming to Rome to see him.

†

DECISIONS

*It seemed that the next minute they would
discover a solution. Yet it was clear that
the end was still far, far off, and that
the hardest and most complicated part was
only just beginning.*

— ANTON CHEKHOV,
"The Lady with the Dog"

CHAPTER 13

†

Into the Twilight

F ather Breslin pulled on thick woolen underwear and socks before buttoning his black shirt and trousers. The predicted first flakes of snow were swirling outside the window. However, it was not as cold as when he had gone to bed a couple of hours earlier, half-frozen, after returning from a fatal accident. By the time he had arrived, the four bodies — two from each car — had been removed to the city morgue. The uniformed sergeant in charge was apologetic. "No need for the oil tonight, Father. They died before they knew it. Sorry to have called you." He resumed measuring skid marks.

Father Breslin stood staring at the carnage, holding the silver container of holy oil, feeling useless among the police and firemen. He wondered if the victims had been drunk or obsessed with speed in some mindless race with time. So many are nowadays. He turned away from the accident, offering a silent prayer for the dead and another for their relatives.

The police car brought him back to the rectory. On its radio he had heard the forecast. He could not remember when it last snowed on the first Sunday in Advent, remembering again that the weather had been perfect for the accident which destroyed his father.

He had been in this bedroom — the only space in the world he could call completely his own — when the news came. His father, one midmorning six months ago, stone-cold sober, had stepped into the path of a car. Father McKenna had driven him at once to the hospital, saying little, but all the more supportive for his silence. He realized again how grateful he was for the old priest's friendship and wisdom.

It was pure accident, said the policeman at the hospital: the driver had no chance; the eyewitnesses all said so. His father's sight and hearing had been deteriorating since they had stood together at the graveside of his mother, at last united through grief. His injuries included brain damage. The doctors said he would never leave the hospital, but he would be able to speak again. It was a dubious blessing. His father used his restored gift to cry out his terror about impending death.

There was something medieval and frightening about the way his slurred speech evoked fears that his mortal sins had forfeited eternity. Death, for him, was a malignant skeletal figure, hovering around his hospital cot.

Father Breslin buttoned up his cassock and looked out of the window. The snow was thickening. But this was his free afternoon and later he would go to the hospital, not from any sense of duty, but out of love. In these past months he had grown closer than ever to his father.

The person who helped to make this possible was a psychiatrist. Father Breslin finally consulted him about his experiences in what they agreed could be termed the twilight zone. The doctor suggested it would help him understand what happened there — the time when he was somewhere between drowsiness and sleep — if he kept a record of his thoughts and impressions. It was one thing to speak about these feelings in the privacy of a consulting room, quite another to put them down on paper. An alternative would be to tape them; that would give them an even more immediate and unedited quality, making them consequently all that more valuable.

At first he found it difficult to speak into a cassette recorder. He did not recognize his voice on the playback and the words sounded stiff and premeditated. But gradually, over weeks, he realized he was able to put on tape his innermost feelings. Listening at regular intervals, he better understood what happened to him in the twilight zone. He told Father McKenna why he was making the tapes, and the old priest said he was lucky to have such a good and caring doctor. He had not pressed, just listened, full of understanding.

Father Breslin went to his desk by the window and stared out at the swirling white, thinking how, on the last tape, he had admitted that he loved the old priest and felt his love in return; or, to be more accurate, they loved each other in their lives together. It was the sort of affection that defied description, impossible to pin down. It was not physical, but neither could it be defined as a mere friendship. It was subtly more. He was still surprised at how naturally Father McKenna ignored the unspoken rule of the priesthood about keeping ministry and friendship separate, showing him that to combine them is not in conflict with the ideal of Christian holiness.

He was warned, before accepting this post, that his superior was cantankerous and given to outbursts. This was true; on such occasions his portly figure would shake and his voice thicken. Either some newspaper item about the Church aroused his ire, or it was Miss Maddox. From the beginning he had enlisted Father Breslin as an ally against the housekeeper. After Father Breslin had first witnessed one of their arguments, making sure she was out of earshot, Father McKenna delivered himself: "A vixen in tweeds. That's what she is. A vixen in tweeds. Nags nonstop. She'll have to go." But she remained entrenched, the sharp point of a triangle of lives in this large rambling house. She had come to recognize that the slight tremble of his hands, mistaken for anger by others, was due to another attack of painful arthritis. This, more than anything else, he admitted, was what drove him to bed early and kept him indoors for most of the winter. Those were the days when Miss Maddox would stoke up the fire in the sitting room and command Father McKenna to sit before it, letting its warmth penetrate his aching body. Then she would march upstairs to place a hot-water bottle in his bed. She would never go. For all the tensions and confrontations between them they, too, belonged together. Theirs was an unspoken affection, different from the one Father Breslin shared with Father McKenna, but equally important for its purity and never to be undervalued.

On the desk top, beside his typewriter on which he prepared all his sermons, was the recorder, which had become a friend. He had spoken into its microphone for over thirty hours already. He kept the tapes in a top drawer of the desk, each cassette containing thoughts he had never thought he would express.

He turned from the window, remembering how on his last tape he had felt strong enough about his own feelings — that he could love in a multiplicity of analogous ways, each of them totally celibate — to be able at last to talk about Mary and other women without feeling his chastity and vocation threatened.

He looked at his watch. It was a little after seven-fifteen. Ian, who had altar-boy duties this week, would not yet have arrived to light the candles. He pulled open the top drawer and removed a tape, numbered and dated like all the others. He inserted it in the recorder.

"If marriage wasn't my vocation, celibacy was to be a life commitment. At this stage, the commitment, as I think I may have mentioned before, was more a denial of sexual pleasure, of a loving wife and the intense pleasure of that. The forgoing of the companionship of an intimate friend to pour out my troubles to and to be there with my slippers and my hot cup of tea when I arrived back after a day's work. That was out as far as I was concerned. The possibility of having my own children. That was gone. All the children of the parish were now mine and I had to love them as a father although I didn't have the same responsibilities...."

He spun the tape forward, thinking that neither marriage nor celibacy was a substitute for the responsibility he had to make his own life. He depressed the button.

"They still rise from the depths, I suppose, of my being, say, in the semiconscious state before sleep or waking up. I'm walking down a country lane with Mary or a girl who doesn't have a name because I don't think it matters. I go home with her or she comes with me...."

His voice stopped. Only the low hiss of the revolving tape was audible.

In all these years, Mary in his mind had not aged a day. Her skin was as tanned and free of makeup as it had been in those last months of the war. At first he tried to send her away, whispering fiercely into the recorder that she had no place in his life.

He remembered how he had sat there, saying that he really did see his celibacy as a positive undertaking, filled though it was with struggle and challenge.

Mary had laughed, that soft beguiling laugh he had last heard almost twenty-five years ago and that remained vividly clear in his head. And, finally, he had not let her go, but allowed her to encourage him, and obeyed her, doing what she told him. Afterward, he was quite certain what had happened.

That finally was what sent him, secretly, every Wednesday afternoon to a consulting room in Dublin. The psychiatrist had questioned him carefully about his childhood, his lack of girlfriends, his early commitment to a vocation, his first nocturnal emission at Clonliffe, what occurred with Brigid and then Mary. He was, he said, looking for a pattern.

The hissing sound was once more replaced by his voice. It was a peculiar sensation, he thought, listening to himself, knowing what was to come, yet surprised at what was revealed.

"...and we make love.... There's the release ... of sexual tension ..."

Another pause. But he knew there was more.

"There are dreams and no guilt is involved. Guilt involves the will, and if there's no will, there's no fault. If I'm asleep, there's no will, I can't be guilty. My only bother is at what stage of consciousness I am at. Am I semiconscious, or am I totally conscious? Or am I kidding myself, trying to pretend to be asleep when I am not? That is the problem. Morality, as far as the Church goes, involves clear knowledge of the intellect and full consent of the will. Passion outside of that is not a sin. . . ."

Such thoughts acted as a trigger for Mary or one of the others to emerge from that part of his subconscious where they dwelt. It was only afterward, when they had returned to their hiding place, that he had been troubled by the fact that these feelings might be inappropriate for a priest.

"... the objective act. First of all there is the objective act. I can say, objectively, that murder, blasphemy, and masturbation are wrong. But when I ask the question, 'Is it a sin to masturbate?' I can't say 'yes' or 'no,' because it has to be decided if this particular act is a mortal sin and that can only be decided by my confession. . . ."

His voice came to a sudden halt. He remembered how difficult it had been to express this simple statement so that it held the exact meaning he wanted. Sometimes he could talk into the machine without any special thought as to what he was saying, the way the psychiatrist had encouraged him to do. But he had dwelt on this matter of objectivity. Even now, listening to the words, he could sense his uncertainty, his searching.

"God is all part of my journey through life. He has shown me that I cannot live my life if I continue to look back, listing afterwards, lest in a sense I turned into a pillar of longing and resentment. I suppose all this is really about that to live my life I have to be free of guilt. Coping with my sensuality is the same as handling my other passions. I have had to control my angers. I can't just get mad because I feel like it. I have been able to bring into line this anxiety I used to have to do others down, which was quite strong. . . . If I can do all that, I suppose I can do the sexual thing in . . . I'm not sure this is very clear. . . ."

He stopped the recording. Father McKenna had once said there is something beyond truth, or at least so far isolated from it, that few people were aware of its existence. When they were lucky enough to discover this quality, they should treasure it. He wondered if he dared hope that he had begun to discern it. He depressed the button again.

". . . seventeen years . . . no, seventeen years, seven months, and five days precisely, this very day, I was ordained a priest. I feel strong and healthy and vigorous enough at forty-one. I am a celibate still, who always tries and remembers it is never meant to be easy to respond to those words which first drew me. 'Come, follow Me.' It is still the most worthwhile challenge I know. . . ."

The tape ran on, but he was no longer listening, thinking there were those moments of such sensory vividness, especially with Mary — and they troubled him deeply.

The psychiatrist had asked questions: Did any of the women persecute him? Did they ask him to do anything he found unpleasant or degrading? Did they torture or abuse him? Did they revile him afterward? Has his willpower been weakened by their presence? Or his faith?

He answered each time: No.

At the end of six weeks in therapy, the conclusion was reassuring.

"Father, you came here full of anxiety. Almost obsessional anxiety. But there's nothing psychologically wrong with you. Quite the reverse. You're an impressive example of a person able to function in the twilight zone, an area between sleeping and waking. We all go through that zone, going in or out of sleep. But you have managed to remain there, perhaps for considerable lengths of time. Certainly long enough for you to fantasize satisfactorily. We do not know that much about the twilight zone. But one thing is certain. While we are in it, we are not guilty of any volition. So you can rest assured you have not committed the mortal sin of cooperation. You are not in breach of your vow of celibacy. You should not feel any guilt, the cause of your obsessional anxiety."

He was relieved and stopped the machine.

*

Buttoning up his cassock, he noticed its hem was stained from the foam the firemen had poured over the cars. Father Breslin was certain Miss Maddox would be awake, just as she had been when he returned from the accident. He had been in the hall, on that first day, his bags at his feet, when she spoke to him with indefinable familiarity.

"I've seen curates come and go for all sorts of reasons, Father. But I've said to them all: I run this place my way. The way Father McKenna likes it run. Three good meals a day. If you're not going to be in, you tell me. If it's an emergency, I'll keep something warm in the oven. You keep a record of all your private telephone calls and settle up once a month. Visitors in the sitting room, but only if Father McKenna is not requiring it. Then you see them in the back parlor. I change the beds once a week, Thursdays, after breakfast. I collect all your washing at the same time. I try to run a happy house and I hope you'll be happy here, Father."

In spite of the turbulent changes affecting the Church as a whole, these past four years as curate had been the happiest and most rewarding of his ministry. He enjoyed the routine of a busy parish, with its rotation of baptisms, weddings, funerals, school meetings, and house visits. There was a hard reality about these people that he admired. They were healthy and human, willing to allow him into their lives. They, for their part, never attempted to go beyond strictly defined limits with him. Even at the most informal of gatherings, he was still *Father*. To them, his celibacy was first and foremost a matter of abstinence; they could not understand self-transcendence: that being a celibate was not a single factor, but a combination of diffuse, complex, and mysterious conditions, in which physical denial was only a part.

He had once asked Father McKenna: "What do they really think we are? Robots in cassocks?"

The parish priest thought for some time. "Best let them think that. People are always more comfortable with their fantasies."

It was perfectly true.

Wrapped against the cold, he left his room, the way he had done for over a thousand mornings, pulling the door quietly behind him and avoiding the squeaking floorboard at the top of the stairs. In the hall he put on his topcoat and scarf and his black priest's hat. He quietly drew the bolts and chains on the front door, a phalanx of barriers placed there by Miss Maddox as a defense against the world. He had often thought it would require a team of burglar-locksmiths to break through these defenses, which every morning required him to perform a slow glissando of openings before he could swing the door open to the world. The snow swirled in his face, and past him into the hallway. Born five hundred miles to the north, driven here by turbulent winds, these particular flakes ended as tiny droplets on the hall floor Miss Maddox waxed and polished daily, as if her life depended on it. He quickly pulled the door behind him and began to walk to the church. Ian was waiting, his face pinched and as white as his surplice. He had walked a mile to get here.

Father Breslin smiled sympathetically, thinking it needed real dedication to turn out on a morning like this. He began to robe, putting first the amice around his shoulders, telling Ian about the accident and asking the boy how he had spent his Saturday night. He had watched another televised debate on Northern Ireland. Reaching for the draped chalice, Father Breslin explained his own feelings on Ulster. "The murders will continue as long as people fail to see the Gospels offer the only solution."

"You should tell my dad that."

"I would — if he came to Mass."

The boy's father was another parent who had lapsed.

✝

When he left Clonliffe twenty-two years ago, it was to join a Church that was a clearly defined ecclesiastical institution, functioning with the same ideological unity which had sustained it for the past fifteen hundred years. The significant statistics spoke for themselves: the number of priests, nuns, monks, and seminarians; of baptisms, inter-Catholic marriages, communions, confirmations, and confessions all showed a Church staunchly faithful and securely on course for a new millennium. Those were the days when no Catholic — let alone priests or nuns — would lobby for divorce, contraception, abortion, and the acceptance of homosexuality. It was still the era when celibacy was rarely mentioned, and then only to have its positive value emphasized and presented as the perfect way for persons in religious life to show they would not be obstructed from their vocations by the demands of the flesh; that their celibacy set them apart, ensuring the continuity of the Church's centralized control and its universality in worship. It made every Catholic monastery, convent, and seminary a special place. There were no autozoic groups, demanding their own freedoms and style of living. It was predominantly the Church of the Passion of Jesus, not of man; where the poor were blessed because they were poor, and the Kingdom of Heaven in Northern Ireland was not yet seen through the sight of a gun. This was still the Church where women's liberation, Catholic yogis, Catholic Pentacostalists, Catholic Proceesans, and Catholic gays were unknown.

He had begun his priesthood when there was no ecumenical movement. The Church stood alone and certain in all it did, as if to say that in spite of its irredentism, it was also capable of almost infinite compromise. Its long history had remained unchanged since Pontius Pilate had asked Jesus, having already condemned Him to death, if He really believed He was a king, and Christ replied: *"Thou sayest it. . . . But my kingdom is not of this world."*

The Church had never forgotten the power of those words and always remembered to use them as part of its killing patience and inexhaustible perdurance.

He had joined a Church he knew with a record of survival no other could match. It had overcome persecution, exile, intemperance, rebellion, syncretism, hate, ostracism, scorn, calumny, war, corruption, greed, weakness, cruelty, heresy, and hypocrisy. It had dealt in slavery, prostitution, and murder. Countless millions had been killed, or died, in its name. But on the issue of its authority it had never given ground. Neither Attila and his Huns, or Luther and his Reformers, or the modernists of a century ago had been able to make Rome yield a single sentence in its interpretation of all it held to be true and holy.

It was a good and secure feeling to belong to such an organization; to share, however modestly, the aphrodisiac of power that reached out from Rome in that glorious summer of 1947, when the twelfth Pope Pius sat on the Throne of Saint Peter.

Those first nine years of his ministry were, he was now certain, a time when he was spiritually nourished by the example of Pope Pius XII, invincible in all he did, ready to excommunicate, to excise, to exorcise. A priest knew where he stood.

Yet, though nobody knew it, the religious arsonists had already begun to build their bonfires. They had worked methodically, the vanguard of a secret army, waiting for Pius to die: eager to divagate into new discussions and concepts, to introduce revolution into theology, turn the Sacred Congregations into politicking caucuses.

That was all still to come when he had taken his place on the lowest ladder of the Church, a priest without a regular job. Graduation from Clonliffe did not automatically guarantee work. He had survived in that first year on Mass stipends, receiving modest sums in return for celebrating Mass in various churches around the diocese. Later he had been appointed chaplain to a Catholic college. Then followed a lengthy spell doing youth work among Dublin's docks. From there he had been appointed to the staff of the Pro-Cathedral, the diocese's imposing center of worship, where the Archbishop regularly celebrated Mass at the high altar.

He had been on the Cathedral staff when Pius XII died and a new and altogether more robust and compassionate successor, John XXIII, had taken his place. The change in papal direction became noticeable at once. In all he had said and done, Pius had demanded that he, as a man, be accepted without question as a pontiff. John went out of his way to show that as Pope, he wanted to remain a man. Visibly mortal, with his belly laugh and passion for jokes, he displayed a determination to shake the very foundation of the Church by calling a Vatican Council, the second in history.

The men with matches sensed, he could now see, their moment had come. The bonfires were already burning out of control when, at the age of eighty-one, John, after one of the longest death agonies on papal record, finally succumbed. Cancer had wasted his body but left his mind contemplating the failure of his brave gamble, to introduce change, to allow the arsonists a free hand.

In 1965, the Archbishop had appointed him Father McKenna's curate. The first thing he discovered was a shared alarm over what had happened, and continued to happen, to the Church they both loved.

Pope Paul VI had, from the outset, shown himself to be a timid pontiff. For a while he successfully hid his weakness behind a call for unity; his charisma disguised his inability to control, let alone stamp out, the raging inferno consuming the Church on every major issue — a pigmy-pope who had allowed his divinely invested authority to slip and fall.

Standing here, in this cold sacristy, with a seventeen-year-old boy glancing at him curiously, wondering why he had hesitated so long after robing, was neither the time nor place to continue pondering such questions. All he could be certain of was that despair was the first and most dangerous sin, the one that leads to all others. He had admitted this on part of his taped record.

†

He smiled at Ian and motioned him forward. Together they stepped into the sanctuary and genuflected to the altar, covered by a starched white cloth, the lights from the candles shimmering before their eyes, bathing the sacristy in a soft glow. The faces of the Holy Family etched into the stained-glass window had a life of their own.

Some things, indeed, did not change.

✝   ✝   ✝

Victoria found the sameness reassuring; so much else had changed; yet, as she expected, the interior of the battered Ford smelled, as the saying went in this part of the country, like a bachelor on Friday: a mixture of Sam's stale tobacco, his body sweat, and his dog. The coonhound curled up in the back seat, asleep. His paws rested on top of the larger of her two suitcases, the one that contained her modified habit. The other was crammed with brochures.

Coming here from Chicago, she had thought of the words of John Brooks about America remembering a dream just lost and resolving to capture it next time. But would there be a next time? And, as the train approached the stop where she had arranged for Sam to meet her, she called to mind the words of Thomas Wolfe. *Remembering speechlessly we seek the great forgotten language, the lost lane-end into Heaven, a stone, a leaf, an unfound door. Where? When? O lost, and by the wind grieved, ghost, come back again.* She felt a little like Willa Cather's lost lady, or whomever Scott Fitzgerald had in mind when he wrote about being borne ceaselessly into the past. Sam met her train, removing his hat and pressing it against his chest. His face was pink.

Victoria wore a light-gray two-piece suit and a blouse with a frilled front. Her makeup was expertly applied. The years had been kind to her. She looked as vital and youthful as she did on the day she became a Bride of Christ. Only she knew the differences; they were all inside her.

Sam had thrust his hat back on his head and grabbed her cases. He was a small hard-bodied man, with proper old-fashioned manners, instinctively uneasy around a woman, more so if she was a nun.

Chicago, like Detroit and Minneapolis–St. Paul, had been a depressing reminder of the hideous attacks on the nation's moral fiber. It was there in the cities, in the very visible lack of respect people showed toward authority: toward the schools, the universities, the family, and, above all for her, toward the Church. This, more than anything, was the difference on this trip: she had seen that the Church, by the behavior of those within it, was no longer guaranteed respect even from its own ranks. When she was last in Chicago, priests and nuns would never have felt able to approach her — a visiting sister, someone they would probably never encounter again — and tell her bluntly that the Archbishop of Chicago, Cardinal John Cody, who ruled over one of the richest dioceses in the Catholic world, was a racist; a financial cheat, using diocesan funds for his personal profit; a lecher, having his way with whatever woman he fancied, taking and discarding her with the abandon of a Borgia pope. And, when she expressed her astonishment and disbelief, they silenced her, providing evidence, fact after fact, until in the end she had been numbed into acceptance. She went to Chicago's impressive cathedral to hear the Cardinal preach, watching him genuflect before the high altar, his massive girth framed by the tiers of candles — she had counted forty to a tier — and later listened to him read a passage from Matthew: *Master, what good deed must I do to possess eternal life?*

Yet, if any who condemned His Eminence knew, what would they have said about *her* behavior?

Though her transgressions were very different from those of the Cardinal, they were, nevertheless, sins. She had not needed a confessor to tell her that — just as she no longer felt a need to confess them. It was the Church, not she, that was out of step. It was no longer enough for it to forbid, to say it has always been so and must remain so. There must be a good reason. The Order educated her to think, yet the Church expected blind obedience to rules devised by men, a long time ago.

What, she wondered, would Sam say if she were to explain why she found masturbation a healthy relief, and that she could cite some of the world's leading clinicians to support her view? What would he think if he knew that in the suitcase in the backseat was a thick notebook containing, in her painfully wrought words, the entire story of her psychosexual development in religious life? The notebook was her most prized possession. She brought it with her on these long trips, when she was away for a month at a time, so that she could retrace her long journey into self-realization. Now fully professed, she had entered her fourteenth year as a nun, destined, she suspected, to hold high office in the Order.

She was as fully committed to her faith as ever, but now never felt a moment's guilt over her sensuality. She was certain she was in no way psychologically maladjusted; that, indeed, she was regarded by the Order as a persuasive representative, able to make girls share her excitement over His words, *Come, follow Me.* If she were to explain any of this to Sam, would he judge her as harshly as they had Cardinal Cody? In his eyes, would there be a difference?

Sam relaxed, talking about the advantages of country life, saying he could not understand why people were leaving the land. She stared out of the window, wondering whether the nation's patience would finally snap with the collapse of Henry Kissinger's latest initiative to extricate America from Vietnam, which had led to Nixon's authorizing, in this Advent week, the most savage retaliation yet launched by the United States in its long, bloody, and inglorious involvement in the war. Even now, as she drove through this peaceful countryside, the radio announced that this week alone no fewer than 1,400 sorties had been flown against Hanoi, leaving the North Vietnamese capital stricken, with vast, densely populated areas laid to waste. The latest destruction, reported the newscast, was an entire school, killing hundreds of children, no different, probably, from the girls she had come to see.

Sam switched to a music channel, and she thought that not for the first time had a President failed to understand the moral outrage of the country. It had come up time and again during this trip. The President should come out here, where common sense mingled with nostalgia; where infinite open spaces, the houses and barns evoking a timeless pastoral simplicity, allowed finite judgments to be made about the surreal images of violence which filled the airwaves. Sam chewed on his unlit cigar — a man close to sixty, who had lived all his life where he was born, with no wish to go anywhere. "It makes no sense. No sense at all. Killing all those kids."

She sensed that he was not especially patriotic, but he had a deeply entrenched sense of what was right. There was an unwavering compass about his life, just as she felt, for different reasons, there was now in hers. Only a week ago, she had written in her notebook:

"Read: 'The Revelation of Hope,' a good description of people wanting to control life because it is too spontaneously uncontrollable. They would rather kill life than become part of it themselves. It is just like the Church. On one level it allows itself to be split down the middle over Vietnam. But inside, it remains unified against any change. It does not listen to all our crises of unfulfilled needs. We are still forced to relegate our sexuality and sexual development to the most strongly guarded basement of our personality structure. The Church expects us to continue as if sexual needs do not exist. I refuse to die because I believe sexuality has a place in any maturing personality. Chastity can only have any value now for me if it is a way of loving, not a means of avoiding love."

This would be the seventh school in a week she had visited. In the next three weeks she would visit a further eighteen, traveling by train and bus or making hops in and out of small municipal airports. Each time she would be brought to the final destination by some committed Catholic like Sam.

Across the country recruiters like her would visit other high schools to give identical talks about vocation. Ten of them had left the Mother House a week ago. Before their departure, Reverend Mother addressed them. She had grown more frail and distant with the passing years, remaining seated behind her desk, her lips bloodless and barely moving as she reminded the group:

"You have a heavy responsibility. Our ranks are not as full as they were. We need new girls to be trained to carry on our mission. We need them badly. And we need a goodly number of them. The percentage, as you well know, is higher now than ever before of those who now leave during, or at the end of, their postulancy. I fear there is no longer the spiritual strength among the young that there once was."

She paused, gathering her thoughts. The nine nuns around Victoria were, like her, young and personable, chosen by the Order as worthy representatives of religious life and trained to promote its benefit. Reverend Mother continued.

"Be careful in your assessment. We cannot afford to continue with a high degree of wastage. It is a drain on our finances. And people wonder why girls don't stay in religious life. You must make it clear to those you think likely candidates that our way of understanding Jesus Christ the Saviour has not changed. At the same time, you must make it sound attractive as a lifelong commitment. Yet please do not stress that they are coming for life. That is our hope. Instead, make it sound as if they can review their future from time to time. The important thing is to get them to come. Once they are here we will endeavor to try to keep them, offering you, among other things, as an example. It is a great responsibility you have. But I am certain you will discharge it with love and care for what you represent in His name."

In her suitcase was the balance of the thousand dollars she had been given to pay motel and food bills. She found it strange at first, handling money after years of being told it was one of the causes of sin. *A sister with a penny isn't worth a penny.* The Mistress once said that. Now, she was no longer called Mistress, but the Director of Formation: yet she still remained the same doctrinaire teacher, her faith as flinty as her voice. At the time of the title change Victoria had jotted in her notebook: "You can't change a lifetime's habit with a new title. Today's girls are that much smarter. They see through that kind of labeling." Is this, she wondered, another reason why this trip so far has been so unsuccessful?

The itinerary this year was more crowded than usual; almost twice as many schools to visit. She had queried the Sister of Administration, a tall, bony woman who had entered religious life rather late, after a career in commerce, about this. Her response had been predictable. "In one word — money. We haven't got it. It's as simple as that. You've got to do twice as much in half the time. If you believe you can do it, you will. Good luck, Sister." She could have been still working for IBM.

Tomorrow Victoria had to be in Minnesota, almost a thousand miles away. There, she suspected, she would face not only competition from pitching sisters of rival orders, but also challenges from industrial recruiters and bemedaled officers of the armed services.

She began to question Sam. How large is the neighborhood's Catholic community? Are they regular churchgoers? What do the girls usually do after leaving school? She drew him out slowly, careful not to step on any small-town sensitivities.

What would Sam make, she wondered, of a Church in which so many of its priests and nuns were confused about their sexual roles? A month ago she had attended a lecture in Philadelphia on the role of androgyny in religious life. The statistical evidence had been shattering: over twice as many priests as laymen, in one sample poll, admitted to feeling and wanting to behave like women.

The town was like a hundred others she had visited these past two years: tacked-on porches; outbuildings; a drugstore; a handful of other shops; perhaps a hundred modest houses scattered on either side of the highway.

Sam stuffed his cigar into a pocket. He pointed at a single-story building with a playing area at the rear: the school.

"Wait, I have to change," she explained.

"Well, seeing as who you are, I'd be honored if you'd use my place."

He swung the Ford across the road. The house was behind the garage. He carried her case, apologizing before he opened the front door.

"My wife died three years ago. Never got over losing our only child. I don't bother much."

She still remembered when her own father died. The pain had lasted long afterward. During those first years in the Mother House she sometimes awoke, imagining his voice. That was before she had learned to call up other male voices, ones able to excite and dominate her fantasies, and finally to satisfy her.

Sam led her into a bedroom. The bed was unmade. He rushed forward, pulling up the coverlet. She smiled as he closed the door behind him. She

301

opened her suitcase and took out her habit. It was made of crease-resistant material. The training sister had explained its importance:

"How you wear it will initially decide how they see you. Wear it in the knowledge that it has stood the test of time. Modified it now is, but it is still a habit, the outward badge of your office. It is special. It's your badge of courage. It shows you have made sacrifices. These are the thoughts you must get across to a class. Courage. Victory. Positive ideas. They are the captivating images."

She changed out of her suit, and in her bra and slip walked over to an old-fashioned mirror on a stand and used a tissue to remove her makeup. She stared for a moment, as she often did nowadays, at her reflection. It was, she knew, not that she was making up for all those years when she had been forbidden access to a mirror. She searched for something else, a confirmation of what she had once written in her notebook.

"I want to be a good nun. But I want to be a fulfilled woman, allowed to behave as I want, openly, without having to hide and pretend. The more I learn, the more I see that it is a convenience for the Church to stamp hard on all forms of sexuality. It is the most powerful way it has to control us. Sexuality is the force of life and all energy. God gave it to us. Why should men take it away from us?"

Just as she had dressed on that first day as a postulant, she now put on her habit, garment by garment, thinking again how, indeed, some things never changed.

† † †

Father McKenna reclined on the sofa, thinking hard. The fire in the sitting-room grate drew noisily. The snow had stopped, but the wind had risen. Father Breslin sat in the armchair to one side, sweltering, wondering how the old priest, directly in front of the hearth, could stand the heat.

Some of his most rewarding moments had been spent in this room, contemplating something Father McKenna said. It was here, for example, that the parish priest pinpointed that the Church's way out of man's moral distress was not the Greek way of knowledge, based on redemption from ignorance. Nor did it echo ancient Egypt's escape from mortality, with its elaborate ritual centered on the embalmed mummy. Nor, again, did it embrace Buddhism's self-elimination set out in the doctrine of Nirvana. Father McKenna said that after a life of ministry, he was as certain now as he had been on the day of his ordination that the Church's doctrine of re-demption is, God is gracious. No more — no less. On other occasions he had shown he could listen, sitting in intent fellowship as Father Breslin explained his own feelings about how God is known, the authority of the Church, of the Bible, and the need for true religious authority to have an essential mystery. Each found in the other, Father Breslin was certain, a great deal more than merely an exchange of ideas. They had from the very beginning spoken to each other from the soul.

The housekeeper commenced dusting on the far side of the room. Father Breslin was reminded again of how she resembled a tree that had grown in the permanent shade. She looked undernourished, gnarled, and pale. Her hair was unnaturally black, as if she dyed it and was indifferent as to whether it complimented her skin: a half-completed vanity, perhaps? Her expression now was, as always, fixed and frozen as if by some terrible mo-ment of long ago. It had aged with her, deepening the lines on her face. It was a suspicious and resigned look.

Father Breslin wondered why Miss Maddox behaved as she did. It was almost as if she got some pleasure in hearing the anger surge in Father McKenna's throat, seeing his face darken and his temples beat. She could drive him in moments to almost speechless fury. And yet, she was happy when his anger abated, and they could be reunited in a silent, but for all that, a strongly bonded union, each aware of the value of his or her space, never encroaching too far. The sofa was undeniably Father McKenna's ter-ritory.

On Sundays after breakfast, Father Breslin went through his sermon point by point with the parish priest, and every time, without fail, Miss Maddox contrived to be present, listening, indicating approval or rejection through facial movements he had come to recognize were as distinctive as any semaphore.

"I thought I'd base it on the text 'needs must I carry my life in my hands'; to show this is the meaning of this Sunday; a new coming, a new call from God to us; time for a renewal, a new time for decision."

Miss Maddox watched him in a mirror. Her lips, by the slightest frac-tion, parted. Approval.

Encouraged, he continued to expound upon the sermon.

"I thought I would tell them about the feasts of the new year of salva-tion —"

"A good phrase. Perfect for the Pro-Cathedral. But a mite highfalutin for here, don't you think?"

"Fair enough." Father Breslin scored out the words.

Miss Maddox's nose twitched, once, so quickly that the movement was almost imperceptible. Disapproval.

One evening last summer, they had sat here, only a few sods of turf glowing in the hearth, and discussed how God can be revealed in, and through, the events of time. Father McKenna had remembered going to bed as a small child and being unable to sleep. He had crept downstairs and peeped into the kitchen. His mother was sitting with some neighbors who had dropped by. That he was for the moment clearly far from her thoughts came to him as a shock. He had until then always assumed as a matter of course that she lived only for him, and really had no substantive identity of her own.

It's the same with God, Father McKenna insisted. "In a way He has a life of His own, one that transcends time in its divine simultaneity." He had leaned forward, his face flowing in the embers.

"Remember, Seamus, our faith has never confessed the ineffable mystery of God's eternal being. It implies it. As priests, we must never forget to preach that man may only worship something that cannot be conceived as being greater. To worship anything less is idolatry. They taught us both that at Clonliffe. But we have to make it work by showing, like my mother showed me, the true and wider meaning of faith to those who would never really understand what I have just said. Always keep it simple, Seamus."

Father McKenna had a further thought.

"When you link Advent and the Resurrection, you must stress why at the beginning of the ritual year, the Lord must come as judge. Advent is the start of our process of judging ourselves."

"I can work that in. Many thanks."

"I said that over forty years ago. They won't remember that now, of course. But nothing's new."

Father Breslin continued reading from his notes, explaining how he wanted to remind the congregation of the high serious character of Advent; of why it is the first great liturgical vision, a reminder of the longing for salvation.

" 'Man cannot achieve it alone. God must come to him. God's Eternal love, drawn by the poverty of man, gives him the pledge of salvation. That, we must see, is the first meaning of Advent.' "

"Excellent. Really quite excellent."

They continued to go through the sermon until the housekeeper reminded them, as she did every Sunday, of the time. Father Breslin went to his room and typed up the notes, reducing them to a series of headings on a single sheet of paper. He put it in his cassock pocket.

It had started to snow again. But he would go, because his father needed him, and he needed to be there, just as he also felt a need to add some further thoughts to the tape he had listened to earlier this morning. It was not only, he reminded himself, another liturgical year that was ending and a new one starting. He was about to begin a further twelve months of struggle within himself. The fact must be recorded as well as additions made to previous explanations. He quickly set up the recorder on his desk and crouched over it.

Intellectually, he could rationalize sin and guilt, judgment and grace. He had always seen their primary and permanent emphasis as ethical; that, if salvation is to be real, God and God alone must offer it.

"What I am trying to say is that I must be perfectly truthful to myself, and to God, when I say afterward there has been no volition. That is the whole key to living a sexual life within this framework, which I fully accept. No question of that. I am not going to start a revolution. Not after something has been going for almost a couple of millennia. All I want to do here . . . is to put down a few thoughts. I think there should be a proper course for every seminarian and for every priest. Yes, why not? For every priest, given by a psychiatrist, not a theologian. All about the twilight zone. The rules need to be clearly set out. At the moment there is nothing. . . ."

He stopped the recording. Righteousness so easily clouded the sin of self-righteousness. Long ago he had learned that there was no sin so subtly dangerous as the self-sufficiency of the morally righteous man. Indeed, all righteousness was suspect. High-sounding moral principles often included a rationalization of self-interest — egotism asserting itself as idealism. Self-righteousness wrapped up in another guise. Was this what he was doing in suggesting guidelines for his fantasies?

He pressed the button.

"I do not know; when I sit here, into my mind come Browning's lines about the reality of our faith. ' 'Tis the faith that launched point-blank her dart/At the head of a lie — taught Original Sin,/The corruption of Man's Heart.' There is a lot more in that than I have first realized . . . and all the great thinkers of modern times . . . I'm thinking especially of Montaigne and Pascal, Kierkegaard, Nietzsche, and Freud . . . not all, by any means in the Church's good books . . . well, they have probed the human heart and told the truth about its strength. But we, as priests, we need to know about how to handle its weakness. It is the submerged rock on which our complacency will be shipwrecked. Sin . . . that is what I am talking about. . . ."

He paused. He had recorded, in these past weeks, a great deal about his views on sin. Much of it was detached, an intellectual reasoning that man's tragic apostasy from God is not something that occurred at one single awful moment: it is always present. The symbolism of the Creation complements the Fall. But now he decided to personalize his argument.

"The very word has an individual reference. I have already said it must be a conscious and responsible act of will each time. This is not a full description of what sin is. There is also a state of sinfulness . . . something that mysteriously forms the empirical side of my character. But it is even more. If I commit a sin, it is not my business alone. My failure is a failure for all priests who are struggling with me. That is why we call it the priesthood . . . our lives are interlocked. That is what Saint Augustine meant by sinful mass, when he spoke about 'each the work of all, in all the work of each.' And it was Dostoyevsky who said that 'we are each responsible to all for all.' And yet, where does the Church help us to understand that below not only our conscious, but also below the unconscious, there is another layer? There live my hidden inborn forces that are in all truth beyond the conscious control of my will. . . ."

There was a knock on the door. He turned, startled; it was Miss Maddox reminding him of the time.

† † †

Victoria waited while the religious teacher, her introduction complete, retired to a chair in a corner of the classroom. For a moment longer she surveyed the girls seated at their desks before her.

"I chew bubble gum, I like French fries and bacon burgers. I also dated when I was your age."

A shivery murmur, a mixture of surprise and delight, the one she expected, swept the class.

"I've also had a call from God. Not collect, but if you like, direct. He dialed into my soul one day, when I was your age, not so long ago now, and

306

here I am. You get a lot of recruiters trying to convince you they hold the answer to your futures. Well, I'm not going to do that. Your future doesn't rest in my hands. Just as it doesn't rest in their hands. It is between you and God. I just want to spend this time explaining why I answered His call, what it means to do so, and why His voice is deep inside me still. That when the going gets tough, He is always there. If anybody thinks this is not what they want to hear, then please feel free to leave."

She paused. The training sister had stressed the need for immediate identification, to be followed by an option. *Give them the chance to get up and walk out. They almost certainly won't — because they will not wish to miss anything. You've got their attention then. It's up to you to hold it.*

Nobody moved.

Victoria defined a vocation and said that from the beginning it had been ordinary boys and girls who had recognized a commitment. She explained that the core of a vocation was renunciation. She dropped in her first scriptural reference: Saint Paul's message to the Corinthians that Christ saw them as ambassadors for Him and that they should renounce their licentious ways.

"For me, it meant giving up dating. But, you know, what surprised me was how quickly I came to see that worldly pleasures really aren't everything. I saw what Saint Augustine had meant when he said he had felt something was still missing by only having a good time. He wanted more in his life. I guess I did."

†

When had she first missed them — all those physical joys she had promised to renounce forever, and believed she could? The question had drifted into her mind again last night as she lay awake in her motel room, blaming the softness of the bed and the strangeness of her surroundings for being unable to sleep. She had lain on her back, naked as she always now slept, her legs apart, her hands by her side, listening to the roar of the trucks on the expressway, reminded of Art and that night in the car. She never tired of his memory, of the last time she had been physically touched by a man. The roughness of his movements had again aroused her, and afterward, when it was over — and she had been able to assuage what she described in her notebook as "this raging hunger that rushes up through me" — she wondered if he was still as she remembered him. Or had marriage and three children calmed his passions?

He had never become a pilot, ending up instead as a salesman with a ball-bearings company. He once traveled a lot; he used to send her post-cards from all over the country, the words carefully innocuous, always signed "love, A.," as if he suspected that his first and only letter had never got beyond the Mistress. The cards had helped to reinforce her fantasies; she imagined she was with him in the places he had posted them from. Then, abruptly, they stopped. She learned much later that he had become a desk-bound executive. It made no difference. In her twilight zone, he still made love to her in his office after the staff had gone home.

Danny was no more — incinerated in an auto crash. Her mother had sent her a newspaper clipping about the incident and she had been filled with guilt that she had been unfair to Danny: she should not have felt soiled because he was the first. She should have been grateful he had been so gentle.

But in her fantasies, she now preferred men to be like Art, forceful and thrusting, almost as if she was being raped and was powerless — convincing her that physical satisfaction was completely possible within her religious life.

✝

The training sister had emphasized the need to be realistic. *Anything that can help them to identify will help you to get across your points. The important thing to stress is that being a nun is not doing something weird, that it is a very natural choice for living.*

She gave them the latest figures for the sisterhood.

"It's a tough life today for many of us. More nuns are being persecuted today than at any other time in history. This is the age of their martyrdom. In Czechoslovakia right now there are over ten thousand nuns in prison."

There were gulps from some of the girls. The idea of women going to prison for their faith always struck a chord.

"What keeps them going is the knowledge Christ promised them His divine protection. No other job offers that. No other employer can, or would, dare say to you that he will guarantee to protect you twenty-four hours a day until you die. Christ does."

A girl in the front row had a faraway look in her eyes. Victoria, for the moment, concentrated on her, explaining that renunciation was never easy; there was always a measure of suffering.

✝

Early on she had faced, and rejected, the idea of leaving the sisterhood. In her notebook she had written:

"That would be the easy option. I believe, unlike Luther, that this is a fight which must be won from within the ranks. If I felt I was alone I would perhaps reconsider and resign. But I am certain there is a growing number of religious like me who feel that renunciation should no longer include an enforced celibacy, that it is psychologically dangerous, sociologically out of step, and theologically dubious. More than any of the other forces continuing to tug and tear at the very foundations of the Church, the issue of sexuality is the one that will actually blow the lid off the pressure cooker. Behind all the formal argument and clash of opinions is the issue of sexual freedom. It, more than anything else, is driving the Church even faster down the religious tube."

She could not understand why the Pope was deaf to what was happening. How could he remain impervious to reason? How could he insist there could be no choice?

✝

She began to explain about choice.

"For most of you here today, it is clearly made. You will get married and raise a family. That's absolutely fine. But perhaps, for one or two of you, the idea of getting married and having children is not everything. This is not your prime consideration."

The sister tutor had been clear: *Always emphasize the concept of being special. That's always important. A girl who is interested could be influenced against feeling she has been called if she thinks everybody else has also been. Always get across the idea that a vocation is something precious. And link it with family pride.*

"No one's locked away — like they show you in the old movies. Those days are gone. Your family get to visit you. You get vacations. If there has to be renunciation, there is also reward."

She inserted another scriptural example, the story of how Saint Paul discovered that while his vocation made stringent demands, there was the compensation of living in Christ.

She waited, at the midpoint of her talk, expertly assessing the impact so far.

The girl with the faraway gaze was a possibility. So was the fair-haired teenager at the back who stared fixedly at her. Perhaps a third potential postulant was the young black in the middle of the class. It was more than she had expected.

She began to explain how the life of any nun was governed by vows, describing the pledges as a way of showing complete trust in God. Each required its own special kind of courage on the path to holy consecration. The vows were an exterior symbol of an inner serenity.

She began with poverty.

"Have you ever thought how much trouble possessions can cause? How many times have you fought with a brother or sister over things? And in the end it isn't worth it. And look how much emphasis everybody puts on possessions. People are measured by what model of car they have, where they go on vacation, which country club they belong to. In religious life we don't value such things. Our convent car is almost as old as Henry Ford himself! None of us ever goes to a country club, except to collect gifts for a tag sale. And, you know, I don't think any of us miss that sort of thing. And yet we don't live like paupers."

She explained that since the Second Vatican Council, the Church had dramatically reassessed its views on poverty. No longer were its ascetic values emphasized: now the emphasis was on seeing poverty as part of living a modest life in religious orders.

"The bottom line with poverty is forgetting our own selfish needs. It is a turning away from our egos. Saint Luke put it very well: '*No man putting his hand to the plough, and looking back, is fit for the kingdom of God.*' To look back is to cling to possessions. Someone very dear to me told me that."

✝

Sister Elizabeth had been dead for three years, never regaining consciousness after being mugged. Her cross and chain, the only items of value on her body, had been torn from her neck. At her funeral Reverend Mother had reminded them that if Satan had a plan Jesus could work through it. Standing at the grave of her old teacher, Victoria recalled it was Sister Elizabeth who taught her, many years ago, that it had once been permissible for faith to use violence to spread its message because, as the Gospel says, "*the Kingdom of Heaven suffereth violence, and the violent bear it away.*"

Victoria felt the Church had adopted this justification now to control those within its ranks who dared oppose its teachings. From the full majesty of its high efflorescence it showed that, no matter what the Council had promised, there could be no room for argument against the suppression of that most basic of all freedoms — that of the body. She believed that by denying this one liberty, it had driven many nuns and priests into sociopolitical activity and activism of all sorts, and she recorded in her notebook that the Church was calling a plague upon itself by its intransigence.

Returning to the Mother House after the funeral, she sat and listened to the early evening news announce that the American Bishops' Conference admitted it had lost another fourteen hundred priests in the preceding year and that vocations had dropped by 48 percent for the priesthood and more than 60 percent for the sisterhood. Next morning the findings of another poll were published. Eight out of every ten priests surveyed across the country under the age of forty-five said they were against compulsory celibacy; one in five claimed he would resign unless there was a change in the rule.

✝

"Now for the vow that makes everybody say: 'Thanks — but not for me.' Chastity."

She waited a long moment. When the excitement had run its course through the room, she asked a question: "How many of you have seen *The Nun's Story?*"

Hands shot into the air.

"I bet you all remember Audrey Hepburn — Sister Luke — going through all that preparation and having it drilled into her that she had to cut herself off from the world forever in an emotional sense. Die to it. You all remember that?"

They did.

"Well, it is, and it isn't, like that anymore. Do you remember how the doctor said to Sister Luke, when they worked together in that hospital in Africa, 'Do you know, Sister, what I most admire in you?' And she asked him, 'What?' And he said, 'Your total faithfulness to Christ.' That is what chastity comes down to in the end. Being faithful."

It had, in the beginning, when she was preparing and rehearsing her talk under the watchful eyes of the tutor sister, taken her weeks to reduce it to this short statement. She had worried over every word, wondering how far what she had said actually reflected what she now thought. But the instructor had been satisfied, repeating her words as a model for the other vocation counselors. *A perfect example of not laying overemphasis. Touch on the subject. Don't hammer at it. Girls today need more time to absorb the idea of chastity. They mustn't be frightened off. Later, when they are here, we can explain to them the deeper realities.*

The final vow to be explained was the one that gave her the least trouble.

"When I was at high school, I was probably the most disobedient in the whole class. I just bucked authority. I thought that was terrific. Later, I saw what my problem was. I just didn't have the faith to be myself, so I was disobedient — trying to be somebody else. You have to be obedient to be a nun. You get asked to do some pretty hard things. Like going off to work with Mother Theresa of Calcutta. Or helping the poor in Africa. We send our people everywhere. It's a bit like being in the army — except we are fighting a far more deadly enemy than even Communism. Every nun is fighting the Devil. That's what it comes down to in the end. Good versus evil. If any of you want to join in that fight, I'll be happy to see you afterward."

She stopped, thinking that perhaps in this room there was one girl who would have made this long journey worthwhile.

† † †

Father Breslin unlocked the door, instinctively stamping the snow off his shoes, and wiped his feet on the doormat, the way his mother had always insisted all the family should before entering the kitchen. Even now, he still thought of it as *her kitchen*. Right to the very end, this had been her domain: his father could occupy it, but she owned it. It had been hers to arrange and rearrange. It was his mother who had agreed to have the old radio and oil lamp sent to auction; the proceeds helped to buy a new television set to stand in their place. It was she who had vetoed having the floor resurfaced with linoleum. Standing in the doorway, the cold of the room almost as icy as the weather outside, he could recall her voice, gentle but firmly insistent, addressing his father. "Kevin, flagstones belong in a kitchen. They keep the place cool in summer and hold the heat in winter."

He closed the door behind him. There was still a faint smell of turf smoke, even though the oven had been converted to gas the year before she died. That was when she also agreed to move the eight-day clock from the sideboard to the front parlor. On a wall hung its replacement, an ugly battery-operated, square-faced timepiece his father had bought in a pub off a crony. It had stopped after six months, at a quarter to four, and its battery had never been replaced. Glancing at it, Father Breslin wondered if it had been morning or afternoon when it had ceased to tick.

Every Sunday afternoon on his way to the hospital, he came here, to check on the house, to make sure it had not been damaged by weather or vandalized now that his father was in the hospital. It would have to be sold eventually; that would be the hardest part, disturbing all these memories. He moved around the kitchen, touching and remembering. Only the week before she died, she had stood at the table and prepared a tea-brac for him, mixing the ingredients from a recipe that had been in her family for over a hundred years. He had driven over to collect it. She was wrapping it in greaseproof paper to keep it fresh, when she had winced and closed her eyes, squeezing back tears of pain. He had wanted to call the doctor or drive her to the hospital; instead, she stopped him, saying very calmly there was no need to waste their time.

He stared at the photographs on the sideboard top. Where once there had been only her children, there were now grandchildren: his sisters had married and produced families of their own. In her last years, his mother had never missed a chance to photograph any member of the family: at Christmas and Easter; outside the house, in its parlor. There was only one snap of her, standing in the kitchen doorway, the pretty print dress hanging on her like a shroud; even then, her legs and arms were like matchsticks. That was a full two years before the end.

He still firmly believed her religion had enabled her to survive so long. He stared around the kitchen, recalling how here they shared some of their most important conversations about the meaning of death. She was never evasive. Her end was coming: she would face it with fortitude. She took medicine to ease the pain; had ample faith to keep at bay any doubt. Her only hope was that she would pass away peacefully in her sleep. "I wouldn't want, Seamus, having you all around the bed, waiting, and me lying there, waiting. I don't want that at all. Besides, I know we will all meet again."

Her words reminded him how firmly she believed in a future existence. She had very definite views. "Our trouble is that we all like to think we are not made to die. All my life I've tried to live by one great truth, the impermanence of this world."

He left the kitchen, walking through to the parlor, remembering the last time he helped her over these few steps. The cancer had forced her to use a stick; when he was there she always preferred to lean on his arm.

The parlor was dark, the curtains drawn. He switched on a light. The room was furnished from another age: a shiny imitation leather sofa, a coffee table, its top scuffed. His father would sometimes sleep off his drinking bouts in an armchair, using the tabletop as a foot rest. The clock on the mantel had long stopped, like its kitchen replacement. The grate was stuffed with old newspapers; the fire hadn't been used for years. The plant-holders were empty; the plants had died when she did. She had said they would: "Your daddy doesn't have green fingers." It was not a judgment, it was more a defense. Here they explored another aspect of death: that it is the sacrament of sin, because it effectively represents opportunities gone forever. She had sat opposite him one afternoon and displayed again, in her own modest manner, that she had more instinctive insights than some theologians he knew, saying that in a way thinking of death was the greatest of all thoughts except thinking of God. He had said that was very profound, and she smiled and said she had not meant to be.

He turned off the light and closed the parlor door. The wind was sighing through the letter box. Long ago, after the break-in, his father had removed the key on its string. A thief, no more than a boy really, had brazenly pulled it out through the letter box, opened the front door, and made off with some loose change on the hall table. He might have gotten away with more if Kevin Breslin had not emerged from the kitchen. He had given chase but lost the youth in a side street. He had not bothered to report the incident to the police; already he had started to suspect them as being incapable of providing the law and order he thought necessary.

Father Breslin checked the top-floor bedrooms. He could not recall ever seeing her in bed, except in the hospital. Even then, surrounded by efficiency, she seemed better able than anybody else to take care of herself. She would wave the nurses away, whispering for them to tend to other patients, saying she wanted nothing. They had been sitting holding hands, not talking, when she had finally given up the fight. She had been dead for some minutes before he realized it. He had wept, dried his tears, and then anointed her. Later he conducted her funeral service. His mother was the first person in his ministry he had buried.

His father had come here from the cemetery, trembling, already in fear of his own mortality.

Father Breslin carefully locked the kitchen door behind him and walked to Father McKenna's car to drive to the hospital. It was one of the oldest in a city of old hospitals. He parked in the front lot, among the doctors' cars, a priest's privilege. The porter at the desk told him the duty doctor would like to see him in his office. Instinctively, he walked faster, past the cafeteria where relatives sat smoking and drinking from Styrofoam cups, waiting for news and decisions. The office was a cubbyhole with a dirty window and a single chair facing the desk. The doctor was young, but already equipped with the voice of professional kindness.

"I'm sorry to have to tell you, he died an hour ago. It happened suddenly.

A total collapse. Heart. Lungs. All at once. Nothing could have saved him. Mercifully, it was all over —"

"May I see him?"

"I'd really advise against that. Try and remember him as he was in life."

"I'd like to see him. Please."

"Of course, Father. I'm sorry, of course you can."

His father had the mortuary to himself, laid out on a gurney in the pajamas he'd given him last Christmas. It was here, at last, that he felt a grief, raw and lacerating.

✝ ✝ ✝

The priest whose name he did not know reminded Father Philippe he must remain silent. Not by so much as a whispered syllable could he offer a word of defense: none was open to him. One black-gloved hand pulled the cowl across the priest's face so that only his eyes were visible, bloodshot and filled with an intensity he found even more terrifying than the man's spectral voice. He was nudged past the papal knights and the Swiss Guards at their posts in the corridors. For months, though he could not be certain for how long, he had been incarcerated in one of the dungeons of the Apostolic Palace in the Vatican. How or who brought him here was a blurred memory. Simone, with the connivance of his doctor, he suspected, must have drugged him. She had, he knew, cooperated in other ways, giving evidence against him, describing the most intimate moments of their life. She had lied, of course; it *was* her fault, all of it. But his judges had not listened. Now, he was being brought from the depths of this stronghold for popes these past six centuries, to hear sentence pronounced. The hooded priest urged him forward up another wide flight of stone steps, icy cold to his bare feet. They reached a great inner courtyard, cobbled and open to the elements. A blistering merciless wind howled around the piazza, chilling the blood in his veins. He was naked under the high-buttoning cassock that hid the absence of his Roman collar. Before leaving his cell, he had been made to burn it in the presence of the priest who pushed him on across the cobbles. The windows of the buildings that boxed in the square were filled with faces. Many he did not know; stone-faced men in the red, black, purple, and white vestments of the Church. But in one window was Frank, peering down at him, talking on the telephone, dressed in medieval clerical garb. Before he could attract Frank's attention, the priest had pushed him forward, past another window. In it, jeweled and bewigged, but nevertheless recognizable, stood his mother. She was shouting at him in a language he did not understand. A few windows beyond was Walter. He wore one of the most splendid of all the Church's uniforms, the full regalia of a Knight of Malta. One hand extended accusingly toward him, the other grasped a copy of Schopenhauer. Walter intoned that he had never wanted to be kissed in the bookstore. At an adjoining window stood Lolo, naked, as she had been when he left her in the Holiday Inn. Suddenly, she opened her mouth and he saw she had no teeth. He traversed the courtyard, his feet scratched and bleeding from the stones. Waiting in a massive doorway, spanned by a lintel of hewn marble, was Father Brannigan. He wore the armor of a Crusader covered with a robe made from hopsack, dyed brown. Under one arm he held his helmet. In the other hand were his sword and shield. He turned and marched into the building, leading the way, shouting in between his tears that this is the time of repentance, that penance is justice, and pardon is possible only after punishment. He led them down a short corridor ending in two of the tallest doors he had ever seen. They must have been thirty feet high. Father Brannigan rapped on them with his sword. Once. Twice. They silently swung open. Father Brannigan and the cowled priest stood aside. He must enter alone. At the far end of this vast hall was a raised platform. With its tiers of candelabra dripping tallow and tall, free-standing crucifixes on white starched cloths, it resembled an altar. But no altar he had seen was as wide as this one, stretching from wall to wall of this hall. Even then the judges seated behind it were bunched together. From a distance they were a mass of purple. But, as he approached, he recognized faces. Mr. Watts was there, as imposing and ascetic-looking as he had been in the banqueting room in Dallas. A few places along toward the center, sat his daughter, her cloak trimmed with gold coins. Between them, she and her father had led that part of the inquisition dealing with Lolo, demanding every detail. There, too, was the priest to whom he had confessed about Lolo, and who had recounted every word of it to the judges. How was it possible, he had interrupted at one stage, for a priest to be allowed to break the sacred secrecy of the confessional? The majestic figure in the center of the tableau, toward whom he was finally approaching, had ordered him to be silent. On the index finger of the figure's right hand was a ring surmounted by a perfectly carved crucifix — the Fisherman's Ring. On his head was a towering conical miter. But just as, earlier, it had been the priest's eyes that had terrified him, now he was petrified by the gaze of the Pope. The pontiff's head perpetually turned to absorb everything that was happening and to indicate, by a nod, that he must stop and kneel before him. At first he could not see Simone, only heard her chanting. Then she emerged from behind the Pope's throne and stood at the pontiff's elbow. She was taller and even more beautiful than when he had last seen her. Simone was dressed in a full habit. He still could not make out the words of her plainchant. Father Brannigan had often warned him to pay more attention to his Latin. Then, with a shock that made him tremble, he realized that each long, divided syllable was an account of his failure to live a celibate life. The Pope finally raised his hand. His voice stunned him. It was that of Judge Dupois. Then, as it began to pass sentence, Father Philippe continued to tear at his skin, drawing blood, spotting the sheets of his bed in the monk's cell, clawing at himself so violently that he surfaced from his twilight zone. Night after night, he experienced the same fantasy — always identical down to the last detail. He had been ordered into this monastery by the Prefect for the Sacred Congregation for the Faith, the Holy Office, which, since 1542, has been responsible for conducting all the Church's inquisitions. In confining Father Philippe to this institution, the Prefect had reminded him he had done so while the Supreme Pontiff, Pope Paul VI, considered his future. The previous evening, Father Philippe learned that a letter, its envelope embossed with the Pope's heraldic coat-of-arms, had been delivered to the abbot. After reading it the abbot went to the monastery chapel to pray. It was this knowledge, the terrible uncertainty over what had been decided would be his fate, that impelled Father Philippe to awaken and kneel on his bed.

CHAPTER 14

†

Beyond the Dawn

Inhaling slowly, the way he had been taught to calm himself after the nightmare, Father Philippe stood at the window, realizing these past months in therapy had been the most painful of his life. The analyst had spoken about a need to locate the psychodynamics that created the nightmare. Sensing his lack of comprehension, the doctor explained he would have to trace and define his *alienation*: what made him continue to resent his mother's rejection; what was at the root of his self-preoccupation, his fears, and anxieties; why he was so emotionally starved; why his infantile ego had never developed an independent identity, giving him that sense of self which would have provided the maturity to live in an adult world.

In these months his psychological needs and deficiencies had been located one by one, the process so hurtful at times he had just sat in the doctor's office and wept copiously. The analyst had pinpointed his obsession with possessions, position, and power, explaining they represented his desperate search to seek selfhood from without, using *things* to serve as a measure of his ego and his definition of identity. That was why he so often had behaved unstably, as inner pressures built up and ran rampant within him, freed of the normal restraints of an integrated personality. Walter had, in that sense, been a *thing*. So had Lolo and marriage to Simone. His adulation of Frank fitted the same pattern. Even his vocation could be seen as a *thing*.

The doctor said therapy must be designed to give him a new ego and a dependable sense of maturity. It would be a long and demanding process, one in which all the implications of the nightmare would be thoroughly explored. He asked him what were the chances of success. The doctor had been honest. "There is no way of knowing. There never is. But let's both always be positive."

He had come a long way, even if the nightmare continued to torment him. It was so vivid that, even fully awake, he could still see that awesome palace and what happened within the walls of his mind. He began keeping a written record shortly after he had telephoned Frank and begged him to help him return to the priesthood. Frank had arranged for him to see the Bishop. The chancellor, saying there could be no question of his returning to his old parish, had dripped poison. "I'm sure you understand it would be difficult for those ladies whose hair you have been shampooing to have you resume ministering to their souls."

The Bishop was sympathetic. "An aberration. That's what you experienced. A genuine aberration. That's why I never forwarded your dispensation to Rome. I just wrote the Holy Office a report. The bare facts. They agreed to wait. We both hoped you would come to your senses."

But there had to be a punishment. For a start, he must agree to be confined in this monastery while the Holy Office considered his future.

The Bishop had been the first to suggest the idea of a record. "Use the time valuably. Think upon your experiences. See the lessons. Put them on paper. It often helps, you know."

The analyst encouraged the idea. Father Philippe had been referred to his office after the abbot learned of the nightmare; a monk in an adjoining cell had heard the shouts.

At first he found it difficult. When he initially tried to record his feelings about his mother, he would feel nauseated. He would walk away from the desk and stand at the window. But slowly, over weeks, he became no longer afraid to dredge the deeper recesses of his mind, and much of his diary was revealing. He had written, among other things, how the wind so often reminded him of a child crying for its mother.

Now, standing at his cell window in the darkness, he again saw the breeze as a living, silent entity. A day's drive away Simone would be asleep, the bedroom window open, the wind tugging at the drapes. The same wind that had touched her now touched him.

He concentrated on the movement of his lungs, forcing himself to inhale and exhale as slowly as possible. About a week after he had arrived, the wind suddenly turned into a howling fury, and he sat on his bed scribbling distractedly that the storm reminded him of the words of Yeats. "The wind blows over the lonely of heart. And the lonely of heart is withered away." He had, he wrote, been scared then, because he had also remembered how his mother would croon, "When the wind blows the children will cry." He used to hate her singing it.

After reading the passage to the psychoanalyst, he was reassured. While the words were further proof of how traumatized he was, his admission about his mother showed that at last he was no longer somebody who obliterated his past. Once that had been the only way his mind could offer self-help; sealing off all unpleasant memories. "In a clinical sense you are a person without a past." He found the doctor's phrase so striking that it went into his record.

There, too, was a full account of the incident the analyst often returned to.

There had been a strong breeze on that night he agreed to meet Simone at a Ramada Inn. It required a bare-faced lie to the abbot before he was given permission to leave the monastery. He told the old monk his mother had taken a turn for the worse. At first he had been filled with foreboding. His divorce lawyer had been quite clear.

"Stay away from her. No contact at all. The fastest way to end this business is to show grounds for incompatibility. It happens more often than you think. A priest falls for a woman's wiles but can't forget he's a priest. Just because you shared a bed with her doesn't mean you forgot your vocation. But no contact with your wife. None at all."

He had been surprised to discover the attorney was a practicing Catholic and was even more astonished to learn that he knew Mr. Watts and handled a lot of the Church's legal problems. He had a reputation, he said, matter-of-factly, for getting priests and nuns divorced faster than probably any other lawyer in the state.

On the day the papers were filed, Simone called him at the monastery, on the pay phone near the front door. He had been pleasantly surprised to hear that her voice was free of the pathos he remembered in their last weeks together. She said she had only wanted to know how he was. He was fine, he told her. How was she? Coping, she said, laughing; she was thinking of going back to teaching Sunday school. Was that a good idea? He had thought for a moment before deciding. It was. She ended by telling him he could always call her. "I'm always here for you. I really want you to believe that."

He should have stopped her there, and told her, firmly, it was over. Instead, a few days later, he telephoned her. It was after an especially hard day of crop-spraying with only a monk as company, talking endlessly about the joys of the contemplative life. He had wanted, then, to hear her voice. They had spoken for a long time, until the campanile bell heralding the Great Silence put an end to the call.

Not only did he know he should not have made the call but also he should have reported the previous one to the analyst; he had promised at their first interview to disclose everything. But the therapy was still at its opening stage.

Just as he had drifted into his relationship with Walter, so he rekindled one with Simone. It became their secret. She would phone him one night, he would call her the next. He would discuss in a loud concerned voice the plight of his mother when one of the monks happened to pass the pay phone. When they were out of earshot, he would explain how the divorce was proceeding from his end: he had asked his lawyer not to press for the return of his possessions. She could keep them: the solid-silver candlesticks, the antique furnishings and paintings he had brought into their home.

He knew they both enjoyed the sensation of fooling their respective lawyers; and, for him, there was the very special pleasure of hoodwinking the abbot. The monk had struck him in those days as being supercilious and condescending. When Simone finally suggested they could meet at the Ramada Inn, he felt no compunction about lying.

Parking the car outside the motel, he had an unsettling moment when Sister Mildred came into his thoughts. He would later swear she had told him to turn back. Instead, he had gone on.

†

The bedroom was a reproduction of every other Ramada room. She had checked in earlier and bathed and put on a nightdress he could not remember seeing before — purple and clingy. He was about to switch on the overhead lights when she told him not to, reminding him how he liked the light to be soft. Her voice was breathy. She took his hand and guided him into the room, closing the door behind them. She embraced him hungrily, trying to kiss away the weeks they had been apart. He inhaled the fragrance of her perfume. The solitary bedside lamp gave her skin a warm pinkish glow. He remembered the first time they had been together like this and he had been on the brink of his first full sexual experience. Then there had been no question of sin or volition, only one of fulfillment. She had made him feel wanted and attractive, eager to give himself to her. He had. He wanted to now. Her lips ignited feelings he thought had died. She undressed him slowly, the way she had always liked to do, laying him down on the bed, leaning over him, caressing and touching, exploring him again, gently, yet with a sure certainty, arousing in him a fever that he had tried to convince himself was dead but that had never been more alive.

He sat on the window ledge, cooled by the wind, remembering how they had reached new heights that weekend. Then, on the Sunday night, as he dressed to come back here, she had looked at him steadily and said, "Come with me. Let's go home."

Even now he could remember his exact response. "Simone, it would not work on a day-to-day basis. I have to go back."

She stared at him. Finally, she asked with a bitterness he had never heard before: "What sort of man are you? What gives you the right to behave like this? You think you can just take me and dump me?"

She had sounded, at that moment, so like Lolo he had thrown his things together into his overnight bag and driven to the monastery. Only back in its keep did he feel calm and able to control the raging panic.

The abbot had sent for him after supper, saying he had called Father Philippe's mother, who said he had not been there. Where had he been?

The monk's voice was suddenly gentle and compassionate. "You can say anything to me and only you will know if it is the truth. Only you, and God. It is not me you will be speaking to, but Him. Please, tell Him the truth. However much it pains you, be assured He will understand."

He made a complete confession.

The abbot pondered. After some time he came to a decision.

"I don't see a need for you to repeat any of this to your lawyer. I am sure your wife will feel the same in her case. For the matter to become known to lawyers could only complicate the situation. No one would wish that. But you must tell your doctor. This is most important. And from now on you will never leave here again except to see him or your lawyer, until a decision is made in Rome. Is that absolutely clear?"

He said it was.

✝

When he recounted the episode to the analyst, Father Philippe dismissed it as having been no more than a whim, insisting there was nothing in it to analyze. Suddenly, he began to shout. "I've been talking for months. Talking, talking, talking, week after week. What good is it all doing me? I'm tired of it, sick and tired of it, of the whole business."

The doctor remained silent, letting him continue for a while, then asked very quietly, had this outburst not reminded him of someone?

He paused, puzzled, demanding to know, still aggressive, who the doctor meant.

The reply sobered him. "You used to say your mother and Simone browbeat you. Now you're trying to do the same to me."

That was when he began to see himself for what he was. All these years he had been blaming others for faults that were his own. He had chosen the masks he would wear, the poses he would assume. In the end he was hungry for manhood, but refusing to move beyond the diet of an infant.

After the doctor's words, he began to cooperate fully and totally, without holding back. Over several sessions he began to understand what had taken him to the Ramada Inn, and he finally admitted the episode was all part of a romanticized, childish belief that he could behave as he liked.

Guided by the analyst, he gained insights into his sexuality. His feeling of rejection went all the way back to his mother's not having suckled him. He had never been maternally fondled or caressed. These omissions, explained the doctor, had contributed to his anxiety, producing a feeling of being unable to trust his sexual organ to a woman. His mother had, at the first opportunity, stopped washing and drying his genitalia. In later years, this had also helped to create an obsessional fear about sex itself. This is why he failed with Lolo, and why even, in spite of the initial pleasure Simone provided, he had been glad to withdraw physically from her. The visit to the motel was, on that level, no more than another desperate attempt to deny what he knew to be the truth.

The doctor questioned him carefully about one particular matter. Each time he had made love in the motel he had gone to the bathroom to urinate. Had he always done this after having sex? He had. What else had he done in the bathroom? He had been puzzled. Well; had he examined himself? Yes, he had. And what had he been thinking when he had done this? That his penis was still whole and unharmed. Another mask had been peeled away, coming closer to his inner core. The process was hastened when the dam of his years of pent-up strain broke. He sobbed, and in between the tears said he was glad somebody finally understood.

He was puzzled that the analyst had not immediately zeroed in on celibacy; he had always seen his inability to live within the vow at the root of the failure of his vocation. He raised the matter several times in those first weeks until the doctor explained: "Chastity is only a symptom. We have to find the cause of its failure in you before we can get some perspective on how you can handle it in the future — or indeed whether you should."

That idea stuck in his mind.

After two months, when he was still going three times a week to the analyst, the doctor asked him whether he felt that the Holy Trinity was a model for any religious celibate who feels lonely and alienated even though deeply committed. The question had excited him and he had expounded that, indeed, the Father, Son, and Holy Ghost formed a union in which each remains autonomous and unique. The analyst listened intently, then interposed to suggest one possible cause for his failure to cope with celibacy. "Listening to you, I have a distinct impression that the Church over-emphasizes the idea that a priest should focus on his intimate relationship with God to the exclusion of all others."

He walked over to his desk, picked up a book, and began to read. " 'Married lovers are not sexual or passionate enough. And what's more, neither are celibate lovers, who should be at least as sexual and passionate as married people. There is no other way to be a really great lover. And if religious men are not great lovers, what hope is there for Christianity?' "

Handing him the book, he said a priest, not a doctor, wrote those words. That night Father Philippe sat up until dawn, reading *Mystical Passion*. For the first time he saw that it was possible to live a life in Christ without enduring an everyday, emotionally barren existence. Indeed, the book showed that the whole purpose of loving God was to develop along healthy spiritual and psychological lines. For a priest, that meant taking a realistic approach to his sexuality. There was one sentence that synthesized exactly how he wanted to be; he copied it on the inside cover of his diary. " 'If as sexual beings we love not only God but human persons, we become living witnesses, passionate witnesses to Him, and alive and joyous to others.' "

Over the following weeks the analyst explored why his relationship with God, to work properly, must begin with an understanding of who he was. Time and again the doctor surprised him by quoting from the Bible to support his arguments. From the Book of Kings he cited the account of Elijah the prophet climbing a mountain to find God. At the summit he was met first by a howling wind, then by a devastating earthquake, and finally by a fire. But Elijah had not found God in any of these forces. Instead, the old prophet had finally heard the voice of God within himself, no more than a tiny, whispering sound, records the Book of Kings. "You see, the only healthy way to talk to God is from within yourself. And you are only able to do that when you are psychologically strong. Then, and only then, does God take His proper place in your life. That is the first thing you must understand about successfully handling your celibacy. It needs a healthy mind."

The analyst quoted the words of Christ to show that mature loving requires integrating sexuality. "Your problem, one for any priest or nun, is that Canon Law does not allow you to express yourselves as healthy sexual persons."

He explained that sexuality and spirituality are not incompatible. The tragedy was that nobody had shown him how both are at the very core of vocation. Instead of encouraging him to integrate them, his tutors now faced him with an impossible choice. He could be either holy or sensual. But not both. Some priests could cope with this ultimatum. He had not been able to. The sexuality at his three seminaries, by being officially denied, was all the more potent and appealing. Over the years denial had stretched him to a psychological breaking point. The doctor gave him a further guideline. "Some tensions are good for you. Those you experienced with celibacy were not, because no one explained how to handle them. No one said that it is healthy for a priest to be sexual."

Once more the doctor turned to the Gospels for support. Jesus spoke far less about sin than about people who had lost their way, only to rediscover it, and God, by opening themselves to full and satisfying human relationships. "Never forget that though you are a priest, you are also a man. You cannot split your sexuality from your faith. You have to see them as one unifying force that makes it possible for you to live your vow and be a human being."

The doctor urged him to see celibacy not as something mysterious, a consecration of himself only to God, but as an intensely human condition.

"Don't try to be an angel at the expense of being a man. That's part of the reason why you lost touch with your own feelings. Your training as a priest repressed them. Your every word and action warned others to keep a distance. It is a psychologically unhealthy thing for a priest to be on a pedestal. You are always 'Father.' You are encouraged to see yourself as 'special' and 'separate.' That worried you from the beginning. The more you tried to integrate, the more isolated you felt. Your former chancellor is a perfect example of what you feared you might become. Finally, sensing you were even beginning to distance your outer self from your inner self, you leaped into bed with Simone."

He had sat for hours rereading the Gospels. Just as the analyst had predicted, he could not find a single reference that sexual feelings in a priest must be suppressed. He had gone back to the notes he made in Israel and added to them, writing that the Church, by suppressing sexuality among its priests and nuns, has allowed it to assume a power it neither has nor deserves.

The next session had been entirely devoted to discussing this point with the analyst, admitting that, in a sense, he had lived for years outside his body. Apart from Walter and Simone, he had never experienced physical intimacy. His time in the priesthood had, he now saw, been a life spent surrounded by ideas and abstractions; an existence based upon theory but no actual involvement. For all its trappings it had been an empty and cold life, filled with thoughts about feelings as opposed to feelings about thoughts. He had become a workaholic, unable to trust his ability to control the messages from his body, confusing him to the point where he had first turned to Walter and then to Simone. That was, he concluded, probably why he had plunged into marriage, lured away from the arid emotional emptiness of his life as a priest. Anything, he said, was better than waking up alone. Only when he shared a bed, in the promised permanency of a marriage, had he realized he'd exchanged one emotional prison for another.

In the gentlest of voices, the analyst had responded to this outburst.

"Too many mea culpas. Many too many. And, you're labeling yourself. Failure, failure, failure. That's what comes through. That's much too black and white. There's no shading in your self-evaluation. That's because you have such a poor opinion of yourself. Behind all the self-indulgence, you are a very insecure person. You were almost certainly never quite as bad as you have painted. You're swinging far too much the other way. And that is another reason why you have had a problem in coping with celibacy. You understand it on an intellectual level. But not on the emotional plane. You keep the two apart. You live by the dangerous principle of dividing yourself up into compartments. Faith in one. Suppressed sex in another. Vocation in a third. A fourth holding your fantasies. And so on. Suddenly the boxes all popped open at once. Everything got mixed up, rather as if you had put off your emotional responses into a clothes drier. They became so entangled that you did not know which way to turn. So, apart from running into a marriage you never wanted, you had to find an excuse for behaving so irrationally. Celibacy seemed to be the most obvious one. You could convincingly put all the blame on it because it was something you genuinely did not understand how to handle. Psychologically, until now, what you have been unable to grasp, you ignore. Hopefully, that can be changed. But it is going to be you, not me, that works out how to live with a new set of values. I'll lay them out for you, especially as far as celibacy goes. But only pick up those you know you can be genuinely comfortable with."

It was, he now recalled, the longest speech the analyst had ever made. But he was beginning to see how celibacy had to be totally rethought. He could no longer pretend to be comfortable with the existing view of the Church, that the only effective way of living his vow was to suppress his sexual drive. For centuries the Church had insisted that one of the strongest forces of the human personality was a sin for a priest. To survive as a man he would have to reject the moral theology perpetuated by other men, who insisted there could be no forgiveness for a priest over sins against celibacy: each offense is a mortal one. For years, it had affected his psychosexual development. It must not, in future, be allowed to do so.

The analyst had raised the question of guilt.

"Part of your problem is that you felt guilty about what you were doing. The Church, after all, had embraced you, even if only on her terms; but you felt you let her down, by behaving in a healthy and normal manner. This produced guilt in you; with sexual freedom came guilt. You will have to learn how not to feel guilty over how you handle your celibacy. Assuming, of course, you want to go on being a priest."

He said he did. Becoming aware of who and why he was, he saw his vocation in a new and positive light. It was one of the few times he could remember the analyst made no comment.

The doctor had constantly reinforced the need for him, as a priest, also to recognize he was only human. He should expect to fail, time after time. The Church would look upon these failures as sins; but in terms of human understanding, they were not. In the analyst's opinion there was no need to confess them. By realizing he could fail, the chances were that his affections — his sexual impulses — would find a natural place in his life. He would not have to go on feeling he was someone composed of two separate entities, a body and a soul; he could become a guilt-free, integrated human being. But the analyst cautioned it might require years of working through before he could be fully comfortable with his ability to live as a fully integrated sexual celibate.

Accepting, he felt like a blind man given back his sight. At his regular session he vented feelings repressed for years against everyone who had ever shown him rejection, resentment, slight, and indifference. He began with his mother and ended with Simone. In the aftermath of this purging, the doctor had explained they were the ones who had particularly forced him into a dependent relationship; his mother by not caring, Simone for caring in the wrong way. Between them, they had never allowed him to develop beyond the stage of childish security.

He had explained that he felt very much better at being allowed to empty himself of such negative feelings. The psychoanalyst returned once again to Simone. Did he think there might be other reasons why, in his nightmare, she continued to be cast as having total responsibility for the marital breakdown?

In the silent isolation of his cell — the only home he now had, hopefully a temporary one, but nevertheless the place where, until Rome decided, he would sleep, wake and wait in an atmosphere of endless endeavor, occasional triumphs, and recurring frustrations — he tried to find answers. He finally filled a half page of a notebook with his answers. The passage, more than any other, was deeply implanted in his mind.

"If I go on blaming her I'm still playing a dangerous game. The least I can say is that I don't think she is all to blame and the least I can say is that I'm not all to blame. It probably falls somewhere in between. Maybe not exactly fifty-fifty, but that doesn't matter. I can't run my life on percentage points. I've done too much of that. All my life, I've been trying to portion things out. So much blame here, so much there. That's not the way it works; not at all. I can see it now, doubly clear, because I couldn't see it then. But this isn't even the issue. It is not one of blame, but something quite different. All my life I have been like a runner who has made a bet with himself to see how far he can push himself. For years now I have been staging this race inside my head. There is a part of me that says I should blame everybody else if I fall. Another part says it would be sensible to see my limitations and to do so is the only way to preserve myself. I really have got to get used to living day by day. That's what it all comes down to: living each day as it comes, trying to grow stronger."

Simone never telephoned again. Four months and twenty-three days after the papers were filed, the divorce was granted. The certificate of dissolution was on the shelf-desk beside his bed. A week later, his mother called with the news that Simone was going to marry Brad. This fact had not been incorporated into his nightmare.

But the nightmare itself continued to weave, like a shuttle on a loom, back and forth through the analysis. The doctor encouraged him to use the dream to examine new possibilities. Was Father Brannigan dressed as a Crusader because he represented an authority to be resented? The presence of Walter in his fantasy allowed their whole relationship to be explored. Did he fear, deep down, he had homosexual tendencies? He admitted he did. The analyst had smiled. "That's the healthiest thing you've said since coming here. Everybody has those feelings. You wouldn't be normal if you didn't."

He remembered that question of Walter's. *What's normal?*

The wind had dropped. On the horizon there was the first reddening of dawn in a cloudless sky. The glow, silent and utterly peaceful, spread, creating a mosaic of color as it touched the fields and walls and roofs of the monastery.

In his room two floors below, the abbot would be awakening to greet the new day. Then, sometime this morning, he would give him the decision from Rome.

By seven o'clock he had dressed in black pants and open-necked white shirt, said his Divine Office, joined the brothers celebrating Mass in the lofty chapel, eaten a light breakfast, and returned to his room. Normally, he would be out in the fields at this hour. But he had been told that he must wait indoors until the abbot was ready to see him.

He had imagined before entering that monastery life, even more than a seminary, could have the effect of stunting personality, reducing initiative and self-reliance, the two essentials of parish work. He expected there would be serious problems with sexual tensions and these would be sublimated through excessive prayer or overwork. His surprise, after only a few days, had been total. There was no hint of covert homosexuality, let alone any attempt to express it physically. Yet he found the monks, far from being exclusively concerned with their own feelings, integrated into a healthy, sharing life; and, though they were totally self-sufficient as far as their worldly needs, they displayed no estrangement from reality.

In the spacious community room, the social hub of the monastery, they debated the wisdom of President Nixon's overtures to China; the media's handling of the revelation that Senator Thomas Eagleton had received electroshock therapy and could no longer be considered a Vice Presidential candidate; the publishing hoax of the century, the faked memoirs of Howard Hughes. Reports of the Dow Jones industrial average were followed as eagerly as news from Rome. The market remained consistently bullish; the news from Rome was increasingly confusing.

The Church seemed undecided where the Kingdom of God began and ended. Pope Paul's visits to Asia, Africa, and the Near East, on each occasion the first pontiff to kiss the soil of these vast areas, had produced little. The more the Vatican tried to become involved on the world stage, the more firmly it was rebuffed. The Pope offered himself as a mediator over Vietnam. Both Hanoi and Washington politely rejected his services. He pled for greater freedoms for Catholics within the Communist bloc; Moscow sharply rebuked him for meddling. In the internal affairs of the church, Pope Paul was becoming increasingly Hamletic. The monks were well informed on the finer points of the arguments still raging throughout the American Church over his papal encyclical on birth control.

Father Philippe noted: "I had not expected an enclosed community to be so well attuned to the issue, with the same quiet passion they would discuss any attempt to interfere with the Holy Trinity."

These past months, he had not only written about his psychological development but also tried to reevaluate his religious outlook. He now felt himself to be a better Catholic and could, given the chance, become a better priest.

He had copied out and thumbtacked over his desk the words of Eudoxius, put down sixteen centuries earlier. "Nature has placed mankind under the grievance of two serving masters, pain and pleasure. It is for them alone to point out what we ought to do as well as to decide what we shall do. On the one hand, the standard of right and wrong; on the other, the chain of causes and effects. They govern us in all we do."

Tacked below that quotation was a striking epigram of Luther's:

"He who merely studies the commandments of God is not greatly moved, but he who listens to God commanding, how can he fail to be terrified by majesty so great?" He had silently contemplated how these words could be adapted to deepen his faith; how they could further energize his life in Christ.

He began to write in his diary.

"Forgiveness in the Old Testament is not a doctrinal statement. It is an explication that man cannot forgive. Only God forgives by calling man for a purpose; without it life has no meaning. God offers forgiveness as part of a divine adventure which nothing, except the reality of what it offers, can really justify. The Old Testament is rich in examples of how God has liberated the oppressed, unshackled those held in bondage, revitalized those who have accepted their fate to the point where they have become stultified. There is not a book of the Old Testament which does not contain its imagery of God enticing rebellion against overwhelming odds, of God offering vast rewards to those who will go where He wants them. He challenges them to listen to His commandments and to His wishes. He wants them to conquer in His name."

He paused, thinking again how once it had been much easier to write about God than himself. The analyst had warned him to expect this.

"In many ways God represents true love to you. Your mother and Simone do not. God you know will always forgive you, no matter what you do. But you have always felt that your mother and Simone could not do so. Trying harder to please them only seemed to pile up the points against you. You were the prisoner of your own best intentions. In that sense your vocation is highly unusual. It is largely based on your desire to seek forgiveness — and to administer it to others. There is nothing wrong with such feelings. But they must be placed in perspective."

He resumed writing.

"The true meaning of forgiveness is to be seen in the way God continually calls us back to our beginnings. Through forgiveness He offers hope and freedom. Forgiveness is in the opportunity that Matthew says should be grasped through sharing a responsibility. It is something active. Those who do not forgive are not forgiven. The Lord's Prayer makes it clear that forgiveness is also of the future. It is not forgetting or discharging the past. The past is dead — only fit to be buried by the dead. The Gospels clearly show that the man who forgoes the opportunity of giving others a chance, failing to appreciate the chance he has been given, has missed out. Anyone who refuses to obey the inspiration of hope can never be forgiven."

He framed a further thought.

"There is nothing moralistic about forgiveness. In life we tend to think it can be used as a means to rectify all damage. We hurt somebody — and we ask to be forgiven. Somebody hurts us — and we expect our pardon to be sought. It has become an easy and convenient way to cope with shortcomings. But what needs to be forgiven is something far more serious, the corruption of our one reason for living, our faith. We are too concerned with superficial moralism to recognize this reality."

The analyst had been very precise.

"Part of the appeal of the Church for you is that it provided answers in a simple and easily digested form. It also offered you a fine, free education, which compensated for the inferiority you felt about your background. Indeed, it even gave you a superiority, in your mind, against which Simone had no chance. You had been given your set of maxims by the Church. As a priest, of course, you were taught a great deal about the rules of a good marriage, but never how personally to live within those rules. You had, in other words, no firsthand experience. A brief fling with Simone beforehand, yes. But living on a day-to-day basis? No. The adjustment was not only a shock, it was a catastrophe for both of you."

Father Philippe developed his theme:

"The New Testament is absolutely clear that sin is unbelief, not immorality. The Gospels contain limitless proof that our sin is our failure to seize upon opportunities. We are sinners, not because we commit some act, or fail to, but because we refuse to follow our faith. All the Gospels are parables of forgiveness. That is the true meaning of the miracles of Jesus. A man is returned to the world. Another has the world returned to him. The blind are made to see, the deaf able to hear again, the dead allowed to walk from the grave. None of this is explained by the laws of man. They have nothing to do with cause and effect. It is all to do with faith. This is the true meaning of forgiveness."

At the end of one session the analyst offered him a thought:

"What makes you a good priest is that the Church permits you to indulge in an aggression that it hopes will not get out of hand. In your case, it finally did. You wanted more 'action.' You wanted to do more; you threw yourself into everything going. There wasn't a parish visit you wouldn't make, a funeral or wedding you wouldn't officiate at. You needed those outlets for your feelings. But in the end, this was not enough, just as Simone was no substitute. You have to understand that maturity is not achieved through sublimation."

There was a time, he remembered, when he had felt the analysis was no longer helping; that it might even be making him worse. He was agitated, prone to tears, unable to eat, filled with confusion. The analyst explained that these responses were all signs that therapy was slowly, but definitely, advancing over his illness.

"In these past weeks, the very substructure of your personality has began to change. You are more positive and secure. You can talk and cry. You can behave like any other human being under great emotional stress. This is a strain for you. Analysis could not be otherwise. You may think you are standing still. But you're not. For the first time you are facing yourself a little more each day. You are looking at yourself and seeing how you have been propping yourself up all these years with neurotic gratification of all kinds. Now you are beginning to grasp the psychodynamics of your illness. Three months ago, I could not have told you what I can tell you now. The fact is you are having a healthy response: you're scared of fouling up. That's what's behind this feeling that you're suddenly not getting anywhere."

Those first months of analysis had been, Father Philippe now saw, an added strain for the doctor because of his tendency to offer interpretation. Finally, the analyst had stopped him.

"The important thing is not to explain. You have been doing that all your life. Deluding yourself with explanations. A lot of your defenses were installed before the age when you could intellectualize. What you are doing now is trying to explain away tensions that are natural to feel. You place a burden of guilt upon yourself that is quite unnecessary. If, for instance, you see your mother's reference to premature ejaculation in those terms, you will begin to see how those words further impressed upon you the idea that sex is something dirty and bound to end in failure. But don't try to make superficial deductions. Work everything through. The answers will come, in time."

He was still considering this when a monk arrived to escort him to the abbot.

The office, like the abbot, was deceptive. Both were larger than they appeared: the office, wider; the abbot, taller, with his stomach pushing out of his monk's habit and the hair on his head close-cropped. There was something about him that called to Father Philippe's mind tales of sensual, well-fed clerics. In reality, as he had known ever since he returned from his weekend with Simone, the abbot was a gentle, kindly man, yet shrewdly penetrating for all that. He exercised his considerable authority benevolently.

"Let us be seated by the window." The abbot motioned toward the armchairs overlooking part of the gardens. "Being inside so much, I never miss an opportunity to gaze upon nature."

He had, thought Father Philippe, a curious way of speaking, as if his elocution had been acquired in an academy a century earlier.

For a moment the abbot remained standing, staring out of the window, then settled himself in his armchair, hands on his knees.

"So we have come to this. I will not hold you in suspense any longer. The Holy Office have no objection, in principle, to having you back."

"I'm very glad —"

"No, wait." The abbot raised his hand. "I have not yet finished. There is no objection from Rome, providing I am satisfied that you are ready to resume your priestly duties. That is why I have asked you here."

"I understand." He realized how the apparatus of power and discipline magnified a man's presence.

"May I begin with a question. What does your doctor say?"

"That I am making good progress. I have also been doing a lot of reading."

"Yes, yes. I understand. They tell me you haunt the library. But your nightmare . . . ?" He leaned forward, shrugging, lifting his hands from his knees for a moment.

"I think my anxiety feeds it. If I'm given back my ministry, I honestly believe it will go away. I really do."

"Yes." The abbot steepled his fingers. "Tell me, have you ever read Sam Keen's *To a Dancing God?*"

"Yes." The analyst had recommended the book, and he had read it, twice.

"Then you will perfectly understand why I ask."

He had found in Keen's words a riveting explanation of his tendency to allow past experiences and future expectations to determine uncritically what he thought at a particular moment. Keen wrote feelingly that he himself had discovered the road to maturity was possible only when he had digested and compensated for the biases and prejudices of his own personal history.

"Keen, would you not concede, is dealing with the concept that self-discipline can only lead to an enlarging of self in spiritual terms?"

"Yes. I accept that completely."

"Why are you so positive?"

"I think I've learned more about being honest with myself since I've been here than I have over the past twenty years."

334

The abbot weighed the responses. "But why does the nightmare persist? Do you really think it is only a question of anxiety?"

"A year ago I would have said something like 'I'm positive.' I try not to use such words now about something like my nightmare."

"That, of course, is commendable. But it still leaves the question unanswered, does it not?"

"Yes. But I've also learned not to expect an answer for everything."

The abbot smiled. "Your response suggests you have learned that any worthwhile living involves a risk, and the more worthwhile you live your life, the greater is the risk. Would you accept that?"

He did.

"And your former wife? How do you see her now?"

"Part of the past."

"Yet she remains, as I understand you, part of your present. Part of your nightmare."

"Yes. I suppose there is still this conflict inside me. But every day it seems to become closer to resolution."

He said that he looked upon his decision to end the marriage and return to Holy Orders as the first really independent step he had ever taken. He finally realized that his dependency on Simone had been a living death for them both, yet he, not she, had blocked any attempt to change the nature of their relationship. That was why he had this conflict. That was part of the cause, too, for the nightmare.

"Yet you continue to blame her totally — at least in your nightmare?"

"Yes. Because part of me still does. But at least I can recognize that now. I'm trying to work through it."

"Could you ever envisage repeating the experience again?"

"No one but God would dare to answer with absolute certainty. But I honestly believe that I would not. I could have gone anywhere when I left her. But I came back to the Church because I felt this is where I belong. I believe I have a place within it. I would go anywhere and do anything to serve it. I'm saying that, not because you have told me what Rome has decided, but because this is what I truly feel. I now see my vocation differently. I understand its deeper meaning. I want to serve. It's as simple as that."

The abbot was silent, thinking. Finally, he walked over to a wall of books and found the title he wanted and riffled through the pages.

"Let me read you this. 'The Crucifixion hurt his feelings; very much; the carved nails; the unfeeling spear. He looked at the picture a long time and

335

then turned the page saying, if God had been there, He would not have let them do this.' " The abbot snapped shut the book. "What do you make of that?"

He had read Richard Jeffries's book *Bevis: The Story of a Boy*, on Walter's recommendation. They had spent an entire Saturday afternoon discussing the dramatic irony of the words. He replied now with what he had said then to Walter.

"The whole point is that God *was* there. The whole of Christianity, the very existence of the Church, depends on the fact that God was there when His Son was crucified."

"Please go on." The abbot placed the book back on a shelf.

"I think the important first point to consider is that Jesus was a man, in the full physiological sense. He ate and drank. He knew thirst, hunger, and what it is like to be tired. He had a sense of humor, yet could be severe."

"What about sin?"

Father Philippe did not hesitate. "I think it is impossible to accept that He was not *capable* of sin. But the important thing is that He was *without* sin. You could argue that He may have been tempted to succumb, such as when He was in the wilderness. But He did not."

"Indeed. He did not. But please, I did not mean to interpose. Please do continue." The abbot remained leaning against the shelves, his arms folded, completely still, his eyes intent upon Father Philippe.

He began to explain how, through the human Jesus — Christ the man — came the loving God. To bring them together is the only way fully to comprehend the Incarnation. Jesus is the amazing grace of God. To reject this fundamental truth is the very meaning of sin.

"To see Jesus in this way is the only critical attitude possible toward the New Testament. Without this content — that Christ is the Son of God who gave His life as a ransom — there is little else of value in the Gospels. Without total acceptance of this one central fact, they become mythologies, become fiction."

The abbot broke the ensuing silence. "I am much reminded, listening to you, of what Calvin said about the Nicene Creed. 'Out of abundance of the heart the mouth speaketh.' "

"I appreciate the compliment." He felt, at last, completely relaxed, caught up in an old and abiding enthusiasm for theological speculation, as he began to put into words the vast evangelical truth that God and Christ are one. Without that, there is nothing. Finally, he was silent.

The abbot's eyes remained fixed on Father Philippe. At last the old monk spoke. "Welcome back, Father. We need you." He reached forward and gripped Father Philippe's arm. "I am glad to be the first to welcome you back into your ministry."

The analyst's office was on the ninth floor of a luxury building.

"Don't you think this is a little too soon? I need to be convinced this is the wisest move. You want to go a long way from here."

The analyst swiveled in his chair, staring momentarily through the large picture window at the high-rises.

"I think I'm ready."

"Why?" He turned back from the view. "Why do you think you are ready?"

"I just feel it."

"Yes?"

"I feel I can cope. It won't be easy. But I can cope. I have a better idea of the risk factors. And I also know myself better."

"What does the abbot say?"

"He thinks I can make it."

"Spiritually, he is better able to judge that than I am. But I am concerned with your psychological safety. Ten months ago you were crashing out of control. A danger to yourself and the Church."

He was almost as tall as the abbot. But there all similarities ended. The analyst looked ten years older than his forty years.

"Have you really thought this through?"

"Yes, I want to go."

"Why do you feel so strongly about going?"

"The challenge. Another chance to take up my calling. A new beginning."

"Labels. You're using labels again." The analyst's cool voice interrupted.

"I'm sorry."

"Try not to use labels. I want you to convince me."

He realized the analyst was watching him carefully. He looked at him steadily.

"I'm not certain I can convince you."

"Why not? Why do you think I can't be convinced?"

"I'm not sure it is important that I do convince you."

"What makes you say that?" The analyst's unperturbed voice framed rather than asked the question.

There was a silence before the doctor once more probed.

"What are you thinking about?"

"I was just wondering why you can't accept."

"If you go, I have to accept. Is this what you want me to do?"

"Yes. I've got to make a new start sometime. You've always said that. You've always said that the real world is out there. That's where I have to make it. Not in here."

"That is perfectly true. But why do you think you are ready? You still have the nightmare."

Father Philippe gave him the same answer he had given the abbot: "If I return to my ministry it will go away."

"That's certainly positive." It was the first sign of encouragement.

Father Philippe asked questions. "How will you ever know when I am ready? How does anyone really know? How will I ever know? I just have to take a chance. Three months ago I wouldn't have risked saying that. Now I feel able to, because I feel strong. Not blindly strong, but quietly strong. And it's not just my strength, but my limitations. I know them. I know, I think, when to stop. But I'll never really know until I go out there and try. I have to face the challenge. The responsibilities. And the risks. If I don't, I'll never know. That's why I think I'm ready."

The analyst resumed.

"Nothing has changed in the priesthood since you came into therapy. There is the same emphasis on compartmentalizing. The same demands to be part theologian, part expert on social justice, part counselor. The same temptations."

"But I'm not the same person. You've shown me the importance of self-nurturing. I've got a new feeling of self-worth. I'm more mature now."

"But maturity and weakness are two sides of the same coin. Yet the Church still does not see that. A priest is supposed to be mature enough to handle anything and have no weaknesses. The Church sees weakness in its priests as some sort of threat. In fact, it's quite the opposite, as we often discussed. How are you going to cope with this inconsistency?"

"Prayer, for a start. That's the most powerful tool I have. Being able to get down on my knees and pray. Only now I'll be praying to keep intact the values you gave me."

"Sitting here and saying it is one thing. Going out there and being alone and coping is another. Supposing you start to feel that the pressures simply do not give you enough time to live up to your obligations as a priest and to have a full prayer life? You will be back to those twelve-, or fourteen-hour days. How are you going to cope with talking to God through prayer and handling all the demands of your ministry?"

"I'm going to try and unite myself with God through my work . . ."

"What about women? The world is full of Lolos and Simones. They'll be waiting, you know."

"I know. But you have shown me how to relate realistically to women. I've got a new perception of reality about them I never had before."

"Are you certain? No doubts at all about what you are saying?"

"No doubts."

"You're sure you won't be tempted to take the easy option and remain unaware of your sexuality? That's the way it still is for lots of priests."

"If I get a chance, I'll try to help them."

"How will you do that?"

"Tell them I've learned not to treat celibacy as a precious pearl or an abstract, but more as an ideal to try to live up to."

"What happens if you fail?"

"I'll try again. And keep on trying. That's really all I can do."

"The Church won't like that."

"No."

Another pause. Then the analyst's voice. "You seem to be very certain. That worries me a little. Growth is not something that generally happens overnight."

"I've had eighty-six sessions, sitting in this chair. Probably for another patient that would equal two or more years in therapy."

There was no response. This time it was Father Philippe who resumed.

"What I'm trying to say is that I've learned that spiritual renewal is impossible without self-knowledge. I'm trying to be like Pope John. Remember what you told me he'd once said? About observing every single detail, disregarding a great number of things, and improving some things a little bit? I'm trying to go forward like that. Leaving here is part of that. I'm not going with any great expectation of being Superpriest. I just want to pray together with parishioners again, sharing with them a personal spiritual profit. I want to serve in a healthy way, using my own experiences as a starting point for a new life. I don't feel blocked anymore. I'm now aware of the emotional experiences going on inside of me."

"You could be aware now, but once more come to ignore them. That would be an understandable defense tactic, given the pressures you will have to face."

"It would. And of course I can't be certain. . . ."

The analyst's voice was reassuring. "That's good. That's understanding limitations. That's very important for you. Don't repress what you feel, especially in the area of sexuality. That will only once more narrow your view of life."

"I know. Oh, believe you me, I know. I've been there. It hurts too much to go back."

The silence stretched before the analyst spoke. "I pushed deliberately hard today. You didn't resist, except for a moment. And that was a perfectly healthy response. You rode with the situation. You didn't charge at it. That's good. Keep on doing that. But don't get overconfident."

He gripped Father Philippe's hand and wished him good luck.

Two days later, Father Philippe was heading eastward in a rented car that held all his possessions. In his jacket pocket was a business car the analyst had given him. Written on the back was the name and telephone number of another psychoanalyst. The doctor had said his colleague was one of the best in the diocese he was going to. Father Philippe had been tempted to throw it away, but the memory of the nightmare stopped him.

† † †

Andrew watched Jane inhale the joint and thought unhappily that her smoking pot was symbolic of the gap between them. He poured wine, remembering she had never smoked during their relationship.

A week ago she had arrived in Rome and, over dinner that first night, produced from her pocketbook a tin crammed with hand-rolled joints. Giles, she said casually, in response to his question, had introduced her to the habit. The revelation confirmed his worst suspicions.

They filled the pages of his diary.

"I shouldn't react like this. I told her at the airport how good I feel about my vocation. I said it has made me more altruistic. She said she'd read that seminary life does that. Yet when she mentioned Giles and produced her joint I just felt angry and depressed. There's no reason, none at all, for me to be like this."

In the past seven days they had repeatedly lunched and dined together in a trattoria near the Quirinal Palace, chosen by him because it was off the beaten track for anyone from the seminary and because he particularly liked the house speciality, spaghetti served al dente and garnished with pieces of bacon.

"I really shouldn't be so self-effacing. But I want to please her. I suppose I'm making a bit of a fool of myself. But I can't help my feelings. I don't think I'm being weak. Quite the opposite. When I'm with her everything is okay. But afterward, when she's gone, I feel this longing. It's quite silly, really, but since she has been here I've not been able to sleep again. I stand in the window knowing she's very close and yet a long way away."

They had quickly established territorial rights to a table in the rear of the *ristorante*, sitting beneath an enlarged still from Fellini's *Satyricon*. On their third visit, when he'd removed the Reserved sign from the table, the owner said he had been an extra in the film. Jane, slightly tipsy from wine, had offered to share her joint. He took the cigarette and murmured he enjoyed the taste of her lipstick on the butt as much as he did the drug.

"I've told her again today that I feel I'm growing in spirituality, why I'm quite certain about my vocation. I've tried to talk to her about this. She listens, but she doesn't seem to want to pursue the matter."

Jane had stared across the table that night and said, "Andy, don't look so severe. You're beginning to act like an old-fashioned priest, sitting there so stiff and disapproving."

She and the owner had finished the joint between them. He had insisted, in return, they should have a complimentary brandy. When they left, the man had kissed Jane on each cheek, and Andrew was shocked to see her response, pressing herself close to the restaurateur. Andrew had confided his feelings to his diary.

"These past days I've begun to wonder if she ever really loved me. She's so casual. She treats me at times like a stranger. That really hurts. But I won't tell her. I'd never do that. She's said more than once how I've changed. She thinks I'm more passive now. I'm not really. When I get back here I can smell her perfume and her body. I'm still attracted to her. Maybe that's why I don't sleep and feel this depression. It comes and goes. When I'm with her it's fine. Then she'll say something which will stick in my mind and the whole past will come back. I can't sleep then."

"What are you thinking?"
"Oh, lots of things."
"You want to share?"

He smiled. The words reminded him of when they lived together and would curl up, reading, in the apartment and he would suddenly look up, struck by something he had just read. And she, instantly, would put aside her book and say: "You want to share?"

"This time tomorrow you'll be back home."

"It's really flown, Andy. I never thought we'd cram in so much. You're a great guide."

"I really am tired. I had the strangest dream last night. I was a priest going through all the motions like a mechanical toy with a key in my back. I told her and she just laughed and said I shouldn't have any doubts about turning out a good priest."

This past week he had shown her Rome and the Vatican. They walked the length of the Corso, gazed upon the Trevi Fountain, stared in awe at the ceiling of the Sistine Chapel, attended Mass in St. Peter's, wandered around the Colosseum, strolled along the Via Veneto, visited the Pantheon, bought fresh fruit at the great market in the Campo Dei Fiori, sipped coffee in espresso bars. He had shown her the Greg, the seminary, and even his room. She had, he knew, noted her photo on the wall, but said nothing. She did, however, comment that the pay phone by the front door was a very public place for any private conversation. He wanted, then, to kiss her on the mouth, to pull her to him, to say he still loved her. Instead, he turned away, trying to hold back the tears.

"I keep on feeling that since she has been here I'm keeping too tight a grip on myself. I'm being too careful in what I say. It's like I'm always walking some invisible line, trying to avoid — avoid what? I suppose it's because I can't allow my feelings to show. I can't allow that to happen. That's why I'm so careful in what I say. Dear Jesus. I do love her. But only You know that. I'm very careful with her."

"I'll miss you, Jane. I really will."

He poured more wine into their glasses.

"She took my arm today, and said she sensed the presence of God for the first time since coming to Rome. We were in a side chapel in St. Peter's. She said how lucky I am to be close to such beauty all the time. I wanted to say how lucky I was to be close to her again. I didn't, of course."

"You've settled in very well, Andy. Giles said you would."

"I wish you would stop talking about him."

She looked surprised. "Why? He's been a great help to me this last term. He got me into the Debating Society and the Dining Club. He's very good on his French wines —"

"I'm jealous."

He hated himself for blurting.

"But, Andy, that makes no sense. Why should you be jealous?"

"Because I am!" He toyed with his glass. "And I wish you were, too —"

"But that's totally irrational. Why should I be jealous? What is there to be jealous about?" She looked at him quizzically. "That sounds even more complicated than all this theology these Jesuits are force-feeding you on! I mean, why should I be jealous?"

"Jane, I'm sorry. I suppose it doesn't make sense."

"Skipped another class. Walked along the Tiber discussing if we are responsible for our actions. She said, yes, always. I couldn't be certain. We argued like the old days. Great fun."

What would she say, he wondered again, if she could see what he had written in his diary these past nights? There, on paper, he had fought with himself.

"I'm glad she has come. It proves something about me. I know I have a lot of qualities as a man that can help me to be a priest. I have an essential presence, aggression, and diverse interests. I am sociable. I love very strongly and I can commit that love to Christ. I love Our Lord. Like Him, I have a passion for people. It is this ability to feel, though, that makes it so hard to be with her. I can feel her closeness. I can feel myself thinking, 'Oh, God, if only, if only.' But then He has called me. I can feel that more each day. But having her here, and not being like it was before is a very strange and unsettling experience. I keep on thinking what would happen if she made a move. How would I cope? Would I run away — or to her? I just don't know. I know that I am still a very sexual person. I can't help my feelings. But I am going to keep on praying to make sure they do not lead me from my path. But is that possible?"

"Andy, don't be sad."

"It's difficult at times not to be."

"Try and remember we had a good time. We can still be friends."

343

"I'd like that, Jane. I really would."

Watching her sip her wine, he thought how impossible it was to exorcise his love for her.

"This afternoon I tried to get a discussion going about love. She kept on avoiding the subject. But this time I did push a bit. I said it was all probably an invention. I was testing her out. We were sitting in a café and she suddenly said she'd like to go shopping. I said I'd come with her. But she said no, she wanted to be alone. Met for dinner. She showed me the leather belt she'd bought for Giles. I felt pretty miserable though I tried not to show it."

"Andy, about Giles . . ."

He knew she was looking at him carefully.

"We're very close."

She reached for his hand, resting her fingers lightly on his knuckles. He could still remember the first time she had done this, in that pub, when she had said she did not like a man who couldn't hold his drink. Giles, he recalled, had a limitless capacity for beer. But how would he cope with the strong Italian wine?

"This morning, she finally asked me how I was coping with celibacy. I said fine. Absolutely no problem. Just a question and my answer. I would have been happy to go into it with her, to try and explain. But once more she didn't want to. I have this feeling that there are some things she just doesn't want to get involved with. That's the time when I feel I don't really know her at all.

"Over lunch today, she said she had just reread *A Burnt-Out Case* and thinks Greene's Father Joseph is right about the sameness of religious life. Didn't that get me down? I said that if life is a bit predictable then it made it easier to lead a full prayer life. She let it drop. There is this gap between us. I can't seem to reach her; it's actually worse now when we are together."

"Andy, did you hear what I said? We're very close, Giles and myself."

His hand tightened over hers. "Please, Jane. Don't. It hurts too much. I still want you."

She pulled her hand away. "Andy, you must understand. That's all over between us. It has to be. You made that choice. And it is the right one."

344

She poured herself more wine. "You really are cut out for the priesthood. They need people like you. Vibrant and aware."

"That's the point, Jane. I *am* aware — of you!"

She put back her hand, stroking his skin gently, murmuring. "Andy. Poor Andy. I think it was a mistake to have come. Giles said it wouldn't help —"

"To hell with him! I still love you!"

He knew the owner was staring at them.

Jane was looking at him across the table, staring into his eyes. There was understanding there, but no hope.

"Andy, you have to be realistic. You're going to be a priest."

"Jane, who knows what the position will be when I'm ordained!" He realized he sounded desperate. "Priests may be able to marry. There could be optional celibacy!"

"Oh, Andy! You know nothing will change. If it did the whole Church would collapse. It's what makes priests special — their celibacy. We both know that."

She pulled her hand away.

"Andy. I think you had better know that Giles has asked me to marry him."

"Marry?" He felt as if his head had been snapped off its spine. "Marry? That's just incredible. Marry? I've never heard anything so unbelievable!"

"No, it isn't. It happens all the time. My God, Andy —"

"Have you accepted?"

"Not yet."

"Well, maybe. . . ."

"He is certain it could work." She looked thoughtful. "We do have a lot in common. He's not the possessive type. I told him about us, and he said that was all in the past. I think that's very healthy."

"He sounds like a budding psychologist."

"Don't be bitchy! Actually, he's going to start his own business."

"Well, good for Giles."

"Oh, Andy, don't be like this —"

"How do you expect me to be? You come to Rome. We spend a week together. I mean, how do you expect me to be . . . ?"

She sat back in her chair, arms folded.

"You haven't changed, have you? You still think you can have everything. Snap your fingers and it's all yours. Life isn't like that, Andy. It really isn't."

It was uncanny, he thought. Two days ago he had predicted this.

"Woke up at four o'clock, sweating all over. Got up and wrote. I could swear she has been in the room, saying what a mess it is. I just put down what I feel. How easy it is to be caught up in what we think. I bet Giles moved in. It's just the sort of trick he would pull. Read the Bible for a while. Then stopped because the meditations didn't lift this depressing feeling. I just suddenly think this past week has counted for nothing. Why did she come? It's difficult to put down my thoughts on paper. It's as if something's dying inside me. The more alive she is, the more dead I feel. I can't explain this feeling. But it hurts. Oh, God, it hurts."

"So . . . you'll get married . . . ?"

"Yes. I think being in Rome has made me realize how much I miss him."

He nodded, unable to think of anything to say.

"I'm sorry, Andy. I couldn't think of any other way of telling you . . ."

"You could have written."

"I could have. But I wanted to tell you myself. I felt that was important."

"Thanks, Jane."

The owner approached. She waved him away.

"Please, Andy, don't spoil our last evening together. Please don't do that."

He pulled himself together. "What did Oscar Wilde say about the past? That no one can buy it back?"

"Yes. But think of your future." She smiled brightly. "You know, maybe in forty years time I'll be able to tell my grandchildren that I had one of the best weeks of my life being shown around Rome by a future pope!"

The gulf, he finally realized, was unbridgeable. Sitting here now, she was already gone.

Trying to smile, he had the first thought of committing an act of aggression against her and himself.

CHAPTER 15

†

Revelations and Responses

C lare huddled among the Christmas shoppers, waiting for a bus as the rain started to lash down again. She was planning her answer to the question set by the lecturer in Mystical Theology on how the Church should evaluate the role of married saints.

Tom had suggested a list of references. The publications filled not only her briefcase but her arms. People around her continued to stare curiously at *Lectionary of Saints, Butler's Lives*, and a copy of *Married Saints*, published in 1935 and still a definitive work on the subject.

He had guided her to new self-awareness — an achievement all the more remarkable, she often thought, because their entire relationship existed only on the campus. The demands and obligations of her new life, even more, she suspected, than of his, would make it virtually impossible for them to meet outside college. Neither had, in fact, raised the question: it remained beyond the dimension of their discussions these past months over lunch, during morning and afternoon tea breaks and study periods in the students' common room. At first, she listened while Tom explained. Later, after she read the books and magazine articles he had recommended, she began to argue and to challenge, with increasing confidence, some of the more revolutionary ideas coming into the Church.

She believed that the Second Vatican Council had produced a range of crises in the Church that profoundly affected traditional values. She found this true particularly in some of the new American and European theological arguments, where so often the emphasis seemed to be on clever critique. She had been surprised at her conservatism in such matters because she now found parts of her own life pointlessly ritualistic and almost offensive. She had come to resent having bus and lunch money doled out by the Deputy; having to ask permission from her superiors to telephone home to inquire about her father; having to accept being treated like a child over such matters as bedtime. She had told Tom these restrictions had contributed to her feeling that the Church she still loved was like a great ship heading for the rocks, out of control, unable to keep pace with events. He had replied that further strictures could be in the offing; the latest news was that the Pope would not live much longer; his successor would undoubtedly want to assert his authority; the present crisis could only deepen. In the meantime, they should enjoy what they had. Who knew how the Church would look upon friendships like theirs in the future?

Months ago, he had taken John's Gospel and shown her what Jesus meant by friendship. "It's the ultimate choice, Clare. A complete giving. Not being possessive or secretive. People fall in love and get married. But the relationship often doesn't work because they have not learned the true value of friendship."

He had added, "You and I know that marriage is out. But we can still be friends. I think that's much more important. Don't you agree?"

She did.

Another time he defined friendship as stated by Aelred de Rievaulx, a twelfth-century Cistercian monk, and applied it to their relationship. "A friend must be chosen, then tried, before being accepted forever as a friend. That's us."

She felt compelled to respond. "Tom, don't forget what else de Rievaulx said. If a friendship has to end, it should be done gently, so as not to cause pain."

He had looked at her and said very quietly, "I hope this won't end. Friendships are very important for us celibates."

She had begun for the first time to read and think seriously about celibacy. There was — of this she now had no doubt — a full-scale sexual revolution sweeping the Church. Within the hierarchies of the United States, Holland, and West Germany it was especially rampant. The most frequent reason given by priests and nuns for abandoning their vocations was celibacy. Those who remained in religious life were engaging in hot and public debate on such controversial issues as how intimate can a friendship be for a nun or priest; what are the limitations of tactility; how could celibates cling to their sacred vows and yet have meaningful sexual identities? There was talk about an entirely new theology of sexuality, based on a reinterpretation of teachings going back to the Yahwist, the Song of Songs, Saint Augustine, and the Gospels of the New Testament. There were even those who claimed that Jesus could be called a sexual celibate.

She saw her own views on chastity must be rethought. She knew she still could never accept the more outspoken American demands for a full sexual life within a vocation. But she realized she had moved a long way from her original perception that chastity was something natural for a nun and therefore easy to cope with.

Tom convinced her that sexual desires were not wrong for a celibate; it was how they were interpreted that mattered. The capacity to love, he stressed, not making love, was what was ultimately important. He argued that to be a celibate did not mean having to be asexual; it meant never having any physical intimacy. In the end celibacy for a religious came down to a realistic understanding of friendship, ministry, and prayer. She found his words far more evocative than anything she had read. They had prompted her to ask him if he meant their lives at present were not now completely fulfilled and he had grinned and refused to be drawn. That, she had come to see, was one of his defenses: when he didn't want to be pursued he retreated behind his grin. It could be very annoying.

He would, she imagined, still be weaving through the traffic, headed for Clonliffe on his motorcycle. She suggested several times he should exchange it for a car, but he always grinned and said he enjoyed the wind on his face.

Her father had liked Tom from the day he dropped in with a pile of magazines and stayed for an hour to talk. He had done this several times since. It was one of the qualities, she knew, that would make Tom a good priest: his caring. He showed it in another way. When she first told him about her father's illness, Tom went to the city's medical school and collected everything available in its library on the disease. He had left the Xeroxed pages for her, with a note saying the more she knew, the easier it might become. The information had been sobering and invaluable: there was no cure for her father; all the family could do was to give him as much loving care as possible. Every time she visited home — the Order had been one of the first to implement the Vatican Council recommendations that nuns should be allowed such visits — her father seemed physically more enfeebled, but his mind, so often affected by the illness, remained clear and alert. He never complained; the more noticeable his symptoms became, the more patience and fortitude he displayed. If he were on his way to the hospital for tests and a bus went by, he would say, "All in good time; there'll be another one along soon."

Tom, on the other hand, reacted very differently. He had it in him to step in the path of a bus, force it to stop, and then charm the driver to allow him on board. He was a born persuader, as, she remembered ruefully, he had shown again today.

He'd suggested she should go to the college library for a report that would be useful in answering the question on married saints; it shouldn't take her long to find, he insisted. She had spent the entire lunch hour searching. She made copies and hurried to the restaurant. By the time she arrived, there were only tea and cheese crackers available. Tom thanked her warmly for his copy and said he'd seen no point in ordering her anything as he had no idea how long she would be. She had thought, again, he could be quite infuriating at times.

On other occasions he could cut her to the core, criticizing an essay with almost brutal frankness or saying that she had asked the wrong question in class. Sometimes he could be intensely personal. How did she cope with living among a lot of old women? What could she possibly talk to them about? She had responded, almost angrily, that convent life was no different from what she imagined life was in Clonliffe. He'd grinned, sensing that he had gone too far.

Yet, she recognized that he had an innate sensitivity. This was probably why from the beginning she had been comfortable with Tom, sparing him few of the details of her upbringing and decision to be a nun. In turn he had made his life equally accessible to her. They had, she discovered, remarkably similar childhoods. His parents had indoctrinated him with identical religious values. Their common memories included trips to the country and home always filled with the smell of baking. They had revealed what led them to vocations. For Tom it was clear-cut. "God loved me. It seemed the most natural thing to work for somebody who loved so totally. I just wanted to love like that."

He had been at Clonliffe six years and in a few weeks' time would be ordained a deacon. There was a reassurance about his future that complemented hers. Or so Clare had once thought.

*

The wind was blowing fresh from the sea as she hurried along the long darkened drive toward the lights of the Mother House. She opened a side door and entered the kitchen. She could see her meal under a warming cover on top of the range. She put down her books and briefcase on a table and lifted the cover, savoring the plate of stew.

The warmth of the kitchen and the smell of food acted like sedatives. She had not realized how tired she was. Putting the plate back on the stove, she removed her topcoat and laid it across the back of a chair, oblivious to the water puddling on the floor. She turned to pick up her meal.

"Sister Mary Luke, what are you doing?"

The Deputy stood in the doorway leading to the main house. Draped around her neck were yards of electric cord and colored lights.

"You know perfectly well no one brings wet clothes into the kitchen! Have you forgotten there's a drying room?" The Deputy grabbed Clare's coat, and carried it, dripping, out of the kitchen. She returned with a mop and pail. "Now, Sister, clear this mess up!"

"Why are you treating me like this, Mother? You never seem to be satisfied —"

"How dare you, Sister Mary Luke! How dare you speak to me like that! First, you're thoughtless, making such an unholy mess. Now you're insolent!"

She stood before Clare, her lower lip trembling with fury, her hand clenching and unclenching.

Clare's eyes filled with tears. "I'm sorry, Mother. I didn't mean to make a mess. I just was so glad to get inside." She mopped up the water, took the mop and bucket to their cupboard, and returned to the kitchen.

The Deputy asked why Clare was there.

"I was about to have dinner, Mother. They'd kept it hot for me —"

"Dinner? At this hour?" The Deputy glared at her. "Where have you been until now?"

"It's the weather, Mother. And the Christmas rush, the buses are all full —"

"Sister Mary Luke, stop making excuses. You are late. You should have been here an hour ago. Now come with me. There's work to be done."

"But, Mother. It won't take me a moment to eat this —"

A new rage convulsed the Deputy. "How dare you continue to argue with me! Is that what they teach you at college? To be insolent to your superiors? How dare you stand there and answer back! Now come with me. This instant!"

She turned on her heels.

351

With a last look at the plate, Clare followed her into the main entrance hall where Dominic and the kitchen nuns were busy erecting the convent's Christmas tree. The Deputy removed the lights festooning her body and thrust them at Clare.

"You know how these go. Or at least you should."

Clare felt the hunger rumbling in her stomach.

"Mother, couldn't I just have a quick bite first, please? It won't take a minute. Then I'll be glad to get —"

"Up that ladder now! Do you hear, Sister? Now!" The Deputy was shaking with renewed anger.

Clare responded in a voice that seemed to come from someone she did not know.

"You're not being fair! I do my share. I always have! But you go on goading me. On and on. You seem to hate me going to college! You go on and on, trying to make me lose my temper! You've done it to others. They couldn't stick it so they left. Well, I'm not going to leave, but I'm sick and tired of your meanness. Leave me alone! Just leave me alone!"

There was a stunned silence around the tree.

"Do you know what you have just said, Sister Mary Luke?"

The Deputy's voice was cold and unemotional. Something about her reminded Clare of an unexploded bomb in a Belfast street: danger embedded in a familiar landmark. She was suddenly too scared to cry. And her heart was racing so fast she was convinced it would obliterate her apology.

"I'm sorry, Mother. I really am. I lost my temper. That is unforgivable." She pressed her hand against her mouth.

The Deputy's heavy breathing filled the silence.

"You must also apologize to all your sisters for causing them to feel such embarrassment."

"Yes, Mother." After apologizing, Clare climbed the steps and began to hang the lights on the tree, her eyes shiny with tears.

The Deputy stood at the foot of the ladder, ordering how the lights should be arranged. Finally, she handed Clare the large silver-painted tin star Sister Dualta had fashioned in her workshop. Clare fixed it on top of the tree. Only after the Deputy had stood back to admire the effect was Clare allowed to climb down. The Deputy looked at her watch.

Clare moved toward the kitchen.

"Sister Mary Luke, where are you going?"

"I thought now I could get my supper —"

The Deputy advanced on her once more, trembling uncontrollably.

"Really, Sister! You and your stomach. Have you so lost touch with life here that you've forgotten chapel? What are they teaching you at college?"

Clare bit her lip. Yet she was no longer angry. She had a new thought: *I'm able to tune her out. It's as simple as that. She really doesn't matter to me anymore. I only wish everything else was as easy.*

Kneeling in her stall for Silent Meditation, Clare felt again the restlessness she thought had gone forever. She could not admit why she felt like this, not even to her confessor. What would he say? That she must resist such feelings? Undoubtedly. That she must pray? Certainly. But she had tried to resist them; had turned to prayer. The feelings would not disappear. How could her confessor make them? How could anyone stop her being a woman? How could she be true to her vows and yet be honest to herself? The questions silently tormented her, ruining again this period of deep inner contemplation, designed to calm a nun's mind at the end of her day. For weeks now, Silent Meditation had been a time when her mind raced instead of being still, when it drifted instead of remaining focused.

Had it, Clare wondered again, become so obvious what she now felt about life outside these walls? She remembered Tom's words. "You look the same, but you're different. It's the way you think. You don't have convent tunnel vision anymore."

They had been walking back to class from lunch, having spent the meal discussing women and power in the Church. Tom had quoted Matthew: "He had it right when he said, if I remember correctly, *'You know that among the pagans the rulers lord it over them, and their great men make their authority felt. This is not to happen among you.'* You can't get away from that."

She countered that while indeed Jesus had taught that no one must seek power for himself or herself, and that to be subservient is a blessed state, to do nothing to ease the oppressive restraints on women in the Church was also wrong. Women were not seeking personal power — only the right to serve the Church better.

Tom responded that the maleness of the Catholic priesthood is part of a God-given symbolism.

She demanded the proofs.

He said none was necessary, because that kind of mystery went beyond the logic of man.

She retorted that in creating woman, God intended her to have the fullest role on earth on His behalf.

Was this why, she wondered, she had finally felt indifferent to the Deputy's behavior; that it was no more than a classic example of what Tom meant — narrow, petty, and pointless? Nor was it the first time it had happened. On several recent occasions the Deputy had rebuked her, publicly and with real anger. Sometimes she had ended with an instruction. "Sister Mary Luke, search your heart. Are you really in communion with Our Lord? Or is there something in you that makes Him unhappy? Pray, Sister, that He restores what is lacking."

She could barely admit, even to herself, what caused her to be so restless. Yet, could it be, she wondered again, that the Deputy had somehow known, all these months, the truth?

Clare opened her eyes. She felt utterly miserable. The tears streamed down her face. She never imagined this could happen to her. She had seen others cry in chapel, but that had always been shortly before they had left the community forever. She knew she did not want to leave. Yet the silence of the chapel, with nuns kneeling in the semidarkness, filled her almost with dread.

Leaving the chapel, Clare slipped through a door between two of the parlors. On visiting days it was normally used by the kitchen nuns bringing tea and cakes to guests. The passage was long, narrow, winding, and pitch-black. She felt her way along the walls, and had gone some distance when she realized she was not alone. She could hear breathing, slow and shallow, as if someone was trying to hide. She hesitated, not knowing what to do, remembering there were several alcoves on either side of the passage, used for storing supplies. Someone was in one of them.

Clare crept forward, placing a hand on the wall to guide her along the cold and faintly dank-smelling passage toward the sound. It was more pronounced. She looked behind her and could no longer see the crack of light under the narrow door. Ahead, the door leading to the kitchen was also not visible. Above her was the refectory, deserted at this hour. She doubted if anyone would hear her screams through the thick walls. For the first time she began to feel frightened.

The breathing was coming from the back of an alcove and she could make out a vague shape in the diffused glow from an overhead grille. She had forgotten that the passage was below ground and the opening provided natural light during working hours.

"Who's there?" Her voice was unusually loud in the confined space.

The shape in the alcove shrank back into a corner.

"Who's there? Come on out."

The shape moved toward her.

354

"Who are you?"

She struggled to keep her voice calm.

"Sister Mary Luke?"

"Dominic!"

Clare leaned against the wall, relieved.

"What on earth are you doing here?"

Dominic whispered. "It's my nip hole. Every time you're all in chapel of an evening I come in here for a quiet tot."

He struck a match, lighting up the alcove. He had a whiskey bottle in his hand.

"But what if Deputy Mother caught you?"

The handyman cackled. "No chance of that, Sister. She's scared of the dark! Won't come down here once the light goes!"

"God, Dominic, you're a case!"

He smiled, his goblin, slightly tipsy smile, the one he had whenever he returned from a wedding.

She led the way into the kitchen. Her meal, she saw ruefully, was a congealed mess and the kitchen nuns had strict orders to lock up everything and hand over the keys to the Deputy.

From a pocket Dominic produced keys on a ring. With unerring instinct he unlocked a pantry and stood aside. Its shelves were laden with food Clare had never seen served in the refectory.

"Deputy's private store. For impressing priests and the like who come visiting her." He grinned. "I don't think she'll miss anything."

Clare hesitated.

"No, you just sit down, Sister. Leave it all to me. No volition then."

He motioned her toward the table. She looked at the dried-up stew on the range and her stomach gave another rumble. That decided Clare. She sat at the table.

Dominic removed a tin of salmon from a shelf and in no time had provided Clare with a substantial supper. He leaned against the sink, watching her eat, taking nips from his bottle. "Sister, if you ask me, you don't look well."

"I'm fine, really, I'm fine." she smiled. "A little tired. Nothing else. And you scared me back there."

He shook his head. "No, that's not it. You have that uncertain look, if you don't mind my saying so ..."

"Uncertain?" She was alert. "I don't feel uncertain about anything ..."

"I hope not, Sister. I really hope not. But I've seen that look in nuns be-

355

fore they even knew they felt uncertain. I always can tell, you know. Been right too many times."

"Well, you're wrong this time, Dominic!" She wished she hadn't sounded so sharp. "There's nothing uncertain about me."

She gathered up her books and briefcase.

"Don't worry about the washing up, Sister. I'll take care of that. You be off now."

He gave her another lopsided smile.

Going to her room, she thought: "Has it become this obvious?"

She loved Tom.

† † †

The amplified metallic voice announced that all flights out of Harrisburg were delayed indefinitely because of severe weather conditions. The same message had come over the loudspeakers every thirty minutes. This was the sixth time Victoria had heard it. The world beyond the concourse windows had disappeared. She heard a ticket agent say it was one of the worst whiteouts he could recall. The blizzard had begun as she left her last high school appointment. By the time she reached the airport, the snowplows were fighting a losing battle to keep the runways clear. Flights had steadily backed up and the airport was crammed with frustrated travelers.

Victoria glanced at her watch. There was no way she could reach the Mother House before the Great Silence. That decided her. She would stay overnight in one of the nearby motels. She walked toward the courtesy telephones; lines were already forming in front of them. She chose the shortest queue and put down her cases. One was empty. She had left the last of her brochures at a local high school. It had been a disappointing tour. Not one girl had made a firm commitment; only eight had given uncertain promises to consider the matter further. She should not, she told herself, be really surprised. Religious life was losing its appeal for American youth. Many of them had become as cynical about God as they were about Watergate as its revelations started to surface.

Matters had not been helped, she knew, by the persistent rumors that in Europe the Church had discreetly trafficked in young Asian girls. It brought them from Vietnam and Cambodia to supplement the falling numbers of vocations, particularly among the teaching and nursing orders of France, Germany, and Holland. The Vatican had conducted an inquiry; while it denied the allegations of widespread nun-running, it did admit that some orders had not been as scrupulous as they might in how they obtained entrants. In spite of this, according to newspaper reports, the practice continued. Asian priests sent half-starving girls to Europe, condemning them into a life from which there was virtually no escape. The orders had paid the girls' air fares and fees to their priest-sponsors. No one knew precisely how many had come this way — some reports suggested as many as ten thousand might have made the long flight from Asia — but one Order in Europe reluctantly admitted paying five hundred dollars for each of the girls. They had been put to work in the convent kitchens or on the land, freeing other sisters to teach or nurse. Questions about the scandal had come up several times on this trip. Victoria answered them by saying this could never happen in the United States. Yet, in the end, it made no difference. There was still a reluctance to commit. On each tour it was getting harder to find vocations.

She was suddenly aware he was watching her, and perhaps had been doing so for some time. He smiled, making him look almost too young for the chestful of ribbons. It was an air force colonel's uniform. She wondered, briefly, if he was on the recruiting circuit. He had the steady gaze and trim figure that would attract graduates into the service.

"Hi."

"Hullo."

He edged his tote bag forward.

"I guess we both made it in time."

He had a pleasant voice; West Coast and well-bred, Art would have said. She had used him again last night. He looked a bit like Art, too: there was that same determination, that same fixing look. She glanced over her shoulders. The lines were steadily lengthening.

In front of her a man was shouting into the telephone. "What do you mean you have no rooms? How is this possible?"

The colonel had reached his courtesy phone.

The man was still yelling. Suddenly he slammed down the phone and stormed away.

Victoria picked up the telephone and a bored voice told her there were no vacancies.

"Are you absolutely certain there just isn't one single —"

The voice cut her off before she could complete her question.

The colonel was looking across at her and speaking into his telephone. He was smiling: a smile, she decided, with no hooks in it. She nodded. The colonel spoke into the phone, just as the loudspeakers paged a passenger. He replaced the receiver, saying he had booked her a room.

"Thank you." She smiled. "But can I afford it?"

"They're all the same rate, ma'am." He picked up his tote bag. "Here, let me take one of these." He motioned toward her cases.

He introduced himself. "Frank Rivers. United States Air Force, ma'am."

She hesitated. "Victoria John. Actually, Victoria Sarah John."

As they waited for the motel bus, the snow swirled around them. She was glad now she was wearing a trench coat and fur hat. He seemed indifferent to the weather.

"You get used to it in Alaska." He had Art's way of cutting out anything superfluous.

"Are you based there, Colonel?"

"Frank, ma'am." He smiled; she could not be certain but there might be a hook. "Was based there, Victoria. Posted now to Manila."

She noticed his left shoulder was slightly hunched.

"Are you a flier?"

"Used to be." He tapped his left shoulder. "Bailed out the wrong side of forty thousand feet. Wrecked a plane and my shoulderblade. Now I fly a desk. Anchorage, Manila. It's the same desk. What line are you in?"

A snowplow roared past. Suddenly, she did not want to say she was a nun. That would only lead to more questions. Why, she often wondered, was it always open season on nuns? Strangers asked her questions they would never put to even their closest friends. "Is it really possible to live without sex? Do some nuns make out with priests? Is it true that nuns still whip each other?" It's astonishing, she thought, the way people associate nuns with all kinds of covert sexuality.

"Oh, I travel . . ."

She had long ago decided it was nice to keep part of herself private; she supposed it had a lot to do with there still being so little privacy in the Mother House. Though each nun now had her own room, they still were very much bound together as a community. The really hard thing was the age gap. What could she possibly say, she wondered, when on infirmary duty, to an eighty-year-old whose last lucid memories were of the Depression?

"You like traveling?"

"You can get to dislike anything on a day like this."

"You work for a big company?"

"Big enough." She smiled, switching roles. "Are you looking forward to Manila?"

"My second tour. A wild place. You can't beat it."

She let the remark pass.

He was still talking about the attractions of Manila when they arrived at the motel. He marched toward the desk and gave his rank and name.

"Yes, sir. Here we are. Colonel and Mrs. Rivers —"

Victoria stepped forward. "I think there's a mistake."

The clerk consulted his list. "No. I have it here. One double with bath. Forty —"

"A double. There is a mistake. Definitely."

The clerk and the colonel looked at each other. Victoria sensed something move between them, short and swift. It was gone in a moment.

"It's the only room right now —"

"Then I'll take it." She smiled at the colonel. "I'm sure you won't mind giving up your room."

He hesitated, crestfallen.

"Well, not at all, Victoria." He turned back to the clerk. "Would you check again, please?" He slipped a five-dollar bill across the counter. "I believe I did reserve two singles."

The clerk shrugged, pocketed the bill, and ran his finger down a list.

"Okay, I have it. Two singles."

The colonel turned to Victoria. "I'm really sorry about this."

"I'm sure it doesn't happen very often to you." She smiled sweetly.

"Will you let me at least buy you dinner?"

"There's no need to, really."

The clerk asked them to register. Victoria leaned forward so he could not see over her shoulder. She slid the form across to the clerk. He looked at it and blinked, then handed over the keys to their adjoining rooms.

"Look, about dinner —"

"Please, Victoria. I'd like you to have dinner with me."

"Well . . . okay. I'll need about fifteen minutes to freshen up."

"Wonderful. That's just wonderful."

She caught him glance triumphantly at the clerk and then look momentarily puzzled when the hotel employee gave him a quick shrug.

She gave herself a final check in the mirror and went down to the bar. The colonel was leaning back on a banquette, sipping a cocktail. She advanced toward his stunned expression, explaining.

"I didn't want there to be any more . . . misunderstandings." She smiled. "Now I'd like a glass of red wine followed by a steak medium rare. And I want to hear more about how wild the Philippines are."

The colonel could only nod, dumbfounded, at Victoria standing in her modified habit and veil.

✝   ✝   ✝

The irony of having help so close to hand, yet so out of reach, filled Andrew with savage, silent rage and self-pity. He sat opposite the spiritual director, counting the minutes until he could escape from the priest's well-meant intentions.

Intellectually, he recognized the emotions. From all he had read — in the hope that understanding would banish these and other feelings, though it hadn't — the anger and self-pity were two symptoms of his reactive depression. For weeks the malaise had held him in its grip.

He could date its onset precisely; fifty-three days ago, the day he received Jane's letter. He had read it several times, not wishing to believe before finally crying himself to sleep, still not able to accept. Next morning he had awakened immeasurably sad. He missed his seminary duties and classes that day, pleading a stomach ailment. By nightfall his depression had deepened and had remained.

Physical numbness and lethargy had been accompanied by interrupted sleep and periods of withdrawn, lengthy silence. The emotional security of his life had been destabilized, and his defense systems, those essential guards for healthy living, had been steadily weakened. In their place came a cunning mingled with shame. No one must know, he decided, how he felt, so he must cover up. He was surprised, at first, how inventive he could be; now, excuses and lies tripped off his lips with no trouble. A strange inner compulsion — a feeling that he dubbed *The Thing* — told him that he must behave like this because no one would really understand his inconsolable mourning.

Nothing, he believed, could fill the vast void that Jane had left in his life.

But, encouraged by *The Thing*, he managed to keep his sense of loss, and the corresponding depression, a secret. His sadness and tears, along with the more irrational of his thoughts, were kept for the privacy of his room. That he spent an ever-increasing amount of time there, he knew, was not a cause for comment. His tutors and the seminary staff had merely assumed he was studying or meditating. At chapel, the Greg, and mealtimes, he managed to conceal the tides of inner sorrow and rage consuming him — just as he did on this cool spring afternoon from his spiritual director. He had not been able ever to mention Jane or her letter and what it had done to him. Andrew was convinced no one could begin to grasp why his heart was broken and his life ruined; no one could possibly understand why he had believed deep down that Jane would always be there for him; that if, by any chance, he was to give up his vocation, she would be waiting; that if he called, she would always come, dropping everything and everybody to be with him, and doing so without questioning. He had clung to that expectation even after she left Rome. Shattering though her revelation over dinner was, she had at least left a tiny crack of hope. Jane had not, then, actually accepted Giles's proposal. But the letter, arriving nine days after her return home, left no hope. She *was* going to marry Giles. Consequently, he realized she would no longer, could no longer, wait for him. Increasingly, he felt not only bereaved but betrayed by her decision.

In his mind, losing her — because that, for him, was what it came down to — assumed such proportions that he was convinced he could never find someone to compensate him for his loss. Jane was an essential dependency factor. Knowing she was somehow there in the background had made it possible for him to plan his life. Without her availability, his personal grand design lay shattered in his mind.

Then why go on living? *The Thing* had planted the thought on one of those nights Andrew had been unable to sleep. The stark, straightforward directness of the question had first frightened him, so much so that he had gone to chapel and tried to pray it away. It stubbornly refused to go, returning at any moment. He would be crossing a road and the idea would occur to him how easy it would be to step in front of a bus or car; he would be leaning out of the window of his room and it would cross his mind it would require little effort to jump to his death. He was no longer, as such, frightened by the concept of suicide. It had a definite appeal. Death, after all, would be a relief from the steady corrosion of his personality, his prolonged and intense feeling of mourning, his hopeless depression for which he was scared to seek help, and which anyway he was sure no one could treat. *The Thing* said, time and again, it was *his* loss, *his* bereavement, caused by *her* betrayal.

This inner voice was very persuasive, urging him to resolve matters by his own hand. At the last moment, another voice, the one that intellectually he recognized as sanity, told him not to obey. Sometimes he was forced, in his room, to shout out loud his wish to go on living.

Then *The Thing* retreated. Andrew had the feeling it was content to bide its time. It was, he suspected, a staged withdrawal into the recesses of his unconscious. That was a scary feeling: not knowing what was going on in the depths of his mind. Because he could not understand it himself, he realized — once more the voice of reason — he could not expect his spiritual director to suspect that his outward calmness was really a way of masking his feeling of being divorced from these familiar surroundings.

"Do you follow, Andrew?" The director was looking at him through the tent of his fingers. "The important thing is to say to yourself that it's quite normal to feel like this." The priest searched for the words he wanted. "I can't think of anyone who has not felt, for want of a better word, out of sorts in their first year here. We fall into a mood, feel gloomy and morose. Just like you say you feel now. But it's common to all our lives. The feeling that everything is getting on top. That little doubts are becoming big ones. The important thing is not to let them grow. You can see that, can't you?"

"Yes." Andrew felt the anger curdling in his stomach. "I didn't mean to sound full of self-pity." His own voice sounded distant to him; just as his body often felt a stranger. The director in trying to be helpful was only making matters worse.

He had borrowed a number of books from the Greg medical library. But he found it was one thing to read about the clinical symptoms of loss, stress, chronic fatigue, sleeplessness, rejection, and uncertainty; it was quite another to interpret them in relation to himself. *The Thing* urged him not to bother, pointing out that no words could cure his pain. Only Andrew could do that.

Yet he knew now that he had lost many of the skills to control his emotional self; that his silent anger, condemnation, acute pessimism, and bursts of crying in his room were matters he could not regulate.

He had read about the dynamics of suicide. Most cultures indignantly reject it as an act of impiety, as indeed does the Church. But the inner voice, velvety, persuasive, *The Thing*, said such an attitude of abhorrence was wrong, based on an ignorance of the real value of suicide in his case. It was in a sense the most meaningful answer he could give to Jane's heartless behavior. His death would be his ultimate triumph. It would show her he had not lost his sense of self-purpose; that he was not halfhearted about matters; that he was not lacking in judgment; that, in taking his life, he was not indulging in some pointless act of self-injury, but displaying a higher form of courage that few aspire to — certainly not Jane. His brave action would make her realize what she had done to him. That, insisted *The Thing*, was what was important: making her aware, and using his death to punish her. She, not he, would suffer. The voice of madness gave suicide an appeal that none of the books he had read understood.

The director's voice finally intruded.

". . . as I was saying, Andrew, the human spirit is a powerful force. I've seen boys come in here and sit where you are, filled with all the woes of life. They weren't getting on with their studies. They felt all the distractions of Rome. Their prayer life seemed to be up the creek. They couldn't relate to their situation. Life, they felt, was a real mess. Yet the more they talked about it, the more they realized they had been letting things build up."

He paused, reflecting and remembering.

"Sometimes they couldn't talk to me. I can understand that. So I suggested they should go to chapel. Find a place in a corner and kneel and pray and have direct contact with God. I can't think of one boy it didn't help. I really can't. I think it would help you. Open yourself to Christ fully. Tell Him that things are a bit difficult right now and that you want Him to guide you through a bit of a bad patch. That's what it is, you know, Andrew. A bit of a choppy sea. There you were sailing along, everything as smooth as the Med in August, and then something probably said, 'What am I doing here?' A very natural reaction. We all wonder that in the beginning. We all think, can it really be that God has called us to His service? But He has, that's why we are here . . ."

"I'm sure you are right."

Andrew had this idea that he was slowly moving away from the world, retreating into a darker private hideaway inside him: a remote, frightening, and unknown realm; a place where common experiences took on an evil numen. In the beginning, trying to interpret the textbooks, he had kept a record of his disturbed sleep patterns. Now he no longer had to. He knew that, without fail, he would awaken around four or five each morning, feeling dull and unrefreshed. Sometimes an intolerable restlessness would then overcome him. He would get up and pace his room, composing in his mind letters to Jane and his parents, explaining why he had no alternative but to take his life. He never managed to complete a letter before once more exhaustion reclaimed him. He would lie on his bed, desperately attempting to get back to sleep. He tried counting back from a thousand, hoping the sheer boredom of the exercise would overcome all else. But nothing worked. Each morning he lay there, waiting for dawn, utterly alone, feeling increasingly upset, and filled with a sense of doom. This, more than at any other time, was when *The Thing* came, saying there was an easy way to end his misery.

It was after one of these mornings that Andrew had crept downstairs to the seminary's storeroom. He brought back a length of rope and hid it under his bed. Afterward, he sat at his desk and read in a medical book, with complete detachment, that hanging was still the second most common method of committing suicide, exceeded only by an overdose of drugs. He could think of no way of acquiring the necessary pills without consulting a doctor. *The Thing* had warned him never to do that. Doctors, he now firmly believed, could not help him.

The director was smiling a him.

"... I realize that when the novelty wears off, the food isn't quite what you are used to at home."

"The food's fine. Really."

Andrew knew now that one of the side effects of his depression was a dislike for eating. It reminded him of Jane. During her week in Rome she had shown her normal healthy appetite: three-course lunches followed by four-course dinners. That silent voice in his head suggested that before he delivered the ultimate punishment he should show her he did not need food.

"I hear you've cut back a bit. Not quite filling your plate the way you used to."

Andrew forced a smile. "I find I don't need so much. I suppose it's the climate."

He hoped the priest would not notice that his depression had created a flatness about all his responses. Since Jane's letter he had turned his back on so many of the excitements of living in Rome. No longer did he explore the city. He had not been to St. Peter's since Jane left; he had avoided even the street where the *ristorante* was. No longer did he go to the *Pesquina*, the only English-language cinema in Rome. Nor did he join the debates in the common room. He virtually stopped writing home, pleading that his studies took up all his time. His mother still wrote twice a week, long, chatty letters about activities in and outside the house. She never mentioned Jane, not since he had telephoned his mother with the news that she was going to marry Giles. He had been dully grateful for his mother's tact, but otherwise her letters left him indifferent and unmoved. They had piled up on his desk, waiting to be answered, along with those from friends. One or two expressed polite surprise that Jane was marrying Giles.

"... but in spite of any little drawbacks with the food, think of the compensations. I do believe we are one of the best-equipped seminaries in the city."

Andrew forced himself to sound positive. "I really do keep quite busy. I like to study alone. I picked up the habit in my last year at university."

"It's a good one. But don't let it take you over. Study is important, I grant you. But a priest, you know . . ." The director hesitated, framing his thought. "A priest needs to be a bit of an all-rounder. Good on the theoretical stuff but also able to make contact. One of the things the Rector is very keen on here is having everybody integrate. He puts great store on that. So, for that matter, does the Cardinal. His secretary was on the phone the other day. He asked how you were getting on."

"That's my mother again."

The director smiled, understanding about the importance of family connections.

Andrew risked a quick glance at the mantel clock. It would soon be over. He did not desire to be remotivated. He did not want to experience what one textbook called an awakening of his psychologic ego function. He only wanted to be left alone.

He looked at the priest. "I'm sorry if I've sounded like some homesick kid away from Mother for the first time. I'm really happy here. I'm certain about my vocation. The Greg is a challenge and it's really . . . well, more than I'd hoped for."

The director nodded, relieved. "That's good to hear. That's very positive. The important thing is not to feel sorry for yourself. It's so easy to drift into . . ." He paused, once more settling the words in his mind. "Once you are adrift, all sorts of things can go wrong."

Andrew waited. The tension brought on a pain in his neck.

The director peered at Andrew over the top of his fingers.

"From time to time seminarians have problems distinguishing between friendship of a nonsexual kind, what I would call a Christian friendship, and other feelings. Some of them find they cannot cope without affection. So they turn to each other for comfort. There is nothing intrinsically wrong with this, providing it remains within a healthy dimension. And that is where no element of sexuality is present. The important thing is to be able to distinguish between a close and loving relationship and one that contains sexual elements. Apart from the serious sinful moral aspect involved in any kind of friendship other than a purely celibate one, there is the very real psychological problem of guilt, which homosexuality can produce in people. The more balanced a person, the more his guilt. Because we live in an all-male community, friendships can take on a more intense meaning. And so the temptation to go that little bit further takes on a new attraction. Freud saw that. So did others after him. The wrongness in homosexuality is for a celibate exactly the same as the wrongness in hetero-sexuality. That is, not in the condition, but in the failure to act responsibly, to show a lack of control and respect, perhaps for the very person we love, or think we love. That is why we have very strict rules. We just could not let anything start —"

Andrew could not contain himself. "You don't think I'm turning gay, do you?"

He wondered what the priest would say if he told him that as well as his zest for food, his sexual drive had diminished correspondingly. No longer did he look at pretty girls in the street; Jane had killed off his feelings of masculinity. Most of the time he felt impotent, finding it hard even to stimulate himself. But the idea of having any homosexual contact was totally repugnant; he felt about homosexuality the way the textbooks defined suicide — as something to be repudiated.

The director's voice remained even. "No. I don't think you are. But if I may say so, you are turning into a bit of a sartorial mess." The priest flexed his fingers and resteepled them. "I'm sorry to be so blunt. But I've always found it best not to mince matters when it comes to self-neglect. There's something about one's outward appearance that's very important. It's one of the reasons a priest's cassock compels respect. No one can look untidy in a soutane."

"I'm sorry. I suppose I must look a bit scruffy at times."

After Jane's letter he had paid less attention to his appearance; sometimes he skipped shaving every day and he shampooed his hair less frequently than he used to. This lack of fastidiousness was another manifestation of his depression, which developed as his self-confidence waned.

The director collapsed his tented fingers and placed his hands on his knees. They sat silently opposite each other. In the past, periods of silence like this had been shared reflective pauses, allowing each of them to consider what had been said, and what further needed to be stated. But now in the numbing silence Andrew was unable to concentrate. It was even an effort to remember how this conversation began.

He was aware of other changes. He used to be very decisive. Recently, he could not make up his mind about the simplest of things. This morning he had stood in his room for some time, unable to decide whether to wear a plain or a striped shirt. Both were equally creased and grubby. In the end, he put on the sweatshirt he was now wearing. He had read that indecision and a loss of willpower are very common in depression. They went with all the other symptoms, especially lack of hope.

He had come here again, wanting to believe in the magic of the priest's spirituality. Somehow, he'd hoped the director would have prompted him to explain this strange feeling that at times he was almost someone else; that it was this stranger who allowed *The Thing* to suggest the best means, the only certain way, to make her realize what she had done. She must be made to feel guilty. And, insisted *The Thing*, there was only one way for him to achieve that.

"I gather you're still doing extremely well at the Greg. We're all very pleased. That's why I think this is no more than a passing mood. If it was serious it would show in your work."

He was certain that nobody, least of all the director, had any idea how distorted his thinking had become; he was aware of it himself only when that voice of reason intervened. But most of the time he was filled with a treacherous pessimism. Those were the occasions when *The Thing* was at its most persuasive, insisting he should give up the burden of living. That was the only way, it told him, to eliminate this agony.

Then there were those spells, always when he was alone in his room, when his mind suddenly began to race from one idea to another, all centered on how he could persuade Jane to give up Giles. He would telephone her. No, write to her. Better still, have his mother call or write to her. No, have his mother visit her. No, much better, have his mother call her mother and join forces to make Jane see reason. He, in the meantime, could appeal to Giles, man to man, to give up Jane. No, not appeal, explain: that Giles had only caught her on the rebound. Then a new thought: why not send a mutual friend to persuade her? But, as the impracticability of each idea became clear, his anger and panic, resentment and guilt, and the awful feeling of futility grew. Once more his mind would begin to dwell on a solution that always seemed to be hovering.

"The important thing, Andrew, is to keep a sense of balance between your studies and your prayer life. I've seen so many boys throw themselves full tilt into class work that going to chapel becomes almost a chore. It's all a matter of planning. Knowing what to take from each which is important. It comes down to proper planning, not playing it by ear."

"I hope I don't do that."

In these past weeks his depression had narrowed his emotional horizons. He seemed to need all his strength to keep his feelings hidden. This, for him, had become of prime importance. At times the effort drove him to tears. Several times he tried to follow a textbook's suggestion. When he started to sob, he stood in front of the mirror and stared at himself. The manual insisted that no one can continue to cry when faced with the sight of one's own tears. It had not worked. He also tried talking to himself, addressing his image in the mirror. The sound of his voice debating his wish to die frightened him even more.

The director was on his feet, his voice mellifluous and sympathetic. "I sense a restlessness in you. Really."

"I can't think why."

The priest nodded, thoughtfully. "Well, perhaps it's my imagination. You know, when I first came out here I imagined I would never settle. Those first couple of years were, to put it bluntly, hell. I used to be always writing home, I just couldn't let go and live my life here. I really wanted both. I wanted to be back in London and I wanted to be here. I used to invite people to come and see me. Then, suddenly, it all fell into place. I accepted that I belonged here. I think that's what we all have to do. Accept something."

"Yes. I suppose so."

The priest smiled. "Rome, in every sense, is far from home. Just come and stand here for a moment and you'll see what I mean."

Andrew followed him to the window. Beyond were the ancient irregularly shaped Roman roofs with their corroded pipe vents and terra-cotta chimney pots.

"Reminds me a bit of Paris, but more foreign." The director peered at the street bustle far below. "Down there we'd be hard pressed to find anybody who understands our language. The Romans are really worse than the English. Can't speak anything but their own lingo, and the rest of Italy says they don't even do that very well."

He turned back into the room. "Every time I look down there it somehow still emphasizes how far from home I am. I suspect you feel the same. That can also make you feel out of sorts."

"Yes." A few weeks ago he would have found the distinctive pungent smells and sounds still invigorating. Now they had no effect.

"Seminary life is different from university. Perhaps it's suddenly even harder for you than for most, coming from all that freedom to here. Could that be it?"

The director's voice was gentle, still trying to pin him down. Yet the more understanding and compassionate he was, the more remote he seemed to become.

"I suppose it could be that." He knew it was untrue.

The director put his hands behind his back, rocking gently on the balls of his feet — a signal he was running late. It meant, thought Andrew, suddenly relieved, that he could leave this sanctum of books and platitudes. Another fifty minutes of his life had gone. *The Thing* had just silently whispered in his mind that he really shouldn't waste any more time.

"I hear your Italian is now fluent. That's really very encouraging. A lot of students never get to grips with the language."

The director was moving toward the door.

Andrew remained standing in the middle of the study. He could almost feel the bubble of pain swelling inside him, a living entity feeding off his emotions, draining him even further.

The priest turned at the door. "Same time in a fortnight?"

"Yes. Fine." He walked toward the door, thinking he would not be here. His suicide would shock his parents. He had no doubt at all about that. This was why he had resisted the impulse: they would be destroyed. But, on the other hand, he could really see how it would be a fitting punishment for Jane. She should carry the memory of what she had driven him to do to her grave. He wondered why he couldn't open himself to the director. He was kind and his interest was genuine.

The priest opened the door. There was a certainty in his eyes and voice. "Remember. Prayer. See you in a fortnight. But drop by any time you feel the need for a chat."

"Thanks." He felt drained, yet triumphant. He had achieved what *The Thing* commanded. He had kept their secret. Nobody yet suspected, he was certain, what was in his mind. His life had taken on a malignancy all of its own. He felt detached from it, as if it had nothing to do with him, this precarious balancing act he was performing within himself.

He reached his room and fell on his bed, burying his face in his pillow. After a while the tears subsided and the pain turned to resolve. He began, again, to compose a farewell letter to Jane.

Nothing had changed. After an hour, and endless attempts, he was still unable to find the right words for Jane. He finally retreated, overcome, to his bed, watching the sky lose its hard blueness and take on a softer paleness. For a while, with the sun gone, an abyss of blackness filled the window, then the stars appeared all at once. And after them, the light of the moon, incandescent, bright enough for him to see the crumpled sheets of paper scattered on the floor around his desk. He had tried so hard. But the words would not come, at least those which would make any sense of what he wanted to do. There was no way of putting on paper the anguish he felt. His thoughts continued to be remote and detached, completely unrelated to his surroundings. He wondered if the Pope was at his window, staring through his telescope into the heavens as he did on most clear nights. And would that telescope be powerful enough to see the gods waiting to punish? He could hear his own whisper. "Please God, help me. Please, God . . ."

Still pleading, he drifted into sleep.

The storm, accompanied by a sudden fierce wind from the north, developed quickly, its lightning jerking Andrew upright. The clap of thunder appeared to be directly overhead. In the next flash of lightning he saw the first drops fall. There was another concerted series of flashes, like artillery fire, then an enormous cataract of water descended from the sky. He rushed to close the window, and turned to the desk. The words began to swirl once more in his head, faster and faster, keeping time with the lightning and thunder. He sat, frozen, his pen poised, unable to close the gap between his mind and paper. *I love her. I hate her. Love. Hate.* He threw down the pen, held his hands over his ears, and clenched his teeth tightly to try to contain this senseless litany.

The Thing was whispering: *You really are a very foolish man. You know you can stop this. All this struggle. It really is quite pointless, postponing what you know is the only sensible solution. There is no pain, you know, with dying. It is over before you even realize. You'll feel nothing, only a relief. No one will think you have behaved wrongly. That's why you don't have to write the letter.*

He rushed to his bed, burying his face under the pillow, trying to blot out the storm and the voice in his head.

"Dear Lord," he prayed again. "Dear Lord, I am being torn apart. I am. I am. I can't go on. Please."

The Thing was back. *You can't run anymore. You've been running for too long. You need to rest. You need to put an end to this pain. You can't take anymore. You must stop now.*

Andrew continued to pray.

Beyond the window the violence of the storm lifted as quickly as it had descended. Tomorrow, he thought, it would be blue again, a new day. It was like being reborn. But not for him. This thought was still uppermost in his mind as the sheer weariness of his body dragged him once more into uneasy sleep.

He lay in the darkness, somewhere between sleep and wakefulness, his twilight zone. The stars were out. The street sounds had returned: shrill voices, an interminable blaring of horns, radios, televisions. But it was all so far away, just as was this feeling that his penis belonged to someone else. Some stranger was handling it.

There had been, he now remembered, a heated discussion after supper a few nights ago, on how self-stimulation could fit into the life of a celibate Christian. He hadn't really paid much attention. One of the visiting Americans, a deacon, started it. He and a few others from their college had been invited over for a meal. The Rector encouraged such interseminary contacts; he felt it broadened outlooks. The deacon had said something about how the latest thinking clearly differentiated among four kinds of masturbation; Freud's infantile exploration of the genital area; the masturbation of puberty; abusive masturbation; adult masturbation to relieve psychological tension.

Someone was touching him. He could feel the hand. The noises outside were receding. He tried to remember what else the deacon had said. Something about psychological disturbance often being a cause of masturbation in grown people. He'd left then and come up to this room to brood. He didn't like it when people started discussing psychology.

Suddenly, as he had known all the time she would be, she was there, exactly as she had looked in the pornographic photographs of his school days. Yet, somehow, in spite of the various positions she could adopt at his command, she still continued to read from *The American Ecclesiastical Review*, one of the more prestigious of the religious publications he subscribed to. How had she obtained a copy? The deacon must have given it to her. That must be it. The deacon and his comforting view that self-stimulation was all right. She laughed as she read.

"Masturbation is objectively a mortal sin. Except in rare cases it is subjectively sinful . . ."

She had done this before. Read to him as she sat at the end of the bed, using her long heavy braid of hair to caress her pubis.

"Masturbation is far from being a simple sexual sin, but it is part of the complex problem of maturation . . ."

The girl laughed again, edging toward him, rubbing herself against his knee, describing what the learned magazine had defined as "the fundamental option view" within the Church on self-stimulation.

"While masturbation is a moral question, it is not necessarily to be regarded as seriously sinful . . ."

She was reading and stroking him at the same time.

"Masturbation is such a normal part of growing up that the only serious evil that can be attached to it arises from the unfortunate guilt feeling that comes from early training and negative attitudes toward sexuality . . ."

He felt his body letting go. He knew he was groaning, but he could no longer control it. She had thrown the magazine aside, concentrating totally on what he was doing. He could hear her voice encouraging him.

The tension surged from him and he lay on the bed drained. On the floor was his copy of *The American Ecclesiastical Review*, with the article on masturbation and its conclusion that while it is possible for celibates to incorporate self-stimulation into their life in Christ, it can only be done when there are no guilt feelings.

Andrew always felt guilty.

The nightly silence of the seminary had fallen when the image of his mother came into his mind. She was dressed in black, standing at the foot of a grave, so new that the mound of flowers had not wilted. On the temporary wooden marker was his name. His mother propped her wreath against the marker. Then another black-coated figure came forward and placed a tiny posy: Jane. She stood back, allowing him a clear view of the card. *R.I.P. Jane and Giles.*

The Thing was no longer in his head. It was at the foot of the bed, shrouded in mist, tall and without a definite face or form, yet with an authoritative presence and voice.

You see, even in death she mocks you. There is only one way to punish such a woman. You must show her you do not fear death.

Andrew begged to be left alone, closing his eyes. Instantly, *The Thing* was back inside his head, ordering him to resume his search. There was an impatience in its words. *You must find a place where you can put an end to this. Take the rope. Take it with you.*

Andrew pleaded that this was not the right thing for him to do. The words struggled up through the consciousness of his mind and escaped from his lips.

To use the rope is not a sign of weakness. It requires a special strength. You must stop resisting. There is no reason to delay any longer. We have had this conversation many times. We both know what must be done. Now is the time to do it.

Beyond the window the blare of traffic faded. Rome was going to sleep.

It is time for you to rest. You are very, very tired. You deserve to sleep.

"I must write Jane a farewell note. I must. You must let me do that." Andrew stumbled to the desk and started to write, first saying the words, then putting them down on paper. "I love you. Good-bye. I love you. Good-bye. I love you. Good-bye."

He filled a page with the repetition.

The Thing was consoling: *You have done everything. There is no more to be done. It really is time to go. There has been too much delay. You are making the right decision. You really are.*

"Jane." Andrew called out her name, as if she would appear and unlock the doors closing his mind. "Jane. Please understand. I love you. Good-bye. I love you."

As he walked toward the door, there was a tightening feeling in his throat, as if he was being choked.

The secret voice commanding him to stop. *Have you forgotten? The rope. You must take the rope.*

The tears welled up behind his eyes. Please, he silently pleaded, not just yet.

Now! There is no time to waste.

"No!" The shout burst from Andrew. "No! No! No!"

Immediately *The Thing* was gone. It hated to be shouted at. He had done so before and it always worked. He continued to do so now. "Go away! Damn you. Go away!"

The tears spilled down his cheeks. He was so weary that he could barely stagger back to bed. He lay there until once more he fell into another exhausted sleep. But even then his mind, isolated and exiled within the pain of his body, could not rest.

He lay in the darkness, now awake, looking at the rectangle of moonlit sky framed in the window. The unknown late-night listener had tuned the radio. The music was beguiling, like *The Thing's* voice, telling him he could leave the rope; that all he should do was to settle on a place where he could hang himself.

Slowly Andrew rose from the bed. He walked to the window, standing there in his shirt and trousers, listening to the music. The air at this hour was cool and sweet-tasting, freed from fumes from the Fiats that crawled past below, most of the time. Somewhere out there, a thousand miles away, beyond the domes and silent campaniles, his parents would be asleep. He loved them, differently, but so much that it suddenly hurt. He wanted so badly for them to understand. But could they? How would they live with the stigma? People would point them out as the poor parents of that boy who committed suicide in Rome. What would it be like for them, in their community? What would Father Patrick say? What would his mother say to the Cardinal? What could anybody say? How would anyone ever begin to understand? How could he understand what he was being asked to do? The insistent voices said he could. His parents would understand. So would Father Patrick and even His Eminence. They would reserve all their anger for Jane. She would be the outcast, not he. She would bear the stigma, the one person who drove him to this. She would suffer eternal damnation, not he.

Andrew knelt before the bed, searching under it with a hand. He pulled out the rope. He fed it through his hands, foot by foot, feeling its thickness and the roughness of the hemp, silently counting as he had done so before. It was eleven feet long. He would need two of those feet to fashion a noose. That would leave him nine feet. A beam or hook ten feet clear of the ground would be ideal. He recoiled the rope.

The voice inside him was silent. But he could sense its approval.

He had reached the Corridor of the Cardinals. He stood, uncertain. The voice reminded him that he had done all this before and in the end failed, allowing his resolve at the last moment to weaken. He must not do so this time. He must find a place.

"I want to feel better. I don't want to die." He whispered the words suddenly. "I want to live. Dear God, I really do."

No, no, no. It's much too late for this. Don't stop now. You have to find a place.

"No! No!" His voice was low, but stronger. But this time *The Thing* did not retreat.

Yes. Yes.

Andrew turned and descended the staircase to the ground floor. He paused near the chapel, thinking there was no loneliness as great as that of utter silence and complete darkness. Standing there, perfectly still, sweat on his skin, his bare feet cold on the tiled floor, he was filled with a medley of thoughts: he was somewhere between Purgatory and Hell; he was overcome by a tremendous primitive fear; and forcing itself up through a bubble of unreality was the one devastating thought, both mad and captivating, that at last he could discover for himself the greatest mystery of life, what lay beyond it.

"I want to live." He spoke the words, feeling the full petrifying presence of death.

But his body, he knew, was obedient only when the mind permitted.

He pushed open the chapel door, the rope in his hand.

CHAPTER 16

†

Ministering

Father Philippe always thought that changes — social, political, and environmental — were more noticeable from his study picture window. It offered an uninterrupted view into the suburb where he did most of his ministering.

Forty years ago the ramshackle area across the street had been countryside, where farming was done by hand and with animal power. Then the postwar boom enticed the developers onto the wornout land. They swiftly set about tearing up pastures with their machines. By the early 1950s, a community had been established. It was comprised exclusively of young, white, professional families whose adults voted overwhelmingly Republican. Their children went to the local Catholic school. Later, when they grew up, they were married in the local Catholic church, St. Mark's, where Father Philippe was assigned as an assistant. When they died they were buried in the neighborhood's Catholic cemetery, segregated even in death from non-Catholics.

Blacks had entered this suburb only to work, the women to clean houses, the men to tend gardens. They arrived and left by bus from places far beyond the railroad, areas white folks avoided.

Then came the 1960s and the civil rights movement. Within a decade, not only politically but in other ways the area was irrevocably changed. In effect the movement rearranged a segregated society. Street by street, house by house, the blacks advanced. Soon there wasn't a white person left in the neighborhood. Every house had been bought by blacks. At local and national election times they filled their windows with Democratic party posters. Formal dinner parties were replaced by Sunday picnics, and soul music was heard where string quartets once filled living rooms. Gardens were no longer so well attended to; houses needed repainting. And the pews of St. Mark's were increasingly filled with black Catholics, who gave thanks to the Church that during the decade of civil unrest supported their cause.

Several years had now passed since Father Philippe had arrived in the diocese. But he had never lost his enthusiasm for helping the black community. In his previous three parishes he had established a deserved reputation for championing the various causes of black people. This in part, he suspected, was why the Bishop had transferred him to St. Mark's, where he had become a familiar figure in the ghetto. Yet he still managed to retain a friendly relationship with his handful of white parishioners. The Bishop had said, again, only the other day, how pleased he was about this.

From the beginning Father Philippe liked the gentle, soft-voiced leader of the thirty thousand Catholics scattered throughout the diocese, with its ten parishes, each with a solidly built church and rectory, schools, counseling centers, and a hospital, the General. The Bishop was a paternal figure, respected both for his office and for the careful way he integrated the Church into civic affairs.

This morning, the anxious voice of Father Ray Nolan continued to issue instructions over the telephone. The parish priest, Father Philippe's superior, was calling from the Bishop's office in the chancellery downtown.

Father Philippe had found the chancellor distant. The monsignor was proud of being "F.B.I." (foreign-born Irish), and in his soft Galway brogue made it clear he knew all about Father Philippe's past, at the same time somehow managing to suggest he was himself a paragon of virtue. Father Philippe now suspected something different; there was more to the chancellor's relationship with a Protestant widow than mere instruction in the faith. Father Nolan had hinted as much.

He now also knew that the parish priest was not, though for very different reasons, what he appeared. Behind the grumbling that he had liked his parish the way it once was, he was a caring and hard-working cleric. His problem, Father Philippe saw, was that Father Nolan was a born worrier and completely unable to delegate. Nor could he always spot a social problem. He was also quirky with women. He would not allow one inside the rectory, except Marcia, the old black woman who had cleaned it since it was built thirty years ago. All other women conducted their business with Father Nolan on the rectory doorstep.

Yet, in many ways, the elderly priest allowed Father Philippe a surprisingly free hand. When he suggested that the old-fashioned confessional should be replaced by a Confession Room situated to one side of the altar, Father Nolan raised no objection, accepting Father Philippe's argument that parishioners would feel more relaxed admitting their sins in comfortable surroundings instead of having to crouch in the darkness of a stuffy box.

The Confession Room was, Father Philippe admitted, rather startling. It had a silver carpet, pale blue walls, and two overstuffed armchairs, covered in crimson velvet, facing each other with a low table in between. The color scheme was his own — just as he was responsible, and proud of it, for the decor of his five-room apartment in the rectory.

The study had a pale pink carpet and lime-colored walls. The living room was richly red, from floor to ceiling, the way he imaged a Renaissance baronial chamber might have looked. His bedroom was the softest of cream: carpet, walls, and ceilings. The kitchen was predominantly dark green with solid oak paneling. The bathroom walls were covered with exotic birds and flowers hand-painted on ceramic tile; it reminded him of a picture he had once seen of the Garden of Eden. Three families from the small remaining white enclave in the parish had, among them, refurbished the entire apartment. Yet another parishioner dropped by soon after Father Philippe moved in and said he would be honored if he would visit his haberdashery to pick out some clothes. The shopkeeper persuaded him to accept as another oblation an entire wardrobe: suits, casual wear, shirts, shoes, even socks, in all some two thousand dollars' worth, enough to fill the closets in the bedroom, its bed adorned by the patchwork quilt stitched by his wife. She still invited him regularly over to morning coffee in her new home, some distance away. But she no longer came to St. Mark's. She could not abide what had happened to the neighborhood.

Father Nolan continued to issue instructions. He had been gone only a couple of hours, yet already had called twice. This morning, because of a diocesan finance committee meeting, he had been forced to hand over his house calls.

"When you get to the Schiff house remember to check on Beth. Her mother says she's always asleep when I call. Try and see her."

He had never visited the Schiffs. They had always been Father Nolan's responsibility. All he knew was that Beth Schiff had been bedridden for some weeks.

Father Philippe continued to stare out of the window while Father Nolan gave further instructions.

"Make sure the church is locked before you go."

"I already did."

A month ago Father Nolan had caught a youth about to prise open the golden door of the tabernacle. He had chased him out into the street, but the teenager escaped. A patrol car had combed the area for an hour while Father Nolan fumed about junkies ready to do anything to get money for a fix. Since then, the church had been locked whenever one of them was not on duty.

"Did Fern East leave off that check?"

"No. But I can go and ask her, if you like."

"No, no. Don't do that."

Father Philippe could see the widow out on the jogging track beyond the church boundaries. She ran every morning, sometimes with her daughter Margot. They made a striking pair in their matching purple track suits, supple and graceful, circling the track for an hour. Fern had told him its therapeutic value for her: keeping her body fit could help her recover from the shock of losing a husband to cancer.

A couple of months before, Fern had asked him, on her way out of the Confession Room, if he would join her on the track. He had accepted and next morning he turned up and Fern approved his sky-blue suit but rejected the sneakers. His feet would soon be a mass of blisters. She had driven him to a sports store and insisted on buying him a pair of jogging shoes. Since then, he had regularly joined her, lapping the track, finding after a while he was fit enough to talk as he ran.

With Fern there was no sexual element involved. She was past fifty, loyal to the memory of her husband, and devoted to her children, all of whom except Margot were married. Her eldest daughter, she explained, was a concern to her. Margot was taking, in her mother's view, an unusually long time to get over a broken engagement. Perhaps one day, she suggested, he could drop by the house and explain she must stop feeling sorry for herself. Perhaps he would, he said.

Fern had not pushed — which was also why he enjoyed her company.

Their morning workouts became occasions when he was able to speak increasingly freely about his past. She listened sympathetically, occasionally interjecting to remind him that his secrets were safe and she felt privileged that he would share them with her. In so many ways, he realized, Fern was the mother he wished he had had.

Not once, in all these months, had the terrifying nightmare returned. While, like anyone else, he still dreamed every night, they no longer suddenly awakened him, bathed in sweat and gripped with fear. From what little he could remember of them, these were happy and reassuring memories, mostly no more than extensions of his working life. They were not filled with dire omens, prophecies, and warnings, nor were they sacrilegious, depressing, or bristling with hostility. Instead, the imagery he could now recall from beyond the threshold of his consciousness was happy and joyful: a sermon preached with particular fervor or an adult Scripture class that had gone extra well. They were dreams about communications: his soul in harmonious contact with others.

People told him his sermons were some of the best they had ever heard preached; that his off-the-cuff speeches at weddings were legendary; that they had never before known a priest who could baptize a baby without making the infant cry; that there was probably not a better priest in the diocese to conduct a funeral.

Father Philippe felt he especially understood death and its effects on the bereaved because he had once come close to a spiritual death. He also knew that, no matter how eloquent his words, their impact fell flat unless they were accompanied by a genuine desire to comfort. He had always tried to make known that their grief was his; that he shared their despair; that he knew no amount of assurances on his part would initially relieve the agony for a family no longer intact. He knew, he reminded himself on these occasions, what it was like to feel lost, broken, and emotionally adrift. Faith, he resolutely believed, his faith, never shaken, was instrumental in bringing him back from his brink of despair. He offered it to others, using words that, for all their repetition, still retained a freshness: "I know what you are enduring. I have a few suggestions that might help. I don't possess any secret knowledge or any special comforting skills. But I can try to show you how to survive."

He had succeeded, time and again, in making people believe that God intended the living to go on with life. This, too, was why these had been such rewarding months. The proof was there in his diary.

*

"Tuesday, October 30. The Bishop introduced me at a deanery meeting. Said I had come to do missionary work. That's why he has given me St. Mark. Spent rest of the day driving around the parish with Ray. He did not say much.

"Saturday, November 10. Getting to know Ray. He's like the Bishop. They both don't say it, but I feel they want to protect me from my past sins. They are good men, but I am certain that in their mind sex is evil. I just feel it. They are very generous to me. But the chancellor is a s.o.b. In his mind I am someone who has come back after doing the unforgivable — getting married and then divorced.

"Monday, November 19. Ray is really a humble man. On the one hand he's the kind of pastor who calls me up to his office and reads the riot act. Last Saturday was typical. He had a whole list of things. I'd left a light burning when I wasn't in a room. Had the radio playing too loud. Made me feel like a kid. Then, he says, okay, don't do it again, and I'm doing a good job. He's happy with my work.

"Monday, December 3. Sat with Mrs. Woodstock all day. She knew she couldn't last until morning. I said to her, 'When you die it'll just be like the candle going out. It'll be very quiet. You'll just die like that.' She was saying her rosary when her candle went out. Her last words to me were 'Oh, my Jesus, save us.' Then she died in my arms.

"Sunday, December 9. I realized again how much I love babies. Held the Lawrence baby for a long time when baptizing him and really felt he was mine. I told his mother. She understood. But Big Dick Lawrence told Paul Kirwan that there's no way a priest can feel like I did. I just took Big Dick aside and told him he was a crock of b.s. if he didn't understand that the person inside the cassock was a man first and a priest second. He looked at me strangely, and I said that was being honest.

"Saturday, December 15. First wedding here. Alan Newton and Jodi Bonham. I was very conscious of how fragile a relationship is. Marrying them, I kept on thinking of a tiny plant that had just been put into the ground. If that sounds dramatic, it's the only way to say what I want to say without being philosophical or theological. Told them they would, like a tiny plant, be buffeted by the wind and pelted by the hail and scorched by the sun, but somehow they should look upon their vows and their prayer life as providing them with shelter and shade to survive. Marriage, I said, was the most tremendous risk and if they could survive they would have a miracle. Any marriage that survives is a miracle."

*

He watched Fern pass once more beneath his window, and decided to make his first call on Beth Schiff and her mother.

Ma Schiff shifted from one foot to another, as if her massive body was searching for a point of equilibrium. Father Philippe estimated she could be between forty and sixty. She had several chins and a purpled goiter on her neck. Her hair was matted, graying and plaited like a child's. Her hands reminded him of ancient trees, gnarled and twisted. Her skin was leathery. Standing on the porch, she towered over him, asking where Father Nolan was.

"He had a meeting, Mrs. Schiff."

"That so?" She dug her hands deep into the pockets of her shapeless dress. It was stained down the front as if she spilled everything she touched. "He ain't missed a call before."

"The Bishop wanted him at the meeting."

She turned abruptly and resumed tugging at a mass of creeper, a dark shady green, curled around one of the porch pillars. It snapped quite suddenly under her strength and she stood for a moment, staring at the clump of tendrils in her hand before tossing it to the side of the porch.

"That so?"

He could see her looking at him, skeptical and suspicious. He knew that gaze: it sometimes came into his mother's eyes before one of her attacks.

From somewhere inside the house came a strange croaking sound, more animal than human.

"Is that Beth?" He tried to sound casual. She did not answer, pausing in her work to stare at him.

"Sounds like she might need some help. Don't you think we should go and see?"

She continued to stand, her eyes narrowing and face blotching with color. He gently repeated the question.

"What's the matter with Beth, Mrs. Schiff?"

She tore at more of the creeper and dumped it. He had a sudden image of her being able to destroy anything with her hands.

"She got problems." Her voice was surprisingly high-pitched. "I can't think why you've come if you don't know the problems."

She examined the pillar from which she was stripping the vine, concentrating totally on the task, tracing the creeper as it climbed around and around the pillar.

He wished Father Nolan had briefed him. But, then, the parish priest believed the core of ministry is personal discovery. Over their first meal in the rectory he had set out his rules. "We're both priests. We know all the regulations and we live and work within them. Strictly. No deviations. But, that apart, no point in my asking you to be my shadow. We just agree here and now that you do things your way, I do things mine."

Behind him dogs were growling around his car. Across the street children paused in their game of whooping and turning cartwheels, silent and wary, watching him. He concentrated on Ma Schiff, thinking how best to proceed, realizing she had probably never been quite in control — of her huge body, of this dilapidated clapboard, of the patch of garden, and possibly of Beth.

"Why don't we go inside and talk?"

She hesitated and then turned and led him into the house.

Stepping out of the light, he needed a few moments to adjust to his surroundings and the prevailing odors of dried urine and cooking. The linoleum, he noted, was torn in several places, as if gnawed by rats. The furniture was oversized and from another age, too broken to have any antique value, too dirty to be sold even as junk. The only wall decorations in the living room were religious symbols: a wooden crucifix and a Madonna framed in plastic. There was a bunch of wax flowers on a table that was littered with dirty crockery.

"I've let things go since my husband died."

"When was that?"

"Ten years ago next May." There was a long silence.

"What happened, Mrs. Schiff?"

Father Philippe stood in the center of the room, feeling her silent anger swelling around her in a great cloud. Finally, she hurled the words at him.

"Auto crash. Father Nolan went out there, right in the middle of the night, and gave him the last sacraments. He died on the way to the General."

She started to rub her face, so hard that she drew tiny flecks of blood, working her hand hard back and forth across her big drooping jaw. It was, he realized, an involuntary habit, not so much nervous as altogether primeval.

"And Beth. She your only child?"

"Yup. Never tried again after her. Saw no point in repeating the mistake."

The sound came again from the adjoining room.

"What happened to Beth?"

She caught her lower lip in her teeth and whispered. "What happened? Nothing happened. She was made like that. God made her like that."

It took a little while before he could bring himself to ask the question. "She has some congenital defect? Is that it?"

"Questions!" She uttered the word almost fiercely. "Don't you come here and try and question me!" She resumed rubbing her face. "Ain't nothing I can do for the child. Ain't nothing anyone can do."

She walked heavily around the room, her foot catching on a hole in the linoleum. She appeared not to notice. She suddenly giggled. "You know, best thing for Beth, she was dead."

"Mrs. Schiff! It's your daughter you're talking about. Your flesh and blood!"

"Yup. But best she was dead."

He looked at her uneasily. "You told Father Nolan this?" He sensed her eyes, dark and accusing.

"Nope."

He took a step back, watching her. "Beth has got to be helped."

"No one can do anything."

"Yes, they can."

"No! No!"

"Yes, Mrs. Schiff. You've got to be sensible."

Suddenly she charged at him, screaming for him to get out. He stepped aside to avoid her rush. She leaned against a wall, sobbing. "I can't stand it! I can't stand it!"

"You can get help, Mrs. Schiff, do you hear? You can get help. Welfare, medical —"

"I don't want no help! You hear, Father? I want no strangers coming in here. Poking around. Minding my business."

Outside, he could hear the children playing once more.

"But, Mrs. Schiff, you need help —"

"No! Who's to say what I need? You come in here and tell me I need help! Who's to say you can do that? Who's to say that, Father? You tell me. God? You think God says you can say that to me? I don't need help, do you hear? No help!"

He waited until she finished shouting.

"Mrs. Schiff, when I go from here, I'm going to go straight down to the town hall and see what can be done —"

"No! Better she dies!"

"Take me to Beth."

"No."

"Why not?"

Suddenly she was on her knees before him, sobbing, the tears running down her jowls.

"Don't you understand, Father? Nobody cares. Nobody cares what happens —"

"I care. I promise you. I care. And God cares."

He kept his voice calm.

"God! You think if He cared, He'd let this happen —"

"God doesn't let things happen, Mrs. Schiff. We make them happen. And then we turn to Him and ask God to help put things right. Don't you see that? You can't shift the blame on to God. You can't do that. God wants to help you. That's why He has sent me. Why Father Nolan comes. But if you won't let us do what God wants, to help you, then you can't start blaming Him."

He reached down and placed his hands on her head, saying nothing, just standing there, hoping to let her feel his support.

"Mrs. Schiff, we're both of us in this together. Let me share the load with you. Let's try to remember that God gave us courage and strength. Let's try and make a new beginning."

After a while she managed to control her sobs. She rose and fetched a candle from the kitchen, lighting it and placing it on the table.

"Don't you think we should see Beth first before I give you Communion?"

"No. Afterward."

"I understand. Do you want to confess anything?"

"No."

She lowered herself on to her knees again, staring up at him. He thought that as well as resignation there was a hint of madness in her eyes.

He removed the wafer from its gold case and made the sign of the cross before her face, and then asked that the Body and the Blood of Jesus Christ should guide her soul into the life everlasting. He placed the wafer on her waiting tongue, watching while she closed her mouth and dissolved the Host. Then she rose to her feet.

The sound came once more from the adjoining room.

"Mrs. Schiff, let's go to Beth."

"No! No, she's resting. She don't want a visit!"

"But you said —"

"What I said and what I mean are different!"

Suddenly she was giggling softly and shivering uncontrollably, pacing the room as if were a cage. He had seen his mother do the same thing.

Father Philippe looked at her levelly. "Mrs. Schiff, you can't hide Beth away like this —"

"I'm not hiding her."

"I think you are, Mrs. Schiff."

He started to move toward the door to the adjoining room.

"You don't go in there! You hear me? You don't! You don't go in there!"

Father Philippe turned and faced Ma Schiff. His voice was gentle but firm. "I only want to help. I'm not going to harm Beth."

"You can't help."

"But I can get help —"

"No! She's better off dead."

"I just want to see her."

"No."

"Yes. She obviously needs help —"

"I've no money to pay for that. Don't you understand, Father? I ain't got a cent to spare —"

"Help needn't cost you money. I can arrange things —"

"I don't want your charity. Now leave. Get outa here!"

Father Philippe's voice was quiet but firm as he delivered his ultimatum. "Mrs. Schiff. Either I see your daughter or I come back here with the proper authority. But I insist on seeing her."

Without waiting, he walked into the adjoining room. Above the bed was another crucifix. The blinds were drawn, but there was enough light for him to see the form curled up beneath the sheet.

"Beth? I am Father Philippe."

He advanced toward the bed.

The form gave another strange sound.

He stood, staring down at the emaciated figure, her face yellow and skeletal.

"You satisfied, Father?" Mrs. Schiff was behind him, trembling. "Father Nolan should have told you. She was born sick. She got sicker and sicker."

"She should be in the hospital."

"She should be dead."

He whirled on her. "God forgive you for that, Mrs. Schiff. I don't know what is the matter with her, but she should be in the hospital."

He pushed past Ma Schiff.

"Where you going, Father?"

She started to follow, then stopped as he ran out of the house.

He could hear her wailing.

Outside, the children had stopped playing and he asked where the nearest telephone was. They backed away from his voice, but one of them pointed. He ran to a door. An elderly black opened it. He explained why he wanted to use the telephone. The man nodded. Father Philippe dialed the General and returned to Ma Schiff. She was standing in the living room, cradling Beth in her arms, crying.

Father Philippe put his arms around them, whispering. "It's going to be all right. She'll get help. And so will you. I'll see to that."

Three hours later, Father Philippe sat with Ma Schiff in the MICU, the medical intensive care unit of the General. They were masked and gowned, as was everybody who worked in or visited this area. Ma Schiff stared vacuously at her daughter, lying in a bed beyond the glass observation window.

Beth was surrounded by equipment. Wires ran from electrodes positioned on her body. Towering over the clutter of machines was a drip stand; a clear liquid from its suspended bottle trickled down a plastic tube and into a vein in her left arm.

Father Philippe had telephoned Father Nolan from Admissions. Fifteen minutes later the priest called back and told the clerk that all bills were to be sent to the chancellery. It had been as simple as that.

"Is my girl going to live?" It was the first question Ma Schiff had asked since coming to the MICU. Her words were muffled by her face mask.

A doctor had replied. "Mrs. Schiff, we'll do all we can. But she is a very, very sick girl."

Father Philippe stared at the monitor on the wall above Beth's head, displaying her heartbeat. Wave after wave of spiky lines pulsed across the screen. He glanced at his watch. It would be dark outside, but in the critical-care area day and night are a continuous even fluorescence. He continued to sit beside Ma Schiff in an alcove near the nurses' station, waiting for news.

An hour ago, a surgeon had visited Beth's cubicle. Afterward he took Father Philippe aside, explaining her condition was deteriorating, because Beth's pneumonia was bilateral: there was an accumulation of purulent mucus in both lungs.

"Let's go home," Ma Schiff said. "Ain't nothing we can do here." She had once more retreated into a world of her own, indifferent to everyone and everything around her.

Later, the surgeon returned and in a low voice explained that Beth was showing signs of being cyanotic, from lack of oxygen in her blood. He was going to perform a tracheotomy to help her breathe. He made an incision just below Beth's Adam's apple and inserted an L-shaped plastic tube through the skin and muscle into Beth's trachea. He returned to report she was now breathing easily.

"Take me home." Ma Schiff stirred in the alcove.

"No. We wait. Both of us." Father Philippe was gentle but insistent.

Another hour passed and he was thinking of what to say at Hildie Simpson's wedding to Garry Grafton, knowing she was four months pregnant, when the loudspeaker system announced.

"Code Three! MICU Seven! Code Three! MICU Seven!"

Seven. That was the number on Beth's cubicle. He was on his feet at once and out in the corridor.

"Goddammit! Get out of the way, Father! Get the hell out of the way!"

Two white-coated men, interns, rushed past him, pushing a cart stocked with equipment. He had noticed it earlier, standing farther down the corridor. Other figures were running toward Beth's room as Father Philippe reached the observation window. The loudspeaker continued its repetitive command.

He had heard doctors talk about this kind of ultimate emergency on previous visits. "He died in Code Three." Or: "We never got the Code Three in time." But he'd never seen it in operation. He remained transfixed at the window. He could not hear anything through the thick plate glass, could see only the controlled efficiency. Somehow the drama was made all the more vivid for him by the lack of sound. The interns around the crash cart were working swiftly, unloading, opening, preparing. A nurse was standing to one side, stopwatch in hand, counting aloud. He remembered there were perhaps only four, never more than six minutes to resuscitate a person in Code 3. He looked at the monitor above the bed. The lines were almost horizontal. Beth was, he suspected, already as close to death as anybody could be.

He fingered the vial in his pocket, filled with its measure of holy oils. He began to pray, that the doctors would triumph, that Beth would be resuscitated, that he would not have to uncap the silver bottle.

The senior surgeon who had performed the tracheotomy burst through the door, taking command, bringing authority to the speed, knowledge, and experience of the medical team.

Father Philippe could feel his heart hammering as he prayed that the feverish activity around Beth's bed would succeed. But part of him was already looking ahead, to dealing with Ma Schiff. She would have to be helped to come to terms with having outlived her child. There would have to be no judgment about her behavior, only support. In her confused mind, he would have to try to implant a fundamental determination: from here on she would have to exchange an existence for a worthwhile life. He prayed God would, if it came to that, show him how best to help her.

A nurse disconnected the last of the electrodes on Beth's body. One of the interns whipped out the plastic prongs from her nose. Another was working the bag attached to the tracheal tube. The monitor above the bed went blank. Instantly, a smaller screen on the crash cart began to pulse. Father Philippe thanked God she was still alive.

Peering through the window, moving from prayer to prayer, Father Philippe remembered the story of another man, a long time ago, who, seeing his son close to death, had changed from his magnificent robes to a hair shirt and forsaken his banqueting to fast, hoping his sacrifices would persuade God to spare the child he dearly loved. For six days he maintained a vigil at the boy's bedside, finally aware that the doctors around him were having difficulty looking into his eyes. On the seventh day, in spite of their devotion, the boy died. Next day, the father put on his finery again and ordered a huge meal. When his family asked how he could do this so soon after his great personal tragedy, he calmly replied he had done everything possible to keep his son alive. Now that he had been returned to God, he must resume his own life. That man, Father Philippe remembered, was King David of the Old Testament. In death, he thought again, eyes intent on the scene in the room, there is always life.

An intern was inserting a tube into a vein in Beth's arm, concentrating totally on the task. The others still worked at speed, yet instinctively avoided jogging or jarring his hand. He attached the tube to a plastic bag on a stand. Father Philippe watched as a nurse felt for a pulse in Beth's neck. He had always believed that to lose someone to death is to lose part of oneself. He did not feel, he knew from conversations with them, like other priests about death. For him, each death was mourned as part of his own mortality.

The surgeon stood poised over Beth's bared breasts, his fist raised and closed. He brought it down swiftly, delivering a hard blow to her breastbone. Father Philippe winced. He had never known until this moment how primitive was a precardial thump.

When he first began to realize he must, as part of his ministry, make death understandable, Father Philippe had come across an ancient Arabian legend. The eldest son of the Caliph of Baghdad had run into his father's room one morning and said he must leave at once for Damascus. His father had sleepily asked the reason for the unseemly haste. The boy, wide-eyed with fear, had cried out that he had just seen Death standing at the window of his quarters. The only way he could live was to flee immediately to the family fortress in Damascus. The Caliph agreed, and gave him his best horse. When the boy was on his way, his father went in search of Death and confronted him about frightening the son of the most powerful ruler in the region. Death, ran the fable, looked in astonishment at the Caliph. He insisted he had made no threat, but had only come to remind the boy they had a rendezvous later that day in Damascus. Father Philippe had often told the story to show that there were certain matters no one could change.

The surgeon delivered two more blows in rapid succession. The monitor on the cart showed Beth's heart was still barely beating. The nurse with the stopwatch continued to count. The surgeon gave new instructions. Both interns turned to the cart and reached for the defibrillator, the machine that could provide an electric shock to the heart. A nurse coated Beth's chest with paste from a tube, smearing it thickly on the skin. One of the interns handed the surgeon two paddle-shaped electrodes attached to the defibrillator. He pressed them onto Beth's chest, one just above her left nipple, the other slightly to the right. He glanced at the second intern, who adjusted a dial on the machine. Everyone stepped back from the bed.

Then, checking that his own body was not in direct contact with Beth's, the doctor pressed down hard on the paddles and at the same time touched a button on each. A measured electrical shock passed through Beth's heart.

Father Philippe closed his eyes as she went into spasm, her spine arching and her legs stiffening as the electricity pierced her body. He opened them as Beth slumped back on the mattress, inert as before. The nurse was counting. Father Philippe remembered it took nine critical seconds for the defibrillator to recharge. The surgeon was keeping time, nodding impatiently. He knew one of the hardest things for any doctor was to realize the inevitability of death. Its impending presence and its feeling, for them, of accompanying failure, could quite often fill the most experienced physicians with a sense of desperation, as if they had somehow failed their calling.

Inside the cubicle, he could see, all eyes were watching the monitor. It showed Beth was still alive. The nurse stopped counting. The surgeon delivered a second powerful shock. Once more Beth's body was galvanized, almost lifted clear of the bed. She dropped back, limp. Nine seconds later, she received a third shock.

The doctor lifted the paddles from her chest, shaking his head. He put them back on the cart. He bent over Beth and closed her eyes. Only then did he glance briefly at the monitor. It had been blank for some seconds. He looked up and saw Father Philippe at the window. The surgeon shrugged and walked out of the cubicle. The team began to switch off the machines.

"She's all yours, Father." The surgeon was at his elbow. "If she had survived she would have been a total vegetable. Sometimes God is merciful."

"Amen to that."

Father Philippe waited until the last nurse had left before entering the room. He used the holy oil to make the sign of the cross on Beth's forehead and murmured the shortened form of Absolution and Extreme Unction.

"You're lucky, Beth." He spoke softly over the bed. "God called you home."

Then, he left the room and walked toward where Ma Schiff was standing, slack-faced, in the corridor. He silently formulated the first all-important words he would say to her.

✝   ✝   ✝

Father Breslin hesitated again over a paragraph in his sermon for the coming Sunday.

It was the one thousand, two hundred and fifty-third he had prepared since his ordination Mass thirty-five years ago. He kept all his sermons in binders on a shelf beside his desk, consulting them regularly, seeking themes that he first had expounded as a young priest, and that over the years he had felt a need to restate. Most dealt with the consistent position of the Church on marriage, sin, morality, social responsibility, hedonism, abortion, catechism, human dignity, fidelity, justice, and the Holy Family.

The sermons marked the passing of his years more so than physical change. Apart from his thining and graying hair and the stronger lenses in his spectacles, he was otherwise now, in late middle age, little different from the way he looked when he first came to Father McKenna's parish, thirteen years ago. His body weight had not varied by so much as a pound; his voice remained clear and expressive. There was still a handsomeness about him the years had not diminished: it was there in his shy smile, his old-fashioned good manners, and a natural vibrancy. He knew women continued to find him attractive — just as he better understood how to handle such danger.

His ever-growing library of tapes, neatly racked beneath the shelf of sermons, contained a great deal about coping at all levels. The tapes, like his sermons, revealed how far he had traveled on his spiritual and emotional road.

Only he knew, by going back through his sermons and tapes, how hard he sometimes found coming to terms with a Church that had changed more since the election of Pope John Paul II than under all the previous pontiffs he had served.

The Polish Pope — his name derives from *Wolt*, the bailiff or person-in-charge — was attempting to regain control, and had tried to do so since the day he assumed office, October 22, 1978. Through his own unyielding values he was trying to haul a battered and bedraggled Church back from the abyss in which now rested so many empty seminaries and convents, and from which continued to emerge an endless procession of lipsticked and short-skirted nuns, Marxist priests, and prelates who behaved like revolutionary politicians.

Like the Pope, Father Breslin felt the battle lines were drawn. The Church of Jesus was at a momentous crossroads. It had been virtually stripped of the last vestiges of political authority and financial power; the constant calls from Rome for cutbacks and the Vatican's disastrous diplomatic failures in Ulster and Central America were, for Father Breslin, sorrowful proof that all the Church had left was its spirituality, which indeed, he comforted himself, was all its founder had asked from it.

Within the diocese, throughout the Irish hierarchy, and beyond, in the vast Catholic empire, Father Breslin saw how far down the road to unacceptable secular values the Church was being dragged. Priests and nuns, some of whom had gone from the diocese to the Third World, continued to align themselves with political extremism, even with Communism and armed revolution. He could not understand them and, from time to time, he challenged their claims to subject Catholic revelation to contemporary anthropology and psychological permissiveness. Some of his most powerful preaching had been against those who wished to rewrite the Gospel message in the light of the latest linguistic discoveries, against those who defended birth control and all kinds of sexual freedoms, above all, against those who gnawed at the very foundations of his Mother Church. This was where his sermons showed how far he had traveled.

On this early summer evening in 1982, he reviewed his long ministry: that period when he lived from Mass stipends and acted as a stand-in confessor; his time as a school chaplain; the years when he worked among the youth of Dublin's docks; his spell on the staff of the archdiocese cathedral; his span as curate in a midtown parish before becoming Father McKenna's assistant. At the completion of each of those stages he had preached a farewell sermon. He must now do so again.

In a week, he would depart for the last time from the parochial house, leaving behind forever Father McKenna and Miss Maddox, and go over the mountains to take charge of the spiritual life of a farming community; some four hundred families scattered over ninety square miles of land. It would, he knew, be very different from urban parish work.

He scratched through the paragraph that had caused him to ponder and started again. "One of the greatest and wisest things in Christian life consists of making all graces as they are revealed and offered throughout the course of the year one's own."

He was genuinely surprised at his appointment. He had long ago concluded that he would end his days as a curate: caring passionately for the lives of these townspeople, gently reminding them of sins they spent so much energy committing and so little time repenting; offering, in his own modest way, himself as a continuing witness; delivering his ministry as an example of simple fidelity.

On the day of his elevation to a parish priest, Miss Maddox delighted him by preparing a magnificent dinner, served not in the kitchen but in the dining room, where Father McKenna and he normally ate only on Christmas Day and Easter Sunday. Waiting until Miss Maddox had taken her place at the table — her presence was another sign of the importance of the occasion — Father McKenna had raised his glass and delivered a short toast. Then, eyes glistening, Miss Maddox rose to her feet and said, her voice unsteady, she had never had a finer curate in her house than Father Breslin.

Looking back, he recalled how they had supported him through his spells of illness and the sorrow over the deaths of those he also loved deeply. As well as his parents, he had lost, in the past ten years, a sister, a nephew, and a niece. The experiences affected him deeply, making that much clearer the importance of not resisting the natural tide of mourning, but also refusing to give in completely to it. There was, he could affirm, no formula or role; every death had been different, each a learning experience, which made him that much better a priest.

He penned a fresh thought. "What does it mean in practice to live as a member of Christ's body? "

He hesitated once more. Father McKenna would say the thought was too erudite. After all these years he was still grateful for the guidance, encouragement, and protection of the parish priest.

Father Breslin reworded the thought: "We must never forget that the glory of God's work will be born from the pain and terror of the Body of Christ."

The sentence would, perhaps, trigger another of Father McKenna's astounding recollections. He always seemed able to sketch with spellbinding accuracy the tiny peculiarities and eccentricities of his parishioners; he could even forecast the character traits of individuals when they were only boys and girls.

The old priest, Father Breslin remembered, had been right about Betty Dolan and Mick Byrne. Betty was five months pregnant and barely seventeen years old. Mick was close to nineteen. Tonight he would see them for the last time until they knelt before him in the morning when he would pronounce them husband and wife.

There was still, after all those years, something about an impending wedding that produced a tension in him. Self-examination, he had found, was a powerful relaxant, so he selected a tape recorded two years earlier, at a time when he was recuperating from another bout of illness. He had lain in this room for five weeks, receiving daily injections from the doctor while Miss Maddox had fed him the most tempting of foods. He inserted the cassette in the recorder and listened, eyes closed.

"It's taken a long time to realize that in the end all that matters is love. Love, which is genuine and noninvolved in any physical sense, but is established in the spiritual and supernatural. It is this kind of love that, hopefully, every day allows me to look at and judge the best in a person. That matters especially in giving guidance on marriage. At first I had not found it easy to sit down with a young couple. The girl often pregnant, the boy more than likely without work, and talk about the practical side of intimate marital life as seen by the Church. The only way to make it work is to sound totally convinced that the teachings are right. There is no other way. But I am also convinced that by being detached from physical sex, it does allow me to judge the rightful place it can have in a person's full life. I can, I think, because of my celibacy, see sex in a clear and objective way. It is not part of my physical life. I am not ensnared in any of its physical aspects. I am, as it were, above it. But being above it as a priest, I must never forget I am not beyond it as a man. While I must appear sexless, in the true spiritual sense of that word, I dare not for a moment pretend to myself that I am an angel, outside the realm of mortal temptation. There is an old say-

393

ing about no man, or for that matter, no woman, being able to judge his or her own case. This is particularly true of the emotions aroused in everyday human relationships like marriage, bringing up a family, paying the bills. Those involved are so close to the everyday issues and the problems their own flesh brings, their passions and demands . . . so close that they do not often have time to see the greater picture. That is where a priest can help. That is certainly where I try to be of assistance. The one thing I have learned in life is to have an overview. Personal emotions do not allow for an objective judgment. Yet those are the judgments which matter. It is the true absolutes that make us all what we should try and be . . . strong in our faith, committed and sympathetic. It is never easy, even now, knowing that celibacy is not, in one sense, a normal condition. God, we all know, intended that a man and woman should be of one flesh. And it is perfectly true that for a priest that was once allowed within the Church. . . ."

He spun the tape forward, his voice suddenly unintelligible, hunting again for evidence of his struggle and acceptance.

"I have come, and it has been a slow process, to realize that in a way my very celibacy can help to protect the sacredness of marriage vows. From the day a child understands what a priest is, he also knows a priest is 'married' to God. Now, if a priest was to be permitted to break that contract with Him and marry a woman, then it would make it just that much easier for the advocates of divorce within the Church to move closer to victory. It would open the gates to even more confusion. I have not met one person who, when the subject has come up, did not say that he or she felt my celibate state was even holier than marriage itself. Of course, there are those who will try and disrupt this situation. There are women who have almost an obsession with trying to seduce priests. There has been one in every parish I have been in. To avoid them is to encourage them further. The only way to handle them is with firmness. . . . I must make it clear that as a priest I am the representative of Christ in the world, and that for her to behave as she does is to betray His teachings. There is no need to get angry or make a great issue of it, though it is not always easy to remain calm. . . ."

Mary drifted into his mind. He felt sleepy and relaxed, only half-listening to the words.

". . . there's a certain Eve in every parish. She has a partiality to forbidden fruit. A collar turns her on. It sort of excites and stimulates . . ."

He fell asleep before any question of volition arose.

Miss Maddox showed Betty and Mick into the sitting room. Father Breslin guided them to the sofa and sat in his armchair. He had awakened to the sound of his recorded voice stressing the conscious decisions he had made.

"I used to be concerned about the effects of my sexuality on my celibacy. I felt pulled and tugged until I began to really understand that love held the key. Loving myself, knowing myself, I could face my sexuality. God gave it to me. He had never meant it should be removed the moment I became ordained. He had intended for me to use my inner resources to face my sexuality. Until I could do so, I have had that constant feeling of panic, that things could get out of control. I always felt a danger of letting emotional feelings dominate personal commitment. The important thing, and it took me a long time, was to understand where feelings and commitment can come together. . . ."

"All set? No backing out? You can still change your mind, you know!" He smiled, teasing. "One or both of you."

These past weeks he had discussed with them his views on Christian love, knowing they had it aplenty. Tonight he planned to remind them of some of the key issues he had raised previously.

"Love is a funny thing. It is not like anger or jealousy or any other emotion. It can come and go much more subtly. And it changes directions as we go through life. But the one rule about love that never alters is one you must always remember. To love each other, you have to love yourself. That is the only way you can give your love to each other — when you have it to give."

They nodded, understanding, just as he understood why he had taped a thought.

"Celibacy and Catholic marriage have a lot in common. They are a life-long contract in response to God's wishes. I cannot say that in all honesty about other forms of marriage, where divorce seems to be a built-in option. But within the Church, marriage and celibacy have similiar bonds. Both demand integrity and a willingness to acquire a deep inner understanding of where God fits in. That's the key, of course: faith. If you have faith, celibacy, like marriage, can work. The faith may be tested, many times, but as long as it is there, you will survive all the risks. . . ."

He addressed Betty, thinking how in these past weeks her baby was visibly growing inside her.

"Loving yourself doesn't mean you have to be like the Queen in *Snow White* and look in the mirror all the time and ask who is the fairest one of all. That is not loving yourself." He smiled at her. "Mind you, Betty, you look very fair to me. I must say, having a baby does suit you."

"Thank you, Father."

"And you, Mick. You've planted a seed that's going to be part of you until you die. You must always see your child as your way of offering new hope in the world. Each baby is. When your first one comes, he or she will be starting a great journey. But what your baby discovers in life depends very much on you both as parents. In the end, your baby's growth will result from how good and loving, how feeling and caring you are to each other. That's what I mean by loving yourself. If you can do that, love yourself properly, then you can really love each other, and your baby will thrive in that love. That's much more important than anything else you can give that child."

Putting it on tape had made it easier.

"Celibacy, like marriage, is a search for a common meaning that life must ultimately focus on God to have any purpose. When that focus is clear, there is complete freedom within both marriage and celibate living. Both are a continuous growing process. There is a great deal of exploration before there can be understanding. It is the growing realization of being human, and therefore why nothing can be perfect. All we can do is try our best. . . ."

He liked the way they sat relaxed, hands entwined. Not embarrassed by anything he said.

"The important thing is never to use love as a label. There's nothing wrong in saying to each other, as often as you like, 'I love you.' But don't let it become an escape. God gave us language so that we could communicate in a different way than animals. Words were our great leap up the tree of evolution. The trouble is, down the centuries, we have taken them for granted, used them as excuses to say what's so often convenient, not what should be meant. Nowhere is this more evident than when we speak of love, loving, and being in love."

At their last visit he had opened a copy of James Joyce's *Ulysses* — now freely available in Ireland — and pointed out how the book ends with Molly's joyous affirmation: "And yes I said yes I will Yes."

He pointed out the significance. "Saying 'yes' is the greatest promise you can make to each other. You'll be saying it tomorrow in your vows. What you will be saying is 'yes' to a life together. 'Yes' to growing together. 'Yes' to being realistic about your life together, like understanding that having differences is natural. But as long as you keep on saying 'yes' to love, you will be able to handle any disagreement, squabble, or cross words. As long as love is there, they will not cause you a problem."

He had put it differently on tape.

"Celibacy, like marriage, founders so often because people embark upon one or the other filled with a naïveté which in any other walk of life they would expect to lead to disaster. . . ."

He had reminded them on other occasions about the practical realities they must incorporate into their love for each other. They should put aside a set sum each week for the baby's future. They should learn to shop wisely. He had told them how, whenever he organized a parish function, he went from one supermarket to another, pricing items before buying.

"From tomorrow each of you will have twice the responsibility — one to the other. It sounds very romantic but it can soon sour if you don't know what is involved. I always say that after the candlelight dinner comes the stale taste of wine the following morning. It must be difficult to think of love when you have that taste in your mouth. Our mouths are the most public part of our body, simply because we speak through them. It's the surest way we can tell the world what we think and feel. So we tend to guard our mouths. And that, too, is a mistake. Another way to ruin a marriage is to be always on guard and never relaxed. That's the quickest way to destroy love before it has had time to take root. And it must have time."

Another taped thought came to him.

"People expect to be always happy in marriage or in their celibate state. That assumes that life is suddenly and magically free of all its frustrations and temptations. The reality is that both marriage and celibacy depend on understanding the deeper meaning of a relationship. It needs a balanced view on friendship, sacrifice, self-discipline, and a willingness to fail and go on trying. That is the most important thing of all: being able to pick up the pieces and go on after failure. . . ."

He thought how young and vulnerable they looked; yet there was also about them a strength that went back through the generations.

"Tomorrow, you will start a journey that, to work, is going to take you back, each one into yourself. You are going to find in yourself that you really do have the faith to guide each other toward a permanent love. Both of you are going to discover that the demands of marriage begin and end with one word — love. But also remember this. To make your marriage work you have not only to go forward hand in hand, but you must also go forward at your own pace. I think it's one of the hardest things to realize that separation and togetherness, in a good marriage, are essential. You must live together, but separately. You must be as one, but remain two distinct individuals. You must grow in the same direction, but accept it will be through a different way. That, in the end, is what a good marriage is: being together — and understanding the importance of being separate."

When he finished, he made the sign of the cross over Betty's abdomen, murmuring as he did so for God to bless and protect her baby.

Father Breslin reverently raised the gold and silver chalice, thinking, as he could still do after all these years, that his one movement placed him gloriously at the center of his faith. He was celebrating his last Mass in the parish. At the memento of the dead he murmured the names of his parents, sister, and other relations. At the memento of the living, he included Father McKenna and Miss Maddox.

He had decided, in the end, to keep his sermon short, taking as his text Matthew 28:19: *Go, therefore, make disciples of all the nations; baptize them in the name of the Father and of the Son and of the Holy Spirit.*

It was his farewell.

Four hours later, with the good wishes and blessing of Father McKenna ringing in his ears and the tears of Miss Maddox long dried on his cheek, he turned a bend in the road. There, up on the hill, beyond the village, he could see the building, steep-roofed and granite-walled.

Throughout the long drive, he had been filled with expectation. Now, warm though the day was, he felt a sudden chill as he drove toward his very own church.

† † †

Staring across the dining table, with Fern at its head, and the rest of her family, daughters, sons, and in-laws, seated around him, Father Philippe realized that something quite extraordinary was happening.

Three hours ago, when he had prepared and cooked the meal — his pre-condition to accepting Fern's invitation to dinner — Margot had been no more than another pair of willing hands in the kitchen, cutting and peeling while he mixed and tasted. She and two of Fern's other daughters had been smilingly press-ganged into acting as his assistants. He had stripped off his clerical collar, donned a butcher's apron and a paper chef's hat, and began to turn the shopping list he had given their mother into a French feast.

While the baking and roasting and basting had gone on, the two other girls had gone back to the living room to sip cocktails. He had poured Margot and himself glasses from the remains of a bottle of champagne he had used in one of the sauces. They had sipped and talked and looked at each other a great deal.

He opened another bottle to prepare the sorbet, refilled their glasses, and suddenly found himself inexplicably nervous. He had forced himself to concentrate on the oven and the pots on the stove. He was behaving, he thought, like a character in a Tennessee Williams play, pacing up and down, starting and rarely finishing a thought, and then racing through a burst of words.

At the start of dinner, he had withdrawn into silence, acknowledging with smiles the praise for his culinary skills, thinking if he ignored the situation it would go away. It didn't work, but he could think of nothing else to do. He sensed that deep down, Margot, like him, was trying to discover some kind of explanation. After all, he had rationalized, they were both normal people, leading normal lives, living by normal rules in their very separate existences: something like this did not happen.

His words began to flow. It wasn't the wine. It was something far more potent, this chain of events being forged in a crucible of small talk. He still doesn't know how it happened. It seemed to him almost cosmic, the way his life-stream established this rapport with hers. She had the greenest of eyes and hair that was burnished dark gold to match her tan. She was wearing a white short-sleeved dress and seashell bangles on one arm.

Fern was looking at him, smiling. Yesterday she had told him, as they did their laps, that she had once fallen in love with a priest; they had skirted around their emotions for six months before one day he had suddenly flown back home to Ireland. Fern had said she didn't really admire that kind of strength; it was much too inhuman. Her judgment had somehow taken away the initial amazement he had felt about her revelation.

An electrifying shock-wave rippled up his spine. His eyes were riveted on Margot. As she raised her glass, he could feel her bare toes exploring inside his trouser leg under the table, rubbing against his skin, working themselves up and down his calf.

CHAPTER 17

†

The Celibate Travelers

Victoria tried to sound consoling as she walked with Sister Cornelia toward the chapel.

"We're all getting older. This is my sixth election."

Every four years the Order voted to reappoint either its present Mother Superior or to elect a new one. In the previous five elections Victoria had cast her vote for the Reverend Mother who had welcomed her into religious life twenty-four years ago. A month ago, the aged nun had died from a brain hemorrhage and as its first collective duty after a period of mourning, the community was about to vote for a new Superior.

Coming out of the Mother House to cross the gardens to the chapel, Sister Cornelia had finished a tirade she began when the Great Silence lifted. Her anger was aroused by the news that another Catholic activist group had launched a new campaign for women to celebrate Mass. With eyes flashing dangerously, she snapped that lack of ordination had not stopped Saint Catherine of Siena or Saint Teresa of Ávila from exercising influence, and besides, all the male saints lumped together counted for nothing when measured against Our Lady, the Blessed Virgin, Queen of Heaven.

"And Poland," Victoria murmured to herself, thinking how once more

Sister Cornelia had magnificently missed the point. But long ago she had discovered it was useless trying to reason with her. Any form of liberalism, in the old nun's eyes, was a malevolent challenge to ancient truths and fundamental values; it was the evil that threatened the good, not only relatively, but absolutely.

"This is my fourteenth election. I don't expect to see another. But if I died tomorrow I'd go knowing that at least our country and our Church are once more in safe hands. Praise be to God."

Victoria calculated that Sister Cornelia must be close to eighty, but she sounded as old as time itself.

"The first time I voted was in nineteen twenty-eight. We put in a strong Mother that year. She used to hold regular all-night vigils. And we had to do a full day's work on top. We had discipline."

"But did it make you a better nun? I'm not sure if praying around the clock makes anyone holier."

"It made us *different*. That was the whole point. We were different. We could do it. We could stay on our knees for a whole day or night, with just short breaks to go to the bathroom or sip some water. We weren't like seculars in those days. Now you can't tell the difference. This place has become like a hotel. Soft beds. Talking at meals. The discipline's gone. We've got a good Pope in Rome at last, but he still probably can't do what Pope Pius did in the first year I voted. He spent a whole week in prayer. Never slept a wink. In those days, we used to get news like that from Rome. Mother would read it out to us as encouragement. But now. . ."

The old nun fell silent once more, locked into events more than half a century earlier.

The year after that, Victoria realized, Pope Pius XI signed the Lateran Treaty with Benito Mussolini, giving the Vatican guaranteed sovereign territorial independence and ninety million U.S. dollars' compensation for the loss in 1870 of the Papal States.

Art had once told her that the Church, in the wake of the 1929 crash, had acquired a large financial portfolio in the United States and launched itself along a new venture of financial manipulation that eventually led to the burgeoning financial scandals currently rocking it. These included the mysterious disappearance of funds from the Chicago archdiocese while under the stewardship of the late Cardinal Cody; the multimillion-dollar machinations of the Vatican Bank under its present governor, Archbishop Paul Marcinkus, and old friend of Cody's; and the links from Cody, Marcinkus, and even Pope Paul VI, to the convicted Sicilian swindler Michele

Sindona. Art had added that no one should be surprised, given the Church's fiscal dealings these past fifty years.

She knew now, after her visits to his hospital bed, that Art was, after three years, completely alert and aware of what was being said to him, but still remained totally paralyzed and unable to speak since his mountain-climbing accident. One of the nurses had told Victoria that it was miraculous he had survived at all.

Victoria had written in her journal: "A miracle that he should be doomed to live the rest of his life like this? That his wife has left him and his children can't bear to visit. That, apart from me, no one ever comes. A miracle?"

She had lost count of the times she had prayed God would show Art mercy.

Sister Cornelia delivered another reminder. "We must choose a strong person to lead us. Someone who can reflect the values we have once more in Rome."

The sudden fierce timbre of the old nun's voice, the tone of absolute authority and command in her words, were like a sudden slap on Victoria's cheek.

"We used to set an example. Now we are the cause of the crisis! We've got to reestablish our position. Show that we can deal with our dissidents before we take on those outside! The Church has always led from within. We have got to go back to that. That's why this vote is so important. We can make a start!"

In Sister Cornelia's voice, there was contempt for anyone who rejected her belief that time not only can be arrested but can actually be turned back.

Her puritanical hatred of consumerism, one of the Pope's own bêtes noires, was reflected in her dress. Her habit was darned and patched in several places; she would go on repairing her shoes for as long as the leather survived. She judged all human relationships by the standards of her personal frugality.

Victoria was conciliatory.

"I think we have to recognize the tremendous pressures building up."

"Because we have allowed them to build! There's been too much blurring of the roles. Too many unchecked challenges to authority! Too much compromise! Too much criticism!"

"Perhaps the answer would be more research into why all this is happening. Maybe the analysis should begin right at the top."

"Nonsense! We've had too much talk of analysis. We've analyzed Vatican Two until I'm sick and tired of hearing about it. No. We need a Superior who will see our vows upheld, now and forever. Freedom is one thing, but recklessness is another. There has been too much of that."

"Well, we'll soon know, Sister Cornelia."

Victoria wished she hadn't started this conversation. She would rather have gone straight to chapel to spend another few minutes thinking of Art. She had told him at the end of her last visit that she would not be able to come anymore because the Order was sending her to San Francisco to complete her course in counseling.

Four years ago, the Order had begun training her to help nuns experiencing emotional trauma from the changes introduced by the Second Vatican Council. She was enrolled in a college course to prepare psychological counselors. She had studied how to measure and classify human behavior, how to observe and investigate the inner worlds of perception, attention, and thinking; how to use various techniques to establish a person's emotional and motivational states of mind. Her academic achievement had been sufficiently high for the Order to send her on to one of the nation's preeminent universities.

She had, on that last visit, held before Art the earrings she had worn at her profession as a Bride of Christ and said she would always treasure them, just as in her heart she would always keep a place for him. He had looked at her, and she had felt closer to him than ever before, knowing there was no question of sensuality or physical satisfaction. She had realized her feelings were infinitely more complicated and rewarding. Art, in his helplessness, was someone uncorrupted and uncorruptible. For all the terrible destruction his injuries had inflicted, they had left him with the silent spiritual strength of life itself — as if he recognized totally he had come from the earth and would return to it, unable to change the unchangeable, accepting, unlike Sister Cornelia.

All around them, nuns converged on the chapel, taking last-minute soundings among themselves. Victoria found the election process to be little different from secular politicking. Throughout the past month there had been discreet lobbying to advance the claims of one or another of the candidates — the *consultation* allowed for under the Rule.

On that last visit to Art, Victoria had explained that her road to spiritual growth was one where she must question, at least to herself, everything. It was her very personal religion, one in which she allowed no room for guilt. Sitting beside his cot — which continuously rocked gently, compensating for Art's inability to move by rearranging his helpless body to avoid bed-sores — she had finally told him, in a voice no louder than a whisper, how over the years she had used her memories of him to satisfy her needs.

His eyes had stared at her.

Then she leaned down and kissed him gently on the mouth. Though there could be no response from his lips, she felt his breath, warm and sweet, and she continued to look into his eyes. "I still love you, Art. I always have and I always will."

On the way back to the Mother House she had a thought, so over-whelming that it brought tears to her eyes: Art came very close to showing her God with a human face — all-seeing, all-comprehending, all-forgiving, yet all-silent.

Sister Cornelia returned to the attack.

"You know what the root of the trouble is? Sex. There is just too much emphasis on it nowadays!"

Victoria smiled. The question of her happiness or unhappiness, she had understood for many years, was in every sense a physical one. Yet each time she emerged from her twilight zone she realized that she had failed to experience what she knew existed — full sexual satisfaction.

". . . you know why we don't get more girls coming in, Sister? We don't offer the same challenge. We should be more demanding. Better to have a few postulants with the right ideas about vocation than all those who come and go. We need old-fashioned leadership to stop the rot."

Leaning on her cane, hobbled by arthritis, Sister Cornelia was a ma-triarchal figure. Oblivious of the dust raised by the first swirls of autumn around the hem of her long black skirt, she continued to harangue Victoria on the sort of qualities the new Superior should have.

Victoria interposed. "In my experience, Sister Cornelia, the reason we don't get girls is because they don't want to live their lives in a system where the Pope is the prisoner of the teaching of previous pontiffs."

The old nun waved her stick.

"You're wrong, wrong, wrong! Look what happened when Pope Paul loosened his grip. On his own doorstep, Italy voted for divorce. The churches of France emptied. West Germany went secular. And here we had religious mayhem. We still do. And it's going to take years to end the rot. I'll be gone before that. But you'll still be here, please God, to see the day when we listen to our Pope speaking about discipline being good for the body and soul!"

Victoria was filled with compassion, wondering what must have happened over all those years to make her fellow sister forever the victim of a religious system where discipline was used as a substitute for love. The harshness she had been subjected to had been based on mechanical repetition of the Rule: total obedience in which there was no room for even the smallest correction or adjustment. It was a ukase handed out without the remotest understanding that the only worthwhile discipline is that which is self-imposed. Victoria knew that could be achieved only by self-caring and a sense of personal value.

Sister Cornelia had been raised by a system that, while it sheltered and provided for every material need, did not care for her as a *person* — any more than, Victoria realized, it had cared for her. Her companion had spent the past sixty years believing herself to be of little value. The only way she could survive was to cling to a discredited idea that discipline was the answer to everything. For her, it was still a small price to pay for safety and protection against a world, beyond the Mother House, which she perceived as a dangerous and frightening place. Victoria doubted if the old nun could even begin to comprehend why she felt a need to secure, through discipline, what she saw as otherwise a dark future: that discipline was, in psychological terms, the only *possession* she had been allowed to retain, an implanted belief that, very likely, had made Sister Cornelia's life even more of an uphill struggle and, in the end, spiritually wasteful.

Victoria smiled sadly at her fellow sister's reactionary attitudes. She had been through this scene so many times with other nuns unable to accept the truth: that their concept of religious life was doomed; that the whole idea of a formal institutionalized life in Christ was on the verge of being swept away. The young did not wish to live in monolithic buildings like the Mother House. While, indeed, a nun's life was still dedicated to God, without thought of reward in this world, but based on the promise of everlasting life, there was an increasing belief that it need not be lived hemmed in by an outmoded Rule and figures of bleak authority.

The way forward, Victoria was convinced, the only hope she saw of survival, was for nuns to be allowed greater personal freedom to live and work as they wished, so that they could dedicate themselves in a far more healthy way to keeping the Church alive. For her, the vow of chastity was infinitely less important than having a mature understanding of psychological stability, and with it an awareness of a wider reality: that the more clearly visible the way of the world, the better equipped was a nun, like anyone else, to deal with it.

Yet, constricted by a lifetime of misconceptions and illusions, Sister

Cornelia, she feared, had cut herself off from any chance of exploring the rewards this reality offered. Her last words as they entered the chapel sadly confirmed this.

"We must elect a disciplinarian."

Through the Mass, Victoria glanced at the printed list of names. With every election it seemed to shorten, reduced by death or resignation. Once there had been two hundred professed nuns eligible for election. During the introit, she had counted only eighty-seven. Two elections ago, every pew had been crowded. Now, here and there only a solitary nun occupied a stall. Where once there had been rows of postulants and novices, there was now only a handful. They could not vote. Only the professed had that privilege. The names were separated by perforated lines, making it easier to remove any one of them. Victoria's name was twenty-ninth on the list, another indication of how over the years she had automatically grown in seniority.

As she joined in the chants and responses, her mind turned again to what she had told Art. Her religious life had become an endless and critical self-examination; she knew no other way to live it. It was part of her own dedication to the truth. That was why, in many ways, living in the Mother House had become a stifling experience; it was like existing under a huge dome in which old ideas were continuously recycled until they created a stagnant atmosphere.

She suspected that the majority of the community was made up of women in whom the tendency to avoid challenge was so ingrained that it had become omnipresent. They continued to accept that the Church had total control over their lives. Indeed, the entire apparatus was designed to control. A Pope as strong-minded as John Paul II controlled the Roman Curia, who controlled the bishops, who in turn controlled the clergy and the sisterhood through a multiplication of sacred congregations and secretariats, pontifical commissions, and archdiocesan offices. Victoria was positive no other organization would be allowed to exercise such authority, which often verged on abuse of social and legal powers.

From the moment she was elected, the Superior's word would be absolute. There could be no appeal against her decisions. The only way to circumvent her commands would be for a nun to resign. It was the same in every Order. Nevertheless, Victoria wondered whether the new Reverend Mother would understand that, to make the system really work, she would have to be aware that women in religious life, as anywhere else, no longer liked to be the victims of power plays; they did require simple recognition that their willingness to work extraordinarily long hours would not be abused or taken for granted. Even under the previous Superior, Victoria had noticed that the greater a nun's commitment, the greater the tendency to extract more from her; and, just as she suspected was true in the Vatican, so it was in the Mother House: there were secret files on each of its members, and spying or informing was not unknown. Would a new Superior abolish this — or maintain the status quo?

That was why she would not vote for Sister Bernadette, whose cause Sister Cornelia had been avidly promoting since the election became necessary. She was in charge of the kitchen, a thin little woman in her late fifties, who bossed her staff like a trail-driver. Sister Bernadette was an arch-exponent of control through manipulation, hiding her actions behind a pretense of dialogue, consultation, and participation. For her, obedience was total: not questioning; not showing a hint of sadness or any other emotion, except complete satisfaction with her cooking; not demanding or defending basic rights. She used her power ruthlessly, dominating her kitchen with the physical aspects of her person: her darting movements, her shrill voice, even her smell, a permanent odor of overcooked vegetables and meats that even now, several pews away, Victoria could distinctly detect.

In many ways, Sister Monica, who worked in Admissions, would be an ideal choice. She was close to fifty, a large, rawboned, cheerful woman who had been one of the first to modify her habit. But her presence was intimidating. Without meaning to, she was physically intrusive, speaking loudly and standing uncomfortably close. Someone so unaware of the importance of personal space might well be insensitive in other ways. She would not win Victoria's vote either.

Sitting across the aisle, Sister Paula was an obvious choice, in spite of her age. At the last election she had forced a second ballot against Reverend Mother. A quiet woman in her late sixties, devoted to her duties, she had given her whole life to supervising the Order's various links with the outside world: its schools, colleges, hospitals, and remedial clinics. Although she had never said more than a few words to her in all those years, Victoria sensed that behind her prim demeanor was someone who recognized the need for change. She would stand somewhere between the complete commitment to change Victoria would like, and the restoration of a past Sister Cornelia yearned for. Her only drawback was a tendency to overagree, shaking her head up and down and making a continuous little clucking sound. A Superior like that could be very wearying.

Victoria's own choice would be Sister Joan, who was seated beside her. She was in charge of the infirmary, a gracious woman who had entered five years before Victoria and who had always shown a calm good humor. She, more than anyone else Victoria could think of, was aware of the need to exercise decision-making with compassion and dignity, dealing as she did with the aged and dying. That had given Sister Joan a level of awareness Victoria felt many others in the community lacked. She would maintain her position against the more conservative forces in the Mother House without producing open conflict. She would understand the real challenges of the day and, with her well-integrated perspective, would ensure a harmonious relationship among all the various factors. She would know how to implement new ideas, without resolutely moving toward the right or the left. She would understand how best to handle the grass-roots thrust for change from the moderates in the Mother House, just as she would know when to ignore some of the wilder rumblings of protest.

Sister Joan would be a marvelous Superior — charismatic in every sense of the word. Nevertheless, Victoria thought, there could be, all told, half a dozen possible contenders for the post. This might mean repeated balloting before a candidate emerged with the required 51 percent of the votes.

The Bishop would not be pleased if it went beyond the lunch hour. Over the years, Victoria had watched him change perceptibly. He had grown bulkier and as purple as his stole, while Father Lowell was almost as pale and delicate-looking as the filigree on his vestments. The two men sat side by side, on identical thrones before the altar. In front of them was a table draped in white. On it was a silver chalice, gleaming in the candlelight. To their left behind another table, also covered in white, sat two nuns. Before each was a silver plate. On the opposite side of the sanctuary was a vacant chair.

The Bishop addressed the community, asking for the roll to be called.

Each nun rose as her name was read aloud by Father Lowell from a list in his hand. When that task was completed, Sister Cornelia hobbled to the sanctuary, removed the Bible from the lectern, and placed it before the Bishop. The Bishop rose and placed his right hand on it.

"I swear by Almighty God to conduct an election without fear or favor and in absolute conformity to Holy Rule."

Father Lowell swore to do all in his power to observe there was no breach of the Rule. The two scrutineers left their seats and solemnly vowed to perform their function under the Rule.

Sister Cornelia addressed the Bishop.

"On behalf of this community, and by the power invested in me as its authorized representative, I swear on this holy Bible and before Almighty God that each one of us will vote solely for the one considered the most suitable to hold the office of Superior and will do so without favor or personal bias, and in the knowledge that each one of us has not been offered, or has engaged in, any pact or favor of any kind; that we are each of us conversant with the Holy Rule and will follow it."

The oath dated from the Middle Ages and was first uttered in the wake of the Crusades and the Inquisition; an age when the Order, like the Pope, ruled with absolute power.

The Bishop remained seated as he spoke.

"May I remind you, dear sisters, that voting must be carried out in absolute secrecy. Consult the list before you and choose your preference. And may the Lord Jesus Christ guide your deliberations."

He extended a hand in benediction.

All over the chapel there was the distinct sound of paper separating and being carefully folded. When each nun had made her choice, she dropped to her knees and silently prayed. Victoria was one of the first to kneel, her vote in her clasped hands.

Only when every sister was kneeling did the Bishop break the silence.

"I call upon the mistress of ceremonies to place her vote before me."

Sister Cornelia rose slowly, her left hand clenched. She stood in front of the two men.

"I call to witness Christ the Lord, who will be my judge that my vote is given to the one who before God I consider worthy of election."

She dropped her tightly folded ballot into the chalice, paused for a moment, genuflected to the altar, and retreated.

Father Lowell called the scrutineers forward, who repeated exactly Sister Cornelia's actions. Then, answering his sonorous voice calling the roll, the nuns rose, one at a time, and cast their votes.

Victoria dropped her ballot into the chalice before walking quietly back to her place to resume kneeling. In a week's time, all this would be a thousand miles behind her. In the end, it would not really matter to her who became Superior. She would continue to lead her own life. When she entered, tradition played its part not only in bringing her into religious life, but also in encouraging her to stay. Now, seventeen years after Vatican Two, the latest figures showed that some fifty thousand nuns had left American convents. Throughout the Catholic world the total loss amounted to more than three hundred thousand sisters. Victoria was sure the figures would have been even higher but for the fact that many nuns, in early middle age or older, felt unable to cope with the secular world. However, for many of those below the age of forty, leaving was no longer a disgrace, or a sign of special courage.

Victoria, peering through her fingers at Father Lowell, thought how this ceremony would better fit into a time when a nun's sense of importance and psychological well-being were accorded no value: then, if for any reason her self-esteem was broken, it was a matter of inconsequence. Those were the days when the supply of young girls willing to die to the world seemed endless. Now, they were almost unobtainable.

Many of the present nuns were in a child-parent situation — still totally dependent for survival upon the Order. She knew that in the chapel there were those who felt a sense of abandonment and with good reason: there was now far more competition for any worthwhile position in the gift of the Order. Its own existence in the world demanded it train the very best teachers, nurses, and administrators for secular work. Those within its ranks who applied for such positions and did not measure up were relegated to more menial posts inside the convent. This often increased their feeling of being threatened and abandoned. That was why she was being trained. But even before she could begin to counsel, she realized that the new Superior would have to show firmness and neutrality; be nonpartisan and above the pettiness of Mother House life. That person would have to be Sister Joan.

Nuns were rising from their knees. Victoria wondered how many realized they had waited too long — that now there was, indeed, little left for them except to anticipate that day when the confessor would anoint them. Yet they, she also suspected, were the ones who would have voted against their memories; prepared to appoint a Superior, who like Pope John Paul's Church, would continue to weigh its decisions in centuries rather than in years.

Sister Cornelia reverently picked up the chalice and placed it before the scrutineers, who commenced counting.

Victoria wondered how many of the silent women around her realized their lives had been impaired by maldevelopment in their psychosexual growth. This in turn might have led to even more serious problems, afflicting, in the end, their essential Christian qualities. For all their repose and stillness, their listening and watching, some of them were going to need her newfound skills to soothe their inner turbulence. Of that she was certain.

Victoria knew that when the time came to counsel, she would focus on the virtues of caring, self-respect, justice, freedom, and love and put firmly aside the rigidity of the Rule. She was certain that the only way to help any nun with sexual problems was to encourage her not to suppress psychosexual growth by remaining faithful to a vow. To achieve this, she would need a Superior who was as enlightened as she was herself.

Sister Cornelia informed the Bishop that the number of votes cast matched that of the electors. He ordered the scrutineers to move to the next stage.

The first teller tipped the slips back into the chalice. Sister Cornelia placed it in front of the second scrutineer. She removed a ballot, opened it, ticked the name on a tally card, refolded the paper, and placed it on her plate. Sister Cornelia took the plate and tilted it so that the vote fell on the other teller's plate. The second scrutineer repeated what her companion had done. Then both checked to see that the name ticked on their tally cards matched.

Sister Cornelia returned to stand over the first teller while she removed another slip. The checking continued. Finally, the old nun took the two identically marked tally cards to the waiting men, handing one to each. They compared the results.

The Bishop rose and in a loud, measured tone began to read.

"Sister Bernadette, thirty-three votes."

"There was a ripple of excitement.

"Sister Paula, twenty-six votes."

Victoria remembered that at the last election she had collected the same number of votes in the first ballot.

"Sister Theresa, nineteen votes."

The murmur turned to an incredulous gasp.

Victoria felt suddenly exultant. Sister Theresa taught in one of the Order's schools. Victoria had excluded her as a likely contender because she had gone to Chicago during Pope John Paul's American tour to join nuns keeping a silent vigil outside the cathedral, protesting the pontiff's attitude over limiting the role of women in religious life. Sister Cornelia had been furious at seeing her on network television news.

"Sister Joan, nine votes."

Victoria sighed. The chance of a dream come true had vanished. The opportunity to elect a moderate, centrist Superior had been rejected. Nor, she thought, would Sister Theresa, in spite of her surprising showing, go much further. But she had been wrong once; she could be again. The next round of voting would be critical.

The Bishop ordered the tellers to collect the first ballot papers and distribute new ones.

Almost an hour later his resonant voice read the result of the second ballot.

"Sister Bernadette, thirty-five votes."

She needed only nine more votes for victory.

Victoria had hoped there would have been enough sisters like her, willing to reject the sort of leadership Sister Bernadette would bring. But she now saw how true was the psychological point that group behavior mirrors individual response. In the end, being an organism, the community tended to operate as an entity. There had been profound forces at work, and probably still were, to bring about a victory for conservatism.

The nuns around her seemed to be calling for an instrument of power. Sister Bernadette would clamp down — hard. She would not bother with any ecclesiastical facade. She would rule through condemnation and demotion. For the first time in religious life, Victoria prayed for someone's defeat: "Dear God, anybody but Sister Bernadette. Anybody — but not her."

"Sister Paula, thirty-four votes."

A renewed concerted murmur swept the chapel. Victoria guessed, suddenly elated, that Sister Paula must not only be drawing votes away from the other candidates but also was blocking Sister Bernadette's advance. She was not mustering votes rapidly enough. She was still the conservative's perennial candidate, but there seemed to be a sudden mood for compromise.

"Sister Theresa, eleven votes."

She had had her moment. The more extreme of the progressive liberals had made their point.

Victoria watched Sister Cornelia. She sat impassively, her cane tapping the floor just once at the end of each of the Bishop's announcements.

"Sister Joan, seven votes."

She, too, had served notice that Sister Bernadette was not the automatic choice of all.

It was going to be a straight fight between Sister Bernadette and Sister Paula: reactionary versus compromiser.

Victoria prayed once more as the Bishop announced the third ballot.

Forty minutes later, he read its result.

"Sister Paula, forty-nine votes."

It's over, thought Victoria. Compromise.

413

"Sister Bernadette, thirty-eight votes."

Victoria smiled. Compromise was better than defeat.

Next morning at Mass, when the newly elected Reverend Mother asked the community to pray for its departing sister, Victoria noticed how, in only a few hours, Sister Paula's voice had assumed the distinct tone of her predecessor.

Victoria's suitcases were waiting by the main door. The Great Silence was in force and those who had said good-bye had done so the night before. The singing of the choir practicing in the chapel was the only sound to break the silence. Victoria knew she would miss the soft and haunting chanting most of all.

Reverend Mother gave her a final embrace.

As Victoria opened the door, on the other side of which a taxi was waiting to take her to the airport, she heard a familiar tap-tap behind her. She looked around. Sister Cornelia embraced her, and broke the Rule by whispering: "Yesterday we had compromise, but never live to regret it — or compromise yourself!"

She turned and hobbled away.

† † †

Clare sensed she was approaching the core of her crisis.

It was past three o'clock in the morning and she was still in the chapel. Yet it was not only the tiredness or the chill of the air at this hour that made her tremble, it was an inner force, sufficiently recognizable for her to have named it *Jiminy*, after the celebrated Disney cricket who was Pinocchio's conscience.

Jiminy — the calming voice of serendipity — was telling her again to recognize and to accept that at last, after months of skirting the issue, she was prepared to face reality.

Her consciousness still told her to resist: that, in spite of all she had endured, to give up now would be completely out of character for her and would display ingratitude. It reminded her that through the Order she had obtained a valued education, culminating in a degree: that though she had been severely tested, it was only because she had had the strength to cope.

But that other force, *Jiminy*, synchronously asked that she look at her recent history from a different perspective. It was true she had a degree, but she had worked extraordinarily hard to achieve it, not complaining about having to study far into the night because it was often the only free time she had. In the end, in spite of all her hard work, and her tutors' feeling that she could achieve further academic distinction, the Order had thought otherwise.

While the way she had handled her trials and tribulations was a credit to her levelheadedness and stamina, it did bring to the fore fundamental questions. Did God really want her to continue the way things were? How could she grow the way He wanted when, until recently, she had not been aware of what she should be growing toward? What did God want of her?

Jiminy told her there was only one answer to these questions: she must allow reality into her life by recognizing that the way to grow as a person and to grow closer to Him was to have complete understanding of her responsibility to herself. There was a little way to go, still more of her recent past to be put into perspective and no longer to be seen as a mysterious and troubling paradox. Her sense of enlightenment had grown, the more she came to understanding her dilemma and how it could be resolved. She suspected *Jiminy* already knew the answer but wanted her to come to it in full awareness: something to be accepted without reservation. He, and the rest of her mind, must be at one.

It was not enough for her to set out the problems; to hope that by honestly and painfully admitting each and every one of these torments, she would banish them. Important though this was, such self-examination would not provide resolution. It required something further. She must allow her unconsciousness to become consciousness. She must fully accept that the greatest wisdom she could know was buried inside her, deep in her unconsciousness. It might well be a supernatural force. The thought of God dwelling within her no longer shocked her.

The concept of His presence guiding her decisions, she now saw, was no different from what the Mistress of Postulants and Novices had instilled right from the beginning, that the Holy Spirit lives in every person. So, having God within her, she was a part of Him all the time. While she had always hoped He had been there — after all, God had called her — it was the highest reassurance she could have, knowing that each decision she came to would be made in His name.

Jung, whom she had read at college, had been right. He likened consciousness to a plant that shoots to the surface, blooms briefly, and then dies — an ephemeral apparition. But that is not the be-all and end-all of life, of thinking, of total awareness. There remains the unknown root system of the unconscious, the rhizome. Accepting that, she had been able to understand her new relationship with God — how and why He was in her and always would be. Familiar words, she realized with total acceptance, could take on a new meaning. *Thy will be done.* What she was asking herself to do was not for herself — but for Him. God was telling her what to do.

She must pause after each recollection and let the conclusions come to her, not impose solutions. She must allow her subconsciousness to enter her consciousness without hindrance; without trickery; without undue hurry or impatience. This was the road to her reality, the one, she suspected, everyone must travel.

From the beginning of her awareness, she had realized it would never be easy to have a relaxed relationship with her own mind. This was why she had created *Jiminy.* It allowed that part of her brain — into which she had dumped all the panic, fear, anxiety, and anger — to have time to assess them; to bring to them a fresh perspective; and to offer her something she never had before: reality. She had come to know herself and God in a completely new way. First and foremost was the understanding of love: that it is the greatest gift she could give. But before daring to offer it, she must first make herself lovable, not in any romantic sense, but in a spiritual one: a condition where loving and being loved were absolutely outside any self-seeking or self-interest. It was the closest human love could come to the love of God.

These past weeks, she had sat here in the chapel many times, often until dawn. At first she thought the prayer life she had been taught would show her the way forward. It had not — at least not by itself. Prayer, certainly, was important, but her search for answers, her quest for meaningful spiritual growth — the avenue by which she could make the one decision from which all others would naturally flow — she realized also needed courage, independence of thought, initiative, and action. There could be no substitute, no surrogate, no shortcut. While her prayers to the saints and her recollection of the words of the prophets had been of help, in the end she had had to journey alone. That was another reason she needed *Jiminy.* He was *her* — a constant self-reminder that, in the end, she must not depend on anyone outside herself. Books provided nothing more than pointers, just as reciting the rosary, fasting, and following all the other rituals of Mother Church would not help in her search to develop a mature consciousness, with a free will that allowed her to make her own choices, in the knowledge that every action was approved by God; that she, in all humility, was His agent, living her life always in His grace.

She did not know yet exactly when this would be achieved. But she sensed she was close.

Now, in the small hours, trembling, realizing what was at the core of her crisis, Clare knew she would leave here only when she had irrevocably settled the matter uppermost in her mind. She knew, from the spiritual strength guiding her instincts, that she must not make her decision the way she had so often acted in the past, when she had taken action without giving thought to the consequences that might flow from it.

In many ways, these past years in religious life had been lived, in spite of all her prayer life and hard work, at an unrealistic level. She had refused to stop and take note of the warnings. Her ego, her consciousness, had told her she could cope and to pay no attention to that other deeper feeling.

The results had been that time at the wedding when she had almost fainted; her defensive response to Sister Imelda's well-meant words; her reaction to the Deputy; her silent anger and frustration. She could now see them for what they were: indications. But at the time she had not been able to interpret them, to grasp they were really a way of telling her that she alone was the only one who could rescue herself. Now, at last, the fragments were coming together. To rush to a conclusion would be to create disaster, and her hopes of achieving spiritual growth would be destroyed.

She had known this from that moment four hours ago when she pushed open the chapel door and bowed low and reverently toward the altar, lit only by the sanctuary lamp. As usual, she had not gone to her stall, but sat in a corner, out of immediate sight of anyone who might also wish to meditate.

The stillness had provided a helpful environment to activate her interior chemical and psychological forces, whose dimensions were so vast that she doubted if there was any way of measuring them. The hush had brought to mind the words T. S. Eliot gave Thomas à Becket in his play *Murder in the Cathedral*: the exhortation to think for a while on the meaning of peace.

Through tears — she had wept many times on this lonely and difficult odyssey — she could see Tom clearly, sitting at their table in the college restaurant, declaiming, amid the roar of voices and clutter of crockery, Becket's speech.

Their table. She still thought of it as *theirs*: the one in the corner near the doors leading to the kitchen. It was identical to all the others, the same four metal tubular legs, the same plastic surface. It was the table he had led her to on that first day, and became the one over which they had exchanged so many ideas about duties and obligations and much, much else. When Tom became especially intense about a subject, he would curl his long legs

417

around one of the metal supports. She had often wondered if that was how he had sat when he wrote her the letter.

On that morning, five months ago, her life had suddenly changed direction. She had as usual awakened to the electric bell shrilling and had risen in the dark, knowing that winter or summer her day would always begin in the pre-dawn. Turning off the low-wattage light in her room — the drive to conserve electricity was the latest money-saving measure — she joined the silent procession to chapel.

Kneeling, she heard the familiar sighs accompanying weary bones being lowered onto stained wood. After silently meditating, she blended her voice with all the others offering the first salute to a new day. Rising at the end of her devotions, she had genuflected again to the altar and then filed through the corridors, keeping close to the walls — another way to demonstrate humility, by not standing out, taking care, like her companions, to move silently like a shadow through the wide hallways. Being Tuesday, breakfast had been a boiled egg, toast, and tea, taken in complete silence. Afterward, she had gone to her pigeonhole in the long line of open-fronted boxes where mail was left by the Deputy. Though she no longer had the right to open and censor letters, Clare knew the nun inspected each envelope carefully before reluctantly parting with it.

Removing the envelope, Clare had glanced at it curiously, not recognizing the neat bold print. She had opened it, still unsuspecting.

She could recall, word-perfect, what Tom had written, how he must have hesitated and deliberated — because she now knew that true love is possible only when it is an extension of oneself, offered in all honesty. She had felt the sheer energy he had expended, trying to express on paper his restless conflict. She realized now how painful it must have been for him to lay himself bare the way he had. At the time, though, she had thought none of these things.

The letter had covered one sheet of the pad he used for note-taking.

My dearest Clare, darling one,

I have wanted to call you that for months. It is only an hour since we last saw each other, yet I miss you desperately. I guess you have known this for sometime, though I have never dared to say so. But I love you. You must wonder why I have written it, instead of telling you. But I did not want to embarrass you by saying this face to face. If it makes me an emotional coward, well yes, I suppose I am. No-

body has ever told me how to handle a situation like this, that is why I'm frightened of my own feelings and the way they pull me between what I feel for you and what I know is also true: I want to be a good priest. I know that. That, I suppose, is why I hesitated over whether you should come to my ordination to the diaconate. It seemed to me that having you there would only make matters worse. It would make the conflict that much harder for me. You came and I was glad. When I stood before our bishop I felt your eyes on my back. I really did. When I turned and walked back to my seat I could see your face. I have never told you this, how could I? But at that moment I felt there was something there. Dare I say it — love? Right then I had an urge to go to you and say what I had felt and what I had seen. Yet, my calling is, like my love for you, a very real matter. There is my conflict. In spite of all we have spoken about these past months, I have not been able to discuss this with you. I have, I suppose, been frightened at how you would respond. I do love you. To pretend otherwise would be to deceive myself. But at the same time I want to go on living my life in the eyes of God, not on the edge but at the very center of my vocation. I know you have a similar feeling about your calling. That is why I will understand if you wish to end our friendship. In one way, as you know, it is already about to be physically separated. Soon I will be ordained. But I wished to share my feelings with you. In a way, I suppose I want a reassurance that you understand them and why I can't walk away from what God has intended for me. Please don't be angry. God bless you, always.

Love,

Tom.

Clare closed her eyes: reminding herself how the letter had left her void of intelligent thought; how she had almost run to her room, abandoning all ideas of going to college, taking to her bed, convincing herself that the pain in her stomach was an attack of food poisoning. All day her mind had given her no peace. She had read and reread every word, driven to distraction, filled with a dread and a strange feeling of excitement. That night, shortly before the Great Silence, she had gone to the kitchen. There, she had read the letter one last time before tearing it into pieces and throwing it into the furnace.

She had returned to college next day, feeling a mounting panic at what she would say to Tom. Waiting for the lecture to begin, she had frequently glanced across at the vacant place where he normally sat with his pad and several freshly sharpened pencils before him; it had then still amused her the way, when taking notes, he suddenly would switch from one pencil to another, and how, concentrating deeply, he gave his left earlobe a little tug. She came to a decision. She would pretend she never received the letter.

Tom had not shown up. He had gone on Retreat. Ten days later, in the great chapel at Clonliffe, he had been received into the priesthood.

For weeks, she agonized over the question of whether or not she should respond to his letter, and if she did, what she should say. She tried several times to put her thoughts on paper, to assure him she did understand: that, like him, she wished there had been proper guidance on how to handle their emotions; that to deny they existed was only to create further problems.

Tom, she now saw, was frightened because he knew where his feelings would lead.

She could face the truth. His love for her, their love for each other, would only have brought him to a situation totally incompatible with celibacy. He would — because he might well not understand what she now did — have been tormented by the passions of his body.

She accepted that over these past months there had been between them an almost consuming need for love, all the more aching because it had, until Tom's letter, not been mentioned. She had always wanted to tell him she understood his deep need to love and be loved. But she had been unable to say so because, then, she had not grasped that discipline, while hard and painful, was not only a matter of self-denial, but a decision to use a different and more meaningful way of showing love: expressing it purely through words. The physical act of making love could, she believed, mean anything: an expression of caring, certainly; but it was often merely a way of obtaining nothing more than sensual relief. Love expressed through words alone could not but have a clearer meaning; it provided its own special psychic rewards for those who uttered and received them.

Tom still might not understand about the deeper reality of commitment and love. That was why she had detected hesitation and deliberation behind his words. He had made an effort but had failed to disguise why he had laid out the choice facing him. In confronting himself, he was really saying he would not change; that the risks were too high for him — but he wanted her to know he was aware of them. In that sense, there was a childlike quality about his letter, as if he were confiding in her more than anything as a mother figure.

She understood this now and did not blame him. She also no longer felt a need to challenge his decision. She had learned that a part of true love is being able to accept and respect. That she could go on loving him was perfectly acceptable; that he had felt it necessary to continue to remain out of contact she could also respect.

Yet she would never confront him with her feelings. To do so would be nothing short of attempting to manipulate his life. The more she had come to understand her responses to the letter and what they had done for her, the more humble she felt. The letter had been the clue that had led her along this path of understanding.

To have responded in any way to Tom would have, in effect, placed her in the position of playing God. If she had given him the slightest encouragement, he might have struggled harder with his conflict. If she had rejected his love by saying she completely understood his sense of vocation, she might have left him uncertain over whether he should have ever confided in her. Whatever she would have done would have been exercising power and attempting to influence. Thankfully, she realized something had warned her of the danger.

Clare now saw that not to respond to his cry from the heart had been the best possible way to show her love. Out of the pain the letter had initially caused had grown an understanding that true love required sacrifice and humility before it could dare be compared to the love of God that was now guiding her.

Six weeks after Tom's letter arrived, her crisis took a further turn.

Following breakfast, she found a note in her box from Reverend Mother ordering her to report to her office that morning instead of going to college.

When she tapped on the Superior's door, she had to press her ear against it to hear the command. "Enter." In the past year, Reverend Mother had aged markedly. She had been hospitalized twice; the first time to have a portion of her stomach removed, the other to have ear surgery, which had left her partially deaf.

Clare had sat on the chair before the desk and for a long moment the Superior simply stared at her. When she spoke, her voice was barely audible. "There has been a change of plan. We are well satisfied with your degree. When your college term ends in three weeks, you will not be returning. Instead, you will commence teaching in our local boarding school. You will sleep there, but must return here every day for meals and to partake in the

Divine Office. It will require abundant energy to cope, but you will, with God's help."

Clare had been too overcome to speak and had merely nodded. After the Superior had given her benediction, she had immediately come here to the chapel, and in its solitude, wept and prayed for God to help her to understand the meaning of the vow of obedience.

She had tried hard: rising an hour earlier to arrive at the Mother House in time for first devotions; gulping her breakfast before hurrying away to spend her morning in the classroom; returning for lunch; hurrying back to the school for the afternoon teaching session; beginning to mark classwork before returning to the Mother House for supper and Compline; afterward rushing away again to supervise bedtime for the children she was responsible for. In her cubicle beside their dormitory, she would continue marking papers and preparing the next day's lessons. It was frequently midnight or later when she climbed exhausted into bed. Even so, she had often been unable to sleep. In three months, she had lost twenty pounds and felt frayed to her nerve ends.

It was then she had started to come to the chapel. Her guilt over her behavior and sense of frustration at what she was being made to endure had only been partially eased by prayer, and this she had found the most distressing of all. For the first time, the harder she prayed the more elusive had been the comfort the familiar words had always brought. God was there — but where? She had to find a way to Him. But even Saint John, who had never failed to show her the value of living a humble religious life, could not assuage her spiritual exhaustion.

Now she understood why the Order was unable to function successfully without squashing feelings and personal wishes. Denial, not desire, was still at the core of all it represented. In spite of all the changes introduced by Vatican Two, certain fundamentals remained unchanged. The Order clung to the belief that its members were like the children to whom she taught religion and art. And, above all, there must be no passion or display of feelings by any sister.

Yet, in insisting that a nun must exemplify the old proverb about still waters running deep, the Order failed to see that, for all the self-control and moderation she exercised, she was a passionate person who found it increasingly hard to identify with a system that relied on the destruction of self. There was something she found obsessional and deeply unacceptable in a way of life that routinely used authority as its prime form of control. Among her fellow sisters she had often detected a fading of willpower or a mood of covert rebellion; she did not wish to end up feeling either.

This was another reason she was in the chapel: she was trying to formulate rules for the self-discipline she knew she would require to act independently.

At the first tinge of creeping gray light where night ended and a new day began, five o'clock by her wristwatch, a Christmas gift from her father, new thoughts dominated her mind.

He was dying. The doctors had assessed he had a year left — two at the most. On her last visit home she and her mother had embraced silently, their tears mingling, both agreeing he need not be told. He had been in a wheelchair for some months; it seemed to grow larger as his body continued to shrink, the skin tightening around his cheekbones and at the wrists. While the illness etched lines of pain deep into his face, his gaze remained clear. Clare realized why. He had accepted. He was not troubled by doubt. He understood himself. Her father had achieved his own inner grace.

He would be pleased, she knew, when she told him of all she had experienced: that now, at last, she had braved the storm. She knew what she must do — and why she must do it. She rose to her feet, totally calm and certain, and walked from the chapel.

Two long days passed. Through the Deputy, she had submitted her request for an interview with Reverend Mother. The first available time, she had been tartly told, would be Thursday evening immediately after Compline. She had spent every available moment in the chapel, kneeling for hours, completely convinced that God was still telling her this was the right decision.

A moment ago, Clare had finished her explanation to Reverend Mother. The aged nun was gently probing.

"Why did you not come before?" The voice was old and faint. "I would have prayed with you."

"I wanted to be certain in my own mind first, Mother. I had to be absolutely certain."

Clare leaned forward to catch the Superior's words.

"We can never be certain. God called you. That is all you can be certain of. That He called you, just as He called each one of us."

"I really feel He understands, Mother. I really do have that feeling after praying."

The Superior's lips moved wordlessly for a moment.

"If you are so convinced, will you at least put your certainty to a test?"

"A test, Mother?"

"Yes. Will you talk to somebody first?"

Clare hesitated.

"Not the chaplain, Mother."

The convent's confessor, for all his good intentions, would not understand.

"No. Not him. A specialist. A priest trained in counseling. Will you see him for me? I will prepare a report of all you have said. I will let him see your file. Will you be willing to talk to him?"

"I think it's too late, Mother."

"It's never too late, Sister Mary Luke. Will you do this for me?"

Clare hesitated once more.

"Mother, I don't want to waste his time."

The Superior shook her head.

"Never see it like that. You are a good sister. You have undertaken many arduous duties and responsibilities. It has not always been easy for you. But Our Lord is clearly in you. Do this, if not for me, for Him."

"Very well, Mother."

The appointment had been arranged for a week from the following Friday. In the intervening period, Clare continued to pray. At four-thirty in the afternoon, she knocked and entered the parlor where, years before, Sister Imelda had sat with her.

The priest invited her to be seated. She sensed his immediate warmth and kindness. He was, she was relieved to see, surprisingly young. He could be barely thirty. She liked the way he came straight to the point.

"Reverend Mother has told me of your feelings. I have read her report. She has great respect for you."

"Thank you, Father."

He smiled.

"Let me say at once that I completely sympathize with your decision. I am not here to try and change it. If there is to be change, it will be a matter for you. I merely wish to act as a catalyst. To see if you have really thought it all through."

"I have, Father. I can assure you I have done more praying about this than anything else."

"Well, that's good. Then you are very certain."

Clare sat back in her chair, relaxing. There was to be no inquisition, only a discussion based on acceptance.

She told him why she wanted to leave religious life. It took her almost an hour to describe her inner conflicts and how she had resolved them.

At the end, he sat deep in thought and then said that while he was most impressed with her arguments, she must recognize her thinking was still only on the fringes of the great upheaval occurring in the world beyond the convent. Not only the commandments and ideas of sin, but God Himself was being challenged. While Ireland appeared to be staunchly Catholic, it was a nation of believers whose ideas about the Church's position in their lives was of the hand-me-down variety.

She interrupted him.

"I know what is happening. I see the changes with the kids at school. I know the attendance at Mass is dropping Sunday by Sunday. And that those who go often do so only because it's been drilled into them. I know all that, Father. But I also know that while I have changed my commitment to a life in religion, I have not changed my religious outlook. My parents gave me values. From the beginning they didn't force them. They just planted them and let them grow. I grew up believing it was the most natural thing for a girl to be a virgin when she married. That may have changed for others, but not for me. Marriage is still a sacred state for me. So are all the teachings of the Church. It's people's attitudes toward them that have changed. It's a matter of adapting the Church's teachings and modifying them here and there. But sin is sin. Right is right. That hasn't changed for me."

The priest looked at her carefully.

"When do you want to leave?"

"As soon as possible, Father."

"I'll ask Reverend Mother to see that all the arrangements are made."

Clare was told by the Deputy that it would take two weeks to complete the arrangements for dispensation. In the meantime, she would continue performing her normal duties. She would have no clear memory of how time passed except that at every free moment she continued to pray.

A fortnight later, the Deputy sent for her. "You will go during the supper hour. We have arranged for a taxi to take you home. Reverend Mother will see you at six-thirty."

After she left her office, Clare realized the Deputy had not addressed her by her title in religion. It was as if she had already been divested of her links with the Order.

The truth, as they both knew, was otherwise. Reverend Mother had offered her a teaching post at one of the Order's schools far from the Mother House.

"Even though you have chosen to leave, we do not wish to lose your experience. And remember, we are always here for you. Always."

She had gratefully accepted. Few nuns returning to the outside world, she suspected, had any form of guaranteed employment.

Astonishingly, apart from Reverend Mother and the Deputy, no one seemed to know she was leaving. Her name was still on the duty roster for next week. At lunch, instead of joining the community for its midday meal, she went to chapel and knelt, knowing this would be the last time she would come here. She finally rose and bowed slowly toward the sanctuary lamp.

She spent the afternoon packing. The previous evening her mother had dropped off a suitcase containing her going-out clothes. By six-fifteen she was dressed in the skirt, blouse, and shoes she had worn a decade earlier. She sat on the edge of her bed, staring at her suitcase. It held everything she possessed: her posters, books, photographs. In the closet she had hung, for the last time, her habit and cape.

There was a knock on the door. She opened it to Dominic.

"Sister Mary Luke. I've come to take your case down while you see Reverend Mother."

He twisted his hands, suddenly embarrassed, the words coming in a rush.

"It's not going to be the same without you. I'm going to miss you. Good luck, Sister."

Clare had a sudden lump in her throat. She reached forward and impulsively kissed him on the cheek.

"Thank you, Dominic."

She would miss him.

Clare left the room without a backward glance.

Reverend Mother and the Deputy stood behind the Superior's desk.

"Come forward, Sister."

Reverend Mother's voice seemed to grow fainter on each occasion she had come here.

Clare stood in front of the desk. On top of the mass of papers, she could see the dispensation documents that had been prepared in the Archbishop's office.

The Deputy stared at Clare glacially.

Reverend Mother's question barely reached across the desk.

"You are certain, Sister Mary Luke, that this is what you wish? Even at this late moment you can reconsider."

"Thank you for the opportunity, Mother. But I am sure. God wants this of me."

The Deputy's harsh words filled the room.

"As I have remarked before, you are truly fortunate to be so definite about God's wishes for you."

Reverend Mother sighed. She picked up the document.

"The moment you sign this paper you are released from your sacred vows. You are then no longer a sister in religion. When you sign, you will hand over your profession ring. You will notice the document is in triplicate. We will witness your signature on all three copies. You will receive one. One will be forwarded to the Archbishop and one will remain in your file."

The old nun paused, searching for the words that would complete her task.

"Finally, you must clearly understand that if, at any future date you wish to reenter religious life, your time here will count for nothing. You will have to begin at the very bottom again, as a postulant. Is that clear to you?"

"Yes it is, Mother."

"Very well. I ask you now. Will you accept and sign this dispensation I hold in my hand?"

"Yes, Mother. I will."

The Superior silently extended the paper, taking care that she did not in any way touch Clare's waiting hand. The Deputy passed her a pen, also avoiding any physical contact.

Without reading the words, Clare signed her name three times. Then she quickly worked loose her ring and placed it on top of the document. The Superior eased the paper and band toward her.

There was a lengthy silence, before Reverend Mother delivered her final whisper.

"May God protect you and keep you in His mercy, Clare."

Apart from that time with Sister Imelda, it was the first time anyone in the Mother House had called her by her baptismal name.

The Deputy brusquely handed Clare her copy of the dispensation document.

"Your taxi is waiting. Good-bye."

Clare addressed Reverend Mother.

"Thank you for all you have done for me. Good-bye, Reverend Mother."

"Go in peace, my child."

Clare walked toward the door. She could not help it, but tears started to well in her eyes.

At the door she turned and looked for the last time at the two nuns, as inert as statues staring at her. Then Reverend Mother raised her hand in benediction.

Instinctively, as she had always done at this moment, Clare bowed, and the question crossed her mind whether she would always be able to think and respond only as a nun.

CHAPTER 18

†

The Power to Be

When he felt the need, Andrew's memory could still summon Jane's voice and recall her skin and touch. But his strange sickness had now gone, the depression driven out of his mind. It had stripped him, but he was rid of it at last, freed now after a year of pain.

It had been replaced by the belief that, more than marriage would have done, living by the rules he had designed would enable him to grow deeper in the love of God. While he realized his was not a life-style based exclusively upon the Church's rules for celibacy, it still required considerable perseverance, determination, understanding, and acceptance. These and other values had been reinstated or instilled once the depression began to lift.

He achieved all this through prayer, using its gift and mystery to expand his ability to love less selfishly and to be a more sensitive person, yet strong enough to handle those negative emotions which once had ruled him completely. Self-analysis and self-discipline had helped. But in the end it was, he was convinced, the power of prayer that had brought him a clear understanding of how to satisfy his particular needs. He now saw that the loss of Jane had paved the way to realization.

He continued to dress for the wedding of two strangers who had a role to play in his pleasant mood. As he carefully fixed his Roman collar, he remembered it had rained on that morning he finally glimpsed a new beginning. Then he had put it more graphically. "I have sighted a landfall rising from the wastes of the spiritual wilderness, which have all but claimed me."

This analogy remained one of the few records of his return from the brink of suicide. But for these words, he would have found it difficult at times to recollect the journey to the edge of hell and back because he was not only mentally but physically transformed.

His hair shone, his fingernails were pared, and his skin was tanned and glowed with vigor. The overall effect gave an even more commanding presence to the cassock he liked to wear, and he had explained why in his diary. "When I was a little boy I once described Father Patrick as a man who wore his collar backward. Now I know better: a priest is still a priest no matter how he dresses. But that first definition has merit: it sets a priest apart."

The diary was peppered with self-revelation; primarily it was an account of what had happened when he went into the chapel intent on ending his life; how with the rope dangling at his feet, he had felt completely detached from himself: experiencing the sensation he was two persons in one body, as if he had achieved a new psychological dimension. It had been inexplicable, that time he had stepped outside himself. The more he thought about it, the more eerie it seemed.

On the other hand, he knew perfectly well why he did not word the telegram he had arranged to be sent in the Pope's name to Jane and Giles on this, their wedding day. The reason had been another moment of awareness to put on paper. "Jane has a choice. She can believe the Holy Father actually sent it. Or she can realize I'm behind it, but I'm keeping her at arm's length."

As he recognized the challenge of growing anew in communion with God, he realized he must develop firm rules for relating to people. On the one hand he must keep a certain distance — with each person it was a matter of fine judgment — but on the other, he must live without suppressing natural desires or blindly enduring privations.

The guilt he used to suffer had gone. He had noted its passing. It was all here, in the brown-covered book on his desk. For the most part, his diary was filled with the extraordinary experiences he had undergone and that now left him happier than he had been since coming to Rome.

He sat at his desk and once again dipped into pages which explained something of the motivations and compulsions that impelled him to attend a wedding on the very day Jane was getting married; to be close to a bride who was a stranger and hear her exchange vows as Jane was doing the same with Giles.

Andrew turned to the page where it all began.

". . . I don't know how long I stood in the chapel, feeling I was somehow looking at myself. I didn't appear like a man about to do away with himself, although I suppose my eyes gave a clue. They were going everywhere: to the arches and the supporting marble columns; anywhere I could fix the rope. The spiritual director once said that if those ancient pillars could speak, what secrets they would reveal. But there was nowhere suitable. Yet I had this feeling of being very set and determined, the way I clenched the rope.

"It was quite extraordinary, standing there, in the sense I'm trying to convey, debating with myself: did I, or did I not, want to commit suicide? It really was as simple as that. I had somehow managed to reduce my entire life to one question. I remember thinking: if only I could do that in moral theology.

"That person I was watching in the chapel, that other me, was quite detached, standing there, considering the question. I really was so absorbed by what I was thinking it made me feel quite giddy. I had to sit down. I wonder how many serious suicides go through this phase of rethinking? I sat there and thought about that for a long time. I had always imagined that being close to death I would feel calm and resigned. But I had that sick feeling that always comes when I'm badly frightened. I used to feel like this as a child. Father Patrick once said, when I was about nine and I'd missed altar-boy duties two days in a row, that I should feel sick and ashamed. Since then, whenever I had done something really bad, I had felt sick — as if it was part of my shame.

"I remember looking at my watch. I'd been sitting for an hour. The thought occurred to me that if I did go ahead, my watch would be ticking for a whole year after my own heart stopped. I'd just put a new battery in it. I wondered why I thought about time in that way. Was it because I realized life would go on after me? That my suicide would not change anything? Jane would still marry Giles. There would be no reason for her not to. My parents would be shattered. That was absolutely certain. They would be the helpless victims of my sin. I would be ruining their lives because I could not manage my own. Is that what I wanted?

"Something said I should go back to my room. That was a conscious decision that I was ready to think the matter through. *The Thing* was very upset and kept saying I was a coward. I told it to shut up. I would have used stronger language but I was in chapel. Even so, I said it quite loudly. Shut up. I suppose I should have realized the significance of this. But I didn't. For one thing, I was still on the edge. I could feel I was walking a tightrope in my mind. But I did get up at last. . . ."

Andrew paused and looked at his watch. He had often wondered what part it had played in that crucial decision to return to this room.

Nowadays, time as such had a new dimension: how long it took to achieve goals. There had been the time needed to understand that while celibacy involved sublimation it could create its own psychic energy. More weeks had passed working out how to handle his sexuality, understanding that it was not a matter of running away from it, but learning how to integrate it into his celibate life.

He required further time before he recognized, and accepted, that his body was always going to confront him with its physical demands, especially now that his sex drive had returned, all the greater for having been dormant for so long. The skill, he realized, was being able to enjoy sensuous pleasures in his mind, accepting his fantasies as an essential part of his newfound mental health and human dignity.

But in that pre-dawn, returning from the chapel, he had had precious little left of either. Coming up the stairs, he had met a newly arrived seminarian, going down to pray. It often happened, someone who could not sleep would go and meditate. Andrew didn't know who had been the more startled, and he had come back here, his mind bubbling, wondering if the youth suspected why he was carrying a rope.

Months of despair passed before the renewal of his prayer life allowed him to pose the question in his diary. "What does a potential suicide look like?"

By then, finding an answer did not unduly concern him; he became preoccupied with more positive discoveries and felt less inhibited in expressing feelings and emotions. He began to explore what role love would play for him in the future. With Jane, he had seen it predominantly, and often exclusively, as a physical pleasure.

Slowly, a deeper, distinct thought took root: celibacy, to have any meaning at all, must be totally related to the right to enjoy genuine human affection; above all, he must love himself before he could love anybody else. He had now built this ideal into his value system, using it as a scale by which to judge his emotional needs and understand how to satisfy them.

Celibacy, in these terms, he saw not as a solution, but merely a means; by itself it is not a whole way of living, only an aspect. It can be woven into the fabric of commitment, but it must not assume a supreme importance. Celibacy cannot be completely rationalized but must retain some of its mystery. Consequently, it can have no hard and fast rules: it must always be a matter of individual interpretation, depending in the end on the quality and extent of his imagination.

He turned a page.

". . . It's been ten days now and I've been back to chapel every night, sitting for hours. My mind filled with sour thoughts. Mostly long periods of feeling a total failure. I couldn't even end my own life. I hadn't the guts to do it. Dark thoughts when *The Thing* was at its most powerful. Then, mercifully, a total blank. It must have been after one of those periods that I realized one night I had come to chapel without the rope. I had this feeling of relief. I was kneeling, eyes closed and fingers so crushed together that they were really hurting when the realization came. I realized I wanted to live. The strange thing was, it didn't mean I wouldn't think about suicide again, but that I was free to make my own choice. *The Thing* had no part to play.

"I came back here and lay on my bed and I examined all those sour thoughts about Jane once more. What she had done and why she had done it. I just lay on the bed consumed by total misery. Then, when things were at their blackest, there was this feeling of being able to go on. I went back to chapel and prayed and prayed. I spent a whole day on my knees. I came up around six in the evening and just dropped into bed. I slept for a straight twelve hours. When I awoke I felt hungry. I didn't realize how important this was. Hunger goes with a will to live. I know that now. . . ."

Andrew turned and looked across the city, remembering that Wednesday dawn — so black. That was the morning he had sunk so deeply into depression again that he was prepared to plunge from this window. Instead, he had dropped to his knees and simply asked over and over again for God to show him how to survive. He had remained like that throughout the day. That night, exhausted, he felt the tiny seed that had saved him once before stirring again from deep within him. It gave familiar words a sudden new meaning. "Choice. Human Needs. Responsibility. Self-image. Self-confidence."

He felt God had spoken to him. From then on, first as a glimmer, then as a growing certainty, he began to see that what Jung said was true: neurosis is always a substitute for legitimate suffering. Neurosis is mental illness: legitimate suffering is part of a healthy mind. He could never reach a state of well-being as long as his mind continued to drive him to extreme action. He must come to terms with the reality of Jane and live without her.

God, he was certain, had suggested the solution. It was too awe-inspiring to have come from anywhere else. God would become his friend. Their relationship would transcend all others: through it, he would see his spirit grow, his ability to face and overcome problems return.

That silent Presence inside his head urged him not to fear pain; it was part of legitimate suffering. He must not procrastinate. Nothing would go away until he dealt with it in a healthy manner. Sucide was the ultimate way of avoiding reality — rather than taking up the challenge of coping with the suffering that led to self-awareness. It would be hard; it was only human, after all, to try to avoid pain and suffering. But this time he would not be alone. God would be there.

The idea of a friendship with Him was not easy to assimilate. Intellectually, he found theological objections. Friends are on a par, giving and receiving in equal measure. Such a relationship with God at its highest value suggested an equality.

He could see what God could give him, but what could he offer in return? How could his finity match divine infinity? How could God come any closer than being a father to a child?

He read his Bible again. In Romans he unearthed his first clue. God the Father, through His beloved Son, and the power of the Holy Spirit, made him a son of God by adoption. The second book of Peter enhanced his status. "You will be able to share *the divine nature*." He turned to Matthew, Mark, and John. He had seen with blinding clarity it was possible to share an *equal* friendship with God because through His grace, God in the fullness of truth, goodness, beauty, and spiritual strength had always been in him. He was, in its most humbling sense, the Trinity. God, Jesus, and the Holy Spirit had never deserted their place inside him. All they were asking was that he should not turn his back on Them.

Then, and only then, did he understand the fullest meaning of prayer.

He had seen it work every day in this room, bringing him face to face with his illness, stripping it away layer by layer and replacing it with legitimate suffering.

The journey back was well documented.

"This is my first entry for sixteen days. I don't really know what has happened to me this past month. It is mostly blank but something happened. The power of something: yes, certainly, the power of something. There is no other way to describe it. I don't feel as if the strings are about to snap anymore. And the most extraordinary thing of all is that when I checked under the bed, the rope had gone. I went down this morning to the lumber room and there it was. I must have brought it back. But I have no recollection of doing so. It is God's doing. . . ."

Beside the diary was an essay, written in flawless Italian, with an unprecedented high mark from his theology professor. It dealt with the Trinity and how its presence is essential to develop a balanced Christian self-image and self-acceptance. It had been hard to put his arguments on paper. But God had urged him to persevere. They had, he realized, become equal partners.

"God never seems to be far away. Today was typical. I just could not get going. I had a whole stack of work from the Greg to catch up on. The work load is now formidable.

"I had three essays. I just sat there, staring at the paper, thinking what a mess life still was. I really got quite down in the dumps. Really low again. I must have plunged quite a bit before something seemed to steady inside me, saying that I had been down here before and had hated it. It was time to continue rebuilding. God is able to bring me back to a level of real emotional security. I suspect I will plunge again. But I know He will be there. That is a very good feeling. . . ."

He had examined others. He read C. S. Lewis's *The Four Loves*, an exploration of affection, and transposed Lewis's rather abstract ideas into the framework of his new life. Affection, he saw in this context, was really a question of shared values and ideas. He had never had that with Jane. But he could experience it here: seminary life was bound up in living and praying together. He could begin to explore the affection and friendship on offer, a kind largely lost to the outside world since the Romantic movement. The world beyond these walls had little time for affection that was neither sentimental nor physically sensuous. But the affection he had in mind could hold its own beauty and rewards. It would have no physical basis. It would be love in its noblest form. In giving and receiving it he would have to take care. There must be no misunderstanding over what he

435

had in mind. But any risk would be more than compensated for by the return. And he would still have his own private inner world intact, using it when required: a very necessary haven. Slowly, he began to feel that inner force, God, increasingly fill him with a quiet goodness, enriching him, allowing him to make calmer judgments, ones in many ways more profound. These, too, had been written down.

"... but I have also begun to realize that for anything to be worthwhile it has to be absorbed before it can be appreciated. It must go through the soul. In making that one decision I have agreed to accept full responsibility for how I would live the rest of my life. I've stopped thinking life should be easy. It is only through the difficulties and the pain of resolving situations that I can ever hope to go on growing. It comes down to what Benjamin Franklin once said: 'Things which hurt, instruct.' I've taken that first timid step toward a profound wisdom. To welcome the problems of living is also to look forward to the happiness which comes from solving them. . . ."

For the first time in months he noticed his room was strewn with clutter. There were finger marks on the wall on either side of the mirror from the times when he had stood and cried at his reflection, hands pressed hard against the wall to try to quell the tears. It took a whole day of cleaning and sorting to get back the comfortable order. He then began to answer his letters. But there had been one problem left to handle.

"This compulsion to hear Jane's voice always comes at night. I try to con myself that I am really going to chapel. But end up at the phone. Nothing can stop me from dialing her number. I hear the ringing tones and I think how a telephone is plugged into one's feelings. I can see her stretching to answer — see her face and the bedroom. I can anticipate the click as the instrument is picked up at her end.

"Early this morning I called her again. Suddenly, as the phone began to ring, I put it back on the cradle, saying to myself I didn't need to hear her voice just then. It was quite a moment. . . ."

He riffled the pages of his diary, turning again to the entry that dealt with his reaction to the news of the wedding from his mother.

Jane had invited his parents. Should they go? His first reaction was that they should not, then he had deliberated further and realized that would be totally selfish. He telephoned home and had a lengthy conversation with his mother, explaining exactly what he wanted them to do.

He looked at his watch. It was time to go.

The church was behind Castel Sant'Angelo in the Parti district of the city, a residential area close to the high walls of the Vatican. He had come across it on one of his first post-depression walks. He had been back several times to sit in its nave, the gloomy silence broken only by footsteps coming and going to the confessionals. After a while, Andrew had come to know the priest who told him about the wedding and suggested he drop by: it would be another Roman experience.

His plan, resulting in the telephone call to his mother, was born out of the invitation. The priest had given Andrew the seat he requested, beside the choir stalls, on the bridegroom's side of the church. His cassocked presence would, he knew, go unremarked. To the congregation he would be no more than another acolyte among those assembling before the altar.

The priest was supervising the robed figures. Satisfied, he led them down the nave to the main doors, which were opened, waiting to receive the bride. The church had been transformed. Tiers of candles flanked the altar, there were flower arrangements in the sanctuary, and every statue had a bouquet. The massive chandeliers shimmered in the light of hundreds of candlelike bulbs. Organ music filled the expectant silence.

The bridegroom and his best man were already standing at the sanctuary rail, nervous blue-suited young men, occasionally glancing over their shoulders toward the open doors.

Andrew was certain that in Jane's parish church, where once he had thought they would marry, the atmosphere would be the same.

He closed his eyes, as if in prayer. . . . *In his mind he could see Giles in formal dress, standing, waiting with his brother, Tony; he was whispering nervously and Tony nodded, reassuringly. He imagined his parents seated as close as possible to the places they would have occupied had he been the bridegroom. They had also agreed to his request to give Jane a set of hand-cut crystal decanters and goblets.*

The music suddenly swelled as the bridal procession slowly made its way up the nave.

He opened his eyes and had his first glimpse of the bride. She was not as pretty as Jane or as tall, but she had, unusual for a Roman, Jane's fair hair.

He closed his eyes. *Jane, as she had once said she would, was wearing a gown with a train long enough to require the support of four bridesmaids.*

She wore the veil off her face and her eyes were shiny with excitement.

Andrew watched the bridegroom nudge his best man and give him a quick relieved smile. The bride took her place beside her future husband and they, too, exchanged smiles.

He closed his eyes. . . . *Jane was smiling at him.* He opened them at the point where the priest blessed the wedding rings. Andrew's gaze was steady as he watched the man place the ring on the girl's finger and the priest pronounce them man and wife. As they knelt in their first act of marital worship, he closed his eyes for a further moment; long enough for him to visualize Jane and Giles performing a similar action.

Then he opened his eyes again and murmured, "Good-bye, Jane, good-bye."

†   †   †

Victoria had a caseload of fourteen nuns. Nine were members of her own Order; the remainder came from three different congregations. Each sister required medium-term therapy, three to six months, before deciding whether or not to return to religious life, and realizing that if she wished to remain there, she must never forget that her ultimate goal was not to avoid healthy pain and suffering, but to integrate it into her total spiritual evolution. Equally, if she wished to leave, she should feel no guilt and Victoria would do everything to help her successfully face that decision.

Sister Catherine, seated in this room on a cold January morning in 1984, had been coming four times a week for five months. This was to be her last session. When it was over, she would not be returning to the Mother House. She would no longer be a sister in religion.

The story of this previously well-balanced and attractive woman seated before Victoria was, she felt in so many ways, typical of the close connections between psychopathology and religion. Victoria suspected there were thousands of nuns like her.

For too many centuries, the Church had avoided its responsibilities. Having embraced future priests and nuns at the level of parochial school and catechism class, it had, until the past decade — yet another positive result of pressure following the Second Vatican Council — virtually ignored their plight. Even today there were cardinals and bishops, men close to the Pope, who insisted there was no link between the increased number of professed religious seeking psychiatric help and the ecclesiastical demands Victoria saw as more appropriate to the Middle Ages. Only when the psychiatric beds in hospitals began to overflow with disturbed religious men and women did the Church finally act. It decided to treat its own. Even then, Victoria thought, its motives were not totally above suspicion. The prime emphasis in many Church-sponsored counseling centers was to get nuns and priests *back* into religious life. This, thankfully, was not the policy of the unit to which she was attached. From the outset, Victoria insisted that if she was to make the best possible use of her long and expensive training, she must have a free hand. That had extended to how she furnished her office in the guidance clinic.

The desk at which she wrote her case reports stood against a wall in one corner. Several plant-holders dotted the room: ivy and ferns climbed and sprouted, creating an impression of a healthy, vigorous atmosphere. The curtains complemented the theme: sunflowers against a summer-blue background. Sister Catherine had said the flowers reminded her of that first time Eddie drove her into the countryside and they had made love in a cornfield. She had sobbed at the memory.

Though Victoria had been taught that it was a tactical blunder openly to show undue sympathy, she had been deeply moved by the nun's unhappiness; without being aware of it she had somehow communicated her compassion. It had been unwise. Sister Catherine mistook Victoria's attitude and reacted predictably, demanding in all sorts of ways more condolence to fuel her self-pity.

It is a common symptom in cases of psychosexual guilt. Paradoxically, having somehow conveyed her sympathy, Victoria was accused by her patient of being cold and uncaring, and at the end of one session, Sister Catherine had suddenly stormed, "What would you know about love? You're just another one the system has sucked dry."

Victoria continued to work to find answers to Sister Catherine's moving dilemma. It was all the more haunting because, for the most part, she unfolded her story in those first few weeks with an almost total absence of histrionics, a calm broken only at times when inner pressures drove her to use Victoria as a safety valve and she hurled frenzied abuse. Her fury spent, she would stare at the sunflowers; a tragic figure in her modified habit and veil.

Victoria, who had seen the changes emerge, still found them rewarding and remarkable. Sister Catherine's face had lost its strained look. Her heavy-lidded blue eyes were once more clear and her nostrils no longer flared in sudden anger. She could laugh and be comfortable with herself.

Sister Catherine now sat relaxed, hands folded in the lap of her silk dress, which she explained Eddie had bought for her months ago. It had been a double present; to mark her twenty-third birthday and to celebrate her abrupt decision to leave religious life and move in with him.

The weeks following that development had been especially grueling. As she worked through her guilt, now released from repression, Sister Catherine's self-esteem, never too high, had ebbed away. Reciting the rosary of her mistakes, she had spared neither herself nor Victoria. Day after day, at the appointed time, between three and four o'clock in the afternoon, she explained why she had literally fled from the congregation in Eddie's car, leaving everything behind in her room in the Mother House.

Eddie had stopped at a liquor store and picked up wine and they had gone to his apartment and made love for days. But, she had confessed, her decision had not brought freedom; her guilt, if anything, had deepened. She knew she had betrayed the Order, deceived Reverend Mother, and caused great anguish to her fellow sisters.

Victoria had remained virtually silent during this purging, interrupting only to ask an occasional question, but always careful never to comment on what Sister Catherine persisted in calling her *sins*. She had remained equally noncommittal as Sister Catherine described the expiatory measures she had used to discharge them. She had turned on Eddie, blaming him for all that had happened. If it had not been for him, she railed in this room, she would still be a nun; he had led her from the path of righteousness. Eddie was responsible for *everything*.

Still Victoria had not commented, not even when Sister Catherine said, through a flood of tears, she wanted to return to the Order.

That evening over dinner with Jim, Victoria had unfolded her plan. As usual, he had listened most carefully.

†

Jim had resurfaced in her life as easily as he had left it almost thirty years ago. That had been the day she had cheered him on as he churned through the water to win the hundred-yard crawl for their high school. He had lifted himself out of the pool, waved at her casually, and loped off to the locker room. Jim had joined her later and over burgers and fries he told her he was going to be a priest. She had been stunned enough to blurt out, her face crimson, that his decision would break the hearts of a lot of girls. He'd looked at her, surprised, and she had added, only half-joking, that perhaps she might have fallen for him herself if Art hadn't been around.

When they had been reintroduced by the unit's director and she had overcome her surprise at seeing Jim, she reminded him of the long-ago incident. Jim had grinned and said it was not too late and they both had laughed.

From then on they had slipped easily and naturally into a relationship. At first it had been confined to the clinic, discussions in the staff room, and lunch in the coffeeshop across the street. But one evening Jim dropped by her office and suggested dinner. He had spent a particularly difficult hour with a young priest with fetishism difficulties — he liked to wear women's underwear — and Jim wanted a break from patients' problems.

Over cocktails she mused whether Jim should refer the case to their superior. Jim had resisted; this was his case and he was going to do his very best to help. His quiet determination impressed her. Over coffee they began to catch up on each other's life. He had ministered in Canada, served for a spell in Rome, then returned to the United States to work in a Church-run clinic in New York and later in Detroit before joining this unit.

When they reached the house in the suburbs she shared with three other sisters, he had leaned across and kissed her gently on the mouth. She had been too startled to resist. Pulling away, she had looked at him carefully and then they had clung together in a silent embrace. He had finally whispered that everything would be fine; that they could handle the situation.

The most surprising thing for her was how easy it had been to do so. It had also, she was convinced, helped her to resolve Sister Catherine's dilemma.

She and Jim had gone to their favorite Chinese restaurant where she explained Sister Catherine's latest change of mind.

"Will they have her back?"

"Of course. But that's not the point, Jim. Catherine is still fundamentally Catherine. This recent shift is no more than a variant of her overall behavior pattern. Going back in is the last thing she should be encouraged to do."

"I can see that in one way she might find it hard to give up the still novel joys of sex with Eddie, but it may be that she's also found a new commitment. It does happen."

"I know, Jim. But I don't think sex, as such, is her problem."

"Oh?"

"No. Her problem is that the Church sold her a bill of goods and she doesn't know how to cash it in. So she has looked for an excuse."

Jim looked thoughtful. "Why doesn't she just quit? Thousands still do."

"Yes, but they don't have her personality structure. She is still a martyr to a simple truth. Deep down inside her she wants to question the authority and wisdom of the whole Church, or at least what she has experienced of it. But she knows she cannot do that. Nobody takes on the Church on that level and wins. So she hopes that by being outrageous she'll get kicked out. That would confirm all her feelings about the Church. But if that happens the same guilt that has driven her from Eddie will drive her to another crisis."

"But surely the Order could refuse to have her back?"

"It could, but the chances are it won't. It will simply see her as somebody who went off the rails, but is now ready to return to the bosom of the Mother House. That's why they sent her to me in the first place. I'm supposed to work the miracle that gets her back into religious life."

"And you're saying you can't?"

"What I'm saying is that it would be wrong for me even to try. The only way to help her is to make her see that she's absolutely right to feel as she does about the Church."

"I'm not sure, Victoria. I mean, it's a hell of a thing to do."

"I think it's the only way. I really do. It's the only way she will ever face herself — by accepting that much of what she has been told about God is wrong for her."

"Jesus, Victoria!"

"I'm serious, Jim. Her guilt, her anger, all her hangups go back to the fact that some smart nun or priest, anxious to score brownie points with the bishop, talked her into becoming a nun. They sold her a glossy package that was about as realistic as saying Heaven is up and Hell is down. That's the level Catherine psychologically operates at. She bought the package blindly and the only way she saw how to unscramble it was by grabbing the first man who looked at her. She's got a strong sex drive, but her fantasies are a childish hodgepodge of the big-black-man-having-sex-with-her variety. With Eddie, she initiated intercourse two or three times every night. He was a sort of sex toy for her. Making up for all those lost years. Common enough, as we both know. But at the root of it, sex is not her problem. It's simply that she should never have become a nun. The only way to help her is to make her see this."

Jim was silent for a long time.

"That's a big gamble you're taking. You could get yourself busted out of the unit. Even here, we don't actually have a mandate to return them to the world."

She had smiled, suddenly realizing how tired she was.

"I know that, Jim. But in Catherine's case, it is the only way. It really is."

So it had begun: the slow and difficult process of exploring Sister Catherine's guilt, which continued to draw her back into a life for which Victoria was convinced she was totally unsuited.

First, she had switched Sister Catherine's appointment hour to the morning, bringing her in at eight o'clock when Victoria would herself be fresh. Victoria had launched, on that very first morning, the battle to make Sister Catherine peel away her defenses; to make her realize either she would have to discard them voluntarily, or they would be gently but firmly taken from her by soft-voiced persuasion.

"Catherine, in every sense, this is a new start for both of us. As from now, I want to hear no more mea culpas. You have done enough confessing. You could probably spend the rest of your life searching for new evidence to support your guilt. But what I want you to think about first of all is this: all these recriminations of yours are only a mask. What we have to do is look behind that mask and see what is really there. To do that you need to have your ego in as good a shape as possible. So no more of these mea culpas."

Each subsequent session held its special terrors for Sister Catherine; each produced its small but significant victory as she began to see herself differently in a hundred ways. Yet, although she began to be polite and cooperative, she was often reluctant to part with intimate details, and Victoria had to extract them by patient and subtle questioning. She saw that for all her newfound courtesy and respectfulness, Sister Catherine still felt antagonistic. Beneath this mark lurked a very real fear. She still believed the Order was all she had left; that, indeed, to return to religious life would be the only fitting punishment for what she had done.

Victoria now found herself in a curious position. Totally believing herself in the value of religious life, she used every possible therapeutic skill to pry loose Sister Catherine from her misguided belief that she was meant to return to that life. At the same time, she set about convincing her that she had a basically well-motivated personality and showed a promise — when she had readjusted her perspective — of being a person well able to take her place in secular society.

To achieve this demanded taking the calculated risk about which Jim had warned. To free Sister Catherine of her desire to rejoin her Order she would not openly disagree with her, hoping that by remaining silent she would eventually bring Sister Catherine to the stage where she herself would question the value of religious life for her.

It had taken weeks to achieve that result.

Victoria had led Sister Catherine all the way back to her childhood, exploring her feelings for her parents, getting her to finally admit that her entire family had been completely dominated by her father. It was largely to escape him, and to earn his rare approbation, that she had allowed herself to follow the advice of her catechism teacher: the priest had said she would make a fine nun.

She had gone, uninformed, into religious life at seventeen. Her father had said it was the proudest day of his life and that his strictness had paid off and led her to a life in Christ. It was in the novitiate that she began to see that the endless restrictions, the commands, and the implacable demands for obedience were how the Church, like her father, held onto power.

She began to experience sexual fantasies and enjoyed them. That was a double sin — having them and enjoying them. Her voice shook as she made the admission. The morning she became fully professed, she awoke to find herself masturbating. The discovery distressed her deeply. She had gone to the communal bathroom and filled a tub with cold water and immersed herself until she could no longer bear it.

At first it seemed to work. The numbing of her body had been sufficient to keep her sexuality at bay. But a week later she had found herself masturbating again. From then on, she had regularly done so and also had sexual fantasies. She had been driven to eliminate them by returning to icy soakings. She stopped only when she developed pneumonia and lay seriously ill for weeks in the Mother House infirmary.

Restored to health, she found her sexual proclivities returned. Her well-established guilt became almost obsessive. Unable to face any more cold baths, she developed a compulsion to wash her hands; the more she did so, the dirtier she felt.

Victoria began to explore Sister Catherine's concept of sin. Why did she believe masturbation was wrong? What made it so? Who had told her that? Why did she think it was wrong to fantasize? Who said so? When she met Eddie and made love with him, why did she feel guilty? Where did she think was the guilt in responding to a normal human emotion? What was love? What was sin? What was the difference between good and evil?

The questions had been carefully spaced and Victoria had allowed Sister Catherine all the time she needed to respond. They had returned time after time to both the questions and her answers.

Gradually, Victoria had led Sister Catherine to the point where she began to ask questions of herself.

Why had she allowed herself to think she had a vocation? Did that even matter? Surely what mattered now was that she could see her mistake. Why hadn't she been able to see that the best thing to do would be to ask for dispensation instead of running away?

Then, an old doubt surfaced. What would her family say? Her father would accuse her of failure. She could not face that —

Victoria had for once interrupted.

"Yes, you can, knowing what you now do. You know now this sort of life is wrong for you. But that doesn't mean you have behaved wrongly. It is what is being asked of you that is wrong. That is important for you to grasp."

"But I'll still feel I've let God down."

"Catherine. Whatever you have done, you have not done that. None of us is big enough to let God down. Not one of us is clever enough even to begin to know His mind. All I can say to you is that the God you describe is not the God I know. You are talking of a punishing God. You are trying to make your God sound like your father and perhaps even the Order. But that is not the way I see Him. He wants you, I am certain, to be happy. He knows you are not a bad person. You have to understand that and believe it, from this moment. Okay?"

It had taken time to nurture the idea. But Sister Catherine had, at last, been able to see her affair with Eddie as a symptom; the root cause began with her father, and was compounded by that catechism teacher and then by the Order, and ultimately by the Church and its doctrine, which she finally found impossible to live with.

Progress, when it came, was dramatic. An important element was the warmth and the security of the contact Victoria set out to establish; she hoped that Sister Catherine would see their relationship — to all intents and purposes part of the secular world — was very different from the one she had had in the Order and before that with her father.

At first Sister Catherine had come to therapy in her habit. But one morning, at the start of her third month, she appeared in a new dress. Somehow it transformed her personality. From then on, each time she came she wore either a dress or casual clothes. Each month she found enough money to add to her wardrobe. The effect of being able to dress as she liked became instantly noticeable.

"The clothes have made me change inside. I not only look different but I feel different. I see God differently. He's still very important to me, but in a new way. And I don't need to worship Him within a framework. You know what I mean?"

Victoria had said she understood perfectly.

Two weeks ago, Sister Catherine had announced that she had applied for formal dispensation. She also had a new man in her life, a buyer in a department store. While she would continue to date him, she would live alone in an apartment she could now afford to rent because of her new job as a sales clerk in a bookshop.

Victoria had asked how she felt about making the first independent decisions of her new life.

"Good. Pretty damn good!"

†

Victoria rose from her chair and handed Catherine her copy of the dispensation she had arranged to be sent from the Mother House.

Catherine stared thoughtfully at the sheet of paper.

"It seems strange, needing all this formality, all these Latin words, to start living." She looked at the document with her name inked in and the end of her religious life affirmed by the flourishing scrawl of the Archbishop. "It's impressive enough to be framed."

Victoria smiled. "We normally only frame things which matter. Today is the first day of your new life."

Catherine nodded, understanding, and thrust the paper at Victoria. "You keep it. A reminder of a difficult patient."

Victoria accepted the document.

For the first part of the flight from New York to Athens, Victoria and Jim had slept, holding hands beneath their blankets.

He was wearing jeans and a shirt open at the neck. She had chosen a linen pantsuit. Each had packed a rosary and missal. Jim also packed his anointing oils and stole. Occasionally his fingers would stroke her profession ring; sometimes her hand would stray and touch his thigh. Both had discovered they were very tactile.

At Orly Airport in Paris, while the jet refueled and the crew changed, they mailed postcards to friends and colleagues at the unit. Victoria hesitated about signing her name next to Jim's.

He laughed. "There's your guilt showing."

She kept her voice level. "I don't feel guilty. I just don't want to make people uncomfortable. Father Julius, for one." He was the medical director of the unit.

"You're forgetting he's a psychiatrist. Anyway, he knows."

She couldn't keep the surprise out of her voice. "You told him?"

Jim shrugged. "Sure. What's there to tell? We're going to spend ten days looking at the ruins of Greece. So?"

"We're also sharing a room. Remember?"

"I haven't forgotten."

"I bet you didn't tell Father Julius that."

Jim laughed. "No. That I didn't tell him. That would really have been pushing things a little too far." There was a bantering tone to his next words. "Of course, you can always switch the reservation."

Victoria looked at him steadily. "Now who's feeling guilty?"

She wished he would drop the subject. The idea for the vacation had come up on a cold night last November, when they sat in his apartment overlooking the water, watching a travelogue about the Greek islands. Pouring more wine, Jim had said they should go. Not really taking him seriously, she had replied, why not? At lunch next day, he surprised her by saying he had made the reservations. She should have remembered; Jim was a person who followed through on his impulses.

That day was exactly a month after she had moved out of the shared house in the suburbs and into the small, comfortable apartment a few blocks from Jim's. He had found it for her after she had called Reverend Mother and said she needed more privacy to work at home on her case notes. Her Superior at once agreed that the Order would furnish and pay the rental on the apartment.

Four nights a week, Victoria reviewed her files, steeping herself in the crises of other nuns. The other three were invariably spent in Jim's company. On Fridays, he cooked for her; on Saturdays they generally ate at the Chinese restaurant. On Sunday evenings, she cooked for him. All but a small portion of their salaries were remitted directly to their orders. In turn, their living expenses were paid for by their congregations. They saved out of their remaining income for extras such as this vacation.

By the time Jim suggested they should go to Greece, they had both realized their relationship was one that had few limitations. From the beginning, they had agreed to explore how far they could go and still remain comfortable with their vows. Walking through the Orly concourse, she reminded herself it was for this very reason she had carefully documented in her journal each step they had taken. She reminded him of the decisions they agreed upon together before the vacation.

"Jim, I don't want to change anything. I told you. I don't see anything morally wrong with sharing a room. Or, for that matter, a bed. Sleeping together in our case is just what it means. Sleeping. Together. It's really no different from sitting close together on your sofa or on my couch. The same emotions are engaged. The same temptations are there. You know that. I know that. We could just have easily made love on a couch as in a bed. So I don't see anything wrong in sharing a room." She smiled, wanting to wind up the matter on a light note. "Besides, it's cheaper. On our budget that's important."

Jim stared at her. "I don't think many people would believe we are doing this because we want to run a test-temptation experiment on the cheap."

"Look, if you want to switch when we get there, fine. But let's not make a production out of this. We both said we want to try it. If you've changed your mind, it's no big deal."

"No, Victoria. I haven't. It's just, well a little scary."

She looked at him. "If it's any help, I'm also scared."

He took her hand, and they walked silently toward the departure gate as their flight to Athens was called.

She had often thought that their entire relationship was as unpredictable, yet revealing, as any case history. She had written that, in many ways, it would be the culmination of a love story no novelist would dare invent: how she and this vigorous-looking priest, his Levi's unwrinkled, despite the long trip, had explored their passions.

Waiting to board the Olympic Airways flight, she recalled the first time they had stood in line together. It was to see a hard-porn movie set in a New York massage parlor, where the masseuses all seemed to be either students at Hunter, NYU, CCNY, or aspiring actresses.

At the time she was beginning Catherine's case and Jim was treating a young priest who regularly went to massage parlors to satisfy a desire to feel a woman's touch. Jim had said he would like to see the movie in the hope he might better grasp the compulsion that drove his patient to such behavior.

The film, for all its tackiness, did unwittingly offer insights into the frustrations of men with sexual difficulties who used the parlor to work out their insecurities by allowing themselves to be aroused with baby oil or talcum, lying naked on their backs, eyes closed, lost for a brief time in a world of their own. Victoria knew the filmmakers did not intend this endless shuttle of men and girls to have any serious psychological significance, but in fact it did: there was a common undertone of guilt about the customers, often only removed when the masseuses would insult, berate, and scold the men for their need to be massaged.

There was also a kinky religious aspect to the movie. One of the regular clients was an Orthodox rabbi who always arrived with a sandwich wrapped in a plastic bag. Having eaten the sandwich while lying on the table, he would then cover his penis with the bag so that he could be masturbated without having the girl's hand come into actual contact with him. One of the girls wore a travesty of a habit, and received her clients in a pseudoreligious atmosphere. At the foot of the massage table was a prie-dieu and an incomplete set of the Stations of the Cross hung on a wall. The camera would pan from the table to the pictures and then back again. But Victoria knew this was not the reason Jim finally became tense over this endless masturbatory activity; it was, she suspected, because it was the first time he, like her, had ever seen fellatio performed.

She later put on paper her reaction and Jim's response when they returned to her apartment.

"I told him I found it sexually exciting. The idea of doing that to a man is a definite turn-on. Part of it, as the film suggested, might well have to do with the power of being able to deny or give pleasure in a very erotic way. That's perfectly natural. I told Jim I would do anything that would give us both pleasure. He gave me a funny look, and reached across and just grabbed at me. But not in a rough way. He's not that sort of man. It was all very gentle. We were fooling around. I guess we both knew what was in our minds. Suddenly, it got very serious, and when we realized how heavy, we pulled back. We had got to the stage where we were touching each other and we knew it was a very close thing. But I didn't feel frustrated. I was, more than anything, curious about my responses. That night, I dreamed of Jim for the first time. It was a wonderful experience. A total climax. I couldn't believe it could be this good . . ."

As they took off, Victoria stroked Jim's hand, thinking how naturally they had fallen into giving and receiving pleasure.

"The first time he touched me in a completely different way was tonight. He pressed his thumb in the palm of my hand. He pushed slowly and firmly and asked me what I felt. It was like electricity. I couldn't believe it. He took my hand and asked me to do the same to him. We sat there, each with a thumb placed on a palm. The effect was doubly electrifying. I could feel the vibes from him and I knew he was feeling mine. We had drunk a lot of wine while we again discussed the movie. Jim kept on going back to specific moments, describing them in a low voice. I could see that he was very aroused. He had been like that since he started to talk. It was a real turn-on for him, and for me — being able to be part of this excitement. It was a whole new dimension and very, very sexy. I could feel what was happening to me and I could see what was happening to Jim. That just increased my own excitement. What made it so pulsating was feeling it all through that one focal point, where our thumbs were touching our palms. Everything was concentrated there. This was sensuous in a way I had never thought possible. All the time Jim talked about sex. He can absolutely make love with words. He drove me to the point where I felt I was losing control. I had never been aroused like this before. I wanted to pull my thumb away, but he said I mustn't. That I must keep going and what was going to happen was absolutely fine. I suddenly felt myself coming. It just shot through me. Then he kissed me on the mouth and we lay down on the couch and curled into each other. When I awoke he had gone home to his apartment. I called and he said, 'Go back to sleep.' His voice is quite hypnotic. I just did like he said. . . .

". . . It has happened again. We'd been to an open-air concert and later I cooked dinner. Afterward, we settled down with a classical tape and a brandy. Then he just took my hand . . ."

She could feel his hand searching for her. "Are you crazy, Jim? Here?"
He looked at her intently, whispering. "It's going to happen in your mind. All of it. We're going to make it happen like that. Nobody's going to know except us. Now give me your hand."

The hotel was in the Kolonaki district of the city, with an unrivaled view of the Acropolis and Mount Lycabettus. They registered and handed the forms back to the clerk. He looked at them for a long time. Then he lifted his eyes and stared solemnly, first addressing Jim.
"You are a priest of religion?"
"I don't know of any other kind."
The clerk nodded to himself, glancing down at the form to make sure he had not misread what Jim had written alongside "Occupation."
He looked at Victoria. "You are a nun?"
She smiled. "Yes."
The man once more nodded slowly, murmuring to himself in Greek. He looked at them both.
"A nun. A priest." He smiled. "But why not? Nothing is impossible today . . ."

He turned and handed them the room key. "Enjoy your stay."

Jim took Victoria by the arm as they followed the bellhop to the elevator.

"It's the only way to be, Victoria. If they'd found out, it would have made us seem furtive and dirty. If we play it out front, people will see we've nothing to hide."

Victoria looked at him. "Jim, don't protest so much. It's no big deal, two adults sharing a room."

They rode up in silence. The room was large, with twin beds several feet apart. The balcony looked across the rooftops of Athens. Victoria motioned toward the beds.

"Which one? Nearest the balcony or the bathroom?"

"I'll take the balcony side."

She put her case on the bed and began to unpack, shaking out the creases in the new nightdress she had bought for the holiday. She noticed that Jim had paused in his own unpacking and was looking at her.

"Something wrong?"

He shrugged. "You know, I thought I'd got it all straight in my mind. But now, here . . ."

She walked over to him, unselfconsciously holding a pair of pants. "Jim, the worst sin is pride. Don't forget that. I know you don't want to be the first to fail. I think I know how you feel —"

"Would you please mind not standing so close?"

She felt the warmth of his body. She stepped back.

"We're still too close —"

"Jim! For God's sake, we can't start like this." She looked at him seriously. "Would you like me to take another room? Maybe next door or across the hall?"

"No. Don't do that. I'll be fine in a minute. It's just . . . seeing you there with your nightie and those pants in your hand . . ."

"I'm sorry, Jim."

"No. It's okay. Really. But try and keep a little distance until I get used to this. Feel more comfortable."

She took another pace back. "Jim, this is not the way I'd hoped it would be. It's turning into an issue. We both agreed we wouldn't want that to happen. If you want to leave while I unpack, then leave. But I can't spend every minute wondering if what I do or say is going to either arouse you or make you feel guilty."

"Jesus, Victoria —"

"Jesus, nothing! Have you ever thought I might also need some space? You're not the only one under vows in this room. But we can't just stand here and calculate how much of a sin it is to unpack our clothes —"

"I'm sorry."

He reached for her, encircled her with his arms, and kissed her.

She started to pull away, but he held her close, murmuring. "Hey, I'm sorry. Kiss me. Kiss me."

She kissed his lips. "Come on, Jim. It's going to be fine." She felt his hardness against her. "Here, give me your hand." She led him to the bed. For the first time, she took the initiative.

The days slipped by. From Athens they had gone to Corfu, the Gulf of Corinth, and Rhodes.

Now, late in the afternoon, a boat was bringing them to their final destination, the volcanic island of Santorini. Tomorrow they would return to Athens to begin the long journey home.

Jim pointed at the spectacular pumice and lava. "Erupted in Minoan times. The whole island shot up inside a day."

She studied the towering cliff faces, with the white-housed town of Thíra perched on the cliffs, usually reached either by mule or by cable car.

"It's a climb of eight hundred steps from the harbor."

"You're a mine of information."

"I read up on it while you were sleeping."

"I wasn't sleeping. I heard you get up. I've heard you get up every night."

"I'm sorry, Victoria. I thought I'd been quiet."

"I guess getting used to having you in my room, I notice when you've gone."

Night after night they had lain side by side, usually on her bed, with Jim kissing her cheeks while she pressed her thumb into his palm. She had seen his erection under his shorts and had come to accept how he would suddenly pull away from her and go to the bathroom.

One night she had asked him what he had done. He told her.

She had looked at him. "Why don't you let me take care of you? I'd like to do that."

From then on she had.

He had asked if he could touch her and she had agreed.

With his thumb pressed against the palm of her hand and his other hand caressing her clitoris, he had brought her even more quickly to orgasm, holding her while her entire body trembled and she sobbed her relief.

Then he would give her a final good-night kiss and return to his bed. After a while she would hear him sigh before he began to murmur a prayer.

Every night she would awaken suddenly, realizing he was not in his bed. At some point he would always rise and sit on the balcony, smoking, the moon bright enough for him to read, staying there until dawn.

Just once, in Rhodes, she had risen and started to go to him. Then she turned and walked back to bed. That morning, while he used the bathroom, she jotted in her journal: "Jim can't really cope because he doesn't understand that he can still be a priest while recognizing he's a man. I can't do any more. He must find himself. It may come before this trip is over. It may take him longer to work it out. He knows a great deal about loving others, but he doesn't know how to love himself."

He had come out of the bathroom and asked her what she was writing. She had smiled at him. "Trying to put on paper something that can't easily be written down."

Riding up in the cable car to Thíra, Jim suddenly said that they should try to get a good night's rest in preparation for the long flight.

"I agree. An early dinner and then bed."

"Why don't we take separate rooms for tonight?"

She looked at him. "Is this what you want?"

"I think so, yes."

"All right. It's no big deal."

"Thank you, Victoria."

Over dinner, in a restaurant dug out of a cliff face, he was already back at work, talking about his caseload.

He said that he would write again to the Vatican to try to get accurate figures on the number of priests who had abandoned their vocations since Pope John Paul II was elected. He needed the information for a paper he wanted to publish, showing a clear correlation between the Pope's strong enforcement of celibacy and the claim of Corpus, a Chicago-based organization, that as many as five thousand American priests had left their calling. Most gave as an overwhelming reason the fact that they found the vow particularly impossible to follow together with all the other regulations the Pope continued to direct at his clergy.

He reminded her, too, that their first social engagement on their return would be as guests of Paul and Mario, a gay couple they were close to. Victoria had helped Paul to come to terms with his homosexuality and encouraged him to join Dignity, an association of Catholic homosexuals.

She realized that the holiday was already over for Jim; that he could not wait to return to where he felt most comfortable: living his life on his terms, seeing her when he wanted to, able to come and go as he liked, free of any of the pressures he had felt on vacation. She understood perfectly.

They kissed outside her room.

"I think it went fine, don't you?"

"Same here. I think it went the way we expected it would."

"Yes." He kissed her once more.

She sat on her bed, expanding her journal of these past days and nights, and concluded with the words:

". . . If Jim completely discovers himself he will be fine. He is in so many ways a magnificent person. All he has to do is find the man in that person, and it will all come together."

† † †

At nine o'clock on a Sunday morning, the dominant sound in the rectory was the tapping of Father Breslin's typewriter as he prepared his sermon. His fingers sped over the electric keyboard, muffling the gurgling of old-fashioned plumbing and the rattle of window frames shaken by another gust of wind blowing in from the sea. The presbytery was more than a century old, a rambling place, gray-walled and slate-roofed. It was built in the days when the parish priest shared it with a couple of curates and a housekeeper. Father Breslin lived alone here.

The house was too large for his needs. There were five bedrooms, a dining room, a living room, and a study. There was a large kitchen in which he ate all of his meals. He slept in the smallest bedroom, leaving the remainder of the house almost undisturbed. Nevertheless, it required a portion of each day to attend to domestic chores. The Archbishop's office had decided he must do without a live-in housekeeper: it was part of the general economy drive within the diocese. A woman from the village came twice a week to dust and do his laundry.

It was a little more than three years since he had first sat in this study, still gripped by that strange chilly feeling that had taken hold as he drove toward the village. That moment was now only a taped memory.

One of the first things he had done on arriving was to sit over his trusted recorder and admit that that feeling was really no more than a reminder to himself of his new and great responsibility: he, and he alone, had full authority for the spiritual welfare — and much else — of his people. The chilly feeling had lifted.

454

From the beginning they had wanted him to see them like that. *His people.* He now knew each one of them by their Christian names: the tradesmen in the High Street, the four publicans, the farmers with surnames that are part of the history of Ireland: Byrne, Kelly, O'Brien, O'Connor, Devlin, Duffy. He knew them as Maeve, Pat, Sean, Joe, Paddy, Biddy. To them he was *Father*, or more formally, *the P.P.*, their parish priest. He was pastor to them all; from old Ned Flynn, eighty-seven next birthday, to the latest Wilson baby, Louise, christened only a week ago. The tiny infant would be there this morning in her mother's arms, crying, no doubt, but he loved the sound of children. It reminded him there would always be a tomorrow. He had told little Louise's aunt Eileen that. She knew now she was dying and, just as he had expected, Eileen's faith was strong enough to sustain her in these closing weeks of her life. This morning, he would ask them all to remember her in their prayers. This afternoon he would visit her again in the hospital.

He continued to transfer his sermon notes onto paper. The new portable typewriter was a gift from his parishioners. They had also bought him a car and a television set.

A chance remark of Eileen's during his last visit had prompted the theme for this morning's sermon. He had sat, holding her hand, the way he had once held his mother's while she was dying and Eileen had whispered how glad she was to be a Catholic — because it gave her a priest with no ties, able to devote himself entirely to his parishioners.

He had never, by so much as a hint, told anybody there had been periods these past three years when the responsibility seemed too heavy a burden to bear. Then the depression, dark and silent and dense, had settled on him. The Bible, he knew, is filled with descriptions of its effects, and how it can strike with sudden savagery, leaving a person helpless and filled with a dread of having lost faith in God and in the future. Realizing, in a completely nonarrogant way, the gap he would leave in the lives of these people, whom he loved as his only family, if his ministry were to be continually interrupted by these debilitating spells, he had returned to the psychiatrist who had once before encouraged him to make the tape recordings and come to terms with his sexual fantasies.

He had hardly recognized him; the man was old and in semiretirement. He suggested Father Breslin should go into the hospital. He had explained his need to carry on. The doctor referred him to a colleague. Instead, Father Breslin had finally contacted a psychiatrist who had been working in Europe and was now a consultant in a Dublin hospital. He had explained that the depression was a chemical happening in the brain that could be

455

successfully treated by drugs to help restore the electrolytic imbalance. The tablets had brought the melancholia under control. At the same time, he had prayed quietly each night that God would spare him so that he could continue his ministry. He was emotionally stronger now than he had ever been. This was why he would preach a sermon about the difference between love and sex.

The church was packed, pew after pew filled with freshly scrubbed faces, country faces, round and shining. The men mostly wore blue or brown suits, the women frocks. This was a part of Ireland where the tradition of dressing up for Sunday Mass persisted.

Standing at the back were the latecomers, mostly young men and women who had slept until the last moment after a Saturday night on the beer. Sometimes he shook his head at their excesses, but he never allowed his own feelings about drink to be foisted on others.

This morning, he had run his eyes over his flock to see who had returned from a holiday or from a spell of illness; who was absent, gone perhaps to the hospital to have an operation or a baby. Mass was another way of keeping track of developments within the parish.

He stood at the lectern to one side of the altar, rearranging his typed notes. He had allowed himself ten minutes, remembering the guidance Father McKenna had given him about brevity.

Three months after he had come here, Miss Maddox had found the old priest dead in bed. A heart attack, the doctor had said. "Not so, Father," she had told him at the funeral. "He died of a broken heart. He loved you like a son. His life was empty without you. The new man's not the same. He's a cleric, not a priest." She herself had died a few months later. He had continued to remember them both in his prayers. He began his sermon.

"Today, I want to speak to you about human love and sexuality. The first thing I want to emphasize is that it is God's wish that men and women should be united with each other through love, and that real love can be truly experienced only through the joy of marriage. This, we all know, does not always fit in with so-called modern thinking."

He glanced at Paddy Nulty sitting with Marie O'Dwyer. They had been living together for two years and had told him they saw no point in getting married because their sense of commitment to each other was all that mattered. He had told them he could not fully accept this view, but they were still welcome in his church. Marie was seven months pregnant, and he had said that, when the time came, he would baptize their child and receive it fully into the church. Then he would make renewed efforts to persuade them to marry.

"There are those of you today who will ask what gives me the right to stand here and speak about love and sex. I can feel the questions forming. 'What does he know about either? How can he tell us? He's only a priest.' Perfectly fair. I am, indeed a priest. But I am also a man. Jesus, too, was a man. In choosing to follow my life in Christ, I have had to make sense of what He meant when He said: it is never going to be easy for anyone to live life the way it is meant to be lived.

"When I marry a couple I do so in the hope that they will live together until death. When I baptize their babies, I know what it is to see love. Marriage and parenthood are things I long ago chose to forgo. But I can share in them. So, yes, you may ask the questions and I can say in all humility that I can answer them.

"I know all about how easy it is to say, 'Oh, well, it doesn't matter. Just this once.' But it always matters. The smallest deviation from what Christ intended for each of us matters. That's the first thing to understand about love. You can't sell it short.

He paused. His next point was marked: "Sex is not love."

He told them the rules that must govern their sexual feelings were those based upon moral goodness and true Christian loving. Sex was not something to be treated casually; it was a powerful and potent force that could be handled only within the sanctity of Christian living. He was talking not only of marriage, but of the benefits accruing from a loving *relationship*.

He hoped Molly Doyle would take note. She sat in the front pew, a buxom widow, fifty and full of vitality. These past six months had been very trying. She had emerged as his parish Eve. He had finally taken her aside and explained that he was perfectly happy to have her visit the parochial house and to accept her invitations to a meal, but these occasions must be spaced out, otherwise the other ladies in the parish would feel he was neglecting them. They had both smiled: an understanding had been reached. The best way to deal with a problem, he knew, was to settle it before it developed.

"Human weakness is something we all experience. Each one of us. But God's grace is powerful and helps us overcome it and grow in His love. We should be as tolerant as Christ Himself was. . . ."

The closer he had tried to come to God, he had realized, the farther away he was from deserving of His love: the longer he traveled his road of realization, the more conscious he became of his sinfulness.

"No one except Jesus and His Mother has ever lived on this earth without sin. We all die with promises to be fulfilled. Healthy people are indeed those with a proper sexual awareness. But they must still look to God to see

457

the conditions under which love may be expressed. The Commandment 'thou shalt not commit adultery' is not a law against love. It is a law that protects love. It is not a law that restricts freedom. It is one that gives real freedom. Married love is shared, unique and untouchable. In that framework sex is a beautiful experience."

He gazed at the silent attentive faces. He had deliberately softened his voice.

"The only love that really works is the kind that can be given and expressed freely, without guilt. It is not something separate from you. It is part of each one of you. You are love. Love is you. There are not different kinds of love. Love is love. The only way it can vary is in how much of it you can give and how much you can receive. You can only do that in a truly loving and Christian relationship. There, and only there, can you see love working as a trusting and accepted reality. The sort of love I am talking about does not need guarantees. Guarantees are what sex is all about. Will something guarantee to be a turn-on? Will something guarantee to titillate and excite? Real love is the Christian joy of mutual sharing in a Christian life. If you do not already have it, leave here and search for it. But don't look for it in your pasts. Or in your futures. Love is something that exists in the moment. Love, in the end, is this moment, in each one of us."

He made the sign of the cross and walked slowly from the lectern to the altar.

CHAPTER 19

†

A State of Grace

Father Philippe lobbed the ball into the basket and again resisted the urge to rush forward to catch it before the ball dropped to the floor of the gymnasium in the Chemical Dependency Unit attached to the General. He managed to restrain himself more during this practice than at any other; it was a further indication of the values Dr. Stanway, the director of the unit, had instilled in him.

For the past two months, Father Philippe had seen the psychiatrist for an hour each day, six days a week. On Sundays, he spent hours in the hospital's chapel, praying and meditating. In between, a sense of self-realization had developed.

He now knew he would never be able totally to quell his passion. His impulsiveness, impatience, lack of forethought would always remain a part of his makeup. Dr. Stanway, at most, had tried to give him a new awareness of not only who he was, but how he could best live with himself. The analyst had stressed he must realize he would always be at risk. Yet, just as he had at last learned not always to lunge for the ball, so he would, he hoped, learn not to be impulsive in an altogether more critical area — his need for affection.

The doctor said he wanted him to develop the discipline *not* to grab the ball before it hit the ground because it would help to strengthen his self-control.

Before he had come to the gymnasium, Dr. Stanway had been frank at this farewell session. There was really no more to offer him. Indeed, to remain here any longer could be therapeutically contrabeneficial. The doctor explained that arrangements had been completed to send him to a Church-run counseling and rehabilitation center. There he would receive guidance about his return to ministering. Dr. Stanway had emphasized that when he did go back to work he must always remember he was one of those individuals with a certain personality pattern, the mechanics of which modern medicine still only dimly understood: psychologically, he was not well equipped to resist sexual impulses that the vast majority of the religious can cope with. This lack of protection for his sexuality did not make him a bad priest. Quite the opposite: it made him human and someone more easily able to identify with the failings of others. But, nevertheless, to survive in the priesthood it was essential that he constantly be aware of the absence of this element in his defense system.

Dr. Stanway had risen from his desk, shaken him by the hand, and led him to the door. "Go play ball, Father. It's still as good a therapy as any to understand what I mean. And remember the mantra I gave you. It synthesizes all I've been trying to say these past weeks."

He stood beneath the net and recited. "I know you. I created you. I have loved you from your mother's womb. You have fled — as you now know — from My love, but I love you nevertheless and not the less, however far you flee."

The words are from "Known," by Charles Robinson, and appeared in the *Duke Divinity School Review*. At first, Father Philippe had doubted whether reciting them, like so much else in the therapy, would work. Now he knew better. The words, like the workout, had helped him to see his dilemma in a clearer light.

Margot had insisted he must love her unconditionally. At the same time, the pull of his vocation demanded he remain completely faithful to his priestly vows. Once more he had been caught in emotional cross fire.

Just as his first analyst had set out to do, Dr. Stanway, by a radically different approach, showed him that self-realization required a continuous creative tension. In the beginning, uncertainty plagued every step. But he recited the lengthy mantra a portion at a time; the analyst advised that whenever he felt he had been deserted, he should do so. The words had been written by another priest who imagined what God would say if they met. They fitted perfectly what Father Philippe would like the Creator to say to him and he now quoted them continuously.

"It is I who sustains your very power and I will never finally let you go. I accept you as you are. You are forgiven. I know all your sufferings. I have always known them."

In the hour between six and seven each evening, he had come to the gymnasium, not only to get the necessary exercise Dr. Stanway said his body needed after the drug abuses to which it had been subjected; but also, by the simple discipline of the workouts, to see a way out of the cottony mush that had surrounded much of his thinking. Controlling his impulse to catch the ball was, in its own small way, a further step toward enabling the cobwebbed world of his unconsciousness to be rewoven into a more acceptable support system for his badly torn consciousness. He recited another portion of the mantra.

"Far beyond your understanding, when you suffer, I suffer. I also know all the little tricks by which you try to hide the ugliness you have made of your life for yourself and others. But you are beautiful. You are beautiful more deeply within than you can see."

Meditating on the words, he turned and walked back to the foul line, tossing the ball from one hand to the other. From the beginning, the analyst had stressed that he was not mentally ill. Confused, certainly; suffering, absolutely. Anxious, fearful, and hurting, no doubt. But not mentally ill. Terming his condition an illness was no more than a convenient label attached by all those other doctors he had seen in the past eighteen months before coming to the CDU.

They had prescribed an arsenal of pills: to make him sleep, to stop him scratching, to keep him calm, to give him energy, to take away his stomach pains, to remove his headaches. But not one tablet had eased that deep inner core of hurting, so agonizing it could make him cry and tremble. These past two months had been aimed at making him see that living with the pain was the only way to achieve maturity. He uttered a further portion.

"You are beautiful because you, yourself, in the unique person that only you are, reflect already something of the beauty of My holiness in a way which will never end. You are beautiful also because I, and I alone, see the beauty you shall become."

The time in the unit had passed in a blur of sudden insights, moments when the truth hurt so much he had wished he could con himself into believing he could resume a double life: shredding himself between the demands of Mother Church and his craving for Margot.

He was honest enough to admit he still missed her and, he hoped, strong enough to live without her. Margot, for all her loving, had been part of a myth. She was wrong to say a priest could also be a man. A priest must always be a priest. He believed he had once more located enough self-discipline to live a life exclusively in Christ, never again to allow that impulse, his driving sexual force, to get the better of him.

Dr. Stanway had kept on saying there was no drug available to cure soul-pain; that he must invent his own, finding the raw ingredients in his head and mixing them together in the laboratory of his mind. If he succeeded, Dr. Stanway had suggested a brand name: *Father Philippe's Growing-up Pill.*

He impetuously lobbed the ball over his shoulder into the net and was unable to check himself from whirling around and rushing to catch it. He groaned aloud as he returned to the foul line.

Dr. Stanway had said that accepting failure was a step toward not repeating it. Self-discipline was a prerequisite for self-love. Without that kind of love he would have no real chance in life; he would be reduced to chasing fleeting moments of pleasure, which would never provide lasting satisfaction.

Margot.

He remembered how she used to croon the John Denver hit "Love Is Everywhere," another of those ballads about life being perfect. It required the acceptance of only one rule: "Come and play the game with me." That was typical of Margot. From the very beginning she had insisted he must play the game by her rules: that he could still be her priest as well as her lover. He didn't blame her. But he also no longer blamed himself.

He began to bounce the ball expertly, thinking how she still loved him, in spite of everything he had done. He wished she didn't. He started to dribble, feinting around imaginary opponents, moving swiftly across the floor, hands and legs moving in perfect unison, his whole body committed — the way it had once been to Margot.

Those past eighteen months had been absorbed with the heady sensations her love had evoked: the way she would look at him, the sensuous contact of her hands, the revelation of her nakedness, which made him draw his breath. Her voice and laugh were only two of a succession of proofs she had given him of her love: each one had its own special bouquet, heady enough for him to have become so helpless he forgot completely he was a priest. He reached the end of his run, the ball at his feet, hands on knees, breathing deeply, remembering other words.

"She is love — with a capital L. She is a marvelous listener, a great conversationalist, a snappy dresser. She is caring, she is certain and carefree. She is LOVE."

He had written that when the affair was only weeks old; before the resultant confusion and inner loneliness set in; before he came to realize that Mother Church, like any dominant mother, was not prepared to give up a son so easily.

In the hospital library he had come across the work of the poet Anne Bradstreet, who had written to her husband, *If ever two were one, then surely we*. He felt that way again about the Church: she absolutely loved him, he absolutely loved her: her rituals, her all-embracing power, her certainty, her pledge of eternal life. He was certain that together they would again voyage forth on new and significant journeys. Through the Church he would once more help people; through Her, God would once more help him. No human relationship could offer that much. Margot, for all her whispered magical words, had not been able to establish such a meaningful relationship as he felt he once had with the Mother of all Churches. He had behaved like a teenager over Margot. That silent, reproachful voice of Mother Church said Margot was no different from Simone. That he would spend the rest of his life unsuccessfully trying to find love outside the Church, but in her bosom he had a love no mortal woman could give.

Dr. Stanway explained that along with his powerful and unpredictable sexual impulse was an equally strong, good joy he gave and derived from his ministry. A few days ago, at the end of another session, the psychiatrist had said that if ever a man was meant to be a priest, he was.

They had spent the entire hour discussing the positive values of celibacy. The analyst had urged, and he had enthusiastically agreed, that celibacy is both an ideal and a challenge. The important thing to understand was that he would never be alone. That behind Mother Church was Jesus Himself. Both His Church and He based their call, *Come, follow Me*, on a very exciting and exclusive concept: to be a celibate is the closest any man can come to living the fullest possible life in Christ, which in the end was what all worthwhile mortal life was about. He had always known this. That was why he had begun silently to question his behavior shortly after Margot started their affair. That was why his itching had returned, and with it, the awesome nightmare; where before Simone had had a starring role in his horrendous dream, it was now Margot who had taken over the part.

He completed the mantra and started another run, zigzagging, shooting the ball toward the backboard, and leaping to catch the rebound.

Through one of the windows he could see the block housing the MICU, where Ma Schiff's daughter had died. Four days after he buried her, he had made love to Margot for the first time.

He hurled the ball against a wall, allowing it to rebound and slam into his midriff, making him gasp, just as he had done when he finally realized his ministry was crumbling around him.

Within weeks of the affair's start, the pain was outwardly visible; his body torn in a hundred places by his fingernails. Those were the times he regretted most of all what he had done and wished he had never met her, the moments when he hated Margot, believing it was her fault entirely that he had pursued her in an erotic, amorous delirium.

He held the ball close to his body for a moment and began once more to repeat the mantra.

He realized now that his road back to holiness had come about through challenging everything about Margot's role in his life. The more he had done so, the more clearly he saw that she had capitalized on the fact that, like many priests, he had not developed any distinctive personal life. Its absence for most was not as critical as it had been for him.

On the nights they had not slept together, he had lain in the darkness of his bedroom, twisting and turning, in spite of medication, his mind filled with a longing for her. Unable to sleep, he would go down to the chapel and kneel on the priest's prie-dieu near the sanctuary lamp as if saying Hail Marys there would somehow be more beneficial. His gaze would wander from the immortal light toward the statue of Our Lady; contemplating the figurine, he would forget Her sanctity and see in Her place only the woman he desired. He would reach out and touch the cold marble folds of the Madonna's robes and in the limitlessness of his imagination would yearn anew for Margot.

He had not dared to acknowledge this behavior when he went to confession. Usually he did so at St. Anthony's, the church across the street from the chancellery. More often than not, it would be the chancellor himself who had heard his contrition. He began to bounce the ball, remembering the reason why he had stopped going there.

✝

After leaving the church one evening, he had, on impulse, sat in his car farther up the street. The chancellor emerged from the sacristy and drove off. He followed. He knew where the monsignor was going: to see Susie Henly. He had heard the gossip about his superior and Susie, widowed at thirty and ten years later still a striking woman. The talk started after a lay secretary working late one evening had gone into the chancellor's office, thinking he had already left, and had not knocked. She found the monsignor talking to Susie on the telephone and masturbating. The girl had fled and resigned next day. The story spread that he regularly called Susie in order to gratify himself when he couldn't drop by to see her.

Father Philippe had watched the monsignor park outside Susie's house. He had driven over to Margot and told her what he had seen. She had laughed softly and said Susie told a lot of people that the chancellor regularly made love to her on the living-room couch.

He had looked at her seriously. "We're all the same. No matter how important we get, we're all the same."

Kissing him and nibbling at his ear, Margot had murmured, how could Mother Church then judge him? That night the intensity of their lovemaking reached a new high.

†

He hurled the ball from him and walked to the locker room, the certainty that she still loved him purling through his mind.

Dan was there, naked, his black skin glistening after a shower. The needle marks on his arms were clearly visible. Even after years of drug taking, he was still magnificently built, without an ounce of fat. His shaven head gave him a skull-like appearance. Like many physically powerful men, Dan was gentle. Behind his back the staff called him the Fairy Hulk.

From the beginning, Father Philippe found Dan had an intuitive way of trimming away all nonessentials. Some patients and staff misunderstood this and thought he was morose and monosyllabic; a dumb jock who liked nothing better than to punch a bag.

He knew better. Dan had shown him that friendship with a homosexual, one that was not based on any physical need, as it had been with Walter, was an important element in any person's adult life.

On the night Father Philippe entered the CDU, Dan came into his room, shy, yet gently forward, as if their being patients in a mental institution should not faze either of them. He had wanted to hug Dan for his offer of sympathy and support. Dan said he shouldn't: they'd tag him as another

gay. He'd explained that some of the staff, in spite of their supposed insights, didn't like homosexuals, adding that what they feared and resented
was their own homosexuality.

He had looked at Dan and said that sounded very Freudian. Dan said it
was Henri Nouwen who had understood that experiencing homosexual
feelings at a certain time of life, or in a temporary fashion, is a perfectly
normal thing; far more dangerous than the experience are the anxiety and
fear it generates. Many men viewed the presence of a homosexual dimension in their personalities as catastrophic. It was not its presence, Dan had
said, that was unhealthy, but the discomfort and self-rejection it generated.

Since then, he had regarded Dan as someone he could talk to.

"How you shooting them?"

"Bull's-eye each time."

"You stick around and you'll make the team."

He started to undress as Dan vigorously toweled himself. Dan was the
first man he had ever felt comfortable with when taking his clothes off.
They had spoken about this when Dan described the panic gays generate
in many men, and how hospitals, like prisons, could strengthen the homosexual dimension of any personality.

They had discussed how, after the faint promise that Pope Paul VI held
out, his successor had reverted to the traditional Catholic view that homosexuality could never be morally acceptable; that there was no possibility
of Rome's accepting, for instance, the recommendation of the Catholic
Theological Society of America that a homosexual engaging in homosexual
acts in good conscience had the same rights to the sacraments as a married
couple practicing Church-approved birth control.

It was the first and only time they had disagreed. Dan had called the
Pope the new Torquemada of the Tiber, trying to drive the Church into a
Procrustean bed modeled after the conservative Polish Church. Father
Philippe had found himself defending the Pope, saying it was wrong to see
him only as an obscurantist, or an unfeeling traditionalist. Afterward, he
had realized how much his own attitude had changed under the influence
of Dr. Stanway.

Dan stood before the shower stall.

Finally, Father Philippe was able to say it. "I'm going to do it, Dan. I
really am."

He had discussed his future plans with Dan, who had urged him to consider most carefully what he was proposing to do. He had said that he
knew he had not completely mastered self-control, but it was equally true

that he had a better chance than before of surviving as a priest. He had received a number of messages from his unconsciousness, giving him new insights into himself, Margot, and the world at large. This awareness was no longer an unwelcome intruder, but a presence totally relevant to his wish once more to lead a celibate life.

"You really thought this through?"

"All day. Nothing else but."

Dan nodded. "Well, you ain't some dumb priest." Father Philippe turned on the shower.

He believed, in full honesty, that he was no longer a house divided within himself. He was willing to admit he must really try again. The next step would be to talk to Margot. These past weeks, in all their telephone conversations, she had not hidden her hope he would decide in her favor. Part of him still wanted to do so. He recognized that — and Dr. Stanway had said it was good he did: he should see it as a sign of his essential humanity. But it was also an indication that he recognized a greater commitment: that the larger part of him knew he must return to be a priest.

"It's the only way, Dan."

"Well . . . it's your life."

Dan walked out of the locker room.

Father Philippe adjusted the temperature control and began to sing. " 'I once was lost, but now am found, was blind, but now I see.' " It was Father Nolan's favorite song, one he sang every morning when he arose.

✝

The words of "Amazing Grace" often had come to him with a sense of irony on those nights when he had walked excitedly up and down Margot's living room, leveling accusations against the Church's demands for celibacy. Why had it forbidden its priests the most natural of satisfactions? How could the Pope really believe that from the moment an old bishop had put his hands on his head — and he remembered how he'd pantomimed his ordination — his hot blood would suddenly run cold? It was dishonest — trying to make people live an impossible life. She had sat and said nothing, her eyes never leaving him, watchful, concentrating, not wanting to interrupt, letting him talk.

Who had invented celibacy? A group of decrepit cardinals shuffling about their monasteries, with about as much sexual drive as eunuchs. When they had convened in Elvira and Nicaea in the fourth century, what had they known about the demands of *his* body sixteen centuries later?

Afterward, Margot had said, her voice calm and certain, that she didn't know what had happened at Elvira or Nicaea, but she did know what was going to happen to him right then.

She had led him into the bedroom.

✝

He turned the shower to cold, letting the stinging water massage his skin. The scratch marks had almost healed; the worst ones, deep and lacerating, had been around his abdomen. From early on in their affair, he had repeatedly torn at his thighs, drawing blood, which dried on his genitalia.

Margot had always wiped him clean and dusted him with medicated powder. For a few nights, until the wounds began to heal, they did not make love, just lay on her bed, holding each other. She had always been comforting, ready to give of herself in any way he wished. When he pretended he wanted to sleep, she had curled up, her back to him. He would wait until her breathing steadied and remain awake, remembering the three evils of the soul — women, the Devil, and the flesh.

Then he began once more to scratch steadily. He had felt the stickiness of his blood. Margot had awakened and gone to the bathroom, returning with a cloth soaked in cold water, and after she cleaned him, she held him in her arms, rocking him gently back and forth. Lulled by the motion, he had been able to concentrate totally on the new thought that came into his head. She was, in a way, his devil, his temptress, his downfall. While he could not do what the saints of old had done, plunging into the burning sands of the desert or seeking the company of wild beasts, he could promise he would never return to her bed. He made such a vow many times.

When he had admitted this, Dr. Stanway had said the incessant tearing at himself and his thoughts about Margot had been his unconsciousness warning about the perils of not being in a state of grace. Once more the doctor had, as he had done on many occasions, explained that while as a man there was nothing intrinsically wrong in his affair with Margot, as a priest it went to the very core of betraying his calling. No matter how much he had tried to justify it, he knew he had mocked Christ's unequivocal statement, *Many are called but few are chosen.* He had been one of those who had been chosen to respond to His call. His physical pain had been a way of reminding himself of his fall from grace. Once he had chosen to seek back that grace, by removing himself from Margot, the wounds had began to heal.

Switching off the shower, letting the water drop from him, he remembered how on each occasion he had been driven to justify his right to love her by turning to ancient texts.

They had been filled with interpretative comfort. Those first Christian martyrs, the bedrock from which the Church had risen, had married one another in the Roman arenas to the acclamation of the crowds before the lions tore them asunder. Even Jesus had not lived continuously in His impossible saintliness. While indeed He had been unsparing and unyielding in the temple and the streets of the City of David, He had in Bethany created His own haven. There, beneath the shade of the trees in the garden of his friend Lazarus, Jesus had Himself put His hand on the head of Mary, the woman He loved, who was sitting at His feet.

Where, in the end, he had asked himself, was the difference? He was guilty of no more than a breach of outmoded Canon Law. In the Gospels, Jesus never mentions celibacy; the only reference to it, in explicit terms, is Paul's mere four lines. Those, he had argued, could be theologically challenged. Where was his sin?

It would outrage the Bishop and the Pope if they knew he was sleeping with Margot. But God, surely, would not be angry: after all, priests in other Christian denominations were allowed to have full sexual lives.

Stepping out of the stall and drying himself, he remembered, too, how each time these arguments had been sufficiently powerful to persuade him to return to Margot, convinced there was nothing wrong in wanting her love, her kisses, and her body. Yet all the time, he now realized, dressing, he had been deluding himself. He had committed the greatest sin a Catholic priest could commit: he had blasphemed against the sacred mystery of the Blessed Sacrament.

When he had revealed that much, Dr. Stanway had once more explained the merits of a celibate life. He made no bones about it: it was an elitist way of living. Very few, in the end, could measure up to the challenge. It required heroic qualities to live it day by day in a world where moral values were increasingly under attack. But those words were the key: *day by day.* That was the only way to remain in the Church's grace: to seek it consciously every day, every hour, and, if need be, every minute. That way of life, and only that, was the road back to grace. That, and no less, was what Mother Church demanded.

He was certain the realization was already in his mind when he spent an entire evening in his study, on the first anniversary of the affair, composing a letter — sixteen pages in all — pleading with her to understand why he could not see her anymore. He had never posted it. Instead, he had returned to Margot's bed.

He had let her control all the aspects of their relationship: they must never be seen alone together in public; at Sunday Mass they would not betray their intimacy by so much as a glance. He now understood why she had insisted on such conditions: Dr. Stanway had said it was almost certainly based on her own fear that if she did not control the relationship, she would lose him. She had completely overwhelmed him, and when it became too much he had run: to doctors for pills; to priests who were strangers, seeking absolution. Each time Margot had drawn him back.

The remarkable part, Dr. Stanway had commented, was that in spite of everything, he had still managed to perform his priestly duties and obligations. Though that was highly creditable, it had, perversely, encouraged him to believe he could have the best of both worlds. The doctor, not for the first time, had surprised him by quoting, in faultless Latin, the dictum of Saint Augustine: "*Dilige et quod vis fac* — be diligent, and do whatever you want." Dr. Stanway said that while indeed that was true, the only way it could have worked in his case would have been to add another quotation: "O Lord, I fear I am not worthy of your trust." The therapist had suggested he should henceforth combine both statements, using them as a reminder that the only way to remain in grace was never to misuse what God had intended; he must always remember He had called him for a very special purpose. In accepting that, he must also accept that he would do his utmost to resist the human tug of his body.

†

One night, after making love, he had waited: his hands locked in his armpits, his eyes nailed to the bedside clock, counting the minutes until he could rise without upsetting her and return to the rectory. The drive across the city in the pre-dawn calmed him enough at least to stop grinding his teeth before he reached the parish house.

He had slipped through the front door to find Father Nolan sitting on the stairs leading to his apartment, a haunted and embarrassed look on his face. He said he did not wish to pry, but this was the third night that week he had been out until this hour; the previous week it had been four nights and the same the week before that. The older priest had asked what was going on.

Without mentioning her name, he had said there was a woman. Father Nolan had risen slowly and stood dumbfounded. He had remained like that for some minutes. Then, sensing he must do something, he had asked if he had tried to pray this away.

He told him he had.

Father Nolan asked if they could pray together, and they had knelt side by side before the altar for almost an hour.

For two nights, he managed to stay away from Margot. On the third, the desire to make love to her had overcome everything else. He had driven from the rectory at dusk and had once more returned in the early hours.

Father Nolan had been waiting. He had uttered just one word: "Why?" They had stood together in embarrassed silence and he had felt the other priest's immense sadness. Next day Father Nolan had given him the news. The chancellor had booked him a bed in the CDU. The Bishop wanted him to know he was praying for him, as they all were. He had felt an overwhelming relief. Mother Church had once more reached out to recover him.

He had entered the unit without telling Margot. In their first session he had revealed her existence to Dr. Stanway. The doctor told Philippe to call her and say where he was, inviting him to use his own telephone. Dr. Stanway had sat listening while Margot pleaded with him to let her visit, and to his firm refusal to allow her. She had finally burst into tears and hung up. The therapist suggested he should wait a few days before calling again; next time he should once more try to explain he was in the hospital because he wanted to remain a good priest, one in a state of grace.

Since then they had spoken frequently on the telephone. Each time Margot had begged to see him; each time he had felt more able to refuse her request. Sometimes she had hung up while he was trying to explain his feelings. He hoped she would not cut him off when he called her now to tell her why he had reached an irrevocable decision.

✝

He walked out of the locker room and past the occupational therapy area, where as part of his rehabilitation he had learned to work in ceramics. He continued down a hall known as Shrink Alley, where the doctors had their offices. He pushed open fire doors and entered a corridor. Here were separate rooms for fifty patients, each colored the same pale green, each with a mirror glazed into the wall and beneath it a washbasin. There had been a similarity about his seminaries.

The bank of pay phones was in a recess beside the nurses' station. He chose the one farthest away and dialed.

He could see now what Dr. Stanway meant. He *had* used sex as a refuge.

Yet his yearning for tender feelings and affection was not based solely on sexual desire, but on a deep-seated longing for an emotional, fondling relationship such as he had never enjoyed as a child with his mother. Margot, like Simone, had satisfied not only this aspect of his sexuality, but had also fulfilled his powerful, instinctive need for female companionship, a longing that had been there from that time, when still a baby, he had experienced what Dr. Stanway called *psychologic separation* from his mother. Her rejection of him, and later her condemnation of his father, especially over their sex life, had created in him *psychic parturition*, a deep-seated anxiety, acquisitiveness, and aggressiveness. While perversely these had helped to make him a good priest — he had shown himself to be concerned, protective, and sheltering, strong-willed and outspoken, on behalf of his parishioners — he had driven himself to seek relief from all those subconscious memories of a loveless childhood. But, concluded the doctors, his distress over what he had done with Margot was even greater than that over the original denial of affection from his mother.

Margot answered the telephone.

" 'Lo."

"It's me."

"Hi, Phil! How are you?"

"Much better."

He hesitated.

"Margot. I have to talk to you . . ."

He felt an inarticulate dread.

"Go ahead."

"I'm sorry about the last time. I guess, well, I was still coming off drugs and I was jumpy."

"That's all right, Phil."

Dr. Stanway had said Margot tried to instill her own very wrong values in him.

"Phil, you should get out of there."

"I'm going to, Margot. I've made a decision. I've thought it all through. I've spent the whole day thinking about it . . ."

"A day? That's not a lot of thinking time."

He had come to see that Dr. Stanway was right: Margot had set out to weaken, rival, question, and finally slight his own ideals by offering her own substitutes. The doctor had called her behavior *paganlike indulgence*: sleeping with a priest.

"Margot . . . could you pack up my things and have your mother drop them off here?"

DECISIONS

In one of Margot's bedroom closets were his sports jackets and pants, some shirts and underwear. He'd brought them over from the rectory in the first month of their affair.

The silence stretched.

"Is this why you've called? For your clothes?"

"Margot, please don't get mad at me . . ."

Dr. Stanway had explored the idea that he had seen all the women in his life as *Goddesses*, punishers and providers. Beginning with his mother, they had shown themselves capable of taking personal offense and revenging themselves on him.

"I'm not mad at you."

A new silence.

"Could you get your mother to bring them over?"

Fern, he was certain, was the only one in the family who knew the full extent of their affair. From the beginning, she had tacitly approved. She had bought his ticket for a secret holiday in the Bahamas with Margot only a month after they had met; she had slipped him an envelope filled with dollar bills to use as spending money; she had spoken to them daily in their shared hotel room; and he was certain she had only pretended to be shocked when Margot told her they needed only one of its double beds.

It was Fern who reminded them to travel back separately; for good measure, Margot had disguised herself behind California-sized sunglasses and a huge beach hat. Next morning, Fern had joined him on the jogging track and said she had come to see him more as a son than as a priest. He had come to think of her as the most remarkably open-minded mother he had ever known.

"I could bring them over."

"I don't think that would be a good idea."

"Okay. I'll ask Mother to drop them off. You want your toothbrush and your razor?"

"No, dump them. I've got new ones."

He had left the toiletries on the shelf below the mirror in her bathroom. He had always been careful to remove any trace of their lovemaking before returning to the rectory.

Dr. Stanway had discussed the thought that Margot, aided and abetted by her mother, had seduced him.

"Margot, are you there?"

473

"I'm here."

"Did you hear what I said?"

"What I hear is a small and frightened voice crying for help."

Her voice sounded as if she was dying and crying inside.

"You hear wrong, Margot. I'm fine. That's why I called. I want you to know I'm fine and I've made up my mind . . ."

Dr. Stanway had said that he must see the relationship with Margot as no more than a substitute for the psychological loss of his mother. The analyst had looked across the desk and said he should regard himself as being fortunate to have been called into the priesthood. The Church offered him insulation from the hunger that lack of maternal affection had created.

Margot's voice was more questioning.

"What have you decided?"

The psychiatrist had suggested he should see himself as her sacrificial victim. Instead of being a personal representative of God on earth, dying for his parishioners, and thus highly honored, he had become an outcast to himself. In appeasing his own needs, he had become what Dr. Stanway had called a *sin offering*. But, thankfully for him, the Church understood about his guilt.

"Margot, I'm leaving in the morning. He's letting me out."

"Phil, that's terrific."

"I'm going to a sort of halfway house, out of state."

"Do you have to go?"

She could not contain her disappointment.

"I don't have to, but I want to. That's the point. I really want to try this time."

"Phil, you've said all this before. Every time you've called you've said it. Then changed your mind. You seem to be always shifting your center of emotional gravity —"

"You're beginning to sound like Dr. Stanway."

Her pain gave way to a sudden surge of anger. "I'm not surprised. Do you know what you sound like every time you call? Like a goddamn shrink! When you're not telling me what they're doing to you and what you feel, you tell me what everybody else is feeling. It's the only conversation we seem to have."

He kept his voice even. "I'd hoped I'd sounded like a priest."

He could hear her sobbing. After each call, she had told him she wept, not able to understand why he had done this, turned inward, away from the world, away from her.

"Goddamn! Each time you call up and say 'I'm a priest!' There has to be a limit."

He had told Dr. Stanway that Margot had said that Catholicism is a neurosis, the last harbor for primitive and unreal thinking. The analyst had smiled bleakly and said that the trouble with women like Margot was that facts which did not fit into their scheme of things are pushed aside. So many good priests had found that out, to their cost.

Her voice was suddenly fierce. He could imagine her gripping the phone until her knuckles were white, tears rolling down her cheeks.

"How many times do you think I've worried myself sick because you've suddenly taken off and I haven't known where you were? Then you call up and say, 'It's all off because I'm a priest.'"

"I had to get away. I thought you understood."

"Understood? What do you think this past year has been about, except trying to understand and help? I love you. Don't you understand? I love you. I love you! Can you understand *that?*"

Dr. Stanway had added, his smile gone, that one of the problems priests find in fending off women who pursue them is that they always present themselves as a beguiling solution to what they claim is the most disturbing element of religious life, the Church's insistence on celibacy.

Margot was pleading once more. "Why are you doing this? Why don't you come here? I'll come and pick you up. Let me drive over. You could be out of there in an hour . . ."

Earlier, when he had been preparing himself, he had believed it would be a matter of calm explanation, self-control, and understanding. She would accept why he had to return to his ministry. Instead, she was gouging into his resolve.

"It's the goddamn dream, isn't it? It really spooked you. Well, think how I feel! That the man I love thinks I want to chop off his pecker because that's the punishment the Pope has ordered! Think how I feel about that!"

"Margot —"

"You think it's nice to know you're part of a nightmare like that? Do you?"

He had told her that over the past year he had once more almost nightly faced in his mind a tribunal presided over by the Pope. The proceedings had always been in an unfamiliar language. The punishment had always been the same: castration.

Her cracking voice revealed the sensitivity he had always found so appealing.

"My mother will help. She wants to. We can find a good analyst. Dr. Stanway's a Catholic. You don't need a doctor with a built-in bias toward the Church!"

"He's not biased."

"The hell he isn't. His funding comes from the Church!"

"That doesn't make him biased."

There was sudden silence.

The psychiatrist had suggested he should see the Crucifixion as an act of *unconditional forgiving*. If he could regard his affair with Margot as his own crucifixion, then he would realize that the Church was anxious only to show him a similar forgiveness. All it wanted was to see him safely returned to his calling.

"Margot, life isn't over."

"Is that all you can say?"

"If you really love me, Margot, let me go. Please."

"Is this what you really want?"

The tension and anger had flown out. Her voice was suddenly resigned.

"Yes. Margot . . . look . . ."

"Hang up. Just leave me alone."

He whispered into the mouthpiece. "Take care, Margot." It took him a moment to realize she had already replaced her receiver.

He walked away from the telephone, murmuring the mantra.

Father Philippe intoned the words of the promise and fulfillment of the Holy Eucharist. The church was small and cold in the first chill of another winter. He had seen it in the faces of his temporary flock, the hundred or so mostly elderly people bowed before him. He had said Mass for them every morning for five weeks. Permission for him to do so had been granted by the Bishop.

It had come after two months in the Church-run counseling center. A priest therapist, Father John, had until then spent most of their time together assessing Father Philippe's readiness to return to a full life in religion. They had explored every aspect of his ministry. Father John had spoken about the need to recognize that spiritual health came only through suffering, in seeing Jesus as the ever-availing victim.

Father Philippe reminded the congregation of the timeless purpose of their presence.

" '*He who eats my flesh and drinks my blood,*' Christ promised, '*lives in me and I live in him. As I, who am sent by the living Father, myself draw*

life from the Father, so whoever eats me will draw life from me. This is
the bread come down from Heaven; not like the bread our ancestors ate:
they are dead, but anyone who eats this bread will live forever.' "

One by one they came forward to receive the Host. He felt in himself a
single-minded devotion to his divine calling. More than ever this past
month, he had felt, through his daily references to the Church's teachings,
that the privilege of being a priest was one of the greatest gifts given to
man, one that even the angels did not possess. Standing here at the sanctuary rail he was *Alter Christus*, Another Christ. His every word and action this morning had once more been performed in the full, sublime, and
majestic knowledge that he was again God's direct instrument.

As he returned the sacred vessels to the tabernacle, he knew too, that
once more he had been given the power to bridge heaven and earth.
Through him, each member of this congregation had, for the moment at
least, understood again the meaning of adoration and the need to yearn for
their eternal home. For them he was not only the glory, but the *true* power.

That, he had told Father Nolan on the telephone last night, was why he
was ready to come back to St. Mark's. He said he had finally worked out
who he was and what he wanted. Father Nolan had said how glad, how
very glad he was to hear that, and he wanted him to know how much he
and his parishioners were looking forward to having him back. Father
Nolan had added that the past was over: it would never be mentioned again
by him.

For fourteen days, he drove himself relentlessly. He had forgotten how
demanding a parish St. Mark's was. In between his regular church duties
there were hospital calls, house visits, and school meetings. There had been
four funerals, three weddings, and two baptisms.

Father Nolan's welcome had been touching; he had put flowers in the
apartment and stocked the refrigerator. A number of people called at the
rectory to welcome him back. Nobody mentioned his spell in the hospital.
He had been grateful they were considerate enough not to pry.

Fern jogged past every morning, and when she saw him standing at his
study window she waved. He had, on that first morning, raised his hand
and continued talking to Harry Turner. The haberdasher had discovered
his eldest son was on drugs. Father Philippe had arranged for the youth to
see Dr. Stanway.

He had spoken to the analyst on the phone a few days after he returned
to the rectory and told him he was completely at peace with himself. Dr.

Stanway asked if he was still practicing with the basketball. He confessed he had not found the time. What about the mantra? Again, he had pleaded pressure of work had made him forget to say it as often as he would have liked. The psychiatrist had grunted and told him to hang in there.

Next day, Fern passed and waved again. This time she had beckoned him down. He had spoken to her at the door of the rectory. She kissed him on the cheek and said how delighted she was to see him around. Keeping his tone casual, he had asked about Margot. Her mother said she was fine. Neither had explored the matter further, and after a few more minutes of small talk, Fern returned to her laps. Before doing so, she had addressed him formally. "See you around, Father."

The fourteenth day began like the others. After celebrating Mass, he met Father Nolan to discuss the day's schedule. Father Nolan would make five hospital calls and four to parishioners ill at home. Father Philippe would handle the seven remaining visits, including allowing an hour at the hospital bedside of Perry Turner. He would also drive out to see Karl Cummings on Forest Avenue and be back in time for duty in the Confession Room.

Father Nolan tapped his list. "Why don't you take Ma Schiff?"

"Sure. How is she?"

Father Nolan gave a small-boy smile. "You go see."

Driving into the ghetto, he noticed there was an even greater despair about the people not present six months ago. Unemployment was higher and so was resentment. He could sense it in the sullen black faces. He would, he decided, talk to Father Nolan; between them they must find more ways to help these underprivileged people.

He did not immediately recognize Ma Schiff's house. The mass of creeper, which had seemed to have a life of its own, writhing and devouring the porch and walls, had gone. In its place the wood was a gleaming, freshly painted white; the front door a dark green.

When she opened it, the change in Ma Schiff herself was even more striking. She was no longer a gross hulk. She must, he guessed, be at least sixty pounds lighter and she certainly looked twenty years younger. Even her goiter seemed to have shrunk. She greeted him warmly and ushered him inside, seating him in a new armchair.

Father Nolan, she said shyly, had arranged it all. Harry Clampit had sent his men over to repaint. Pete Power let her have the furnishings and carpets on extended credit.

She took his hands and led him into the room where her daughter had lain. It had also been repainted and carpeted. Before the window was an artist's easel and palette.

"I do landscapes."

For all their rawness, there was a vital quality about the paintings leaning against the wall. Through her pictures she was saying she was prepared to acknowledge herself as the sole author of her behavior, and no longer lived her life as a subperson.

He suddenly remembered all those years ago, sitting in the bookshop with Walter, discussing the idea that a truly personal life is not secondhand or a reflection; its originality is in its sincerity.

"This is wonderful, Mrs. Schiff. This is really wonderful."

She stood before him, once more holding his hands. "I owe it to my girl. I really owe her that much."

Father Philippe shook his head. "You owe yourself."

In a society that so often discouraged individual initiative and encouraged passivity, the change in Ma Schiff offered an important reminder: she had known how to search out her own truth. Yet what had happened to her, he thought, was also powerful evidence that Christian living is not a matter of human achievement, but fundamentally a question of divine grace. Without it nothing can be achieved.

Three hours later, two more house visits done, he was at the bedside of Perry Turner. He held out a box of tissues. The youth's swollen eyes and nose were dripping; his face sallow and sweating.

"If you want to cry, that's okay. Tears are good for all of us."

The boy took some tissues.

His room in the CDU was only a few doors away from the one Father Philippe had himself occupied.

"Did my dad send you?"

"No. Nobody sent me. I came because I want to try to help you."

Perry trembled uncontrollably. "My dad doesn't understand." Still in the early stages of withdrawal, he was racked by another spasm.

"I think he does, Perry. I know he wants you to live."

Broken, dry sobbing came from Perry. The boy so tragically typified the age of increasing confusion, an era where the line of least resistance was to have no standards at all.

"May I sit down?"

The boy nodded between his pains. Father Philippe sat on the chair. "Do you want to talk about it?"

Perry shook his head. "I want to die. I feel I want to die."

"You feel like that now. But tomorrow you'll feel a little stronger. And a little more the day after that. It'll get a little easier each day."

Another spasm shook the boy's body. "I'm scared, Father. I'm scared."

Father Philippe sat on the edge of the bed. "Would you like me to hold you?"

Perry nodded, tears streaming down his face. Father Philippe cradled him in his arms, letting the boy bury his head against his shirt.

"I can't take any more. I can't. It's killing me. I need a fix. Christ, I need a fix. It's killing me."

Not only had material values changed — there was a report on the morning news that the cost of packaging now added another 40 percent to the price of food — but moral values even more. The same news show reported that thirty years ago there had not been a known teenage drug addict in the state; now there were tens of thousands.

The effects of addiction were only too clear in this hospital cot with its demoralized and frightened teenager who had rejected the philosophy of his own father: that the best way to live was by the old teachings of self-control and self-denial. Harry Turner still swore that to do without things today was worthwhile for a better tomorrow. Perry was a person who believed that with a five-dollar bill in his pocket, the one thing he could be certain of was that if he did not spend it today, it would be worth that much less tomorrow.

He held the boy tight, feeling his trembling. "Don't be afraid."

"I want to die."

The boy put his arms around him.

Father Philippe kept his voice and tone certain. "God wants you to live, Perry."

For a while they remained locked in silent embrace. Gradually, he felt Perry calming.

"Perry, I want you to listen to me very carefully. You understand?"

After a lengthy pause a muffled voice answered. "Yes."

"There is no magic. No pill. Nothing. Only you can get through this. Cold turkey is hell. It's the pits. But it's better than dying. You must believe that. You have to. I'm going to close my eyes now and I want you to do the same. And then we're both going to pray. Will you do that with me?"

The answer was whispered. "Yes."

He felt desperately sorry for the youth. He was a prime example of the disillusionment and cynicism of the 1970s. Authority, both external and internal, had been shrugged aside. Riddled by egalitarianism, riven with doubts and self-doubts, believing nothing and able to honor no one, the likes of Perry Turner stood on nothing and could stand for nothing. The drug culture battened on him and his sad belief that everybody was entitled, almost as a birthright, to experiment.

"Let's say the Our Father together. It's the best prayer I know."

They recited it slowly.

The boy stopped crying, though his body continued to shiver spasmodically.

He thought how ironic it was that this boy had used his wealth and privileges to seek his own reality in a needle. Somewhere along the way he had forgotten that personal values were prerequisites for a meaningful life. He would try to instill them now.

Father Philippe gently disengaged himself and looked at Perry. He took a clean tissue and wiped the boy's face.

"Now I want to teach you something. A very wise man wrote these words. I want you to listen very carefully. I want you to not only hear what I'm going to say, but feel the words."

Father Philippe recited the mantra.

Heading south, he was preoccupied with Perry Turner. The boy might not have the willpower to break the hold the drug had on him. He left the parkway and joined the interstate. Dan had landed a job somewhere out here, tending the lawns at one of the office complexes carefully sculpted into the contours of the land. It occurred to him that Dan could be the answer. He, better than anyone, could act as Perry's mentor. He'd call Dr. Stanway and suggest it; then he'd find Dan, and together they would go and see Perry. It really could work, he thought, as he slowed to take the exit to the country road where Karl Cummings lived.

Karl was a widower who had taught carpentry at Holy Family, one of the diocesan schools. When he retired two years ago, he had opened a shop selling reconditioned farm furniture, and had built up a good business.

Six months ago he'd gone into the General for minor surgery. A malignant tumor was discovered in his abdomen. He had undergone a major operation and follow-up chemotherapy and radiation treatment. All had failed to halt the cancer. Four weeks ago, Karl insisted on coming home to die. Every day, either Father Nolan or Father Philippe had come out to see him.

Karl sat on a rocker on the porch. His bald head seemed too large for his scrawny neck.

"How are you doing, Karl?"

"Fine, just fine, Father. The new shots help a lot."

A nurse called every day to administer increased doses of painkiller.

Father Philippe sat opposite him. "I ordered the book you wanted. The school's sending it over."

Karl had asked for a Holy Family yearbook to complete his set covering the twenty-five years he taught there.

"Thanks, Father. Nineteen sixty ..." He gave a fragile cough. "... that was the year public schools began to desegregate. I had a couple of my old students wounded when they joined a march on the governor's mansion ..."

Father Philippe had noticed before that the closer a person who knows death is imminent comes to it, the clearer was the recall of the past.

"That was a bad time for us all, Karl."

The old man nodded.

"Worse now. We didn't have a big problem then. Now kids in sixth grade are hooked. Look at the Turner boy."

They spoke about the case. Karl had taught Perry the rudiments of carpentry.

"His dad dropped by this morning. I guess Harry was trying to find out how the boy got started ..."

Father Philippe had often felt that the needs of today's generation were no different from previous ones: the freedom to experiment in a healthy way; the need to seek out challenging experiences and the security of dependable personal relations. Sadly, Perry Turner felt he did not have that with his own father; it was something to work toward. But he could experience it through his wise old teacher.

Karl stared out across the land to where a tractor left a wake of dust on the skyline.

Father Philippe described his visit to Perry.

"He's pretty sick. He says he wants to die."

Karl fixed his eyes on Father Philippe. "He's a good boy, Father."

"I know."

They both watched the tractor turn and begin another run, plowing a fresh, richly dark furrow.

"I told Harry I'd like to talk to his boy."

Father Philippe nodded.

He could see Karl before the boy as someone, who, in all kinds of ways, had found his true self. Example was always worth a great deal more than precept and Karl's courage offered a shining version of the human spirit at its heroic best.

482

"I'll speak to Harry."

The dying teacher could be offered as a perfect oblation. Perry had to make a choice — give up drugs and return to living. Karl, too, would benefit. Right to the end, his life would have an even deeper purpose.

The tractor passed and continued on up an incline.

"What would you say to Perry, Karl?"

Karl gave another weak cough. He said it was a side effect from his injections.

"What would I tell him? That he's got a whole life of living to do. That God didn't intend him to mess it up like this. And if he wants to talk about dying, I'll tell him what it's like to wait to die. I'll tell him it's not easy."

"I know, Karl."

The old man nodded. "I was scared as a jackrabbit until you and Father Nolan talked to me. But you're right. A man has to learn to die."

Between them, and without relying only on overwhelming religious beliefs, they had encouraged Karl to accept that he must die and that he should not blight his life with doubts about his end.

"Like I said, Karl, for each of us the end of the race is not dying. It's the beginning."

The old man's voice was soft. "Let me see the boy. I want him to win out, too."

Father Philippe nodded. "I'll drop by the hospital on the way back and fix it. In the meantime, I'd like to pray with you."

For a moment, they remained with heads bowed and eyes closed. Then Father Philippe delivered the words of the Apostle John.

"Christ said, '*Peace I bequeath to you, my own peace I give you, a peace the world cannot give. I have told you all this so that you may find peace in me. In the world you will have trouble, but be brave: I have conquered the world.*' May God bless you, Karl, now and forever."

Driving back into the city, he thought that Karl's courage was proof that the gifts of the Spirit were available only through unconditional discipleship. For those who were less than fully certain in their faith, there was a terrible reality in Christ's teaching that could be disturbing. John had been right. Christ had conquered the world.

So, in his own way, had Karl.

Turning onto the state highway, he had no inkling that in just minutes — the time it would take him to drive one and two-thirds of a mile along the highway to the shopping mall — he would discover his own response to the words Jesus gave his Apostles: "I have conquered the world."

At three-seventeen on this cloudless afternoon, beneath a late fall sky that people around these parts called "vibrant," he realized he was hungry, and he parked his car outside the Home Bakery. He was free until seven, when the Confession Room opened.

Just as he climbed out of the car and locked the door, a voice rooted him to the spot.

" 'Lo, Phil." Margot was standing to his left. She had come out of a boutique and was wearing the green pantsuit she had bought on their last day in the Bahamas.

His initial response was a silent entreaty: *Jesus, don't desert me now. Jesus, not now.*

"How are you, Margot?"

An interminable span of time elapsed; he was certain it could only have been seconds.

Through his mind flashed the memory of how he had struggled in the CDU gymnasium to check himself from lunging to catch the ball. He remembered, too, Dr. Stanway had said the only way a priest can live by Saint Augustine's maxim was to couple it with that other dictum. Under his breath he recited: *"O Lord, I am not worthy of your trust in me."* Standing here, he knew his fearfulness was suddenly very real.

Margo was smiling at him, her eyes fixed on his.

"I'm fine. Mother said you were back. You look terrific."

He felt himself desperately trying to remember.

It was Matthew who wrote, "Many are called but few are chosen." But what does that mean here and now, on this sidewalk, at this moment? How can I fit that into this shattering realization that all these months I have experienced a real aloneness? I have missed her. There is no use denying it. I have, more than I ever realized.

He stood there, staring at her expression of almost childlike delight. The look, he remembered, was a part of her; she wore it the way other women wore makeup. He had forgotten how feminine, soft, and desirable it could make her.

He managed to keep his voice calm. "Thanks. So do you."

She moved toward him, and he could smell the perfume of her body. She touched him on the arm, then quickly withdrew her hand.

He continued to be intensely aware of his every response.

Touching has always been important to me. I've always felt that one of the great mistakes of the priesthood has been to make a sin of tactile pleasures. There has always been this unhealthy emphasis on the dangers of tactility. But Christ had been highly tactile. There is plenty of Gospel evidence to show He gave and received pleasure through touching.

"Phil, it's great to see you."

"Same here."

He waited for her to say more. He noticed her clasped hands were gripping themselves hard. His own were behind his back, clenched; his mind remembered all those times, after they had made love, when there would be silence between them and the absence of words would contain its own special sort of contact. She had said that words, at such times, held no meaning for her; they acted only as a barrier to her own deeply felt emotions. These silences, she had said, were especially uplifting; a very special kind of intimacy.

She stared at him.

She still had, he thought, the most beautiful eyes he had ever seen in a woman. He smiled at her.

I know I'm rushing for the ball. But I can't help it. I'm human. That's always been my trouble. I'm flesh and blood inside this priest's suit. To deny that would be to deny my own self-realization. Everyone wants to be loved. And loving is no longer being frightened, but understanding. "O Lord, I fear I am not worthy of your trust in me" really means that as a man I am able to give and receive love. I still love her.

"Where are you going?" Her voice had a cadence he had always found exotic.

"To eat."

Chastity is part of the virtue of temperance, the state that controls the pleasures of touch: eating, drinking, and sexual satisfaction. But a virtue to have any meaning must not be repressive. A virtue is meant to humanize living in Christ. I've always believed that any control over my passions is even less possible when I'm condemned to pretend they don't exist. I'm not running a police state in my head, where everything is suppressed. I've always tried to let my mind govern me democratically. I don't think any virtue can work if it's repressive.

She smiled. "Why don't you follow me and I'll cook you a steak?" Her eyes, framed by those incredibly long lashes, looked at him. She repeated her offer. "Medium rare and a salad. With some wine. How does that sound?"

It was a statement rather than a question. He had forgotten, until this moment, that she had this knack of bypassing the nonessential and homing in on what mattered.

Only pleasure based on evil intent is evil. I don't have a bad thought in my head. I'm human. It's the Church that isn't. Instead of forcing me to suppress my feelings it should help me Christianize my sexuality.

He touched her arm, saying to himself he was expressing a basic human need; that affectionate, tactile stimulation was essential for him to function as a healthy, emotional, integrated priest. It was more than merely physical. Through this one touch he wanted her to know he felt other and altogether more powerful emotions.

"Sounds terrific."

As he drove down the highway, he went over all the things she could have said. Why had he not written from the halfway house, or called since he'd been back? He remembered it was not her style. She'd always said recriminations were negative.

It had been so long, seven months now, and yet here he was, once more, driving to her apartment, thinking whoever said people can change had it all wrong.

Margot hadn't changed. There was about her the extraordinary ability to show a vulnerable modesty while at the same time allowing an open hungry look on her face: it was there in her eyes and the sexy pout of her mouth. It was, he said to himself, watching her drive ahead of him, an absolutely magical combination. Times can change, so can circumstances, but never people. Certainly not Margot. Nor, he realized, himself. He looked in his mirror. It was there again, that scared-little-boy look. Suddenly it was gone.

He knew he had never stopped believing that sexual fulfillment and chastity were not incompatible, just as he had always known that the Church would continue to reject this reality. Margot had been right. A priest is a man. His sexuality was a gift from God, a sign of His love for him as a man and as a priest. He was certain now that there could be no honest distinction. There was not one kind of sexuality for celibates and another for everybody else. A priest is a man. What he must do was integrate his feelings into his Christian ministry, using them to live a full and satisfactory life.

Until now, he had not realized how much he had grown up in himself; undoubtedly not the way the Church of Dr. Stanway would approve, but that, in the end, did not matter. He was his own person, driving behind the woman he had never stopped loving. That was the reality. That was his honesty.

Easing out of the traffic to park behind Margot's car, he knew he would no longer be ambivalent and hesitant, but eager and certain to show himself he could manage. He recognized that he was behaving impulsively and doing everything that Dr. Stanway had said he must not. But he was equally certain he would accept responsibility for his action. That, too, he saw as a sign of his newfound self-realization of who he was and what motivated him. He had never felt more comfortable.

Watching her fumble with the key in the lock of the apartment door, he had no feeling of shame or failure. Instead, he was filled with an overwhelming desire to recapture moments that he had thought lost. He was full of love and grace.

As she turned the key, he reached forward and held her by the shoulders, turning her to face him.

"You're looking very, very beautiful — more beautiful than I've ever seen you."

She laughed.

Inside him the excitement mounted.

She turned and opened the door. He kicked it shut after them. His arms were around her waist, holding her to him.

Margot removed his hands and they stood staring at each other until the silence became unendurable. She asked him a question.

"Are you thinking what I'm thinking?"

"You better believe it."

She drew him to her and he knew from the way she kissed him that she was feeling what he felt and again the sense of exaltation, more wonderful than anything he could ever remember experiencing, swept over him.

Margot led him into the bedroom.

He hesitated for a moment in the doorway, staring at the king-size bed.

She kissed him lovingly on the mouth. Then she whispered. "I didn't change a thing since you left. I guess I just knew you'd come back."

"I never went away. Not really." He reached to undo the zipper on her suit. "Show me. I want to see you."

She stepped out of the suit, murmuring there was no right or wrong: there was only now. There was only them. She was naked except for her panties.

He reached down and touched her gently as she undressed him, slowly, the way he had always liked, first removing his priest's collar, then unbuttoning his black clerical shirt, pressing her lips against his chest, keening softly with pleasure. She unbuckled his belt and his priest's pants fell to the carpet. He stepped out of them, kicking off his shoes. She bent down and removed his socks. As she rose, she pulled down his shorts. He felt he was on fire as she took him in her hand, and guided him to the bed. He pressed his face against her neck, moaning under her touch.

"Wait. Don't be in such a hurry."

"I've missed you, Margot. I've missed you so much."

Her voice matched his whisper. "I've missed you, too. I want this to be beautiful. I want to make you happy again." Her hands were everywhere, touching and exploring him.

He was kissing her eyes, her lips, her neck, her nipples, her stomach, the moistness between her legs.

She softly commanded him to wait, pushing him on his back, touching his lips with the tip of her tongue. Then, in the way she knew he enjoyed, she lowered her head and he felt her gentle sucking mouth absorbing him. He writhed and groaned.

Her head continued to rise and fall steadily. Suddenly she gasped, rolling on her back, ready for him.

Father Philippe lay on the bed, listening to the sounds from the kitchen, talking to Harry Turner on her bedside phone, explaining why he wanted Karl and Dan to see Perry.

Once more, the words of Saint Matthew drifted into his mind. *Many are called, but few are chosen.* He still felt he had a vocation and was full of God's grace. Making love to Margot had not changed anything. It had been a beautiful human experience. It did not make him less of a priest. What had happened was striking proof that he could not live a worthwhile life in Christ without taking into account his sexuality. Making love with Margot this time had been a joyful and meaningful experience; the start of recultivating their friendship. It had been an essential element of his deep need to show affection and to receive it. He had made love with the same essential sacredness as the erotic, human, passionate, and sensual lovers in the Old Testament's Song of Songs.

Margot was back, standing naked at the bedside, holding two goblets of chilled wine. She handed him one and curled up beside him, laying her head on his shoulder, listening to him tell Harry why a dying old man and a reformed junkie might be able to help his son.

He put down the phone and looked at her.

She placed a finger on his lips. "Don't say anything. Don't spoil it. It's going to be fine."

After they drank the wine, he buried himself once more in her soft flesh and she welcomed him, matching each of his thrusts with an arched response. He had never remembered their lovemaking reaching such indescribable heights.

Margot returned to the kitchen to cook their steaks. Lying on the bed, listening to her singing, he reminded himself that the Bible is full of the real appreciation of sexuality; making love is the ultimate way to express feelings that no words could satisfy. The underlying message of the Song of Songs is that physical lovemaking is the final affirmation of a healthy relationship between two persons who genuinely love each other.

Just as the relationship between the biblical lovers was not based solely on the physical enjoyment, but on deeper meanings, so he would work hard to ensure that his relationship with Margot would have an endurance, permanence, and fidelity to the kind of ongoing, strong, and committed love which the Song of Songs so evocatively describes. Its sexuality is unsullied by the rules of man. Through its verses, he was convinced, can be heard the authentic voice of God. Only aeons later had a Pope in Rome, purely for expedient political reasons, decided that celibacy would become the sacrifice; that the cult of virginity for priests would be the most acceptable form of Christianity for the Roman Empire. But it was still a man-made law. It had nothing to do with God. That was why he felt he was secure in His grace.

He called Dr. Stanway to suggest how Dan and Karl could help Perry. The doctor was totally in favor.

"Philippe, that's what makes you such a good priest. You really care."

They ate in bed. He talked to her about his time in the CDU and at the halfway house, and what he had been thinking from the time they met again. It felt so natural and good to speak so freely. He told her he felt closer to her in mind as well as body than he ever had before. Finally, he turned and looked at her seriously. "It's going to be okay this time, Margot. It really is."

Her hand moved possessively over his face. "You better believe it. This time you better had."

For thirty-two days Father Philippe lived a dual life. The priestly side of him was more devoted than ever to his ministry. The man in him was never more evident than when he was with Margot.

He located Dan and brought him to see Perry. He sat with them while Dan described what it was like to come up from addiction. He had driven over to Karl and brought him in to see the boy, and again listened while the teacher quietly explained why Perry must fight for his survival.

Every day he had offered the sacrifice of the Mass, distributed Communion, and delivered penances in the Confession Room. Once, he had administered Extreme Unction. In all he said and did in dispensing the grace of the sacraments, he was endowed with the power of the Holy Ghost and visibly filled with spiritual excellence.

Every night he had luxuriated in the smell of Margot's body and the joys of her bed.

He had resolved this paradox by telling himself there was nothing to resolve. There was no theological rule that any longer made sense to him about grace. The "state of grace" the Church spoke of was, he further believed, a poor substitute for the greater grace God offered. It was as simple as that.

He resumed jogging with Fern. She had looked at him appraisingly but said nothing. The unspoken message was clear: he, and he alone, must walk his own tightrope.

Never once after making love had he felt a compulsion to scratch himself. He had slept deeply, not disturbed by a return of the nightmare. He found this reassuring proof that God understood him.

What had once seemed an impossibility — living without guilt because of his love for Margot — had become a joyous certainty. He could have a full, loving relationship with her, and at the same time, live a full life in Christ. The Bishop, the Pope, the Church, and Canon Law: all, he accepted, would challenge his right to behave like this. But, he had told himself, his superiors and their man-made rules did not trouble him anymore; God had made it clear there was space for both his ministry and Margot in his life; that indeed, through her, he had become an even better priest. Loving her had released a vast and unsuspected dam of love within himself. He was so filled with love that it touched everything he saw and did. Discovering this, he had discovered how much more he could still give to others.

One night, driving back from her apartment, he dropped by the CDU to see Perry. The boy was making slow but noticeable progress. He had been off drugs for six weeks and was no longer crying for a fix. Slowly, rung by rung, he too, was climbing his own ladder to self-realization.

Together they said the mantra. Then Father Philippe told the boy the story of what Christ said to Nicodemus, about hearing the wind, but not knowing from where it came or where it was bound. He told Perry that

God was like that. "We just don't know on whom He will next bestow this light from Heaven."

At a little after six-thirty on his thirty-third morning, the telephone rang at his bedside in the rectory. He picked up the receiver. It was Margot.

"Can you come over? I need to talk to you."

"Are you okay?"

"Come over. Please?"

She hung up before he could answer. He did not know why, but he felt suddenly apprehensive.

Forty minutes later, he faced her across the breakfast table. She sobbed again in response to his question. Her period was two weeks overdue. Heavy tears continued to roll down her cheeks.

Staring into her face, he felt as though the kitchen door to the great world beyond had been wrenched open by a gust of icy wind, blowing into his mind the realization that his familiar old guilt complex was back. From outside came the sound of morning traffic: people going to work, life going on. He asked her again if she was convinced she was pregnant.

Margot nodded. "I can't be absolutely sure, but I've never been this late with my period before."

For a moment he closed his eyes. As quickly as it came, the chill wind had gone. The moment of guilt passed. All the time he had known the risk of this happening.

Her voice was so soft that it was a mere thought. She asked him what they were going to do. He opened his eyes, a feeling of goodness coming over him. He walked to her chair. She pressed against him, and he felt his blood begin to surge and his entire body come alive as he experienced the vital force of himself fuel this feeling of goodness, enriching it and himself. He asked her what she would like to do.

She stared at him for a while.

"I'll get a test kit from the drugstore." The words came from her lips as a dull moan, and with them a release of new tears.

He went to her, cradling her head against his waist, endlessly smoothing her hair. He started to sing her favorite song, "Love Is Everywhere."

She put her arms around his waist, hugging him to her. When he had finished singing, he bent down and murmured the words of Anne Bradstreet. "If ever two were one, then surely we."

Then he began to speak, his voice low and compelling, saying the most important thing of all was that they loved each other. Everything else they would decide would stem from that; loving each other must be their base line for all decision-making. But there was time to reflect on what was best for both of them. He had, he realized, placed the gentlest of emphasis on "both." He wanted her to understand this would not be his decision alone, but they would make it together. The first step, he concluded, would be to get the pregnancy test kit. He would go to the drugstore.

Margot looked up at him wonderingly. "But, Phil. You're a priest. You just can't walk in and buy a test kit. The whole town will know."

He smiled down at her. "I'll disguise myself."

She suddenly started to laugh.

He knew he had successfully negotiated a dangerous moment, showing her he was prepared to act decisively. For the moment, all she needed was reassurance; later, they could discuss the reality.

Driving back to the rectory, Father Philippe reviewed their options. He swiftly rejected an abortion. Both of them had always felt it was morally reprehensible. The psychological damage it would do to Margot made him shiver. The idea of having the baby surgically destroyed must, he was sure, be responsible for the sudden panic that swept over him, bathing him in sweat. He pulled over and sat, willing himself to be calm.

After a while he felt able to drive on. He considered another possibility. The baby could be adopted. But that, too, would be emotionally unsettling for them both. They would always know that somewhere was their child, alive but abandoned to its own fate. And, for Margot there would be the additional trauma of having to endure the pointing fingers in the community. She was not a teenager, but a mature woman, close to thirty: the speculation about who the father was would be that much more intense. It was true that, with Fern's money, she could go away and wait out her confinement, but that, too, would be stressful. Margot would feel abandoned, having to move away to wait for a baby she would then have to give away. Besides, leaving the area would not end the gossip. People would guess; they almost always did. Yet, he could hardly admit fatherhood and expect to remain in active ministry. While he still believed he was in God's grace, he was quite certain the Church would show no mercy. Then there was Fern. For all her charm, he suspected, she could be tough. Once more he was bathed in perspiration.

Arriving at the rectory, he considered a third option. Margot could face the gossip, keep the child, and raise it as a single parent. Its paternity would be their secret.

He entered his apartment, thinking that if Margot kept the baby he could see their child growing. He would continue to visit her and though outwardly he would seem no more than a caring priest, they would both know he was there as the child's father, first playing with it, and then later, educating it. Their child. He could be both a priest to his flock and a father to his child.

The more he thought about it, the more possible it seemed: he would give their child all the things he had himself been denied: parental love, security, understanding, support, encouragement. He was suddenly very excited. He still could have the best of both his worlds.

He started to disguise himself. He put on a sweatshirt and Levi's and sandals. From a dresser drawer he removed a box that contained greasepaint and cotton wool. A while ago, an actor had given him the makeup as a memento of a backstage visit. Wadding cotton wool into balls, he inserted them inside his mouth, appreciably changing the shape of his face. Then he darkened his skin with the greasepaint. From a closet he took a battered fedora. On his last visit home, years ago, his mother had insisted he accept it. The hat had belonged to his father; the only time he had worn it was at his funeral. He completed the transformation by putting on a pair of silver-tinted sunglasses.

He suddenly realized the absurdity of the situation. There really was no need for him to disguise himself. What possible suspicion would be aroused by a priest buying a pregnancy test kit for a parishioner? It was an impulsive fear that had made him try to hide; he also knew that a part of him wanted to run from the situation. He shrugged at his reflection. At least he could admit that. It was more than he had been able to do in the past.

As he drove across town, a new idea occurred to him. Margot could refuse to raise their child alone. What then? He drove for a half-hour before he saw that if this were to be her reaction, he would have to marry her. He felt stricken. While he loved her, he also knew he was deeply committed to his ministry.

He groaned aloud and started once again to go over all the options. He had found no acceptable solution when he entered the drugstore. The clerk handed him the kit, her voice suddenly low and conspiratorial.

"She'll need an early morning specimen. Then she must wait an hour. If the test is negative, the specimen will be cloudy. If it's positive, it will show clear. You remember to tell her. Fuzzy — and she's fine. Clear — and she starts knitting."

He repeated the instructions.

*

At a little after six-fifteen the following morning, his bedside telephone rang. Yesterday morning when she had called he had instantly felt apprehensive. Now he felt exhausted.

Until the early hours of this morning he had sat with Margot, discussing their options. She had constantly changed her position. One minute she wanted to have the baby adopted, the next she had decided to raise it herself. For a while she had spoken about moving to another part of the country and starting a new life. Then she had said she would remain and brave the gossip. Each time he thought she had come to a final decision, Margot had reversed it. But not once had she even hinted they should marry. Nor had he raised the idea. Finally, around two o'clock this morning he had said they could not really decide anything until she knew absolutely if she was pregnant.

He had returned to the rectory and spent what was left of the night letting his thoughts rise and fall, peaking with the hope that she had made a mistake, plunging at the idea of having to give up the priesthood. Finally falling asleep barely an hour ago, he had remembered the story he had told Perry about what Christ said to Nicodemus. Grace, indeed, did come in all sorts of mysterious and unpredictable guises. For a moment longer he let the telephone ring, already seeing her face, their bed, where they had started a new life. He picked up the receiver, his pulse quickening.

She told him the result was positive. He reminded himself that everything must be absorbed before decisions could be made. Then he realized she had asked him again what they would do.

From the apartment across the hall he could hear the strong and unmistakable baritone of Father Nolan starting his day with "Amazing Grace." He listened for a moment, absorbed in the words John Newton wrote two hundred years ago.

Amazing grace! How sweet the sound
That saved a wretch like me!
I once was lost, but now am found,
Was blind, but now I see."

Father Philippe felt a surge of confidence. "Margot, listen. It's going to be okay. We'll work it out. Together."

"Oh, Phil. I'm so glad . . ."

The voice from across the hall had grown louder.

'Twas grace that taught my heart to fear,
And grace my fears relieved;
How precious did that grace appear,
The hour I first believed!

He spoke into the telephone. "Margot. We're going to keep the baby. I want that."

She started to weep. He reassured her he would find a way. Father Nolan's voice was bellowing out the words of the song.

"Margot. I want to sing to you."

"What?"

He started to sing, his voice united with that of Father Nolan's.

Through many dangers, toils, and snares,
I have already come;
'Tis grace hath brought me safe thus far,
And grace will lead me home.

He asked her to join in the last verse. Together over the telephone they sang.

The Lord has promised good to me,
His word my hope secures;
He will my shield and portion be,
As long as life endures.

There was silence from across the hall and over the telephone. Then Father Philippe told Margot he loved her and would see her shortly.

Dressed in his rabat, trousers, jacket, and white collar, his chalice case in one hand, he knocked on the door of Father Nolan's apartment. From within came slow, shuffling footsteps. The door opened. Father Nolan stood there in his bathrobe and slippers. For a long moment he stared at Father Philippe, his eyes going from the chalice case to his face and back again. Father Philippe said he would like to speak with his superior.

Father Nolan opened the door wider, his eyes firmly fixed on the chalice case, and led the way into his sparsely furnished living room, motioning to a chair. Father Philippe placed the case on the carpet.

Father Nolan went to the kitchen and returned with a coffeepot and two cups. He busied himself pouring, saying nothing. He handed Father Philippe a cup, staring once more at the chalice case. The only sound was the ticking of a wall clock.

"What's going on, Philippe?"

"I'm leaving."

Father Nolan stared, not comprehending.

Father Philippe repeated he was leaving, this time adding he was doing so to get married. He explained why and what had happened.

When he was finished, Father Nolan sat, slumped in his chair, a finger moving back and forth over his lower lip.

Father Philippe waited, steeling himself for the rain of reproach.

Father Nolan rose to his feet and said he would get hot coffee.

Father Philippe went to the window and looked out. Fern was starting her laps.

Behind him, in the kitchen doorway, Father Nolan spoke. "Have you thought this through? You're a fine priest. The Church needs men like you to do God's work."

He turned and faced Father Nolan. "The Church is run by men, Ray. A man in Rome decides what is fallible or infallible. I can't live my life any longer like that. I can't have other men split me down the middle about such an important matter as being a man. I can't go on living with myself, pretending."

Father Nolan walked back to his chair. "They'll never release you. There's hardly been a dispensation since this Pope came to office. You won't get one. As long as he stays on, you'll still be a priest. Don't you see that?"

"Ray, listen to me. I know you mean well. You always have. And I'm grateful for that. I really am. But don't you understand? I want to live with my own passion for the first time, not the handed-down passions of the Church. I can't go on living under the sort of regulations which are destructive to me as a man. That's what I don't want to live with anymore. Having to pretend my collar acts as a totem that keeps me from having normal healthy responses."

Father Nolan looked away. "But you made a vow —"

Father Philippe interrupted. "Don't lay that one on me, Ray. When I took that vow, I didn't know what it really meant. You probably didn't. I doubt if a goddamn priest in the whole Church knows. We get sucked along with the idea we are better than the angels. Then one morning we wake up and find we're human, with human responses. That we can actually love in a human way. Care in a human way. Feel in a human way. That we're not just hiding behind our collar —"

"Watch it, Philippe. Calm down."

Father Philippe shook his head. "Oh, sweet Jesus, Ray, I'm sorry. But don't you understand that what we are asked to do has nothing to do with God? It's all to do with men. God didn't say I could be a good priest only if I'm celibate. God didn't invent the Blessed Mother. Men did. God didn't say we have to live outside our bodies to do His work. Don't you see, Ray? It is men who took away our passions. It is men who make us cheat on ourselves. It is men who created this whole myth of celibacy. Don't you see that?"

Father Nolan stared at him. Finally, he spoke.

"It's what makes the priesthood different from all the others. We weren't meant to have it easy, like the Protestants, the Jews, and the Moslems. We were meant to be singled out. We are priests forever."

For a moment Father Philippe stood still. Then he walked over to his chalice case and handed it to Father Nolan.

"I don't need this anymore, to be in God's grace."

He turned and walked toward the door.

Father Nolan's whisper stopped him.

"God bless you."

†

IMAGES
TODAY

It is not our part to master all the tides
of the world, but to do what is in us for the
succour of those years wherein we are set, uprooting
the evil in the fields that we know, so that those
who live after may have clean earth to till. What
weather they shall have is not ours to rule.
— J.R.R. TOLKIEN, *The Return of the King*

CHAPTER 20

†

Certainties

Waiting now in an empty classroom, Clare realizes she can no longer be certain when she stopped merely coping and learned to accept. Though there have been definite markers, they were not conveniently placed with the evenness of milestones, allowing decent intervals between the end of one experience and the onset of another. Sometimes events had been bunched together.

She went to her first party just days after leaving the convent. She bought a new dress for a neighbor's twenty-first birthday celebration and had looked forward to the evening. But being asked to dance, having a man hold her close, one hand on her bottom, the other drooped around her shoulder, his face buried in her neck, had made her stiffen in panic. She had abruptly pleaded a headache and gone outside so that no one would see her shaking. Her cousin found her there, and being both quick and understanding, smiled sympathetically and said what Clare needed was a drink. Several whiskeys later, she allowed her cousin's husband to dance with her. He grinned disarmingly and said some men could be very cloddish. She had found herself smiling gratefully for his understanding. The burden of not knowing how to respond to that other man seemed that much lighter.

Weeks had elapsed between leaving and actually starting to teach. When she finally telephoned the Mother House, her former Superior said she should use the time to readjust. Reverend Mother's voice had been barely audible, as if she was speaking from another world. "I expect you're finding it very strange out there?"

She had said she was finding it difficult.

The more well-meaning people were, the harder it was to adjust. On that first evening, after the taxi deposited her outside her parents' home, her mother had led her upstairs to her old room and thrown open the door, her voice filled with pride. "I didn't change anything since you went in."

The books she had read as a teenager, the records she had played, the bed with a crucifix above it, her chair: the past all surged back as she remembered how she had left here, a slip of a girl filled with a certainty that she would never return and that God had chosen her to live in His image. Aware her mother was watching, knowing she was eager for a response, she had experienced that first moment of somehow having failed to live up to His expectations.

She had turned and smiled brightly and said how great it was to see everything just as she remembered it. The other feeling was hers to share with no one.

In those first weeks out, she was filled with guilt. Rationally, she knew there were no grounds for it. She *had* come to the right decision. There *had* been no rush to judgment or even the mildest of criticism of religious life. Instead, she defensively insisted to her family and friends who worked hard to welcome her back, that while going to the movies and pubs and being able to go to bed as late as she liked or being allowed to sleep in on weekends and to wear the latest fashions were certainly new experiences, life inside had not all been silence and solitude.

She had at those times felt the pull of the recent past most of all. The Rule, for all its strictness, had developed her sense of purpose, her prayer life, her ability to do without so many of the things others found important. She didn't really mind what she ate or drank and wasn't anxious to buy some new items of clothing every week. She didn't need to be invited out on dates. Her family had listened silently when she said she still liked to spend a portion of her day alone and enjoyed going early to bed, awakening in the dark at the convent hour, waiting for them to get up.

No one was aware that in those pre-dawn hours she would lie in her bedroom, filled with uneasiness, thinking. God really had called her because she had a vocation. She *had* been accepted by the Order and that, too, was further evidence of her calling. It had been made clear to her by the Mistress of Postulants and Novices that only those with a definite vocation were admitted. Those were still the boom days when every Irish family would expect to give a son or daughter to God, and only the most committed were chosen. And so she had lain there and wondered. Had she after all done the right thing? In the first light of a new day the image of Reverend Mother dispensing her with immeasurable sadness from her sacred vows would frequently float into her consciousness.

In the weeks that followed — in between registering with a doctor and the tax office and placing herself on numerous bureaucratic lists — she faced realities.

Living a spiritual life in a world where all forms of religious values were under attack was the greatest of challenges. While her own home remained a bastion of faith, beyond it there was a more profound upheaval than she had ever imagined.

Before, she had always been able to retreat into the convent, to enjoy a common life of the spirit, to experience the same joy of united prayer, to share a communal sense of reverence in worship, a feeling of selfless obligation to mankind in which mere mortal things had no solid importance and were a gossamer curtain through which the outer world was dimly seen.

Prolonged contact with that inner world had given her values she suddenly found were in confrontation with the demands of temporal life. Her love of God — the key to all the wisdom she knew — had been the only way she had known how to live. Now, she suddenly found herself plunged into the midst of a theological eruption, which daily challenged dogma and morals she had hitherto believed to be immutable. There was no shelter from its fallout; it assailed her on all sides.

Nearly all the women she knew, single or married, were practicing some form of contraception — in a country where birth control is still proscribed. More Catholic girls than ever before, among them a high percentage of schoolgirls, were going to England for abortions. Marriage itself was under attack. In the circle she was introduced to — middle-class, hardworking Dubliners — there were numerous couples living together who were either both single, or with one partner having deserted a husband or wife to live with someone else. Sex at every level was a casual matter.

Until now, she had never had unrestricted access to television, radio, and films. In the convent, viewing was still controlled. But at home, able to watch and listen when she liked, she was stunned at the emphasis on sex: its crudeness, its explicitness, the frankness of its language. She felt at times she had been transported into an alien culture where the emphasis seemed to be on nakedness and sensual pleasure. It was a shock to see the elaborate structure of her theological and moral doctrine crumble before her eyes.

Some of the changes have been intensely personal. Her years of chastity had conditioned her always to remember what the Rule said were the *dangers* of touching. It is strange to be embraced and kissed by her parents and sisters and to be called casually *darling* by one of her brothers-in-law, when for so long she has been called *Sister;* and that had never been used as a form of endearment.

Even dancing with her cousin's husband reached deep into the no-touch asceticism of the Order. For years she had been drilled that there was no value in human tactility; that it had no part to play in her affectionate and emotional life; that it could not make her grow as a person.

But this new world she has entered is filled with people who caress, hug, hold, pet, cuddle, stroke, embrace, and fondle. No one seems able to survive without tactile stimulation. It is, she realizes, with a dawning sense of wonder, a natural way of showing love.

Initially, she found it almost stifling at times to live in the small space of her parents' home after the vastness of the Mother House. It needed a daily effort to adjust to the sheer *closeness* of everybody; to accept this continuous feeling of being crowded.

It will take, she realizes, time to accept that beyond the convent walls not everything is superficial. It is only different. Knowing that, she can continue to reach out, from within herself, above time and space, into God's eternity and immensity. But it will be done in a *different* way. She will have to be clear about the division between her empirical self and her spirit. One would be occupied with the business of living; the other would allow her to continue to enjoy peace with God. With a sense of relief she sees that she can live the life she wants if she remembers that Saint John of the Cross had said that the higher and lower portions of the soul are meant to be apart, but that they can be united by the fertile and creative presence of God.

She no longer requires a constant reminder to accept the simplest of freedoms: not having to wait until being spoken to; realizing it is natural for people cheerfully to interrupt each other and talk whenever they feel like it.

She finds it strange not to have rules and regulations at mealtimes. They are now casual and relaxed occasions, with the television on, or one of her sisters more often than not playing a tape of hard rock in the kitchen. She had forgotten what a noisy place the world was.

She taught for six months before she moved out of her parents' house to a home of her own. She had successfully negotiated a mortgage, opened a bank account, and learned how to handle a weekly budget. It is a strange feeling, being able to spend what she has, and not having to rely on the Deputy for bus fares and lunch money.

Most evenings on the way from school, she would drop in to see her father, confined to his daybed downstairs. He indicated that preparing properly to die holds its own rewards. Once, his solicitor came to the house and they spent an hour together alone in his room. Afterward her father breathed a small sigh and said how glad he was to have settled his will.

More than anyone else, he had been responsible for marking that first all-important milestone in her journey into a new life, allowing her to see it is wrong to judge a response as a single entity; rather, to regard it as part of an accumulation of new emotions and feelings. It was he who gave her a peacefulness she had not before experienced.

With him, more than with any other member of the family, she explored her spiritual needs. He readily understood that she could live no other way than at that apex of which mystics speak, a life of radical volition that comes directly from God. But even after a year out, she would find herself pausing to pray silently seven times a day as she had done in the convent and continue to discover spiritual truth.

Truth, she told her father, is neither less true because it is old, or truer because it has been recently discovered. God for her is still now; Eternity His instant.

Finally, one evening he looked at her for a long moment and said that while he so admired her values, she must not devote all her life to this constant inner searching. She had done her share of that. God wanted her to do something else; she should relax. He motioned her to sit on the chair beside his bed. Holding her hand, the way he had when she was a child, he had spoken gently.

"I can feel the guilt in you. This idea that you've let your mother and myself down, and above all, God. You've no need to feel like that. The Order is getting what it wants. You spend almost three hours a day traveling to and from school. You work the sort of day that some people would call exploitation. You've nothing to feel guilty about. God wanted you back in the world, Clare. He really did."

She remembers how she had held him close, laying her face against his, feeling his hand softly stroking her hair.

A month after she came out, Tom telephoned and asked if they could meet. She had hesitated, knowing that his part in her life had ended before it even had a chance to begin; the words of his letter were forever etched in her memory. The past, the might-have-been, was done. He was an old dream, he might once have become a fairy-tale prince, but she was too old to believe in fairy tales, and besides her prince was now a priest. He had quietly pressed and his tone, though still soft, held something new, a protective hardness. Perhaps there would be no harm. She had finally agreed, knowing she would be comfortable.

Coming into the coffeeshop, she had recognized him at once; he was wearing the same sports jacket she had last seen him in. He embraced her quickly and over tea and cakes he told her he was in a parish in the suburbs as a curate to an old priest: a petty tyrant whose meanness was equaled only by that of his housekeeper.

She had spent the afternoon laughing at his stories of life in the parochial house. Toward the end, Tom asked why she had left. She told him. He had looked reflective. He said he never thought she would have *quit* over an issue like obedience. "Chastity, maybe. But not obedience."

For a moment the softness and kindness were gone from his voice. In one of those moments of insight — blindingly clear, cuttingly sharp and dreaded — she realized there was a distance between them. Yet in spite of it she felt glad their lives had once more intertwined, and it had been on the tip of her tongue to mention his letter. But she decided the past should remain as undisturbed as possible.

He told her, after she insisted on settling the bill between them, that he was coming up to town next weekend. Could they go and see a film together? She said, why not?

So it had begun. They met on weekends, going to a movie or a play, to eat out, to visit an art exhibition, or to a Sunday concert. He often would drop by to see her father, spending an hour being amusing at his bedside.

Sometimes Tom brought troubling news, as on the day he came from a diocesan conference with the report that the number of vocations had now reached a record low, not only in the diocese but throughout the country. Clonliffe and Maynooth, the other great Irish seminary, were virtually deserted tombs; convents often only had a handful of aging nuns. Tom said that if present trends continued, by the end of the century Ireland, one of the great bastions of Catholicism, would be a vocational desert.

Her father shook his head and replied that while there were priests like Tom the Church was still in safe hands.

Tom had begun to speak, with a passion she had never heard him use before, arguing that there were still too many within the Church ready to jettison old values. This could lead only to its doom.

She had studied him in the deepening twilight of the sickroom. Softened by the shadows, he looked more boyish than ever, more like a teenager than a man in sight of middle age. A voice within her pleaded for him not to change, not to grow too set in his ways, grow too priestly, pretending that being a man didn't matter anymore for him.

She had known from the very first meeting that she still loved Tom. But she had been so careful, so self-protective of him. Sometimes she had been tempted to tell him, honestly, how she felt, but she knew, instinctively, that would be wrong. There were also those times when she knew she would be able to live without him, just as on those occasions she was not at all sure she wished to. Yet, being with him somehow made it all that much harder, the realization that much more painful, knowing there could be no end because there would be no beginning. Worst of all was having to endure it alone. There was, she knew, nobody she dare tell that the man she loves is a priest.

She had, just once, almost admitted it to her father. It had been shortly before his death. They had been speaking about friendship and how difficult it was to maintain. Her father had gently held her face between his hands and whispered, his voice now husky from his painkillers, that, like him, she had very powerful emotions. Then, his words barely reaching her, he had said that Tom, for all his priest's carapace, was also filled with feelings. He had looked at her for a moment, his gaze as steady and searching as she remembered when it had held her as a child. Then he had asked her to be careful; for a woman, a friendship with a priest was very special — and unusual, when the woman was as young and as pretty as she was. That was the moment she had almost said what was in her heart. Instead, she had told him he must not worry, because her faith would always guide her conscience. He had hesitated a moment; then, his voice rallying, he replied he had never for a moment meant to imply he thought otherwise.

*

A week later her father died. It happened while she was on the bus coming home from school. Her mother met her at the door and broke the news. Clare had gone to her father's bedside and knelt in prayer, half-listening to her mother explaining he had been wondering what little bit of news Tom would bring next, when he suddenly closed his eyes and composed his face so that those he loved would see he had suffered no pain.

She carefully copied out her leitmotiv from Corinthians and placed it in his coffin, resting the words about love on top of her father's hands, clasping his rosary.

One of the first photographs she took with the new camera she bought from her teacher's salary was of her father's grave.

The following Saturday she snapped Tom on the steps of the art museum. He had been reluctant to pose, and over dinner she had finally raised the question of their relationship, insisting he must never think she would expect more than he could give. He had given her a quick smile and changed the conversation. That night she had written in her diary. "Now, here, today — they are all that matter."

Increasingly, he spoke to her about his growing certainty that he could face his own inner needs; that he positively enjoyed being able to turn away from the world from time to time, either through short periods of solitary prayer or on Retreats. He constantly said he did not feel a need for any other life than the one he shared with God.

She said that while that was quite wonderful and she felt much the same, she did wonder whether at times he did not feel lonely. He shook his head, almost angrily, and said he had never been lonely.

She sensed it would be wrong to press the matter. But in herself she wondered if he understood that perhaps his suppressed anger was linked to his stifled sexuality. In making her own adjustments she had recognized the truth that a celibate person will try to brush aside any negative feeling. It had taken her months to be able to admit that any form of healthy intimacy — her now easygoing relationships with her family and her fellow teachers — can sometimes produce hostility. Ambivalence, she had finally learned, was very much part of her personality, but undoubtedly no more or less than anybody else's. There were times, just like everyone, when she both loved and hated people simultaneously. There was nothing wrong, she has discovered, in allowing these emotions to coexist. It was a sign of maturity to recognize that this was possible.

She so badly wanted to say to Tom that for any relationship to have more than a superficial meaning, there must always be present an element of risk; to give oneself to another person was the most selfless of all love-giving; but present with it is an element of threat. The more deeply felt the love given, and received, the more important it is to face the anger it can sometimes bring. But she said none of these things. Once more she realized to do so would change nothing.

She began to notice certain other traits about Tom. When she held his arm, she could feel his body become rigid and see his eyes cloud over, al-most as if he was hurting; as if her femininity was alien, and it was wrong of her to want to be so close to him.

One time she made a brave effort to argue that tactility is healthy and need not always be in a sexual context. She said it could also demonstrate affection, caring, support, and selfless loving. In saying so, she realized how far she had come from those lonely nights in chapel when she had thought that only through words could love be expressed.

She told him, holding his arm, that chastity should not preclude touch-ing. He had flushed and asked her, please, to take her arm away. From then on, she stopped touching him, feeling a sense of personal defeat that she had been unable to make him see that touching was a positive sign of his sexuality; that in not being tactile he was creating a way to suppress far more powerful and potentially explosive emotions. She was certain that touching, in full awareness of the limitations imposed, could be an integral part of religious life.

After they had been seeing each other for about six months, he began to develop blinding headaches and crippling pains in his back. Then he started to break dates, phoning usually on a Friday evening, when she was beginning to anticipate what they might do over the weekend, saying he felt too unwell or that a sudden parish commitment had come up.

She noticed in particular, then, that he had a priest's way of talking, making *commitment* sound as if it was something very special, a pact he shared with God, something he had been asked to discharge on earth for Him. Finally came that dreadful discovery that to save himself, Tom had lied to her. On that particular weekend he had not been ill, as he said, but had gone away with another priest.

Two weeks later, he drove her out into the countryside and said they could no longer go on meeting. Through the pounding in her head she had thought afterward, *Once a priest, always a priest.*

She never heard from Tom after that Saturday when her loneliness and aloneness became one. Much later, with a new Archbishop in the diocese, she heard Tom had been given his own parish. That he was now a full shepherd to his flock made no difference. She still loves him. She expects she will go on loving him for the rest of her days.

The classroom door opens.

Marion comes in. The tall, graceful eighteen-year-old is the winner of this year's Scripture prize for her essay on Saint John being the Disciple Jesus loved above all the others.

"I'm sorry I'm late, Miss."

Clare smiles. "That's okay. What did you want to see me about?"

Marion's voice is very certain. "Miss. I want to be a nun."

In the momentary silence, Clare has a sudden vivid memory of that other time and other classroom when she had confided to Sister Imelda her own wish to enter religious life.

She realizes she has come full circle. The girl she had been stares into her eyes.

"Miss . . . why are you smiling like that?"

The question hits at her mind, along with a thought a moment ago she would never have believed possible.

"Come and sit down, Marion. We've got a lot to talk about."

This girl will be her way back in. She will be her mentor; Marion her phoenix. Clare knows with quiet certainty she can now have the best of both worlds. Her way forward has assumed a new perspective, one strong enough to sustain her for the foreseeable future.

That this girl even wants to enter religious life is striking proof of God's continuing self-revelation, of Christ abiding above the ever-flowing race of time. At the very period when the prospect for Catholic liturgy is darkening, all is not lost. Gone, it is true, is the Psalter, the compendium of Old Testament Scripture, once the common prayer of Christians and Jews, recited in its entirety by the Church's priests. Vanished, too, is so much else: the Divine Office has been shorn in all manner of means. And yet, in a way, none of this matters. Here, in this trusting, wide-eyed teenager, is the exquisite promise of tomorrow. She, too, wants to be part of the ultimate Mystery, not explain it away. There is hope for them both.

Clare begins to explain why she is smiling.

† † †

Through his developing connections to the Vatican, Andrew has secured good places for himself and Nancy, the petite, dark-haired girl at his side. They are seated close to the stage where Pope John Paul II will shortly address the vast gathering in St. Peter's Square at his regular Wednesday audience.

Nancy is openly impressed with his influence. In his soutane and gleaming Roman collar, Andrew is a commanding figure, leading her confidently past the armed City of Rome policemen who, after they have checked their passes, motion them forward with their machine pistols. She was even more admiring of the smart salutes the Papal Swiss Guards gave him at their checkpoint, and the deferential bow from the Vatican court usher as he led them to their seats below the podium.

Seated here, a few feet from the papal throne, he reminds Nancy, that though their Church is plagued with change, the exquisite beauty of the Mass remains undimmed. It can still produce in him the most satisfying religious happiness he knows, taking part, as they will do shortly, in the solemn ritual and hieratic responses.

She stares around, fascinated at the spectacle, as he knew she would be. There are already a dozen cardinals on the platform, and perhaps another fifty Church dignitaries; middle-aged men in red, purple, gold, and green: the colors of Roman clerical power.

He knows why she wanted to come: to be here, so close to the very center of the power of the Church, the Pope, is to be in the presence of what she sees as the inexplicable mystery of the Church. In many ways Nancy thinks of Catholicism as a kind of magic, which is at the command of those who know the right incantations. She would never understand, he is certain, however much he explained, that the gifts of the Spirit are available only to those who accept unconditionally. If he told her that in Christ's teachings he has found a terrifying reality, she would probably look at him blankly. For all her education and her position with a United Nations relief organization based in Rome, when it comes to religion Nancy has very definite limitations. For her the papal Mass is really little different from Academy Awards night back home in the States. There is no point in telling her that Catholicism requires courage and, for him, is never dull.

In her own special way, he freely concedes, she has enlivened his life.

It would be hard for anyone, he knows, to recognize in this pretty girl, so demure and delectable in her modest long-sleeved dress, the one who sat opposite him in the *ristorante* where once Jane had said she was considering marrying Giles. Last night Nancy had worn a halter and skirt and her eyes had been fixed on him continually, challenging him by her detailed recounting of her newest conquest, an Italian businessman. A few months ago, he would have been aroused by her words. But not anymore. He can listen to them now with the same detachment he imagines in the years to come he will show when hearing confession.

Interpreting his faith, telling himself that like the Apostle Paul he has acquired a new set of beliefs and values that satisfy him more effectively than the old ones, is the reason he feels so stable. He has created for himself an acceptable life-style, which has enhanced his psychosexual development. Within this complex framework he can distinguish between pure sexual desire and love.

He no longer needs Nancy to satisfy his intense sexual feelings. He has outgrown that demand on her. Now she is the woman friend he has always wanted. In becoming so, she has helped him better understand all kinds of emotions.

He knows that getting angry, when the occasion demands, is not only releasing but healthy because he can handle it constructively. Jesus, he has told himself, often became very angry; the Gospels are filled with His sudden and justifiable fury. Far from being un-Christian, anger is a very Christian response. He knows that part of the cause of his depression came from not being able to express his natural anger and frustration at losing Jane. The tensions and the headaches had all been associated with suppressed hostility. Once he realized that, they disappeared, never to return.

Many of his fellow seminarians practice a conscious denial of anger. This is especially true in the area of their sexuality. They simply refuse to concede they are angry because there is no optional celibacy. Instead, unlike him, they pretend it does not matter, not recognizing, he believes, the damage this does to their personal growth. For his part he has become a champion for optional celibacy. At every opportunity he can he has raised it within the seminary and at the Greg. The more intense the opposition the more relaxed and fulfilled he feels. There is nothing better, he has told Nancy, to release tension than the swift and deadly cut-and-thrust of clerical debate. The next best outlet, he has added, is listening to her.

Doing so has also helped him to cope with jealousy — one of the curses of seminary life. He is no longer, unlike so many of his companions, hypersensitive; rather, he accepts that it is positive for him to feel jealous, not about Nancy's exploits, but when they sometimes remind him of his lovemaking with Jane. He rarely thinks of her nowadays. One of the rewards of being able to live with his jealousy is that he feels better able to accept and trust. He is certain these will be important insights when he becomes a priest.

There is a sudden distant cheer from the far side of the square. The roar grows. He lifts her onto her seat so that she can get a better view. In the distance, the *campagnola*, the white-painted "Popemobile," is slowly driving around the edge of the plaza. Nancy bends down to say something. Andrew cannot hear her above the cheering. She turns back to watch the vehicle, moving at its two miles an hour, the Pope turning from side to side, waving and smiling at the tens of thousands in the square.

The cheering has now reached a nonstop roar as the *campagnola* stops before the podium. Flanked by his aides, the Pope slowly climbs the steps to the massive throne. He turns before it to raise his hands. So swift it seems to have been rehearsed, silence falls over the square.

Nancy whispers to Andrew. "He doesn't need anything else with that power. It must be the biggest turn-on ever."

Andrew grins. "That's why I'd like to be Pope." He winks at her.

Then the powerful voice of Pope John Paul II, amplified by scores of loudspeakers, booms across the square.

"Our beloved predecessor, Pope Paul the Sixth, said that priestly celibacy has been guaranteed by the Church for centuries as a brilliant jewel, and retains its value undiminished . . ."

Nancy, Andrew believes, has shown him that he has inner strengths he had never before recognized. His sexuality no longer controls and dominates him but has found its place in his overall personality. God, he is now certain, never intended his sexuality should be suppressed; He only expected he would control it. How he chose to do it was his business. God, he is certain, would not object to what he is doing with Nancy, any more than He would condemn the explicit sexuality of the Songs of Songs.

Through Nancy he has learned — and he feels it has been a truly joyous and creative experience — that he can allow himself, as a celibate, increasingly to experience his sexuality and still retain full control over his behavior. Though he has felt at moments he would like to make love to her, he has never so much as broached the subject. For him his attitude is no different from those times he has felt he could hit someone who has made him angry. But he knows he never would. All he is experiencing, he has told himself, in both cases is an essential proof of his self-control. With Nancy he can balance his sexual feelings on the midway point between having them repressed and seeing them destroy him.

Having established that control, he is fully convinced that whether or not at some stage the Church introduces optional celibacy, it will make no difference to him. There will always be a Nancy in his life, to allow him to be a rational priest who will never repress his feelings or act on them blindly. He will enter his ministry knowing exactly who he is, able to identify his emotions clearly and calmly, and to justify each one, especially in the sexual arena, without fear or guilt. No man could want more. No priest should expect less.

† † †

It's Victoria's turn to cook breakfast. She fries the eggs over easy, the way Jim likes them. She can hear him singing in the shower. She slips the eggs onto a plate. Checking that the coffee is percolating, she goes to the bathroom. She tells him he had better hurry as she will have to leave in fifteen minutes. Her first patient is Sister Ann, whom she is convincing to understand that her lesbian feelings do not in any way diminish her religious commitment; that what she must do is recognize that her deep spirituality remains the core of her life. She has been trying for weeks to wean Sister Ann from her doubts and make her see that being lesbian need not be the end of her life in religion.

Victoria goes to the bedroom door. Jim has made the double bed. He told her, after he started to sleep over, that he is first-rate at domestic chores. He had finally accepted his sexual awakening, realizing it is his ability to love, totally and without preconditions, as she loves him, that is important to them both. The physical release they both enjoy is really no more than a very small part of their loving relationship. They have both discussed, and agreed, that if actual sexual intercourse were to occur they would afterward feel unhappy and dissatisfied with the experience. They would almost certainly wish to try again, undoubtedly with the same dissatisfying result. Rather than risk such unhappiness they will continue to handle their sexual feelings in a way that leaves them both content.

They have been operating under this arrangement since shortly after returning from Greece. He has said he wanted to try to see if he could spend an entire night with her without getting up. That first night they had fallen asleep cradled together, his legs locked around hers, almost as if he wanted to anchor himself. She had awoken next morning to find him beside her. He had grinned and said he'd go and run her bath.

He now spends on average a couple of nights a week here; she invariably sleeps at his place on the weekends. He never stays over when he has early Mass duty next morning.

They feel no guilt, no loss of control, no panic, no repression, no unhealthy curiosity. Instead, there is a common shared commitment, an honesty, an affection, and an excitement they do not fear but cherish. They recognize all their responses as natural between persons who care deeply for each other. They have decided that whatever the Church would do if it discovered the true nature of their relationship, God never insisted that sexlessness and coldness are prerequisites for holiness.

She believes their relationship has helped them both to grow in their desire to be caring people, comfortable with their sexuality, ready to question and examine every aspect of it, and always able to place it within their total and everlasting commitment to their faith.

Both agreed this is how it should remain until she returns to the Mother House. A month ago, Reverend Mother telephoned to say the Order wished her to return and counsel there. Victoria explained that she must first follow through her present cases. With Sister Ann now beginning to show definite progress, Victoria believes she can be back in the convent by early summer.

Jim is staying on at the unit. They have promised to remain in touch, and for their next vacation, they plan to go to Rome. They have invited Paul and Mario to accompany them. It was Jim's idea. She does not mind. She recognizes there is an element of homosexuality in both Jim and herself. Victoria knows it will always be there.

Because there is a self-imposed limitation on their sexual desires, she believes they have achieved a higher form of love than normal married couples. By transcending full physical intercourse — often with its attendant strains when one partner is more demanding than the other — she is convinced their emotional attachment is deeper and less destructive, more free of tension and consequently more loving.

The fundamental dishonesty of the Church, she said, and Jim agreed, is that it has always known that psychosexuality is at the very core of the private life of every person, and yet for every nun and priest the vows they must take to fulfill their vocations makes that privacy a matter of public speculation.

In her view it is totally wrong that her ability to help other religious who have not been able to come to terms with their sexuality is dependent on her concealing her commitment to Jim and his to her. She is certain that if they were not so psychologically integrated, and if both had realized that celibacy is something they will never feel comfortable with, they would have given up vocations to which they feel deeply committed.

In their opinion, the dishonesty is not theirs, but that of the Church. It still takes no real account of normal human responses. They, and they suspect many others, have been forced to hide perfectly healthy relationships because of a decision made centuries earlier and one which, from a modern psychological standpoint, is unsupportable. Yet to dare to challenge that decision, to suggest that perhaps tens of thousands of nuns and priests are forced to live part of their lives in Christ as a subterfuge, to have their emotional growth arrested and their emotions traumatized, would lead to swift and savage punishment. The Church under its present Pope, she believes, could do worse than ponder the early sayings of the fathers.

Judge not him who is guilty of fornication, if thou arte chaste: or thou thyself wilt offend a similar law. For He who said thou shalt not fornicate said also "Thou shalt not judge."

She has already mailed a copy of that quotation to His Holiness Pope John Paul II. She wonders if it has ever reached him.

But she is absolutely certain that sharing her life with Jim has made living her life in Christ that much more meaningful. She is sure that to be a good nun first requires that she be a fully aware and sexually integrated woman.

† † †

Shortly before eleven o'clock, Father Philippe parks outside St. Mark's.

He has remained steadfast to his faith and he believes that in spite of now being the father of two children he is entitled to receive the Blessed Sacrament. The Bishop and chancellor will concelebrate Sunday Mass with Father Nolan as the Bishop makes a final round of the diocesan churches before he retires.

Many of his former parishioners still greet him as Father Philippe. Others ignore him. A few are openly hostile. Some of the priests in the diocese are embarrassed when they encounter him, but Father Nolan remains a steadfast friend and ally. He came to the General to see Margot after Cap was born and, two years later, Daniel. He was one of the first guests invited to dinner when they had bought a house with money Fern lent them. Father Philippe is closer to his mother-in-law than he has ever been to his own mother.

Married life with Margot has, after an initial period of adjustment, run surprisingly smoothly. She is a loving, caring wife and mother, imbued with a fierce loyalty. She refuses to take any interest in the Church, feeling that somehow it alone has been responsible for the years of trauma her husband endured.

His only disappointment is that Margot will not partake in Communion with him. Sitting in the car provided by the company he now works for as a sales executive, Father Philippe tries again to persuade his wife to accompany him.

"Just this once, Margot."

She shakes her head firmly. "No, Phil. I don't need all that. I don't mind your taking Cap and Daniel. But it's not for me. Not while they've got men like the chancellor and this new Bishop running the show."

On the day the Bishop had arrived in the diocese, a sociological survey confirmed that still the biggest single factor for priests and nuns in deciding to leave religious life is their unwillingness to accept the vow of celibacy. Almost half of those surveyed said they found the vow unrealistic and distasteful.

Father Philippe is certain that the local situation reflects a national trend. More than half of those who have abandoned their religious calling throughout the nation since the start of the 1980s have been in their mid-thirties to their late forties. All said they originally entered because they believed God called them; they came in during the late 1950s to the middle 1960s, a period when the specially trained priests and nuns could still expect a rich haul from their vocation pitching.

The great majority who abandoned Holy Orders have also turned their back on the Church. Many have sought other faiths and cults. Judaism has been a popular choice. More thought-provoking has been the admission by many nuns and priests that they have turned to paganism, goddess worship, astrology, or Oriental meditation. They have often redesigned their old Church rituals for the worship of solstices, equinoxes, and full moons.

The Bishop-elect had dismissed the survey as further evidence of a dangerous conspiracy by a handful of liberals to convince the faithful that their findings represent those of the majority. He has already installed himself in the chancellery, flexing his ecclesiastical muscles, sending out word that from the day he is inaugurated, he wants all his priests and nuns to dress and behave strictly as Rome commands.

The techniques remain as rigid as always for intellectual and emotional control. Yet behind the continual flow of encyclicals, apostolic letters, and commands from the Pope and the Prefects of his Sacred Congregations, there is, thinks Father Philippe, a tragic mistake; totally absent from all the Vatican's outpourings is any understanding that the only way out of the most serious crisis the Church has ever faced is to recognize that change is inevitable and that nothing can alter the forward momentum. Rather than bleak condemnation and a narrowness that is at times enforced with medieval harshness, Rome and prelates like the Bishop-elect should recognize that an ever-increasing number of American nuns and priests are going to reassess their religious position when it comes to sexuality. They will place it, as he has, within the context of the society in which they live.

In the five years since he has left, scores of other religious men and women have abandoned their vocations throughout the diocese. The nuns have been freed from their vows. But not a single priest has received dispensation. Those, like Father Philippe, who have married know they have committed mortal sin. Their unions are not recognized and their children are, in the eyes of the Church, bastards.

They are pained by such odium. Yet, just as over two centuries ago their forebears bore arms in the pursuit of liberty against an English king, so now they do battle with their Roman pontiff and his legions of enforcers. Those who resist these powerful forces do so with the only weapon they have — a passionate belief that what they have done is right; that being driven from the Church, they have not for a moment lost the protection of God.

Lost forever to Rome, damned in the eyes of the Pope — angrily dismissed by his men for failing to live up to the pontiff's idea that priests and nuns should be always docile and fearful and invariably glad to be governed — Father Philippe suspects that, like him, the great majority still care deeply about their faith and their Church.

Its future, at least in the United States, depends on the Vatican's recognizing that behind the rebellion and the vocal dissatisfaction of the religious press, there is an ever-increasing number of serious-minded religious men and women who are prepared to stand in direct conflict with the ecclesiastical establishment.

Though the Pope has recently stiffened the hierarchy with bishops of his own conservative persuasion, many senior American churchmen are displaying a respectful tolerance — very similar to that for the German and Dutch hierarchies — when it comes to listening to the growing call for optional celibacy. While the chancelleries remain largely insensitive to human needs — predominantly filled as they are with clerics of bureaucratic impersonality, concerned with fund-raising and economic planning — some of the occupants of the episcopal palaces are no longer prepared to bend to the winds from Rome. They are the bishops who are beginning to see that the Church's survival as a global entity is doomed and that whether it can continue to claim total and binding authority is increasingly problematical. They are the still small but growing number of senior prelates who now see that the greatest of all the errors of the Church is to perpetuate papal infallibility.

Less than a decade ago, when Father Philippe had first come to St. Mark's, the issue of religious sexuality, at best, had been raised in a speculative way, and then only behind firmly closed ecclesiastical doors. Now there is not a diocese in the country without its determined revisionists, fully equipped with alternative theologies to integrate sexuality and celibacy. With growing vigor they are demanding a full investigation into the validity of their claims.

The traditionalist bishops sense what is happening and are trying to stamp out the emotional fires burning in their priests and nuns. But the louder they thunder that behind the calls for sexual freedoms is a direct Satanic-inspired challenge to the magisterium, the more every aspect of Catholic teaching is being thrown into question.

Serious issues of theology are under attack; the severity of the conflict grows apace with the intransigence of Rome and its American supporters who insist on abiding by traditional values. They wince as issues are fully discussed in print; they mourn that the old etiquette, where everything was implicit rather than explicit, has gone. With it has also vanished the cautious, tentative approach to any controversial issue, in which it was mandatory to express docility to the authority of Rome and to agree unconditionally that important matters finally be settled there.

The once accepted rules have been totally swept away in the case of celibacy. No longer is radical religious sexual speculation kept away from the eyes of the secular faithful; no longer is any idea about redefining celibacy submitted first to the scrutiny of superiors; no longer is there an acceptance that if an idea for sexual freedom is rejected those advocating it will retire silently to mull over their mistake. The issue of celibacy — whether it should be optional or should be entirely scrapped — has seen those comfortable rules go. Father Philippe knows that the issue of celibacy is going to be a fight to the finish.

Father Philippe tries one last time to persuade his wife to accompany him and their children to Mass.

She shakes her head.

He nods, not in defeat, but finally accepting. He picks Daniel up with one arm and takes Cap by the hand and walks toward St. Mark's.

Margot calls after him. "You still walk like a priest."

He turns and replies that he supposes he always will.

In his heart he knows it will need a miracle to make the Church understand the normal sexual needs of committed men and women. He knows if there was optional celibacy he would resume his ministry this very day. He would give up a well-paid job, and all its attendent fringe benefits and return to fourteen-hour, seven-day weeks — if he could also still have Margot, Cap, and Daniel as part of his life. But the Church remains obdurate. In his eyes, on the question of celibacy it continues to be the Church of stultification, of dogmatism, of rigid cruelty, of self-righteousness, of inhibition, of fear, of morbid guilt, of hypocrisy, of ignorance, of superstition, of insensitivity, and of self-destruction.

It is not God who is responsible for any of this, but men who claim to act in His name for their own ends. He is now certain that nowhere can they cite infallible Scripture to support their premise that a priest must deny his sexuality to do God's work. Nowhere has he been able to find in the Bible a passage that says abnegation of his sexuality is a healthy and psychologically balanced way to live. The inhibitions imposed on him as a priest came from without, ultimately from another priest. Given his personality, he can now see that that sort of control, from the very beginning, had no hope of succeeding: he is the sort of person who only really responds to self-imposition. Ultimately it is the rules he has given himself that matter.

That is why he can walk with confidence and certainty into St. Mark's, in spite of knowing that the Church regards his wife as his concubine and their children as illegitimate, because he also knows that his life is still Christologically based, but no longer on the unrealistic expectation that he would follow the celibate life of Jesus of Nazareth, but that he will continue to live his life in Christ fully, as a man. He will almost certainly remain, on the Roman books, a priest until he dies. That is an administrative fact. But far more important to him is that he knows that God is a continuous part of his personal history. God has made him what he is. He will remain what God wants. The Church is the ultimate loser in failing to allow him to integrate his sexuality into the service of the Kindgom of God.

† † †

Driving through the hills from a house call, listening to a midmorning radio talk show, Father Breslin realizes another year has slipped by. This pleasant day is the start of the fortieth year of his ministry. The anniversary falls at a time when the Church is besieged by priests and nuns who want to turn it into a worldwide managerial system, a religious multinational, with the Pope presiding over God Incorporated and his bishops acting as divisional heads with special responsibilities for finances, baptisms, bequests, betrothals, and burials. There are others who want the Church to abolish the sins of masturbation, fetishism, and transvestism: to allow women to be ordained; to turn dogmatic and moral theology, and Canon Law itself, inside out, no longer a matter of total obedience, but something for constant argument. But the most vocal of all demands is for an alteration in the sacred vow of celibacy.

He crosses the road where, a few miles farther along, Mary had died almost a year ago, killed instantly in a head-on collision with a farmer's truck. He had gone to the funeral, standing behind the mourners, a solitary figure in black. Watching the coffin being lowered into the earth, he knew he would go on loving her, until they would meet one day in that other world on which the Church, more than on any of its other assurances, has rested its promise.

On the car radio a priest is insisting that the pontiff's latest pronouncement has brought the Church ever closer to confrontation. The soft persuasive voice says the Church is moving into the twilight with the pontiff's thunderous declaration that he will never allow optional celibacy, let alone totally break the bond linking chastity and the priesthood. The radio priest poses a question.

"If the golden law of sacred celibacy is to remain, what reasons are there to show it is holy and fitting?"

He switches off the radio, more sad than angry, more aware than ever that the anarchy is spreading from within.

He has often thought how celibacy has been singled out to be isolated and scrutinized, more than any other sphere of religious human acitivity. It has somehow become the new challenge to a Pope who has shown that tough leadership need not be unimaginative and insensitive. In a world ruled by empty leaders — actors, politicians who have been groomed for television, men and women who will promise anything in exchange for power — the pontiff has shown it is possible to govern without compromise, that to heed the clamor for change is to only increase the sense of insecurity; that to offer new hope is to remember old truths. The Pope has shown it is possible to lead without having constantly to pause to count success, converts, or votes; he is mercifully free of the domination of the measurable. He has shown that he is ready to take risks, with his life, and with the Church he leads; that he is prepared to fail sincerely instead of achieving victory at the expense of his beliefs. He will neither compromise for the sake of easy unity, nor deny the nagging of experience. He is not a man like his predecessors, ready to appease the doubters, or to change his mind, or to forget that his responsibility is steeped in tradition. He will never sell out original aspirations, but will continue to bear witness to a truth that for centuries has been strong enough to sustain itself, but now requires every available defender against those who would undermine one of its pillars — celibacy.

Father Breslin has come to see how unimportant, in the end, is the issue of whether celibacy should be optional or scrapped. He feels immeasurable compassion for all those nuns and priests who have left the Church either to marry or to live their lives with others; those seminarians who dream impossible dreams of changing the unchangeable; those religious who remain in holy life by cheating only themselves: that unless they are allowed fully to explore themselves, and each other, sexually, they cannot do His work. He thinks how tragic it is for them that they cannot see how they have made celibacy a scapegoat for their own helplessness, pettiness, neglect, and failure. All too easily, those who wish to see the vow of celibacy whittled down or abolished are resigning themselves to extinguishing their own inner creative forces. His great hope is that in the fullness of time they, like him, will see celibacy is part of a miraculous process; it is a reminder that here on earth they must search, as he continues to do so, for a righteousness he also realizes most certainly he will never achieve.

He has now, after a life of frequent pain and continuous struggle, earned the wisdom that aging sometimes brings, and he recognizes that a hunger for the merely physical can never provide lasting pleasure. The years have allowed him to ease himself into a purely aesthetic enjoyment of the gifts of others. His great pleasure nowadays is to read of the agonized wrestling of the saints and to steep himself further in the meaning of life and death.

More clearly than ever he sees that his priestly celibacy represents both hope and a promise for the future if he can show in his life three things: that he can live by the unique experience of a deeply personal communion with God and neither squander his vital energies elsewhere nor allow his intimacies to become barren by concentrating them on any one person; that for him a celibate life is a passionate turning and returning time and again to the beginning of his own commitment; that for him life is an unquestioning acceptance of failure and an active longing to redeem it. If he can do all this, he has decided, then it is a worthwhile reward indeed for having resolutely turned away from any compromise. A full life in Christ is one based on the certain knowledge that the first and only intended goal of celibacy is to enhance spiritually those who have voluntarily accepted it.

Celibacy for Father Breslin is neither desire nor denial. It is acceptance.

For the moment:

Father Breslin is still a parish priest in Ireland.
Victoria is in Paris on attachment from her Order.
Clare is a regular visitor to her former Mother House to see Marion.
Father Philippe is still waiting for dispensation.
Andrew is close to ordination.

†

Selected Bibliography

Abraham, Karl. "Manic-Depressive States and the Pre-Genital Levels of the Libido." In *Selected Papers*. London: Hogarth Press, 1949.

Addis, W. E., and T. Arnold. *A Catholic Dictionary*. London: Virtue & Co., 1955.

Adler, Alfred. *The Practice and Theory of Individual Psychology*. London: Kegan Paul, Trench, Trubner, 1924.

———. *Superiority and Social Interest*. Evanston, IL: Northwestern University Press, 1964.

Aelred of Rievaulx. *On Spiritual Friendship*. Paterson, NJ: St. Anthony's Guild Press, 1948.

Altheim, Franz. *Der unbesiegte Gott: Heindentum und Christentum*. Hamburg: Ernest Rowolth Verlag, 1957.

Anastasi, Anne, and J. P. Foley, Jr. *Differential Psychology*. Rev. ed., New York: Macmillan, 1949.

Andics, Margarethe M. von. *Suicide and the Meaning of Life*. London: Hodge & Co., 1947.

Ansbacher, Heinz. "The Structure of Individual Psychology." In *Scientific Psychology: Principles and Approaches*, edited by Benjamin Wolman. New York: Basic Books, 1965.

SELECTED BIBLIOGRAPHY

Arintero, Juan G. *The Mystical Evolution in the Development and Vitality of the Church*, translated by Jordan Aumann. 2 vols. St. Louis: B. Herber Book Co., 1949–51.

Arnold, Vernon. *Roman Stoicism.* New York: Humanities Press, 1958.

Audet, J. P. *Structure of Christian Priesthood: Home, Marriage and Celibacy in the Pastoral Service of the Church.* New York: Macmillan, 1968.

Augustine, Saint. "Against Julian." In *The Fathers of the Church*, vol. 35. New York: Fathers of the Church, Inc., 1957.

Barclay, Andres. "Sexual Fantasies in Men and Women." In *Medical Aspects of Human Sexuality* 7 (1973): 204–216.

Barron, F. *Creativity and Psychological Health.* New York: Van Nostrand, 1963.

Bernstein, Marcelle. *Nuns.* London: Collins, 1976.

Berkinsopp, Joseph. *Celibacy, Ministry, Church.* New York: Herder & Herder, 1968.

———. *Sexuality and the Christian Tradition.* Dayton: Pflaum Press, 1969.

Bonhoeffer, Dietrich. *The Cost of Discipleship.* New York: Macmillan, 1948.

Branden, Nathaniel. *The Disowned Self.* New York: Bantam Books, Inc., 1973.

———. *The Psychology of Self-Esteem.* New York: Bantam Books, Inc., 1971.

Brown, J. A. C. *Techniques of Persuasion.* London: Pelican Books, 1963.

Brown, Raymond. "The Problem of the Virginal Conception of Jesus." In *Theological Studies* (1972): 3–25.

——— *The Virginal Conception and Bodily Resurrection of Jesus.* New York: Paulist Press, 1973.

Budzynski, Thomas H. "Some Applications of Bio-feedback-produced Twilight States." Paper presented at American Psychological Convention, Washington D.C., 1971.

Bultmann, Rudolf. *Neues Testament und Mythologie.* Hamburg; Reich & Heinrich, 1948.

Bunnik, Rudd J. *Priests for Tomorrow.* New York: Holt, Rinehart & Winston, 1969.

Burrows, Millar. *The Dead Sea Scrolls.* New York: Viking Press, 1955.

Caspar, E. *Geschichte des Papsttums von den Anfängen bis zur Höhe der Weltherrschaft.* 2 vols. Tübingen: J.C.B. Mohr, 1930–33.

Cole, William Graham. *Sex in Christianity and Psychoanalysis.* New York: Oxford University Press, 1955.

Dahlgren, K. G. *On Suicide and Attempted Suicide.* Lund, Sweden: Lindstedts, 1945.

Davis, Katherine Bement. *Factors in the Sex Life of Twenty-two Hundred Women.* New York: Harper, 1929.

Delhaye, Philippe. "History of Celibacy." In *The Catholic Encyclopedia,* vol. 3. New York: McGraw Hill, 1967.

Delmonte, M. M. Short collection of papers on pre-sleep states (unpublished). Health Care and Psychosomatic Unit, St. James' Hospital, Dublin.

Denzler, G., ed. *Päpste und Papsttum.* Stuttgart: A. Hiersemann, 1971–.

Dodd, Charles Harold. *The Interpretation of the Fourth Gospel.* Cambridge: Cambridge University Press, 1953.

Driver, Tom. "Sexuality and Jesus." In *New Technology No. 3,* edited by Martin Marty and Dean Peerman. New York: Macmillan, 1966.

Eissler, K. R., *The Psychiatrist and the Dying Patient.* New York: International Universities Press, 1955.

Farnell, Lewis R. *Attributes of God.* Oxford: Oxford University Press, 1925.

Finegan, Jack. *Light from the Ancient Past.* Princeton: Princeton University Press, 1946.

Foss, Brian M. *New Horizons in Psychology.* London: Pelican Books, 1966.

Frankl, Viktor. *The Doctor and the Soul.* New York: Stanton Books, 1967.

Frein, George H., ed. *Celibacy, the Necessary Option.* Symposum on Clerical Celibacy, Univ. of Notre Dame 1967. New York: Herder & Herder, 1968.

Freud, Sigmund. *The Complete Psychological Works of Sigmund Freud.* London: Hogarth Press, 1964.

Fromm, Erich. *The Art of Loving.* New York: Harper & Bros., 1956.

Goergen, Donald. *The Sexual Celibate.* New York: Seabury Press, 1974.

Greenberg, Jerrold, and Francis Archambault. "Masturbation, Self-esteem and Other Variables." In *Journal of Sex Research* 9 (1973): 41–51.

Grelot, Pierre. *Man and Wife in Scripture.* New York: Herder & Herder, 1964.

Haller, J. *Das Papsttum: Idee und Wirklichkeit.* 2nd ed. 5 vols. Basle: B. Schwabe, 1950–53.

Heiler, Freidrich. *Die Religionen der Menscheit in Vergangenheit und Gagenwart.* Stuttgart: Reclam Verlag, 1959.

Hendrickson, Paul. *Seminarian.* New York: Summit Books, 1983.

Hinton, John. *Dying.* London: Penguin Books, 1967.

Jeffreys, M. V. C. *Personal Values in the Modern World.* London: Pelican Books, 1962.

Jeremias, Joachim. *Die Gleichnisse Jesu.* Zurich: Swingli Verlag, 1947.

Jung, C. G. *The Soul and Death. The Collected Works of C. G. Jung.* London: Routledge & Kegan Paul, 1934.

Kazantzakis, Nikos. *The Last Temptation of Christ.* New York: Simon & Schuster, 1966.

Keller, Werner. *Und die Beibel hat doch Recht.* Hamburg: Reich & Heinrich, 1955.

Kennedy, Eugene, and Victor Heckler. *The Catholic Priest in the United States — Psychological Investigations.* Washington, D.C.: United States Catholic Conference, 1971.

Kiesling, Christopher. *Celibacy, Prayer and Friendship.* New York: The Society of St. Paul Press, 1977.

Kinsey, Alfred. *Sexual Behavior in the Human Male.* Philadelphia: W. B. Saunders, 1948.

Kübler-Ross, Elisabeth. *Living with Death and Dying.* New York: Macmillan, 1981.

Lasor, William S. *The Dead Sea Scrolls and the New Testament.* Grand Rapids. MI: Wm. B. Eerdmans, 1972.

Lea, Henry C. *History of Sacerdotal Celibacy in the Christian Church.* London: Watts & Co., 1932.

Legrand, L. *The Biblical Doctrine of Virginity.* New York: Sheed & Ward, 1963.

Leowenich, Walter von. *Der moderne Katholizismus.* Witten/Ruhr: Luther Verlag, 1948.

Machen, John Gresham. *The Origins of Paul's Religion.* New York: Macmillan, 1921.

McCary, James. *Human Sexuality.* New York: Van Nostrand Reinhold, 1967.

Mann, H.K. *The Lives of the Popes in the Early Middle Ages.* 18 vols. London: Kegan Paul, Trench, Trubner, 1902–32.

Martin, Malachi. *Three Popes and the Cardinal.* New York: Doubleday, 1972.

Maslow, Abraham. *Religions, Values, and Peak Experiences.* New York: Viking Press, 1970.

May, G. *Social Control of Sex Expression.* London: Allen & Unwin, 1930.

Mehta, Ved. *The New Theologian.* London: Weidenfeld & Nicholson, 1966.

Mirbt, C. *Quellen zur Geschichte des Papsttums.* 4th ed. Tübingen: J. C. B. Mohr, 1934.

Nouwen, Henri. *Intimacy.* Notre Dame: Fides Press, 1969.

O'Neill, David P. *Priestly Celibacy and Maturity.* New York: Sheed & Ward, 1965.

Peck, Scott M. *The Road Less Travelled.* New York: Simon & Schuster, 1978.

Plato. "The Last Days of Socrates," In *The Apology,* translated by H. Tredennick. Harmondsworth: Penguin Books, 1954.

Ple, Albert. *Chastity and the Affective Life.* New York: Herder & Herder, 1967.

Reich, Wilhelm. *The Murder of Christ.* New York: Farrar, Straus & Giroux, 1953.

Saunders, C. *Care of the Dying.* London: Macmillan, 1959.

Schillebeeckx, E. *Celibacy.* New York: Sheed & Ward, 1968.

Schmidt, Wilhelm. *Ursprung und Werden der Religion.* London: Methuen, 1931.

Schwarz, Gerhart. "Devices to Prevent Masturbation." In *Medical Aspects of Human Sexuality,* 7 (1973): 140–153.

Stengel, E. and Cook, N. G. *Attempted Suicide.* Oxford: Oxford University Press, 1958.

Suttie, Dian D. *The Origins of Love and Hate.* London: Routledge and Kegan Paul, 1955.

Tanner, J. M. *Growth at Adolescence.* Oxford: Blackwell, 1962.

Taylor, Vincent. *The Historical Evidence of the Virginal Birth.* Oxford: Clarendon Press, 1920.

Unger, Merrill F. *Guide to the Bible.* Wheaton, IL: Tyndale House, 1974.

Unwin, J. D. *Sexual Relations and Human Behaviour.* London: Williams & Norgate, 1933.

Wilson, Robert McLachlan. *The Gospel of Philip.* London: Mowbray, 1962.

Wong, Mary G. *Nun.* New York: Harcourt Brace Jovanovich, 1983.